The C  dbook of
Epilepsy

It is becoming increasingly recognised that epilepsy is no longer the sole domain of the medical profession. In particular, over recent years the contribution made by psychologists to the understanding and treatment of this disorder has developed enormously. *The Clinical Psychologist's Handbook of Epilepsy* addresses those psychological aspects of epilepsy that are important for both assessment and management.

Following a brief introduction to epilepsy, its causes, classification and investigation, the topics addressed in detail by the book include: neuropsychological assessment; memory deficits in epilepsy, their assessment and rehabilitation; the impact of anti-epileptic medication on cognition and behaviour; psychological disturbance associated with epilepsy; behaviour problems in children with epilepsy and the impact of epilepsy in people with learning disabilities.

The book contains contributions from experts in the field and provides a review of the latest research findings. It will be a valuable handbook and a practical guide for all clinical psychologists, and other clinicians, working in, or new to, the field of epilepsy.

Christine Cull is a Clinical Psychologist with the Learning Disabilities Service, Mid Anglia Community Health NHS Trust. **Laura Goldstein** is Senior Lecturer in Neuropsychology at the Institute of Psychiatry and Honorary Consultant Clinical Psychologist for the Neuropsychiatry/Epilepsy Unit, Maudsley Hospital, London. Both have published widely in the field of epilepsy.

The Clinical Psychologist's Handbook of Epilepsy

Assessment and Management

Edited by Christine Cull
and Laura H. Goldstein

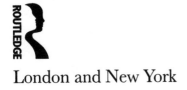

London and New York

First published 1997
by Routledge
11 New Fetter Lane, London EC4P 4EE

Simultaneously published in the USA and Canada
by Routledge
29 West 35th Street, New York, NY 10001

© 1997 Christine Cull and Laura H. Goldstein, selection and editorial
matter; individual chapters, the contributors.

Typeset in Baskerville by Routledge
Printed and bound in Great Britain by Creative Print and Design
(Wales), Ebbw Vale

British Library Cataloguing in Publication Data
A catalogue record for this book is available from the British Library

Library of Congress Cataloguing in Publication Data
The clinical psychologist's handbook of epilepsy: assessment
and management/edited by Christine Cull and Laura H. Goldstein.
Includes bibliographical references and index.
1. Epilepsy – Psychological aspects. 2. Clinical psychology.
I. Cull, Christine, II. Goldstein, Laura H. (Laura Hilary).
RC372.C55 1997   96–52980
616.8'53 – 21   CIP

ISBN 0–415–13050–6 (hbk)
ISBN 0–415–13051–4 (pbk)

Contents

Illustrations

Contributors

Gus Baker graduated from the University of Liverpool with a Masters Degree in Clinical Psychology in 1988 and completed his PhD in 1992. He is a Clinical Lecturer in Neuropsychology and Health Psychology at the University Department of Neurosciences in Liverpool. Dr Baker is also a Consultant Clinical Neuropsychologist at the Walton Centre for Neurology and Neurosurgery, where he works in a multidisciplinary team providing both clinical and surgical services for people with epilepsy. He has published widely on the psychosocial consequences of living with epilepsy, and is a member of the Outcomes Commission for the International League Against Epilepsy and executive member of the Mersey Region Epilepsy Association.

Christine Cull is a Clinical Psychologist with the Mid Anglia Community Health NHS Trust in the Learning Disabilities Service. She is also an Honorary Senior Lecturer in Clinical Psychology at the Institute of Psychiatry, London. Dr Cull has worked with people with epilepsy in a variety of clinical settings, and currently is particularly interested in the psychosocial sequelae of epilepsy in people with learning disabilities. She has published on a variety of topics, including anti-epileptic drug effects on cognition and behaviour, behaviour problems in children with epilepsy, and seizure self-control.

Colin Espie is Professor of Clinical Psychology in the Department of Psychological Medicine, University of Glasgow, where he is also Course Director of the West of Scotland post-graduate training course in clinical psychology. Current research interests include the assessment and management of sleep disorders in various populations, health issues in people with learning disabilities, and the measurement of outcomes in people with epilepsy. Professor Espie has held numerous research grants and published widely in these areas.

Maria Fowler has worked extensively in the field of epilepsy and behaviour as Principal Educational Psychologist at St Piers Lingfield in Surrey, a school for children and young adults with epilepsy and other special needs. She has specialised in learning disabilities with an interest in developmental and cognitive neuropsychology, and has undertaken research on the effects of anti-epileptic drugs on behaviour. Other interests include rehabilitation in frontal lobe dysfunction, education and subtle seizures, self-control of seizures and cognitive slowing in epilepsy. She has published in all these areas.

Ruth Gillham holds an Honorary Senior Clinical Lectureship at the University of Glasgow. She is also a Consultant Neuropsychologist at the Institute of Neurological Sciences in Glasgow, where she is involved in the assessment and treatment of people with neurological problems. Dr Gillham's research interests and publications in the field of epilepsy include the effect of anti-epileptic drugs on cognition and the psychological management of seizures.

Laura Goldstein is a Senior Lecturer in Neuropsychology at the Institute of Psychiatry in London. She is also an Honorary Consultant Clinical Psychologist at the Bethlem Royal and Maudsley NHS Trust, where she has provided a clinical psychology service to the Neuropsychiatry/Epilepsy Unit for over nine years. Dr Goldstein previously worked in the epilepsy surgery programme at the Maudsley Hospital. Her epilepsy-related research interests include neuropsychological and psychosocial sequelae of epilepsy as well as psychological treatments for people with epilepsy, and she has published in these areas. She is involved in the post-qualification training of clinical psychologists and runs the Diploma in Clinical Neuropsychology course at the Institute of Psychiatry.

Anna Kendrick completed her PhD (*Repertory Grid Technique in the Assessment of Quality of Life*) at the Institute of Neurology, London. Her main research interest has been in the development of an epilepsy-specific measure of quality of life. She has also conducted research on the effects of anticonvulsant medication and nutrition on cognition and mood. She has recently published on the use of repertory grid technique as a model for assessing quality of life. Dr Kendrick is currently employed as an Associate Lecturer with the Open University in Wales, teaching on the post-foundation 'Introduction to Psychology' course.

Susan Oxbury, a Consultant Clinical Psychologist, is head of the Department of Clinical Neuropsychology at the Radcliffe Infirmary,

Oxford. She has developed the neuropsychology service to the Oxford Epilepsy Surgery programme for both adults and children. Her particular interests are temporal lobe surgery and the relationship between hippocampal pathology and neuropsychological function, long-term neuropsychological and psychosocial outcome in children following surgery for epilepsy, and studies of severe amnesia. She has published in all these areas.

Audrey Paul is a Research Psychologist in the Epilepsy Unit of the Western Infirmary, Glasgow. She is currently writing up her PhD on stereotyped behaviours in people with learning disabilities and epilepsy and has recently produced an educational video on epilepsy for use with clients. She was the 1996 winner of the Gowers Prize for young health professionals working in the field of epilepsy.

Pamela Thompson is Head of Psychology and Rehabilitation Services at the National Society for Epilepsy, Honorary Consultant Psychologist at the National Hospital for Neurology and Neurosurgery, and Lecturer in Psychology at the Institute of Neurology, University of London. From 1978, her clinical and research activities has been devoted to psychological aspects of epilepsy. Research work has included memory problems, neuropsychological and psychosocial aspects of surgical treatment and, more recently, family stress. She has also co-written a book for people with epilepsy, their families and carers.

Preface

Epilepsy is a relatively common neurological disorder, which tradition-ally has been the domain of the medical profession (general practitioners, neurologists, neurosurgeons and psychiatrists). However, it is becoming increasingly clear that other professional groups have a valuable role to play in the assessment and treatment of epilepsy and its psychosocial sequelae. In this particular text we are concerned with one of those professions, namely, clinical psychology.

Clinical psychologists have been working in this field for many years, and from the work carried out to date, it is clear that, as a profession, we can make a major contribution to the understanding of epilepsy, its assessment and treatment. Our aim, therefore, in editing this volume is to bring together current expertise and knowledge in order to provide a readily accessible source of information for psychologists coming to the field for the first time, for those with some experience, and for other interested professionals.

CC
LHG

Acknowledgements

We would like to take this opportunity to acknowledge our debt to Professor Michael Trimble (Institute of Neurology, London) and Dr Peter Fenwick (Institute of Psychiatry, London), who, within our respective careers, have stimulated our interest and influenced our work in the field of epilepsy.

We are also extremely grateful to Gail Millard for her good-natured and efficient processing of numerous modified manuscripts. It is thanks to her that this book is seeing the light of day. Of course, the support and encouragement of our respective husbands (Roger and David) and families has been incalculable.

CC
LHG

Introduction

Clinical psychologists work in a variety of settings where they may encounter individuals with epilepsy (e.g. child guidance clinics, child development clinics, general practice, services for older people and learning disabilities) as well as in child or adult neurology and neuro-surgery services. Traditionally, in a clinical setting, psychologists have been asked to carry out assessments of neuropsychological functioning and to repeat assessments over time to evaluate cognitive decline. However, clinical psychologists are increasingly being asked to become involved in the treatment of individuals with epilepsy, in particular those who are thought to display seizures for which there are identifi-able psychological factors. They are also becoming involved in the treatment of people with non-epileptic seizures. In addition, in the last twenty years, psychologists have been undertaking epilepsy-related research from an increasingly wide range of perspectives. These have involved the assessment of anti-epileptic drug effects on behaviour and cognition, investigations into the psychosocial sequelae of epilepsy, examinations of the relationship between environment and seizure occurrence, non-medical (i.e. psychological) approaches to seizure management, the assessment of cognitive and psychosocial functioning pre- and post-surgery for epilepsy, and the factors that affect the quality of life of those with epilepsy.

Our aim here is to present a collation of this work, reviewing the available literature to date and highlighting its broad-ranging implica-tions. In this way it is hoped that this text will be of value to researchers and practising clinicians alike.

We start off with those areas which have traditionally been the domain of the clinical psychologist, and about which relatively more is known, notably neuropsychological assessment (Chapter 2); epilepsy and memory (Chapter 3) and assessment related to surgery (Chapter 4).

Chapter 4 considers not only what is known about pre- and post-operative cognitive/neuropsychological procedures, but also what is known about changes in psychosocial functioning and assessment of this. In any assessment, part of the clinician's skill is to evaluate the reliability of their findings, and the extent to which factors other than the critical variable of interest may have a contributing role to play. In this respect, in Chapter 5 we consider one of those factors, the impact of anti-epileptic drugs on cognitive functioning and behaviour. This is also of importance, as claims that AEDs do not have adverse effects on behaviour and cognition are an important marketing strategy for drug developers.

Chapter 6 addresses the relationship between epilepsy and psychological disorders in adults, reviewing the literature and exploring the psychologist's contribution to the assessment/treatment of such disorders.

It is becoming increasingly clear in the literature that seizure occurrences, be they spontaneous epileptic seizures or pseudoseizures (non-epileptic seizures) may be affected by factors in both the person's external and internal environments, and that psychological approaches can be used beneficially in both the assessment and management of such seizures, as can be seen in Chapter 7.

A diagnosis of epilepsy can have a major impact on the individuals themselves – their self-image, their expectations for the future, not to mention their family and friends and, in the broadest sense, on their quality of life. It is only in recent years that this issue has been addressed in relation to epilepsy, and this is the topic of Chapter 8.

Thus far we have concerned ourselves mainly with epilepsy as it affects adults. The next two chapters deal with children. The first is on neuropsychology and cognitive assessment (Chapter 9), as the assessment of children presents a different set of challenges and the need to use different measures to that of adult neuropsychology. Behaviour problems are commonly associated with a diagnosis of epilepsy in childhood, and can be of such severity that residential schooling may seem the only solution to an apparently insurmountable problem. Chapter 10 deals with this issue, focusing on assessment and management, having considered the prevalence and aetiology of such problems.

Epilepsy occurs more commonly in people with learning disabilities than in the normal population, and most frequently in those with severe/profound learning disabilities. Surprisingly, this group has been the focus of very little research interest. In an attempt to redress the balance, research is reviewed in Chapter 11 with respect to the psychological implications of epilepsy for people with learning disabilities, and its contribution to our understanding of epilepsy in people with learning disabilities is highlighted. The practical implications for psychologists working with individuals with both learning disabilities and epilepsy are explored. In Chapter 12 we summarise issues raised in the book and consider future developments. Finally, as several chapters discuss the use of neuropsychological tests, we provide the reader with an Appendix containing names and sources of materials referred to, especially those in Chapters 2, 3, 4 and 9. However, before all of this, we felt that it would be of value to present in Chapter 1 a brief overview of the disorder of epilepsy itself.

We have endeavoured throughout the text to use terminology that is not pejorative or demeaning. For example, we refer to 'people with epilepsy' rather than 'epileptics', since, while the term may be an appropriate description of seizures, it only serves to perpetuate inappropriate stereotypes when applied to people.

Christine Cull
Laura H. Goldstein

Chapter 1

An introduction to epilepsy

Christine Cull and Laura H. Goldstein

WHAT IS EPILEPSY?

Epilepsy is . . .

> a chronic disorder characterised by recurrent seizures
>
> (Gastaut 1973)

and a seizure is . . .

> an occasional, an excessive and a disorderly discharge of nerve tissue
>
> (Hughlings Jackson in Taylor 1958)

that is, an episode of altered behaviour and/or consciousness, which can take many forms, but which results from an abnormal electrical paroxysmal discharge in cerebral neurones. Types of epileptic seizures will be described later in this chapter but, a clinical diagnosis of epilepsy is made if two epileptic seizures occur within a two-year period.

EPIDEMIOLOGY

Epilepsy is a common neurological disorder, occurring in 5:1000 children (Cowan *et al.* 1989) and in 4–7:1000 adults (Hauser and Annegers 1993), such that in the UK it has been estimated that there are approximately 350,000 people with a diagnosis of epilepsy (Brown and Betts 1994). The prevalence of epilepsy is reported to be ten times that of multiple sclerosis and a hundred times that of motor neurone disease (Brown *et al.* 1993).

New cases reported each year are in the region of 20–70 per 100,000 (Hauser and Annegers 1993), the highest rates occurring in infants and young children and in the elderly (Brown *et al.* 1993). The incidence is consistently found to be higher in males than females, although in most studies the difference fails to reach statistical significance (Hauser and Annegers 1993).

CAUSES OF EPILEPSY

Everybody has the potential to have an epileptic seizure. When considering the aetiology of seizures, Lishman (1987) emphasises however that epilepsy must be thought of as a symptom rather than a disease. He also indicates that for many people the cause of the disorder may never be identified. The proportion of cases of unknown aetiology may account for as many as two-thirds of cases (see Lishman 1987). He indicates that the majority of such seizures are generalised (either absence or tonic-clonic) in nature, and that in most cases the presence of a focal component to the seizures will indicate the existence of a discrete structural brain lesion. In addition, an hereditary component is found more commonly for seizures of unknown origin than for seizures that occur in the presence of readily identifiable brain lesions.

Where causes can be identified, they may be varied in nature. Lishman (1987) reviews these causes, and categorises them as seizures due to birth injury or congenital malformations, due to brain damage, infections, cerebrovascular disease, tumours, neurodegenerative disorders, drugs or toxins, or metabolic disorders. Chadwick (1994) distinguishes between acute symptomatic seizures that are the result of some metabolic disorder or cerebral insult, and remote symptomatic seizures that reflect some form of persisting brain damage. Hopkins (1987), on the other hand, considered two main classes of aetiology – predisposing and precipitating factors – and this subdivision will be used here.

Predisposing factors

When considering predisposing factors, it is important to remember that these may not be independent of each other. Thus, a genetic predisposition towards epilepsy may involve either the inheritance of a convulsive threshold, or of a condition associated with epilepsy (see Anderson and Hauser 1993). Lishman (1987) indicates that family loadings seem to be more marked with certain types of seizures, but he cautions that the potential to have an epileptic seizure is present throughout the population, given the right precipitating circumstances.

Developmental brain abnormalities that predispose to seizures may or may not be inherited. Porencephaly, microgyria (and other abnormalities of the cortex), tuberous sclerosis and arteriovenous malformations are other congenital malformations that may be associated with the development of epilepsy. In addition, the person may have acquired structural brain abnormalities that then predispose to epilepsy. With respect to epilepsy arising from birth injury, Lishman (1987) indicates that pregnancy and delivery complications may produce brain damage and lead to epilepsy. Particularly relevant here is damage that produces anoxia or cerebral haemorrhage. Illnesses early in infancy (e.g. cardiorespiratory disorders, infections or metabolic disorders) may also produce seizures. The occurrence of febrile convulsions, possibly with status epilepticus, may give rise to anoxic damage and the formation of scar tissue. This so-called 'mesial temporal sclerosis', which consists of gliosis of mesial temporal lobe structures, is commonly found in patients with temporal lobe epilepsy. Whilst this was initially thought to occur unilaterally in most cases, data revealing the more frequent bilateral presence of abnormality is now appearing (Incisa della Rochetta et al. 1995).

In terms of post-traumatic epilepsy, head injury carries a high risk for the subsequent development of seizures. In cases of closed head injury, the underlying neuropathology may include the formation of scar tissue (gliosis) with focal cerebral atrophy. The incidence of epilepsy will be about 5 per cent once the immediately post-traumatic seizures have been excluded (Jennett 1975). Post-traumatic seizures may not appear for several years after injury even though more than half of those going on to develop epilepsy after head injury will do so in the first year post-injury. Where there has been an open head injury, with skull penetration or fracture, there is a much higher incidence of post-traumatic epilepsy (e.g. Russell and Whitty 1952). Post-traumatic seizures may prove difficult to treat, and have important implications for rehabilitation following head injury. Their development must be considered when estimating compensation following head injury.

Certain infections of the central nervous system are likely to be associated with the development of epilepsy. Thus encephalitis or cerebral abscesses are more likely to lead to the development of epilepsy than is meningitis (Lishman 1987). In certain parts of the world, parasitic cysts play an important role. Epilepsy may also develop as a consequence of subtle brain involvement during childhood mumps or whooping cough, although this may be hard to determine in individual cases. In older patients, neurosyphilis should be ruled out as a cause of seizures.

Again, in older patients, cerebral arteriosclerosis and episodes of hypertensive encephalopathy may be important aetiological factors.

Lishman (1987) indicates that a cerebral embolus is more likely to lead to epilepsy than are either a thrombosis or a cerebral haemorrhage; however, any cerebral infarct may provide a focus for the subsequent development of seizures. With ageing, the increased incidence of dementia may also be accompanied by the development of epilepsy, and seizures may occur in 25–33 per cent of cases of Alzheimer's disease and in Huntington's and Creutzfeldt-Jakob disease (see Shorvon 1988). Demyelinating neurodegenerative disorders such as multiple sclerosis may accompany seizure onset in adults, whereas in children degenerative disorders such as tuberous sclerosis may be causative. The development of seizures in a previously healthy adult may reveal the existence of a brain tumour. Sumner (1969) indicated that in 20 per cent of cases of cerebral tumour, the first symptom may be the onset of seizures.

Precipitating factors

A number of factors can be shown to precipitate seizures. Many of these are due to toxic conditions or metabolic disturbances, with an interaction between these. Thus, in addition to alcohol and rapid withdrawal from other drugs, Lishman (1987) notes the wide range of substances that may be associated with seizures. These include barbiturates, amphetamines, ergot alkaloids and steroids, as well as exposure to lead and the chlorinated hydrocarbons found in some pesticides. In addition, certain antipsychotic and antidepressant agents may lower seizure thresholds, thus making them more likely to occur.

A wide range of metabolic causes have been found for seizures. These may include porphyria, and occasionally hypoglycaemia, as well as uraemia, hypernatremia and hypercalcaemia. Electrolyte disturbances, such as those occurring in eclampsia may also be associated with seizure occurrence.

Certain external stimuli may precipitate seizures. Thus, there are accounts of reading, music, flashing lights, TV screens, loud sounds and other such events precipitating seizures (see Chapter 7 for further discussion of so-called reflex epilepsies).

Changes in the sleep–wake cycle have also been shown to precipitate seizures, as has sleep deprivation, and some seizures occur on waking. For seizures which occur in sleep and arise from the frontal lobes, the precipitating factor is the transition between different stages of sleep. Rapid alterations in arousal level in the waking state may also be associated with seizure occurrence (see Chapter 7).

In some women with epilepsy, seizure occurrence is related to the menstrual cycle. So-called catamenial epilepsy, where there is an increase in seizure frequency pre- or perimenstrually in the majority of menstrual cycles, has been shown to occur in anything from 9–72 per cent of women with drug resistant epilepsy (Crawford 1991).

Other precipitating factors may take the form of illnesses and inter-current infections. The possibility that psychological factors may influence seizure occurrence will be considered in Chapter 7.

Overall in terms of the epidemiology related to aetiology, Sander *et al.* (1990) found that in newly diagnosed patients with seizures, tumours were a rare cause of seizures in people younger than 30 years of age, accounting for only 1 per cent of the sample studied; however in adults between the ages of 50 to 59 years, 19 per cent of cases were attributed to the presence of a tumour. Vascular disease accounted for 49 per cent of cases of epilepsy in elderly individuals. In general, cerebral infection was the cause in 2 per cent of cases and traumatic brain injury was found in 3 per cent of the sample. Alcohol was the most likely single cause of what Chadwick (1994) termed acute symptomatic seizures, accounting for 6 per cent of these, with the highest incidence occurring in adults aged between 30 and 39 years old.

PROGNOSIS

Chadwick (1994) reviewed a number of studies that have considered prognostic indices for seizure remission. Prognostic factors may include age at onset of epilepsy, duration of epilepsy before the onset of treat-ment, seizure type and aetiology and although Chadwick indicated that none of the studies to date permit adequate quantification of the rela-tive weights that each of these factors may play in overall prognosis, age at onset of seizures seems to be the most important factor, with seizures beginning in the first year of life carrying a poor prognosis. In addition, the absence of early brain damage and the absence of evidence of generalised seizure activity are positive indications of good outcome. The interested reader is referred to his useful paper for more details.

It is important to note that a diagnosis of epilepsy carries with it increased risk of mortality, perhaps some two or three times higher than expected for the general population (Chadwick 1994). The risk is highest in the first year of life, and in individuals with tonic-clonic and frequently occurring seizures. Sudden unexpected death in people with epilepsy is a matter of concern as is accidental death due to drowning, with patients with epilepsy needing to take precautions over bathing and swimming arrangements. Accidents involving falling or burns as a result of seizures are problematic but rarely result in death.

CLASSIFICATION OF SEIZURE DISORDERS

Different classification systems of seizure disorders exist, focusing either on the type of seizure or on the type of epilepsy. One is therefore symptom-based, while the other is disorder-based.

The classification of seizures by the International League Against Epilepsy (ILAE) ignores underlying anatomical features of seizures and does not take into account age and gender in its seizure classification (see Neppe and Tucker 1992). It broadly divides seizures into partial (simple and complex), generalised and unclassified epileptic seizures. For a fuller discussion of seizure classification, see Dreifuss and Henriksen (1992) and Chadwick (1994).

Partial seizures

Partial seizures are subdivided into simple and complex partial seizure types. In simple partial seizures there is no alteration of consciousness. Seizures begin in a localised brain area with the sensations evoked dependent upon the part of the brain that is involved. Simple partial seizures are subdivided into *motor* (any part of the motor cortex can be involved), *somatosensory* (with sensory, somatosensory, gustatory or vertiginous symptoms), *autonomic* (with vomiting, flushing, sweating) and *psychic* (dysphasia, dysmnesia, déjà vu, jamais vu) seizures.

In complex partial seizures, there is a characteristic alteration of consciousness, and the person demonstrates automatic behaviour (automatisms), which takes the form of more or less co-ordinated involuntary activity occurring either during the seizure or immediately after it, and for which the person is usually amnesic. Automatic behaviour may take the form of eating actions (chewing, swallowing), gestures, ambulation and verbal utterances. Complex partial seizures most commonly arise from the mesial temporal lobe structures, although approximately one-third of such seizures have their origin in the frontal lobes. Prior to a complex partial seizure, the person may experience an aura, which is a simple partial seizure and which often serves as a warning of a more serious impending seizure. Auras for seizures arising in the temporal lobes include epigastric auras, described as a feeling that starts in the stomach and which rises up to the throat, feelings of fear, déjà vu and jamais vu. Both simple and complex partial seizures can develop into generalised seizures with the resulting seizures being known as secondary generalised seizures.

Generalised seizures

There are a number of types of generalised seizures. Primary generalised seizures manifest themselves immediately and there is a simultaneous spread of the seizure throughout the cortex.

In *absence seizures* (previously called petit mal), there is an abrupt onset with cessation of ongoing activity and the person may demonstrate a vacant appearance, either with or without an upward movement of the eyes. The attacks may last for up to thirty seconds, with an abrupt end and no postictal confusion. Occasionally, automatisms such as lip-smacking or chewing may occur, causing confusion with complex partial seizures.

Tonic-clonic seizures (previously called grand mal) are rarely preceded by a warning, although there may be a prodromal change in mood in some cases. There is a sudden contraction of muscles with tongue biting, urinary incontinence and absence of breathing, and this is then followed by clonic convulsive movements which are symmetrical, rhythmic, and which decrease in amplitude over time. Seizures will last no more than 2–3 minutes. Following tonic-clonic seizures, the person may remain unconscious for a variable length of time and may then sleep deeply. *Tonic seizures* may occur without the clonic component, and similarly *clonic seizures* may occur on their own.

Myoclonic seizures take the form of single/multiple jerking movements, which may be generalised to the face, trunk or one or more limbs or muscle groups. These contractions occur especially on falling asleep or waking, and occur as part of an idiopathic generalised epilepsy or as part of a mixed seizure disorder such as the Lennox-Gastaut syndrome. They are also seen in Creutzfelt-Jakob disease.

Atonic seizures are characterised by a decrease in muscle tone such that there will be head drop, jaw slackening, and the person will fall to the ground. These are often known as drop attacks but need to be distinguished from drop attacks that occur in narcolepsy/cataplexy.

Of particular concern in individuals with generalised seizures is the development of Lennox-Gastaut syndrome, usually presenting between the ages of one and six years, and which is accompanied by the existence of learning difficulties. It may follow on from infantile spasms (also a form of generalised seizures), but the aetiologies are manifold. The seizure types seen in this disorder may typically include atonic and absence seizures, but they may also be myoclonic in nature. As the person gets older, complex partial and generalised tonic-clonic seizures may become the predominant symptom pattern. Multifocal spikes and spike-wave disturbance are seen on EEGs in individuals with Landau-Kleffner syndrome, which, like Lennox-Gastaut syndrome, presents in childhood and is characterised by acquired aphasia.

A number of types of seizure are unclassified, resulting from insufficient data, and these may include many of the seizure types occurring in infancy. Of particular importance is the need to distinguish epileptic seizures from non-epileptic seizures, especially as both types may occur in the same person. Non-epileptic seizures may take a number of forms (see, for example, Betts and Boden 1992), although disagreement over this exists. There is consensus that such seizures may occur when environmental gains are present (although motivation is likely to be unconscious) and they are frequently triggered by stress. They often look similar, but not identical, to epileptic seizures and seldom result in injury. Diagnosis requires careful post-seizure neurological examinations (checking pupillary and plantar reflexes), the measurement postictally of the hormone prolactin in the blood, and a careful analysis of the function of these attacks in the person's life. Some studies suggest raised incidence of a history of sexual abuse in females with non-epileptic seizures (see Chapter 7).

The occurrence of *status epilepticus* is of particular importance. This refers to continuous seizure activity with no recovery between successive tonic-clonic seizures. As a consequence of the cessation of respiration during the tonic phase of the seizure, the person is at risk of anoxic brain damage and cognitive deterioration (see Chapters 2 and 3). Occasionally, absence status or complex partial status may occur and may also require verification by EEG monitoring (see Treiman 1993 for more details).

In contrast to the ILAE classification of seizures, a classification of epilepsies was approved by the same body in 1970 and revised in 1989. As discussed by Dreifuss and Henriksen (1992), the classification distinguishes primarily between *idiopathic* or *primary epilepsy* (i.e. genetic epilepsy) and *symptomatic* or *secondary epilepsy* resulting from structural or metabolic disorders. In cases of idiopathic epilepsy, there may be a family history of a similar disorder, age at onset of seizures may be young, there will be no structural abnormalities, and the background EEG will be normal.

The term cryptogenic epilepsy is used within this classification to describe secondary epilepsy of unknown cause. Cryptogenic and symptomatic epilepsies are less benign than idiopathic types. Dreifuss and Henriksen (1992) indicate that partial and generalised seizures may fall into either category of idiopathic or symptomatic epilepsies, and describe several examples of these.

INVESTIGATIONS

EEG

The electroencephalogram or EEG, as it is commonly referred to, is a record of cerebral electrical activity measured via electrodes. The standard procedure is a scalp recording, where sixteen to twenty electrodes are placed on the scalp in a standard pattern (or montage) covering both hemispheres and all surface regions of the brain. The activity of the brain is recorded as wave tracing which varies in form, amplitude and frequency, and the EEG provides information about the pattern of activity emanating from each part of the brain. This information can be used to confirm a diagnosis of epilepsy and may contribute to the seizure classification. Recordings of this kind generally take place over a short period of time (less than one hour) during which the subject has to keep quite still, and will rarely coincide with a seizure happening. When there is still doubt about the diagnosis and/or seizure type, recordings during sleep or longer recordings may be preferred, and the latter recordings may involve video-EEG monitoring (telemetry), or ambulatory EEG monitoring.

Telemetry takes place in a controlled environment, where the subject is free to move around with the electrodes in place, but is constantly monitored by a video camera. Thus, behavioural observations can be matched with changes occurring in the EEG. Alternatively, the EEG can be recorded on to a tape in a portable cassette recorder; a smaller number of electrodes are used, which are placed very unobtrusively so that individuals can carry on with their normal daily activities. This ambulatory monitoring allows for much longer periods of recording, although the quality of the information gathered is less detailed.

When surgery is being considered, more invasive recordings may be made, either on the surface of the cortex itself or from deeper structures in the brain (depth recordings), as these will yield more reliable 'noise free' information and permit recording of EEG changes that may not be detectable from routine scalp recordings.

For a more detailed discussion of the EEG, the reader is referred to Binnie (1993).

Brain imaging

In most cases, EEG investigations will be sufficient. However, where an organic aetiology needs to be identified or excluded, or where surgery is being considered, further information will be required. There are a number of methods by which 'images' of the brain, in respect of structure and function, can be obtained.

Both CT (Computerised Tomography) scans and MRI (Magnetic Resonance Imaging) can be used to detect abnormalities of structure – such as tumours, vascular lesions and atrophy – that may be of aetiological significance, although it is generally accepted that MRI is superior in this respect (Polkey and Binnie 1993). In particular, MRI is being used increasingly to examine abnormalities of the hippocampus often found in complex partial seizures arising from mesial temporal lobe structures.

PET (Positron Emission Tomography) and SPECT (Single Photon Emission Computerized Tomography) are used to investigate cerebral function and measure blood flow (PET also measures metabolic rate). Their use includes demonstrating functional abnormalities in affected areas of brain, demonstrating the point from which focal seizures emanate (Polkey and Binnie 1993), and in some instances distinguishing between types of abnormality with similar structural presentations (Kendall 1993).

TREATMENT

It is perhaps worth pointing out that not all epilepsies/seizures will necessarily be treated, for example, if the particular epilepsy syndrome diagnosed is self-limiting, if the seizures are not severe or debilitating, or if the patient does not wish to receive treatment (Richens and Perucca 1993).

Drugs

For those where treatment is indicated, the first approach considered is pharmacological management. The drugs currently in use in the UK are shown in Table 1.1. While some drugs are more effective for particular seizure types than others, and other drugs may be contraindicated in particular types of seizure/epilepsy, the drug–seizure match is actually very limited and, in practice, research suggests that most drugs work for most seizure types. As far as possible, prescribing will be guided by seizure type in the first instance, followed by considerations regarding side effects (Richens and Perucca 1993). Where possible, a single drug will be used, but it may sometimes be necessary to use a second drug if none of the appropriate medications work effectively as a sole treatment. In situations where this is the case, the present trend is towards 'rational polypharmacy' – that is, using two drugs with different modes of action, rather than ones which target the same neurotransmitter system (Brown and Betts 1994). It is now accepted that three drugs are likely to be of little benefit over two (Richens and Perucca 1993). The reader interested in the mechanism of action of anti-epileptic drugs (AEDs), or a more detailed discussion of prescribing habits, is referred to Richens and Perucca (1993).

Although doses of AEDs will be quoted in drug trials and patients' notes, what may be important when judging the effectiveness of AEDs in controlling seizures in an individual case is the blood serum concentration of the drug. This will usually be quoted with reference to a therapeutic range. Whether or not drug serum levels fall in this range may depend upon patients' metabolism, compliance in taking the medication, and the interaction between that AED and other AEDs or other drugs being taken concurrently. Occasionally, serum levels will be too high and the patients will become 'toxic', demonstrating a wide range of side effects specific to the AED. A reduction in drug dose should reverse such symptoms, which may well include cognitive impairment and double vision.

Table 1.1 Drugs currently used to treat epilepsy in the UK

	Generic name	Trade name
Licensed for monotherapy use	Phenobarbitone	Gardenal
	Primidone	Mysoline
	Phenytoin	Epanutin
	*Carbamazepine	Tegretol
	*Sodium Valproate	Epilim
	Ethosuximide	Zarontin
	Clonazepam	Rivotril
	Lamotrigine	Lamictal
Licensed for add on use only	Vigabatrin	Sabril
	Gabapentin	Neurontin
	Topiramate	Topamax
	Clobazam	Frisium

* Also available in slow-release preparations.

In any one individual, serum drug levels are known to vary throughout the day when the AED is taken in a divided dose regimen. Thus, drug levels will be at their highest (or peak) value soon after drug ingestion, and at their lowest (or trough) level just before the next dose is due. The introduction of controlled release preparations, necessitating only a single dose per day, minimises the degree of variation in serum drug levels.

For some patients, adverse effects of AEDs (e.g. skin rashes with carbamazepine, low sodium levels) may precipitate drug changes in the same way as might poor seizure control. Clinical experience indicates that patients' seizure control may often initially improve following admission to hospital because medication is taken more regularly than at home, and stress levels may be lower.

The effectiveness of AEDs has improved over the years and new drugs are being developed all the time; however, seizure control is obtained in only approximately 80 per cent of those people being treated for epilepsy (Richens and Perucca 1993), leaving the remainder who continue to display refractory seizures despite optimal drug treatment, some 7,000 new patients each year (Brown and Betts 1994).

For those patients who continue to have seizures, there are two alternatives to be considered. The more conventional consideration is surgery, while a newer alternative being explored is the area of psychological approaches to the treatment of seizures. This is discussed in detail in Chapter 7.

Surgery

As mentioned, surgery may be an option for some patients with intractable seizures which are drug resistant. The aim of surgery is to control the seizures by removing the area of pathology and surrounding tissue (resective surgery). This may involve sections of the temporal lobes, or (less commonly) the frontal lobes, or may necessitate a full lobectomy. The alternative is to limit the impact of the seizures by altering the function of the brain in some way (functional surgery) – for example, by removing a whole hemisphere, or by cutting the links (or part of the links) between the two hemispheres, i.e. the corpus callosum (callosotomy).

The careful selection of patients for surgery means that outcome for surgery is improving, but it is not without its drawbacks that may occur in some patients, such as short-term or lasting neurological complications, cognitive deterioration, and behavioural deterioration. Furthermore, in some patients, seizures may continue unchanged.

Success rates vary, depending in part on the type of surgery under-taken. Thus, approximately 40 per cent of patients may be seizure-free after temporal lobe resection, and approximately 60 per cent of patients will experience at least a 50 per cent reduction in seizure frequency following callosotomy. For a fuller discussion of surgical procedures and outcome, the reader is referred to Polkey and Binnie (1993).

Despite the improving success rates of surgery, it is clear that it is not a successful procedure in a substantial minority of patients, and further, there is another group of people for whom surgery is not a viable option. Again, psychological approaches to seizure management may be appropriate for these people (see Chapter 7).

CONCLUSIONS

The broad-ranging impact of epilepsy in terms of its aetiology, investi-gation, treatment and effect on daily life indicates the potential scope of involvement for clinical psychologists. These issues will be dealt with in greater detail in the following chapters.

REFERENCES

Anderson, V. E. and Hauser, W. A. (1993) 'Genetics', in J. Laidlaw, A. Richens and D. Chadwick (eds) *A Textbook of Epilepsy* (4th edn), Edinburgh: Churchill Livingstone.

Betts, T. and Boden, S. (1992) 'Diagnosis, management and prognosis of a group of 128 patients with non-epileptic attack disorder: Part 1', *Seizure* 1: 19–26.

Binnie, C. D. (1993) 'Electroencephalography', in J. Laidlaw, A. Richens and D. Chadwick (eds) *A Textbook of Epilepsy* (4th edn), Edinburgh: Churchill Livingstone.

Brown, S. and Betts, T. (1994) 'Epilepsy – a time for change?', *Seizure* 3: 5–11.

Brown, S., Betts, T., Chadwick, D., Hall, B., Shorvon, S. and Wallace, S. (1993) 'An epilepsy needs document', *Seizure* 2: 91–103.

Chadwick, D. (1994) 'Epilepsy', *Journal of Neurology, Neurosurgery and Psychiatry* 57: 264–77.

Cowan, L. D., Bodensteinder, J. B., Leviton, A. and Doherty, L. (1989) 'Prevalence of the epilepsies in children and adolescents', *Epilepsia* 30: 94–106.

Crawford, P. (1991) 'Catamenial seizures', in M. R. Trimble (ed.) *Women and Epilepsy*, Chichester: Wiley.

Dreifuss, F. E. and Henriksen, O. (1992) 'Classification of epileptic seizures and the epilepsies', *Acta Neurologica Scandinavica* 86 (Suppl. 140): 8–17.

Gastaut, H. (1973) *Dictionary of Epilepsy*, World Health Organisation: Geneva.

Hauser, W. A. and Annegers, J. F. (1993) 'Epidemiology of epilepsy', in J. Laidlaw, A. Richens and D. Chadwick (eds) *A Textbook of Epilepsy*, Edinburgh: Churchill Livingstone.

Hopkins, A. (1987) 'The causes and precipitations of seizures', in A. Hopkins (ed.) *Epilepsy*, London: Chapman and Hall.

Incisa della Rochetta, A., Gadian, D. G., Connelly, A., Polkey, C. E., Jackson, G. D., Watkins, K. E., Johnson, C. L., Mishkin, M. and Vargha-Khadem, F. (1995) 'Verbal memory impairment after right temporal lobe surgery: Role of contralateral damage as revealed by 1H magnetic resonance spectroscopy and T2 relaxometry', *Neurology* 45: 797–802.

Jennett, B. (1975) *Epilepsy After Non-missile Head Injuries* (2nd edn), London: Heinemann.

Kendall, B. (1993) 'Neuroradiology', in J. Laidlaw, A. Richens and D. Chadwick (eds) *A Textbook of Epilepsy* (4th edn), Edinburgh: Churchill Livingstone.

Lishman, W. A. (1987) *Organic Psychiatry* (2nd edn), Oxford: Blackwell Scientific Publications.

Neppe, V. M. and Tucker, G. J. (1992) 'Neuropsychiatric aspects of seizure disorders', in S. C. Yudofsky and R. E. Hales (eds) *The American Psychiatric Press Textbook of Neuropsychiatry* (2nd edn), Washington: American Psychiatric Press.

Polkey, C. E. and Binnie, C. D. (1993) 'Neurosurgical treatment of epilepsy', in J. Laidlaw, A. Richens and D. Chadwick (eds) *A Textbook of Epilepsy* (4th edn), Edinburgh: Churchill Livingstone.

Richens, A. and Perucca, E. (1993) 'Clinical pharmacology and medical treatment', in J. Laidlaw, A. Richens and D. Chadwick (eds) *A Textbook of Epilepsy* (4th edn), Edinburgh: Churchill Livingstone.

Russell, W. R. and Whitty, C. W. M. (1952) 'Studies in traumatic epilepsy. 1: Factors influencing the incidence of epilepsy after brain wounds', *Journal of Neurology, Neurosurgery and Psychiatry* 15: 93–8.

Sander, J. W. A., Hart, Y. M., Johnson, A. L. and Shorvon, S. (1990) 'Newly diagnosed epileptic seizures in a general population', *Lancet* 336: 1267–71.

Shorvon, S. D. (1988) 'Late onset seizures and dementia: a review of epidemiology and aetiology', in M. R. Trimble and E. H. Reynolds (eds) *Epilepsy, Behaviour and Cognitive Function*, Chichester: Wiley.

Sumner, D. (1969) 'The diagnosis of intracranial tumours', *British Journal of Hospital Medicine* 2: 489–94.

Taylor, J. (ed.) (1958) *Selected Writings of John Hughlings Jackson, Vol. 1: On Epilepsy and Epileptiform Convulsions*, New York, Basic Books.

Treiman, D. M. (1993) 'Status epilepticus', in J. Laidlaw, A. Richens and D. Chadwick (eds) *A Textbook of Epilepsy* (4th edn), Edinburgh: Churchill Livingstone.

Chapter 2

Neuropsychological assessment

Laura H. Goldstein

The rich literature dealing with different aspects of neuropsychological assessment in epilepsy stems particularly from the need to evaluate patients carefully prior to neurosurgical treatment of their seizures (see Chapter 4). For patients not being considered for neurosurgery, a neuropsychological assessment of a patient with epilepsy is most likely to focus on the delineation of the person's intellectual strengths and weaknesses, with respect to a particular brain lesion, possibly evaluating potential cognitive deterioration (Goldstein 1991). The need may remain, in the absence of good neuroimaging data, to corroborate evidence gained from electroencephalograms (EEGs) with neuropsychological data to predict the location of an epileptic focus. The difficulties in making such predictions will be discussed below. In addition, the factors that may affect neuropsychological performance will be discussed, and suggestions will be made for developing a testing protocol.

MEMORY AND TEMPORAL LOBE LESIONS

Whilst a detailed account of the memory impairments to be found in patients with epilepsy is provided in Chapter 3, the current discussion will outline the limitations in trying to identify the lateralisation of an epileptic focus on the basis of memory impairments.

The literature on memory deficits in individuals with complex partial seizures arising from mesial temporal lobe structures, previously classified as temporal lobe epilepsy (TLE) has parallels with data from neurosurgically treated individuals who have had varying but unilateral excisions of mesial temporal lobe structures. Summaries of surgical outcomes suggest that after unilateral left and right temporal lobectomy there is decreased ability to learn and recall verbal and visuospatial material respectively (e.g. Jones-Gotman 1987). However, this situation is not always replicable in patients with TLE, and a number of studies have failed to find between-groups material-specific deficits dependent upon the side of epileptic focus (Goldstein 1991). Reasons for such failures may have included the difficulty in preventing the verbalisation of visuospatial material (Berent *et al.* 1980) or having used too simple test materials (Loiseau *et al.* 1983). Many studies use subject groups being evaluated for surgery and the exclusion of patients with well-controlled seizures may also have affected results.

More recently, Lee *et al.* (1989) noted that the Verbal and Visual Memory Indices of the Wechsler Memory Scale-Revised (WMS-R) do not differentiate right- from left-TLE patients, and that Visual Paired Associates of the WMS-R do not discriminate between patients with lateralised brain lesions (Chelune and Bornstein 1988). Further, they found that some visuospatial tests (delayed recall of the Rey-Osterreith complex figure and Form Sequence Learning, involving recognition of a series of unfamiliar geometric shapes from an array containing the target and distracter designs) were not very sensitive to the effects of right temporal lobe (TL) damage. The use of complex, unfamiliar, difficult-to-verbalise visuospatial test materials is advocated when attempting to elicit right TL effects.

Loring *et al.* (1989) also criticised the Verbal-Visual Index discrepancy of the WMS-R in that it incorrectly predicted the laterality of a previous temporal lobectomy in an unsatisfactorily high number of cases. Accuracy for left temporal lobectomy cases was higher than for right-sided ones. This may result from the verbalisable nature of the Visual Paired Associates stimuli.

Loring *et al.* (1988) attempted to predict side of onset of seizures in temporal lobectomy candidates, using tests reported by Lee *et al.* (1989). Accurate predictions of laterality of focus were more likely to be achieved when there were consistent dissociations between performance on verbal and visuospatial tasks for all the measures of material specific learning, rather than for single measures. Thus, a comprehensive battery must be employed if lesion lateralisation is to be attempted with any reliable chance of success. In a similarly cautionary manner, Williamson *et al.* (1993) reported that neuropsychological assessment yielded predictions of lateralisation that were in agreement with the side of seizure origin in only 73 per cent of cases. When testing produced discordant or non-lateralising results, patients tended to have right TL foci. The greater accuracy in predicting left-sided foci was attributed to the strong verbal (i.e. left hemisphere) nature of most assessments.

A substantial number of studies, however, do provide evidence of material specific deficits in lateralised TLE. Often delayed recall memory tasks reveal between-groups differences where immediate recall measures do not (see Goldstein 1991), although immediate, as well as delayed, recall and per cent retention of the Logical Memory passages from the old Wechsler Memory Scale (WMS) were found to be impaired in patients with left- as opposed to right-TL seizure foci (Sass et al. 1992a). Saling et al. (1993) found that patients with left rather than right hippocampal sclerosis (HS) were particularly impaired on learning the hard pairs of the Paired Associate Learning Test; the right-sided group scored essentially within normal limits. No between-groups differences were found on immediate or delayed recall of the Logical Memory passages.

In several studies, the Selective Reminding Test (SRT: Buschke 1973) has yielded promising results. Westerveld et al. (1994) recommended its use for identifying patients with dominant TLE, as they are reported to perform more poorly than patients with right TLE (Sass et al. 1990; Ribbler and Rausch 1990). Similarly Lee et al. (1989) found that verbal learning measures (SRT, supra-span learning) were sensitive to the effects of left-sided pathology.

Despite difficulties in designing adequate testing materials, visuospatial memory deficits have been detected in right-TLE patients. Helmstaedter et al. (1991) employed a visual design learning test, wherein nine 5-line hard-to-name designs had to be reconstructed using wooden sticks, within six learning trials. Patients with right- or bilateral-TL foci showed poorer immediate recall and learning capacity than left-TLE individuals. Sass et al. (1992a) found that patients with right TLE were impaired relative to left-TLE subjects on the immediate recall of the WMS Visual Reproduction subtest, although between-groups differences were not found on delayed or per cent retained measures.

Recognition memory in patients with TLE has also been examined. Seidenberg et al. (1993) focused on the types of recognition errors made on the California Verbal Learning Test (CVLT). Unoperated TLE patients with left-sided focus were less able than right-sided patients to discriminate target words from distracters, they had a positive response bias and made more false positive errors. Ellis et al. (1991) found that TLE subjects did not differ from controls in their ability to recognise words using the Recognition Memory Test, whereas right- and left-sided TLE patients were impaired relative to controls (but not to each other) on the face recognition subtest. Right-sided TLE patients were impaired at recognising familiar faces; the left-sided group had difficulty naming them.

Although it is not usually good practice to undertake a neuropsychological assessment shortly after a patient has suffered a seizure, this may assist in the identification of the side of focus. Andrewes *et al.* (1990) tested verbal and visuospatial recognition memory in patients with left or right TLE. Interictal measures (obtained at least twenty-four hours after a seizure) failed to show between-groups differences, whereas in eight patients subsequently tested within one hour of a seizure, seven showed a pattern of deficits that would be expected on the basis of the side of lesion.

Language functions and the temporal lobes

Mayeux *et al.* (1980) had suggested that what some patients report as memory impairments may in fact be word-finding difficulties. They compared small groups of patients with left or right TLE or generalised seizures on the WAIS, the WMS, the Benton Visual Retention Test, the Rey-Osterreith figure, the Boston Naming Test (BNT) and the Controlled Oral Word Association test. Whilst the groups did not differ on the memory measures, the left-TLE group was weak in terms of confrontation naming. Several measures of memory and intelligence were found to be highly correlated with naming ability.

In addition, Mungas *et al.* (1985) reported that left-TLE patients were impaired on phonemic-cued recall, and hypothesised that linguistic deficits might affect verbal memory performance in left TLE. Ellis *et al.* (1991) found that left-TLE patients were impaired relative to right-TLE and control subjects on the National Adult Reading Test and that although both patient groups were impaired on the Graded Naming Test, the left-TLE group was more impaired than the right-sided group. On the Test of Reception of Grammar (TROG), both patient groups were impaired relative to controls, with a trend for greater impairment to be seen in the left-TLE group.

Sass *et al.* (1992b) reported an impairment on the BNT and slightly lower Verbal IQs in left-TLE individuals. Immediate and delayed recall on the Logical Memory passages correlated with BNT scores for the left-TLE subjects but not for the right-sided group. Hermann *et al.* (1988a) examined patients with dominant lobe TLE; performance on the CVLT was generally predicted by scores on the BNT and verbal fluency. Aural and reading comprehension also influenced CVLT scores.

In a further study by Hermann *et al.* (1992), left-TLE patients scored significantly lower than right-TLE patients on visual naming, sentence repetition, reading and aural comprehension and on the Token Test, but not on verbal fluency and spelling, although the findings were in the same direction. Poorer performance on visual naming was associated with poorer memory in both TLE groups.

It is important to distinguish between those memory tests that are and are not correlated with performance on language tests. Saling *et al.* (1995) noted that unrelated paired associates and the post-interference trial of the Rey Auditory Verbal Learning Task do not correlate with results of language assessment; these tests may differentiate better between patients with left and right HS than those that correlate with language skills.

Hermann *et al.* (1988b, 1992) suggested that while naming ability does seem to influence performance on verbal memory measures, anomia is unlikely to account for poor memory ability. Rather, they suggested that underlying both impairments is a general retrieval difficulty. They concluded that there is a distribution of language competence across right- and left-TLE groups, with the left-TLE group overall doing worse, but that the effects of the variability in language competence (particularly visual naming) in the two groups are similar in terms of the consequences for memory functions.

EXECUTIVE FUNCTIONS AND FRONTAL LOBE LESIONS

Considerably less has been written about executive functions and their disruption by frontal lobe epileptic foci.

Corcoran and Upton (1993) compared performance on tests of verbal fluency and on the Stroop Test between patients with frontal epileptic (FE) foci or TL foci, or who had HS. Impairments on both of these tests were expected in the FE group. A significantly poorer performance was found for the word fluency measures (but only in comparison to the HS group – the frontal and temporal groups performed equivalently) with the left-frontal patients producing fewer words than the right-frontal patients. There was only a non-significant trend for the FE group to be less efficient on the Stroop test, with a further non-significant trend for the left-frontal patients to have longer interference condition response times.

More has been written about the Wisconsin Card Sorting Test

(WCST). This test has traditionally been considered sensitive to damage to dorsolateral prefrontal and orbitofrontal cortex. Studies have also shown this test to reflect the presence of TLE. Thus Hermann *et al.* (1988a) reported that 74 per cent of the non-dominant TLE patients and 39 per cent of the patients with dominant TLE foci performed on the test in a manner that would usually be characterised as 'frontal'. High numbers of WCST perseverative errors by TLE patients (irrespective of lateralisation of focus) were reported by Horner *et al.* (1996).

Corcoran and Upton (1993), using Nelson's modification of the WCST, found their patients with HS took longer than the other groups to complete the task, and made more perseverative and category errors than the temporal and frontal groups, and temporal group alone respectively. The HS group also completed fewer categories than the temporal but not the frontal groups. Seventy-five per cent of the HS cases were classified as performing in a 'frontal' manner, making at least 50 per cent perseverative errors. Right-sided HS was associated with more category errors and a longer task completion time than left-sided HS. Corcoran and Upton attributed the poor performance of the HS patients to the working memory component of the WCST, and the poor classification of the FE group's performance as 'frontal' to the mixed location of their foci within the frontal lobes.

Factors affecting WCST performance in TLE patients have also been noted to include side of focus, age at onset of epilepsy (Strauss *et al.* 1993) and mood (Seidenberg *et al.* 1995).

It has also been demonstrated that word fluency, the number of questions (total and pseudo-constrained) asked in the Twenty Questions test, Stroop test interference time, bimanual gestures, motor sequencing and performance on the Trail Making Test are sensitive to left FE, while cost estimation, Porteus Maze completion time, the number of category errors made on the modified WCST, and in an increased number of errors on Part B of the Trail Making Test are more sensitive to right FE (Upton and Thompson 1996).

The assessment of cognitive deficits of patients with FE is, therefore, problematic. Some of this difficulty may result from variable lesion location within the frontal lobes and from the recognition that seizure activity may generalise rapidly from one frontal lobe to the other, so that an epileptic focus in one hemisphere may produce dysfunction in the other. In addition, the similarity in performance between patients with FE and TLE may be explained by the connections between the temporal and frontal regions and by the fact that temporal lobe seizures may spread via the frontal regions, producing dysfunction of these areas. Clinicians must therefore be cautious in using so called 'frontal-lobe' tests when trying to localise an epileptic focus (Corcoran and Upton 1993).

INTELLECTUAL ABILITY

In relatively unselected patients with epilepsy, IQ is generally found to be within or just below the average range, unless it is known that more widespread brain damage exists. Data on IQ is rather confounded in many studies where the samples are being worked-up for temporal lobectomy (see Chapter 4).

Some attention has been paid as to whether the discrepancy between Verbal and Performance IQ is particularly informative in cases of epilepsy (e.g. Ossetin 1988). Brain damage, medication or subclinical epileptic activity (see below) may slow response on timed tests, and may thereby reduce Performance IQ measures. An early age at onset of epilepsy may well result in disrupted schooling, and consequently in lowered Verbal IQ. A tendency towards lower Verbal IQ with left TLE and towards lowered Performance IQ with right TLE may nonetheless be found (Goldstein and Polkey 1993). IQ measures may however be more useful as background measures of functioning than for predicting the localisation of an epileptic focus.

COGNITIVE DETERIORATION

Assessments may be undertaken to evaluate the presence or otherwise of cognitive decline. Whilst this is not necessarily found (Selwa *et al.* 1994), Brown and Vaughan (1988) have described an 'epileptic dementia'. They suggested that in a highly selective group of patients with severe epilepsy, males may be at a higher risk than females of showing significant cognitive deterioration. This may be a 'fronto-temporal' type decline in cognitive abilities, particularly involving the left cerebral hemisphere. Specific neuropathological conditions may also underlie cognitive decline in epilepsy (e.g. Lafora Body disease, progressive myoclonic epilepsy or Rasmussen's encephalitis – see Dreifuss 1992), as may *status epilepticus* (see below). Judicious use of test psychometric properties must be used in evaluating true cognitive decline in the context of the person's medical history.

OTHER FACTORS INFLUENCING COGNITIVE PERFORMANCE

Mood and age at onset of epilepsy can influence neuropsychological profiles, as can a number of other factors although together these may not have enormous predictive value (Hermann *et al.* 1988a; Strauss *et al.* 1995).

Neuropathology

Understanding the impact that differing types of neuropathology can have on test performance may help the interpretation of patients' otherwise confusing test profiles. Thus, for example, the presence of HS has been shown to be associated with a history of febrile convulsions, an earlier onset of regular seizures and with poorer IQ levels when compared with tumour-like malformations or non-specific pathology in patients undergoing temporal lobectomy (McMillan *et al.* 1987). In addition, whereas individuals with right- or left-sided HS did not show any between-groups differences on limited measures of verbal or visuospatial memory (see also Saling *et al.* 1993), patients with left-sided tumour-like malformations displayed performance consistent with the side of the pathology. Thus, patients who suffered febrile convulsions as children and later developed TLE may have intellectual deficits as adults. Oxbury (see Chapter 4) considers in greater detail studies of memory impairment in adults with unilateral HS. It is difficult to separate out the longer history of seizures and the presence of HS when trying to identify the cause of the cognitive deficits, but for individuals with a longer history of intractable epilepsy and possibly increased severity of brain damage, there may be less opportunity for functional reorganisation (Goldstein 1991).

Seizure-related variables

Generalised seizures have been associated with greater cognitive impairment than partial seizures (e.g. Giordani *et al.* 1985), and multiple seizure types are more detrimental than single seizure types (Seidenberg *et al.* 1986). Aldenkamp *et al.* (1992), using computerised assessments found that patients with generalised seizure activity were impaired on tests of language, whereas patients with partial epilepsy or whose seizure classification was unclear were most impaired in terms of response speed. A lifetime total of more than 100 tonic-clonic seizures or a single lifetime episode of *status epilepticus* has been associated with a lowering in IQ and other cognitive functions (Dodrill 1986).

In terms of seizure frequency, Dikmen and Matthews (1977) indicated that high frequency of partial seizures was associated with poorer performance on a range of measures from the Halstead Reitan battery and the WAIS. At worst risk for poor performance were individuals with a long history of seizures; early age at seizure onset has generally been found to be associated with weaker cognitive abilities (see Dodrill 1992; McMillan *et al.* 1987; Strauss *et al.* 1995, but see also Chapter 3). It is important to note, however, that even at the time of the first few seizures, prior to the commencement of treatment, memory and sustained attention may be compromised (Kälviäinen *et al.* 1992). Both in groups and individual cases, a reduction in seizure frequency is accompanied by an improvement in cognitive performance (Seidenberg *et al* 1981; Goldstein *et al.* 1992) Over a prolonged period of retesting, there is no clear evidence that patients with TLE will necessarily show a deterioration in cognitive functioning (Selwa *et al.* 1994).

Neuropsychological assessment results may also be affected by the presence of interictal discharges. When these can be shown to affect cognitive processes, this is known as Transitory Cognitive Impairment (TCI). The demonstration of TCI depends upon the type of neuropsychological task employed and on the nature of the discharges. Binnie and Marston (1992) report that in most studies concerned with this phenomenon, about 50 per cent of patients with frequent subclinical discharges were found to demonstrate TCI (cf. Aldenkamp *et al.* 1992). This is more likely to be seen with demanding tasks that test the patient at the level of their ability and may include choice reaction time, signal detection, information processing, short-term memory and memory span tasks (ibid.). In addition, generalised 3 Hz spike-and-wave discharges of at least three seconds duration are most likely to lead to detectable TCI.

TCI is most likely to occur when the discharges are present during or possibly just before the stimulus presentation (Binnie and Marston 1992, but see Provinciali, *et al.* 1991). Binnie (1988) and Kasteleijn-Nolst Trenité *et al.* (1990) have demonstrated a significant association between the localisation of discharges (e.g. right versus left TL) and the material specificity of the impairment (visuospatial versus verbal). TCI is of relevance during neuropsychological assessment since the pattern of deficits elicited may not be 'permanent' and may be amenable to pharmacological treatment (Binnie and Marston 1992). A range of abilities such as speed and accuracy of reading and mental arithmetic (Kasteleijn-Nolst

Trenité *et al.* 1988), performance on subtests of children's intelligence tests (Sieblink *et al.* 1988) and even driving (Binnie 1993) have been shown to be affected by subclinical discharges.

Therefore, test interpretation may be affected by TCI. However, the practical difficulties of trying to evaluate such a phenomenon in routine clinical practice via simultaneous video and EEG recording, and then analysis of EEG traces corresponding to testing phases, will generally rule out such purity of test interpretation. Careful observation of the patient during testing, in particular for lapses in performance, may at least help with the identification of previously undetected minor seizures.

It is also conceivable that some cognitive tasks, in selected individuals, will induce epileptic activity. These 'secondary psychogenic seizures' (Fenwick and Brown 1989) are discussed in Chapter 7, but include examples of arithmetic-induced seizures as well as reading epilepsy. Finally, not only may epileptic activity affect neuropsychological performance, but the converse may also be true (e.g. Boniface *et al.* 1994).

Other variables

Strauss *et al.* (1995), in a multicentre study, found that Full Scale IQ was 1.35 times higher in patients with extratemporal as opposed to temporal lobe disturbance. Patients with left-sided seizures were 1.6 times more likely to be intellectually impaired than those with right-sided seizures. Atypical speech representation was also associated with decreased performance.

PRACTICAL GUIDE

In interpreting test results, one needs to take into account the patient's mood, underlying neuropathology and seizure related variables as discussed above. In addition, it is important to consider the patient's anti-convulsant medication as discussed in Chapter 5, as well as the psychometric properties of the tests and their sensitivity to change. The absence of adequate norms for people with learning difficulties may impede this process.

The purpose of the assessment will be important in determining the components to be included. An initial assessment after a new diagnosis of epilepsy will establish a baseline against which any future assessments can be compared. Thus, it should assess a wide range of cognitive abilities. All assessments should be informed by the results of investigations such as EEGs and neuroimaging, to determine whether the cognitive profile is consistent with what is known about the patient's epilepsy. Qualitative as well as quantitative interpretations of performance will be needed (Goldstein 1991).

All assessments should include a general measure of intelligence in addition to specific tests of cognitive functioning.

In terms of memory assessment, measures of recognition, recall and learning (where possible of verbal and visuospatial material) should be included. However, local norms are needed in order to be confident about identifying deficits. Comparison of performance across tests may be problematic because of the incomparability of normative samples. This is relevant, for example, when comparing scores on the WAIS-R and WMS-R (Atkinson 1991) and between other memory tests such as the WMS-R and the CVLT (Randolf *et al.* 1994). Without taking such differences into account, inconsistencies in deficient performance may be obtained. While the list learning task from the Adult Memory and Information Processing Battery does not include the recognition components of the CVLT, British norms have been collected. Its ability to distinguish between the effects of right and left TLE remains to be investigated. The SRT offers promise, although non-American norms may not be widely available. A new test of recognition memory, the Doors and People Test may be valuable for patients with lateralised TLE, on the basis of post-lobectomy data (Morris *et al.* 1995). The Rivermead Behavioural Memory Test is not sufficiently sensitive to lateralised memory deficits due to epilepsy (Goldstein and Polkey 1992a), but includes useful measures of prospective memory.

It is important to include measures of language, such as reading, naming, fluency and comprehension. Newer tests such as the Speed and Capacity of Language Processing require evaluation in patients with epilepsy. Measures of attention, and in particular the more ecologically valid Test of Everyday Attention may also have a role to play. Executive dysfunction assessment might include the tests discussed earlier and the Behavioural Assessment of Dysexecutive Syndrome.

Evaluation of mood (anxiety, depression) is also important in this context, particularly because of the high association between anxiety, depression and epilepsy. Mood questionnaires (e.g. the Hospital Anxiety and Depression Scale, Zigmond and Snaith 1983) should be selected that do not contain too many items that refer to physical symptoms that could be due directly to epilepsy.

One increasingly available option for neuropsychological assessments is the use of computerised test batteries. These offer the advantages of precise timing of stimulus presentation and response, improved scoring and the possibility of an increased range of scores, although the qualitative data from an interactive assessment is lost (Thompson 1991), as is scope for being able to break down instructions or 'test the limits' of ability. Many batteries do not yet have sufficient reliability and validity data. Thompson (1991) regards computerised neuropsychological assessment as extending the range of assessment techniques rather than replacing traditional methods. A particularly useful application has been for the detection of TCI, where simultaneous assessment and EEG/video recording can make possible the precise determination of the effect of discharges on cognition (see also Rugland *et al.* 1991).

A computerised battery widely used in Europe for patients with epilepsy is FePSY (e.g. Alpherts and Aldenkamp 1990). This includes simple and choice reaction time tests, rhythm discrimination, finger tapping, a visual search task, measures of vigilance, a WCST-like test, spatial and verbal memory tests and split visual field tasks. Increasingly, good normative data are becoming available, although none are yet available for the effects of lesion laterality as opposed to overall type of epilepsy. There are no parallel versions of the tests.

Finally, it may be helpful to obtain an impression of the patients' own perceptions of their cognitive impairment. This may be done using questionnaires, which have generally focused on memory, such as the Subjective Memory Questionnaire (Bennett-Levy *et al.* 1980; Goldstein and Polkey 1992b), the Head Injury Postal Questionnaire (Sunderland *et al.* 1983) adapted for patients with epilepsy (Corcoran and Thompson 1992) and the Memory Observation Questionnaire (McGlone 1994). A broader-based Multiple Ability Self-Report Questionnaire (MASQ: Seidenberg *et al* 1994) focuses on five domains of cognitive function, (i.e. language, visual memory, verbal memory, visuoperception and attention) and has been validated for use with patients with unilateral TLE; between-groups differences arise on the language and verbal and visual memory subscales. Modest but significant correlations were reported between MASQ scores and objective performance, particularly for left-TLE patients. Other questionnaires such as the Cognitive Failures Questionnaire (Broadbent *et al.* 1982) and the DEX (part of the Behavioural Assessment of Dysexecutive Syndrome), assessing behaviour problems characteristic of the dysexecutive syndrome, require validation for use with patients with epilepsy.

CONCLUSIONS

The neuropsychological assessment of a person with epilepsy remains complex and requires the clinical psychologist to have both a working knowledge of the disorder and the available test materials in order to design and interpret an assessment that will be of help for the patient. Further studies are needed that compare performance of patients across a range of similar tests in order to help the practitioner know which scores really constitute evidence of cognitive impairment.

REFERENCES

Aldenkamp, A. P., Gutter, T. and Beun, A. M. (1992) 'The effect of seizure activity and paroxysmal electroencephalographic discharges on cognition', *Acta Neurologica Scandinavica* Suppl. 140: 111–21.

Alpherts, W. C. J. and Aldenkamp, A. P. (1990) 'Computerised neuropsychological assessment of cognitive functioning in children with epilepsy', *Epilepsia* 31 (Suppl 4): S35–40.

Andrewes, D. G., Puce, A. and Bladin, P. F. (1990) 'Post-ictal recognition memory predicts laterality of temporal lobe seizure focus: comparison with post-operative data', *Neuropsychologia* 28: 957–67.

Atkinson, L. (1991) 'Concurrent use of the Wechsler Memory Scale-Revised and the WAIS-R', *British Journal of Clinical Psychology* 30: 87–90.

Bennett-Levy, J., Polkey, C. E. and Powell, G. E. (1980) 'Self-report of memory skills after temporal lobectomy: the effect of clinical variables', *Cortex* 16: 543–57.

Berent, S., Boll, T. J. and Giordani, B. (1980) 'Hemispheric site of epileptogenic focus: cognitive, perceptual and psychosocial implications for children and adults', in R. Canger, F. Anglieri and J. K. Penry (eds) *Advances in Epileptology*, New York: Raven Press.

Binnie, C. D. (1988) 'Seizures, EEG discharges and cognition', in M. R. Trimble and E. H. Reynolds (eds) *Epilepsy, Behaviour and Cognition*, Chichester: Wiley.

—— (1993) 'Significance and management of transitory cognitive impairment due to subclinical EEG discharges in children', *Brain and Development* 15: 23–30.

Binnie, C. D. and Marston, D. (1992) 'Cognitive correlates of interictal discharges', *Epilepsia* 33 (Suppl. 6): S11–17.

Boniface, S. J., Kennett, R. P., Oxbury, J. M. and Oxbury, S. M. (1994) 'Changes in focal interictal epileptiform activity during and after the performance of verbal and visuospatial tasks in a patient with intractable partial seizures', *Journal of Neurology, Neurosurgery and Psychiatry* 57: 227–8.

Broadbent, D. E., Cooper, P. F., Fitzgerald, P. and Parkes, K. R. (1982) 'The cognitive failures questionnaire (CFQ) and its correlates', *British Journal of Clinical Psychology* 2: 1–16.

Brown, S. W. and Vaughan, M. (1988) 'Dementia in epileptic patients', in M. R.

Trimble and E. H. Reynolds (eds) *Epilepsy, Behaviour and Cognitive Function*, Chichester: Wiley.

Buschke, H. (1973) 'Selective reminding for analysis of memory and learning', *Journal of Verbal Learning and Verbal Behaviour* 12: 543–50.

Chelune, G. J. and Bornstein, R. A. (1988) 'WMS-R patterns among patients with unilateral brain lesions', *The Clinical Neuropsychologist* 2: 121–32.

Corcoran, R. and Thompson, P. (1992) 'Memory failure in epilepsy: retrospective reports and prospective findings', *Seizure* 1: 37–42.

Corcoran, R. and Upton, D. (1993) 'A role for the hippocampus in card sorting?' *Cortex* 29: 293–304.

Dikmen, S. and Matthews, C. G. (1977) 'Effects of major motor seizure frequency on cognitive-intellectual function in adults', *Epilepsia* 18: 21–9.

Dodrill, C. B. (1986) 'Correlates of generalised tonic-clonic seizures with intellectual, neuropsychological, emotional and social function in patients with epilepsy', *Epilepsia* 27: 399–411.

—— (1992) 'Interictal cognitive aspects of epilepsy', *Epilepsia* 33 (Suppl. 6): S7–10.

Dreifuss, F. E. (1992) 'Cognitive function – victim of disease or hostage to treatment?' *Epilepsia* 33 (Suppl. 1): S7–12.

Ellis, A. W., Hillam, J. C., Cardno, A. and Kay, J. (1991) 'Processing of words and faces by patients with left and right temporal lobe epilepsy', *Behavioural Neurology* 4: 121–8.

Fenwick, P. C. B. and Brown, S. W. (1989) 'Evoked and psychogenic epileptic seizures. I. Precipitation', *Acta Neurologica Scandinavica* 80: 535–40.

Giordani, B., Berent, S., Sackellares, J. C., Rourke, D., Seidenberg, M., O'Leary, D. S., Dreifuss, F. E. and Ball, J. T. (1985) 'Intelligence test performance of patients with partial and generalised seizures', *Epilepsia* 26: 37–42.

Goldstein, L. H. (1991) 'Neuropsychological investigation of temporal lobe epilepsy', *Journal of the Royal Society of Medicine* 84: 460–5.

Goldstein, L. H. and Polkey, C. E. (1992a) 'Behavioural memory after temporal lobectomy or amygdalo-hippocampectomy', *British Journal of Clinical Psychology* 31: 75–81.

—— (1992b) 'Everyday memory after unilateral temporal lobectomy and amygdalo-hippocampectomy', *Cortex* 28: 189–201.

—— (1993) 'Short-term cognitive changes after unilateral temporal lobectomy or unilateral anygdalo-hippocampectomy for the relief of temporal lobe epilepsy', *Journal of Neurology, Neurosurgery and Psychiatry* 56: 135–40.

Goldstein, L. H., Patel, V., Aspinall, P. and Lishman, W. A. (1992) 'The effect of anti-convulsants on cognitive functioning following a probable encephalitic illness', *British Journal of Psychiatry* 160: 546–9.

Helmstaedter, C., Pohl, C., Hufnagel, A. and Elger, C. E. (1991) 'Visual learning deficits in nonresected patients with right temporal lobe epilepsy', *Cortex* 27: 547–55.

Hermann, B. P., Wyler, A. R. and Richey, E. T. (1988a) 'Wisconsin Card Sorting Test performance in patients with complex partial seizures of temporal lobe origin', *Journal of Clinical and Experimental Neuropsychology* 10: 467–76.

Hermann, B. P., Wyler, A. R., Steenman, H. and Richey, E. T. (1988b) 'The interrelationship between language function and verbal learning/memory performance in patients with complex partial seizures', *Cortex* 24: 245–53.

Hermann, B. P., Seidenberg, M., Haltiner, A. and Wyler, A. R. (1992) 'Adequacy of language function and verbal memory performance in unilateral temporal lobe epilepsy', *Cortex* 28: 423–33.

Horner, M. D., Flashman, L. A., Freides, D., Epstein, C. M. and Bakay, R. A. (1996) 'Temporal lobe epilepsy and performance on the Wisconsin Card Sorting Test', *Journal of Clinical and Experimental Neuropsychology* 18: 310–13.

Jones-Gotman, M. (1987) 'Commentary: Psychological evaluation – testing hippocampal function', in J. Engel Jnr (ed.) *Surgical Treatment of the Epilepsies*, New York: Raven Press.

Kälviäinen, R., Äikiä, M., Helkala, E-L., Mervaala, E. and Riekkinen, P. J. (1992) 'Memory and attention in newly diagnosed epileptic seizure disorder', *Seizure* 1: 255–62.

Kasteleijn-Nolst Trenité, D. G. A., Bakker, D. J., Binnie, C. D., Buerman, A. and van Raaij, M. (1988) 'Psychological effects of subclinical epileptiform discharges. I: Scholastic skills', *Epilepsy Research* 2: 116–8.

Kasteleijn-Nolst Trenité, D. G. A., Sieblink, B. M., Berends, S. G. C., van Strien, J. W. and Meinardi, H. (1990) 'Lateralised effects of subclinical epileptiform EEG discharges on scholastic performance in children', *Epilepsia* 31: 740–6.

Lee, G. P., Loring, D. W. and Thompson, J. L. (1989) 'Construct validity of material-specific memory measures following unilateral temporal lobe ablations', *Psychological Assessment* 1: 192–7.

Loiseau, P., Strube, E., Broustet, D., Battelochi, S., Gomeni, C. and Morselli, P. L. (1983) 'Learning impairment of epileptic patients', *Epilepsia* 24: 183–92.

Loring, D. W., Lee, G. P., Martin, R. C. and Meador, K. J. (1988) 'Material specific learning in patients with partial complex seizures of temporal lobe origin: convergent validation of memory constructs', *Journal of Epilepsy* 1: 53–9.

—— (1989) 'Verbal and visual memory index discrepancies from the Wechsler Memory Scale-Revised: cautions in interpretation', *Psychological Assessment* 1: 198–202.

McGlone, J. (1994) 'Memory complaints before and after lobectomy: do they predict memory performance or lesion laterality?' *Epilepsia* 35: 529–39.

McMillan, T. M., Powell, G. E., Janota, I. and Polkey, C. E. (1987) 'Relationships between neuropathology and cognitive functioning in temporal lobectomy patients', *Journal of Neurology, Neurosurgery and Psychiatry* 50: 167–76.

Mayeux, R., Brandt, J., Rosen, J. and Benson, D. F. (1980) 'Interictal memory and language impairment in temporal lobe epilepsy', *Neurology* 30: 120–5.

Morris, R. G. M., Abrahams, S., Baddeley, A. D. and Polkey, C. E. (1995) 'Doors and People: visual and verbal memory following unilateral temporal lobectomy'. *Neuropsychology* 9: 464–9.

Mungas, D., Ehlers, C., Walton, N. and McCutchen, C. B. (1985) 'Verbal learning differences in epileptic patients with left and right temporal lobe foci', *Epilepsia* 26: 340–5.

Ossetin, J. (1988) 'Methods and problems in the assessment of cognitive function in epileptic patients', in M. R. Trimble and E. H. Reynolds (eds) *Epilepsy, Behaviour and Cognitive Function*, Chichester: Wiley.

Provinciali, L., Signorino, M., Censori, B., Ceravolo, G. and Del Pesce, M. (1991) 'Recognition impairment correlated with short bisynchronous epileptic discharges', *Epilepsia* 32: 684–9.

Randolf, C., Golds, J. M., Zorora, E., Cullum, C. M., Hermann, B. P. and Wyler, A. (1994) 'Estimating memory function: disparity of Wechsler Memory Scale-Revised and California Verbal Learning Test indices in clinical and normal samples', *The Clinical Neuropsychologist* 8: 99–108.

Ribbler, A. and Rausch, R. (1990) 'Performance of patients with unilateral temporal lobectomy on selective reminding procedures using either related or unrelated words', *Cortex* 26: 575–84.

Rugland, A-L., Henriksen, O. and Bjørnes, H. (1991) 'Computer-assisted neuropsychological assessment in patients with epilepsy', in W. E. Dodson, M. Kinsbourne and B. Hiltbrunner (eds) *The Assessment of Cognitive Function in Epilepsy*, New York: Demos.

Saling, M., O'Shea, M. and Berkovic, S. F. (1995) 'Verbal memory in temporal lobe epilepsy: cognitive influences on task-specific effects', *Epilepsia* 36 (Suppl. 3): S93–4.

Saling, M., Berkovic, S. F., O'Shea, M. F., Kalnins, R. M., Darby, D. G. and Bladin, P. F. (1993) 'Lateralisation of verbal memory and unilateral hippocampal sclerosis: evidence of task-specific effects', *Journal of Clinical and Experimental Neuropsychology* 15: 608–18.

Sass, K. J., Spencer, D. D., Kim, J. H. Westerveld, M., Novelly, R. A. and Lencz, T. (1990) 'Verbal memory impairment correlates with hippocampal pyramidal cell density', *Neurology* 40: 1694–7.

Sass, K. J., Sass, A., Westerveld, M., Lencz, T., Rosewater, K. M., Novelly, R. A., Kim, J. H. and Spencer, D. D. (1992a) 'Russell's adaptation of the Wechsler Memory Scale as an index of hippocampal pathology', *Journal of Epilepsy* 5: 24–30.

Sass, K. J., Sass, A., Westerveld, M., Lencz, T., Novelly, R. A., Kim, J. H. and Spencer, D. D. (1992b) 'Specificity in the correlation of verbal memory and hippocampal neuronal loss: dissociation of memory, language and verbal intellectual ability', *Journal of Clinical and Experimental Neuropsychology* 14: 662–72.

Seidenberg, M., Beck, N., Geisser, M., Giordani, B., Sackellares, J. C., Berent, S., Dreifuss, F. E. and Boll, T. J. (1986) 'Academic achievement of children with epilepsy', *Epilepsia* 27: 753–9.

Seidenberg, M., Haltiner, A., Taylor, M. A., Hermann, B. B. and Wyler, A. (1994) 'Development and validation of a Multiple Ability Self-Report Questionnaire', *Journal of Clinical and Experimental Neuropsychology* 16: 93–104.

Seidenberg, M., Hermann, B., Haltiner, A. and Wyler, A. (1993) 'Verbal recognition memory performance in unilateral temporal lobe epilepsy', *Brain and Language* 44: 191–200.

Seidenberg, M., Hermann, B., Noe, A. and Wyler, A. R. (1995) 'Depression in temporal lobe epilepsy: interaction between laterality of lesion and Wisconsin Card Sort Performance', *Neuropsychiatry, Neuropsychology and Behavioural Neurology* 8: 81–7.

Seidenberg, M., O'Leary, D. C., Berent, S. and Boll, T. (1981) 'Changes in seizure frequency and test-retest scores in the WAIS', *Epilepsia* 22: 75–83.

Selwa, L. M., Berent, S., Giordani, B., Henry, T. R., Buchtel, H. A. and Ross, D. A. (1994) 'Serial cognitive testing in temporal lobe epilepsy: longitudinal changes with medical and surgical therapies', *Epilepsia* 35: 743–9.

Sieblink, B. M., Bakker, D. J., Binnie, C. D. and Kasteleijn-Nolst Trenité, D. G. A. (1988) 'Psychological effects of subclinical epileptiform EEG discharges in children II. General intelligence tests', *Epilepsy Research* 2: 117–21.

Strauss, E., Hunter, M. and Wada, J. (1993) 'Wisconsin Card Sorting performance: effects of age of onset of damage and laterality of dysfunction', *Journal of Clinical and Experimental Neuropsychology* 15: 896–902.

Strauss, E., Loring, D., Chelune, G., Hunter, M., Hermann, B., Perrine, K., Westerveld, M., Trenerry, M. and Barr, W. (1995) 'Predicting cognitive impairment in epilepsy: findings from the Bozeman epilepsy consortium', *Journal of Clinical and Experimental Neuropsychology* 17: 909–17.

Sunderland, A., Harris, J. E. and Baddeley, A. D. (1983) 'Do laboratory tests predict everyday memory? A neuropsychological study', *Journal of Verbal Learning and Verbal Behaviour* 22: 341–57.

Thompson, P. J. (1991) 'Integrating computerised and traditional neuropsychological assessment techniques', in W. E. Dodson, M. Kinsbourne and B. Hiltbrunner (eds) *The Assessment of Cognitive Function in Epilepsy*, New York: Demos.

Upton, D. and Thompson, P. J. (1996) 'General neuropsychological characteristics of frontal lobe epilepsy', *Epilepsy Research* 23: 169–77.

Westerveld, M., Sass, K. J., Sass, A. and Henry, H. G. (1994) 'Assessment of verbal memory in temporal lobe epilepsy using the selective reminding test: equivalence and reliability of alternate forms', *Journal of Epilepsy* 7: 57–63.

Williamson, P. D., French, J. A., Thadani, V. M., Kim, J. H., Novelly, R. A., Spencer, S. S., Spencer, D. D. and Mattson, R. H. (1993) 'Characteristics of medial temporal lobe epilepsy: II. Interictal and ictal scalp electroencephalography, neuropsychological testing, neuroimaging, surgical results and pathology', *Annals of Neurology* 34: 781–7.

Zigmond, A. S. and Snaith, R. P. (1983) 'The hospital anxiety and depression scale', *Acta Psychiatrica Scandinavica*, 67: 361–70.

Chapter 3

Epilepsy and memory

Pamela J. Thompson

MEMORY COMPLAINTS

An association between epilepsy and memory disorders has been reported for centuries. Indeed, early commentators perceived memory decline as an inevitable consequence of having seizures:

> unless the disease be arrested we soon discover that the intellectual faculties begin to fail. The memory is one of the first that shows impairment.
>
> (Sieveking 1861)

Today, while memory difficulties are not seen as an invariable symptom of epilepsy, complaints of disturbed memory represent the most frequently reported cognitive problem by patients. Broughton *et al.* (1984) reported that 50 per cent of a sample of outpatients with epilepsy complained of significant memory problems. In a larger survey involving 760 people with epilepsy we found 54 per cent rated their memory as a moderate or severe nuisance. This contrasted with a nuisance rating of 23 per cent in a control group (Thompson and Corcoran 1992).

A complaint of poor memory, however, may represent different things to different people. In our survey, this became clear from the individual comments made by participants. For instance, one woman wrote of her memory:

> Events that happen involving me which stick out in other people's minds, I have no recollection of at all much to the surprise of friends because that particular event could only have been a year ago.

Another person commented:

> Much can be done to hide the memory problems but the difficulty of

remembering names is so embarrassing and it makes socialising difficult.

All participants in our study completed a questionnaire relating to the frequency of everyday memory failures. The major difficulties reported by subjects and their observers were similar in the epilepsy and the control group, although the frequency was greater for the respondents with epilepsy. The most troublesome failure reported was the 'tip of the tongue' phenomenon, followed by having to go back to check and then losing items (Thompson and Corcoran 1992). Inspection of the responses suggested other cognitive problems, including language difficulties and organisational problems, may underlie or contribute to some of the reported difficulties. Even where a breakdown of memory underlies everyday failures, many different types of deficit might be implicated, as memory is not a unitary phenomenon (see Table 3.1; Baddeley *et al.* 1995).

Most of the formal studies of memory functioning in epilepsy have involved assessing the formation of long-term memories. The majority of these report some impairments in epilepsy groups compared to controls or normative test data. For instance, Halgren and colleagues (1991) report findings from sixty-one general neuropsychological referrals. Twenty-three were reported as having selective memory deficits for verbal or non-verbal material, while twelve were assessed to have a global memory deficit. In an earlier, larger study, Loiseau *et al.* (1988) also reported a high level of memory problems.

Table 3.1 Memory systems

Name	Characteristic
Episodic	Memory for personally experienced events
Short-term memory	Small capacity < 30 sec
Long-term memory	Vast capacity > 30 sec
Semantic	Stored knowledge about the world = facts, rules, concepts, independent of time
Implicit/Procedural	Acquisition and recollection does not require conscious recall, e.g. motor skills
Remote Memory	Experiences from distant past
Prospective Memory	Remembering to do things in the future

RISK FACTORS

Investigators have attempted to assess what factors place individuals with epilepsy at risk for memory difficulties.

Aetiology

Brain damage is probably the most potent factor underlying memory problems. Epilepsy can be caused by a variety of pathological processes (see Chapter 1). Some of these clearly cause memory impairments independently of seizures. With improved neuroimaging techniques, an increasing number of cases are found to have brain pathology, for example, cortical dysgenesis and hippocampal sclerosis.

Not surprisingly, pathologies involving temporal lobe structures have been most frequently associated with memory deficits and laterality of pathology with material specific memory deficits. Although this theme is developed further in Chapters 2 and 4, the most consistent finding is a verbal memory deficit in association with dominant temporal lobe pathology (Hermann *et al.* 1987); some authors report deficits with right sided cases, although this is less consistently reported (Helmstaedter *et al.* 1991; Cohen 1992).

Type of epilepsy

Early studies reported that patients with complex partial seizures of temporal lobe origin were more impaired on tests of memory than individuals with generalised epilepsy. This finding may well be related to the underlying pathology, but also to other aspects of the seizure disorder. In our recent research, individuals with frontal lobe epilepsy demonstrated memory disturbance on formal testing. The memory test performance of seventy-four patients with frontal lobe epilepsy was compared with fifty-seven patients with temporal lobe epilepsy. Memory tests included measures of recall, learning and recognition for both verbal and visuospatial information. The scores on the verbal version of the Recognition Memory Test significantly differentiated the groups, although scores on other memory measures did not. Furthermore, the left frontal and right temporal groups were equally impaired on the Design Learning test from the Adult Memory and Information Processing Battery.

Age at onset and duration

Early studies reported an inverse relationship between age at onset and impairment on memory tests. Dikmen *et al.* (1975) studied two groups of patients who were matched for duration and frequency of tonic clonic seizures, but differed with regard to age at onset. Patients with onset below five years were more impaired on the majority of tasks. Kalska (1991) reported that subjects whose epilepsy started below ten years had lower memory quotients and lower IQs than those with later onset.

Some studies have not found any relationship between age of onset and memory function (Delaney *et al.* 1980; Halgren *et al.* 1991; Hermann *et al.* 1988). Loiseau *et al.* (1988) found that onset during adolescence was associated with the greatest risk of memory impairment. Corcoran and Thompson (1993) noted patients who complained most about their memory were significantly older at seizure onset than patients who did not complain. Halgren *et al.* (1991) found that twelve patients with a global memory deficit were seventeen years older when they developed epilepsy than patients with normal memory.

The duration of epilepsy is obviously related to the age of onset. Delaney *et al.* (1980) reported longer duration of epilepsy was associated with greater impairments on memory tests. Hermann and colleagues (1988) did not find any relationship between tests of verbal memory and duration of epilepsy. Clearly, the impact of these variables will be influenced by other factors such as aetiology and seizure control (see also Chapter 2 for further discussion).

Seizures

Memory loss for the duration of a seizure is a feature of most complex partial and generalised attacks. Where seizures occur several times daily, they may be expected to disrupt an individual's ability to register information and form memories for ongoing events.

Disturbances of memory may also arise in association with brief epileptic discharges, so called subclinical seizures, which may have no visible features but are detectable on EEG recordings. This has also been discussed in Chapter 2. These can occur frequently, with hundreds or thousands of episodes a day. Clearly, in such cases, disruption of memory and other functions is to be expected. Furthermore, there is some evidence that epileptic discharges from mesial temporal structures detectable only via implanted depth electrodes have a disruptive impact on memory. Bridgeman *et al.* (1989) reported five patients who underwent memory testing while such discharges were recorded during implantation. Impairments were noted on memory tests, but not on other measures of cognitive functioning.

There are reports in the literature of amnesic seizures, defined as recurrent paroxysmal memory loss with an alteration in consciousness. During the attack the person appears normal and continues activities, including speaking, and personal identity would be retained. Such episodes, however are reported retrospectively and may be difficult to distinguish from transient global amnesia (Kapur 1993).

Recovery from seizures can be variable and in some individuals, neuropsychological assessment undertaken in close proximity to complex partial seizures or generalised attacks may underestimate an individual's memory functioning. Halgren et al. (1991) described how patients assessed as much as two days following a bout of complex partial seizures performed significantly less well on tests of learning and memory than two weeks following the episodes (see also Chapter 2).

Whether seizures themselves accelerate forgetting, however, is less clear. In a recent investigation we attempted to explore this issue (Bergin et al. 1995). Fifty-eight patients with refractory partial seizures under-going video EEG telemetry were administered memory tests shortly after the telemetry commenced; memory was reassessed two days later. Thirty patients had at lease one seizure during this period. Patients who had seizures forgot no more than patients who had no seizures. There was no correlation between memory performance and the timing of seizures, or the number of seizures. These findings indicate isolated seizures do not generally cause patients to forget material they have recently learned.

Other research studies have assessed the relationship between esti-mates of seizure frequency and memory test performance. Loiseau et al. (1983) divided 200 subjects into those who had been seizure free for two or more years, those with no more than one seizure in the past two years, and finally those who had had twelve or more seizures in the past year. The authors concluded that seizure frequency analysed in this way was not a factor which influenced memory ability.

Kalska (1991) reported little memory decline in a longitudinal study with a ten year follow-up. During the course of the study, 40 per cent of the patients experienced generalised seizures, twenty-one had ten or fewer seizures and seven patients did not have any seizures. All patients underwent seven subtests of the Wechsler Memory Scale. The mean initial Wechsler Memory Quotient was 91.9 and at ten years 96.8.

Improvement occurred in 30.4 per cent of the patients, while only 5.8 per cent deteriorated.

In addition to Dodrill's (1986) finding that patients who had experienced more than one hundred tonic-clonic seizures, or who had experienced an episode of convulsive *status epilepticus*, performed less well than other patients on a variety of tests, including some measures of memory, Treiman and Delgado-Escueta (1983) reported patients experiencing severe memory problems after an episode of non-convulsive status. One case, a 53-year-old man, experienced a week-long episode of complex partial status after abrupt discontinuation of carbamazepine. Even four months later he had severe memory problems. Victor and Agamamolis (1990) reported a 65-year-old man who suffered an episode of generalised *status epilepticus*. On recovery, he was found to have a moderately severe anterograde and retrograde amnesia which persisted until he died thirty months later.

During absence and partial *status epilepticus*, a range of cognitive disturbances have been reported. Outwardly, an individual may not seem to be behaving too abnormally. Detailed assessment, however, can reveal gross memory disturbance. Such states are more frequent than previously thought; as many as fifteen per cent of individuals with intractable epilepsy may experience at least one episode (Shorvon 1994).

Individuals with atonic and tonic seizures are at risk for head injuries resulting from their seizures. Over time, repeated minor head injuries result in changes in brain function, particularly of the frontal regions which may produce memory deficits. In patients with intractable epilepsy, we have found an association between head injuries and deterioration in intellectual ability and memory.

Anti-epileptic drugs

In recent years there has been much research on the effects of anti-epileptic drugs on cognitive abilities, including memory functioning. Overall, medication in high dosages or when prescribed in combination may influence test performance, although it is the author's impression that this is secondary to more general cognitive effects rather than a specific effect on memory processing (Thompson and Trimble 1996; this volume Chapter 5).

Surgery

A number of surgical options exist for patients with intractable epilepsy. Temporal lobectomy represents the most frequently undertaken procedure and research exists spanning many decades on its impact on memory functioning. (Thompson and Trimble 1996; this volume Chapter 4).

Mood

Depressed mood and elevated levels of anxiety have been reported in patients with epilepsy. There is evidence from other psychological research that negative mood can have an impact on neuropsychological test performance (Calev et al. 1986). We have found higher levels of depression to be a predictor of poor memory test performance, particularly on measures of verbal recall (Corcoran and Thompson 1993).

OTHER MEMORY STUDIES

Remote memory

Surprisingly little research has been undertaken assessing the ability of patients with epilepsy to retrieve past memories. Ratti et al. (1992) tested fifteen patients with temporal lobe epilepsy on a remote memory questionnaire, and compared their response with fifteen controls matched for age and educational level. The authors report that remote memory was impaired in the epilepsy group, with no difference between patients with right or left temporal lobe seizures. Barr et al. (1990) tested remote memory in patients who had undergone anterior temporal lobe resections. Subjects were tested for recognition of famous faces, recognition of names of television programmes, recall of generic and specific factual knowledge and memory for public events that had occurred after the subjects had reached the age of ten. They were also given questions relating to autobiographical knowledge. The left temporal lobectomy group performed significantly less well than the right lobectomy and control groups.

Upton et al. (1992) tested autobiographical remote memory in thirty-five patients with the Autobiographical Memory Interview (AMI; Kopelman et al. 1989). In this investigation, no significant correlation was found between memory test performance and subjective ratings of memory competence scores. The data were not analysed in regard to seizure variables such as nature or frequency of attacks. Tests of autobiographical memory such as the AMI provide a qualitative assessment of the richness of an individual's memories. It can be difficult, however, to verify answers or quantify the amount of detail remembered. Furthermore, many questions on the AMI do not have relevance for younger subjects as it was standardised on an older sample (mean age 55 years).

Bergin *et al.* (in preparation) recently explored the performance of three groups of patients with epilepsy on a remote memory questionnaire. The questionnaire assessed knowledge of public events which had occurred since 1980. The epilepsy groups comprised thirty-three patients with temporal lobe seizures, thirty-three with extratemporal lobe seizures and ten with primary generalised seizures. Thirty control subjects were also tested. Patients with temporal lobe epilepsy performed significantly less well on the questionnaire than all other groups. Patients with extratemporal primary generalised epilepsy did not differ from controls. Performance on the questionnaire was not determined by verbal IQ, educational achievement or drug treatment, but was related to the number of generalised convulsions which had occurred since 1980. Moderate correlations existed between scores on the questionnaire and performance on tests of verbal memory.

Prospective memory

In our survey of everyday memory problems in epilepsy, it was clear from replies received that patients reported some prospective memory errors, for example, forgetting to undertake tasks they had intended to do, and forgetting to take their tablets. This is probably a common sort of memory complaint which subjects volunteer to their clinicians. Prospective memory is very important, but it is seldom tested clinically in patients with epilepsy. This is partly because it is logistically difficult to devise tests that match the complexities of real life situations.

Bergin and colleagues (in preparation) studied forty patients with intractable temporal lobe seizures who were undergoing a period of video EEG telemetry as part of their pre-surgical assessment programme. The prospective memory task given to the subjects was to answer a written question regarding likely seizure occurrence at four predetermined times (9.30, 12.30, 3.30 and 6.30). Patients were asked to fill in the chart as close as possible to the allocated time. Completion of the task was undertaken in full view of the camera and video tapes were subsequently reviewed to determine when charts were filled in. A scoring system in percentages was devised, with patients gaining maximum points if they made the entry within ten minutes of the appropriate time, and with a reduction in score with time elapsed from this time. Three patients failed to make any predictions and all subsequently confirmed that they had understood the requirements of the study but had completely forgotten about the task. Twenty-five patients scored more than 50 per cent, and the remaining twelve patients less than this.

All three patients who failed to make any prediction had right temporal lobe epilepsy, and patients with right temporal lobe epilepsy as a group tended to perform more poorly than other patient groups. Eighteen patients had one or more seizures during the three-hour period immediately preceding the scheduled entry. The likelihood of the chart being completed, however, was not affected by a seizure occurring during this time period. Indeed, twelve of the patients actually scored as well or better for the entries after an attack than they did following periods when they did not have seizures. Patients who reported weak memory in response to three everyday memory questions tapping memory tended to perform poorly on the prospective task described above. No control group was included in the study; this would have been logistically difficult. For this reason, we have no evidence regarding the efficacy of our patients' memory in relation to other individuals.

Memory questionnaire studies

Some studies have explored memory functioning in epilepsy using subjective questionnaires via which the respondents report the nature and frequency or severity of everyday failures. We use a version of the Everyday Memory Questionnaire (EMQ) devised by Sunderland et al. (1983) in our studies referred to in this chapter. Bennett-Levy et al. (1980) employed the Subjective Memory Questionnaire (SMQ) in patients who had undergone unilateral temporal lobectomy. Patients rated their memory as poorer than controls.

Memory questionnaires, however, have been criticised as only weak correlations are reported with more traditional neuropsychological tests (Hermann 1984). We found a significant relationship between the EMQ and measures of verbal recall, but not with other memory measures (Corcoran and Thompson 1993). However, memory questionnaire content does not always seem to be tapping the same functions as memory tests and a better relationship has been reported between questionnaire scores and more behavioural measures of memory (Goldstein and Polkey 1992).

REHABILITATION

There are few research studies in the literature which focus upon the effectiveness of rehabilitation. This seems surprising given the importance of an efficient memory for the optimum management of a person's epilepsy. Patients have to remember appointments, to take tablets, to document seizure frequency and to monitor the effectiveness of treatment. If an individual's memory is unreliable, then the physician may be presented with a less than accurate picture of the individual's seizure control on clinic visits. People with epilepsy may be a good target for memory training as generally memory problems are less devastating than for amnesic cases, which have been the main focus of studies in the rehabilitation literature. In addition, patients with epilepsy generally retain insight into their difficulties. Many people with epilepsy live independently and are less likely than more severely affected patients to have a 'carer' at hand to act as an external support for a weak memory.

Reports on memory training in epilepsy are scarce. Aldenkamp and Vermeulen (1991) report group sessions which involve training in the use of memory aids. The group met for six sessions every two weeks. The authors note that the nature of the group changed over time, initially being quite didactic and later taking on a more supportive therapeutic role. Small improvements in memory functioning were noted, but the authors conclude that even small changes in memory can result in a significant increase in a person's level of independence.

Corcoran and Thompson (in press) have undertaken a study which explored the usefulness of a self-help manual based on the nature of a patient's own memory complaints. Within the study, they explored whether a tailor-made self-help memory manual was effective and whether there was any advantage to having some therapist contact as part of the programme. Twenty-seven subjects participated in the study. All had rated their memory as being a moderate or serious nuisance in a previous study. An eighteen-item checklist of everyday memory failures was used as the main outcome measure and also a relative or an individual who came into daily contact with the subjects completed comparable memory scales. In addition, rating scales of mood were employed. The outcome of the intervention was a little disappointing, as not all of the subjects completed the various parts of the study.

Overall, it did seem certain patients benefited more than others. In particular, those individuals reporting moderate memory difficulties seemed better able to utilise the memory training strategies outlined than individuals who had serious memory problems and those who were depressed.

MEMORY ASSESSMENT

The nature of any memory assessment will depend on the question being asked. This may relate to whether a memory deficit exists which is compatible with a known lesion, or with electrophysiological lateralising data in a prospective surgical candidate (Chapter 4). The question may relate to whether a drug-induced memory difficulty exists (Chapter 5). In this chapter, I will focus on memory assessment in an individual who is complaining of memory problems, with a view to some rehabilitative input.

Where there is any concern that ongoing epileptic activity may be a relevant factor, memory testing is best undertaken with simultaneous EEG recording. Furthermore, to obtain a measure of an individual's emotional state, a screening questionnaire of mood is useful. We routinely employ the Hospital Anxiety and Depression Scale (Zigmond and Snaith 1983).

Assessment for rehabilitation purposes needs to include a broad range of measures of memory. It will be important to look at what aspects of memory are impaired, if any, but more important to see what system or systems may be working well. The majority of memory tests available to the clinician measure the learning and retention of new information (Baddeley *et al.* 1995; this volume, Chapter 2). Focusing on the formation of new memories, measures employed should tap immediate and delayed registration of material and also learning capacity over trials. Ideally, this should include memory for different types of material, although usually this is limited to verbal and visuospatial information. A drawback of many of the available tests is that few are available in more than two parallel forms which reduces the reliability of repeated assessments.

Below are a number of commercially available tests (mentioned also in Chapters 2 and 4). We routinely employ the Adult Information Processing Battery and the Recognition Memory Test. More details, therefore, are given for these measures.

The Wechsler Memory Scale – Revised (WMS-R)

The Wechsler Memory Scale represents the most widely-used memory test battery. The original version was criticised on a number of grounds, and the scale has been revised and many of the shortcomings have been addressed, but only one version of the test is available.

Recognition Memory Test

This recognition memory test is quite widely used in the UK. It has two subtests, one involving memory for words and one for faces. The test is easy to administer and the recognition paradigm has an advantage over measures of learning and recall in that test performance is less suscep-tible to the adverse influence of anxiety and depression. Weaknesses of the test include the photographic detail that could be coded verbally (Kapur 1987), the tendency for subjects to perform close to ceiling level on the verbal version (Mayes 1995), and recent evidence that the word or face discrepancy scores do not necessarily discriminate between right- and left-sided temporal lobe lesions (Morris *et al.* 1995a).

The Adult Memory and Information Processing Battery

This test consists of four measures of memory and two of concentra-tion and information processing. The measures of memory can be subdivided into those tapping verbal memory (prose recall and word list learning) and non-verbal memory (abstract design recall and abstract design learning). The verbal learning test uses the same format as the Rey Auditory Verbal Learning Test. The entire battery is available in two versions and the measures of design retention and story retention have a delayed recall component. Norms for a UK sample are available, although there is some criticism that the standardisation sample is rather small.

The California Verbal Learning Test

This test provides a number of measures, not only of learning capacity, but also of organising strategies and susceptibility to different kinds of interference. There is also a recognition measure.

The Rivermead Behavioural Memory Test

Designed to have more ecological validity than most other memory tests, subtests of this measure include recalling a name, story recall, recognition of faces and of pictures, route learning and recall in addition to questions on personal orientation. It is not specifically materially sensitive however to lateralised temporal lobe lesions (Goldstein and Polkey 1992).

Doors and People Test

This new battery provides measures of learning, recall and recognition of visual and verbal material. Data relating to its sensitivity in surgically-treated patients with epilepsy are now available (Morris *et al.* 1995b).

Other tests

Whichever memory measures are selected, they should never be administered in isolation. It is necessary to assess other aspects of cognitive functioning, including language ability, perceptual skills and organisational and attentional capacity. Reported memory deficits may be secondary to other problems such as organisational difficulties. In addition, if rehabilitative input is being planned, then a memory deficit may be reduced when other cognitive resources are assessed to be well developed.

Remote memory

Adequate assessment of remote memory is difficult and there are fewer tests available.

Autobiographical Memory Interview (AMI)

This measure consists of two subtests. One taps personal memories, including facts about background, childhood, young adulthood and the recent past. Questions include names of schools attended, friends, addresses, journeys, and so forth. The second part focuses on autobiographical incidents and taps event memory using a cuing technique.

The Dead or Alive Test

This is a measure of memory for famous people. Subjects have to indicate whether a given person is dead or alive, and if dead, to indicate how and when they died. Currently it includes famous people from the 1960s to the 1990s (Kapur *et al.* 1989).

Memory questionnaires

A useful complement to memory assessment is the administration of an everyday memory questionnaire. We routinely employ one originally designed by Sunderland *et al.* (1983). Responses obtained provide an idea of the nature and extent of memory deficits experienced on a daily basis. A relatives' version also exists. Other questionnaires are mentioned in Chapter 2.

INTERVENTION

The results of any memory assessment need to be discussed with the patient and their family. This feedback in itself can have a beneficial impact. Individuals may be relieved by the confirmation that a memory difficulty does exist, but that it is not going to get progressively worse. For instance, this would be the case in an individual with well-controlled seizures, but with known left hippocampal sclerosis. For the young person who is struggling academically to achieve a standard comparable to their siblings, confirmation of a memory deficit may result in a reappraisal by the family and redirection to courses with little or no reliance on written examinations.

Sessions can be offered to focus on strategies which might help reduce the impact of a weak memory. Strategies are usually divided into internal and external measures (Baddeley *et al.* 1995). The former include the use of visual imagery whereby individuals may imagine mental pictures involving the information to be remembered. This can be useful in individuals with a verbal memory impairment, particularly where their assessed visual memory is good. Mental imagery can be helpful for remembering a few important names, for example, a bizarre image can be made in association with a name. Other visual strategies include the method of loci and the peg method. Verbal rhymes and first letter mnemonics may be helpful for some people. In general, internal strategies can be mentally taxing and, in my experience, patients find them difficult to employ in their everyday lives. However, it can be fun in rehabilitation sessions to focus on some of these strategies. For instance, a young woman with a post-surgical verbal memory deficit had great difficulty learning lists of words, even with repeated trials. She was, however, able to learn a list of ten things to do – such as go to the dentist, buy some pasta, return a book to the library, etc. – by utilising the method of loci. She would visualise the rooms in her parent's house and make a bizarre image in each room to do with the item to be remembered. Two months after this she was still able to recall all ten items!

External memory aids are the most widely used and are generally the most valuable for patients with epilepsy. Techniques can be divided into aids to assist information storage and cuing devices which prompt people to remember to do things. It is surprising how many patients with impaired memory do not use diaries. Training in the use of a diary or filofax can have a significant impact on their everyday lives. The young woman with the verbal memory deficit discussed above has significantly reduced the impact of her memory deficit by at least daily reference to her filofax. Another young man with significant memory difficulties found his handicap lessened by using a computerised diary and personal organiser.

One of the most valuable external memory aids for people with epilepsy is the drug wallet. Many people find this device helps them remember to take their tablets and also not to take too many. Drug wallets usually consist of seven small containers, one for each day of the week. The compartments can be filled once a week at set times. The seven individual containers are removable so that if the person goes out for the day they do not have to take the complete container with them. Drug wallets can be obtained from local chemists and are not expensive.

For others with memory difficulties, the results of the broader neuropsychological assessment may be of help. For instance, a young man who has a very weak memory, but who has good planning and organising abilities, undertook a year's residential placement which was aimed at improving his independent living skills. On his rehabilitation programme, explicit steps were taken to improve his memory by capitalising on his good organisational skills (see Appendix to this chapter).

CONCLUSIONS

Memory loss is a feature of most epileptic seizures. Many individuals with epilepsy experience difficulties inter-ictally, and complaints of poor memory represent the most frequent reason for a referral for a neuropsychological assessment. In this chapter, research studies were reviewed which have demonstrated memory difficulties in at least subgroups of patients. Most studies focus upon the ability to remember new information, with much less work exploring other aspects such as remote and prospective memory or the efficacy of rehabilitative work. In the second part of the chapter, assessment techniques were presented and rehabilitation strategies discussed. Much more rehabilitative work is needed to enable patients to reduce the negative impact of a memory deficit upon their capacity for independent living.

APPENDIX

An example of a memory rehabilitation programme

John has significant memory difficulties; he finds it hard to remember things he has done and things he has talked about. Despite this he possesses good planning and organisational skills.

Proposed management strategies

1 John is encouraged to take notes of key points of discussions during meetings so that he can remember the work he has done from one week to the next.
2 John now has a filofax/personal organiser which has been personally tailored. This includes the following sections:
   Programme sheets on which he records his daily activities alongside a record of his seizures.
   'Don't Forget' sheets on which he makes notes of things he needs/wants to remember to do.
   A section in which he records the actions he agrees to do during programme review meetings.
   A section in which he records key notes from meetings and work-shops.
   Accounts sheets on which he records his daily spending as part of his budget plan.
   Names, addresses and telephone numbers.
   John is encouraged to make frequent use of this organiser as a memory aid.
3 John has a number of identified places in which he keeps important papers/documents.

4 As John finds remembering large chunks of information difficult, important information should be presented in a simple, precise and sequenced way. Discussions should also be concluded by a summary of key points.
5 John needs structure to his day in order for things to become routine and so that the development of his organisational skills can be further encouraged.

REFERENCES

Aldenkamp, A. P. and Vermeulen, J. (1991) 'Neuropsychological rehabilitation of memory function in epilepsy', *Neuropsychological Rehabilitation* 1: 199–214.

Baddeley, A. D., Wilson, B. A. and Watts, F. N. (1995) *Handbook of Memory Disorders*, Chichester: Wiley.

Barr, W., Goldberg, E., Wasserstein, J. and Novelly, R. (1990) 'Retrograde amnesia following unilateral temporal lobectomy', *Neuropsychologia* 28: 243–55.

Bennett-Levy, J., Polkey, C. E. and Powell, G. E. (1980) 'Self-report of memory skills after temporal lobectomy: the effects of clinical variables', *Cortex* 18: 513–57.

Bergin, P. S., Thompson, P. J., Fish, D. R. and Shorvon, S. D. (1995) 'The effect of seizures on memory for recently learned material', *Neurology* 45: 236–40.

—— (in preparation) 'Prospective memory in epilepsy'.

Bridgeman, P. A., Malamut, M. A., Sperling, M. R., Saykin, A. J. and O'Connor, M. J. (1989) 'Memory during subclinical hippocampal seizures', *Neurology* 39: 853–6.

Broughton, R. J., Goberman, A. A. and Roberts, J. (1984) 'Comparison for psychosocial effects of epilepsy and narcolepsy/cataplexy: a controlled study', *Epilepsia* 25: 423–33.

Calev, A., Konn, Y., Shapira, B., Kugelmass, S. and Lever, B. (1986). 'Verbal and non-verbal recall by depressed and euthymic affective patients', *Psychological Medicine* 16: 789–94.

Cohen, M. (1992) 'Auditory, verbal and visuospatial memory in children with complex partial epilepsy of temporal lobe origin', *Brain and Cognition* 20: 325–6.

Corcoran, R. and Thompson, P. (1993) 'Epilepsy and poor memory. Who complains and what do they mean?', *British Journal of Clinical Psychology* 32: 199–208.

—— (in press) 'Memory difficulties in epilepsy: assessing the benefit of self-help procedures', *Seizure*.

Delaney, R. C., Rosen, A. J., Mattson, R. H. and Novelly, R. A. (1980) 'Memory function in focal epilepsy: a comparison of non-surgical, unilateral and temporal lobe and frontal lobe samples', *Cortex* 16: 103–17.

Dikmen, S., Matthews, C. G. and Harley, J. P. (1975) 'The effect of early versus late onset of major motor epilepsy upon cognitive intellectual performance', *Epilepsia* 16: 73–81.

Dodrill, C. B. (1986) 'Correlates of generalised tonic clonic seizures with intellectual, neuropsychological, emotional and social function in patients with epilepsy', *Epilepsia* 27: 399–411.

Goldstein, L. H. and Polkey, C. E. (1992) 'Behavioural memory after temporal lobectomy or amygdalo-hippocampectomy', *British Journal of Clinical Psychology* 31: 75–82.

Halgren, E., Stapleton, J., Domalski, T., Swartz, B. E., Delgado-Escueta, A. V. and Walsh, G. O. (1991) 'Memory dysfunction in epilepsy: patient as a derangement of normal physiology', in D. Smith, D. Treiman and M. Trimble (eds) *Advances in Neurology, Vol. 55: Neurobehavioural Problems in Epilepsy*, New York: Raven Press.

Helmstaedter, C., Pohl, C., Hufnagel, A. and Elger, C. E. (1991) 'Visual learning deficits in non-resected patients with right temporal lobe epilepsy', *Cortex* 27: 547–55.

Hermann, D. J. (1984) 'Questionnaires about memory', in J. E. Harris and P. E. Morris (eds) *Everyday Memory, Actions and Absent-mindedness*, London: Academic Press.

Hermann, B., Wyler, A., Richey, E. and Rea, J. (1987) 'Memory function and verbal learning ability in patients with complex partial seizures of temporal lobe origin', *Epilepsia* 28: 547–54.

Hermann, B. P., Wyler, A. R., Steenman, H. and Richet, E. T. (1988) 'The interrelationship between language function and verbal learning/memory performance in patients with complex partial seizures', *Cortex* 24: 245–53.

Kalska, K. (1991) 'Cognitive changes in epilepsy. A ten year follow-up', in L. Nordberg (ed.) *The Finnish Society of Sciences and Letters. Commentationes Screntarun Socialium* 44.

Kapur, N. (1987) 'Some comments on the technical acceptability of Warrington's Recognition Memory Test', *British Journal of Clinical Psychology* 26: 144–6.

—— (1993) 'Transient epileptic amnesia – a clinical update and reformulation', *Journal of Neurology, Neurosurgery and Psychiatry* 56: 1184–90.

Kapur, N., Young, A., Bateman, D. and Kennedy, P. (1989) 'A long term clinical and neuropsychological follow-up of focal retrograde amnesia'. *Cortex* 25: 671–80.

Kopelman, M. D., Wilson, B. A. and Baddeley, A. D. (1989) *Autobiographical Memory Interview*, Bury St Edmunds: Thames Valley Test Co.

Loiseau, P. and Signoret, J. L. (1988) 'Memory and epilepsy', in M. R. Trimble, and E. H. Reynolds (eds) *Epilepsy, Behaviour and Cognitive Function*, Chichester: Wiley.

Loiseau, P., Struber, E., Broustet, D., Battellochi, S., Gaueni, C. and Morselli, P. L. (1983) 'Learning impairment in epileptic patients', *Epilepsia* 24: 183–92.

Mayes, A. (1995) 'The assessment of memory disorders', in A. D. Baddeley, B. A. Wilson and F. N. Watts (eds) *Handbook of Memory Disorders*, Chichester: Wiley.

Morris, R. G., Abrahams, S. and Polkey, C. E. (1995a) 'Recognition memory for words and faces following unilateral temporal lobectomy', *British Journal of Clinical Psychology* 34: 571–6.

Morris, R. G., Abrahams, S., Baddeley, A. D. and Polkey, C. E. (1995b) 'Doors and people: visual and verbal memory following unilateral temporal lobectomy', *Neuropsychology* 9: 464–9.

Ratti, M., Galimberti, C., Manni, R. and Tantara, A. (1992) 'Remote memory impairment in temporal lobe epilepsy', *Seizure* 1 (suppl. A): 14/11.
Shorvon, S. D. (1994) *Status Epilepticus. Its Causes and Treatment*, Cambridge: Cambridge University Press.
Sieveking, E. H. (1861) *On Epilepsy and Epileptiform Seizures*, London: John Churchill.
Sunderland, A., Harris, J. E. and Baddeley, A. D. (1983) 'Do laboratory tests predict everyday memory? A neuropsychological study', *Journal of Verbal Learning and Verbal Behaviour* 22: 341–57.
Thompson, P. J. and Corcoran, R. (1992) 'Everyday memory failures in people with epilepsy', *Epilepsia* 33 (Suppl. 6): S18–20.
Thompson, P. J. and Trimble, M. R. (1996) 'Neuropsychological aspects of epilepsy', in I. Grant and K. Adams (eds) *Assessment of Neuropsychiatric Disorders* (2nd edn), San Diego: Oxford University Press.
Treiman, D. M. and Delgado-Escueta, A. V. (1983) 'Complex partial status epilepticus', in A. V. Delgado-Escueta, C. G. Wasterlain, D. N. Treiman and R. J. Porter (eds) *Advances in Neurology. Vol. 34: Status Epilepticus*, New York: Raven Press.
Upton, D., Corcoran, R., Fowler, A. and Thompson, P. J. (1992) 'Autobiographical memory in epilepsy', *Seizure 1* (Suppl. A): 14/10.
Victor, M. and Agamamolis, D. (1990) 'Amnesia due to lesions consigned to the hippocampus: a clinical pathological study', *Journal of Cognitive Neuroscience* 34: 246–57.
Zigmond, A. S. and Snaith, R. P. (1983) 'The Hospital Anxiety and Depression Scale', *Acta Psychiatrica Scandinavica* 67: 361–70.

Chapter 4

Assessment for surgery

Susan Oxbury

INTRODUCTION

Of the 0.5 per cent of people with active epilepsy in the UK, 20 per cent continue to have seizures despite adequate treatment with anti-epileptic drugs. Of these, it is estimated that 30–40 per cent have focal seizures, i.e. about 15–20,000 people. Surgical treatment will be an option for some of them.

Focal seizures arise from over-activity in a group of neurones (the focus), which is often the site of structural pathology or abnormal brain tissue. Much of the surgical treatment of epilepsy is based on the concept that if the focus can be removed, the seizures will cease. Surgery is only offered to those people who have disabling, medically resistant seizures, (the definition of disabling will vary according to the individual's circumstances and lifestyle) and in whom removal of the pathology/epileptogenic zone will not cause unacceptable neurological or neuropsychological deficit.

Types of surgery

Various operations are increasingly being performed (see Table 4.1 compiled from Engel's (1993) published data). The first three operations in the table are designed to remove the source of the epilepsy, whereas corpus callosotomy is intended to interrupt fibres and hence to inhibit the spread of seizure activity.

The number of children included in Engel's survey is not reported. However, there is increasing emphasis on earlier surgery for epilepsy at younger ages in the hope of giving freedom from the deleterious effects of seizures and medication during the formative years.

Table 4.1 Numbers of surgical procedures carried out before 1985 and between 1986–1990

	Before 1985	1986-1990
Total operations	3,446	8,234
Types: Temporal lobe excisions	68%	67%
Extra-temporal excisions	24%	18%
Hemispherectomy	3%	5%
Corpus callosotomy	6%	10%

Pre-operative investigations

The offer of surgery depends upon the outcome of investigations undertaken by a multi-disciplinary team. Investigations are directed towards establishing firstly the probability that surgery will markedly reduce seizure frequency, and the likelihood of producing a deleterious effect on the patient's physical, cognitive and/or behavioural state. A wide range of investigations are available (Table 4.2). Which are used, depends upon various factors including the type of surgery under consideration, the probable nature of the pathology underlying the epilepsy syndrome, and the age and cognitive ability of the patient. Different epilepsy surgery groups use different investigational programmes (Engel and Ojemann 1993) but seem to achieve similar outcome from surgery.

The contributions of neuropsychological assessment and sodium amytal tests are discussed in detail below.

THE CONTRIBUTION OF NEUROPSYCHOLOGICAL ASSESSMENT

The aims of neuropsychological assessment in epilepsy surgery programmes are broadly: (a) to determine whether the neuropsychological profile is consistent with the lateralisation and localisation of the pathology and/or the epileptogenic area to be excised; (b) to predict the risk to memory and other cognitive functions of the proposed surgery; (c) to evaluate neuropsychological outcome; (d) to contribute information relevant to psychosocial or educational issues; and (e) for audit and research to further knowledge relating to all these issues. Most psychologists would agree that (b), the prediction of neuropsychological outcome

Table 4.2 Pre-operative investigations

Area of investigation	Types of investigation
Clinical Neurology (What is the nature of the epilepsy syndrome?)	Clinical History Physical Examination
Electroencephalography (Do seizures start from a consistent focus?)	Routine scalp recording – awake and asleep Recording with special extracranial electrode placements (e.g. sphenoidal) +/- drug activation Ictal recordings - ambulatory using cassette recorder - seizure/EEG correlation using video-telemetry with extracranial or intracranial extracerebral (subdural strips or extradural pegs or foramen ovale) or intracranial-intracerebral (depth) electrodes
Brain Imaging (Where is the pathology likely to underlie the epilepsy?)	Magnetic Resonance Imaging (MRI) - routine for gross pathology (e.g. tumour) - thin slice contiguous for 'subtle' pathology (e.g.dysplasia) and volumetrics - T2 relaxometry - spectroscopy Computerised Tomography (CT) - mainly for detecting calcification
Functional Imaging (Where are the focal metabolic brain changes associated with seizure onset?)	Single Photon Emission Computed Tomography (SPECT) - for detecting focus of seizure onset (increased uptake of isotope injected at seizure onset) Positron Emission Tomography (PET) using radioactive glucose - for detecting interictally hypometabolic cerebral areas indicative of dysfunction Functional Magnetic Resonance Imaging (MRI-f) - for mapping cortical areas subserving major functions (e.g. hand movement, language) - for mapping seizure onset zone
Neuropsychiatry (Are there pre-operative features which increase the risk of post-operative depression or psychosis?)	Clinical history
Neuropsychological Assessment	
Sodium Amytal Tests	Intracarotid injections Selective injections such as posterior cerebral artery

and the risks to cognitive and memory function, is a fundamental and crucial part of their role.

SPECIFIC SURGICAL INTERVENTIONS AND PRE- AND POST-OPERATIVE NEUROPSYCHOLOGY

Our knowledge of brain and behaviour relations has gained much from post-operative studies of cognitive function in patients who have undergone surgery for epilepsy. However, findings from post-operative studies alone cannot be taken to mean that impairment found post-operatively is always the result of surgery, since it may have been present before; or, on the other hand, that the same pattern must be apparent pre-operatively for the neuropsychological profile to be concordant with the site and side of the proposed surgery.

In this chapter, I shall concentrate on pre-operative neuropsychology and on those post-operative studies which include pre-operative assessment and are thus able to reflect change over operation, including the different surgeries for both adults and children.

Temporal lobe (TL) excisions

TL operations may differ in the extent of removal of neocortex and medial structures (hippocampus, amygdala, hippocampal gyrus). The most common procedure is en bloc anterior temporal lobectomy, whereby 4–6 cm of the anterior TL is excised together with medial structures in a single block. In some centres, removal is somewhat smaller in the language dominant side, sparing the superior temporal gyrus. Excisions may be tailored to the individual either by mapping EEG abnormalities and/or areas which disrupt language during surgery, or according to the presence of known pathological tissue. Selective amygdalohippocampectomy (SAH) removes the epileptogenic medial TL areas (hippocampus, amygdala and parahippocampal gyrus) with minimal disruption of neocortex. A small anterior lobectomy giving access to medial structures for removal is sometimes advocated (anteromesiotemporal lobectomy).

Intelligence

IQ is usually in the average range in TL surgery patients. Some centres have considered an IQ below seventy a contraindication to surgery as it suggests more widespread or multifocal damage and thus poor localisation of seizure onset, but this restriction is now less often applied.

Verbal/Performance IQ discrepancies do not consistently distinguish between left and right TL surgery patients (Hermann *et al.* 1995a; see also Chapter 2). Oxbury and Oxbury (1989) found that groups of patients with left or right hippocampal sclerosis (HS) had Performance IQ slightly but not significantly higher than Verbal IQ, with the difference somewhat greater in the left group. A large discrepancy in favour of Verbal IQ in a patient with left TL pathology is probably unusual.

Post-operatively modest increases in IQ may be observed, particularly when seizure outcome is good, possibly more frequently after non-dominant than dominant TL surgery. This may reflect improved function of the non-operated hemisphere (Powell *et al.* 1985).

Cerebral dominance and language function

Determining side of language dominance is important because atypical language dominance will influence interpretation of pre-operative neuropsychological findings and prediction of cognitive outcome from surgery, thereby affecting decisions about whether surgery is safe. It is accomplished by means of intracarotid sodium amytal testing (ISA), which is used routinely in TL surgery candidates in 80 per cent of centres (Snyder *et al.* 1990).

Approximately 90 per cent of right-handed TL patients, and 75 per cent of those with left- or mixed-hand preference, have left hemisphere language dominance (Loring *et al.* 1990). The others have either right hemisphere language dominance or bilateral language representation. The latter is inferred if there is significant language disturbance after both injections and is partly a matter of criteria for definition. It does not necessarily imply equal representation of language in both hemispheres, or that the same functions are represented in both hemispheres (Oxbury and Oxbury 1984; Snyder *et al.* 1990).

Temporal lobectomy candidates do not usually have clinically obvious language disturbance or dysphasia. When this is present, damage beyond anterior TL structures is possible. Some patients, prior to left temporal lobectomy, particularly those with severe HS, appear much less competent linguistically than visuospatially. However, some pre-operative comparisons of left and right TL groups have not revealed significant differences on the Boston Naming Test (BNT), verbal fluency or individual subtests of the Multi-lingual Aphasia Examination (MAE) (Davies *et al.* 1995; Hermann and Wyler 1988;

Hermann *et al.* 1991; Stafiniak *et al.* 1990), although Hermann and Wyler's left TL group was more impaired than the right when subtests were grouped (see also Chapter 2).

In general, lasting disturbance of language function does not follow dominant temporal lobectomy. Thus, Hermann and Wyler (1988) and Hermann *et al.* (1991) found no significant losses on the MAE, but improvement in the comprehension and verbal fluency subtests; Davies *et al.* (1995) found no loss on the BNT and improved verbal fluency. There may be a mild, usually brief, post-operative dysnomia immediately post surgery. Stafiniak *et al.* (1990) using the BNT reported significant decline at two to three weeks after left temporal lobectomy in patients without early risk to brain function (e.g. febrile convulsions, perinatal distress).

Six to 10 per cent of patients do, however, develop persistent aphasia after dominant temporal lobectomy (Pilcher *et al.* 1993). Mostly this is attributable to some people having language zones extending more anteriorly than others. Intra-operative functional mapping can define the anterior limit of the language zones so that the resection can then be tailored. Smaller lobectomies or SAH should also lessen the risk.

Memory

The importance of medial TL structures in anterograde memory function has long been established. The case of HM who developed severe and lasting amnesia after bilateral removal of these structures (Scoville and Milner 1957) is well known. It is also well established that laterality and material specific deficits are seen in patients after unilateral TL surgery. Thus, verbal memory deficits are reliably found in patients who have had left dominant operations (Frisk and Milner 1990) and non-verbal memory deficits in those who have had right non-dominant operations (Smith and Milner 1981), but less reliably so. The extent of hippocampal removal and the type of test paradigm are important factors related to these findings (Jones-Gotman 1991).

In recent years, TL epilepsy research has focused on two main questions. First, what is the status of memory function in patients with unilateral HS (Sagar and Oxbury 1987), since this is the most common single pathology underlying TL epilepsy, and can neuropsychological assessment aid in the diagnosis of this condition? Second, in what circumstances do aspects of memory deteriorate as a result of surgery and can this be avoided (Dodrill *et al.* 1993)? Verbal memory has been studied to a much greater extent than non-verbal memory. Verbal memory decline after left TL surgery may sometimes be quite marked and troublesome; in contrast, patients seldom complain of spatial memory impairment.

The first question can be addressed by investigating the relationship between pre-operative memory and *either* neuronal loss in the hippocampus, which can be established by histopathological examination of the excised specimen post-operatively, *or* by various hippocampal measures seen on pre-operative brain imaging (MRI). These methods have been reviewed by Baxendale (1995). Attempts to answer the second question have investigated the relationship between pre- and post-operative change in memory scores and such factors as pathology, extent and site of removal, pre-operative neuropsychological status and seizure outcome.

The specific nature of the task must be taken into account when considering the relationship between verbal memory and the laterality of HS (Saling *et al.* 1993). The tests most frequently used are those requiring recall of semantically related verbal material usually presented only once (story recall) and those involving learning over several trials of word pairs or word lists which include unrelated material. Several studies have reported no pre-operative difference in immediate or delayed story recall between groups with left or right HS, (McMillan *et al.* 1987; Oxbury and Oxbury 1989; Saling *et al.* 1993) or no relationship between prose recall and degree of HS in either left or right groups (reviewed by Saling *et al.* 1993), although the left HS group was inferior to the right on delayed recall in the study by Miller *et al.* (1993).

Some studies have examined the relationship using neuronal counts in specific hippocampal subfields. Sass *et al.* (1992) found no correlation between immediate and delayed story recall and hippocampal subfields, but in the left group per cent retained correlated with both CA3 and the hilar zones (see Figure 4.1). Matkovic *et al.* (1995a) found a correlation between delayed paragraph recall and CA1 in the right group. MRI hippocampal volume and story recall were not correlated in the study of Trenerry *et al.* (1993). Lencz *et al.* (1992) found a correlation with left hippocampal volume only for per cent retained.

Verbal learning tasks have been more promising in distinguishing patients with left or right HS. Thus, Matkovic *et al.* (1995a), Miller *et al.* (1993), Rausch and Babb (1993) and Saling *et al.* (1993) have all reported differences between left and right groups with varying degrees of HS on paired associate learning and Sass *et al.* (1994) on the Selective Reminding Test. Neuronal counts correlated with verbal

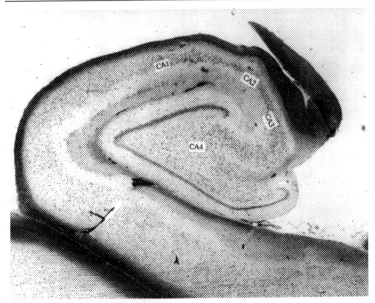

Figure 4.1   A photomicrograph of the hippocampus to show the subfields CA1, CA2, CA3 and CA4

learning in left hippocampus but not right: counts in CA3 and hilar (CA4) zones correlated with selective reminding (Sass *et al.* 1994); CA4 counts correlated with paired associate learning (Matkovic *et al.* 1995a). Although MRI volumes did not correlate with the Rey Auditory Verbal Learning or with the Selective Reminding Test (Trenerry *et al.* 1993; Lencz *et al.* 1992), a left versus right difference in patients with HS defined by MRI volume was found in a word list learning task (Jones-Gotman 1996).

Overall, verbal learning appears to be more specifically associated with left (dominant) hippocampus than does story recall, which frequently fails to distinguish left and right HS groups.

Differences between left and right HS patients in non-verbal memory are rarely reported. However, Matkovic *et al.* (1995b) found a specific correlation between CA4 in the right hippocampus, but not the left, and Benton Visual Retention Test scores. Delayed Rey figure recall correlated with hippocampal neuronal counts in both left and right groups. MRI hippocampal volumes correlated with neither visual reproduction nor a spatial learning task (Lencz *et al.* 1992; Trenerry *et al.* 1993). However, Jones-Gotman (1996) found a right versus left difference between HS groups defined by MRI volumes, on her design learning task.

The risk of reduced verbal memory resulting from left dominant TL surgery is well documented, whereas reduction in non-verbal memory after right TL surgery is less consistently reported (Chelune *et al.* 1991). For left dominant operations, patients with the most intact pre-operative verbal memory appear to be most at risk (ibid.). This is related to the pathological status of the excised tissue. If the excised hippocampus is severely sclerotic, the patient will be likely to have impaired verbal memory prior to surgery and to experience less change over surgery. Conversely, a more intact hippocampus is associated with better pre-operative verbal memory and its excision with a more significant decline (Hermann *et al.* 1995b; Oxbury and Oxbury 1989; Sass *et al.* 1994). Hermann *et al.* found extent of verbal memory loss after left temporal lobectomy to be related to age of onset of epilepsy. This is also likely to be related to pathology, since early onset epilepsy is frequently associated with severe HS (Sagar and Oxbury 1987). Comparable relationships for pathology in right TL and non-verbal memory are not clearly established, but Trenerry *et al.* (1993) demonstrated an association between post-operative decline in visual learning and excision of a relatively non-atrophic right hippocampus, as judged by MRI volumetrics.

Memory change has not been found to be associated with extent of TL excision for total resection, or for extent of medial or cortical resection (Katz *et al.* 1989; Wolf *et al.* 1993). Nevertheless, smaller excisions, if effective for the epilepsy, would seem to be desirable. SAH was designed for this reason and shown to be successful for patients with severe HS. For verbal memory, Verbal IQ and non-verbal memory, Oxbury *et al.* (1995) found better neuropsychological outcome in left HS surgery patients after SAH than after temporal lobectomy, although the better verbal memory has subsequently proved to be the least robust of these findings. Goldstein and Polkey (1992) found no difference in self-reported memory between groups of patients who had undergone SAH compared to standard temporal lobectomy. Goldstein and Polkey (1993) found SAH resulted in slightly less impairment in some cognitive functions than did temporal lobectomy. Improvement in function thought to be mediated by the opposite hemisphere was less after the smaller resection. In these latter two studies, unlike the Oxbury *et al.* study, the two surgical groups were not entirely comparable since they were not matched for pathology, and the criteria for selection for type of operation included pre-operative neuropsychology.

Severe amnesia

There is a small risk that unilateral temporal lobectomy will cause a severe amnesic syndrome (Loring *et al.* 1994; Scoville and Milner 1957). It is associated with a pre-existing abnormality in the medial structures of the non-operated TL (Warrington and Duchen 1992). Pre-operative ISA memory tests are now used to investigate the memory function (and thereby the pathological status) of the not-to-be-operated TL. If memory is inadequate when the side of proposed surgery is inactivated by amytal, then excision of the medial structures may be contraindicated.

Children and temporal lobe excisions

Although many centres now report outcome of TL surgery in children from two to sixteen years of age, remarkably little has been published on detailed pre- and post-operative neuropsychological evaluation. Exceptions are Meyer *et al.* (1986) and Adams *et al.* (1990).

Pre-operatively, neither Meyer *et al.* nor Adams *et al.* found discriminating neuropsychological differences between left and right TL children in either IQ patterns or memory. In the latter study, both left and right groups had a Performance IQ greater than Verbal IQ, particularly those whose excision specimens showed HS. Both groups were poor at verbal paired associate learning, story recall and delayed recall of the Rey figure.

Meyer *et al.*'s group consisted of fifty children followed up after periods ranging from six months to ten years. They reported no overall IQ change, but a shorter interval between seizure onset and surgery was associated with IQ increase. There were no changes in IQ in Adams *et al.*'s forty-four children at six months after en bloc temporal lobectomy. Later follow-up, however, has shown small gains in IQ in those with good seizure outcome (the majority).

Language was assessed in the Adams *et al.* study. Six weeks after left surgery, children had slightly, but significantly, lower scores than pre-operatively on the Oldfield Wingfield naming test. This had recovered at six months. No changes were evident on the Test of Reception of Grammar or Shortened Token Test. In the right group, significant improvement was seen on TROG at six months.

The WMS Memory Quotient did not change overall in Meyer *et al.*'s series, but girls improved while boys worsened slightly. Verbal and nonverbal subtests, however, were not analysed separately in relation to laterality of surgery. Adams *et al.* (1990) found decreased verbal memory following left operation, but no change in either group on delayed reproduction of the Rey figure. Later follow-up has shown more improvement than deterioration in memory scores, not necessarily predictable in terms of laterality or modality. Nevertheless, as in adults, verbal memory is at risk in children having left TL surgery. Preoperative level and pathology are relevant factors. A significant post-operative decrement can be a continuing disability in schooling.

Frontal lobe (FL) and other extra-temporal excisions

FL excisions constitute the largest single group of extra-temporal operations, but are less frequently performed than TL excisions: 18 per cent and 11 per cent in the series of Penfield and of Olivier, respectively, as compared to 56 per cent and 74 per cent TL operations (Olivier and Awad 1993). Based on post-operative studies alone, FL excision patients show several impairments, for example, in conditional learning (Petrides 1990) and impulsive behaviour (Miller 1992).

Few studies have systematically studied frontal lobectomy patients both pre- and post-operatively. Furthermore, different areas or subsystems within the FL are likely to be associated with different functions, making the problem harder to dissect. Milner (1988) reported preoperative test performance and post-operative seizure outcome in patients who underwent FL removals. Pre-operative deficits were not consistently seen except in word fluency in the left group, whose seizures were subsequently controlled by surgery.

The author is not aware of any specific pre- and post-operative reports which help to identify those patients who are particularly vulnerable to decline following surgery. An important factor, as with other excisions, is likely to be that of whether the tissue removed is pathological, or intact and functional.

Pre- and post-operative studies of children having FL surgery are also lacking. Jones-Gotman (1990) describes a children's design fluency task and gives examples of abnormal performance in children tested post-operatively only: highly perseverative prolific output, highly perseverative low output, and rule breaking. She suggests this task be used pre-operatively.

Non-frontal extra-temporal excisions form even smaller groups. Neuropsychological assessment should start with standard broad-based evaluation and be expanded to cover functions known to be associated with the area to be excised. Where this encroaches upon language areas, functional mapping is essential.

Hemispherectomy

Most of those undergoing hemispherectomy are children with a history of infantile hemiplegia and intractable epilepsy or who have acquired Rasmussen's syndrome. The rationale is that the massively damaged non-functional hemisphere from which the epilepsy is coming can be removed without increasing the pre-existing neurological impairment. There are several different surgical techniques, from complete anatomical removal to leaving the hemisphere in situ but disconnecting it from the rest of the brain (functional hemispherectomy); some combine partial removal with partial disconnection.

Hemispherectomy for early static damage

These children have severe damage to one hemisphere from an early age (including foetal). Cognitive function has developed in the good hemisphere with generally most functions represented but usually below the average range. The Oxford series has shown no particular Verbal/Performance IQ pattern prior to surgery and usually little discrepancy between these scores. Intractable seizures are often accompanied by difficult behaviour and both behaviour and cognitive function may be deteriorating by the time surgery is considered. Family life is often seriously disrupted (Beardsworth and Adams 1988).

An early review of ten cases of Adams' modified hemispherectomy (Beardsworth and Adams 1988) showed seizure outcome to be good, motor function largely unaffected, and behaviour and family life improved with cessation of seizures. Some children showed significant and continuing cognitive gains with the passage of time and behavioural improvements were recorded at clinical follow-up in approximately 75 per cent (Oxbury et al. 1995).

Rasmussen's syndrome

This syndrome, which affects previously normal children, usually begins in the first decade of life with uncontrolled focal seizures and progresses over a variable period of time with development of hemiplegia and cognitive deterioration. The disease is considered to affect one hemisphere only, but generalised cognitive deterioration usually occurs. If the onset is in the left hemisphere before the age of six, language usually develops in the right hemisphere, but may make less satisfactory 'transfer' after this age. Taylor (1991) discusses the dilemma of whether to proceed to left surgery before full transfer of speech to the right hemisphere, with the hope of alleviating the continuous seizures, or whether to wait until transfer has happened, while the child suffers the detrimental effects of seizures.

Corpus callosotomy

This operation disconnects the cerebral hemispheres, rather than excising pathology or epileptogenic tissue, and thereby inhibits the rapid generalisation of seizure activity from one hemisphere to the other. This may reduce the frequency of seizures, especially drop attacks, but rarely abolishes them. Callosotomy may be partial or total, anterior or posterior. Usually the anterior two-thirds is divided first, followed by later completion of callosotomy if seizures are not improved.

Adults

Pre-operative abilities span a wide range, from normal to considerably impaired. There is no particular pattern and there may be damage to, or epileptic foci in, either hemisphere. Therefore, neuropsychological assessment needs to be broad-ranging, carefully evaluating those functions at risk. ISA is essential to establish cerebral dominance.

Neuropsychological features of the various disconnection syndromes resulting from callosal section include diminished speech or mutism, apraxia or neglect of left limbs, hemispheric competition in which the two hands may act antagonistically ('alien hand'), and the classical posterior disconnection syndrome in which visual or tactile information entering the non-dominant hemisphere cannot be responded to verbally. Factors related to the occurrence and permanence of these syndromes are discussed by Pilcher *et al.* (1993).

Memory decline may occur following posterior, but not anterior, section, and may be associated with inclusion of the hippocampal commissure in the posterior section (Phelps *et al.* 1991).

Children

Lassonde *et al.* (1990) concluded that corpus callosotomy in children does not affect long-term cognitive, social or motor behaviour, and that neuropsychological improvement was associated with seizure control. The absence of long-term sequelae of the classical disconnection deficits in children operated under 12 years of age suggests that the young brain adjusts more easily to callosotomy.

PRACTICAL GUIDE

It will be clear from the previous sections (and Chapter 2) that assessment of patients prior to surgery for epilepsy must be a broad-based neuropsychological examination covering tests of general intelligence, language function, visuospatial and perceptual ability, frontal lobe/executive/attentional tasks and several aspects of memory and learning in both the verbal and the non-verbal domains. Jones-Gotman *et al.* (1993) have compiled an exhaustive list of the tests used by psychologists from many centres.

Adults

The following is a suggested protocol for use with adults:

1 Wechsler Adult Intelligence Scale – Revised (WAIS-R).
2 Tests of language function: Multilingual Aphasia Examination (MAE) or selected subtests, e.g. Sentence Repetition, Word Association, augmented by a naming test, Oldfield-Wingfield Object Naming, Graded Naming Test or Boston Naming Test, and a comprehension task such as the Shortened Token Test.
   Reading and Spelling – e.g. Schonell Graded Word Reading and Spelling tests.
3 Where indicated, additional visuospatial perceptual tasks, such as the Visual Object and Space Perception Battery (VOSP).
4 Tests intended to examine executive function, such as Wisconsin Card Sorting Test, Trail Making, Stroop, Cognitive Estimates.
   Every psychologist is aware of the behavioural and personality problems experienced by some individuals with FL damage, the most florid syndrome resulting from bilateral damage with a milder picture seen after unilateral damage. Thus, it is important to assess, even informally, a patient's ability to plan and structure his or her activities and to interact with others, so that post-operative change or

lack of it may be recorded. An interesting single case showing a strategy application disorder after unilateral lobectomy, is described by Goldstein *et al.* (1993).

5   Tests of memory and learning (important for all patients, especially for TL patients). In the verbal domain: immediate span, both digits and sentences (from WAIS-R or MAE); story recall (e.g. Logical Memory from WMS) with delayed recall; verbal learning, list learning such as the Selective Reminding Test, Rey Auditory Verbal Learning Test, or California Verbal Learning Test (CVLT), Paired Associates from WMS. In the non-verbal sphere: immediate recall, Corsi block tapping span and Benton Visual Retention; Rey Osterrieth figure or Taylor equivalent with delayed recall; ideally, a non-verbal learning task such as design or maze learning.

The choice of a test battery is important. Only when this has been used over a period of time will the psychologist begin to build up experience with different types of patients, so it is important to stick with one's original set at least for a period of time.

Children

Similar principles, with additional considerations, apply for assessment of children. The extent to which the aims of neuropsychological assessment, as discussed earlier in this chapter, are appropriate or can be met will differ depending on the age and developmental level of the child. Since present knowledge of long-term neuropsychological outcome from surgery in children is scanty, the possibility of making predictions is reduced. Educational attainment tests should be added to the battery, to give an indication of the effect of the epilepsy and/or the underlying pathology on the child's school progress.

In very young, or very delayed children the aim of pre-operative assessment may be careful baseline assessment of developmental level, perhaps with special emphasis on language development. Alternatively, the initial aim may be to monitor development over a period of time and to document developmental arrest or regression. These may be important factors in the decision to recommend surgery, since concern about possible cognitive effects of operation will be less potent if a child with intractable seizures is already losing skills. Indeed, in such cases it is hoped that the removal of pathology, and cessation or amelioration of seizures, will halt the decline, so allowing the child to make progress.

In children between the ages of six and twelve years and of average intelligence much less is known about the degree to which psychological functions are lateralised or localised than it is in adults. Language is usually thought to have lateralised by the age of six and earlier damage may affect cerebral dominance. Little is known about surgical risks to memory, cognition and their future development in this age group. The concept of greater plasticity in the child, and hence an improved chance of recovery from cognitive deficit resulting from surgery attributable to other brain areas taking over function, is often raised in discussion of young children. However, plasticity is unlikely to be abso-lute and the 'crowding' effect may place limits on the final level of cognitive development. In the child over twelve years, the neuropsycho-logical issues can reasonably be assumed to be similar to those in adults. These issues and a range of suggested tests have been reviewed else-where (Oxbury 1997).

A test battery should include:

1   Tests of general developmental level or intelligence such as Griffiths or Bayley Developmental Scales, WPPSI-R or WISC-III, depending on age and developmental level.
2   Tests of language function: Naming, Verbal fluency, STT and/or TROG, comprehension vocabulary, British Picture Vocabulary Scale; possibly additional children's language tests, e.g. Clinical Evaluation of Language Fundamentals (CELF).
3   Additional visuospatial tests, e.g. from the British Ability Scales.
4   Children's norms are available for the Wisconsin Card Sorting Test and Trail Making. Whether these tasks measure FL function in chil-dren is not known. Children may fail for a variety of reasons, and in any case these functions may develop fairly late in maturation. Nevertheless, results could be of interest, especially in the context of long-term follow-up.
5   Memory tests are important and should cover the same ground as in adults. The Wide Range Assessment of Memory and Learning (WRAML) has several suitable subtests but the disadvantage of no equivalent forms. Story recall (Beardsworth and Bishop 1994) is useful. Spreen and Strauss (1991) give children's norms for several verbal learning tasks (e.g. Paired Associates and Selective Reminding). The non-verbal memory tests suggested for adults are standardised for children (see also Chapter 9).

Sodium amytal tests

These tests are designed to anaesthetise one hemisphere (or part of one hemisphere) while language and memory functions of the other hemisphere are assessed. Cerebral language dominance must be established prior to surgery. Adequate memory function of the not-to-be-operated hemisphere must be demonstrated when TL surgery is proposed. In addition, memory failure, when the side of proposed surgery is tested (by injection into the contralateral hemisphere), is taken to confirm pathology in the hippocampus on this side (Carpenter et al. 1996).

The usual method is to inject sodium amytal into the internal carotid artery through a catheter inserted via the femoral artery – intracarotid sodium amytal (ISA). ISA causes contralateral hemiplegia and, in the dominant hemisphere, aphasia lasting a few minutes. Test protocols vary very considerably in terms of dose, whether both hemispheres are tested on the same day or separate days, tests of language and memory, and interpretation of results (see Rausch et al. 1993). Protocols for testing language and memory are described in Oxbury and Oxbury (1984) and Carpenter et al. (1996).

In Oxford, ISA is routinely used in patients over twelve years. Children under twelve tolerate the procedure less well (Jones-Gotman 1990). When crucially important, language dominance can usually be tested in younger children, but results of memory tests, particularly after dominant hemisphere injection, are unreliable (Williams and Rausch 1992).

Post-operative assessment

Full post-operative neuropsychological follow-up is important and its usefulness as a measure of outcome depends upon the quality of the pre-operative assessment. For both adults and children the measurement of any changes, deficits or improvements, will add to knowledge about the risks and benefits of surgery. They are also useful in psychosocial or educational counselling. Assessments should be repeated at intervals, ideally over several years in the case of children, to monitor development and long-term effects. The implications for research are obvious. Without both pre- and post-operative evaluation, knowledge relating pre-operative neuropsychological factors to lateralisation, localisation and type of pathology, or to predict neuropsychological, developmental and other outcomes cannot advance (Hermann 1990; Dodrill et al. 1993).

Methodological considerations must be borne in mind. Effects of practice on test performance and use of alternative test versions are important issues. This constitutes a very real problem in the case of assessment of memory since previous exposure to material purporting to measure new learning may falsify the results. Developmental issues are important. The question remains as to whether it is possible to devise tests for children which can reliably measure the neuropsychological functions evaluated in adults or, perhaps more appropriately, chart the development of these functions over time.

The Oxford protocol includes full pre-operative neuropsychological assessment, including ISA, brief re-assessment of language and memory at six to eight weeks after surgery, and full post-operative neuropsychological assessment at six months, two years and five years.

PSYCHOSOCIAL ISSUES

Consideration of surgical outcome goes beyond that of seizure relief and cognitive outcome. Broader psychosocial functioning should also be evaluated. Areas investigated in studies of psychosocial function vary considerably but commonly include: employment; dependency/independence; interpersonal relationships, inside and outside the family; personal adjustment factors such as self image, sexual functioning (see Dodrill *et al.* 1991). Methodological problems make comparison between studies difficult. These include different areas evaluated; types of measurement (questionnaire, rating scales, factual information); variable follow-up intervals both within and between studies. Nevertheless, some general conclusions may be drawn.

The factor most related to improved psychosocial outcome is relief from seizures. Some studies have found significant improvement only in those patients who experience complete seizure relief. Although others have found the degree of improvement related to the degree of seizure control (Vickrey *et al.* 1991), Hermann *et al.*'s (1992) study re-emphasises the greater beneficial effect of complete seizure relief as compared to 75 per cent reduction in seizure frequency.

Other factors related to improved psychosocial outcome are pre-operative employment status, with those chronically unemployed least likely to benefit, degree of family support and adequacy of pre-operative psychosocial adjustment (Hermann *et al.* 1992).

As for children, Lindsay *et al.*'s (1984) study describing the benefits of seizure relief in all areas of psychosocial adjustment remains a classic. In our more recent Oxford series of children having TL surgery before leaving school, 80 per cent of those who had left education and were seizure free at the five-year follow-up were employed, compared to only 23 per cent of those who still experienced seizures.

Finally, virtually all of these studies have involved patients having TL and, to a lesser extent, other focal resections. Findings may not be applicable to those having other procedures such as hemispherectomy or callosotomy.

REFERENCES

Adams, C. B. T., Beardsworth, E. D., Oxbury, S. M., Oxbury, J. M. and Fenwick, P. B. C. (1990) 'Temporal lobectomy in 44 children: outcome and neuropsychological follow-up', *Journal of Epilepsy* 3 (Suppl. 1): 157–68.

Baxendale, S. A. (1995) 'The hippocampus: functional and structural correlations', *Seizure* 4: 105–17.

Beardsworth, E. D. and Adams, C. B. T. (1988) 'Modified hemispherectomy for epilepsy: early results in 10 cases', *British Journal of Neurosurgery* 2: 73–84.

Beardsworth, E. D. and Bishop, D. (1994) 'Assessment of long term verbal memory in children', *Memory* 2: 129–48.

Carpenter, K. N., Oxbury, J. M., Oxbury, S. M. and Wright G. D. S. (1996) 'Memory for objects presented early after intra-carotid sodium amytal: a sensitive clinical neuropsychological indicator of temporal lobe pathology', *Seizure* 5: 103–8.

Chelune, G. J., Naugle, R., Lüders, H. and Awad, I. A. (1991) 'Prediction of cognitive change as a function of pre-operative ability status among temporal lobectomy patients', *Neurology* 4: 477–85.

Davies, K. G., Maxwell, R. E., Beniak, T. E., Destafney, E. and Fiol, M. E. (1995) 'Language function after temporal lobectomy without stimulation mapping of cortical function', *Epilepsia* 36: 130–6.

Dodrill, C. B., Batzel, L. W. and Fraser, R. (1991) 'Psychosocial changes after surgery for epilepsy', in H. Lüders (ed.) *Epilepsy Surgery*, New York: Raven Press.

Dodrill, C. B., Hermann, B. P., Rausch, R., Chelune, G. J. and Oxbury, S. (1993) 'Neuropsychological testing for assessing prognosis following surgery for epilepsy', in J. Engel Jnr (ed.) *Surgical Treatment of the Epilepsies* (2nd edn), New York: Raven Press.

Engel, J. (1993) 'Overview: who should be considered a surgical candidate?', in J. Engel Jnr (ed.) *Surgical Treatment of the Epilepsies* (2nd edn), New York: Raven Press.

Engel, J. and Ojemann, G. A. (1993) 'The next step', in J. Engel Jnr (ed.) *Surgical Treatment of the Epilepsies* (2nd edn), New York: Raven Press.

Frisk, V. and Milner, B. (1990) 'The relationship of working memory to the immediate recall of stories following unilateral temporal or frontal lobectomy', *Neuropsychologia* 28: 121–35.

Goldstein, L. H. and Polkey, C. E. (1992) 'Everyday memory after unilateral temporal lobectomy or amygdalohippocampectomy', *Cortex* 28: 189–201.

—— (1993) 'Short term cognitive changes after unilateral temporal lobectomy or unilateral amygdalohippocampectomy for the relief of temporal lobe epilepsy', *Journal of Neurology, Neurosurgery and Psychiatry* 56: 135–40.

Goldstein, L. H., Bernard, S., Fenwick, P. B. C., Burgess, P. W. and McNeil, J. (1993) 'Unilateral frontal lobectomy can produce strategy application disorder', *Journal of Neurology, Neurosurgery and Psychiatry* 56: 274–6.

Hermann, B. P. (1990) 'Psychosocial outcome following focal resections in childhood', *Journal of Epilepsy* 3 (Suppl. 1): 243–52.

Hermann, B. P. and Wyler, A. R. (1988) 'Effects of anterior temporal lobectomy on language function: a controlled study', *Annals of Neurology* 23: 585–8.

Hermann, B. P., Wyler, A. R., and Somes, G. (1991) 'Language function following anterior temporal lobectomy', *Journal of Neurosurgery* 74: 560–6.

Hermann, B. P., Wyler, A. R. and Somes, G. (1992) 'Pre-operative psychological adjustment and surgical outcome are determinants of psychosocial status after anterior temporal lobectomy', *Journal of Neurology, Neurosurgery and Psychiatry* 55: 491–6.

Hermann, B. P., Gold, J., Pusakulich, R., Wyler, A. R., Randolph, C., Rankin, G. and Hoy, W. (1995a) 'Wechsler Adult Intelligence Scale-Revised in the evaluation of anterior temporal lobectomy candidates', *Epilepsia* 36: 480–7.

Hermann, B. P., Seidenberg, M., Haltiner, A. and Wyler, A. R. (1995b) 'Relationship of age of onset, chronological age, and adequacy of pre-operative performance to verbal memory change after anterior temporal lobectomy', *Epilepsia* 36: 137–45.

Jones-Gotman, M. (1990) 'Presurgical psychological assessment in children: special tests', *Journal of Epilepsy* 3 (Suppl): 93–102.

—— (1991) 'Presurgical neuropsychological evaluation for localisation and lateralisation of seizure focus', in H. Lüders (ed.) in *Epilepsy Surgery*, New York: Raven Press.

—— (1996) 'Psychological evaluation for epilepsy surgery', in S. Shorvon, F. Dreifuss, D. Fish and D. Thomas (eds), *The Treatment of Epilepsy*, Oxford: Blackwell Science.

Jones-Gotman, M., Smith M-L. and Zatorre, R. J. (1993) 'Neuropsychological testing for localising and lateralising the epileptogenic region', in J. Engel Jnr (ed.) *Surgical Treatment of Epilepsies* (2nd edn), New York: Raven Press.

Katz, A., Awad, I. A., Kong, A. K., Chelune, G. J., Naugle, R. I., Wyllie, E., Beauchamp, G. and Lüders, H. (1989) 'Extent of resection in temporal lobectomy for epilepsy. II. Memory changes and neurologic complications', *Epilepsia* 30: 763–71.

Lassonde, M., Sauerwein, H., Geoffroy, G. and Décarie, M. (1990) 'Long-term neuropsychological effects of corpus callosotomy in children', *Journal of Epilepsy* 3 (Suppl. 1): 279–86.

Lencz, T., McCarthy, G. and Bronen, R. A. (1992) 'Quantitative magnetic resonance imaging in temporal lobe epilepsy: relationship to neuropathology and neuropsychological function', *Annals of Neurology* 31: 629–37.

Lindsay, J., Ounsted, C. and Richards, P. (1984) 'Long-term outcome in children with temporal lobe seizures. V. Indications and contraindications for neurosurgery,' *Developmental Medicine and Child Neurology* 26: 25–32.

Loring, D. W., Meador, K. J., Lee, G. P., Murro, A. M., Smith, J. R., Flanigin, H. R., Gallagher, B. B. and King, D. W. (1990) 'Cerebral language lateralization: evidence from intracarotid amobarbital testing', *Neuropsychologia* 28: 831–8.

Loring, D. W., Hermann, B. P., Meador, K. J., Lee, G. P., Gallagher, B. B., King, D. W., Murro, A. M., Smith, J. R. and Wyler, A. R. (1994) 'Amnesia after unilateral temporal lobectomy: a case report', *Epilepsia* 35: 757–63.

McMillan, T. M., Powell, G. E., Janota, I. and Polkey, C. E. (1987) 'Relationships between neuropathology and cognitive functioning in temporal lobectomy patients', *Journal of Neurology, Neurosurgery and Psychiatry* 50: 167–76.

Matkovic, Z., Oxbury, S. M., Hiorns, R. W., Morris, J. H., Carpenter, K. N., Adams, C. B. T. and Oxbury, J. M. (1995a) 'Hippocampal neuronal density correlates with pre-operative verbal memory in patients with temporal lobe epilepsy', *Epilepsia* 36 (Suppl. 3): S121.

Matkovic, Z., Oxbury, S. M., Hiorns, R. W., Morris, J. H., Carpenter, K. N., Adams, C. B. T. and Oxbury, J. M. (1995b) 'Hippocampal neuronal density correlates with pre-operative non-verbal memory in patients with temporal lobe epilepsy', *Epilepsia* 36 (Suppl 3): S93.

Meyer, F. B., Marsh, R., Laws, E. R. Jr. and Sharbrough, F. W. (1986) 'Temporal lobectomy in children with epilepsy', *Journal of Neurosurgery* 64: 371–6.

Miller, L. A. (1992) 'Impulsivity, risk-taking, and the ability to synthesize fragmented information after frontal lobectomy', *Neuropsychologia* 30: 69–79.

Miller, L. A., Munoz, D. G. and Finmore, M. (1993) 'Hippocampal sclerosis and human memory', *Archives of Neurology* 50: 391–4.

Milner, B. (1988) 'Patterns of neuropsychological deficit in frontal lobe epilepsies', *Epilepsia* 29: 221.

Olivier, A. and Awad, I. A. (1993) 'Extratemporal resections', in J. Engel Jnr (ed.) *Surgical Treatment of the Epilepsies* (2nd edn), New York: Raven Press.

Oxbury, J. M. and Oxbury, S. M. (1989) 'Neuropsychology, memory and hippocampal pathology', in E. H. Reynolds and M. R. Trimble (eds) *The Bridge between Neurology and Psychiatry*, London: Churchill Livingstone.

Oxbury, J. M., Adams, C. B. T., Oxbury, S. M., Carpenter, K. N. and Renowden, S. A. (1995) 'En bloc temporal lobectomy v. selective amygdalohippocampectomy as treatments for intractable epilepsy due to hippocampal sclerosis', *Journal of Neurology, Neurosurgery and Psychiatry* 59: 200.

Oxbury, S. M. (1997) 'Neuropsychological evaluation – children', in J. Engel and T. A. Pedley (eds) *Epilepsy: A Comprehensive Textbook*, Philadelphia: Lippincott-Raven.

Oxbury, S. M. and Oxbury, J. M. (1984) 'Intracarotid amytal test in the assessment of language dominance', in F. C. Rose (ed.) *Progress in Aphasiology: Advances in Neurology 42*, New York: Raven Press.

Oxbury, S. M., Zaiwalla, Z., Adams, C. B. T., Middleton, J. A. and Oxbury, J. M. (1995) 'Hemispherectomy in childhood: serial neuropsychological follow-up and prolonged improvement', *Epilepsia* 36 (Suppl. 3): S24.

Petrides, M. (1990) 'Nonspatial conditional learning impaired in patients with unilateral frontal but not unilateral temporal lobe excisions', *Neuropsychologia* 28: 137–49.

Phelps, E. A., Hirst, W. and Gazzaniga, M. S. (1991) 'Deficits in recall following partial and complete commissurotomy', *Cerebral Cortex* 1: 492–8.

Pilcher, W. H., Roberts, D. W., Flanigan, H. F., Crandall, P. H., Wieser, H. G.,

Ojemann, G. A. and Peacock, W. J. (1993) 'Complications of epilepsy surgery', in J. Engel Jnr (ed.) *Surgical Treatment of the Epilepsies* (2nd edn), New York: Raven Press.

Powell, G. E., Polkey, C. E. and McMillan, T. M. (1985) 'The new Maudsley series of temporal lobectomy. I: Short term cognitive effects', *British Journal of Clinical Psychology* 24: 109–24.

Rausch, R. and Babb, T. L. (1993) 'Hippocampal neuron loss and memory scores before and after temporal lobe surgery for epilepsy', *Archives of Neurology* 50: 812–17.

Rausch, R., Silfvenius, H., Wieser, H-G., Dodrill, C. B., Meador, K. J. and Jones-Gotman, M. (1993) 'Intra-arterial amobarbital procedures', in J. Engel Jnr (ed.) *Surgical Treatment of the Epilepsies* (2nd edn), New York: Raven Press.

Sagar, H. J. and Oxbury, J. M. (1987) 'Hippocampal neurone loss in temporal lobe epilepsy: correlation with early childhood convulsions', *Annals of Neurology* 22: 334–40.

Saling, M. M., Berkovic, S. F. and O'Shea, M. F. (1993) 'Lateralization of verbal memory and unilateral hippocampal sclerosis: evidence of task-specific effects', *Journal of Clinical and Experimental Neuropsychology* 15: 608–18.

Sass, K. J., Westerveld, M. and Buchanan, C. (1994) 'Degree of hippocampal neuron loss determines severity of verbal memory decrease after left anteromesiotemporal lobectomy', *Epilepsia* 35: 1179–86.

Sass, K. J., Sass, A., Westerveld, M., Lencz, T., Novelly, R. A., Kim, J. H. and Spencer, D. D. (1992) 'Specificity in the correlation of verbal memory and hippocampal neuron loss: dissociation of memory, language and verbal intellectual ability', *Journal of Clinical and Experimental Neuropsychology* 14: 662–72.

Scoville, W. and Milner, B. (1957) 'Loss of recent memory after bilateral hippocampal lesions', *Journal of Neurology, Neurosurgery and Psychiatry* 20: 11–21.

Smith, M. L. and Milner, B. (1981) 'The role of the right hippocampus in the recall of spatial location', *Neuropsychologia* 19: 781–93.

Snyder, P. J., Novelly, R. A. and Harris, L. J. (1990) 'Mixed speech dominance in the intracarotid sodium amytal procedure: validity and criteria issues', *Journal of Clinical and Experimental Neuropsychology* 12: 629–43.

Spreen, O. and Strauss, E. (1991) *A Compendium of Neuropsychological Tests*, New York: Oxford University Press.

Stafiniak, P., Saykin, A. J., Sperling, M. R., Kester, D. B., Robinson, L. J., O'Connor, K. J. and Gur, R. C. (1990) 'Acute naming deficits following dominant temporal lobectomy', *Neurology* 40: 1509–12.

Taylor, L. B. (1991) 'Neuropsychologic assessment of patients with chronic encephalitis', in F. Andermann (ed.) *Chronic Encephalitis and Epilepsy, Rasmussen's Syndrome*, Boston: Butterworth–Heinemann.

Trenerry, M. R., Jack, C. R., Ivnik, R. J., Sharbrough, F. W., Cascino, G. D., Hirschorn, K. A., Marsh, W. R., Kelly, P. J. and Meyer, F. B. (1993) 'MRI hippocampal volumes and memory function before and after temporal lobectomy', *Neurology* 43: 1800–5.

Vickrey, R. D., Hays, R., Rausch, R., Engel, J. Jr and Brook, R. H. (1991) 'Quality of life after surgical treatment of epilepsy', *Epilepsia* 32 (Suppl. 1): 57.

Warrington, E. K. and Duchen, L. W. (1992) 'A re-appraisal of a case of persistent global amnesia following right temporal lobectomy: a clinico-pathological study', *Neuropsychologia* 30: 437–50.

Williams, J. and Rausch, R. (1992) 'Factors in children that predict memory performance on the intracarotid amobarbital procedure', *Epilepsia* 33: 1036–41.

Wolf, R. L., Ivnik, R. J., Hirschorn, K. A., Sharbrough, M. D., Cascino, G. D. and Marsh, W. R. (1993) 'Neurocognitive efficiency following left temporal lobectomy: standard versus limited resection', *Journal of Neurosurgery* 76: 76–83.

Chapter 5

The role of anti-epileptic drugs
Their impact on cognitive function and behaviour

Ruth Gillham and Christine Cull

A common concern voiced by people with epilepsy is that their anti-convulsant medication is affecting their memory. This is reflected in the growing interest in the impact of anti-epileptic drugs (AEDs) on aspects of behaviour other than seizures. Indeed, all new AEDs are now evaluated for cognitive/behavioural side effects, and the lack of such effects is a major selling point for manufacturers.

While epilepsy can be associated with a variety of cognitive/behavioural deficits, the clinical psychologist may be asked to comment on the extent to which an AED may be compromising an individual's functioning on formal cognitive testing or on a day-to-day basis, over and above the effects of the seizure disorder itself. The psychologist may be asked to evaluate the impact of any drug change, or to contribute to the planning of drug trials evaluating the effects of new AEDs, in addition to which, the person with epilepsy may wish to discuss the impact of their medication.

In order to make sense of the available literature, the interested clinician needs to be aware of the issues involved in the investigation of drug effects, and the different study designs that have been employed, which we will consider before presenting a brief review of the area.

INVESTIGATION OF DRUG EFFECTS

Study designs

The investigation of drug effects in individuals with epilepsy is problematic. First, this is because one has to take into account all the other variables which may also effect cognition/behaviour such as aetiology, age at onset and duration of the seizure disorder, seizure type and frequency, and type of EEG abnormality. Second, the type of study design that one might use is constrained by ethical issues and the clinical needs of the patient.

Studies of *normal volunteers* eliminate the impact of potentially contaminating epilepsy variables, and allow for methodologically sound designs, often using double-blind placebo cross-over comparisons. However, these are usually single dose studies, or, at most, conducted over a period of two weeks' constant usage at subclinical doses. Thus, there are clearly difficulties in generalising the results to individuals who have to take the drugs for many years. Any effects noted may be transient, but in normal volunteer studies there is no way of evaluating this. A healthy volunteer is not analogous to a patient with epilepsy in that there must be differences between their underlying neural and neurochemical substrates, or both would be producing seizures. Thus, extrapolation from this group to a neurologically different group may not be warranted. Therefore, while such a design has predominantly methodological advantages, the applicability of the results to patients with epilepsy is questionable.

In view of this, the most useful information is likely to come from studies of people with epilepsy, where a number of different designs (longitudinal, cross-over, cross-sectional, or drug/dose concentration studies) are used.

All *longitudinal designs* share in common the use of repeated assessments over time, with individuals acting as their own controls. The most common of these is an *add-on* study in which a new AED is added to a regimen which already includes at least one other AED.

Such designs are often adopted in the investigation of new compounds, used as adjunctive therapy in patients with a refractory seizure disorder. However, since about 80 per cent of patients have their seizures effectively controlled (Brodie 1985), this group is a minority. Many such patients will have complex partial seizures which, by definition, will be associated with focal pathology and may have neuropsychological sequelae. In addition many subjects will have experienced numerous changes in dose and drug combination, which themselves may produce cognitive impairment. Thus, any generalisations made from this group of patients with epilepsy must be tentative. In addition, results may be contaminated by the effect of the new drug on seizure frequency, and by any interaction between the drugs.

It is possible to examine the effects of medication in previously untreated individuals who are taking an AED for the first time. Although the results may be contaminated by the effect of the drug on seizure frequency, such patients do not have a long neuropsychological-deficit producing history and have no previous history of AED treatment, which is clearly advantageous.

Conversely, *drug deletion* studies may be undertaken, involving rationalisation of a multi-drug regimen (which may bring about an improvement in seizure frequency), or, alternatively, the complete withdrawal of AEDs in individuals who have been seizure-free for two years or more, so eliminating the effects of seizure type and frequency. Improvements in performance following withdrawal are taken as evidence that the withdrawn AED was affecting cognitive functioning.

Other longitudinal studies have explored the effect of a change in medication *(drug substitution)*, presumably in an attempt to improve seizure frequency and this may be a confounding factor. While any change in functioning may be attributable to the new drug, it is equally possible that it is the result of the withdrawal of a more toxic or sedative compound.

All of the above designs may be placebo controlled where a matched group of subjects are given a placebo rather than the active medication (although this would not be ethically acceptable in studies of newly diagnosed patients). Both patient and investigator are required not to know who is on what particular regimen (i.e. to be blind). While this is a more methodologically rigorous approach, there are practical issues in maintaining 'blindness' and ethical issues about not allowing patients access to a potentially effective treatment, which means that such studies can only be of limited duration. In studies of new patients, however, it is possible to undertake a double-blind comparison of different drugs.

The simplest study is *cross-sectional* and compares groups of subjects on different AEDs without any treatment changes. However, sources of bias are large: there may well be reasons why a patient has been prescribed one drug and not another, such as the clinician's beliefs about efficacy, previous treatment failures, and even age and gender. For example, sodium valproate (which can produce weight gain) and phenytoin (which can produce facial changes) may be less popular amongst younger women than carbamazepine. Sample sizes must be large, or groups carefully matched, to control for variables such as aetiology, lifetime seizure frequency and previous drug history. The advantage of this design is that it can be carried out in any epilepsy clinic, with the person assessing cognitive factors being blind to treatment, but no complex blinding procedures being necessary. As tests are administered once, learning and practice effects are not an issue. At the end of the day, however, even if there are significant differences between the groups, it will still be difficult to be sure that these are attributable to the drug and the drug alone (Dodrill 1992).

The most methodologically sound design is a *double-blind randomised cross-over* study in which patients are randomly assigned to treatment with one or another drug, or placebo, with both investigator and patient being blind. After a set period of time the new treatment is removed, there may be a brief wash-out phase, and the alternative treatment is then introduced for the same length of time. Assessments take place before any drug is introduced and after a period of time on each agent. Such studies usually involve the use of add-on drugs and thus suffer from the disadvantages outlined previously in terms of the generalisability of the results. Again, ethical and clinical demands dictate that these can only take place over a limited period of time.

A further approach to exploring the cognitive/behavioural impact of AEDs is to look at drug dose/concentration effects (as determined by the concentration of the drug in blood serum (see Chapter 1)). Thus, patients on the same drug but at different serum blood levels may be compared, or performance within the same individual at low and high serum levels. Alternatively, correlational analyses may be carried out between the performance measure and serum levels.

From the above, therefore, it can be seen that there is a wide variety of designs that can be used, none of which are without disadvantages.

Assessment tools

It is also important to take into account the measures used. Early reports in the literature were largely anecdotal. However, as interest in the area grew, so more standardised tests have been used. Cognitive measures have included IQ tests such as the Wechsler scales, or neuropsychological batteries such as the Halstead-Reitan (used predominantly in the USA). Clearly, there are potential difficulties with such measures in a longitudinal study, depending on the test–retest interval and the contribution of practice effects to the outcome. Further, the use of tests designed primarily as neuropsychological measures may yield limited information, as the effects of drugs may be different to those of structural brain damage. Consequently, many investigators have developed their own test batteries resulting in as many different batteries as there are studies, hindering between study comparison.

Most cognitive test batteries try to incorporate measures of memory, psychomotor performance and information processing. The aspects of memory easiest to measure are short term tasks such as Digit Span, which can be repeated without too much learning effect. Recall of passages of prose or word list learning require alternative forms to be available for repeated use. 'Psychomotor' is defined variously: studies from the USA have tended to use it as a composite term, meaning cognitive function, with speed and motor skill included. In Europe, it tends to be reserved for motor tasks such as simple or choice reaction time, and tapping rate. In general, psychomotor tasks, require equipment and this causes a great deal of variability between centres, hindering generalisations from one study to another. 'Information processing' or 'central processing' is an even looser term that subsumes a great many functions and is tested in many different ways. Common tasks which might be included in this category are the Stroop Test and the Digit Symbol subtest from the WAIS-R.

Problems in interpretation of studies

Further complicating matters, Dodrill (1992) asserts that impairments in cognitive functioning may have been wrongly attributed to drug effects because of inappropriate data analysis methods. These include a lack of appreciation of the *selection factors* operating in cross-sectional studies (as described previously), which consequently are not taken into account in the final analysis; *statistical errors* can also contribute to a misinterpretation of the data (including, particularly, the erroneous use of parametric tests, giving credence to a few statistical differences that may have occurred by chance, and running too many statistical tests for the number of subjects or the number of measures). The impact of *seizure frequency* is rarely evaluated in these studies and may in fact be more significant than the AED effects. Dodrill also asserts that the type of *psychological measure* used may determine whether significant results are found or not, in that timed tasks are more likely than untimed tests to be sensitive to drug effects.

In many of the earlier studies there was an implicit but untested assumption that patients were actually taking their medication. More recent studies often report serum drug level concentrations, which may be one way of assessing compliance, and, as mentioned previously, may be a parameter of interest in itself.

The implications of all this are that in reading published studies of cognitive/behavioural effects of AEDs, the clinician should:

- read the whole study thoroughly, not just the results, in order to identify any methodological problems;

- read more than one study to gain a balanced perspective;
- consider the generalisability of the results to the particular issues being addressed.

REVIEW OF DRUG EFFECTS

As there are a number of recent reviews on this topic (Aldenkamp and Vermeulen 1995; Devinsky 1995; Dreifuss 1992; Kälviäinen *et al.* 1996), this review will be limited and will be used to illustrate some of the problems described above.

Older anti-epileptic drugs

Phenobarbitone (PHB)

Historically, phenobarbitone has been associated with behavioural problems, including excitement, aggression, hyperactivity, short attention span, irritability, distractibility, tearfulness and increased motor activity (Hirtz and Nelson 1985), which can occur in up to 75 per cent of those taking this medication (Committee on Drugs 1985). However, in terms of the impact of PHB on cognitive function, the picture is much less clear, partly because very few studies have actually been carried out despite the fact that PHB has been in use since 1912.

Sixteen seizure-free patients (adults and children) were assessed on ten measures of intelligence, vigilance, attention, memory, learning, manual dexterity, sensory discrimination and visuomotor performance (Gallassi *et al.* 1992) before withdrawal from PHB, six months later following a 50 per cent reduction in dose, and again three and twelve months after withdrawal. Only on the Trail Making Test, and before withdrawal, was their performance significantly worse than that of normal volunteers.

Phenytoin (PHT)

Phenytoin is a frequently used AED; it is relatively cheap and widely available in the developing world.

Dodrill (1975) studied seventy patients on PHT monotherapy, who completed the Halstead-Reitan battery, WAIS, Trail Making Test, name writing and strength of grip tests. Comparisons were then made between individuals with low (N=34) as opposed to high (N=36) serum drug levels, and between those who were showing clinical signs of toxicity (N=24) and those who were not (N=46). Groups with high serum levels, or who were clinically toxic, performed more poorly on all tasks than the low and non-toxic groups. Statistical differences were found on eight measures in the serum level comparison, and four in the toxicity comparison, all of which had a major motor component. This data was reanalysed by Dodrill and Temkin (1989), covarying for motor speed, as a result of which the previously obtained statistically significant differences disappeared, suggesting that PHT primarily has its effect on motor speed.

Studying the withdrawal of PHT in patients on a polytherapy regimen, Duncan *et al.* (1990) administered a battery of tests – including the Digit Symbol Substitution Task, a Letter Cancellation Task, Digit Span, Serial Subtraction and Tapping rate – at a practice session prior to study entry, at baseline, at the end of the drug reduction period, and four weeks after withdrawal. The twenty-one subjects showed a significant improvement on a Letter Cancellation Task and Tapping rate. The authors concluded that removal of PHT is associated with an improvement in attention, concentration and simple co-ordinated hand movements.

Gallassi *et al.* (1992) also reported on seven individuals being withdrawn from PHT, using the same design as described previously. Significant differences in favour of the control group were found on two measures prior to withdrawal, and one measure following a 50 per cent reduction in PHT, but no differences after withdrawal.

Thus studies suggest that PHT may have detrimental effects on performance, although the extent to which this may be just a motor speed effect is not always evaluated.

Interestingly, undesirable effects have been reported at serum levels well within, and even at the low end of, the therapeutic range, whereas it has previously been accepted that such effects are more likely to be seen at high serum drug levels (Thompson and Trimble 1982). A more recent study of children disputed this. Aman *et al.* (1994) tested fifty children, whose seizures were well controlled on PHT, at high and low serum level concentrations. Once extraneous factors such as age and seizure type were controlled by statistical modelling, fluctuations in PHT in the order of 50 per cent appeared to have no statistically significant effect on performance.

Sodium valproate (VPA)

Recent studies exploring the impact of withdrawing VPA from either seizure-free patients or those on a polytherapy regimen suggest that VPA may have some detrimental effects. In the studies reported by Gallassi *et al.* (1992), VPA was withdrawn from twelve seizure-free patients. Before withdrawal a healthy control group performed better on a Reaction Time task, the Trail Making Test, Finger Tip Number Writing and Digit Span. After 50 per cent withdrawal, a difference was still apparent on the Trail Making Test and, three months after withdrawal, on a spatial memory task. However, Duncan *et al.* (1990) found that removal of VPA was associated only with improvement on one measure, a tapping task.

A comparison between conventional and controlled release (VPA-CR) preparations has been undertaken in children, comparing their performance on tests of vigilance and attention while taking VPA, and then after four weeks of treatment with VPA-CR. There were no significant differences between the two conditions, and furthermore there was no correlation between performance and plasma drug levels for either VPA or VPA-CR (Brouwer *et al.* 1992).

Carbamazepine (CBZ)

Of all the AEDs mentioned so far, CBZ has been thought to be the least detrimental, in terms of cognitive functioning. Thus, in Gallassi *et al.*'s (1992) study, eleven patients were completely withdrawn from CBZ, and at each of the four assessments there were no differences between the performance of this group and that of a control group.

Duncan *et al.* (1990) found an improvement in tapping rate in fifteen patients having CBZ withdrawn from their AED regimen. However, a significant increase in seizure frequency in this group makes the results difficult to interpret.

Reinvang *et al.* (1991) studied twenty-two subjects on a stable CBZ monotherapy regimen. They were tested twice (following a pre-test) at 8 a.m. or 8 p.m. and noon when the serum concentrations were significantly higher than at 8 a.m. or 8 p.m. Measures included the WAIS, motor speed, reaction time, attention, and memory. Few significant differences between the high and low serum level conditions were found, but there were faster response times in the high serum level condition on two measures, suggesting improved functioning. Interestingly, Aman *et al.* (1990) have also found an improvement in relation to peak serum concentrations of CBZ on tests of attention and motor steadiness in children.

The slow release preparation of CBZ has been studied by Aldenkamp *et al.* (1987) in a single-blind cross over comparison with conventional CBZ. They found a tendency toward consistently higher performance in the slow release condition, especially on tests of memory and visual information processing. On a small battery of automated tests that were administered four times on each day of testing, there were also less fluctuations in performance with the slow release than the conventional preparation, thus resulting in a more stable pattern of performance throughout the day.

Benzodiazepines

There is an extreme paucity of information on the effects of the benzodiazepines most commonly used in epilepsy, notably clonazepam and clobazam.

Scott and Moffett (1986) tested thirty patients on the Stroop test before the initiation of clobazam at 20–30 mg/day as adjunctive therapy, and thereafter at one month, three months and six months, at which times there was a significant improvement in test performance. This was attributed to the addition of clobazam. Interpretation is hampered by the marked reduction in seizure frequency and the role of practice.

No significant change in cognitive function or mood was observed in seventeen people with uncontrolled seizures who were being withdrawn from clonazepam by Chataway *et al.* (1993).

To the authors' knowledge, there are no other recent studies in people with epilepsy. There is thus a need for further research since both clobazam and clonazepam have been associated with behavioural difficulties in some children with epilepsy (Commander *et al.* 1991; Sheth *et al.* 1994).

Newer anti-epileptic drugs

The difficulty in interpreting many of these studies is that the AED is being used as adjunctive therapy in patients with refractory epilepsy; thus, the effect on seizure frequency is unlikely to be negligible.

Vigabatrin (VGB)

Cognitive effects

McGuire *et al.* (1992) compared the performance of fifteen patients taking add-on VGB with fifteen patients whose AEDs remained the same. Over a four-week period no significant cognitive effects of VGB were noted. Gillham *et al.* (1993) also found no significant difference between VGB and placebo in twenty-one patients who participated in a double-blind randomised crossover trial, where VGB or placebo was added to their existing regimen. Subjects were assessed on a battery of nine measures, four times over a twelve-week period in each phase of the study.

A few detrimental effects have been reported, but these may not be clinically significant. Thus, Grunewald *et al.* (1994) compared twenty-two subjects before and twenty weeks after taking VGB, with twenty-three subjects before and twenty weeks after placebo, and reported significantly poorer performance in the VGB group on two measures (motor speed and memory) despite an improvement in seizure frequency. However, this was out of a total of sixteen possible comparisons and it is unclear whether the authors controlled for Type One errors.

Perhaps the largest study carried out to date, in terms of subject numbers, has been that of Dodrill *et al.* (1995). Subjects were assessed before and eighteen weeks after treatment with 1g VGB (N=36), 3g VGB (N=38), 6g VGB (N=32) or placebo (N=40) on eight tests. A worsening performance was found with increasing doses of VGB on one task only, a Letter Cancellation Test.

No detrimental effects were found in fourteen patients who had taken VGB over a period of eighteen months by Bittencourt *et al.* (1994); however, seizure control also improved over this time.

So far, vigabatrin would appear to have no significant effects on cognitive function, at least in patients with difficult-to-control seizures. However, well-controlled double-blind studies are still needed to compare the cognitive effects of VGB with other AEDs (Meador 1995).

Behavioural effects

The impact of VGB on behaviour has been assessed predominantly by self-rating scales/questionnaires, including the General Health Questionnaire (Gillham *et al.* 1993); a mood adjective checklist and the

Hospital Anxiety and Depression questionnaire (Grunewald *et al.* 1994), and mood rating scales, the Profile of Mood States, and the Washington Psychosocial Seizure Index (Dodrill *et al.* 1995). In none of these studies were any of the scales significantly affected in the subjects taking VGB. Thus, in the majority of subjects, VGB appears to have no detrimental effects. In some patients, however, there is an idiosyncratic adverse reaction, whereby they may develop a psychotic-like state, or other severe behaviour disturbance (Sander and Hart 1990; Brodie and McKee 1990). Indeed, in Grunewald *et al.*'s (1994) study, two patients had to discontinue treatment because of depression although this condition was reversible on discontinuation of treatment.

Lamotrigine (LTG)

Cognitive effects

Lamotrigine is the newest AED to be licensed in the UK for monotherapy, but the majority of studies have been carried out using LTG as adjunctive therapy in seizure refractory individuals.

Smith *et al.* (1993) undertook a randomised double-blind crossover study comparing LTG with placebo taken for eighteen weeks each in eighty-one patients (children and adults). Cognitive assessment took place before treatment and at the end of each treatment phase using the Stroop test, number cancellation, Critical Flicker Fusion, and a choice reaction time task. There were no differences between LTG and placebo on any measures. Similarly, Banks and Beran (1991) found no evidence that LTG produces undesirable cognitive side-effects.

One major area of interest with LTG has been its suppression of interictal spiking. In up to 50 per cent of patients with sub-clinical epileptiform discharges, recordable by EEG, there is associated Transitory Cognitive Impairment (TCI) (Binnie 1994); LTG provides effective control over subclinical seizures without adversely affecting cognitive function and therefore, if TCI is prevented, a general improvement in cognitive function might be expected. A study is in progress to evaluate this further.

There are anecdotal reports that LTG may have beneficial effects on the cognitive functioning of children and young adults with severe learning disabilities (Hosking *et al.* 1993; Uvebrant and Bauziene 1994), although such reports are difficult to evaluate, as they are also associated with improved seizure frequency.

Behaviour

Lamotrigine also appears to have beneficial effects on well-being and quality of life. Smith *et al.* (1993) asked patients to complete a variety of mood and self-esteem measures. Subjects reported being significantly more happy and having a greater sense of perceived control when on LTG than placebo, independently of any improvements in seizure control.

Gillham *et al.* (1996) have observed that patients taking LTG report significantly less depression and negative mood than those not on LTG, as assessed by a newly devised self-rating scale.

Beneficial effects of LTG on the behaviour of children with learning disabilities have been reported both anecdotally (Uvebrant and Bauziene 1994), and in studies using standardised rating scales (Fowler *et al.* 1994).

Other new AEDs

Only very preliminary results of the cognitive/behavioural effects of other new AEDs in people with epilepsy are available at the time of writing.

Oxcarbazepine has been available for almost ten years, but is not licensed in the UK. In one UK study, McKee *et al.* (1994) did not demonstrate any significant cognitive effects.

Gabapentin has been evaluated by Arnett and Dodrill (1995), again with no evidence of cognitive effect; preliminary results for Topiramate (Brooks *et al.* 1995) are also negative.

Finally, Tiagabine is currently being evaluated in a multi-centre monotherapy study in the UK and Australia, using cognitive tests and quality of life measures. Results of this study will not be available until 1997, but in a previous add-on study Sveinbjornsdottir *et al.* (1994) showed no cognitive effect.

While initial results for the newer AEDs look promising, more time is needed to evaluate them fully.

Drug comparisons

While it is of some value to examine the effects of individual AEDs, it is difficult to make comparisons between drugs on this basis, although such information is likely to be of more use to both clinicians and patients. It is easier to make sense of studies where comparisons between drugs have been undertaken within the same time frame, using the same test battery, administered by the same personnel.

A number of such studies have been undertaken, and the AEDs most frequently used include PHB, PHT, CBZ and VPA.

To compare CBZ, PHB and PHT, Meador *et al.* (1990) carried out an ambitious randomised, double-blind, triple crossover comparison. Fifteen subjects with complex partial seizures received each drug for three months each. At the beginning of each phase, subjects were withdrawn from their pre-existing medication and started on gradually increasing doses of the drug for that treatment phase. Psychological testing was carried out at the end of each treatment phase consisting of Digit Span, Selective Reminding Test, Digit Symbol Substitution Test, Finger Tapping, Grooved Pegboard and Choice Reaction Time. In the analysis, AED blood levels and seizure frequency were used as covariates, and the only significant difference that emerged was on the Digit Symbol Substitution Test, performance of which was significantly worse in the PHB group. The authors concluded that CBZ, PHT and PHB are comparable in respect of their neuropsychological effects.

In their study of withdrawal of PHT, CBZ and VPA, Duncan *et al.* (1990) also reported that there were no significant differences between the three groups in terms of changes in performance over time. Thus, all three drugs may adversely affect motor function, although there was also a suggestion that PHT is more likely to affect attention and concentration than CBZ or VPA.

The effects of CBZ and VPA have also been found to be comparable after twelve months of treatment in newly diagnosed children, with no significant changes in either cognitive function or behaviour (Stores *et al.* 1992).

Three further studies have also reported no differences, or insignificant differences, between such AEDs and their effects on cognitive function (Craig and Tallis 1994; Meador *et al.* 1993; Verma *et al.* 1993).

However, differences have also been reported. Gillham *et al.* (1990) compared patients taking CBZ, or VPA or PHT with each other, with untreated patients with epilepsy, and with control subjects without epilepsy. CBZ tended to produce the greatest psychomotor impairment and PHT produced the most memory impairment. The biggest differences tended to be between the patients with epilepsy and the control subjects without epilepsy, an indication that whatever effects AEDs might have on cognitive function, they are of less significance than the effect of the disorder itself.

Forsythe *et al.* (1991) randomly assigned sixty-four previously untreated children to either CBZ, PHT or VPA treatment and administered a battery of psychometric tests at baseline, and on three subsequent occasions during the following year. CBZ was associated with poorer scores on memory tests than either PHT or VPA. The study was not blind and the influence of seizure frequency is not clear.

In a study by Bittencourt *et al.* (1992), patients taking PHT or VPA performed worse than controls on a memory test, and patients on CBZ performed worse on the Stroop Test. The authors concluded that the results indicated relatively minor effects of the AEDs on cognitive function.

A major contribution to the evaluation of cognitive function in epilepsy has been the development of a computerised battery specifically for patients with epilepsy. Aldenkamp *et al.* (1994) used FePSY (see Chapter 2) to compare PHT and CBZ in an open, non-randomised, parallel group study. Results showed lower performance in the PHT group on tests measuring motor speed and speed of central processing systems, and information processing.

A study of newly diagnosed patients randomly allocated to treatment with either PHT or CBZ also showed differences. Pulliainen and Jokelainen (1994) tested patients before treatment and after six months, comparing the practice effect with a control group being tested on the same schedule. Both AEDs, but the PHT group in particular, showed a much smaller practice effect.

It will be seen from the above that the evidence for specific profiles for the three first-line drugs is equivocal. The studies reviewed are very different in design, in sample type, and in test battery, and so it is difficult to make an overall generalisation.

Monotherapy versus polytherapy

Drug reduction has been found to have beneficial effects on cognitive function and behaviour, although it is most likely that this has been mediated through beneficial effects on seizure frequency, rather than the AEDs per se (e.g. Ludgate *et al.* 1985). It is further asserted that adverse effects are more likely to be seen with polytherapy rather than monotherapy (Meador 1994), although the impact of drugs used in rational combinations has yet to be evaluated.

CONCLUSIONS

Meador (1994) summarises current opinion with regard to the cognitive effect of AEDs thus:

> all of the established AEDs can produce cognitive side effects, which are both increased with polypharmacy and with increasing dosage and anticonvulsant blood levels. However, cognitive side effects are usually modest with AED monotherapy . . . Further, these effects are offset in part by reduced seizure activity . . . there is no convincing evidence of clinically significant cognitive side effects of AEDs.
>
> (Meador 1994: S12)

Even so, it is still possible for individuals to experience idiosyncratic adverse effects that might not be expected from reading the literature, and it is important to be alert to the possibility of these.

Many of the studies available to date focus on a fairly limited range of subjects, as was alluded to earlier, and do not explore the impact of AEDs in the elderly or people with learning disabilities, and thus the applicability of results to these not insubstantial groups of people is not known. However, it is hoped that in the future, along with improving methodology, such issues will be addressed.

IMPLICATIONS FOR CLINICAL PRACTICE

Any evaluation of the impact of AEDs on the functioning of a particular individual (whether it be a change in the drug or dose of the drug) will inevitably mean that at least two assessments have to be undertaken. This should be taken into account in the choice of tests to be used as they need to be suitable for repeated administration. It will also be important to separate out motor speed from other cognitive measures, to ensure that any effects are not wrongly attributed. Any assessment should include some investigation of aspects of behaviour and quality of life. Clearly any measures used should be appropriate to the developmental level of an individual.

In interpreting test results, the clinician needs to be aware of all medications that a patient is taking, whether they are in a controlled release preparation or not, the dose, and time between drug ingestion and assessment in order to identify whether the AED is at a peak or trough level. A serum drug level assay of blood taken at the time of testing would also be very useful as a way of assessing compliance, and whether or not the levels are within or above the therapeutic range, as a toxic blood level can have detrimental effects on functioning, such as lethargy and slowness. The clinician should also take into account any change in seizure frequency between assessments and the time between the last seizure and test administration.

We would suggest that the challenge now for clinical psychologists is to make a constructive contribution to discussions concerning the impact of AEDs on an individual's functioning, which should be based not just on the literature but on evidence gained directly from their own assessments.

REFERENCES

Aldenkamp, A. P. and Vermeulen, J. (1995) 'Phenytoin and carbamazepine: differential effects on cognitive function', *Seizure* 4: 95–104.

Aldenkamp, A. P., Alpherts, W. C. J., Moerland, M. C., Ottevanger, N. and Van Parys, J. A. P. (1987) 'Controlled release carbamazepine: cognitive side effects in patients with epilepsy', *Epilepsia* 28: 507–14.

Aldenkamp, A. P., Alpherts, W. C., Diepman, L., van't-Slot, B., Overweg, J. and Vermeulen, J. (1994) 'Cognitive side-effects of phenytoin compared with carbamazepine in patients with localization-related epilepsy', *Epilepsy Research* 19: 37–43.

Aman, M. G., Werry, J. S., Paxton, J. W. and Turbott, S. H. (1994) 'Effects of phenytoin on cognitive–motor performance in children as a function of drug concentration, seizure type, and time of medication', *Epilepsia* 35: 172–80.

Aman, M. G., Werry, J. S., Paxton, J. W., Turbott, S. H. and Stewart, A. W. (1990) 'Effects of carbamazepine on psychomotor performance in children as a function of drug concentration, seizure type, and time of medication', *Epilepsia* 31: 51–60.

Arnett, J. L. and Dodrill, C. B. (1995) 'Effects of gabapentin on cognitive functioning and mood', *Epilepsia* 36 (Suppl. 3): S32.

Banks, G. K. and Beran, R. G. (1991) 'Neuropsychological assessment in lamotrigine treated epileptic patients', *Clinical and Experimental Neurology* 28: 230–7.

Binnie, C. D. (1994) 'Cognitive impairment – is it inevitable?' *Seizure* 3 (Suppl. A): 17–21.

Bittencourt, P. R. M., Mazer, S., Marcourakis, T., Bigarella, M. M., Ferreira, Z. S. and Mumford, J. P. (1994) 'Vigabatrin: clinical evidence supporting rational polytherapy in management of uncontrolled seizures', *Epilepsia* 35: 373–80.

Bittencourt, P. R., Mader, M. J., Bigarella, M. M., Doro, M. P., Gorz, A. M., Marcourakis, T. M. and Ferreira, Z. S. (1992) 'Cognitive function, epileptic syndromes and anti-epileptic drugs', *Arquivos de Neuro-Psiquiatria* 50: 24–30.

Brodie, M. J. (1985) 'The optimum use of anticonvulsants', *The Practitioner* 229: October.

Brodie, M. J. and McKee, P. J. W. (1990) 'Vigabatrin and psychosis', *Lancet* 335: 1279.

Brooks, J., Sachedo, R. and Lim, P. (1995) 'Topiramate: neuropsychometric assessments', *Epilepsia* 36 (Suppl. 3): S273.

Brouwer, O. F., Pieters, M. S. M., Edelbroek, P. M., Bakker, A. M., VanGeel, A. A. C. M., Stijnen, Th., Jennekens-Schinkel, A., Lanser, J. B. K. and Peters, A. C. B. (1992) 'Conventional and controlled release valproate in children with epilepsy: a cross-over study comparing plasma levels and cognitive performances', *Epilepsy Research* 13: 245–53.

Chataway, J., Fowler, A., Thompson, P. J. and Duncan, J. (1993) 'Discountinuation of clonazepam in patients with active epilepsy', *Seizure* 2: 295–300.

Commander, M., Green, S. H. and Prendergast, M. (1991) 'Behavioural disturbances in children treated with clonazepam', *Developmental Medicine and Child Neurology* 33: 362–4.

Committee on Drugs (1985) 'Behavioural and cognitive effects of anticonvulsant therapy', *Paediatrics* 76: 644–7.

Craig, I. and Tallis, R. (1994) 'Impact of valproate and phenytoin on cognitive function in elderly patients: results of a single-blind randomized comparative study', *Epilepsia* 35: 381–90.

Devinsky, O. (1995) 'Cognitive and behavioral effects of anti-epileptic drugs', *Epilepsia* 36 (Suppl. 2): S46–65.

Dodrill, C. B. (1975) 'Diphenylhydantoin serum levels, toxicity, and neuropsychological performance in patients with epilepsy', *Epilepsia* 16: 593–600.

—— (1992) 'Problems in the assessment of cognitive effects of anti-epileptic drugs', *Epilepsia* 33 (Suppl. 6): S29–32.

Dodrill C. B. and Temkin, N. R. (1989) 'Motor speed is a contaminating factor in evaluating the "cognitive" effects of phenytoin', *Epilepsia* 30: 453–7.

Dodrill, C. B., Arnett, J. L., Sommerville, K. W. and Sussman, N. M. (1995) 'Effects of differing dosages of vigabatrin on cognitive abilities and quality of life in epilepsy', *Epilepsia* 36: 164–73.

Dreifuss, F. E. (1992) 'Cognitive function – victim of disease or hostage to treatment?' *Epilepsia*, 33 (Suppl. 1): S7–12.

Duncan, J. S., Shorvon, S. D. and Trimble M. R. (1990) 'Effects of removal of phenytoin, carbamazepine, and valproate on cognitive function', *Epilepsia* 31: 584–91.

Forsythe, I., Butler, R., Berg, I. and McGuire, R. (1991) 'Cognitive impairment in new cases of epilepsy randomly assigned to either carbamazepine, phenytoin, or sodium valproate', *Developmental Medicine and Child Neurology* 33: 524–34.

Fowler, M., Besag, F. and Pool, F. (1994) 'Effects of lamotrigine on behavior in children', *Epilepsia* 35 (Suppl. 7): 69.

Gallassi, R., Morreale, A., DiSarro, R., Marra, M., Lugaresi, E. and Baruzzi, A. (1992) 'Cognitive effects of anti-epileptic drug discontinuation', *Epilepsia* 33 (Suppl. 6): S41–4.

Gillham, R. A., Blacklaw, J., McKee, P. J. W. and Brodie, M. J. (1993) 'Effect of vigabatrin on sedation and cognitive function in patients with refractory epilepsy', *Journal of Neurology, Neurosurgery and Psychiatry* 56: 1271–5.

Gillham, R. A., Williams, N., Wiedmann, K. D., Butler, E., Larkin, J. G. and

Brodie, M. J. (1990) 'Cognitive function in adult epileptic patients established on anticonvulsant monotherapy', *Epilepsy Research* 7: 219–25.

Gillham, R., Baker, G., Thompson, P., Birbeck, K., McGuire, A., Tomlinson, L., Echersley, L., Silveira, C. and Brown, S. (1996) 'Standardisation of a self-report questionnaire for use in evaluating cognitive, affective and behavioural side-effects of anti-epileptic drug treatments', *Epilepsy Research* 24: 47–55.

Grunewald, R. A., Thompson, P. J., Corcoran, R., Corden, Z., Jackson, G. D. and Duncan, J. S. (1994) 'Effects of vigabatrin on partial seizures and cognitive function', *Journal of Neurology, Neurosurgery and Psychiatry* 57: 1057–63.

Hirtz, D. G. and Nelson, K. B. (1985) 'Cognitive effects of anti-epileptic drugs', in T. A. Pedley and B. S. Meldrum (eds) *Recent Advances in Epilepsy*, New York: Churchill Livingstone.

Hosking, G., Spencer, S. and Yuen, A. W. C. (1993) 'Lamotrigine in children with severe developmental abnormalities in a paediatric population with refractory seizures', *Epilepsia* 34 (Suppl. 6): 42.

Kälviäinen, R., Äikiä, M. and Riekkinen Sr, P. J. (1996) 'Cognitive adverse effects of anti-epileptic drugs', *CNS Drugs* 5: 358–68.

Ludgate, J., Keating, J., O'Dwyer, R. and Callaghan, N. (1985) 'An improvement in cognitive function following polypharmacy reduction in a group of epileptic patients', *Acta Neurologica Scandinavica* 71: 448–52.

McKee, P. J., Blacklaw, J., Forrest, G., Gillham, R. A., Walker, S. M., Connelly, D. and Brodie, M. J. (1994) 'A double-blind, placebo-controlled interaction study between oxcarbazepine and carbamazepine, sodium valproate and phenytoin in epileptic patients', *British Journal of Clinical Pharmacology* 37: 27–32.

Meador, K. J. (1994) 'Cognitive side effects of anti-epileptic drugs', *Canadian Journal of Neurological Science* 21: S12–16.

—— (1995) 'Cognitive effects of vigabatrin', *Epilepsia* 36 (Suppl. 3): S31.

Meador, K. J., Loring, D. W., Huh, K., Gallagher, B. B. and King, D. W. (1990) 'Comparative cognitive effects of anticonvulsants', *Neurology* 40: 391–4.

Meador, K. J., Loring, D. W., Abney, O. L., Allen, M. E., Moore, E. E., Zamrini, E. Y. and King, D. W. (1993) 'Effects of carbamazepine and phenytoin on EEG and memory in healthy adults', *Epilepsia* 34: 153–7.

McGuire, A., Duncan, J. and Trimble, M. R. (1992) 'Effects of vigabatrin on cognitive function and mood when used as add-on therapy in patients with intractable epilepsy', *Epilepsia* 32: 128–34.

Pulliainen, V. and Jokelainen M. (1994) 'Effects of phenytoin and carbamazepine on cognitive functions in newly diagnosed epileptic patients', *Acta Neurologica Scandinavica* 89: 81–6.

Reinvang, I., Bjartveit, S., Johannessen, S. I., Hagen, O. P., Larsen, S., Fagerthun, H. and Gjerstad, L. (1991) 'Cognitive function and time-of-day variation in serum carbamazepine concentration in epileptic patients treated with monotherapy', *Epilepsia* 32: 116–21.

Sander, J. W. A. S. and Hart, Y. M. (1990) 'Vigabatrin and behaviour disturbances', *Lancet* 335: 57.

Scott, D. F. and Moffett, A. (1986) 'On the anticonvulsant and psychotropic properties of clobazam: a preliminary study', *Epilepsia* 27: S42–4.

Sheth, R. D., Goulden, K. J. and Ronen, G. M. (1994) 'Aggression in children treated with clobazam for epilepsy', *Clinical Neuropharmacology* 17: 332–7.

Smith, D., Baker, G., Davies, G., Dewey, M. and Chadwick, D. W. (1993) 'Outcomes of add-on treatment with lamotrigine in partial epilepsy', *Epilepsia* 34: 312–22.

Stores, G., Williams, P. L., Styles, E. and Zaiwalla, Z. (1992) 'Psychological effects of sodium valproate and carbamazepine in epilepsy', *Archives of Disease in Childhood* 67: 1330–7.

Sveinbjornsdottir, S., Sander, J. W., Patsalos, P. N., Upton, D., Thompson, P. J. and Duncan, J. S. (1994) 'Neuropsychological effects of tiagabine, a potential new anti-epileptic drug', *Seizure* 3: 29–35.

Thompson, P. J. and Trimble, M. R. (1982) 'Anticonvulsant drugs and cognitive functions', *Epilepsia* 23: 531–44.

Uvebrant, P. and Bauziene, R. (1994) 'Intractable epilepsy in children. The efficacy of lamotrigine treatment, including non-seizure – related benefits', *Neuropediatrics* 25: 284–9.

Verma, N. P., Yusko, M. J. and Greiffenstien, M. F. (1993) 'Carbamazepine offers no psychotropic advantage over phenytoin in adult epileptic subjects', *Seizure* 2: 53–6.

Chapter 6

Psychological responses to epilepsy
Their development, prognosis and treatment

Gus A. Baker

INTRODUCTION

In this chapter, the various psychological problems associated with a diagnosis of epilepsy will be considered. Such responses can include high levels of anxiety and depression, low self-esteem, poor sense of control, aggression and some more serious disturbances such as psychosis. The prevalence of such problems will be examined, evidence about their aetiology will be reviewed, and consideration will then be given to the contribution of the clinical psychologist to their assessment and treatment. The focus of this chapter will be upon adults with epilepsy; consideration of behavioural problems in children with epilepsy are discussed in Chapter 10. Rather than providing an exhaustive account of these variables, which would fill a book on its own, this chapter will serve as an introduction, highlighting the main issues.

There are a number of possible reasons why people with epilepsy may develop behavioural and emotional problems and these can be summarised as follows:

(a) the effects of a damaged brain;
(b) the adverse effects of anti-epileptic medication;
(c) the effects of living with a stigmatising disorder.

Historically, the emphasis has tended to be on searching for relationships between structural brain damage and dysfunction as causes of behavioural problems, for example, between psychopathology and specific seizure types, epilepsy duration and seizure localisation (Gibbs *et al.* 1948; Gastaut *et al.* 1955; Gloor *et al.* 1982; Leiderman *et al.* 1990). However, Hermann and Whitman (1991), reviewing a multiaetiological model of psychopathology in epilepsy (see Table 6.1), conclude that the explanatory power of what they term the 'neuroepilepsy' factors is only modest.

Recently, increasing emphasis has been placed on the adverse effects of anti-epileptic drugs as contributory factors in the development and maintenance of behavioural disorders in epilepsy (Dodrill and Batzel 1986; Cull and Trimble 1989). The least researched explanation for behavioural problems in epilepsy relates to the impact of living with a chronic illness, particularly one which is stigmatising and to which a negative social label is attached (Scambler and Hopkins 1986; West 1986; Conrad and Schneider 1992; Jacoby 1994).

It is difficult to disentangle the relative effects of these factors, but if we accept the idea that structural brain damage underlies all

Table 6.1 Potential multiaetiological risk factors for psychosocial and psychiatric consequences of epilepsy (adapted by Hermann and Whitman 1986)

Neurobiological	Psychosocial	Medication
Epilepsy - related		
Age at onset	Locus of control	Monotherapy versus polytherapy
Duration of disorder	Fear of seizures	
Seizure type	Adjustment to epilepsy	Presence/absence of barbiturates
Degree of seizure control	Parental overprotection	
Ictal/interictal EEG changes	Perceived stigma	Folate deficiency
Seizure severity	Perceived discrimination	Hormonal/endocrine
Presence/absence of structural effects brain changes		Medication-induced alterations in monoamine metabolism
Phenomenological aspects of seizures	*Non-epilepsy related*	
	Stressful life events	
	Financial stress	
Neuropsychological	Employment status	
functioning	Social support	Medication-induced alterations in cerebral metabolism
Efficiency of cerebral metabolism	Years of education	
Alterations in neurotransmitters		CNS dose-related side effects of medication

behavioural problems, then the clinical psychologists' role in their treatment is limited. However, given the accumulating evidence of the importance of medication and social variables, then the clinical psychologist has a significant part to play in the assessment and amelioration of such problems.

PREVALENCE OF PSYCHOLOGICAL PROBLEMS IN EPILEPSY

Epilepsy and anxiety

For a number of years, anxiety has been cited as a common, if not the most common, consequence of the unpredictable nature of some epilepsies (Arnston *et al.* 1986; Collings 1990). A number of studies investigating the incidence of anxiety in people with epilepsy using the Hospital Anxiety and Depression (HAD) Scale (Zigmond and Snaith 1983) have reported rates of between 25–33 per cent in patients with resistant epilepsy (Smith *et al.* 1991; Baker *et al.* 1996). Betts (1992) has argued, however, that although many patients are fearful of their seizures only a relatively small number develop a true phobic anxiety resulting in social isolation. Further, a number of studies which have investigated the relationship between epilepsy and anxiety have been confounded by failure to define or differentiate between state and trait anxiety (Betts 1981). Many patients experience anxiety as a result of the diagnosis of epilepsy and the ensuing adjustment. Anxiety may also occur as an integral part of the pre-ictal, ictal and post-ictal aspect of an individual's seizure. Some patients have attacks that are associated with, or precipitated by, anxiety (Betts 1981).

The link between epilepsy and anxiety may be understood in terms of a number of potential sources: first, the fear of having a seizure and the belief that seizures may lead to death (Scambler and Hopkins 1986; Mittan and Locke 1982); second, the stigmatising condition of epilepsy may result in higher levels of anxiety and depression. Arnston *et al.* (1986) found their measure of perceived stigma to be related to a number of psychological variables including anxiety, although a causal link is yet to be established (Scambler 1989). In a recent community study there was clear evidence of a relationship between level of seizure activity and psychological functioning, with individuals with frequent seizures having significantly higher rates of anxiety and depression than those with infrequent or no seizures (Jacoby *et al.* 1996). Tenuous links have also been made between perceived discrimination, adjustment to epilepsy and psychopathology, with some patients experiencing anxiety as a result of their determination to conceal their condition.

Anecdotal evidence would suggest a reciprocal relationship between anxiety and epilepsy in that the more anxious the patient is the more likely they are to have a seizure, and the more seizures they have the more anxious they become.

Epilepsy and depression

A series of studies on the relationship between epilepsy and depression in patients with resistant seizures report that depression is more common among people with epilepsy than normal controls or other neurological conditions (Robertson *et al.* 1987). Rates of depression in a population without epilepsy have been reported to vary between 2–4 per cent (Sullivan 1995). Recent studies of a hospital-based and a community-based population report incidence rates of clinical depression, using the Hospital Anxiety and Depression scale, of between 10–15 per cent (Smith *et al.* 1991; Baker *et al.* 1996), while a previous hospital-based study of 666 patients attending a neurology clinic suggested a rate of 16 per cent, including 5 per cent who later committed suicide (Currie *et al.* 1971). Indeed, suicide in people with epilepsy is approximately four to five times more common than in the general population, and twenty-five times more common in people with temporal lobe epilepsy (Matthews and Barabas 1981).

Determining the causes of this depression has been troublesome, with a number of conflicting studies implicating either biological or environmental predisposing factors. Some authors have proposed that depression is as a result of abnormalities in neurochemical functioning, for example, dopamine, noradrenalin, or folic acid levels (Robertson *et al.* 1987), while others have suggested that it is a reaction to living with a stigmatising disorder (Scambler and Hopkins 1986). Dodrill and Batzel (1986) argue that depression is more common in people with multiple seizure types and frequent seizures, whereas Smith *et al.* (1991) have argued that patient-perceived seizure severity may be more important than seizure frequency or seizure type in predicting depression. In patients with resistant epilepsy, what might be important therefore is not the frequency of seizures but their severity. Betts (1992) has argued that reactive and endogenous depression may coexist in people with epilepsy, and as such there may be a number of causes for depression. The potential relationship between epilepsy, depressive feelings and depressive illness may be classified in the following way.

- Depressive reaction to acquiring the label of epilepsy;
- Depressive reaction to social/family problems of epilepsy;
- Prodromal depressive feelings before a seizure;
- Depressive feelings as an aura;
- Depressive feelings as an ictal experience;
- Post-ictal depressive feelings;
- Depressive twilight state;
- Epileptic depressive delirium;
- Endogenous depression unrelated directly to seizures, but possibly to their increase in frequency;
- Depressive symptoms occurring in association with other mental illnesses particularly a paranoid or schizophrenic psychosis.

The depressive symptoms reported by people with epilepsy have been both somatic and psychotic, but a study comparing depressed people with epilepsy and depressed controls using the Hamilton rating scale and a brief psychiatric rating scale found that the epilepsy subjects reported similar prevalence rates of endogenous depressive traits (e.g. psychomotor retardation), but more psychotic behaviours (e.g. hallucinations) and fewer neurotic traits (e.g. somatisation) (Mendez *et al.* 1986).

Depression can be self-reinforcing and the associated sequelae, such as loss of confidence, low self-esteem and agoraphobia, can also be disabling and last longer than the depression itself. In addition, it has been noted that the effects of anticonvulsant drugs may impair learning and therefore interfere with normal coping responses to stress, including depression (Betts 1981). In a recent study by Jacoby *et al.* (1996), later age at onset of seizures, seizure activity and duration of epilepsy were significant predictors of depression suggesting that, for many adults developing seizures, there are important social consequences of becoming labelled 'epileptic', for example, in relation to their ability to function in the role of an employee or family supporter. These recent findings will have implications for determining how we address the problem of depression in people with epilepsy.

Epilepsy and aggression

Historically, aggression has been associated with epilepsy, despite the lack of well-controlled studies investigating the incidence and prevalence of aggressive behaviour in this condition (Fenwick 1986). Previous studies investigating interictal aggressive behaviour have been flawed by a number of methodological problems including poor design, unclear definitions and lack of standardisation (Thompson 1988). A current review of the literature would suggest that there is no evidence that directed aggression may occur as an ictal behaviour manifestation. Where violence has been witnessed in adults with epilepsy, it has usually been as a response to constraint by others during the post-ictal stage of a stereotypical seizure. Nor is there any evidence to suggest that epilepsy is more common in violent or aggressive people, or that violence or aggression are more common in people with epilepsy (Treiman 1990). Given that aggression is not necessarily a consequence of epilepsy, it would seem important to determine the antecedents, behaviour and consequences of aggressive acts and treat them as any other behavioural problem.

Epilepsy and psychosis

There has been a number of conflicting studies investigating the incidence and prevalence of psychosis in people with epilepsy. In a study of fourteen general practices, Pond and Bidwell (1959) found 29 per cent of their sample had a history of psychiatric illness, but none had been, or were, psychotic. In contrast, a number of outpatient studies (Currie *et al.* 1971) reported an incidence of between 2–5 per cent. In an earlier study of sixty-nine patients with a schizophrenia-like psychosis, 80 per cent were found to have focal EEG abnormalities in the temporal lobe (Slater and Beard 1963), leading the authors to conclude that the characteristics of the psychoses accompanying epilepsy were distinct from functional psychosis. This finding has not, however, been confirmed in subsequent prospective studies (Perez and Trimble 1980) although there have been a number of case reports where patients have presented with a post-ictal psychosis following excessive seizure activity involving the limbic system (Waxman and Geshwind 1975). Such psychotic episodes tend to be of limited duration and may be prevented by the prophylactic use of anti-psychotic medication. Alternatively, Landolt (1958) proposed a theory of 'forced normalisation' where an improvement in interictal epileptiform activity was found to be correlated with the initation or exacerbation of psychosis, although the number of reported cases are few.

The relationship between epilepsy and psychosis is unclear (Devinsky 1992) and this has resulted from a number of methodological problems in previous research, including selection bias and a lack of homogeneity in the psychosis syndrome (Toone 1981). Undoubtedly, this has led to an overestimation of the incidence and prevalence of psychosis in epilepsy (Hauser and Hesdorffer 1990). A small number of people with epilepsy will present with psychoses and there is a suggestion that their symptoms may well be as a result of an underlying epileptic process linked with lesions in the limbic system structures (Trimble 1988). Devinsky (1992), reviewing the behavioural consequences of epilepsy, has suggested that there are a number of risk factors for psychosis, and these include left temporal seizure focus, bilateral seizure foci, structural pathology and left-handedness. Further controlled population-based research is clearly necessary to overcome such pitfalls and clarify the relationship between psychosis and epilepsy.

Epilepsy and self-esteem

Low self-esteem is well recognised as a clinical component of several psychiatric conditions including anxiety and depression, and self-esteem has been found to be significantly lower in people with epilepsy than those without (Collings 1990). Scambler (1989) has suggested that this is a result of the perceived level of stigma associated with the condition. For instance, a number of authors have demonstrated how perceptions of stigma of epilepsy were more strongly influenced by self-perceptions than by other more objective measures of epilepsy (e.g. seizure frequency), although in some of the studies the patient groups were hospital-based and samples may have been biased (Stanley and Tillotson 1982; Ryan *et al.* 1980). Jacoby (1994) indicated that people with well-controlled epilepsy were still stigmatised by their condition suggesting that the diagnosis, and not necessarily the frequency or severity of seizures, is important in understanding the stigma in epilepsy. Collings (1995), in a community study, has proposed that people with epilepsy tend to evaluate themselves negatively and this may be related to 'perceived stigma' as a result of the physician's diagnosis which converts them from a normal person to an 'epileptic' (Scambler 1989). Collings (1995) found that there was significant evidence of low self-esteem among patients with epilepsy specifically in terms of people with epilepsy downgrading themselves for success, competence and adaptation to life. Many of those surveyed reported that their self-esteem would be improved if they did not have epilepsy; whilst intuitively this makes sense, there had been no opportunity to test this belief. Particular areas of low fulfilment in this group were social relationships, peace of mind and employment. In contrast, Hills and Baker (1992) found that people with epilepsy reported higher levels of self-esteem than a normative sample. One explanation for their findings is that people with epilepsy are able, through a series of psychological processes, to protect themselves from the stigmatising effects of their condition. A second explanation may relate to the differences in the clinical populations studied, particularly in the frequency and severity of seizures. Low self-esteem in epilepsy may be the result of a number of potential sources including overprotection, perceived stigma and the failure to fulfil expectations.

Epilepsy and mastery (locus of control)

As has been repeatedly emphasised, epilepsy is a disorder characterised by a loss of control (Matthews *et al.* 1982). For a significant number of people with epilepsy, seizures may occur anywhere, at any time, with little or no warning. The threat of a sudden and unpredictable loss of control (and consciousness) has been thought to comprise an essential dimension of epilepsy (Matthews and Barabas 1981; Arnston *et al.* 1986). Indeed, compared with other chronic conditions, epilepsy is associated with a significantly greater external locus of control (Matthews and Barabas 1981). A small number of people will be able to predict their seizure occurrence and for them behavioural management techniques may be of help (see Chapter 7).

Having epilepsy may predispose an individual to develop an external locus of control (Zeigler 1982; Hermann and Whitman 1991). Unpredictability and the associated psychological complications of epilepsy may induce the sufferer to believe that they have little real control over many important and basic events in their lives, perceiving events to be attributable more to the effects of luck, chance, fate or others. Research indicates that such beliefs may render the individuals more susceptible to psychopathology, particularly clinical depression (Lefcourt 1976), which reduces the ability to manage the demands of everyday living. Wallaston and De Villas (1980) reported that patients with epilepsy perceived themselves as having significantly lower levels of internal locus of control when compared with a group of people without epilepsy, while Matthews and Barabas (1981) found high levels of external locus of control to be associated with anxiety, low self-esteem, feelings of helplessness and a higher risk of suicide in people with epilepsy.

Whilst evidence demonstrates the relationship between epilepsy and an external locus of control, there is little understanding of its development or maintenance. It seems reasonable to hypothesise that parenting behaviour, the severity and frequency of seizures and the patients' perceptions of themselves and their disorder all play an important role in understanding why many patients with epilepsy have an external locus of control. A recent study by Gehlert (1994) investigated the relationship between seizure control and perceptions of control and found that, in a sample of 143 people with epilepsy, seizure control could predict attribution style for bad events but not for good events. The author concludes that for people with epilepsy the occurrence of seizures may be so pervasive that it can negatively influence the way they perceive many events in their lives, and that a good event is any event not marred by a seizure. This finding supports previous research that highlights the impact that an unpredictable event (seizure) can have on an individual's perceived control over many aspects of their lives.

THE CONTRIBUTION OF THE CLINICAL PSYCHOLOGIST TO THE MANAGEMENT OF PSYCHOLOGICAL PROBLEMS IN EPILEPSY

Managing all the various psychological factors associated with epilepsy is crucial to making a positive adjustment to the condition. Such emotional and behavioural problems may become important determinants of motivation to comply with anti-epileptic medication and successful adaptation to a change in lifestyle. Little attention has been paid to the non-medical management of epilepsy, but this may be as a result of the small number of specialist centres world-wide providing a multi-disciplinary approach to the assessment and treatment of epilepsy, and the methodological flaws of studies determining the efficacy of such an approach (Goldstein 1990). Non-medical/surgical approaches to the management of epilepsy can be divided into two broad categories: those aimed at reducing seizure frequency and those which target the psychological adjustment of the individual with epilepsy. Techniques aimed at reducing seizure frequency through non-medical approaches will be discussed in Chapter 7.

The importance of the role of the clinical psychologist as a member of a multi-disciplinary team in the assessment and treatment of epilepsy has been well documented although at what stage they should intervene is less clear. Given that some people will develop psychological problems as a result of the diagnosis of epilepsy, then it would seem appropriate that psychological intervention should be made available at that point. For some families it may not be until several years later that difficulties arise as a result of the impact of the epilepsy, and therefore, a psychological service should be routinely available in epilepsy out-patient clinics.

People with epilepsy should be fully investigated to consider what factors may be important in determining the development and maintenance of psychological problems associated with their condition. Obviously some factors will be amenable to psychological treatment, whereas other more severe symptoms may require pharmacological treatment in addition to psychological therapy.

Clinical anecdotal evidence suggests that the most appropriate treatment for people with epilepsy is cognitive behavioural therapy, but this and other treatment programmes, including long term psychotherapy, have yet to be investigated. Indeed, studies of the efficacy of psychological treatments is warranted, although these should be conducted in the context of a randomised clinical trial as opposed to small group studies or single case studies. Although the evidence for the efficacy of psychological treatment programmes in epilepsy is limited, there is evidence for the success of behavioural treatments in other chronic conditions (Illis 1994). Some studies have shown that psychoeducational programmes of two and seven days duration have proved to be effective (Helgeson *et al.* 1990). In this chapter, the author will concentrate on approaches to improving psychosocial adjustment.

Psychological assessment

In order to establish the nature of the psychological problems that are being presented, in-depth clinical interviewing will be necessary and this may involve the individual and their family, as many behavioural problems associated with epilepsy will occur in the context of the family home. There are a number of psychological assessments used routinely that may be helpful in the initial assessment these are listed in Table 6.2.

Anxiety management

A variety of relaxation strategies might be applied in the management of seizures because of the recognition that anxiety may act as a seizure precipitant and that people with epilepsy are more likely to have increased rates of anxiety when compared with the normal population. Progressive muscle relaxation techniques have been used, with some success, in patients who are able to identify heightened physiological arousal prior to seizure onset and who experience anxiety interictally (e.g. Rousseau *et al.* 1985, see Chapter 7). While there is substantial

Table 6.2 Assessment of behavioural functioning in people with epilepsy

Measure	Authors
Hospital Anxiety and Depression Scale	Zigmond and Snaith 1983
Self Esteem Scale	Rosenberg 1965
Family Environment Scale	Moos & Moos 1981
Impact of Epilepsy Scale	Jacoby *et al.* 1993
Profile of Mood Scale	McNair *et al.* 1981
Cognitive Effects Scale	Aldenkamp *et al.* 1995
Minnisota Multiphasic Personality Inventory	Dikmen *et al.* 1983
Mastery Scale	Pearlin & Schooler 1978

anecdotal evidence that people with epilepsy will benefit from anxiety management, there are few substantial randomised studies to support the efficacy of such techniques in the management of this condition.

Individual counselling and education

The process of adjusting to epilepsy is complex with people with epilepsy having to make many changes as a result of the diagnosis and subsequent treatment. According to Scambler (1993), there are five dimensions to the process of adjustment: accommodation, rationalisation, concept of self, sociability and fulfilment. In the course of adjustment, people with epilepsy will have to deal with the fear of their seizures, make sense of their medical history (sometimes having to generate their own theories about its cause) and try to minimise the negative impact of epilepsy on their own self-worth. For some people with epilepsy, the condition may have adverse effects on their relationship with others, and for this reason they may conceal their condition and at the same time compromise any potential achievements in a number of social roles.

It is important, therefore, for people with epilepsy and their families to have a greater understanding about their epilepsy and demystify any beliefs they might have about their condition. Thus, clinicians have a significant role in influencing the process of accommodation by being aware of the timing of the communication of a diagnosis of epilepsy, as often the diagnosis marks the beginning of a protracted and sometimes lifelong process of adjustment to having epilepsy. A number of authors have highlighted the role of the clinician in the adjustment process, through rational drug therapy combined with treatment for the possible psychological or psychiatric sequelae of epilepsy (Hermann and Whitman 1991; Scambler 1993).

A number of concerns that people with epilepsy have about their condition could be resolved if acknowledged and discussed. It is important to ensure that the person with epilepsy and their family are encouraged to discover for themselves much of the necessary information they require to make sense of their condition and its management; this process of empowerment will be beneficial in the process of adjustment (Mittan 1986). The epilepsy support agencies will also have a role in educating and supporting the individual with epilepsy and their family. There are both local and national organisations covering the whole of the United Kingdom.

The importance of recognising the connections between people's misconceptions about seizures and psychosocial functioning has been well documented (Mittan 1986). Hills and Baker's (1992) research is also relevant in this context in that they demonstrated how possession of accurate information about epilepsy was significantly related to levels of well-being. People with epilepsy who were better informed about the management and treatment of their condition perceived themselves as being in more control and subsequently had significantly better psychological profiles than those who were less informed.

Cognitive-behavioural therapy

Cognitive-behavioural therapy involves shaping the way people think, feel and behave. The rationale for using this approach for people with epilepsy would be to help them minimise the impact of their condition on their daily lives. Interventions aimed at the cognitive level emphasise the importance of providing new information about the illness or its management. Cognitive behavioural techniques are also implemented to modify the underlying core beliefs that people have about their condition which may cause psychological impairments. Interestingly, Tan and Bruni's (1986) use of group-based cognitive behavioural therapy resulted in an increase in ratings of well-being in patients with epilepsy. This author has found that short-term cognitive behavioural treatment can be particularly helpful in assisting people with epilepsy come to terms with their diagnosis, particularly when this is accompanied by clear and precise information about the condition. Families should also be considered as important targets for modifying beliefs about the epilepsy, its cause and its management.

While the general practitioner will be able to provide some information regarding the nature and management of epilepsy, counselling is likely to be undertaken by paramedical staff. Where the psychological consequences of the epilepsy are disabling for the individual, then referral to a clinical psychologist is likely to be the most appropriate referral.

Family therapy

For some families, education and counselling may be sufficient, but for others, where the impact of the epilepsy and its treatment are significant, formal family therapy may be necessary. With this approach, the role of the family is seen as important in the development and maintenance of psychological problems that may have arisen for many reasons, including overprotection, rejection and concealment by family members. In family therapy, the whole of the family are invited to explore and modify communication systems and behavioural functioning in order to minimise the negative aspects of the epilepsy. While there is little evidence of the efficacy of this approach in families with epilepsy, there is substantial evidence of its usefulness in other conditions (Minuchin 1974).

SUMMARY

While much is known about the clinical course of epilepsy, less is understood about the aetiology and prognosis of behavioural problems associated with it. More knowledge is required in order to disentangle the various contributory factors. It is only by increasing our understanding in this area that specific treatment programmes can be designed to ameliorate the often disabling psychological consequences of this condition.

It is clear from recent studies that a significant number of people with epilepsy will have well-controlled seizures with minimum side effects and few behavioural consequences (Jacoby *et al.* 1996). For this group of patients, the need for psychological input will be minimal. For those with behavioural problems associated with the diagnosis of epilepsy, there is evidence to suggest that not enough attention is given to the non-pharmacological management of their condition (Jacoby, personal communication). Evidence from single case and group studies have highlighted the benefits of using psychological techniques, including anxiety management, counselling and psychotherapy (Helgeson *et al.* 1990). Addressing the psychological consequences of this condition will undoubtedly help to improve the quality of life of people with epilepsy, although there is still a need for randomised clinical trials to demonstrate the efficacy of the various behavioural treatment strategies.

ACKNOWLEDGEMENTS

I would like to thank Ann Jacoby for her helpful comments on an earlier draft of this manuscript.

REFERENCES

Aldenkamp, A. P., Baker, G. A., Pieters, M. S. M., Schoemaker, H. C., Cohen, A. F. and Schwabe, S. (1995) 'The Neurotoxicity Scale: the validity of a patient-based scale, assessing neurotoxicity', *Epilepsy Research* 20: 229–39.

Arnston, P., Drodge, D., Norton, R. and Murray, E. (1986) 'The perceived psychosocial consequences of having epilepsy', in S. Whitman and B. P. Hermann (eds) *Psychopathology in Epilepsy*, New York and Oxford: Oxford University Press.

Baker, G. A., Jacoby, A. and Chadwick, D. W. (1996) 'The associations of psychopathology in epilepsy. A community study', *Epilepsy Research* 25: 29–39.

Betts, T. (1981) 'Depression, anxiety and epilepsy', in E. H. Reynolds and M. R. Trimble (eds) *Epilepsy and Psychiatry*, New York: Churchill Livingstone.

—— (1992) 'Epilepsy and stress', *British Medical Journal* 305: 378–9.

Collings, J. (1990) 'Epilepsy and well being', *Social Science and Medicine* 31: 165–70.

—— (1995) 'The impact of epilepsy on self-perceptions', *Journal of Epilepsy* 8: 164–71.

Conrad, P. and Schneider, J. W. (1992) *Deviance and Medicalisation: From Badness to Sickness*, Philadelphia: Temple University Press.

Cull, C. A. and Trimble, M. R. (1989) 'Effects of anticonvulsant medication on cognitive functioning in children with epilepsy', in B. Hermann and M. Seidenberg (eds) *The Childhood Epilepsies: Neuropsychological, Psychosocial and Intervention Aspects*, New York: Wiley.

Currie, S., Heathfield, K. W. G., Henson, R. A. and Scott, D. F. (1971) 'Clinical course and prognosis of temporal lobe epilepsy: A survey of 666 patients', *Brain* 94: 173–90.

Devinsky, O. (1992) *Behavioural Neurology: 100 Maxims*, London: Edward Arnold.

Dikmen, S., Hermann, B., Wilensky, A. and Rainwater, G. (1983) 'Validity of the MMPI to psychopathology in patients with epilepsy', *Journal of Nervous and Mental Disease* 171: 114–22.

Dodrill, C. B. and Batzel, L. W. (1986) 'Interictal behavioural features of patients with epilepsy', *Epilepsia* 27 (Suppl. 2): S64–72.

Fenwick, P. (1986) 'Aggression and behaviour', in M. R. Trimble and T. G. Bolwig (eds) *Aspects of Epilepsy and Psychiatry*, Chichester: Wiley.

Gastaut, H., Morrin, G. and Leserve, N. (1955) 'Study of the behaviour of psychomotor epileptics during the interval between seizures', *Annals of Medicine and Psychology* 113: 1–27.

Gehlert, S. (1994) 'Perceptions of control in adults with epilepsy', *Epilepsia* 31: 81–8.

Gibbs, F. A., Gibbs, E. L. and Fuster, B. (1948) 'Psychomotor epilepsy', *Archives of Neurology and Psychiatry* 60: 331–9.

Gloor, P., Olivier, A., Quesney, L. F., Andermann, F. and Horowitz, S. (1982) 'The role of the limbic system in experiential phenomena of temporal lobe epilepsy', *Annals of Neurology* 12: 129–44.

Goldstein, L. H. (1990) 'Behavioural and cognitive-behavioural treatments for epilepsy: a progress review', *British Journal of Clinical Psychology* 29: 257–69.

Hauser, W. A. and Hessdorfer, D. C. (1990) *Epilepsy, Frequency, Causes and Consequences*, Maryland: Epilepsy Foundation of America.

Helgeson, D. C., Mittan, R., Tan, S. A. and Chayasirisobhon, A. (1990) 'Sepulveda epilepsy education: the efficacy of a psychoeducational treatment programme in treating medical and psychosocial aspects of epilepsy', *Epilepsia* 31: 75–82.

Hermann, B. P. and Whitman, S. (1986) 'Psychopathology in epilepsy: a multiaetiological model', in S. Whitman and B. P. Hermann (eds) *Psychopathology in Epilepsy: Social Dimensions*, Oxford: Oxford University Press.

—— (1991) 'Neurobiological, psychosocial and pharmacological factors underlying interictal psychopathology in epilepsy', in D. Smith, D. Treiman and M. Trimble (eds) *Advances in Neurology. Vol 55: Neurobehavioural Problems in Epilepsy*, New York: Oxford University Press.

Hills, M. D. and Baker, P. G. (1992) 'Relationships among epilepsy, social stigmas, self-esteem and social support', *Journal of Epilepsy* 5: 231–8.

Illis, L. S. (1994) *Neurological Rehabilitation*, Oxford: Blackwell Scientific.

Jacoby, A. (1994) 'Felt versus enacted stigma: a concept revisited', *Social Science and Medicine* 38: 269–4.

Jacoby, A., Baker, G. A., Smith, D. F., Dewey, M. and Chadwick, D. W. (1993) 'Measuring the impact of epilepsy: the development of a novel scale', *Epilepsy Research* 16: 83–8.

Jacoby, A., Baker, G. A., Steen, A., Potts, P. and Chadwick, D. W. (1996) 'The clinical course of epilepsy and its psychosocial correlates: findings from a UK community study', *Epilepsia* 37: 148–61.

Landolt, H. (1958) 'Serial electroencephalographic investigations during psychotic episodes in epileptic patients during schizophrenic attacks', in L. de Haas (ed.) *Lectures on Epilepsy*, New York: Elsevier.

Lefcourt, H. (1976) *Locus of Control: Current Trends in Research and Theory*, New York: Wiley.

Leiderman, D. B., Csernanky, J. G. and Moses, J. A. (1990) 'Neuroendocrinology and limbic epilepsy: relationship to psychopathology, seizure variables and neuropsychosocial function', *Epilepsia* 31: 270–4.

McNair, D., Lorr, N. and Dropplemann, L. (1981) *Manual for the Profile of Mood States*, San Diego: Educational and Industrial Testing Service.

Matthews, W. S. and Barabas, G. (1981) 'Suicide and epilepsy: a review of the literature', *Psychosomatics* 22: 515–24.

Matthews, W. S., Barabas, G. and Ferari, M. (1982) 'Emotional concomitants of childhood epilepsy', *Epilepsia* 23: 671–81.

Mendez, M. F., Cummings, J. L. and Benson, D. F. (1986) 'Depression in epilepsy. Significance and phenomenology', *Archives of Neurology* 43: 766–70.

Minuchin, S. (1974) *Families and Family Therapy*, London: Tavistock Publications.

Mittan, R. J. (1986) 'Fear of seizures', in S. Whitman and B. P. Hermann (eds) *Psychopathology in Epilepsy: Social Dimensions*, New York: Oxford University Press.

Mittan, R. J. and Locke, G. E. (1982) 'Fear of seizures: epilepsy's forgotten symptom', *Urban Health* 11: 30–2.

Moos, R. and Moos, B. (1981) *The Family Environment Scale Manual*, Paolo Alta CA: Consulting Psychologists Press.

Pearlin, L. and Schooler, C. (1978) 'The structure of coping', *Journal of Health and Social Behaviour* 19: 2–21.

Perez, M. M. and Trimble, M. R. (1980) 'Epileptic psychosis-diagnostic comparison with process schizophrenia', *British Journal of Psychiatry* 137: 245–50.

Pond, D. A. and Bidwell, B. H. (1959) 'A survey of epilepsy in 14 general practices. II. Social and psychological aspects', *Epilepsia* 1: 285–9.

Robertson, M. M., Trimble, M. R. and Townsend, H. R. A. (1987) 'Phenomenology of depression in epilepsy', *Epilepsia* 28: 364–72.

Rosenberg, M. (1965) *Society and the Adolescent Self-image*, Princeton NJ: Princeton University Press.

Rousseau, A., Herman, B. P. and Whitman, S. (1985) 'Effects of progressive relaxation on epilepsy: analysis of a series of cases', *Psychological Report* 57: 1203–12.

Ryan, R., Kempner, K. and Emlen, A. C. (1980) 'The stigma of epilepsy as a self concept', *Epilepsia* 21: 433–44.

Scambler, G. (1989) *Epilepsy*, London: Tavistock.

—— (1993) 'Coping with epilepsy', in J. Laidlaw, A. Richens and D. W. Chadwick, D. W. (eds) *A Textbook of Epilepsy* (4th edn), Edinburgh: Churchill Livingstone.

Scambler, G. and Hopkins, A. (1986) 'Being epileptic: coming to terms with stigma', *Social Health and Illness* 8: 26–43.

Slater, E. and Beard, A. W. (1963) 'The schizophrenic-like psychosis of epilepsy', *British Journal of Psychiatry* 109: 95.

Smith, D. F., Baker, G. A., Dewey, M., Jacoby, A. and Chadwick, D. W. (1991) 'Seizure frequency, patient perceived seizure severity and the psychosocial consequences of intractable epilepsy', *Epilepsy Research* 9: 231–41.

Stanley, P. J. and Tillotson, A. (1982) *Epilepsy in the Community*, Leeds, UK: Leeds School of Social Studies, Leeds Polytechnic.

Sullivan, M. D. (1995) 'Depression and disability from chronical medical illness', *European Journal of Public Health* 5: 40–5.

Tan, S-Y. and Bruni, J. (1986) 'Cognitive-behavioural therapy with adult patients with epilepsy: a controlled outcome study', *Epilepsia* 27: 225–33.

Thompson, P. J. (1988) 'Methods and problems in the assessment of behaviour disorders in epileptic patients', in M. R. Trimble and E. H. Reynolds (eds) *Epilepsy, Behaviour and Cognitive Function*, Chichester: Wiley.

Toone, B. K. (1981) 'The psychosis of epilepsy', in E. H. Reynolds and M. Trimble (eds) *Epilepsy and Psychiatry*, Edinburgh: Churchill Livingstone.

Treiman, D. M. (1990) 'Epilepsy and aggression', in D. B. Smith (ed.) *Epilepsy: Current Approaches to Diagnosis and Treatment*, New York: Raven Press.

Trimble, M. R. (1988) 'Anticonvulsant drugs mood and cognitive function', in M. R. Trimble and E. H. Reynolds (eds) *Epilepsy, Behaviour and Cognitive Function*, Chichester: Wiley.

Waxman, S. G. and Geshwind, N. (1975) 'The interictal behaviour syndrome of temporal lobe epilepsy', *Archives of General Psychiatry* 32: 1580.

Wallaston, K. A. B. S. and De Villas, R. (1980) 'Development of multi-dimensional health locus of control scale', *Health Education Monograph* 6: 160–70

West, P. (1986) 'The social meaning of epilepsy. Stigma as a potential explanation for psychopathology in children', in S. Whitman and B. P. Hermann (eds) *Psychopathology in Epilepsy: Social Dimensions*, New York: Oxford University Press.

Zeigler, R. G. (1982) 'Epilepsy: individual illness, human predicament and family dilemma', *Family Relations* 31: 435–44.

Zigmond, A. S. and Snaith, R. P. (1983) 'The Hospital Anxiety and Depression Scale', *Acta Psychiatrica Scandinavica* 67: 361–70.

Chapter 7

Psychological control of seizures

Laura H. Goldstein

In recent years a major development of the role of clinical psychologists working with people with epilepsy has been in psychological management of seizures including spontaneous, self induced and non-epileptic (or pseudo) seizures.

THE BEGINNINGS OF A PSYCHOLOGICAL UNDERSTANDING OF SEIZURE OCCURRENCE

Fenwick and Brown (1989) adopt a model whereby epileptic seizures are precipitated or inhibited depending upon the relative excitation of groups of neurones in and around the damaged area of brain. Group One (G1) neurones, at the centre of an epileptic focus, are damaged and show continuously abnormal patterns of activity. Surrounding these are Group Two (G2) neurones, which are only partially damaged and function either normally or abnormally in terms of paroxysmal epileptic activity. During a focal seizure, G1 neurones recruit G2 neurones into their abnormal pattern of activity. If G2 neurones then recruit normal neurones into their abnormal firing, the seizure generalises. Fenwick and Brown (ibid.) state that the level of electrophysiological activation of G2 neurones, and of normal brain tissue surrounding the focus, determines whether seizure activity is subsequently inhibited or enhanced. There appears to be a relationship between behavioural, physiological and psychological states and the probability of seizure occurrence such that seizures do not occur in a vacuum (ibid.).

Epileptic seizures that are associated with psychological events are called 'psychogenic' seizures by Fenwick and Brown (1989) and are divided into two broad classes.

Primary psychogenic seizures are triggered by the individual engaging deliberately in an activity which they have previously found induces a seizure. For example, a 36-year-old man had learned that by allowing feelings of sadness (which had developed when his father had died during his adolescence) to persist, a seizure would occur; he used this phenomenon to induce seizures in later life when facing personal difficulties.

Secondary psychogenic seizures (Fenwick and Brown 1989) are precipitated by attending to a specific mental task which activates a local epileptogenic brain area without the deliberate intention on the part of the subject to cause a seizure and without an evoking peripheral stimulus. These are also referred to as the 'thinking epilepsies' (Fenwick 1994). Fenwick and Brown (1989) describe a 23-year-old woman with a left temporal lobe epileptic focus, who often experienced auras when doing crossword puzzles and other word retrieval tasks. Other examples include four people whose generalised seizures were triggered by mental or written calculations, card games or board games (Striano *et al.* 1993; see also Goossens *et al.* 1990). Game playing and tasks requiring strategic thinking produced significant EEG changes in a woman with generalised seizures (Siegel *et al.* 1992).

Fenwick and Brown (1989) also discuss 'evoked seizures'. These have external precipitants and include the reflex epilepsies (musicogenic, photogenic, movement evoked seizures, somatosensory evoked seizures and pattern stimulation). Such epilepsies may be very trigger-specific; a 20-year-old man experienced seizures during a hot bath, and on one occasion during a hot shower, but neither heat nor steam alone would provoke a seizure if he was not bathing (Lisovoski *et al.* 1992). Photosensitivity may be relevant in cases of video-game induced seizures (Ferrie *et al.* 1994). However non-photic factors such as excitement, tiredness, lack of sleep and cognitive processing may be relevant especially in non-photosensitive subjects, indicating that sometimes it may be difficult to distinguish between psychogenic and evoked seizures.

Cutting across these classifications of seizures, Cull (in preparation) discusses the self-induction of seizures that occurs in a small percentage of people with epilepsy. Most often reported for individuals with photosensitive epilepsy, seizures may be induced by a number of motor behaviours (e.g. blinking, deliberately looking at vertically striped objects, and waving fingers in front of the eyes in bright sunlight). These methods of seizure induction involve both evoking stimuli and the knowledge that certain actions in the presence of such stimuli will induce seizures (see also Chapter 11).

Extending the idea of predicting seizure occurrence, several studies have considered whether people with epilepsy can identify high and low risk situations for epileptic activity, seizure provoking factors, and whether they could self-induce or abort seizures. The pattern of results is similar across different studies. Thus, Antebi and Bird (1993) and Spector *et al.* (1994) found that the most common factor associated with an increase in seizure frequency was tension/anxiety. Løyning *et al.* (1993) also indicated that stress was the most common 'high-risk-for-seizure occurrence' situation. Spector *et al.* (1994) documented the negative effect of anger and unhappiness on seizure occurrence, happiness being associated with decreased seizure occurrence (Antebi and Bird, 1993). Of interest also are those individuals who can induce seizures at will. Of Løyning *et al.*'s sample, nearly 8 per cent said they could produce seizures, 3 per cent of Antebi and Bird's sample (1993) claimed they could produce a seizure at will and nearly 23 per cent of patients attending a psychiatric clinic for their epilepsy reported deliberately inducing seizures (Finkler *et al.* 1990). Seventeen per cent of patients attending a psychiatry clinic and over 12 per cent attending a neurology clinic reported sometimes being able to induce a seizure. In contrast, nearly 53 per cent and 39 per cent of these groups respectively could sometimes abort seizures; 88 and nearly 81 per cent respectively could identify at least one high risk-for-seizure occurrence situation (Spector *et al.* 1994). The ability to self-manage seizures (e.g. Pritchard *et al.* 1985) is not limited to adults (Cull *et al.* 1996) and has the potential to be formalised into systematic treatment plans.

APPROACHES TO THE PSYCHOLOGICAL MANAGEMENT OF SEIZURES

Clinical seizure frequency (sometimes including auras as evidence of ongoing seizure activity) has been used as the most common target of intervention (Goldstein 1990). Self-control approaches using cognitive-behavioural techniques are directed at psychogenic seizures, whereas classical conditioning procedures have been used successfully with evoked seizures (e.g. Forster 1969, 1972; Forster *et al.* 1969).

Early studies suffered from methodological problems (Mostofsky and Balaschak 1977; Krafft and Poling 1982) and even more recent studies (see Goldstein 1990) demonstrate persisting difficulty in matching treatments to seizure types, being able to make comparisons across different studies in terms of techniques and outcome measures, and rely on self-report of seizure frequency when considering effectiveness. The following sections will review the various cognitive and/or behavioural approaches that have been applied to seizure management, but they should be considered in the light of previous criticisms. For reviews of reward management approaches, see Powell (1981) and Mostofsky (1993).

Altering levels of arousal

Given the self-reported high association between seizure occurrence and stressful situations, it is informative that a number of published studies have used relaxation training as their therapeutic intervention.

Studies employing Progressive Muscular Relaxation (PMR) have varied in sample size and complexity of design, but have shown a similar tendency to produce a decrease in seizure frequency (Rousseau et al. 1985; Whitman et al, 1990; Puskarich et al. 1992). In all cases, subjects were not trained to use the relaxation in stressful situations, although at least twice daily practice was required. The question remains as to which patients will benefit most from relaxation training (Goldstein 1990; Puskarich et al. 1992).

Relaxation has been included in the treatment interventions examined by Dahl and colleagues, who have used variants of systematic desensitisation. Her group emphasised the need to train people to become accurately aware of seizure occurrence in order for treatment to be effective. Dahl et al. (1987) compared the use of 'contingent relaxation' (CR) to an attention placebo and waiting-list control group. CR involved the application of PMR in each individual's own high-risk-for-seizure-occurrence situations and when they were aware of early signs of an impending seizure. In addition, subjects identified low-risk-for-seizure-occurrence situations. Subjects were trained in fantasy, role play and in vivo to imagine or experience high-risk situations and then switch to a relaxed state combined with imagining a low-risk scene. Only subjects trained in CR showed a significant reduction in seizure frequency, with effects being maintained after thirty weeks. The mechanism behind the seizure reduction remained unclear.

Dahl et al. (1988) suggested that not only might the absolute level of arousal be important for seizure genesis but so might be a sudden change in arousal. Three children with refractory epilepsy underwent training that included CR, biofeedback training in early awareness of seizure signals, countermeasures for arousal level, and positive reinforcement for appropriate behaviour. Countermeasures (see below), which were designed to reverse the arousal level experienced at seizure onset were more effective than the CR and positive reinforcement in reducing seizures. Overt seizure behaviour and EEG paroxysmal activity were reduced by countermeasures. The rather intrusive and intensive treatment package, however, may only be justifiable with individuals with very frequent seizures.

In terms of long-term effectiveness of treatment, Dahl *et al.* (1992) evaluated children who had been studied eight years following a behavioural intervention, which comprised teaching the children, their parents and teachers to recognise pre-seizure events and to reinforce seizure control techniques and appropriate behaviour (Dahl *et al.* 1985). The children were also taught to apply CR in high-risk-for-seizure situations. Only those in the treatment group had shown a reduction in seizure index (frequency x duration of seizures) which was maintained at the eight-year follow-up; the control groups showed no change from baseline.

None of the studies that have employed relaxation indicate whether *inter alia* relaxation training focused on breathing patterns (Goldstein 1990). Fried (1993) explained how hyperventilation induces epileptic seizures, and the role that stress may play in this. Fried *et al.* (1984) employed diaphragmatic breathing with biofeedback of the per-cent-end tidal level of carbon dioxide in subjects with refractory generalised tonic-clonic, absence and psychomotor seizures, who also demonstrated chronic hyperventilation. Eight of their ten subjects showed normalisation of their EEG power spectra and reduction in the severity and frequency of seizures. Simply adjusting the rate of respiration via diaphragmatic breathing was insufficient to produce lasting seizure reduction; it was the knowledge of the effect that such breathing produces on blood carbon dioxide levels that was necessary for improvement to be maintained (Fried 1993). The unavailability of biofeedback should not, however, discourage the teaching of diaphragmatic breathing as part of a relaxation training programme; hyperventilation may be associated with other symptoms of anxiety and possibly with EEG dysrhythmia (ibid.).

Brown and Fenwick (1989) successfully combined the use of cue-controlled relaxation with systematic desensitisation in imagination. They exposed individuals to an aura in imagination, and while in a relaxed state they were then taught to associate the relaxed state with a cue word which could subsequently be used to recreate the feeling of relaxation, thereby preventing the development of a seizure and, by association, the aura.

As noted earlier, for some people it is a change in arousal that may precipitate a seizure (e.g. from an aroused to a relaxed state, such as after a day's work or after strenuous exercise). Such people may need to arouse themselves when a seizure is imminent. This would concur with some self-reported strategies for seizure abatement (Pritchard *et al.* 1985). Brown and Fenwick (1989) have successfully combined cue-controlled arousal with relaxation.

Thus while relaxation, either alone or in combination with other approaches, can be effective, the opposite may sometimes be required. Consequently, a detailed analysis of the seizure precipitants for a particular individual is essential.

Countermeasures

If cue-controlled (or contingent) relaxation or arousal serve to reduce the likelihood of seizure occurrence by altering states of arousal in pools of neurones, then other activities may also serve to counteract a seizure if they can alter the activity of the G2 and surrounding neurones. Dahl *et al.* (1988) have termed these actions countermeasures, which may include shouting aloud, increasing physical activity or concentrating on something such as the last thing that has been seen or said (Pritchard *et al.* 1985: 266; Fenwick 1994). Dahl *et al.* (1987) noted that thirteen of their eighteen subjects had spontaneously developed countermeasures. It is not clear whether the spontaneous development of these techniques interacts positively with other treatment techniques, or whether their use was discouraged during treatment studies (Goldstein 1990). It is also unclear why these self-generated techniques do not always seem to work, and why people persist in trying to use them (Betts *et al.* 1995a).

Betts *et al.* (1995b) used aromatherapy as a countermeasure. Here, an oil selected by the patient was initially paired with an autohypnotic suggestion to relax or to become more aroused. Subsequently, the oil was used in relaxing or arousing situations. Smelling the oil and, subsequently, the memory of the oil's smell were later used as countermeasures. Of thirty patients, at one year's follow-up, nine had complete seizure control and thirteen had achieved at least 50 per cent reduction in seizure occurrence. These promising findings require replication.

Multi-component psychological approaches

Gillham (1990) administered a short out-patient treatment package to individuals with inadequately controlled seizures. She examined the effectiveness of two treatment approaches, self-control of seizures and alleviation of psychological disorder, applied in a counterbalanced order. Each was undertaken over a five-week period, involving four hours of patient contact. Self-control of seizures focused on factors that might be involved in precipitating seizures; avoidance strategies, seizure interruption, countermeasures or use of relaxation and breathing exercises were encouraged. Alleviation of psychological disorder focused on problems such as anxiety associated with phobic avoidance of leaving home, mild depression and family disagreements. Relaxation training was not used to help alleviate these problems. Both groups showed a significant decrease in seizure frequency that was maintained after six months, with significantly reduced self-ratings of anxiety and depression.

The two treatments, which were equally effective, both taught subjects coping skills. Gillham (1990) suggested that the reduction in anxiety following from the improved sense of self-control is probably more important than whether the coping skill derived from treatment is primarily concerned with seizures or with psychological difficulties. She concluded that brief psychological treatments aimed at developing coping skills can be offered on an out-patient basis for people without marked psychopathology.

The importance of teaching coping mechanisms has been considered by other researchers. Tan and Bruni (1986) focused on the use of cognitive-behaviour therapy (CBT) because of the extent to which anxiety and depression are commonly associated with epilepsy. Their group-based CBT was applied over eight, two-hour-long weekly sessions and was directed towards training in coping skills for stress and seizure control. Their Supportive Counselling control group had a similar number of sessions of supportive and non-directive group counselling which did not encourage the use of coping strategies. A waiting list control group was also included. Therapists' global ratings of patients' adjustment improved for both active intervention groups, pre- to post-treatment, although the CBT group also maintained this difference after four months. There was only a non-significant tendency for improvement in seizure frequency to have been most sensitive to CBT. Tan and Bruni suggested that CBT might be more effective on an individual basis and that their coping-skills-based group therapy might only be effective for people already predisposed towards self-help skills. With respect to the former point, Brown and Fenwick (1989) report a single case in which the use of CBT for depression was accompanied by an abatement of seizure activity. It is also possible that a more focused approach, as used by Gillham (1990), is a more effective means of reducing seizure frequency.

A comprehensive self-control of seizures programme, with a very strong emphasis on coping strategies, was developed by Reiter *et al.* (1987) for individual patients. There are twelve stages in their programme, intrinsic to which is record-keeping, both in terms of seizures and thoughts associated with the programme requirements. Having decided at the outset that taking control is what the person wants to do, the patient has to identify a support person who will accompany them to some sessions and facilitate the process of taking control, which includes the patient fully understanding the consequences of taking anti-convulsants. Learning to identify seizure precipitants, pre-seizure auras and prodromes is emphasised. Participants are trained to deal with negative emotions and situations, external stresses and internal conflicts. The element of the programme not readily available in all settings is the use of biofeedback to train the brain to produce alpha waves, which in many cases will be incompatible with seizure genesis.

Individuals may proceed through the programme at different rates (Reiter *et al.* 1987). Andrews and Schonfeld (1992) evaluated retrospectively the records of eighty-three adults with initially uncontrolled seizures who underwent their treatment programme between 1980–5. Of these, sixty-nine achieved control of their seizures by the time treatment ended. An initially low seizure frequency was an important positive predictor of ultimate seizure control. Earlier age at onset of epilepsy, more years during which the person suffered uncontrolled seizures and higher seizure frequency at treatment onset, predicted the need for a greater number of treatment sessions. Overall, however, the ability to predict the number of sessions required was poor. Andrews and Schonfeld (ibid.) stress the continuing need to determine why the programme works and who might benefit in particular.

Our own preliminary attempts at reducing seizure frequency have adopted a group format, and have essentially followed Reiter *et al.*'s (1987) programme. For practical reasons, we omitted the biofeedback component, yet, with a total of eight, two-hour-long weekly highly-structured sessions run by a psychologist and a senior occupational therapist, we have shown a reduction in mean seizure frequency in seven adults with epilepsy who had a mean epilepsy duration of over nineteen-and-a-half years, in comparison to waiting list controls (Spector *et al.* 1995). Although the participants were a highly selected sample of our clinic population, in terms of motivation and availability to participate in the group, findings suggest that even chronic epilepsy may be amenable to self-control.

Biofeedback

A relatively brief account of the use of EEG biofeedback in the control of seizures will be given, since this is unlikely to be available for use by many clinical psychologists. Its relevance, however, is that it relates well to the model of seizure genesis expounded above and deals directly with the alteration of electrical activity in the brain. Sterman (1993) reviews his centre's work in training patients to alter the sensorimotor rhythm (SMR: 12–16 Hz) to normalise EEG patterns. Enhancement of this EEG activity can increase seizure threshold and reduce clinical and EEG epileptic activity. His review indicates the success of this method over placebo treatments; successful SMR training may also result in improved cognitive and motor functioning. Particular anti-convulsants and the nature of the epileptic pathology may render the process more difficult, but the crucial factor in undertaking such training is its very intensive nature and the commitment required from the patient. This applies to the training of other EEG patterns as well.

Reiter et al.'s (1987) biofeedback training of alpha activity in their self-control programme was facilitated by relaxation training. They suggest that training will require anything from four weeks to two months of weekly thirty-minute biofeedback sessions for alpha control to be achieved, with subsequent 'refresher' sessions as required. Their programme does not permit the specific evaluation of this form of biofeedback on treatment outcome.

NON-EPILEPTIC SEIZURES

The clinical psychologist's contribution to the management of seizure disorders also includes non-epileptic seizures (NESs). As with epileptic seizures, terminology has been confusing, and 'psychogenic seizures', 'hysterical seizures', and 'pseudoseizures' have been used to describe 'paroxysmal episodes of altered behaviour resembling epileptic attacks but devoid of characteristic epileptic clinical and electrographic features' (Liske and Forster 1964). Most NESs resemble tonic-clonic seizures, but there is also confusion between seizures arising from the frontal lobes and NESs. It is also important to distinguish between NESs that are thought to have an emotional basis (which are the subject of present interest) from disorders that have other medical causes (see Betts and Boden 1991).

Diagnosis of NESs requires a combination of video/EEG monitoring, blood prolactin and careful clinical observations, combined with the use of 'seizure' recording systems (see below). The diagnostic induction of NESs by suggestion can be a relatively sensitive procedure, although many ethical issues are raised (Lancman *et al.* 1994).

As many as 37 per cent of patients admitted for investigation of epilepsy may have NESs (Betts and Boden 1992a). However, many such patients will have a concomitant diagnosis of either a history of, or active, epilepsy (see also Scheepers *et al.* 1994) so that 20–24 per cent have only NESs (Ramani 1986; Betts and Boden 1992a, but see Montgomery and Espie 1986). With time and further clinical information, diagnoses may change, with major implications for management of such individuals.

A history of sexual abuse is likely to be found more often in females with NESs than with epilepsy or other psychiatric disorders (Betts and Boden 1992b; Litwin and Cardena 1993), which may explain the higher prevalence of NESs among females (Kristensen and Alving 1992; Betts and Boden 1991, but see McDade and Brown 1992). The development of NESs after rape has been conceptualised as an example of Post Traumatic Stress Disorder (e.g. Cartmill and Betts 1992) with the paroxysmal behaviour representing the acting out of intrusive, vivid memories of the rape. Other women with NESs and a history of abuse may have characteristic flashbacks of the abuse or may be reminded of it by external cues. Betts and Boden (1991, 1992a, b) describe different forms of NESs. They call these 'Swoons', 'Tantrums' and 'Abreactive Attacks'. This last type of attack is said to be particularly common in sexually-abused women. However, not all authors (see Scheepers *et al.* 1994) have been able to associate these types of NESs with the precipitants or psychopathology suggested by Betts and Boden. This may reflect how the history of abuse is elicited. The role of sexual abuse in precipitating NESs may need to be disentangled from the role of such abuse in the aetiology of genuine epilepsy in predisposed individuals (Betts and Boden 1991; Greig and Betts 1992).

Management of NESs is poorly described in terms of details of therapeutic intervention, but similar themes emerge. Scheepers *et al.* (1994) counsel against treating these patients as a homogeneous group. An eclectic approach to treatment is recommended since patients' responses to diagnosis will vary considerably. Scheepers *et al.* (1994) and Betts and Boden (1992a, b) stress above all that the patient must not feel rejected once the diagnosis is made, and should preferably be treated in the same service as people with epileptic seizures. Hostile reactions from staff must be avoided (Ramani and Gumnit 1982). No doubt must remain over diagnosis, since this is easily communicated to the patient and will undermine treatment. Some individuals may lose their NESs once diagnosis has been made; others may show 'symptom substitution'. Reactions of families should also be taken into account, since family pathology may well be involved in the development and maintenance of NESs (Moore *et al.* 1994). Understanding the functions of the seizures and their maintaining factors, as well as what was happening to the person when the NESs first started, is important since this may reveal unresolved stresses. Potential interventions include anxiety management, relaxation, and marital therapy, family therapy or individual supportive psychotherapy or counselling, operant conditioning and the occasional use of tranquilisers as appropriate (Betts and Boden 1992a, b; Scheepers *et al.* 1994). Anxiety management directed towards recognising and, in particular, predicting the occurrence of NESs may be beneficial as may cognitive-behaviour therapy to assist patients modify thought patterns which may predispose towards NES occurrence. In all of these respects, treatment of NESs is similar to the treatment of epileptic attacks.

In terms of direct treatment of NESs, minimal attention is given to the NESs without appearing uncaring, accompanied by reinforcement of 'seizure' free behaviour with early generalisation to the family (Ramani and Gumnit 1982). McDade and Brown (1992) explain to patients that a way of helping bring the attacks under control is to start by others paying as little attention to them as possible and by dealing with any emotional problems.

Families must avoid scapegoating the patient, even if they feel that the patient has been 'putting it on', since the lack of recrimination, and the ability of the person to 'save face' will affect outcome. Families may need assistance in coming to terms with a new lifestyle once the person no longer experiences NESs. When discussing the treatment of NESs sufferers with a history of sexual abuse, Betts and Boden (1992a, b) emphasise the need for the disclosure to come from the patient; treatment may need to continue on an out-patient basis for a long time.

Good prognosis with respect to outcome may depend upon having a history of epilepsy and anxiety attacks alongside the NESs (rather than the 'tantrum' or 'abreactive' types of NESs [Betts and Boden 1992a]), or on having an IQ of above eighty and no past history of violent behaviour (McDade and Brown 1992, but see Montgomery and Espie

1986). Almost two-thirds of Betts and Boden's (1991) patients were 'seizure' free on discharge from hospital, but relapses were common. Krumholz and Niedermeyer (1983) found complete absence of NESs after a five-year follow-up in 29 per cent of patients, whereas Kristensen and Alving (1992) noted that, with a median follow-up of nearly six years, 45 per cent of patients became free from NESs and epileptic seizures, compared to 64 per cent of patients with only epileptic seizures. Of Ramani and Gumnit's (1982) nine patients, one of whom was lost to follow-up, seven showed a marked reduction in NES frequency over a four-year period. Future evaluations require comparisons to be made across very different treatment settings having different referral biases and philosophies regarding aetiology and treatment.

PRACTICAL GUIDE

Whether one is formulating a treatment plan for spontaneous or self-induced epileptic or non-epileptic seizures, detailed behavioural analysis of the seizure behaviour will be required.

Identification of seizure occurrence and recording the antecedents and consequences of the seizure should form the first stage in seizure management. Dahl *et al.* (1985) recommended that treatment methods be developed for the type and function of epilepsy as revealed by careful *functional analysis* of seizure behaviour. Seizure logs or charts or structured interviews have been described by Dahl (1992) and Reiter *et al.* (1987) but can be developed by any practitioner who is skilled in assessing problem behaviours. The practitioner should not predict in advance what factors are likely to increase seizure frequency (e.g. Webster and Mawer 1989; Neufeld *et al.* 1994).

Seizure recording systems should include assessment of the following points:

(a) *The antecedents to the behaviour*, i.e. where the person was, who they were with, what they were doing, thinking, feeling, the time and day on which the seizure occurred, useful medical information such as whether the person was ill, or if female, whether they were pre- or peri-menstrual, whether they had not been sleeping well or have missed a dose of anti-convulsant medication or have been drinking alcohol. Antecedents may be construed as relating to events or feelings occurring in the immediate run-up to a seizure, such as during a thirty minute pre-ictal period.

Premonitory symptoms such as irritability, depression, headache and 'funny feelings' may occur more than thirty minutes before a seizure in patients with partial epilepsy (and possibly to a lesser extent in patients with generalised seizures) and can last for anything between ten minutes and three days (Hughes *et al.* 1993). Here, an informant's view may be crucial in identifying a seizure prodrome. The identification of such premonitory symptoms may provide an opportunity for a therapeutic intervention to counter the prevailing mood preceding the seizure.

(b) *What the seizure was like* (with a detailed description if there was an independent witness). This is important since many people have different types of seizures. Auras without subsequent full seizures must be recorded in addition to full seizures. Seizure duration should also be recorded if possible since a seizure index (*frequency x duration*; Dahl *et al.* 1985, 1987, 1988) may be a more sensitive treatment outcome measure. For NESs the nature of the attack may provide some clue as to its aetiology (Betts and Boden 1991, 1992a, b).

(c) *What happened after the seizure.* This should include the person's own, as well as other people's, reactions to the seizure, how he/she felt, whether additional medication was given, and how long it took the person to recover.

It may be necessary to train patients in record keeping. The clinician must also be fully conversant with the patient's recording system; one of our patients recorded his complex partial seizures as HPOs, which stood for 'Harry passes out'. Since seizure recording is a crucial part of both assessment and treatment, it may need to continue for some weeks before the clinician is satisfied that it will provide the information that is required to formulate a treatment plan.

It may be easier to work with people who have clear auras at their seizure onset, especially if one is attempting to train the person in the use of countermeasures, but the identification of a prodromal mood change may also permit a successful treatment plan to be developed. Even the more general use of relaxation training, however, has proved effective (e.g. Puskarich *et al.* 1992).

The clinical assessment of both epileptic and non-epileptic seizures should also address wider issues such as the impact of the person's epilepsy on their lifestyle and the lifestyle of those with whom they live or have close contact, support from others for the current treatment programme (Reiter *et al.* 1987), resources that are present for planning a life without (or with less severe) epilepsy, as well as the person's general perception of what constitute high- and low-risk situations for seizure occurrence, and whether avoidance of high-risk situations places undesirable restrictions on the person's lifestyle (Taube and Calman 1992). The guidelines about providing careful reassurance to patients and family about the meaning of gaining control will apply irrespective of the type of seizure.

CONCLUSIONS

Clinical psychology has a key role to play in the non-medical treatment of epilepsy, a role which is likely to increase as more sophisticated therapeutic techniques are developed. The effectiveness of the treatment, however, will depend on the inclusion in the programme of all interested and significant people in the person's life (Mostofsky 1993) to ensure complete generalisation of the treatment approach to everyday life.

REFERENCES

Andrews, D. J. and Schonfeld, W. H. (1992) 'Predictive factors for controlling seizures using a behavioural approach', *Seizure* 1: 111–16.

Antebi, D. and Bird, J. (1993) 'The facilitation and evocation of seizures. A questionnaire study of awareness and control', *British Journal of Psychiatry* 162: 759–64.

Betts, T. and Boden, S. (1991) 'Pseudoseizures (non-epileptic attack disorder)', in M. R. Trimble (ed.) *Women and Epilepsy*, Chichester: Wiley.

—— (1992a) 'Diagnosis, management and prognosis of a group of 128 patients with non-epileptic attack disorder. Part I', *Seizure* 1: 19–26.

—— (1992b) 'Diagnosis, management and prognosis of a group of 128 patients with non-epileptic attack disorder. Part II. Previous childhood sexual abuse in the aetiology of these disorders', *Seizure* 1: 27–32.

Betts, T., Fox, C. and MacCallum, R. (1995a) 'Assessment of countermeasures used by people to attempt to control their own seizures', *Epilepsia* 36 (Suppl. 3): S130.

—— (1995b) 'An olfactory countermeasures treatment for epileptic seizures using a conditioned arousal response to specific aromatherapy oils', *Epilepsia* 36 (Suppl 3): S130–1.

Brown, S. W. and Fenwick, P. B. C. (1989) 'Evoked and psychogenic epileptic seizures: II. Inhibition', *Acta Neurologica Scandinavica* 80: 541–7.

Cartmill, A. and Betts, T. (1992) 'Seizure behaviour in a patient with post-traumatic stress disorder following rape'. Notes on the aetiology of 'pseudoseizures', *Seizure* 1: 33–6.

Cull, C. A. (in preparation) 'Self-induction of seizures: the nature of the problem and a model of the development and maintenance of behaviour'.

Cull, C. A., Fowler, M. and Brown, S. W. (1996) 'Perceived self-control of seizures in young people with epilepsy', *Seizure*, 5: 131–8.

Dahl, J. (1992) *Epilepsy. A Behaviour Medicine Approach to Assessment and Treatment in Children. A Handbook for Professionals Working with Epilepsy*, Göttingen: Hogrefe and Huber.

Dahl, J., Brorson, L-O. and Melin, L. (1992) 'Effects of a broad-spectrum behavioural medicine treatment program on children with refractory epileptic seizures: an 8 year follow-up', *Epilepsia* 33: 98–102.

Dahl, J., Melin, L. and Leissner, P. (1988) 'Effects of a behavioural intervention on epileptic behaviour and paroxysmal activity: a systematic replication of three cases with intractable epilepsy', *Epilepsia* 29: 172–83.

Dahl, J., Melin, L. and Lund, L. (1987) 'Effects of a contingent relaxation treatment program on adults with refractory epileptic seizures', *Epilepsia* 28: 125–32.

Dahl, J., Melin, L., Brorson, L-O. and Schollin, J. (1985) 'Effects of a broad spectrum behavior modification treatment programme on children with refractory epileptic seizures', *Epilepsia* 26: 303–9.

Fenwick, P. B. C. (1994) 'The behavioral treatment of epilepsy generation and inhibition of seizures', *Neurologic Clinics* 12: 175–202.

Fenwick, P. B. C. and Brown, S. W. (1989) 'Evoked and psychogenic seizures: I. Precipitation', *Acta Neurologica Scandinavica* 80: 541–7.

Ferrie, C. D., De Marco, P., Grunewald, R. A., Giannakodimos, S. and Panayiotopoulos, C. P. (1994) 'Video game induced seizures', *Journal of Neurology, Neurosurgery and Psychiatry* 57: 925–31.

Finkler, J., Lozar, N. and Fenwick, P. (1990) 'Der Zusammenhang zwischen spezifischen Situationen emotionalen Zuständen und Anfallshäufigkeit: Vergleich einer psychiatrischen mit einer nichtpsychiatriaschen Population von Epilepsiepatienten', in D. Scheffner (ed.) *Epilepsie 90*, Berlin: Einhorn Presse.

Forster, F. M. (1969) 'Conditional reflexes and sensory-evoked epilepsy: the nature of the therapeutic process', *Conditional Reflex* 4: 103–14.

—— (1972) 'The classification and conditioning treatment of the reflex epilepsies', *International Journal of Neurology* 9: 73–86.

Forster, F. M., Hansotia, P., Cleeland, C. S. and Ludwig, A. (1969) 'A case of voice-induced epilepsy treated by conditioning', *Neurology* 19: 325–31.

Fried, R. (1993) 'Breathing training for the self-regulation of alveolar CO_2 in the behavioural control of idiopathic epileptic seizures', in D. I. Mostofsky and Y. Løyning (eds) *The Neurobehavioral Treatment of Epilepsy*, New Jersey: Lawrence Erlbaum.

Fried, R., Rubin, S. R., Carlton, R. M. and Fox, M. C. (1984) 'Behavioural control of intractable seizures: I. Self-regulation of end-tidal carbon dioxide', *Psychosomatic Medicine* 46: 315–31.

Gillham, R. (1990) 'Refractory epilepsy: an evaluation of psychological methods in out-patient management', *Epilepsia* 31: 427–32.

Goldstein, L. H. (1990) 'Behavioural and cognitive-behavioural treatments for epilepsy: a progress review', *British Journal of Clinical Psychology* 29: 257–69.

Goossens, L. A. Z., Andermann, F., Andermann, E. and Remillard, G. M. (1990) 'Reflex seizures induced by card or board games, and spatial tasks: a review of 25 patients and delineation of the epileptic syndrome', *Neurology* 40: 1171–6.

Greig, E. and Betts, T. (1992) 'Epileptic seizures induced by sexual abuse. Pathogenic and pathoplastic factors', *Seizure* 1: 269–74.

Hughes, J., Devinsky, O., Feldmann, E. and Bromfield, E. (1993) 'Premonitory symptoms in epilepsy', *Seizure* 2: 201–3.

Krafft, K. M. and Poling, A. D. (1982) 'Behavioural treatments of epilepsy: methodological characteristics and problems of published studies', *Applied Research in Mental Retardation* 3: 151–62.

Kristensen, O. and Alving, J. (1992) 'Pseudoseizures – risk factors and prognosis. A case-control study', *Acta Neurologica Scandinavica* 85: 177–80.

Krumholz, A. and Niedermeyer, E. (1983) 'Psychogenic seizures: a clinical study with follow-up data', *Neurology* 33: 498–502.

Lancman, M. E., Asconape, J. J., Craven, W. J., Howard, G. and Penry, J. K. (1994) 'Predictive value of induction of psychogenic seizures by suggestion', *Annals of Neurology* 35: 359–61.

Liske, E. and Forster, F. (1964) 'Pseudoseizures: a problem in the diagnosis and management of epilepsy patients', *Neurology* 14: 41–9.

Lisovoski, F., Prier, S., Koskas, P., Dubard, T., Stievenart, J. L., Dehen, H. and Cambier, J. (1992) 'Hot-water epilepsy in an adult: ictal EEG, MRI and SPECT features', *Seizure* 1: 203–6.

Litwin, R. G. and Cardena, E. (1993) 'Dissociation and reported trauma in organic and psychogenic seizure patients', *Psychological Hypnosis* 2.

Løyning, Y., Bjørnæs, H., Larsson, P. G., Areng, S., Aronsen, R., Bragason, A., Kloster, R. and Lossius, R. (1993) 'Influence of psychosocial factors on seizure occurrence', in D. I. Mostofsky and Y. Løyning (eds) *The Neurobehavioral Treatment of Epilepsy*, New Jersey: Lawrence Erlbaum.

McDade, G. and Brown, S. W. (1992) 'Non-epileptic seizures: management and predictive factors of outcome', *Seizure* 1: 7–10.

Montgomery, J. M. and Espie, C. (1986) 'Behavioural management of hysterical pseudo seizures', *Behavioural Psychotherapy* 14: 334–40.

Moore, P. M., Baker, G. A., McDade, G., Chadwick, D. and Brown, S. W. (1994) 'Epilepsy, pseudoseizures and perceived family characteristics: a controlled study', *Epilepsy Research* 18: 75–83.

Mostofsky, D. (1993) 'Behavior modification and therapy in the management of epileptic disorders', in D. I. Mostofsky and Y. Løyning (eds) *The Neurobehavioral Treatment of Epilepsy*, New Jersey: Lawrence Erlbaum.

Mostofsky, D. and Balaschak, B. A. (1977) 'Psychobiological control of seizures', *Psychological Bulletin* 84: 723–50.

Neufeld, M. Y., Sadeh, M., Cohn, D. F. and Korczyn, A. D. (1994) 'Stress and epilepsy: the Gulf War experience', *Seizure* 3: 135–39.

Powell, G. E. (1981) *Brain Function Therapy*, Hampshire: Gower.

Pritchard, P. B. III, Holstrom, V. L. and Giacinto, J. (1985) 'Self-abatement of complex partial seizures', *Annals of Neurology* 18: 265–7.

Puskarich, C. A., Whitman, S., Dell, J., Hughes, J., Rosen, A. J. and Hermann, B. P. (1992) 'Controlled examination of progressive relaxation training of seizure reduction', *Epilepsia* 33: 675–80.

Ramani, V. (1986) 'Intensive monitoring of psychogenic seizures, aggression and dyscontrol syndromes', in R. Gumnit (ed.) *Advances in Neurology. Vol. 46: Intensive Neurodiagnostic Monitoring*, New York: Raven Press.

Ramani, V. and Gumnit, R. J. (1982) 'Management of hysterical seizures in epileptic patients', *Archives of Neurology* 39: 78–81.

Reiter, J., Andrews, D. and Janis, C. (1987) *Taking Control of Your Epilepsy. A Workbook for Patients and Professionals*, Santa Rosa: The Basics Publishing Company.

Rousseau, A., Hermann, B. and Whitman, S. (1985) 'Effects of progressive relaxation on epilepsy: analysis of a series of cases', *Psychological Reports* 57: 1203–12.

Scheepers, B., Budd, S., Curry, S., Gregory, S. and Elson, S. (1994) 'Non-epileptic attack disorder: a clinical audit', *Seizure* 3: 129–34.

Siegel, M., Kurzrok, N., Barr, W. B. and Rowan, A. J. (1992) 'Game-playing epilepsy', *Epilepsia* 33: 93–7.

Spector, S., Foots, A. and Goldstein, L. H. (1995) 'Reduction in seizure frequency as a result of group intervention for adults with epilepsy', *Epilepsia* 36 (Suppl. 3): S130.

Spector, S., Goldstein, L. H., Cull, C. A. and Fenwick, P. B. C. (1994) Precipitating and inhibiting epileptic seizures: a survey of adults with poorly controlled epilepsy. London: International League against Epilepsy.

Sterman, M. B. (1993) 'Sensorimotor EEG feedback training in the study and treatment of epilepsy', in D. I. Mostofsky and Y. Løyning (eds) *The Neurobehavioural Treatment of Epilepsy*, New Jersey: Lawrence Erlbaum.

Striano, S., Meo, R., Bilo, L., Soricellis, M. and Ruosi, P. (1993) 'Epilepsia arithmetices: study of four cases', *Seizure* 2: 35–43.

Tan, S-Y. and Bruni, J. (1986) 'Cognitive-behaviour therapy with adult patients with epilepsy: a controlled outcome study', *Epilepsia* 27: 255–63.

Taube, S. L. and Calman, N. H. (1992) 'The psychotherapy of patients with complex partial seizures', *American Journal of Orthopsychiatry* 62: 35–43.

Webster, A. and Mawer, G. E. (1989) 'Seizure frequency and major life events in epilepsy', *Epilepsia* 30: 162–7.

Whitman, S., Dell, J., Legion, V., Eibhlyn, A. and Statsinger, J. (1990) 'Progressive relaxation for seizure reduction', *Journal of Epilepsy* 3: 17–22.

Chapter 8

Quality of life

Anna Kendrick

INTRODUCTION

Quality of Life (QoL) is a generic term encompassing an individual's feelings of satisfaction with a complex amalgam of areas of functioning. It is broadly accepted that QoL needs to address (at a minimum) satisfaction with physical, cognitive, emotional, social and economic functioning (WHO 1980; Hornquist 1982; Wenger *et al.* 1984, Spitzer 1987; Ware 1987; Fallowfield 1990).

The way in which an individual determines their level of satisfaction within these key areas remains a matter for debate. The philosophical approach to QoL introduces concepts such as the attainment of life goals (Hornquist 1982; Cohen 1982), achievement–aspiration discrepancy (Campbell *et al.* 1976; Calman 1984; Staats and Stassen 1987) and social–relational models (WHO 1980). It is beyond the scope of this chapter to cover such issues in detail. A full review of these concepts can be found in Kendrick (1993). Such concepts are pertinent to the clinician as they provide practical ways of improving a person's perception of their QoL, for example, through increasing patient self-awareness, adjusting patient goals and ensuring that patients set realistic expectations. For example, the achievement–aspiration discrepancy model suggests that it is the discrepancy between actual achievements and aspirations/expectations that play a critical role in determining an individual's feelings of satisfaction with their QoL. Health professionals can temper patient expectations and prepare them for changes and limitations that will occur as disease progresses, thus avoiding frustration and maximising QoL.

QoL is a complex phenomenon with the following key attributes: it is a multidimensional concept influenced by performance in, and satisfaction with, a number of life domains; it is an individual phenomenon in which an individual's beliefs, desires and perceptions play an integral role; it is a relational phenomenon in which an individual makes comparisons (conscious or unconscious) between their current life situation and some external criteria (for example, past abilities, peers); the discrepancy between actual situation and expectations or aspirations is an important component in the determination of QoL by an individual, and it is a fluctuating phenomenon, with changes being related both to objective circumstances (for example, deteriorating physical health) and subjective perceptions (for example, changing expectations).

QUALITY OF LIFE AND THE PATIENT WITH EPILEPSY

There are various medical (Duncan 1990), social (Thompson and Oxley 1988; Scambler 1990) and psychological factors (Vining 1987; McGuire and Trimble 1990) which may influence the QoL of the person with epilepsy (see Table 8.1).

The occurrence of recurring, unpredictable seizures is undoubtedly a major factor affecting the life of a person with epilepsy. Seizure frequency, fear of seizures and self-perception of epilepsy have been shown to be predictors of well-being in people with epilepsy (Leonard 1989; Collings 1990a, b, c; Chaplin *et al.* 1990). These findings are supported by research showing that health is an important mediator of QoL (Edwards and Klemmack 1973; Campbell 1981; Okun *et al.* 1984; Levitt *et al.* 1987) and, in particular, that self-rated health appears to be more predictive of QoL than objective health (Diener 1984). It is

Table 8.1 Contributory factors to impaired QoL in people with epilepsy

Factor	Specific items
Medical	Seizure occurrence (frequency, severity) Medication (intrusion/side effects) Hospitalisation (in-patient/out-patient)
Social	Stigmatisation (felt/enacted) Family dynamics (overprotection) Employment difficulties Legal restrictions (driving)
Psychological	Cognitive deficits (memory, concentration) Intellectual decline Psychiatric (depression, anxiety, behaviour disturbance)

unclear, however, whether ill-health directly affects life satisfaction or whether the association is due to the secondary effects of ill-health on other aspects of life that are important to QoL – for example, not being able to work, having reduced activity levels and limited social opportunities.

The diagnosis of epilepsy can bring with it many problems over and above that of experiencing recurrent seizures. Stigmatization, social isolation, psychological problems, educational and employment difficulties have all been documented in people with epilepsy (Dodrill *et al.* 1984a; Scambler and Hopkins 1986; Thompson and Oxley 1988; Levin *et al.* 1988). It is of interest that many of these areas have been shown to be predictive of QoL. Factors associated with increased feelings of wellbeing include being married (Cameron 1975; Campbell 1981; Costa *et al.* 1987; Mookherjee 1987), having high social status (Cameron 1975; Potter and Coshall 1987), having high levels of social support (Levitt *et al.* 1987), having high levels of activity – with activities involving a high degree of social integration which are in the individual's control being particularly desirable (Steinkamp and Kelly 1987; Reich *et al.* 1987) – and feelings of personal control and high self-esteem (Campbell 1981; Lewis 1982; Diener 1984; Levitt *et al.* 1987). Disadvantage in any of these areas is likely to result in lower feelings of satisfaction with QoL.

In summary, the person with epilepsy may face psychosocial difficulties in a range of areas of life-functioning that are likely to adversely influence feelings of satisfaction with their QoL. Given the far-reaching consequences that the diagnosis of epilepsy may have on a patient's QoL, it is interesting that few studies have attempted to objectively examine the impact of epilepsy on QoL. Whilst there has been a long-standing interest among researchers in areas relevant to quality of life (for example, adequacy of cognitive, emotional and behavioural status, ability to work, social functioning, self-esteem), research work has tended to concentrate on assessing the incidence of these problems and their relationship with epilepsy-related variables (seizure frequency, medication, seizure type – Harrison and Taylor 1976; Rodin *et al.* 1979; Dodrill *et al.* 1984b) rather than the impact of these difficulties on the individuals QoL. Hermann (1992) provides a review of QoL work in epilepsy and a useful summary can be also be found in Meador (1993).

Recent years have, however, seen an increased interest in formal studies of QoL in this group of patients (Hermann 1992), as evidenced by increased attempts to develop epilepsy-specific measures (Vickrey *et al.* 1992; Baker *et al.* 1993; Perrine 1993) and to examine determinants of QoL in this group of patients (Leonard 1989; Chaplin *et al.* 1990; Collings 1990a, b, c).

The development of epilepsy-specific scales is reviewed later in this chapter. In relation to the areas of functioning considered important to (or predictive of) QoL in patients with epilepsy, a number of recent studies have produced some interesting findings. Leonard (1989) used a fifty-item questionnaire to determine which items were considered most important to the QoL of patients living in a residential centre. Opinions were sought from twenty-five relatives, 135 staff and twenty-five residents. In general, broad agreement across the three groups was seen, with the greatest importance being given to:

1 basic physical needs (warm, dry accommodation, adequate diet, clothing, availability of medical care);
2 seizure frequency;
3 independence (having personal possessions, opportunity for privacy, being ambulant);
4 social relationships/occupation (availability of close friends, facilities to encourage socialising);
5 intellectual/creative needs.

Some interesting differences, however, were apparent. Residents themselves placed greater importance on being in good spirits, being able to get out of the centre (for shopping/day trips, etc), having close friends, having the opportunity for sexual relationships and having their own room than the other groups surveyed (relatives and staff).

Chaplin *et al.* (1990) interviewed patients about the impact and consequences of epilepsy and its treatment on their lives. They identified twenty-one areas of concern to people with epilepsy, covering medical, emotional, social and employment aspects (see Table 8.2).

Collings (1990a, b, c), in a study of factors related to general well-being in a group of patients with epilepsy, found that it was patients' perceptions of themselves (their self-image) and their epilepsy that were more predictive of overall well-being. In addition, he noted that it was the discrepancy between an individual's perception of their current self (with epilepsy) and an anticipated self (without epilepsy) that was important in producing a greater sense of well-being. Other factors that were important to well-being were employment status, seizure control, diagnostic certainty and age.

In summary, the person with epilepsy may face difficulties in a range of areas of life-functioning pertinent to QoL. To date, however, little is known about the impact that these problems have on the quality of

Table 8.2 Areas of concern identified by patients with epilepsy

Area	Specific concern
Medical	Attitude towards accepting epileptic attacks Attitude towards label 'epilepsy' Fear of having seizures Problems with chronic medication Misconceptions about epilepsy Lethargy/lack of energy Sleep disturbance Distrust of the medical profession
Emotional	Lack of confidence in the future Change of outlook on life/self Depression of emotional reactions
Social	Concern about sexual relationships Concern about housing Lack of confidence surrounding travel Adverse reactions in social life Adverse reactions in leisure pursuits Difficulty in communicating with family Feelings of increased isolation Concern about platonic relationships
Employment	Fear of stigma in employment Concern about performance at work

(Source: Chaplin *et al.* 1990)

everyday life of the individual with epilepsy. One of the major obstacles to answering these questions has been the lack of a QoL measure designed specifically for use in patients with epilepsy.

MEASUREMENT OF QOL IN PATIENTS WITH EPILEPSY

Recent years have seen increasing attempts to measure QoL as an outcome measure for clinical interventions. This has been paralleled by an increasing sophistication in our understanding of the QoL concept and measurement methods, as evidenced by the reviews of Najman and Levine (1981) and Hollandsworth (1988).

While there is a wide acceptance of the need to assess QoL in patients with epilepsy, there is no 'gold standard' measure in existence for so doing. Although there are a myriad of generic and disease-specific measures of QoL in existence (see Clark and Fallowfield 1986; McDowell and Newell 1987; Fletcher *et al.* 1987; Fallowfield 1990 for reviews), it is only in the past five years that a number of epilepsy-specific measures have been developed and these are reviewed here.

Washington Psychosocial Seizure Inventory – WPSI (Dodrill *et al.* 1980)

The WPSI was developed in the 1970s as a measure of the impact of epilepsy on a patient's psychosocial functioning. The original scale is a 132-item questionnaire covering seven areas of functioning: family background, emotional adjustment, interpersonal adjustment, vocational adjustment, financial status, adjustment to seizures and medical management. It is based on patient self-perceptions using self-report assessment and has been widely used both to define psychosocial problems in patients with epilepsy (Dodrill 1983; Dodrill *et al.* 1984a, b; Tan 1986) and to examine the influence of epilepsy-related and other variables on psychosocial functioning (Dodrill 1984; 1986). It has demonstrated acceptable levels of internal reliability, test–retest reliability and validity (Dodrill *et al.* 1980). A WPSI QoL scale has recently been developed (Dodrill and Batzel 1995) consisting of thirty-six items of the WPSI which correlated significantly with an independent QoL measure (the QoLIE-31 Inventory: Cramer 1995).

The WPSI, however, was not designed to provide as broad an assessment of areas of life-functioning important to QoL as generic measures of this concept (for example, the Sickness Impact Profile: Bergner *et al.* 1981), and its use as a measure of the broad impact of epilepsy on QoL has been questioned (Langfitt 1995). This scale is likely to be most appropriate in situations where information about the psychological and social facets of QoL is of primary importance.

The Liverpool Initiative (Baker *et al.* 1993)

This is a battery of measures developed specifically to assess QoL in patients with epilepsy. The battery covers physical, social and psychological functioning and incorporates previously validated measures including the Nottingham Health Profile (Hunt *et al.* 1980), a measure of activities of daily living (Brown and Tomlinson 1984), the Social

Problems Questionnaire (Corney and Clare 1985), the Hospital Anxiety and Depression scale (Zigmond and Snaith 1983), the Profile of Mood States (McNair *et al.* 1981), and measures of self-esteem (Rosenberg 1965) and mastery (Pearlin and Schooler 1978). In addition, three novel epilepsy-specific scales have been developed: a Seizure Severity Scale (Baker *et al.* 1991), an Impact of Epilepsy Scale (Jacoby *et al.* 1993) and a Life Fulfilment Scale (Baker *et al.* 1994). This approach has been used successfully to examine the effects of anti-epileptic treatment (Smith *et al.* 1993) and seizure severity (Smith *et al.* 1991) on the quality of life of patients with epilepsy. Other applications include when to start medication, when to discontinue medication, which medication to prescribe and how best to deliver medical services to people with epilepsy (Jacoby *et al.* 1995).

The Epilepsy Surgery Inventory – ESI-55 (Vickrey et al. 1992; Vickrey 1993)

This scale has been developed in the USA specifically to assess changes in QoL following epilepsy surgery. It is a self-report measure covering eleven dimensions of health-related QoL. It consists of a generic core of thirty-five items (covering eight dimensions: general health perceptions, energy/fatigue, social function, emotional well-being, role limitations due to emotional problems, physical function, role limitations due to physical problems, pain) based on the RAND thirty-six item Health Survey (SF-36: Ware and Sherbourne 1992). The SF-36 is a generic measure of functional status and well-being and has been subjected to extensive psychometric development. This is supplemented by nineteen epilepsy-specific items covering three dimensions (cognitive function, role limitations due to memory problems and overall QoL). In addition, the scale includes one item relating to change in health. Data from 200 patients who had undergone surgery for their epilepsy provide evidence of internal consistency and validity (content, construct, convergent) (Vickrey *et al.* 1992).

The Quality of Life in Epilepsy – QOLIE Project (Perrine 1993)

This is a USA-based, multicentre study which began in late 1991 with the aim of developing and validating an epilepsy-specific inventory for patients with mild to moderate epilepsy.

The test battery is based on the ESI-55 (Vickrey *et al.* 1992), but expanded to have a broader application. The initial inventory consisted of ninety-eight items, with the RAND 36-item Health Survey (SF-36) (Ware and Sherbourne 1992) forming a generic core to which epilepsy-specific items were added (based on a literature review and expert opinion as to the areas of importance to people with mild to moderate epilepsy). The epilepsy-specific items added covered ten dimensions: specific health perceptions, worry about seizures, attention and concentration, memory, language, working and driving limitations, medication effects, social support, social isolation and overall QoL. This ninety-eight-item scale was tested in 304 adults with epilepsy and also completed by patient proxies on two occasions with a one month test–retest interval. Patients also completed tests of neuropsychological function and mood status. The initial scale was reduced to eighty-nine items using multitrait scaling analysis methods.

The final version (QOLIE-89) consists of seventeen scales covering four domains (derived by factor analysis): epilepsy-targeted (seizure worry, medication effects, health discouragement, work/driving/social function), cognitive (language, attention/concentration, memory), mental health (overall QoL, emotional well-being, role limitations – emotional, social isolation, social support, energy/fatigue) and physical health (health perceptions, physical function, role limitations – physical, pain). Preliminary data suggest this scale is reliable and valid (Hermann 1995).

Two further versions have been developed: a 31-item version (QoLIE-31), which consists of seven scales focusing on those areas most pertinent to the person with epilepsy (seizure worry, cognitive function, work, energy, emotional well-being, driving, medication effects) and excluding some of the more general QoL scales covered by the QoLIE-89 (physical function, role limitations, pain, health perception, social support and social isolation). The QoLIE-31 takes less time to complete than the QoLIE-89 and is therefore particularly suited to research protocols in which multiple scales and tests are to be used. A QoLIE-10 version is also available, designed as a quick screening tool for use in clinical practice (Cramer 1995).

Quality of Life Assessment by Construct Analysis – QoLASCA, (Kendrick 1993)

This is a 70-item questionnaire based on repertory grid technique. Five areas of life functioning are covered (physical, cognitive, emotional, social and economic/employment). Within these areas, specific items are elicited for each respondent via a semi-structured interview.

Respondents are then asked to rate how much of a problem they view each item at the moment, using a five-point rating scale ranging from 'not a problem' to 'a severe problem'. In addition, patients are asked to rate a variety of situations ('as you were before having epilepsy', 'as you would like to be', 'as you expect to be', 'a close friend', 'the best possible life', 'the worst possible life'). This approach enables the relational aspects of QoL to be tapped. Scoring is based on the discrepancy between current situation ('as you are now') and expectations ('as you would like to be'), with aggregate and profile scores available. The psychometric properties of this scale were established in a group of patients with chronic epilepsy who were assessed on several occasions over a six-month period. Analysis of these data suggest that this scale is reliable, sensitive, valid and acceptable to patients (McGuire 1991; Kendrick 1993).

A cardinal feature of this scale is that it allows an individualised assessment of QoL. Two case histories are presented here to illustrate the benefit of an individualised approach to the assessment of quality of life.

Case history 1: EE

At the time of initial assessment, EE was a 66-year-old gentleman who had lived at a residential centre for a number of years. He had not had a seizure for seven years and led a relatively independent life, living in one of the houses for more able residents. In the ensuing six months he experienced a further seizure. He commented 'I had forgotten that I had epilepsy. This has made me realise that it is still there'. Figure 8.1 shows his overall QoL scores (a high score indicates greater dissatisfaction with QoL). A clear deterioration is seen. During interview the individualised areas he considered important to his quality of life were: to be seizure free, not to be tired, to be able to remember things, to be able to think quickly, to be in control of temper, not to be anxious, not to be lonely, to have confidence, to have job satisfaction and to have enough money for basic needs. Figure 8.2 plots the scores for these areas at the initial assessment and six months later. These profile scores show that the decrease in his overall satisfaction with life (Figure 8.1) seems to be primarily due to the occurrence of a seizure after being seizure free for a number of years. This is evidenced by higher scores (hence greater dissatisfaction) for the areas of seizures (being seizure free) and anxiety (not being anxious). These objective data fit well with his subjective reports of being worried about having another seizure.

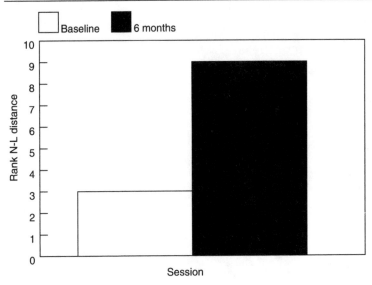

Figure 8.1 Global evaluation (Case 1)

Case history 2: SR

SR was a 27-year-old man who was resident at an independent hostel for people with epilepsy. At initial assessment he was very concerned about his lack of a girlfriend and felt that his lack of confidence and shyness would prevent him from forming such a relationship. He was also unhappy in his job. The specific areas he considered important to his QoL were: his seizures being under control, having a good memory, being able to concentrate, not being aggressive, overcoming shyness, having confidence, having a girlfriend, not being lonely, having job satisfaction and having sufficient money. Figure 8.3 shows the change in his overall evaluation of his QoL six months later. The improvement seen corresponds with major changes in his lifestyle. During these six months he achieved full independence, moving to living in private rented accommodation. He felt that this move noticeably increased his confidence. During the same period he also formed a close relationship with a girl and was given more responsibility at work. These changes are highlighted in his profile scores (Figure 8.4) where the largest changes (in terms of increased satisfaction) can be seen for shyness, confidence, lack of partner and job satisfaction.

A shorter version of the QoLASCA scale has been developed and has been used to compare drug treatments and evaluate surgery

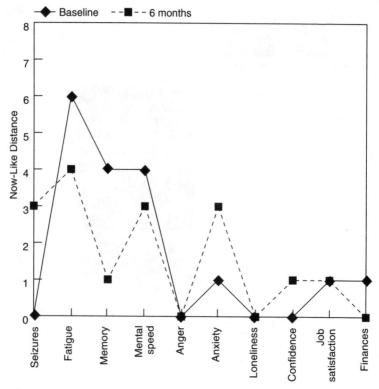

Figure 8.2 Individual profile (Case 1)

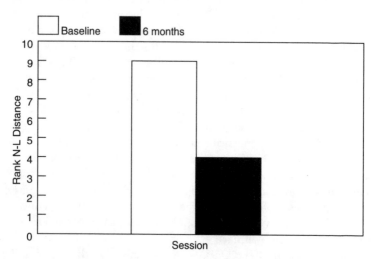

Figure 8.3 Global evaluation (Case 2)

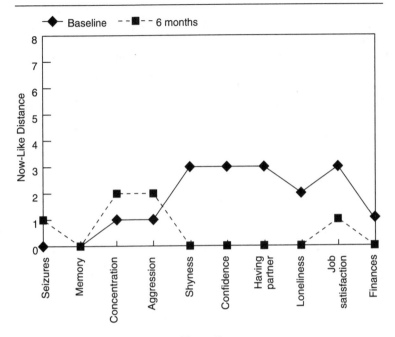

Figure 8.4 Individual evaluation (Case 2)

has been used to compare drug treatments and evaluate surgery outcome in patients with epilepsy (Selai and Trimble 1995).

Non-epilepsy-specific measures of QoL

There are a number of existing QoL measures which may be suitable for use in patients with epilepsy. One of the main advantages of using an older, existing measure is the increased availability of psychometric data relating to reliability, validity and sensitivity allowing increased confidence in interpreting data. Their obvious drawback is that they do not include items specific to the patient with epilepsy.

Psychosocial Adjustment to Illness Scale – PAIS (Morrow *et al.* 1978; Derogatis 1986)

The PAIS is a 45-item questionnaire which assesses adjustment to illness in seven domains: health care orientation (attitude/expectations of doctors and treatments), vocational environment (disruption to job performance, satisfaction with job and adjustment to work following illness), domestic environment (family relationships, communication and impact on finances), sexual relationships (quality, frequency, sexual satisfaction), extended family relationships (communication, interaction, degree of dependency), social environment (level of participation, level of interest) and psychological distress (anxiety, depression, guilt, hostility). Ratings are made on a four-point scale and summed to give scores for the seven domains as well as an overall adjustment score based on the forty-five items. Scores are converted to standardised T-scores (given in the PAIS handbook) which can be compared to published norms. Norms are available for the PAIS in four patient groups: lung cancer, renal dialysis, acute burns and hypertensive patients. Psychometric data is available to support internal consistency, inter-rater reliability, content validity, construct validity and predictive validity (Morrow et al. 1978).

This scale is of possible use in patients with epilepsy due to its comprehensiveness. However, its current use is limited by the unavailability of norms for epilepsy patients.

Nottingham Health Profile – NHP (Hunt and McEwen 1980; Hunt et al. 1985)

The NHP was designed to measure perceived health problems and the extent to which these impinge on the everyday activities of the patient (Hunt 1984). There are two parts to the questionnaire. Part I consists of thirty-eight statements grouped into six areas of functioning: sleep (five items), physical mobility (eight items), energy level (three items), pain (eight items), emotional reactions (nine items) and social isolation (five items). All statements require a yes or no response from the respondent. A weighted score (patient-based) is obtained for each of these areas with a high score indicating greater problems/difficulties. A simpler, unweighted scoring system is also used in which the number of affirmative responses in each area is counted (McDowell and Newell 1987). Part II consists of seven statements relating to areas of life most often affected by health. Patients are asked (using a yes/no response format) whether their health is causing problems with their paid employment, social life, home life, looking after the home, interests and hobbies, sex life or holidays. Statements in Part II are scored one for an affirmative response and zero for a negative reply. This measure has undergone extensive psychometric testing and has been used in a variety of patient populations (Hunt et al. 1985).

The main drawback to its use in patients with epilepsy is the large proportion of statements relating to physical problems (mobility, pain, etc). Such concerns are not usually considered to predominate the life of the patient with epilepsy, who is more likely to experience difficulties with social and emotional aspects of functioning. It may, however, be of value as an assessment of the impact of physical functioning on QoL in the patient with epilepsy as suggested by the Liverpool Initiative (Baker *et al.* 1993), which includes the NHP as a validated measure within the physical functioning domain.

Sickness Impact Profile – SIP (Bergner *et al.* 1981)

This is a comprehensive, generic, 136-item scale covering twelve areas of functioning: sleep and rest, eating, work, home management, recreation and pastimes, ambulation, mobility, bodycare and movement, social interaction, alertness behaviour, emotional behaviour and communication. Patients are asked to tick any item which describes them as they are today and is related to their health. Scores are weighted then summed and transformed to a percentage score to provide individual category scores. In addition, composite scores of physical, psychosocial and overall functioning can be computed. The higher the score on the SIP, the more dysfunctional the patient.

This scale has been widely used in a variety of patient populations and it is well researched with a wealth of published data relating to reliability and validity (Bergner *et al.* 1976; Pollard *et al.* 1976; Carter *et al.* 1976, Bergner 1988). It provides a good coverage of cognitive, emotional and social aspects of functioning, areas likely to be of concern for the person with epilepsy. In addition, internal consistency, reliability and validity have been established in a group of patients with epilepsy (Langfitt 1995).

SUMMARY

Epilepsy is a heterogeneous disease which can affect an individual's life in a variety of ways. The use of QoL as a health status indicator is of particular importance in epilepsy where treatment is often not curative and can be associated with adverse side effects. Information concerning an individual's QoL may be of value to the clinician in a number of ways. At the individual level, it can provide relevant information about how the illness and its treatment impacts on the QoL of the individual. Assessment of QoL can allow areas of concern to a patient to be identified and treatment planned accordingly. In addition, it may be used to monitor over time a patient's response to treatment or reaction to the illness. At group level, it may be used to compare the intrusiveness of different treatments on the individual's everyday life, thus providing a scientific rationale in the choice of treatment enabling a balance between seizure reduction and QoL to be achieved.

The availability of rigorously tested, epilepsy-specific measures of QoL will enable clinicians and researchers to assess the impact of epilepsy and its treatment on the QoL of the person with epilepsy in greater detail. Such measures have already been used to evaluate the impact of novel medication in adults (Smith *et al.* 1993) and children with epilepsy (Smith *et al.* 1995), to examine the relationship between QoL and seizure severity (Smith *et al.* 1991) and other epilepsy variables (age of onset, duration of epilepsy, seizure type) (Kendrick 1993) and to investigate agreement between patient and patient-proxy reports of QoL (Hays *et al.* 1995). It is hoped that wider use of these measures will improve our understanding of the factors relevant to QoL in people with epilepsy and ensure that treatment is tailored to maximise the QoL of all people with epilepsy.

REFERENCES

Baker, G. A., Jacoby, A., Smith, D. F., Dewey, M. E. and Chadwick, D. W. (1994) 'The development of a novel scale to assess life fulfilment as part of the further refinement of a quality-of-life model for epilepsy', *Epilepsia* 35: 591–6.

Baker, G. A., Smith, D. F., Dewey, M., Morrow, J., Crawford, P. M. and Chadwick, D. W. (1991) 'The development of a seizure severity scale as an outcome measure in epilepsy', *Epilepsy Research* 8: 245–51.

Baker, G. A., Smith, D. F., Dewey, M., Jacoby, A. and Chadwick, D. W. (1993) 'The initial development of a health-related quality of life model as an outcome measure in epilepsy', *Epilepsy Research* 16: 65–81.

Bergner, M. (1988) 'Development, testing and use of the Sickness Impact Profile', in S. R. Walker and R. M. Rosser (eds) *Quality of Life: Assessment and Application*, Lancaster: MTM Press.

Bergner, M., Bobbitt, R. A., Carter, W. B. and Gilson, B. S. (1981) 'The Sickness Impact Profile: development and final revision of a health status measure', *Medical Care* 19: 787–805.

Bergner, M., Bobbitt, R. A., Pollard, W. E., Martin, D. P. and Gilson, B. S. (1976) 'The Sickness Impact Profile: validation of a health status measure', *Medical Care* 14: 57–67.

Brown, S. W. and Tomlinson, L. L. (1984) 'Anticonvulsant side effects: a self-report questionnaire for use in community surveys', *British Journal of Clinical Practice* 18: S147–9.

Calman, K. C. (1984) 'Quality of life in cancer patients: an hypothesis', *Journal of Medical Ethics* 10: 124–7.

Cameron, P. (1975) 'Mood as an indicant of happiness: age, sex, social class and situational differences', *Journal of Gerontology* 30: 216–24.

Campbell, A. (1981) *The Sense of Well-Being in America: Recent Patterns and Trends*, McGraw-Hill: New York.

Campbell, A., Converse, P. E. and Rodgers, W. L. (1976) *The Quality of American Life*, New York: Russell Sage Foundation.

Carter, W. B., Bobbitt, R. A., Bergner, M. and Gilson, B. S. (1976) 'Validation of an interval scaling: the Sickness Impact Profile', *Health Services Research* 11–12: 1976–7.

Chaplin, J. E., Yepez, R., Shorvon, S. and Floyd, M. (1990) 'A quantitative approach to measuring the social effects of epilepsy', *Neuroepidemiology* 9: 151–8.

Clark, A. and Fallowfield, L. J. (1986) 'Quality of life measurements in patients with malignant disease: a review', *Journal of the Royal Society of Medicine* 79: 165–9.

Cohen, C. (1982) 'On the quality of life: some philosophical reflections', *Circulation* 66 (5 Part 2): III 29–33.

Collings, J. A. (1990a) 'Epilepsy and well-being', *Social Science and Medicine* 31: 165–70.

—— (1990b) 'Psychosocial well-being and epilepsy: an empirical study', *Epilepsia* 31: 418–26.

—— (1990c) 'Correlates of well-being in a New Zealand epilepsy sample', *New Zealand Medical Journal* 103: 301–3.

Corney, R. H. and Clare, W. (1985) 'The construction, development and testing of a self-report questionnaire to identify social problems', *Psychological Medicine* 15: 637–49.

Costa, P. T., Jr, McCrae, R. R. and Zonderman, A. B. (1987) 'Environmental and dispositional influences on well-being: longitudinal follow-up of an American national sample', *British Journal of Psychology* 78: 299–306.

Cramer, J. (1995) 'Development of the Quality of Life in Epilepsy Scales', *Epilepsia* 36: S219.

Derogatis, L. R. (1986) 'The Psychosocial Adjustment to Illness Scale (PAIS)', *Journal of Psychosomatic Research* 30: 77–91.

Diener, E. (1984) 'Subjective well-being', *Psychological Bulletin* 95: 542–75.

Dodrill, C. B. (1983) 'Psychosocial characteristics of epileptic patients', *Research Publication of the Association for Research into Nervous and Mental Disorders* 61: 341–53.

—— (1984) 'Number of seizure types in relation to emotional and psychosocial adjustment in epilepsy', in R. J. Porter and A. A. Ward Jnr (eds) *Advances in Epileptology. The xxth Epilepsy International Symposium*. New York: Raven Press.

—— (1986) 'Correlates of generalised tonic-clonic seizures with intellectual, neuropsychological, emotional and social function in patients with epilepsy', *Epilepsia* 27: 399–411.

Dodrill, C. B. and Batzel, L. W. (1995) 'The Washington Psychosocial Seizure Inventory: new developments in the light of the quality of life concept', *Epilepsia* 36: S220.

Dodrill, C. B., Batzel, L. W., Queisser, H. R. and Temkin, N. R. (1980) 'An objective method for the assessment of psychological and social problems among epileptics', *Epilepsia* 21: 123–35.

Dodrill, C. B., Beier, R., Kasparick, M., Tacke, I., Tacke, U. and Tan, S. Y. (1984a) 'Psychosocial problems in adults with epilepsy: a comparison of findings from four countries', *Epilepsia* 25: 176–83.

Dodrill, C. B., Breyer, D. N., Diamond, M. B., Dubinsky, B. L. and Geary, B. B. (1984b) 'Psychosocial problems among adults with epilepsy', *Epilepsia* 25: 168–75.

Duncan, J. S. (1990) 'Medical factors affecting quality of life in patients with epilepsy', in D. Chadwick (ed.) *Quality of Life and Quality of Care in Epilepsy*, Royal Society of Medicine Round Table Series 23, Oxford: Alden Press.

Edwards, N. J. and Klemmack, D. L. (1973) 'Correlates of life satisfaction: a re-examination', *Journal of Gerontology* 28: 134–43.

Fallowfield, L. (1990) *The Quality of Life. The Missing Measurement in Health Care*, London: Souvenir Press.

Fletcher, A. E., Hunt, B. M. and Bulpitt, C. D. (1987) 'Evaluation of quality of life in clinical trials of cardiovascular disease', *Journal of Chronic Disease* 40: 557–66.

Harrison, R. M. and Taylor, D. C. (1976) 'Childhood seizures: a 25 year follow-up: social and medical prognosis', *Lancet* 1: 948–51.

Hays, R. D., Vickrey, B. G., Hermann, B., Perrine, K., Cramer, J., Meador, K., Spritzer, K. and Devinsky, O. (1995) 'Agreement between self reports and proxy reports of quality of life in patients with epilepsy', *Quality of Life Research* 4: 159–68.

Hermann, B. P. (1992) 'Quality of life in epilepsy', *Journal of Epilepsy* 5: 153–65.
—— (1995) 'The evolution of health-related quality of life assessment in epilepsy', *Quality of Life Research* 4: 87–100.

Hollandsworth, J. G., Jr, (1988) 'Evaluating the impact of medical treatment on the quality of life: a 5-year update', *Social Science and Medicine* 26: 425–34.

Hornquist, J. O. (1982) 'The concept of quality of life', *Scandinavian Journal of Social Medicine* 10: 57–61.

Hunt, S. M. (1984) 'Nottingham Health Profile', in N. K. Wenger, M. E. Mattson, C. D. Furberg and J. Elinson (eds) *Assessment of Quality of Life in Clinical Trials of Cardiovascular Therapies*, New York: Le Jacq Publishing.

Hunt, S. M. and McEwen, J. (1980) 'The development of a subjective health indicator', *Sociology, Health and Illness* 2: 231–46.

Hunt, S. M., McEwen, J. and McKenna, S. (1985) 'Measuring health status: a new tool for clinicians and epidemiologists', *Journal of the Royal College of General Practitioners* 35: 185–8.

Hunt, S. M., McKenna, S. P., McEwen, J., Backett, E. M., Williams, J. and Papp, E. (1980) 'A qualitative approach to perceived health status: a validation study', *Journal of Epidemiology and Community Health* 34: 281–6.

Jacoby, A., Baker, G. A., Smith, D. F. and Chadwick, D. W. (1995) 'Quality of life in epilepsy: the Liverpool initiative'. *Epilepsia* 36: S219.

Jacoby, A., Baker, G., Smith, D., Dewey, M. and Chadwick, D. (1993) 'Measuring the impact of epilepsy: the development of a novel scale', *Epilepsy Research* 16: 83–8.

Kendrick, A. M. (1993) 'Repertory grid technique in the assessment of quality of life in patients with epilepsy', unpublished PhD thesis, University of London.

Langfitt, J. T. (1995) 'Comparison of the psychometric characteristics of three quality of life measures in intractable epilepsy', *Quality of Life Research* 4: 101–14.

Leonard, I. (1989) 'Quality of life in a residential setting', *Psychiatric Bulletin* 13: 492–4.

Levin, R., Banks, S. and Bero, B. (1988) 'Psychosocial dimensions of epilepsy: a review of the literature', *Epilepsia* 29: 805–16.

Levitt, M. J., Clark, M. C., Rotton, J. and Finley, G. E. (1987) 'Social support, perceived control and well-being: a study of an environmentally stressed population', *International Journal of Aging and Human Development* 25: 247–57.

Lewis, F. M. (1982) 'Experienced personal control and quality of life in late-stage cancer patients', *Nursing Research* 31: 113–9.

McDowell, I. and Newell, C. (1987) *Measuring Health: A Guide to Rating Scales and Questionnaires*, Oxford: Oxford University Press.

McGuire, A. M. (1991) 'Quality of life in women with epilepsy', in M. R. Trimble (ed.) *Women and Epilepsy*, Chichester: Wiley.

McGuire, A. M. and Trimble, M. R. (1990) 'Quality of life in patients with epilepsy: the role of cognitive factors', in D. Chadwick (ed.) *Quality of Life and Quality of Care in Epilepsy*, Royal Society of Medicine Round Table Series 23, Oxford: Alden Press.

McNair, D. M., Lorr, N. and Droppleman, L. F. (1981) *Manual for the Profile of Mood States*, San Diego: Education and Industrial Testing Service.

Meador, K. J. (1993) 'Research use of the new Quality of Life in Epilepsy Inventory', *Epilepsia* 34 (Suppl. 4): S34–8.

Mookherjee, H. N. (1987) 'Perception of life satisfaction in the United States: a summary', *Perceptual and Motor Skills* 65: 218.

Morrow, G. R., Chiarello, R. J. and Derogatis, L. R. (1978) 'A new scale for assessing patients' psychosocial adjustment to medical illness', *Psychological Medicine* 8: 605–10.

Najman, J. M. and Levine, S. (1981) 'Evaluating the impact of medical care and technologies on the quality of life: a review and critique', *Social Science and Medicine* 15F: 107–15.

Okun, M. A., Stock, W. A., Haring, M. J. and Witter, R. A. (1984) 'Health and subjective well-being. A meta analysis', *International Journal of Aging and Human Development* 19: 111–31.

Pearlin, L. and Schooler, C. (1978) 'The structure of coping', *Journal of Health and Social Behaviour* 19: 2–21.

Perrine, K. R. (1993) 'A new quality-of-life inventory for epilepsy patients: interim results', *Epilepsia* 34 (Suppl. 4): S28–33.

Pollard, W. E., Bobbitt, R. A., Bergner, M., Martin, D. P. and Gilson, B. S. (1976) 'The Sickness Impact Profile: reliability of a health status measure', *Medical Care* 14: 146–55.

Potter, R. B. and Coshall, J. T. (1987) 'Socio-economic variations in perceived life domain satisfactions: a South-West Wales case study', *Journal of Social Psychology* 127: 77–82.

Reich, J. W., Zautra, A. J. and Hill, J. (1987) 'Activity, event transactions and quality of life in older adults', *Psychology and Aging* 2: 116–24.

Rodin, E. A., Shapiro, H. L. and Lennox, K. (1979) 'Epilepsy and life performance', *Rehabilitation Literature* 38: 34–9.

Rosenberg, M. (1965) *Society and the Adolescent Self-Image*, Princeton NJ: Princeton University Press.

Scambler, G. (1990) 'Social factors and quality of life and quality of care in epilepsy', in D. Chadwick (ed.) *Quality of Life and Quality of Care in Epilepsy*, Royal Society of Medicine Round Table Series 23, Oxford: Alden Press.

Scambler, G. and Hopkins, A. (1986) 'Being epileptic: Coming to terms with stigma', *Sociology, Health and Illness* 8: 26–43.

Selai, C. E. and Trimble, M. R. (1995) 'Quality of life based on repertory grid technique', *Epilepsia* 36: S220.

Smith, D. F., Baker, G. A., Jacoby, A. and Chadwick, D. W. (1995) 'The contribution of the measurement of seizure severity to quality of life research', *Quality of Life Research* 4: 143–58.

Smith, D. F., Baker, G. A., Dewey, M., Jacoby, A. and Chadwick, D. W. (1991) 'Seizure frequency, patient-perceived seizure severity and the psychosocial consequences of intractable epilepsy', *Epilepsy Research* 9: 231–41.

Smith, D. F., Baker, G. A., Davies, G., Dewey, M. and Chadwick, D. W. (1993) 'Outcomes of add-on treatment with lamotrigine in partial epilepsy', *Epilepsia* 34: 312–22.

Spitzer, W. O. (1987) 'State of science 1986: quality of life and functional status as target variables for research', *Journal of Chronic Disease* 40: 465–71.

Staats, S. R. and Stassen, M. A. (1987) 'Age and present and future perceived quality of life', *International Journal of Aging and Human Development* 25: 167–76.

Steinkamp, M. W. and Kelley, J. R. (1987) 'Social integration, leisure activity and life satisfaction in older adults: activity theory revisited', *International Journal of Aging and Human Development* 25: 293–307.

Tan, S. Y. (1986) 'Psychosocial functioning of adult epileptic and MS patients and adult normal controls on the WPSI', *Journal of Clinical Psychology* 42: 528–34.

Thompson, P. J. and Oxley, J. (1988) 'Socioeconomic accompaniments of severe epilepsy', *Epilepsia* 29 (Suppl. 1): S9–18.

Vickrey, B. G. (1993) 'A procedure for developing a quality of life measure for epilepsy surgery patients', *Epilepsia* 34 (Suppl. 4): S22–7.

Vickrey, B. G., Hays, R. D., Graber, J., Rausch, R., Engel, J. E. and Brook, R. H. (1992) 'A health-related quality of life instrument for patients evaluated for epilepsy surgery', *Medical Care* 30: 299–319.

Vining, E. P. G. (1987) 'Cognitive dysfunction associated with anti-epileptic drug therapy', *Epilepsia* 28 (Suppl. 2): S18–22.

Ware, J. E. (1987) 'Standards for validating health measures: definition and content', *Journal of Chronic Disease* 40: 473–80.

Ware, J. E. and Sherbourne, C. D. (1992) 'The 36 item short-form health survey (SF-36). I. Conceptual framework and item selection', *Medical Care* 30: 473–83.

Wenger, N. K., Mattson, M. E., Furberg, C. D. and Elinson, J. (eds) (1984) *Assessment of Quality of Life in Clinical Trials of Cardiovascular Therapies*, New York: Le Jacq Publishers.

World Health Organisation (1980) *International Classification of Impairments, Disabilities and Handicaps*, Geneva: WHO.

Zigmond, A. S. and Snaith, R. P. (1983) 'The Hospital Anxiety and Depression Scale', *Acta Psychiatrica Scandinavica* 67: 361–70.

Chapter 9

Neuropsychological and cognitive assessment of children with epilepsy

Maria Fowler

The assessment of neuropsychological and cognitive function of children with epilepsy is complicated by alterations in consciousness, drug side-effects and emotional factors. For every one of these children there is a set of intricately linked parameters affecting their cognitive function and test performance. This chapter will address this relationship, its importance and how it influences the choice of methods of assessment and interpretation of test results.

COGNITIVE FUNCTION OF CHILDREN WITH EPILEPSY

General intellectual ability

Many studies have addressed the question of the effects of seizures on children's ability to learn and on their general intellectual development (see Cull 1988; Seidenberg 1989). The overall agreement is that there is wide variability in intellectual ability among children with epilepsy, and having epilepsy is not an adequate predictor of future academic performance on its own. The National Child Development Study (Ross *et al.* 1980) found that two-thirds of the children with epilepsy were in mainstream schools, and a number of other studies have found average or higher than average IQ scores in children with epilepsy who were no different from matched controls in this respect (Bourgeois *et al.* 1983; see also Cull 1988).

Academic achievement

Although most children with epilepsy are of average intelligence, evidence suggests that they underachieve in comparison with their peers in mainstream schools. Indeed, as many as 50 per cent of children with epilepsy have been found to be seriously underachieving to a greater degree than their peers without epilepsy (Holdsworth and Whitmore 1974).

Farwell *et al.* (1985) found that the academic achievement of a group of children with epilepsy (aged six to fifteen years) was behind grade placement more often than in a control group. Similarly, Seidenberg *et al.* (1986) reported that 122 children with epilepsy were making less academic progress than expected for their age and IQ.

Most studies have found reading to be an area where these children often underachieve (see Aldenkamp *et al.* 1990a). For example, in the Isle of Wight Study, Rutter *et al.* (1970) found that a group of fifty-nine children with 'uncomplicated' epilepsy (i.e. with no identifiable brain pathology) had a mean average IQ, but their reading age was about twelve months behind their chronological age. Further, 18 per cent were two, or more, years behind in their reading as compared to 6 per cent of children without epilepsy. Corbett and Trimble (1983) suggested that about one in five children with seizures was likely to show a severe reading deficit.

In their study, Seidenberg *et al.* (1986) found that academic weaknesses were greatest in arithmetic, followed by spelling, reading, comprehension and word recognition. Thompson (1987) reported that only 17 per cent of those with epilepsy in ordinary schools were rated by their teachers as high in mathematical skills compared to 31 per cent of those with no seizures.

Areas of specific cognitive impairment

Aldenkamp *et al.* (1990a) have suggested that the cognitive deficits seen in children with epilepsy fall into three wide but specific categories: (a) 'memory deficit' group, implicating short-term memory and memory span impairments, usually related to temporal lobe dysfunction; (b) the 'attention deficit' group, underachieving in several academic skills and associated with high-frequency tonic-clonic seizures; and (c) a 'speed factor' category which is associated with slowing of information processing and which also affects arithmetic skills. This last group also lacked ability to 'problem-solve', which is a higher order skill associated with verbal reasoning and logical thinking. Indeed, most of the studies highlight that academic underachievement is related to language difficulties, memory and attention deficits. The importance of these findings is not in any way disputed, but it would appear that they may, to some extent, have perhaps overshadowed the existence of other cognitive deficits of equal importance, i.e. perceptual and visuospatial problems. Focal discharges often result in differential influences on cognitive dysfunction. Morgan and Groh (1980) suggested that children with partial seizures are at a greater risk of having impaired visuoperceptual abilities than those children with primary generalised seizures. Such deficits, of course, may play a very important role in reading acquisition skills and in learning from 'doing' or observing, affecting academic skills and scholastic performance in a variety of different ways. They may also cause a child to become 'awkward' in games and sport activities, underachieving in physical education and missing out in peer interaction.

THE MULTIFACTORIAL FRAMEWORK OF DISABILITY

The task of explaining the cognitive and academic difficulties in childhood epilepsy is a complex one as many factors may be involved. These factors could be directly or indirectly related to the condition and these will now be addressed under the following headings:

(a)   Aetiology;
(b)   Epilepsy-related factors;
(c)   Treatment-related factors;
(d)   Factors indirectly-related to epilepsy.

Aetiology

One very important single factor in influencing cognitive development in childhood epilepsy is the presence or absence of coexisting brain damage and its severity (Rodin 1989). In general, children with seizures associated with an identifiable brain pathology i.e. 'symptomatic' or 'complicated' epilepsy, tend to show greater impairment of cognitive function than those with seizures without underlying brain damage or identifiable cause, that is those with 'idiopathic' or 'uncomplicated' epilepsy (Dikmen 1980; Cull 1988). Children with 'symptomatic' epilepsy therefore, tend to be at a disadvantage regarding the prognosis of intellectual ability and have significantly lower IQs, than those with 'idiopathic' epilepsy (Sofijanov 1982; Bourgeois et al. 1983). The literature is well in agreement that neurological as well as psychosocial variables are very important in influencing the cognitive development of children with epilepsy (Bourgeois et al. 1983; Rodin et al. 1986; Thompson 1987; Seidenberg 1989; Sabers 1990). The effects are often complex and multifactorial and a serious attempt to identify these factors is extremely important for the formulation of intervention programmes and for rehabilitation.

Epilepsy-related factors

Factors directly related to the condition affecting cognitive functioning in children with seizure disorders may include age at onset of epilepsy, frequency of seizures, type of seizure, localisation of epileptic focus and epileptic syndrome. It should be understood, however, that these factors are more likely to affect function in combination with each other and with other factors to be discussed later, rather than in isolation.

Age at onset

The literature is in agreement that early onset of seizures is associated with a poor intellectual prognosis (O'Leary et al. 1981; Corbett et al. 1985; Cull 1988; Aldenkamp et al. 1990a; Hermann 1991). However, although early onset is implicated in cognitive difficulties it is not quite clear whether the deficits may also be the result of a combination of factors such as seizure severity, chronicity and polypharmacy. The chronicity of the condition in itself may, of course, be an indication of its severity and the need for polypharmacy when the seizures remain difficult to control. All of these factors will have an accumulative negative effect on cognitive function.

An early onset of seizures can be detrimental to the acquisition of functions as they start to develop and may become implicated in a reorganisation of some of these functions within the young brain. The 'relateralisation' of function and the effects of the plasticity of the brain (Rourke et al. 1983) have important implications, particularly for the assessment of children with epilepsy being considered for neurosurgery.

Seizure frequency

As with adults, studies of children have observed a steady rise in IQ for those persons whose seizures are controlled, with the opposite effect for those with poor seizure control (Rodin 1968; Seidenberg et al. 1981; Bourgeois et al. 1983; Rodin et al. 1986). Evidence tends to indicate that good seizure control is important for improved learning ability and that seizure frequency may be related to educational attainment (Cull 1988; Marston et al. 1993).

Type of seizures and epileptic syndrome

Both of these factors have been found to influence intellectual ability to various degrees. Dam (1990) concluded that seizures can affect the intellectual ability of children with epilepsy when they occur continuously (*status epilepticus*) and when they occur singly. Frequent and prolonged seizures are typically linked with more severe cognitive deficits, especially in the presence of brain damage associated with specific epileptic syndromes such as the West and the Lennox-Gastaut syndromes (Guzzetta *et al.* 1993). Poor prognosis associated with these syndromes is again linked to pre-existing brain pathology (Dam 1990).

Research has also shown that left-sided foci are associated with verbal deficits, right hemisphere foci with spatial problems, centrencephalic foci with attentional deficits and memory problems are linked to psychomotor seizures (Binnie *et al.* 1990; Piccirilli *et al.* 1994).

Transitory cognitive impairment (TCI)

One other interesting disturbance in cognitive functioning, which is also rather difficult to observe, is caused by the effects of subclinical epileptic discharges and has been termed transitory cognitive impairment (TCI). These are very brief disruptions in attending to incoming information. TCI can disrupt cognitive processing in a significant way affecting attention, immediate memory and speed of reaction (Binnie *et al.* 1990; Marston *et al.* 1993).

Treatment-related factors

These are usually factors involving anti-epileptic medication (AED) and surgery. Most studies are in agreement that some drugs such as phenytoin may impair cognitive function in children with epilepsy (Trimble and Thompson 1985). Forsythe *et al.* (1991), investigating a group of sixty-four children with newly diagnosed epilepsy, reported a clear impairment in memory skills and specifically in 'recent recall' after the children had been taking carbamazepine for six months. Speed of information processing was also found to be affected after only one month on carbamazepine and phenytoin. However, these effects were transitory and reversible. The importance of this with regard to assessment will be discussed later.

Anti-epileptic drugs differ in the way they may affect cognitive function. The most important issue, nevertheless, as far as drug treatment and cognitive function is concerned, appears to be not so much which drugs are used, but rather how they are used (Cull and Trimble 1989). It is now universally accepted that dose, absence of toxicity and monotherapy are very important for avoiding adverse effects of the drugs on cognition and behaviour. The improvement that often occurs in attention and learning when epileptic activity is suppressed (Marston *et al.* 1993) suggests that these deficits are linked primarily to seizure occurrence and their control. The suggestion then is that a delicate balance exists between medication, seizure control and cognitive function. A recent study of the neuropsychological effects of anti-epileptic drugs (Nichols *et al.* 1993) confirms that polypharmacy and higher AED blood levels can upset the balance between the beneficial results of the reduction of seizures and the detrimental side effects on cognitive function. In the treatment of children in particular, the effects of the drugs on learning may have an especially negative effect on the development of cognitive skills, and may result in these children becoming delayed at school. Although this may well be a reversible process, the damage might take a long time to be corrected and the psychological scars might be even more long-lasting. Some drugs produce fewer side effects than others (Cull 1988) and, with the newer AEDs such as lamotrigine being increasingly widely used, further studies in this field are certainly needed.

Although the primary treatment of epilepsy in childhood consists of the control of seizures by AEDs, an increasing number of children with difficult-to-control epilepsy however are now being considered to be suitable for surgical treatment (see Chapter 4). Improved and more sophisticated surgical techniques make it more likely that children with difficult-to-control epilepsy will benefit from neurosurgery. Most studies emphasise the importance of presurgical evaluation and agree that the improvement in seizure control achieved by surgical treatment is usually reflected in improvement in cognitive function (Wyler 1989; Dreifuss 1992).

Factors indirectly related to epilepsy

Psychosocial factors are well recognised as influencing the educational achievement of children with epilepsy (Hartlage and Green 1972; Long and Moore 1979; Seidenberg 1989). The literature confirms and emphasises the impact of the lowered expectations of teachers and parents, which may be producing a 'self-fulfilling' prophecy and also influence the children's self-concept, their self-esteem, attitudes to learning, acceptance of failure and general aspirations. The author's own experience is that many of these children often underachieve in formal psychometric assessments because of a readiness to accept failure and to give up all too easily, without even trying.

Other equally important factors affecting scholastic performance associated with the condition, but not neurologically linked, include the actual loss of schooling due to hospitalisation or poor health, the child being sent home from school after a seizure because of the teacher's anxiety and/or ignorance (Stores 1980; Gadow 1982) and last, but not least, the effects of labelling and isolation from the peer group. School then becomes an unpleasant and negative environment, generating a number of damaging effects on the child's well-being. Academic and interpersonal difficulties often generate anxiety, which may cause more seizures leading to more social isolation, rejection, school problems and damaged self-esteem. A number of children could get trapped in a vicious circle of seizures leading to social and learning problems, in turn leading to more seizures.

ASSESSMENT OF CHILDREN – PRACTICAL CONSIDERATIONS

So far we have examined the factors which influence cognitive function in children with epilepsy and the complex relationship between these parameters. The literature agrees that for these children there is a greater than expected prevalence of learning difficulties (Madge *et al.* 1993), and that detailed assessment of specific learning profiles is beneficial both as a diagnostic measure and as a basis for rehabilitation programmes. Full details of test publishers are given in the Appendix.

Why assess?

It is apparent that the cognitive development of children with epilepsy depends on a multitude of factors and there is no specific pattern of neuropsychological dysfunction (Seidenberg 1989). Psychological assessment is invaluable, therefore, in terms of establishing the child's strengths and weaknesses. The findings can then be utilised to put together individual learning programmes so that those strengths can become the main pathways for more effective learning. Assessments of cognitive function are also important for monitoring development and the effects of treatment, for determining the impact of seizures on performance, and for evaluating specific learning and functional deficits.

Issues in the assessment of cognitive function and interpretation of results

Variability in repeated test administration

With respect to the test–retest variability of psychometric testing of children with epilepsy, Rodin *et al.* (1986) found that test results may fluctuate widely over time, and in some there may be a trend towards deterioration. A ten-point change, up or down, was not unusual and verbal and performance changes were not necessarily in the same direction. This may indicate that because differential gains and losses in scores may offset each other, Full Scale IQ might not be a reliable measure and that study of the detailed profile of scores will provide a far more reliable measure of function. In a later study on the test–retest reliability of WISC-R subtest profiles, Aldenkamp *et al.* (1990b) found a relatively stable pattern of cognitive performance over, on average, a four-year period. The increased stability in scores may have been partly due to fewer subjects than in previous studies being on the older drugs such as phenytoin and phenobarbital. This last study reported a specific pattern of cognitive weakness consistently reflected on the Vocabulary, Coding, Information and Digit Span subtests.

Deterioration versus slow learning

Besag (1988) suggested that for a small sub-group of children with epilepsy who show cognitive deterioration, the severity of the condition and pre-existing cerebral pathology are almost always contributing factors. However, a progressive fall in IQ scores does not necessarily indicate a deterioration or loss of skills. In many cases, it is the result of a slowing down in developmental progress, indicating a slower than normal rate of learning. Since scaled scores are age-correlated, a decrease in IQ scores may have arisen because the child, although still progressing, is a slow learner and has failed to acquire the new skills at a normal rate. It is extremely important, therefore, to examine carefully the raw scores and compare them over time in order to determine whether a child has continued to learn, albeit at a slow pace, has reached a plateau, or has lost abilities.

Developmental delay

In trying to examine the relationship between epilepsy and cognitive function, it is important to assess the extent to which cognitive impairment may be permanent, transient or state-dependent or due to a developmental delay. In the assessment of children with epilepsy, the latter is of particular importance and may present a special problem as one sometimes might be making assumptions about abilities that are not as yet fully developed, and whose deficits are due to a rather more global cognitive delay. The particular considerations for this group are not only related to the interpretation of the results, but also to the choice of tests to be used. Neuropsychological assessments are often regarded as a measurement of change from a premorbid state, and they are also used as a diagnostic measure of specific brain dysfunction. For this particular group, however, it is important to differentiate between whether a deficit is due to a specific and localised brain impairment or whether it is reflecting the absence of abilities which have never been developed. This delay, of course, may almost certainly be due to a pre-existing impairment, but not necessarily be indicative of a specific or localised lesion.

Impact of seizures

It is imperative that the skills of children with epilepsy are not judged lightly and only on the strength of one isolated assessment, often given by a professional who may have little prior knowledge of the child. Careful consideration is required in examining whether any deficit registering on any one assessment is of a transient or state-dependent nature due to seizure related (peri-ictal) influences affecting awareness and/or alertness. Such a state may vary tremendously between individuals, and temporary disturbances in cognitive functioning may be either very brief, or they may last for hours or even days and to varying degrees of intensity (Deonna 1993). These cognitive difficulties do not represent a permanent deficit and they should not be interpreted as such. Prior knowledge of a child's pattern of any pre or post-seizure difficulties would be beneficial in determining the best time for conducting assessments. Nevertheless, it would be interesting to ascertain whether such a transitory deficit may exist which could explain the occurrence of some day-to-day problems, and which, if anticipated and understood, may be of great help in the planning of interventions.

The role of EEG

Epileptic activity in the brain can affect functioning without any obvious seizures, as in the case of 'absence' epilepsy. Failure to perform then may be due to a temporary disturbance of information processing skills and not a real loss of skill. The use of split-screen video/EEG recording during psychometric testing can detect subtle epileptiform discharges as they occur and point to how they may be affecting cognitive function and task performance, even in the absence of obvious seizures. A small portable EEG cassette recorder is now available for use in 'real life' situations, such as a classroom, and can record spike-wave discharges over longer periods (Besag *et al.* 1989). The EEG recording can be analysed later and compared with activities occurring during that period, enabling a comparison of fluctuations in performance with discharges during the recording. Although such intensive assessments are not always possible, and perhaps are only done in special epilepsy centres, it is important that the professionals involved with these children are aware of such changes in cognitive function and performance. Psychologists should always be alert to any small tell-tale signs of brief changes in attention, blank expression or gaps in the reception of auditory information, which may be indicative of subtle seizure activity interfering with attention and response execution. This may also partly explain the variability in test performance mentioned earlier.

The influence of drugs

The transient and reversible side-effects of anticonvulsants on aspects of cognitive functioning (Forsythe *et al.* 1991) should be kept in mind when assessing children with epilepsy, especially when evaluating changes in performance, given the many transitory factors related to the condition and its treatment. It will be helpful for the psychologist to be aware of any specific effects of anti-epileptic drugs on performance, and take that into consideration when interpreting results.

Motivation and test behaviour

In addition to assessing cognitive function through psychometric testing, direct observation of the test behaviour is extremely important in order to evaluate any interaction between epilepsy and cognitive deficit, as well as reactions to the problem-solving situation of the assessment. As mentioned earlier, it is important that the assessor remains sensitive to any signs of possible subtle epileptic activity. Other factors equally important which can influence test performance are whether the child is motivated to work on the tasks and is willing to try without excessive sensitivity to failure. Motivation is also important in ensuring coopera- tion and gaining reliable results.

Throughout this discussion, the deficits in cognitive functioning and the academic underachievement of the children with epilepsy have been discussed. For the children themselves, however, it is of extreme importance that we pay at least equal, if not more, attention to their cognitive strengths. It cannot be emphasised enough how important it is to identify and to capitalise on the talents of the child – however small these may be – and help him or her celebrate success. Neuropsycho- logical assessments can be a valuable guide to the areas of function most likely to help these children succeed.

The choice of measurements

The majority of the tests used to assess cognitive function in children with epilepsy are the traditional intelligence test batteries and tests of specific cognitive skills. For the younger children and for those whose cooperation is difficult to engage or sustain, developmental checklists may be a more appropriate tool. An important consideration when choosing assessments, is whether the tests to be used are sensitive enough to the needs of the child. A test must start at the level where it is easy for the child to achieve. This will boost his or her self-confidence and make the child try harder and for longer. It will also serve to estab- lish a baseline of success. For the younger children, or those with limited concentration, very short tasks are essential to capture their potential within their brief attention span. An assessor may often use a variety of subtests taken from different batteries of tests to try and tap as accurately as possible the strengths and deficits within a child's cogni- tive development.

General ability

The Wechsler Intelligence Scale for Children (WISC-III UK) is always a useful tool, provided that attention is focused on the results of the individual subtests and their sensitivity to the various cognitive areas of function, rather than to the overall IQ score. The independent measurement of verbal and performance skills can potentially indicate differential development of skills and their effects on cognitive function.

One other quite useful measure of specific cognitive impairment, and one particularly related to the measurement of attention, is that of the distractibility factor (Gilandas *et al.* 1984). The Freedom from Distractibility index (FD) for the WISC-III is calculated from the Arithmetic and Digit Span scores (Kaufman 1994). As attention is sensitive to seizure activity, such an index can be a useful measure of the interaction between seizures and cognitive deficits. The Leiter International Performance Scale is another useful tool for measuring cognitive development. It covers a wide spectrum of developmental levels starting at two years. It is a non-verbal test and can be used with children who have language and speech problems or do not have a good command of the English language. The purely visual format of the test is useful with children whose attention may be disrupted by frequent epileptic activity. A particularly 'child-friendly' non-verbal measure of general ability is the Draw-a-Person test which provides a quick, efficient and fun way for screening a child's cognitive skills and general development.

Language skills / development

The Test for Reception of Grammar (TROG) assesses language comprehension and is of value in screening language disorders in children. Other assessments investigating language and verbal communication skills include:

(a) The British Picture Vocabulary Scale which is an easy-to-administer test measuring receptive vocabulary;
(b) The Token Test for Children which is a useful test for identifying the presence of subtle receptive language dysfunction within a good range of developmental levels;
(c) The Children's Category Test, which is a measure of more complex intellectual functioning such as concept formation, memory and learning from experience, and is easy and quick to administer.

It is important, however, that examiners make sure that language tests using visual materials do not yield results which may be contaminated through any visuo-perceptual difficulties which may be present in the child.

Visuo-perceptual skills

Tests for the measurement of perceptual and visual skills include the Bender Visual Motor Gestalt Test, which is a diagnostic evaluation of developmental deficits in children. The Benton Visual Retention Test has norms for children of eight and above and assesses visual perception and visual memory. The WISC-III and British Ability Scales subtests also provide good measures for the assessment of visuoperceptual skills.

Memory

Memory deficits feature highly in childhood epilepsy and the assessment of memory problems is important. Some of the tests mentioned earlier provide scores for verbal or visual memory. Some specific subtests from the Wechsler series, the British Ability Scales or the Luria-Nebraska Battery children's version can be useful for screening for memory difficulties. The new California Verbal Learning Test for Children measures verbal learning and memory in children aged five years and older. The children's version of the Rivermead Behavioural Memory Test assesses functional memory, and was also standardised on a group of children with epilepsy. Rourke *et al.* (1986) give a comprehensive list of tests used with children (see also Chapter 4).

The assessment of children with developmental delay

As mentioned earlier, it is very important to choose the right tests to suit the needs of the child. Children with developmental delay present some special problems regarding the choice of assessments, as they usually have limited attention span and attend best to short, simple and mostly visual tasks. The Griffiths Mental Development Scales is a good comprehensive test for this group. The Stanford-Binet (Form L-M), although generally considered old-fashioned nowadays, is useful in the assessment of more severely delayed children as it has tasks which are short, change in quick succession, and keep the interest of the developmentally young. The Symbolic Play Test, which assesses early concept formation and abilities developing alongside early language, is suitable for special needs assessment for such children. Developmental checklists, like the Portage, may also be of use for assessing the general development of those who may not be able to cooperate effectively within a test situation. The Pre-Verbal Communication Schedule assesses communication skills of children who are either non-verbal or scarcely verbal and is valuable when working with severely delayed individuals. Finally, observation of the child's interaction with his or her environment and information from parents/carers will help to complete the picture.

Real-life measures of functioning

These are important supplementary measures to help identify any discrepancies between potential and performance, or gaps in children's functioning. Apart from measures of academic performance, i.e. reading, spelling, arithmetic, real-life measures of children's function are few. The Vineland Adaptive Behaviour Scales, scored through information given by a respondent, are useful in identifying areas of strength and need in four areas of development (communication, socialisation, daily living skills and motor skills) measuring personal and social sufficiency from birth to adulthood.

Computerised assessment

Computerised assessments have become much more available and are used for neuropsychological evaluation in epilepsy (Aldenkamp *et al.* 1990a; Thompson 1991). They may include measures of visual and auditory reaction, speed processing, vigilance and speed of learning as in Corsi-type blocks tests. Rugland and her colleagues have developed a computerised neuropsychological test battery to assess the impact of subclinical EEG discharges in patients with epilepsy. The same battery of tests has been useful in examining attention deficit in children with epilepsy (Rugland *et al.* 1991). One of the main advantages of these tests is that most children are well motivated by computer game-like assessments and enjoy doing them. The timing and scoring are also more accurate. Disadvantages include the fact that these tests are not, as yet, adequately validated and more reliability studies are needed (Alpherts and Aldenkamp 1990). Nevertheless, this is an exciting new area in cognitive testing, with potential to develop and expand its application.

CONCLUSION

Neuropsychological and cognitive assessments in children with epilepsy are useful, not only for the identification of strengths and weaknesses and evaluation of potential academic achievement, but also for developing interventions and rehabilitation programmes. The process of this evaluation, however, is complicated by different variables directly and indirectly linked to the epilepsy which have to be taken into consideration. For every child with epilepsy, there is a wide variation in the type of seizures, degree and nature of their learning disability, and psychosocial experiences which affect their cognitive function. This relationship should be investigated and understood for the evaluation to be as accurate as possible. Global measures such as IQ are not usually totally appropriate for evaluating the presence of specific cognitive deficits and more detailed investigation is required. The most difficult task for the examiner is to decide how these multifactorial influences affect performance.

The choice of measures should be flexible and adapted to suit the needs of the individual. New technology is useful in detecting deficits caused by transient or prolonged states of altered abilities due to the epilepsy.

REFERENCES

Aldenkamp, A. P., Alpherts, W. C. J., Dekker, M. J. A. and Overweg, J. (1990a) 'Neuropsychological aspects of learning disabilities in epilepsy', *Epilepsia* 31 (Suppl. 4): S9–20.

Aldenkamp, A. P., Alpherts, W. C. J., De Brune-Seeder, D. and Dekker, M. J. A. (1990b) 'Test–retest variability in children with epilepsy – a comparison of WISC-R profiles', *Epilepsy Research* 7: 165–72.

Alpherts, W. C. J. and Aldenkamp, A. P. (1990) 'Computerized neuropsychological assessment of cognitive functioning in children with epilepsy', *Epilepsia* 31 (Suppl. 4): S35–40.

Besag, F. M. C. (1988) 'Cognitive deterioration in children with epilepsy', in M. R. Trimble and E. H. Reynolds (eds) *Epilepsy, Behaviour and Cognitive Function*, Chichester: Wiley.

Besag, F. M. C., Mills, M., Wardale, F., Andrew, C. M. and Craggs, M. D. (1989) 'The validation of a new ambulatory spike and wave monitor', *Electroencephalography and Clinical Neurophysiology* 73: 157–61.

Binnie, C. D., Channon S. and Marston, D. (1990) 'Learning disabilities in epilepsy: Neurophysiological aspects', *Epilepsia* 31 (Suppl. 4): S2–8.

Bourgeois, B. F. D., Presky, A., Palkes, H. S., Talent, B. K. and Busch, S. G. (1983) 'Intelligence in epilepsy: a prospective study in children', *Annals of Neurology* 14: 438–44.

Corbett, J. A. and Trimble, M. R. (1983) 'Epilepsy and anti-convulsant medication', in M. Rutter (ed.) *Developmental Neuropsychiatry*, New York: Guilford Press.

Corbett, J. A., Trimble, M. R. and Nicol, T. C. (1985) 'Behavioural and cognitive impairments in children with epilepsy: the long term effects of anticonvulsant therapy', *Journal of the American Academy of Child Psychiatry* 24: 17–23.

Cull, C. A. (1988) 'Cognitive function and behaviour in children', in M. R. Trimble and E. H. Reynolds (eds) *Epilepsy, Behaviour and Cognitive Function*, Chichester: Wiley.

Cull, C. A. and Trimble, M. R. (1989) 'Effects of anticonvulsant medications on cognitive functioning in children with epilepsy', in B. P. Hermann and M. Seidenberg (eds) *Childhood Epilepsies: Neuropsychological, Psychological and Intervention Aspects*, Chichester: Wiley.

Dam, M. (1990) 'Children with epilepsy: the effect of seizures, syndromes and etiological factors on cognitive functioning', *Epilepsia* 31 (Suppl. 4): S26–9.

Dikmen, S. (1980) 'Neuropsychological aspects of epilepsy', in B. P. Herman (ed.) *A Multidisciplinary Handbook of Epilepsy*, Springfield IL: Charles C. Thomas.

Deonna, T. (1993) 'Cognitive and behavioural correlates of epileptic activity in children', *Journal of Child Psychology and Psychiatry* 34: 611–20.

Dreifuss, F. E. (1992) 'Cognitive function – victim of disease or hostage to treatment?', *Epilepsia* 33 (Suppl. 1): S7–12.

Farwell, J. R., Dodrill, C. B. and Batzel, L. W. (1985) 'Neuropsychological abilities of children with epilepsy', *Epilepsia* 26: 395–400.

Forsythe, I., Butler, R., Berg, I. and McGuire, R. (1991) 'Cognitive impairment in new cases of epilepsy randomly assigned to carbamazepine, phenytoin and sodium valproate', *Developmental Medicine and Child Neurology* 33: 524–34.

Gadow, K. D. (1982) 'School involvement in the treatment of seizure disorders', *Epilepsia* 23: 215–24.

Gilandas, A., Touyz, S., Beumont, P. J. V. and Greenberg, H. P. (1984) *Handbook of Neuropsychological Assessment*, Sydney: Grune and Stratton.

Guzzetta, F., Crisafulli, A. and Isaya-Crino, M. (1993) 'Cognitive assessment of infants with West Syndrome: how useful is it for diagnosis and prognosis?' *Developmental Medicine and Child Neurology* 35: 379–87.

Hartlage, L. C. and Green, J. B. (1972) 'The relation of parental attitudes to academic and social achievement in epileptic children', *Epilepsia* 13: 21–6.

Hermann, B. P. (1991) 'Contributions of traditional assessment procedures to an understanding of the neuropsychology of epilepsy', in W. E. Dodson, M. Kinsbourne and B. Hiltbrunner (eds) *The Assessment of Cognitive Function in Epilepsy*, New York: Demos Publications.

Holdsworth, L. and Whitmore, K. (1974) 'A study of children with epilepsy attending ordinary school. Their seizure patterns, progress and behaviour in school', *Developmental Medicine and Child Neurology* 16: 746–58.

Kaufman, A. S. (1994) *Intelligent Testing with the WISC-III*, New York: Wiley.

Long, C. G. and Moore, J. R. (1979) 'Parental expectations for their epileptic children', *Journal of Child Psychology and Psychiatry* 20: 299–312.

Madge, N., Diamond, J., Miller, D., Ross, E., McManus, C., Wadsworth, J. and Yule, W. (1993) 'Children with persisting convulsive disorders', *Developmental Medicine and Child Neurology* 35 (Suppl. 68): 78–88.

Marston, D., Besag, F., Binnie, C. D. and Fowler, M. (1993) 'Effects of transitory cognitive impairment on psychosocial functioning of children with epilepsy: a therapeutic trial', *Developmental Medicine and Child Neurology* 35: 574–81.

Morgan, A. M. B. and Groh, C. (1980) 'Visual perceptual deficits and young children with epilepsy', in B. M. Kulig, H. Meinardi and G. Stores (eds) *Epilepsy and Behaviour 79*, Lisse: Swets and Zeitlinger.

Nichols, M. E., Meador, K. J. and Loring, D. N. (1993) 'Neuropsychological effects of anti-epileptic drugs: a current perspective', *Clinical Neuropharmacology* 16: 471–84.

O'Leary, D. S., Seidenberg, M., Berent, S. and Boll, T. J. (1981) 'Effects of age of onset of tonic-clonic seizures on neuropsychological performance in children', *Epilepsia* 22: 197–204.

Piccirilli, M., D'Alessandro, P., Sciarma, T., Cantoni, C., Dioguardi, M. S., Giuglietti, M., Ibba, A. and Tiacci, C., (1994) 'Attention problems in epilepsy: possible significance of the epileptogenic focus', *Epilepsia* 35: 1091–6.

Rodin, E. A. (1968) *The Prognosis of Patients with Epilepsy*, Springfield IL: Charles C. Thomas.

—— (1989) 'Prognosis of cognitive functions in children with epilepsy', in B. P. Hermann and M. Seidenberg (eds) *Childhood Epilepsies: Neuropsychological, Psychosocial and Intervention Aspects*, Chichester: Wiley.

Rodin, E. A., Schmaltz, S. and Twitty, G. (1986) 'Intellectual functions of patients with childhood onset epilepsy', *Developmental Medicine and Child Neurology* 28: 25–33.

Ross, E. M., Peckham, C. S., West, P. B. and Butler, N. R. (1980) 'Epilepsy in childhood: findings from the national child development study', *British Medical Journal* 1: 207–10.

Rourke, B. P., Fisk, J. L. and Strang, J. D. (1986) *Neuropsychological Assessment of Children*, New York: Guildford Press.

Rourke, B. P., Bakker, D. J., Fisk, J. L. and Strang, J. D. (1983) *Child Neuropsychology – An Introduction to Theory, Research and Clinical Practice*, New York: Guilford Press.

Rugland, A-L., Henriksen, O. and Bjørnæs, H. (1991) 'Computer-assisted neuropsychological assessment in patients with epilepsy', in W. E. Dodson, M. Kinsbourne and B. Hiltbrunner (eds) *The Assessment of Cognitive Function in Epilepsy*, New York: Demos Publications.

Rutter, M., Graham, P. and Yule, W. (1970) 'A neuropsychiatric study in childhood', *Clinics in Developmental Medicine* 35/36, London: Heineman.

Sabers, A. (1990) 'Cognitive function and drug treatment', in M. Sillanpaa, S. Johannessen, G. Blennow and M. Dam (eds) *Paediatric Epilepsy*, Petersfield: Wrightson Biomedical Publishing.

Seidenberg, M. (1989) 'Academic achievement and school performance of children with epilepsy', in B. Hermann and M. Seidenberg (eds) *Childhood Epilepsies: Neuropsychological, Psychosocial and Intervention Aspects*, Chichester: Wiley.

Seidenberg, M., O'Leary, D. S., Berent, S. and Boll, T. (1981) 'Changes in seizure frequency and test–retest scores on the WAIS', *Epilepsia* 22: 75–83.

Seidenberg, M., Beck, N., Geisser, M., Giordani, B., Sackellares, J. C., Berent, S., Dreifuss, F. E. and Boll, T. J. (1986) 'Academic achievement of children with epilepsy', *Epilepsia* 27: 753–9.

Sofijanov, N. G. (1982) 'Clinical evolution and prognosis of childhood epilepsies', *Epilepsia* 23: 61–9.

Stores, G. (1980) 'Children with epilepsy: psychosocial aspects', in B. P.

Hermann (ed.) *A Multidisciplinary Handbook of Epilepsy*, Springfield IL: Charles Thomas.

Thompson, P. J. (1987) 'Educational attainment in children and young people with epilepsy' in J. Oxley and G. Stores (eds) *Epilepsy and Education*, London: Medical Tribute Group.

—— (1991) 'Integrating computerised and traditional neuropsychological assessment techniques' in W. E. Dodson, M. Kinsbourne and B. Hiltbrunner (eds) *The Assessment of Cognitive Function in Epilepsy*, New York: Demos Publications.

Trimble, M. R. and Thompson, P. J. (1985) 'Anticonvulsant drugs, cognitive function and behaviour', in E. Ross and E. Reynolds (eds) *Paediatric Perspectives on Epilepsy*, Chichester: Wiley.

Wyler, A. R. (1989) 'The surgical treatment of epilepsy', in B. P. Hermann and M. Seidenberg (eds) *Childhood Epilepsies: Neuropsychological, Psychosocial and Intervention Aspects*, Chichester: Wiley.

Chapter 10

Assessment and management of behaviour problems in children

Christine Cull

Behaviour problems are frequently associated with a diagnosis of epilepsy in children who are not intellectually impaired (for review, see Cull 1988). Significantly more children with epilepsy display behaviour disorders than do their own siblings (Epir *et al.* 1984), same age and ability peers (Clement and Wallace 1990), and children with other chronic diseases such as diabetes (Hoare and Mann 1994). Recent studies of children of normal intellectual ability attending epilepsy out-patient clinics suggest that approximately 50 per cent display some degree of behavioural disturbance as assessed by rating scales (Hoare and Kerley 1991; Austin *et al.* 1992). However, these rates can be even higher for children in specialist residential schools (Stores 1982).

In the literature, the terms 'behaviour disorder/problem/distur-bance' and 'psychiatric disorder' have all been used interchangeably. This is in part a function of the measures used, which invariably have been broad-based rating scales or checklists. Thus, in talking about behaviour problems, many authors are making reference to the frequency and intensity of behaviours rather than to particular behaviours. Specific problems have been identified and include: poor self-esteem, excessive dependency, immaturity (Lothman and Pianta 1993); neurotic disorders, hyperactive disorders (Hoare and Kerley 1991), mixed conduct/emotional disorders (Harvey *et al.* 1988); anxiety and depression (Urion 1991); and autistic features (Harvey *et al.* 1988). Conversely, it has been suggested that children with epilepsy are less likely to show antisocial (Hoare and Kerley 1991) or delinquent (Rantakallio *et al.* 1992) behaviour although physical and verbal aggres-sion, self-injurious behaviour, non-compliance, and disinhibition have all been reported (Besag 1995). It is clear, however, that specific 'epileptic behaviours' do not exist (ibid.).

The reasons for this increased risk of behaviour disorder are difficult to determine as epilepsy is not a unitary disorder, but may differ along a number of dimensions. Thus, Besag (1995) suggests that possible epilepsy-related causes may include: the seizure disorder itself, its treatment, the impact of associated brain damage, and the reactions to a diagnosis of epilepsy. Hermann and Whitman (1991) have proposed a multi-aetiological model for considering the role of epilepsy-related risk factors associated with the development of behaviour disorders, which fall into three main categories: neurobiological, pharmacological and psychosocial. Cull and Brown (1992), in contrast, have emphasised the importance of environmental factors in the development and maintenance of behaviour problems.

In order to explore this further, a brief review of the literature pertaining to the impact of different epilepsy-related factors on behaviour will be considered, using Herman and Whitman's (1991) framework, which also encompasses the potential causes suggested by Besag (1995). This will concentrate in the main on studies published since 1988, as studies up to this time have been reviewed by Cull (1988) and this review will be referred to as necessary.

NEUROBIOLOGICAL FACTORS

Included in this category are any variables pertaining to the biological status of the individual, as follows.

Aetiology

It has previously been concluded that 'the little available evidence shows only trends in the direction of an association between organic aetiology and behaviour disturbance' (Cull 1988), and that would still seem to be the case. In more recent studies, where aetiology has been investigated, it does not appear as a significant contributory factor to the development of behaviour disorder (Clement and Wallace 1990; Austin et al. 1992).

Age at onset of epilepsy

Studies reviewed up to 1988 yielded conflicting findings (Cull 1988), as do more recent investigations. Thus, it has been reported that children with onset of epilepsy before four years of age are more likely to show behaviour disturbance than those with a later age at onset (Hoare and Kerley 1991; Hoare and Mann 1994). In other studies, however, age at onset has not been found to be a significant factor, either individually (Clement and Wallace 1990; Austin *et al.* 1992), or as part of an overall medical risk score (Lothman and Pianta 1993). There are also conflicting findings with respect to the duration of epilepsy (Cull 1988).

Seizure/epilepsy type

In the past, claims have been made for an association between a particular seizure type and an increased rate of behavioural problems, although these have not been fully substantiated (Cull 1988). There is still uncertainty as to whether some seizure types predispose to behaviour problems while others do not, and this is reflected in the literature. Thus, there may be no relationship between seizure type and scores on a behaviour rating scale (Clement and Wallace 1990; Austin *et al.* 1992; Lothman and Pianta 1993; Hoare and Mann 1994).

More in the way of positive results appear when the epilepsy syndrome, rather than just the seizure type are considered, such that children with Temporal Lobe Epilepsy may show more psychopathology than healthy children, but this may be no different to children with asthma (Apter *et al.* 1991). Further, identification of the relevant epilepsy syndrome may well be of prognostic significance with respect to behaviour disorder. For example, Nolte and Wolf (1992) studied fifteen children with Myoclonic Astatic Epilepsy, which typically starts between the ages of 2 and 5 years and is characterized by the presence of primary generalized seizures (myoclonic or astatic) in children who are thought to be genetically predisposed. They reported that in the majority behavioural problems were apparent before seizure onset; these increased with seizure onset and frequent seizures, but decreased after seizure remission, and further decreased or disappeared after the cessation of medication.

Seizure frequency

In keeping with the contradictory findings of past studies (Cull 1988), more recent investigations are also conflicting in that some studies have reported a clear association between frequent/uncontrolled seizures and more behavioural problems (Hoare and Kerley 1991; Austin *et al.* 1992; Nicholas and Pianta 1994), whereas others have found no such relationship (Clement and Wallace 1990; Hoare and Mann 1994).

EEG activity

An abnormal EEG per se does not seem to be implicated in an increased rate of behaviour disturbance, but the type of abnormality may be a factor (Cull 1988). It has been suggested that focal abnormalities are more likely to be associated with behaviour disturbance than generalised ones (Hoare and Kerley 1991), although no significant relationship has also been reported (Clement and Wallace 1990).

Subclinical EEG discharges which result in Transitory Cognitive Impairment may contribute to impaired psychosocial performance and behaviour problems (Marston et al. 1993). Behaviour problems have also been found to be associated with continuous spike-and-wave activity during sleep in a small sample of children with severe learning disabilities and a frontal epileptic focus (Roulet Perez et al. 1993).

Other behaviour disorders

In trying to tease out the impact of epilepsy on functioning, an alternative approach is to look at the impact of epilepsy on behaviour within the confines of a particular syndrome. Thus, Kinney et al. (1990) compared children with attention deficit disorder with and without epilepsy and found no difference between the two groups with respect to the occurrence of behaviour disorder.

Seizure/behaviour relationship

What is at times confusing about many of the studies investigating the relationship between behaviour and epilepsy is that they do not make clear whether or not the behaviour is inter-ictal and/or ictal, i.e. directly related in some way to the ictus or seizure itself. Such a distinction is important in terms of differentiating whether the aberrant behaviour is part of the seizure and possibly less likely to be under an individual's control, or whether it may be more related to the sequelae of having a diagnosis of epilepsy, since this may well have implications for treatment.

Behavioural changes that are intimately linked with seizure occurrence can occur at any point in the seizure's progress, although, to the untrained eye, it will not necessarily be clear whether seizure activity is imminent, ongoing, or has just ceased. In this respect, Besag (1995) has produced a useful aetiological classification of ictally-related behaviour changes as follows:

- Behavioural changes including, for example, irritability or changes in mood may be observed in the *prodrome* (that period of time leading up to the seizure) which invariably remit once the seizure has occurred.
- The *aura* (a form of simple partial seizure) may affect behaviour if the subjective experience is of an unpleasant emotional sensation such as extreme fear or anxiety.
- *Automatisms* are movements or actions occurring in the ictal or post-ictal phase of which the individual is unaware, and over which he or she has no voluntary control.
- *Focal discharges* may be manifest as odd and apparently bizarre behaviours which are not within the individual's control.
- *Frequent subtle seizures* may not be accompanied by any obvious clinical manifestations, but will inevitably interrupt an individual's stream of consciousness and impair their ability to make sense of what is going on around them and to respond appropriately.
- In the *post-ictal* phase a child may remain in a confused or sleepy state for some considerable period of time, as a result of which their powers of reasoning and understanding may be much reduced.

It is likely that the above variables may have some combined effect, rather than operating in isolation. Therefore, rather than asking whether one factor – for example, seizure frequency – exerts an effect, a more appropriate question may be to ask what is the effect of seizure frequency in children with X seizure type who have Y epilepsy syndrome. Such studies remain to be undertaken.

PHARMACOLOGICAL FACTORS

The majority of children with epilepsy will share in common the taking of anti-epileptic medications (AEDs) to control their epilepsy, and may well be affected by the type of medication they are taking, its relative effective strength as determined by dose and blood level, and the number of different medications taken. This is a major area of research in its own right, and unfortunately space does not allow for a comprehensive review of the literature. The reader is directed to a review by Cull and Trimble (1989); in the space available here the focus will be on more recent findings.

Type of AED

The current literature is remarkably consistent with that reviewed by Cull and Trimble (1989) in that behaviour disorders are more likely to be found with phenobarbitone (Domizio *et al.* 1993) and phenytoin (Clement and Wallace 1990), although adverse responses to primidone and sodium valproate have also been reported (Nolte and Wolf 1992). Interestingly, in newly diagnosed children, phenytoin was not found to affect behaviour significantly after six months of treatment (Berg *et al.* 1993) suggesting that time may be a factor in the development of adverse effects. By contrast, in the same study, those children on carbamazepine or sodium valproate displayed some minor behavioural difficulties after one month of treatment, which was resolved by six months (ibid.). Clonazepam has been associated with behavioural deterioration in some children (Commander *et al.* 1991), and aggressive behaviours have been observed in some children taking clobazam (but predominantly in those with learning disabilities) (Sheth *et al.* 1994). However, it would appear that in all cases such adverse effects are reversible on cessation of the medication (Commander *et al.* 1991; Domizio *et al.* 1993; Sheth *et al.* 1994). It is also possible that a small number of children may display a quite idiosyncratic adverse response to an AED – as, for example, carbamazepine (Silverstein *et al.* 1982).

The impact of the newer AEDs, in particular vigabatrin, lamotrigine and gabapentin, needs to be fully evaluated. Thus far, vigabatrin has been associated with behavioural disturbance in some children, while the behaviour of children taking lamotrigine improved (Besag 1995), although the mechanism by which this was brought about was not clear.

Number of AEDs

Although it has been asserted that combined drug treatments are likely to be more behaviourally toxic than treatment with a single drug (Cull and Trimble 1989; Hermann *et al.* 1989; Hoare and Kerley 1991), a recent report has found that a monotherapy/polytherapy distinction was not of any predictive value with regard to the occurrence of child behaviour problems (Austin *et al.* 1992). However, further research is clearly needed here, as this may well depend on the total number of drugs used and their interactions.

As was mentioned in Chapter 1, there is now a move towards rational polypharmacy in the treatment of epilepsy, the impact of which on behaviour has yet to be evaluated.

Dose/serum level

Drugs given at doses that are too high, or at body concentrations that are toxic may well adversely affect behaviour too, although these effects should be reversible (Cull and Trimble 1989).

PSYCHOSOCIAL FACTORS

The focus of attention in this section are the psychosocial sequelae of a diagnosis of epilepsy. Included are the psychological characteristics of the child with epilepsy, and the impact of the diagnosis on the family.

Child

Children with epilepsy are reported to have a self-image and self-esteem which is significantly poorer than healthy controls or children with diabetes (Matthews *et al.* 1982; Hoare and Kerley 1991), and an external locus of control (Matthews *et al.* 1982), all of which may be associated with behavioural disturbance (Matthews and Barabas 1986). Thus, the lower a child's own rating of self-esteem, the more behaviourally disturbed the child is, as rated by the parent (Hoare and Mann 1994). In respect of skills, children who have good academic performance do not differ from their healthy peers, whereas poor school performance can be associated with behaviour disorder (Sturniolo and Galletti 1994).

Family

A range of family-related variables have been associated with behavioural problems and emotional disturbance in the child with epilepsy. These include: stresses and strains within the family (Hoare and Kerley 1991; Austin *et al.* 1992), a past history of maternal psychiatric treatment (Hoare and Kerley 1991), ill-health among siblings (Hoare and Kerley 1991); a lack of support from relatives (Austin *et al.* 1992), and a perceived lack of control over family events and outcomes (Austin *et al.* 1992). See also Cull 1988.

Interactions

Child–parent relationships are claimed to be important predictors of adjustment (Lothman and Pianta 1993). Indeed, it has been further asserted that these relationship variables are predictive of behaviour problems independently of, and to a greater extent than, epilepsy variables (Pianta and Lothman 1994).

The question then arises as to what are the factors that may impinge on this relationship. Perhaps, first and foremost, there is the epilepsy itself. Parents may feel anxious and uncertain about how to deal with the occurrence of seizures, or even fearful of provoking seizures. The pervasive nature of the perceived stigma associated with epilepsy has been emphasised, as it impinges on the functioning of the whole family (Ziegler 1981; Bagley 1986; West 1986). In addition, it would seem that parents expect different things of a child with epilepsy than of their siblings. For example, they anticipate that the child with epilepsy will be less reliable, less able to make friends, perform more poorly at school, and is more likely to be unpredictable, moody and to develop emotional problems (Long and Moore 1979; Ferrari 1989).

Given the above, it is not surprising perhaps that parents respond differently to their child with epilepsy. Thus, they may become overprotective (Munthe-Kaas 1981; Ritchie 1981), restrict the child's social activities (Long and Moore 1979; Munthe-Kaas 1981; West 1986), exert control over the child in a strict and autocratic manner (Long and Moore 1979; Ritchie 1981), and behave in a more dominant fashion towards the child with epilepsy than to other offspring (Long and Moore 1979).

By contrast, good adjustment in the child is more likely to be associated with parental responses that are, for example, contingent on the child's behaviour and that display warmth, sensitivity and positive regard for the child (Pianta and Lothman 1994).

Additional factors

Thus far, the literature review has been concentrating on those variables that are directly related to the seizure disorder itself and its psychosocial sequelae. What has not been considered here are all the possible explanations for the occurrence of behaviour/psychiatric disorders in children who do not have epilepsy. This is not within the scope of this chapter; however, as has been stressed by Besag (1995), the reader should remember that these factors may be just as relevant for the child with epilepsy, separate from or in combination with the epilepsy-related variables.

THE MULTI-AETIOLOGICAL APPROACH

From the foregoing review, it would appear that at least one variable within each of the dimensions considered may be an important contributor to the development of behaviour disorder in the child with epilepsy. The aim of the multi-aetiological approach is to identify the relative contributions of a variety of individual variables. For example, in an earlier study of their model, Hermann and Whitman (1986) reported that the biological variable (in this instance, seizure control) was the most predictive, followed by psychosocial factors and then medication-related variables. Demographic variables did not have any predictive value at all. Seizure frequency (as one of four epilepsy-related variables) was also found to be predictive of behaviour disorder by Austin *et al.* (1992), whereas two out of three family-related variables (family stress and family mastery) were also predictive, suggesting that much greater weight should be attached to these. It is of interest that, in their study, one demographic variable – female gender – also had a predictive role; this is in contrast to much of the literature regarding gender effects, which, if anything, have implicated boys (Cull 1988). Lothman and Pianta (1993) also highlight the importance of parent–child interactions over and above the impact of biological variables.

Reasons for disparate findings in studies

It is hard to draw any conclusions regarding the reasons for the high rate of behavioural problems found in children with epilepsy, given that there are some inconsistent and conflicting findings with respect to potential aetiological factors. There are a number of possible reasons for such discrepancies, as follows:

- Source of subjects is an important factor, with some subject groups coming from neurology out-patient clinics and others coming from specialist epilepsy out-patient clinics. It is likely that such groups may well differ with respect to the severity and complexity of their seizure disorder, and the results thus obtained are unlikely to be generalisable to other groups of children with epilepsy.
- The presence, absence, or indeed, severity of intellectual impairment may be another confounding factor, and while some studies restrict themselves to children who do not have global intellectual impairments (Apter *et al.* 1991; Clement and Wallace 1990; Lothman and Pianta 1993; Nicholas and Pianta 1994), others are more wide-ranging and do include children with intellectual disabilities

(Clement and Wallace 1990; Hoare and Kerley 1991; Hoare and Mann 1994). The inclusion of those with learning disabilities is rarely, if ever, controlled for.

- Further, many studies fail to be explicit about whether they are looking at all aberrant behaviours, ictally-related behaviours only, or inter-ictal behaviours only. These are important distinctions to make when it comes to thinking about assessment and treatment, as we shall see later.

It is apparent that these factors may well operate together and their relative contribution is hard to disentangle. For example, children with difficult-to-control epilepsy are likely to have multiple seizure types, occurring frequently. When asked to complete questionnaires pertaining to their behaviour, it is likely that some of what is reported will be concerned with ictally-related behaviours unless the respondent is asked specifically about inter-ictal behaviours. Conversely, in children whose seizures are well controlled, ictally-related behaviours will not be an issue, and the resulting information will be largely concerned with inter-ictal behaviours. Consequently it is hard to draw overall conclusions.

ASSESSMENT AND TREATMENT: CLINICAL CONSIDERATIONS

In this respect, the available literature has little to offer. The course of action depends, in part, on how one attributes any presenting problem.

Assessment of potential aetiological factors

Thus, the first step is to attempt to distinguish between medical and psychological factors. If it can be clearly established that the aberrant behaviour is in some way directly related to the seizure disorder itself, and/or is part of the seizure (as in Besag's (1995) classification system), and/or is related to medication variables, intervention should fall within the remit of the physician responsible for the management of the child's epilepsy. It is also important to exclude the possibility of any formal psychiatric disorder which may require additional pharmacological treatment. In this respect, the clinical psychologist can contribute much to such an assessment by undertaking a thorough behavioural analysis of the situation in collaboration with other professionals. The purpose of such an assessment would be to develop some hypotheses concerning the relative contributions of different variables, which can then be tested. Such a procedure is essential as there are dangers in making assumptions about causes of the behaviour. Thus, some parents report that their child's disruptive behaviour is wholly attributable to the epilepsy, implicit in which is the belief that nothing further can be done to change this until the epilepsy stops. Alternatively, carers may discount the impact of the seizure disorder, in their belief that X is just being difficult. One consequence of this may be the inappropriate punishment of a behaviour that is ictally-related, or unsuccessful attempts to reason with a child who is in an ictally-related state, for example, post-ictal confusion. It is possible that it may not be an all-or-nothing phenomenon, and consequently it would be important to distinguish between ictally-related and inter-ictal behaviours.

Typically, however, one may be confronted by a child whose behaviour disorder persists in the presence of a well-controlled seizure disorder and optimal medical treatment (Cull and Brown 1992) or, alternatively, where a potentially behaviourally-toxic drug is being used, but because the seizure disorder is well controlled, it is unlikely that any drug change will take place. The question arises as to what then?

Clearly, it is important to identify those areas which are amenable to change and for which, as a clinical psychologist, one has the necessary assessment and intervention skills. In this respect, the literature has quite a lot to offer with regard to potential targets for intervention.

For example, the importance of environmental factors in the development and maintenance of inter-ictal behaviour disorders has been emphasised by Cull and Brown (1992) with respect to the contingencies that operate around the behaviour. From this perspective, the logical target for intervention is the behaviour itself, using procedures derived from a behaviour-analytic framework. Alternatively, other investigations have concluded that family-related variables are of particular importance, and their recommendations for intervention include family work and, more specifically, dealing with family stress (Austin *et al.* 1992), family counselling (Sturniolo and Galletti 1994) and targeting aspects of the child–parent relationship (Lothman and Pianta 1993; Nicholas and Pianta 1994).

These different approaches will now be discussed in more detail.

Behaviour analysis

The effectiveness of behaviour-analytic approaches has been amply demonstrated in individuals with learning disabilities, but, as yet, its value for children with epilepsy has not really been explored. The essence of behaviour-analytic approaches is to arrive at as detailed an understanding of a behaviour as possible, incorporating its parameters and contingencies, and identifying its purpose for the individual concerned. This is combined into what is called 'Functional Analysis', which, as the name suggests, is aimed at understanding the function(s) or purpose of a particular behaviour (e.g. to escape from an unpleasant activity or to gain access to desired objects or activities). The methods of assessment are many and varied and will probably be familiar to most readers. A useful overview of the method and summary of approaches is available in a chapter by Durand and Crimmins (1991), which, although concerned mainly with individuals with severe learning disabilities, is clearly applicable in a wider range of settings. In brief, the assessment may involve interviews with the child and teachers/carers, direct observation, completion of questionnaires and checklists, and possibly the use of analogue investigations as originally described by Iwata *et al.* (1982). As part of such an assessment, it would be important to explore carers' attributions of the behaviour, as this itself may need to be a target for intervention and may have implications for the success of any intervention.

Within the field of behaviour analysis, it is now accepted that interventions should be constructional (Goldiamond 1974), focusing on developing skills, incorporating reward-based strategies and other non-aversive procedures, rather than punishment (LaVigna and Donellan 1986), in order to equip the individual with behaviours which will fulfil the same functions as the undesirable behaviour – i.e. developing functionally equivalent responses (Durand and Crimmins 1991).

Such an approach may need to be carried out in combination with some contingency management (i.e. rewarding the occurrence of appropriate behaviours), ecological management (i.e. changes in the environment), and some means of dealing with the problem behaviours when they occur (McGill and Toogood 1994). Cull and Brown (1992) have reported on the successful application of a simple contingency management scheme in two adolescent males, whereby tangible rewards of each boy's choosing were given for an absence of inappropriate behaviours. In both cases the behaviours were of long-standing duration, seizures were few, and the resulting improvements were of such a degree that medication used for controlling behaviour (haloperidol and thioridazine) was completely withdrawn within one year of the scheme starting.

While intervention strategies may vary, one common feature is the involvement of the child's parents/carers in the assessment of the behaviour and planning and carrying out the intervention. The need to involve parents/carers is clear from the perspective of treatment generalisation and maintenance and the prevention of future problems, not to mention enabling the stretching of scarce professional resources (Cunningham 1985; Callias 1987). In cases where there are clearly difficulties within the parent–child relationship, however, it may be important for these to be addressed initially, either alone, or as part of a more comprehensive approach.

Parent–child relationships as a target for change

Parent–child relationships are probably best assessed by means of direct observation, for example, during the course of a problem-solving task (e.g. Lothman and Pianta 1993), or within a less structured free-play setting (e.g. Forehand and McMahon 1981), which would also yield information about parent behaviours and child behaviours.

Subsequent interventions would focus on parental behaviour towards their child, attitudes and feelings about their child and ways in which these are communicated, and their response to the child and child-initiated behaviours. One such technique – the Parent/Child Game – was pioneered in the UK at the Maudsley Hospital and is based on the work of Forehand and McMahon (1981) with non-compliant children. The aim of this approach is to modify maladaptive parental interactions with their child by teaching more effective reinforcement strategies, how to use commands appropriately, and the use of behaviour contingent time-out procedures (Jenner 1988). Such an approach has been found to be of value in improving the skills of parents of non-compliant children (Forehand and McMahon 1981), parents who have abused their children (Jenner 1988), and the parent of a child with learning disabilities (Rix 1988); the behaviours of the children also improved.

Parents' groups

An alternative approach to working with parents has been in the use of parent groups as a forum for providing education and counselling regarding their potential role as behaviour-change agents for their child (Callias 1987), particularly for the parents of children with a chronic illness or disability. It would seem that such an approach might well be applicable to the families of children with epilepsy. However, in one recent study attempting to evaluate such an approach, the outcome was highly disappointing because of the very small number of parents who actually participated. Hoare and Kerley (1992) hoped to investigate the impact of a 'parents group counselling programme' on the 'psychosocial morbidity of children with epilepsy and their families' (ibid.: 760). However, of the 108 families who originally expressed an interest in such an intervention only fourteen attended the first session, with an increasing attrition rate as the sessions progressed. Consequently, the authors were unable to evaluate the intervention. It is of interest that the parents themselves subsequently said that they would have preferred individual counselling. It remains to be seen whether other parents of children with epilepsy share this reticence to participate in a group.

Family interventions

The prominent role that family variables appear to play in multi-aetiological models of behaviour disturbance in children with epilepsy (Austin *et al.* 1992) suggests that this may be another target for intervention. Indeed, the potentially useful role of family-centred interventions has been stressed by a number of authors (Austin *et al.* 1992; Sturniolo and Galletti 1994). However, at this time, published studies regarding the efficacy of family-based interventions are distinctly lacking. In order to explore the range of possible models on which to base such an intervention, the interested clinician need look no further than the wealth of material available within the family therapy field.

FUTURE DEVELOPMENTS

Clearly there is much scope for further work that aims to identify those children who are most at risk for developing behavioural disorders. If this were possible, then a range of early intervention-type programmes could be developed, aimed at the child, parents and/or family, with a view to preventing the development of further problems. Improved counselling of the child and parents following the initial diagnosis of epilepsy may well have a role to play in this. Investigations of the prevalence of specific disorders would be of value.

As has been made clear above, there is also an outstanding need for much more in the way of evaluative research of differing interventions for behaviour problems in childhood epilepsy.

To date, much of the literature has concentrated on children of at least average intellectual ability. Further work is clearly needed in exploring the presence (or otherwise) of behaviour problems in children who have learning disabilities.

REFERENCES

Apter, A., Aviv, A., Kaminer, Y., Weizman, A., Lerman, P. and Tyano, S. (1991) 'Behavioral profile and social competence in temporal lobe epilepsy of adolescence', *Journal of the American Academy of Child and Adolescent Psychiatry* 30: 887–92.

Austin, J. K., Risinger, M. W. and Beckett, L. A. (1992) 'Correlates of behavior problems in children with epilepsy', *Epilepsia* 33: 1115–22.

Bagley, C. (1986) 'Children with epilepsy as a minority group: evidence from the National Child Development Study', in S. Whitman and B. P. Hermann (eds) *Psychopathology in Epilepsy: Social Dimensions*, New York: Oxford University Press.

Berg, I., Butler, A., Ellis, M. and Foster, J. (1993) 'Psychiatric aspects of epilepsy in childhood treated with carbamazepine, phenytoin or sodium valproate: a random trial', *Developmental Medicine and Child Neurology* 35: 149–57.

Besag, F. M. C. (1995) 'Epilepsy, learning and behavior in childhood', *Epilepsia* 36 (Suppl. 1): S58–63.

Callias, M. (1987) 'Teaching parents, teachers and nurses', in W. Yule and J. Carr (eds) *Behaviour Modification for People with Mental Handicaps* 2nd edn, London: Croom Helm.

Clement, M. J. and Wallace, S. J. (1990) 'A survey of adolescents with epilepsy', *Developmental Medicine and Child Neurology* 32: 849–57.

Commander, M., Green, S. H. and Prendergast, M. (1991) 'Behavioural disturbances in children treated with clonazepam', *Developmental Medicine and Child Neurology* 33: 362–4.

Cull, C. A. (1988) 'Cognitive function and behaviour in children', in M. R. Trimble and E. H. Reynolds (eds) *Epilepsy, Behaviour and Cognitive Function*, Chichester: Wiley.

Cull, C. A. and Brown, S. W. (1992) 'A socio behavioural perspective for understanding and managing behaviour problems in children with epilepsy', *Behavioural Neurology* 5: 47–51.

Cull, C. A. and Trimble, M. R. (1989) 'Effects of anticonvulsant medications on cognitive functioning in children with epilepsy', in B. P. Hermann and M. Seidenberg (eds) *Childhood Epilepsies: Neuropsychological, Psychosocial and Intervention Aspects*, Chichester: Wiley.

Cunningham, C. C. (1985), 'Training and education approaches for parents of children with special needs', *British Journal of Medical Psychology* 58: 285–305.

Domizio, S., Verrotti, A., Ramenghi, L. A., Sabatino, G. and Morgese, G. (1993) 'Anti-epileptic therapy and behaviour disturbances in children', *Child's Nervous System* 9: 272–4.

Durand, V. M. and Crimmins, D. (1991) 'Teaching functionally equivalent responses as an intervention for challenging behaviour', in B. Remington (ed.) *The Challenge of Severe Mental Handicap*, Chichester: Wiley.

Epir, S., Renda, Y. and Baser, N. (1984) 'Cognitive and behavioural characteristics of children with idiopathic epilepsy in a low-income area of Ankara, Turkey', *Developmental Medicine and Child Neurology* 26: 200–7.

Ferrari, M. (1989) 'Epilepsy and its effects on the family', in B. P. Hermann and M. Seidenberg (eds) *Childhood Epilepsies: Neuropsychological, Psychosocial and Intervention Aspects*, Chichester: Wiley.

Forehand, R. and McMahon, R. (1981) *Helping the Non-compliant Child: A Clinician's Guide to Parent Training*, New York: Guilford Press.

Goldiamond, I. (1974) 'Toward a constructional approach to social problems', *Behaviorism*, 2: 1–84.

Harvey, I., Goodyer, I. M. and Brown, S. W. (1988) 'The value of a neuropsychiatric examination of children with complex severe epilepsy', *Child: Care, Health and Development* 14: 329–40.

Hermann, B. P. and Whitman, S. (1986) 'Psychopathology in epilepsy: a multietiologic model', in S. Whitman and B. P. Hermann (eds) *Psychopathology in Epilepsy: Social Dimensions*, New York: Oxford University Press.

—— (1991) 'Neurobiological, psychosocial, and pharmacological factors underlying interictal psychopathology in epilepsy', in D. Smith, D. Treiman and M. Trimble (eds) *Advances in Neurology* vol. 55, New York: Raven Press.

Hermann, B. P., Whitman, S. and Dell, J. (1989) 'Correlates of behavior problems and social competence in children with epilepsy, aged 6–11', in B. P. Hermann and M. Seidenberg (eds) *Childhood Epilepsies: Neuropsychological, Psychosocial and Intervention Aspects*, Chichester: Wiley.

Hoare, P. and Kerley, S. (1991) 'Psychosocial adjustment of children with chronic epilepsy and their families', *Developmental Medicine and Child Neurology* 33: 201–15.

—— (1992) 'Helping parents and children with epilepsy cope successfully: the outcome of a group programme for parents', *Journal of Psychosomatic Research* 36: 759–67.

Hoare, P. and Mann, H. (1994) 'Self-esteem and behavioural adjustment in children with epilepsy and children with diabetes', *Journal of Psychosomatic Research* 38: 859–69.

Iwata, B. A., Dorsey, M. F., Slifer, K. J., Bauman, K. E. and Richman, G. S. (1982), 'Toward a functional analysis of self-injury', *Analysis and Intervention in Developmental Disabilities* 2: 3–20.

Jenner, S. (1988) 'Assessing parenting skills', paper presented at a conference held December 1988 entitled *When Families Fail: Research and Practice in Child Abuse*, London: Institute of Psychiatry.

Kinney, R. O., Shaywitz, B. A., Shaywitz, S. E., Sarwar, M. and Holahan, J. M. (1990), 'Epilepsy in children with attention deficit disorder: cognitive, behavioral, and neuroanatomic indices', *Paediatric Neurology* 6: 31–7.

LaVigna, G. W. and Donnellan, A. M. (1986) *Alternatives to Punishment: Solving Behaviour Problems with Non-Aversive Strategies*, New York: Irvington Publishers.

Long, C. G. and Moore, J. R. (1979) 'Parental expectations for their epileptic children', *Journal of Child Psychology and Psychiatry* 20: 299–312.

Lothman, D. J. and Pianta, R. C. (1993) 'Role of mother–child interaction in predicting competence of children with epilepsy', *Epilepsia* 34: 658–69.

McGill, P. and Toogood, S. (1994) 'Organizing community placements', in E. Emerson, P. McGill and J. Mansell (eds) *Severe Learning Disabilities and Challenging Behaviours: Designing High Quality Services*, London: Chapman and Hall.

Marston, D., Besag, F., Binnie, C. D. and Fowler, M. (1993) 'Effects of transitory cognitive impairment on psychosocial functioning of children with epilepsy: a therapeutic trial', *Developmental Medicine and Child Neurology* 35: 574–81.

Matthews, W. S. and Barabas, G. (1986) 'Perceptions of control among children with epilepsy', in S. Whitman and B. P. Hermann (eds) *Psychopathology in Epilepsy: Social Dimensions*, New York: Oxford University Press.

Matthews, W. S., Barabas, G. and Ferrari, M. (1982) 'Emotional concomitants of childhood epilepsy', *Epilepsia* 23: 671–81.

Munthe-Kaas, A. W. (1981) 'Education of the family', in M. Dam, L. Gram and J. K. Penry (eds) *Advances in Epileptology: XIIth Epilepsy International Symposium*, New York: Raven Press.

Nicholas, K. K. and Pianta, R. C. (1994), 'Mother–child interactions and seizure control: relations with behavior problems in children with epilepsy', *Journal of Epilepsy* 7: 102–7.

Nolte, R. and Wolff, M. (1992) 'Behavioural and developmental aspects of primary generalized myoclonic-astatic epilepsy', *Epilepsy Research* Suppl. 6: 175–83.

Pianta, R. C. and Lothman, D. J. (1994) 'Predicting behavior problems in children with epilepsy: child factors, disease factors, family stress, and child–mother interactions', *Child Development* 65: 1415–28.

Rantakallio, P., Koiranen, M. and Möttönen, J. (1992) 'Association of perinatal events, epilepsy, and central nervous system trauma with juvenile delinquency', *Archives of Disease in Childhood* 67: 1459–61.

Ritchie, K. (1981) 'Research note: interaction in the families of epileptic children', *Journal of Child Psychology and Psychiatry* 22: 65–71.

Rix, K. (1988) 'Teaching a mother to attend differentially to her mentally handicapped child's behaviour', *Behavioural Psychotherapy* 16: 122–32.

Roulet Perez, E., Davidoff, V., Despland, P. A. and Deonna, T. (1993) 'Mental and behavioural deterioration of children with epilepsy and CSWS: acquired epileptic frontal syndrome', *Developmental Medicine and Child Neurology* 35: 661–74.

Sheth, R. D., Goulden, K. J. and Ronen, G. M. (1994) 'Aggression in children treated with clobazam for epilepsy', *Clinical Neuropharmacology* 17: 332–7.

Silverstein, F. S., Parrish, M. A. and Johnson, M. V. (1982) 'Adverse behavioural reactions in children treated with carbamazepine (Tegretol)', *Journal of Paediatrics* 101: 785–7.

Stores, G. (1982) 'Psychosocial preventive measures and rehabilitation of children with epilepsy', in H. Akimoto, H. Kazamatsuri, M. Seino and A. Ward (eds) *Advances in Epileptology: XIIIth Epilepsy International Symposium*, New York: Raven Press.

Sturniolo, M. G. and Galletti, F. (1994) 'Idiopathic epilepsy and school achievement', *Archives of Disease in Childhood* 70: 424–8.

Urion, D. K. (1991) 'Psychiatric aspects of epilepsy in children', in O. Devinsky and W. H. Theodore (eds) *Epilepsy and Behavior*, New York: Wiley.

West, P. (1986) 'The social meaning of epilepsy: stigma as a potential explanation for psychopathology in children', in S. Whitman and B. P. Hermann (eds) *Psychopathology in Epilepsy: Social Dimensions*, New York: Oxford University Press.

Ziegler, R. G. (1981) 'Impairments of control and competence in epileptic children and their families', *Epilepsia* 22: 339–46.

Chapter 11

Epilepsy and learning disabilities

Colin A. Espie and Audrey Paul

The co-presentation of epilepsy and learning disabilities is a very neglected area in respect of both research and clinical expertise. This chapter attempts to highlight some key issues in this complex area. However, other parts of this handbook also have much to contribute to understanding in this specialist field.

THE PREVALENCE OF EPILEPSY IN LEARNING DISABILITIES

There are few problems associated with learning disabilities which present as commonly and as persistently as seizure disorders. Around 20 per cent of people with learning disabilities have epilepsy, with prevalence rates rising sharply to 50 per cent where learning disabilities are severe or profound (Bicknell 1985; Coulter 1993). In terms of numbers, it has been estimated that 200 people per 100,000 population will have a learning disability and epilepsy (Brown *et al.* 1993). Furthermore, the administration of anti-epileptic drugs remains very high. A recent large national survey reported that approximately 53 per cent of children and adults with a learning disability were receiving at least one anti-epileptic drug (Hogg 1992). Whereas monotherapy is the treatment of choice in epilepsy, practice in learning disabilities demonstrates that 40 per cent of people are on polytherapy (Espie *et al.* 1990; Singh and Towle 1993). Encouragingly, where practices have been revised, there is evidence both of improved seizure control and of reductions in behavioural and social problems (e.g. Fischbacher 1985).

This tendency to over-medicate is in part due to the intractability of seizures in this population. Although it has long been recognised that the presence of additional neurological, psychological and social handicaps is associated with a more adverse prognosis (Rodin 1968), it is only recently that formal definition of complex presentations has been attempted. The term *epilepsy plus* has now been applied to those 30–40 per cent of patients who continue to require access to specialist services because of seizures continuing at an unacceptably high rate, despite treatment or the diagnosis remaining uncertain, or having additional neurological problems or psychiatric illness or learning difficulties (Brown *et al.* 1993). People with severe learning disabilities may present with all of these additional problems.

THE SEQUELAE OF EPILEPSY IN LEARNING DISABILITIES

Any significant degree of learning disability is invariably associated with permanent cerebral damage. Although brain damage is not a necessary precondition for the development of epilepsy, it is nonetheless a sufficient one. Thus, epilepsy and learning disabilities may be regarded as synergistic.

The coexistence of learning disabilities and epilepsy presents a particular challenge to the practitioner who is seeking to identify and resolve problems, or at least to reduce their impact. Answers to certain key questions are required. Does a person with learning disabilities and epilepsy necessarily have significant additional problems and, if so, what are they? What are the effects of seizures and of their treatment in day-to-day life? How can seizure events be differentiated from other behaviours, and what does this imply for management? In addition, self-induction of seizures and non-epileptic events may be a greater problem in people with learning disabilities. The following sections will review the available literature in each of these areas, prior to more specific guidelines for good practice in epilepsy and learning disabilities being presented and discussed.

Behaviour and psychological well-being

Rates of behavioural disturbance and psychiatric disorder are significantly elevated in populations of people with epilepsy (Hoare 1984; Lund 1985) and in populations of people with learning disabilities (Bouras and Drummond 1992; Mansell 1993). Although the presentation of a 'dual disability' might increase the frequency and/or severity of such problems, very few studies of this area have been undertaken.

Our earlier studies reported that people with a 'dual disability' demonstrated poorer life-skills than their peers with no epilepsy, particularly on measures of independent functioning and language development. Behavioural disturbance (aggression, inappropriate social manners, self injury) was particularly associated with frequent seizures and with anti-epileptic polytherapy (Espie *et al.* 1989, 1990; Gillies *et al.* 1989).

Despite the enormous research and clinical interest in 'challenging behaviours' over the past two decades very little specific attention has been directed to this sizeable sub-group of people to investigate possible relationships between epileptic phenomena and behaviour. Equally, interest in the social 'meaning' of epilepsy, clients' perceptions of themselves and of 'control', their coping strategies and the interrelations of all these with the functional analysis of behaviour patterns could be extremely productive.

Learning potential

An information-processing model is useful when considering learning processes of people with intellectual impairments (see Figure 11.1). In this model, deficits in performance of day-to-day tasks are mediated by prior states of arousal and selective attention. The integration of the individual's central nervous system and its capacity to respond to the external environment, the quality of his or her stream of consciousness and the overall capacity and efficiency with which the processing system works, will affect the desired learning and performance.

People with learning disabilities have particular problems, both with the sufficiency of the attentional resources available to them and with

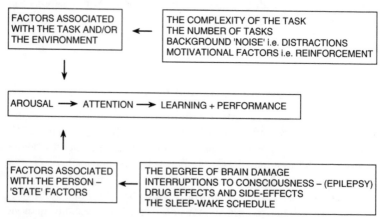

Figure 11.1 A conceptual model of factors influencing learning

the allocation of such resources, particularly when in competition with distracting environmental factors (Carr 1984; Merrill 1990). Figure 11.1 illustrates the interaction between a stimulus-control paradigm and an information-processing model whereby task/environment factors and central-state factors both influence the selective attention processes. Thus, conditions are favourable for attention and learning when the individual is wakeful, with senses focused and engaged on a task, in an environment with minimal competing stimulation. Epilepsy may be a significant contributory factor to the process for a number of reasons.

First, epilepsy typically interrupts consciousness, both during the seizure itself (the ictus) and probably during the interictal period. Although loss of consciousness may be characteristic of some types of seizures, an altered state of consciousness features in other seizure types. It should also be noted that absence seizures, sometimes regarded in clinical practice as relatively less important, may be extremely disruptive, since brief but recurring gaps in awareness may completely destroy the quality of attention available, as our example illustrates.

C was a 42-year-old woman with severe learning disabilities. Lengthy ambulatory EEG assessment revealed numerous bursts of epileptiform activity, ranging from one to thirty-two seconds in duration. Detailed examination of several random hours from the waking trace revealed an average of fifty-five bursts per hour.

The preoccupation with seizure frequency as an outcome measure, both in pharmacological research and in clinical practice, has led to a lack of recognition of the potential importance of interictal well-being, (see Espie et al. under review (a), for detailed discussion). 'Sub-clinical' activity may be of considerable qualitative importance in relation to the maintenance of a satisfactory stream of awareness and consciousness. Similarly, post-ictal adjustment and recovery time may be critical variables in determining suitable care plans.

Second, anti-epileptic drugs have an impact upon arousal. Each of the established anti-epileptic drugs (carbamazepine, sodium valproate, phenytoin) is regarded as predictably causing drowsiness (Brodie 1990); polypharmacy produces further cognitive impairment (Reynolds and Shorvon 1981). This should be viewed against the possibility that people with epilepsy already have an enhanced daytime sleep tendency (Palm et al. 1992).

Finally, it is important to recognise that the majority of both clinical and educational practice is based upon observation of clients, without access to EEG facilities to permit extrapolation of epileptic or sleep phenomena. With this fact in mind, the growing amount of work done in recent years on 'behaviour state analysis' may in time prove invaluable. Coding systems with behavioural criteria have been developed to define and discriminate between various states of optimal and suboptimal functioning ranging from 'sleep states' to 'preferred awake states' (Guess *et al.* 1990). In these analyses, behavioural evidence of arousal and orientation is seen as indicating alertness and greater receptivity to learning, although Green *et al.* (1994) have indicated that apparently non-alert students will not necessarily be unresponsive to training. Behaviour state coding systems include seizures as a separate category, perhaps because seizures are regarded as relatively uncommon. Indeed, in our own studies of twenty-eight adults with severe learning disabilities and epilepsy, we observed only eleven seizures during 1,388 one-minute videotaped observation samples. However, such data almost certainly reflect some actual failure to detect or discriminate and, therefore, underestimate the true frequency of epileptic events in this population.

In conclusion, epilepsy potentially constrains learning potential and learning outcome. An information-processing model may be uniquely adapted to the profiling of neuropsychological status in people with epilepsy and learning disabilities, and assessment may be complemented by the use of behaviour state analysis, particularly if it develops greater assessment reliability and attested validity in the classification of interictal arousal states.

Quality of life

Epilepsy and quality of life (QoL) is discussed in Chapter 8 of this book. Little is known about perceived importance of factors such as social stigma, difficulty in obtaining paid employment and driving restrictions to people with learning disabilities or to their carers. Attempts have been made to define, describe and quantify QoL for people with epilepsy, but it may not be valid to extrapolate themes or norms from such assessment scales to those with learning disabilities. Furthermore, the published measures are in self-report format and they require literacy skills, in addition to comprehension generally beyond those with intellectual disability.

Under the auspices of the West of Scotland Epilepsy Research Group, we ran a series of recent carers' workshops to identify what carers wanted from epilepsy services for people with learning disabilities. Thirty-nine participants, nineteen of whom were family carers, took part in four workshops. Carers were first asked to consider and write down their three main concerns about their family member/client having epilepsy. Second, small groups were formed to enable carers to share these concerns. The small groups then reported their findings to the entire workshop. The final stage in the process was for carers to consider revising their personal lists in the light of hearing how others felt. In this way, we hoped to distil the most strongly felt personal concerns affecting carers' quality of life.

The main themes which emerged were medication and side effects, further damage caused by seizures, risk of injury, client independence, social restrictions, mood change and carer responsibility. From the carer's perspective, 'quality of life' reflected concerns over some very basic issues. An Epilepsy Outcome Scale has now been developed and tested (Espie *et al.*, under review (b)).

Differentiating seizure behaviour from other behaviours

Questions arise in clinical practice about whether a behaviour could be seizure-related. Simple partial and absence seizures may be missed altogether, as of course may nocturnal seizures; myoclonic seizures may be difficult to differentiate from habits and stereotypies. Complex partial seizures are most likely to be labelled 'behavioural'. Primary and secondary generalised tonic-clonic seizures may be less ambiguous but can pass unobserved by carers. Non-epileptic seizures may present and these usually occur in people who also have genuine epileptic attacks. None of these problems is unique to learning disabilities, but three important factors contribute to additional difficulties in detection and classification.

First, clinical practice generally relies heavily upon the patient's self-report. Even when detailed EEG assessment has been conducted, actual seizures are rarely observed by the clinicians. However, patients may have unusual sensations, or be aware of altered consciousness immediately prior to attacks. They may be able to identify seizure events which can be verified electrophysiologically, but which involve extremely modest behavioural change, for example, a chewing movement or a blank stare. Furthermore, many seizures last only a matter of seconds but may be perceptible to patients in retrospect. They may conclude that they must have had a seizure because they dropped something, stumbled, or are in a recognisable post-ictal recovery state. The person with learning disabilities is likely to be less able to interpret and communicate any of this information effectively.

The second factor is the high rate of presentation of other similar behaviours such as movement disorders, automatisms, tics and tremors and drug-induced (especially neuroleptic) movements and postures. Stereotyped behaviours, which have been reported to be present in up to two-thirds of institutionalised people with severe learning disabilities (Berkson and Davenport 1962; Repp and Barton 1980), perhaps best illustrate the differential classification problems. The essential defining features of stereotypy are idiosyncratic, repetitive, invariant and frequent movements. They range in form from body rocking and pacing to more complex fine motor movements, posturing and vocalisation. Head jerking and arm waving are common characteristics, but the range of potential behaviours is quite extensive, particularly in specific disorders such as Rett Syndrome and autism (Paul, 1997).

Third, seizure events have to be differentiated from 'challenging behaviours' where the individual's actions are difficult to manage effectively in the care setting (Emerson *et al.* 1987; Mansell 1993). The usual assessment methodology here is functional analysis (e.g. Owens and Ashcroft 1982), a data gathering and hypothesis-testing approach designed to establish the setting conditions and maintaining factors for the behaviour. Self-injurious behaviour, for example, can be stereotyped and confused with ictal movement.

Another area of overlap is in the expression of emotionality. Although the association of aggression with temporal lobe epilepsy (complex partial seizures) remains speculative (Fenwick 1991), displays of emotion post-ictally are common and there is some evidence that maintenance of a steady state of emotion and avoidance of excitation can abate seizures for some (Betts 1989; Devellis *et al.* 1980). We have noted anecdotally that some carers try to avoid upsetting or pressuring clients in the belief that such emotional states can precipitate seizures. There are clear parallels in the relationship between challenging behaviours and mood (e.g. Novaco 1975).

Non-epileptic events

This topic is addressed in more detail in Chapter 7. Non-epileptic seizures may be symptomatic of other physical or psychological disorders, such as cardiogenic syncope, metabolic disorder and transient ischaemic attacks. The great majority of research work in this area has been on non-learning disabled populations (Stephenson 1990; Porter 1991) and the prevalence is not known for people with learning disabilities.

The association between psychological trauma and pseudo-neurological presentation has been summarised elsewhere (Gates *et al.* 1991).

There is evidence that non-epileptic seizures may represent emotional distress such as sexual abuse (Cascino *et al.* 1987), and this area continues to be an active focus of clinical research in general psychiatry (Greig and Betts 1992). In spite of a burgeoning literature in the learning disabilities field on the identification and management of sexual abuse, the authors are unaware of specific references to non-epileptic seizures within this literature.

Non-epileptic seizures may also represent a reinforced behaviour pattern where 'illness behaviour' has acquired the capacity to provide secondary gain (Gates *et al.* 1991). Montgomery and Espie (1986) describe in detail a case study of a woman with learning disabilities whose 'seizure' frequency was markedly reduced after behavioural intervention. Clearly, the treatment approach will vary markedly between these types of psychologically-based non-epileptic seizures. A psychotherapeutic approach is preferred for the former with a more strictly behavioural regime being advocated for the latter (Gates *et al.* 1991). Further research-based study is required to identify accurately prevalence rates amongst people with learning disabilities and also the efficacy of treatment outcomes.

Self-induced seizures

A small proportion of people with epilepsy demonstrate unambiguous seizure activity in response to sensory stimulation. The most studied area has been that of photosensitivity which occurs in 2–5 per cent of all individuals with epilepsy (Kasteleijn-Nolst Trenité 1989). It has been suggested that people with learning disabilities may be more likely to engage in self-stimulatory behaviour leading to photosensitive seizures. Kasteleijn-Nolst Trenité (ibid.) reported that eleven out of sixteen subjects with significant learning disabilities evidenced self-induction. Despite this small sample, the potential importance of the phenomenon is amply illustrated and beckons further systematic research study. Other forms of self-stimulation have also been reported in the literature, for example, hyperventilation (Fabisch and Darbyshire 1965), bilateral compression of the carotid arteries (Lai and Ziegler 1983) and chewing (Binnie 1988). The most promising avenue to an explanation of these phenomena would be through functional analysis to identify possible determinants and/or consequences of the behaviour for the individual. It would also be useful to consider the hypothesis that people with learning disabilities fail to inhibit behaviours liable to trigger seizures, rather than 'actively' engaging in them. The arousal mediation hypothesis (after Leuba 1955) may be an explanation for a number of poorly understood behavioural patterns, such as stereotyped behaviours, self-injurious behaviours, other challenging behaviours, and potentially self-induced seizures.

Summary

People with learning disabilities often present with epilepsy. This co-presentation potentially affects the individual's learning, behaviour, mood and their quality of life and that of their carers. A more sophisticated conceptual understanding of the mechanisms underlying co-morbidity and behavioural presentation is required. Methodologies of assessment and intervention in previous research have often been crude, and it continues to be an understudied area which is managed largely on a pragmatic basis. We hope the next section will guide practitioners towards improved assessment and treatment practices.

THE ROLE OF THE CLINICAL PSYCHOLOGIST IN THE PRACTICAL MANAGEMENT OF PEOPLE WITH EPILEPSY AND LEARNING DISABILITIES

It has been suggested that clinical psychologists and neuropsychologists should be core members of an 'epilepsy plus' team (Brown *et al.* 1993). Indeed, clinical psychologists see many people with epilepsy and learning disabilities within a general caseload, although rarely does the epilepsy, or the issues arising from a dual disability, become the focus of intervention. However, skilled input is required in each of the areas of diagnosis and classification, assessment methodology, the monitoring of treatment effects, preparation for surgery and evaluation of its outcome, adjunctive behavioural management and carer support. Each of these areas will be addressed briefly in turn.

Diagnosis, classification and behavioural analysis

A diagnosis of epilepsy is commonly a product of clinical observation and EEG confirmation; such observations should be structured and recorded by an agreed method. Behavioural descriptors should be written for each of the common seizure presentations exhibited by an individual on the front page of a seizure diary, which then requires carers only to enter a code letter and time at each presentation of the seizure, rather than having to make a classification decision. An example may be helpful to explain the use of this coding system.

W was a 25-year-old man with severe learning disabilities. His epilepsy started with infantile spasms and he had chronic, refractory seizures of four differing types. These could be described behaviourally for recording purposes and they reflect tonic-clonic, atonic, myoclonic and absence attacks respectively.

Code Behavioural Description

A W suddenly collapses, his whole body jerks quite violently, his eyes may appear to 'roll' and he will vocalise quite loudly.

B W's whole body becomes rigid, he shrieks and he falls either backwards or forwards (still upright) on to floor.

C There is an abrupt brief jerking of one or more limbs.

D W stares straight ahead without blinking for a short period (appears quite vacant).

Given that many carers are informal and are not trained in the classification of epilepsy, such a simple system would appear to be accurate, reliable and economical. The seizure diaries can then be presented to clinicians and are likely to provide the critical information required for diagnostic and treatment purposes.

The psychologist is uniquely placed to develop such systems and can relate these to parallel systems recording other behaviours which may be non-epileptic in origin, such as stereotyped behaviours. Thus, the hypothesis-testing model employed in the functional analysis of behaviour can be extended to include epileptic behaviours and to differentiate their nature and function. Where possible, recording of events on videotape can be extremely helpful in functional analysis and diagnosis. Indeed, many EEG departments make use of video telemetry in order to correlate clinical evidence with EEG deflections. There is tremendous scope, therefore, for closer collaboration between clinical psychologists and EEG specialists in the interpretation of data. The use of ambulatory monitoring equipment with event-marking facilities also has distinct advantages in that it allows the client to remain in the natural environment, thus facilitating behavioural analysis of any setting conditions, triggers or responses which affect the presentation of the disorder.

Assessment and management of challenging behaviours

Whilst this chapter will not concentrate upon challenging behaviour per se, several helpful parallels may be drawn between the study of challenging behaviour and the study of epilepsy.

First, challenging behaviour is 'behaviour which is likely to seriously limit or delay access to and use of ordinary community facilities' (Emerson *et al.* 1987). There has been a marked shift away from the concept of 'behavioural problem', which tended to ascribe responsibility for the behaviour to the individual concerned, towards an interactional view where context has to be taken into account. 'Seizure behaviours' often represent challenging behaviours which similarly restrict access to experience and to ordinary settings. There is a disproportionately high prevalence of severe epilepsy in institutionalised populations of people with learning disabilities (Corbett 1981) and epilepsy continues to represent a foremost health concern in community care planning (Welsh Health Planning Forum 1992; Department of Health 1995). The wide range of behavioural and emotional triggers and sequelae, coupled with these service issues, suggests that, for at least a proportion of people, epilepsy constitutes a 'challenging behaviour'.

Second, methods of assessment, developed in relation to behavioural analysis, may be readily applicable to the study of seizure behaviour, its antecedents and its consequences. Examples are functional analysis (Iwata *et al.* 1990), naturalistic observation (Repp and Felce 1990), analogue methodology (Oliver 1991) and validated questionnaires (Durand and Crimmins 1988). Relevant here is the earlier discussion of the use of behavioural descriptors with coding systems to minimise the inaccuracy of misclassifying seizures as they occur.

Third, conceptual models of challenging behaviour and the treatment techniques emanating from them have, potentially, much to offer to the understanding and management of those seizure disorders which are related to a stimulus control or instrumental learning model. Furthermore, effective treatment of challenging behaviours often depends upon providing services which are able to maintain the individual in the long term, and to support carers adequately. Similarly, people with learning disabilities and epilepsy often depend upon such a management strategy, rather than a curative one.

Assessment and monitoring of neuropsychological functions

The psychologist's potential assessment role does not end with diagnosis and need not be confined to the measurement of seizures alone. As previously stated, epilepsy affects the stream of consciousness and it can be useful to measure the individual's cognitive functioning in relation to the information-processing model presented in Figure 11.1. For example, what is an individual's span of attention in a given circumstance, and does it change for the better (or worse) with the prescription of an anti-epileptic drug? Although seizure control may improve, drowsiness may increase. Another example would be to monitor the impact of a change to anti-epileptic monotherapy from polytherapy, or the implementation of a new anti-epileptic, over a range of cognitive functions (see also Chapter 5).

The particular tools for assessment must be selected on an individual basis since conventional neuropsychological tests may prove either inappropriate due to the degree of learning disability, or insensitive as repeated measures to monitor the specific functions which are of interest. The most accurate assessments here are likely to be quite labour-intensive but may yield useful results. For example, we have found that a simple choice-reaction timer can be used even with people with severe learning disabilities to provide information on vigilance, attention span and eye–hand coordination. Similarly, behaviour state, as defined earlier, can be sampled to provide information on arousal and alertness levels.

Carers are often highly motivated to participate in monitoring changes in neuropsychological status. Side-effect profiles of anti-epileptic drugs should be regularly rated, and targeted outcomes can be derived for 'quality of life' dimensions on an individual basis. In our experience, visual analogue scales are user-friendly for these purposes.

Formal neuropsychological tests usually cannot be used with reference to published norms. However, as part of the clinical appraisal process, and for monitoring of change over time, we would recommend using appropriate sub-tests from the Wechsler Scales or the British Abilities Scales which will not yield floor and ceiling effects for the client in question. The development of standardised instruments for the assessment of cognitive functions in people with severe intellectual impairments is long overdue.

Monitoring drug treatment

Psychologists are commonly involved in clinical trials of new anti-epileptic drugs. Clinical psychologists working in the field of learning disabilities should become familiar with these studies, since changes in status or function may disproportionately affect the person with learning disabilities whose intellectual resources are intrinsically less. Monotherapy is generally the treatment approach of choice, with the discontinuation of all anti-epileptic medication where possible. (Alvarez 1989; Collaborative Group for the Study of Epilepsy 1992). The benefits of rationalisation of drug treatment are social, cognitive and medical, making it important for the psychologist to be in a knowledgeable enough position to advocate for improved functioning in these respects. The profiles of the newer anti-epileptic drugs (especially lamotrigine) appear more favourable in protecting psychological functions (Brodie 1996), although vigabatrin has been associated with psychotic phenomena, which may present as behaviour disturbance in people with learning disabilities (Grant and Heel 1991). The authors are unaware of any sizeable well-controlled comparative trial of anti-epileptic drugs specifically in people with learning disabilities.

Surgery

Surgical intervention for patients with refractory epilepsy has greatly increased in recent years (see Chapter 4). Although, currently, selection criteria for surgical treatment would generally exclude people with severe learning disabilities (Turmel *et al.* 1992), cases of corpus callosotomy in people with mild learning difficulties have been reported (Sass *et al.* 1992). The primary indication for the procedure appears to be for atonic seizures. Psychologists working in learning disabilities should be aware, therefore, of potential future involvements in the work-up to surgical procedures and in the monitoring of post surgical well-being.

Psychological treatment of seizures

There is some evidence that patients can learn seizure abatement strategies to control, or at least delay, the presentation of seizures (see Chapter 7). Such procedures are generally dependent upon the existence of an aura and the individual's ability to intervene prior to the development of the full seizure. Little is presently known about the potential for such an approach in people with learning disabilities, but a preliminary starting point would be to gather information on the frequency with which auras are recognised. Anecdotally, we can report on one man with severe learning disabilities, with no speech, who routinely sat down on the floor or on a couch immediately prior to a seizure to reduce injury. This was initially thought to be evidence of non-epileptic seizure behaviour, but it transpired (after ambulatory EEG monitoring and videotape analysis) that he did this in response to an aura.

Reference was made earlier to non-epileptic seizures evoked by psychological factors, or maintained as illness behaviours, that presumably attract some secondary gains. The psychologist's role in assessment (Hermann and Connell 1992) and treatment have been reviewed elsewhere (Gates *et al.* 1991). However, little of this pertains directly to people with learning disabilities. Further well-documented reports and controlled trials are needed. Similarly, the possible self-induction of seizures would fit well within a behavioural paradigm since the function(s) of such apparently self-stimulatory behaviours might be established through detailed observational analysis and pave the way for intervention using, for example, stimulus control models.

There is an outstanding need to consider the relationship between emotional state, thinking and behavioural response in the care and management of people with learning disabilities plus epilepsy. Cognitive (schema-based) theory potentially has much to offer with its emphasis upon 'internal states'. It does not seem unreasonable to hypothesise that people with learning disabilities will have greater than usual difficulty in understanding their epilepsy, its symptoms and its effects and in developing appropriate coping strategies. However, recently, concepts such as epilepsy knowledge, self-efficacy and locus of control orientation have been touched upon within this client group (Espie *et al.* 1990; Jarvie *et al.* 1993 a, b; Jarvie 1994). There is available a video-based training package which is the first to be designed specifically for use with people with learning disabilities (Paul, 1996). The field is wide open to consider the adaptation of models and methods from general adult psychology.

Carer support and management

Frequent seizures and anti-epileptic polytherapy tend to be associated with poorer social outcomes in people with learning disabilities, including lower levels of independence and higher levels of behavioural difficulty (Espie *et al.* 1989; Espie *et al.* 1990). Many adults with learning disabilities have difficulties in achieving their optimal level of independence from carers, and it seems likely that the added complication of epilepsy is associated with a strengthening of this dilemma.

From our studies it seems clear that carers are looking for improved control over epilepsy, reductions in side effects, reassurance that further damage is not taking place, limitation to the risk of injury, and, against the background of these, an increase in client independence and a reduction in social restriction. Carers experience difficulty in coping with post-ictal aggression or fear. A very common finding, however, was the sense of personal responsibility and anxiety which many carers felt they had and were likely to keep indefinitely. Common views were that other people were unable or unwilling to cope, and were liable either not to react or to over-react. Services must therefore face up to the reality of such consistently expressed concerns and provide psychological support and help to carers.

A therapeutic service to carers could start with information and education, provide training in anxiety management strategies, develop buddy systems between paid and family carers, and support groups, and could involve more specific individually-tailored help during times of social transition. Meeting these needs, along with the specific needs of the individual with epilepsy, will probably interact to produce the best outcomes since family dynamics can prove powerful inhibitors or facilitators of positive change.

CONCLUSION

Psychological factors play an important part in the presentation, assessment and care management of the person with epilepsy and his or her family. The psychologist can apply conceptual models which shed light upon the overall integration of the individual's personal functioning, and of their functioning within a social context. Importantly, the psychologist potentially has more to contribute to working with people with epilepsy than has traditionally been thought. There remains an outstanding need for well-documented clinical research to evaluate both theoretical and practical aspects of such psychological work.

REFERENCES

Alvarez, N. (1989) 'Discontinuance of anti-epileptic medications in patients with developmental disability and diagnosis of epilepsy', *American Journal on Mental Retardation* 93: 593–9.

Berkson, G. and Davenport, R. K. (1962) 'Stereotyped movements in mental defectives. I: Initial survey', *American Journal of Mental Deficiency* 66: 849–52.

Betts, T. A. (1989) 'Psychological aspects of epilepsy', in J. Marshall (ed.) *Focus: Epilepsy in Childhood*, St Ives: Chase Webb.

Bicknell, D. J. (1985) 'Epilepsy and mental handicap', in C. Wood (ed.) *Epilepsy and Mental Handicap. Royal Society of Medicine Round Table Series* No. 2, London: RSM.

Binnie, C. D. (1988) 'Self induction of seizures: the ultimate non-compliance', *Epilepsy Research* 1 (Suppl.): 153–8.

Bouras, N. and Drummond, C. (1992) 'Behaviour and psychiatric disorders of people with mental handicaps living in the community', *Journal of Intellectual Disability Research* 36: 349–57.

Brodie, M. J. (1990) 'Established anti-convulsants and treatment of refractory epilepsy', *Lancet* (Review): 20–5.

—— (1996) 'Lamotrigine – an update', *Canadian Journal of Neurological Sciences* 23 (Suppl. 2): S6–S9.

Brown, S., Betts, T., Chadwick, D., Hall, B., Shorvon, S. and Wallace, S. (1993) 'An epilepsy needs document', *Seizure* 2: 91–103.

Carr, T. H. (1984) 'Attention, skill and intelligence: some speculations on extreme individual differences in human performance', in P. H. Brooks, R. Sperber and C. McCauley (eds) *Learning and Cognition in the Mentally Retarded*, New Jersey: Lawrence Erlbaum.

Cascino, G., Woodward, A. and Johnson, M. (1987) 'Sexual and/or physical abuse occurring in association with psychogenic seizures', *Epilepsia* 28: 632.

Collaborative Group for the Study of Epilepsy (1992) 'Prognosis of epilepsy in newly referred patients: a multicenter prospective study of the effects of monotherapy on the long-term course of epilepsy', *Epilepsia* 33: 45–51.

Corbett, J. A. (1981) 'Epilepsy and mental retardation', in: E. H. Reynolds and M. R. Trimble (eds) *Epilepsy and Psychiatry*, London: Churchill Livingstone.

Coulter, D. L. (1993) 'Epilepsy and mental retardation: an overview', *American Journal on Mental Retardation* 98: S1–11.

Department of Health (1995) *The Health of the Nation; A Strategy for People with Learning Disabilities*, Wetherby: Department of Health.

Devellis, R. F., Devellis, B. M., Wallston, B. S. and Wallston, K. A. (1980) 'Epilepsy and learned helplessness', *Basic and Applied Social Psychology* 1: 241–53.

Durand, V. M. and Crimmins, D. B. (1988) 'Identifying the variables maintaining self-injurious behaviour', *Journal of Autism and Developmental Disorders* 18: 99–117.

Emerson, E., Barratt, S., Bell, C., Cummings, R. G., McCool, C., Toogood, A. and Mansell, J. (1987) *Developing services for people with severe learning disabilities and challenging behaviours*, University of Kent at Canterbury: Institute of Social and Applied Psychology.

Espie, C. A., Gillies, J. B. and Montgomery, J. M. (1990) 'Anti-epileptic polypharmacy, psychosocial behaviour and locus of control orientation among mentally handicapped adults living in the community', *Journal of Mental Deficiency Research* 34: 351–60.

Espie, C. A., Kerr, M., Paul, A., O'Brien, G., Betts, T., Berney, T., Clark, J.,

Jacoby, A., and Baker, G. (under review (a)), *Learning disabilities and epilepsy 2: A review of available outcome measures and position statement on development priorities.*

Espie, C. A., Pashley, A. S., Bonham, K. G., Sourindhrin, I. and O'Donovan, M. (1989) 'The mentally handicapped person with epilepsy: a comparative study investigating psychosocial functioning', *Journal of Mental Deficiency Research* 33: 123–35.

Espie, C. A., Paul, A., Graham, M., Sterrick, M., Foley, J. and McGarvey, C. (under review (b)) 'The Epilepsy Outcome Scale: the development of a measure for use with carers of people with epilepsy plus learning disabilities.'

Fabisch, W. and Darbyshire, R. (1965) 'Report on an unusual case of self-induced epilepsy with comments on some psychological and therapeutic aspects', *Epilepsia* 6: 335–40.

Fenwick, P. (1991) 'Aggression and epilepsy', in O. Devinsky and W. H. Theodore (eds) *Epilepsy and Behaviour; Frontiers of Clinical Neuroscience* Vol. 12, New York: Wiley-Liss.

Fischbacher, E. (1985) 'Mental handicap and epilepsy: are we still over treating?' in C. Wood (ed.) *Epilepsy and Mental Handicap. Royal Society of Medicine Round Table Series* No. 2, London: RSM.

Gates, J. R., Luciano, D. and Devinsky, O. (1991) 'The classification and treatment of non-epileptic events', in O. Devinsky and W. H. Theodore (eds) *Epilepsy and Behaviour, Frontiers of Clinical Neuroscience* Vol. 12, New York: Wiley-Liss.

Gillies, J. B., Espie, C. A. and Montgomery, J. M. (1989) 'The social and behavioural functioning of people with mental handicaps attending adult training centres: a comparison with those with and without epilepsy', *Mental Handicap Research* 2: 129–36.

Grant, S. M. and Heel, R. C. (1991) 'Vigabatrin: a review of its pharmacodynamic and pharmacokinetic properties, and therapeutic potential in epilepsy and disorders of motor control', *Drugs* 41: 889–926.

Green, C. W., Gardner, S. M., Canipe, V. S. and Reid, D. H. (1994) 'Analyzing alertness among people with profound multiple disabilities: implications for provision of training', *Journal of Applied Behavior Analysis* 27: 519–31.

Greig, E. and Betts, T. (1992) 'Epileptic seizures induced by sexual abuse. Pathogenic and pathoplastic factors', *Seizure* 1: 269–74.

Guess, D., Siegel-Causey, E., Roberts, S., Rues, J., Thompson, B. and Siegel-Causey, D. (1990) 'Assessment and analysis of behavior state and related variables among students with profoundly handicapping conditions', *Journal of the Association for Persons with Severe Handicaps* 15: 211–30.

Hermann, B. P. and Connell, B. E. (1992) 'Neuropsychological assessment in the diagnosis of non-epileptic seizures', in T. L. Bennett (ed.) *The Neuropsychology of Epilepsy*, New York: Plenum Press.

Hoare, P. (1984) 'The development of psychiatric disorder among school children with epilepsy', *Developmental Medicine and Child Neurology* 26: 3–13.

Hogg, J. (1992) 'The administration of psychotropic and anti-convulsant drugs to children with profound intellectual disability and multiple impairments', *Journal of Intellectual Disability Research* 36: 473–88.

Iwata, B. A., Vollmer, T. R. and Zarcone, J. R. (1990) 'The experimental (functional) analysis of behaviour disorders; methodology, applications and limitations', in A. C. Repp and N. N. Singh (eds) *Perspectives on the Use of Nonaversive and Aversive Interventions for Persons with Developmental Disabilities*, Sycamore IL: Sycamore Publishing Company.

Jarvie, S. (1994) 'Self-perception and psychosocial functioning in people with intractable epilepsy', unpublished Ph.D thesis, University of Glasgow.

Jarvie, S., Espie, C. A. and Brodie, M. J. (1993a) 'The development of a questionnaire to assess knowledge of epilepsy. 1: General knowledge of epilepsy', *Seizure* 2: 179–85.

—— (1993b) 'The development of a questionnaire to assess knowledge of epilepsy. 2: Knowledge of own condition', *Seizure* 2: 187–93.

Kasteleijn-Nolst Trenité, D. G. A. (1989) 'Photosensitivity in epilepsy: electrophysiological and clinical correlates', *Acta Neurologica Scandinavica* 80 (Suppl. 125): 1–149.

Lai, C. W. and Ziegler, D. K. (1983) 'Repeated self-induced syncope and subsequent seizures', *Archives of Neurology* 40: 820–3.

Leuba, C. (1955) 'Toward some integration of learning theories: the concept of optimal stimulation', *Psychological Reports* 1: 27–33.

Lund, J. (1985) 'Epilepsy and psychiatric disorder in the mentally retarded adult', *Acta Psychiatrica Scandinavica* 72: 557–62.

Mansell, J. L. (1993) *Services for People with Learning Disabilities and Challenging Behaviour or Mental Health Needs*, London: HMSO.

Merrill, E. C. (1990) 'Attentional resource allocation and mental retardation', *International Review of Research in Mental Retardation* 16: 51–88.

Montgomery, J. M. and Espie, C. A. (1986) 'Behavioural management of hysterical pseudoseizures', *Behavioural Psychotherapy* 14: 334–40.

Novaco, R. W. (1975) *Anger Control: The Development and Evaluation of an Experimental Treatment*, Lexington MA: Lexington Books.

Oliver, C. (1991) 'The application of analogue methodology to the functional analysis of challenging behaviour', in B. Remington (ed.) *The Challenge of Severe Mental Handicap: A Behaviour Analytic Approach*, Chichester: Wiley.

Owens, R. G. and Ashcroft, J. E. (1982) 'Functional analysis in applied psychology', *British Journal of Clinical Psychology* 21: 181–9.

Palm, L., Anderson, H., Elmqvist, D. and Blennow, G. (1992) 'Daytime sleep tendency before and after discontinuation of anti-epileptic drugs in preadolescent children with epilepsy', *Epilepsia* 33: 687–91.

Paul, A. (1996) *Epilepsy and You*, Brighton: Pavilion Publishing.

—— (1997) 'Epilepsy or stereotypy? Diagnostic issues in learning disabilities', *Seizure* 6 (in press).

Porter, R. J. (1991) 'Diagnosis of psychogenic and other non-epileptic seizures in adults', in O. Devinsky and W. H. Theodore (eds) *Epilepsy and Behaviour: Frontiers of Clinical Neuroscience* Vol. 12, New York: Wiley-Liss.

Repp, A. C. and Barton, L. E. (1980) 'Naturalistic observations of institutionalized retarded persons: a comparison of licensure decisions and behavioral observations', *Journal of Applied Behavior Analysis* 13: 333–41.

Repp, A. C. and Felce, D. (1990) 'A microcomputer system used for evaluative and experimental behavioural research in mental handicap', *Mental Handicap Research* 3: 31–2.

Reynolds, E. H. and Shorvon, S. D. (1981) 'Monotherapy or polytherapy for epilepsy?', *Epilepsia* 22: 1–10.

Rodin, E. A. (1968) *The Prognosis of Patients with Epilepsy*, Springfield IL: Charles C. Thomas.

Sass, K. J., Spencer, S. S., Westerveld, M. and Spencer, D. D. (1992) 'The neuropsychology of corpus callosotomy for epilepsy' in T. L. Bennett (ed.) *The Neuropsychology of Epilepsy*, New York: Plenum.

Singh, B. K. and Towle, P. O. (1993) 'Anti-epileptic drug status in adult outpatients with mental retardation', *American Journal on Mental Retardation* 98: S41–6.

Stephenson, J. (1990) 'Fits and faints', *Clinics in Developmental Medicine* No. 109, Oxford: MacKeith Press.

Turmel, A., Giard, N., Bouvier, G., Labrecque, R., Veilleux, F., Rouleau, I. and Saint-Hilaire, J. N. (1992) 'Frontal lobe seizures and epilepsy: indications for cortectomies or callosotomies', in P. Chauvel, A. V. Delgado-Escueta, E. Halgren and J. Bancaud (eds) *Frontal Lobe Seizures and Epilepsies, Advances in Neurology* Vol. 57, New York: Raven Press.

Welsh Health Planning Forum (1992) *Protocol for Investment in Health Gain: Mental Handicap (Learning Disabilities)*, Welsh Office: NHS Directorate.

Chapter 12

The way forward

Laura H. Goldstein and Christine Cull

The aforegoing chapters of this volume have laid out for the reader the current state of knowledge and practice of psychological matters that relate to epilepsy. It will be patently clear, however, that there is scope for enormous development in terms of the research and clinical practice that could be undertaken by clinical psychologists. This is essential in order for practitioners to be able to work from a sound evidence base.

The purpose of this final chapter, therefore, is to look at the role that psychologists can play in furthering our understanding of epilepsy and its sequelae by highlighting gaps in our present level of knowledge. Much of this will have been alluded to in the previous chapters and our task here is to pull that information together, as well as to add some thoughts of our own.

Neuropsychology

As will have been seen from Chapters 2, 3 and 4 (with respect to adults) and Chapter 9 (regarding children), much work has been undertaken to document the neuropsychological sequelae of epilepsy and how these might relate to outcome following neurosurgery. As will also have been apparent, however, it has been difficult to describe an entirely consistent pattern of cognitive deficits in patients with epilepsy who have not received, or who have not been candidates for, surgical treatment for their seizures. Whether this is the result of inconsistent criteria for subject or test selection, or is inherent in the disorder itself, is not clear; certainly there is a need for clinical psychologists working in the field to continue the painstaking process of neuropsychological test development, with rigorous test standardisation and validation (e.g. Baxendale and Thompson 1996; Walton *et al.* 1996). This is in order for the process of corroborating cognitive profiles with the results of neuroimaging and neurophysiological test data to be most beneficial for the patient, and to permit accurate descriptions of cognitive strengths and weaknesses to be made. More work is needed to compare the sensitivity of existing tests to detect neuropsychological deficits in patients along the lines of that undertaken by Randolf *et al.* (1994). Such work needs to be done equally in the field of computerised assessments as in the field of standardised pen and paper tests.

An increasing amount of neuropsychological work has involved the correlation of neuropsychological test performance with volumetric measures of temporal lobe structures using Magnetic Resonance Imaging (MRI). Some of this work has been discussed in passing in Chapters 2 and 4. Since the practice of neuropsychology is increasingly less diagnostic and increasingly more descriptive and corroborative, the scope for clinical psychologists working in the field of epilepsy to become involved in neuroimaging work is growing. Thus, for example, Kirkpatrick *et al.* (1993) have used a combination of verbal recognition memory testing and single photon emission computerised tomography (SPECT) to determine the locus of mediation of verbal recognition memory, in patients being worked-up for epilepsy surgery. This study served to demonstrate the difficulty in trying to make a simple localisation of cognitive function in people with epilepsy and demonstrates the value of having clinical psychologists involved in the design and interpretation of neuroimaging studies. With the development of functional MRI, the need for well-designed cognitive paradigms has become even more important, especially given the potential for repeated testing of patients with this technique, in contrast to the restrictions imposed when using scanning procedures involving radiation such as SPECT and Positron Emission Tomography. Thus, imaging during the performance of a neuropsychological test could be undertaken pre- and post-epilepsy surgery, providing the opportunity to monitor the effects of surgery on the mediation of cognitive function. The value of other types of neuroimaging techniques such as Magnetic Resonance Spectroscopy has already been demonstrated in providing an understanding of unexpected patterns of cognitive abilities following surgery (Incisa della Rochetta *et al.* 1995).

The neuropsychological investigation of children is a relatively recent development; however, there is a great need for refined assessment measures to enable us to fully understand the neuropsychological profiles of children with epilepsy. This also applies to those (adults and children) with learning disabilities and epilepsy. Clearly, this is not just an issue for clinical psychologists working in epilepsy but for those working in learning disabilities, since few of the assessment measures usually used to assess patients with epilepsy have norms that are appropriate for people with learning disabilities. It may be that the clinical psychologist with an interest in epilepsy has much to offer to the development of such measures.

Thompson (see Chapter 3), has outlined some approaches to cognitive rehabilitation; these are largely concerned with memory training procedures and, like Aldenkamp and Vermeulen (1991), Thompson has begun to discuss their use for people with epilepsy. Whilst this is a valuable contribution, strategies also need to be developed to help people with epilepsy to overcome significant cognitive impairments other than memory, for example language (see Chapter 2) or executive functions. In view of the possible existence of deficits in executive functioning in patients (see Chapters 2 and 4 in particular), which may be manifested for example in planning and reasoning deficits and also in response disinhibition, it will also be important for clinical psychologists to assess the applicability to patients with focal epilepsy of behavioural management techniques (e.g. von Cramon *et al.* 1991; von Cramon and Matthes-von Cramon 1994; Alderman 1996) which have recently been developed in other fields of neuropsychological rehabilitation. This may be especially relevant in view of the potentially negative cognitive–behavioural consequences of frontal lobe epilepsy surgery (e.g. Goldstein *et al.* 1993). The interaction between treatment designs and epilepsy variables (e.g. seizure type, frequency, age at onset) needs to be defined, as does the potential contribution, positive or negative, posed by anti-epileptic medication. The interaction between one particular anti-epileptic drug, carbamazepine, and behaviour modification techniques has been discussed in the field of head injury (e.g. Wood and Eames 1981). The importance of rehabilitative programmes in children has been alluded to in Chapter 9, but this is an area that has yet to be developed.

If it is possible to identify prospectively those individuals (children or adults) who are likely to experience difficulties in cognitive functions, it may be feasible to establish early intervention programmes that would aim to help individuals develop appropriate strategies and hopefully modify the sequelae of any serious cognitive dysfunction.

Psychological interventions – for patients with epilepsy and associated psychological disturbance and/or to reduce seizure frequency

People with epilepsy are at risk from developing any one of a variety of psychological problems. However, what has yet to be determined are the vulnerability factors that make it more likely that an individual will develop particular problems.

Despite the range of psychological problems that may accompany a diagnosis of epilepsy (see Chapter 6), the range of studies that have considered the value of psychological interventions in alleviating such disorders is remarkably small. Indeed, most accounts of psychological interventions are with single patients (adults and children), are largely psychodynamic in treatment orientation (e.g. Ragan and Seides 1990; Mathers 1992; Miller 1994) or have used counselling approaches (e.g. Usiskin 1993), and have little if any formal evaluation to indicate the rigour of treatment success. However, some attempt has been made to evaluate the effect of educational or self-help epilepsy groups on psychological disorders and psychosocial status (Helgeson et al. 1990; Becu et al. 1993). There is also some evidence that, as a spin-off of psychological interventions designed to reduce seizure frequency, patients' psychological state may improve (e.g. Rousseau et al. 1985; Tan and Bruni 1986; Gillham 1990). The lack of literature dealing with the treatment of seizure-related phobias and anxieties remains of concern, and is a clear area of potential work for clinical psychologists working with patients with epilepsy. It will be important to identify those factors that hinder or facilitate the use of psychological treatment programmes for each individual. For example, what impact would frequent seizures have? Would it matter what the seizure type was? Would the type of AED be of relevance (particularly in view of some of the reported well-being enhancing effects of the newer drugs, see Chapter 5)? Equally, if it is possible to identify those individuals who are most at risk of developing psychological problems, there is scope for developing early intervention programmes which aim to help people with recently diagnosed epilepsy to cope with the disorder, and hopefully avoid the development of more serious psychological disorders. A further area to be developed is the facilitation of adjustment to life without epilepsy for patients whose previously intractable seizures have relatively suddenly become well controlled through neurosurgical or pharmacological means.

In Chapter 7, we have illustrated the range of studies that have been undertaken to demonstrate the effectiveness of psychological interventions in reducing seizure frequency. Many questions remain untackled, most notably the identification of particular patient sub-groups most likely to benefit from psychological interventions for seizure control. Although literature exists on issues of self-control in patients with epilepsy, there is only now some attempt being made to identify any personal characteristics that might single out those patients with epilepsy who believe they can control their seizures from those who do not (Spector-Oron *et al.* 1993). DiIorio *et al.* (1994) have considered the role of self-esteem, self-efficacy, social support and regimen-specific support in epilepsy self-management, and Gehlert (1994) has looked at the relationship between attributional style and seizure control; Tan and Bruni (1986) suggested that individuals predisposed to self-control approaches in their everyday lives might respond to a cognitive–behavioural treatment approach geared towards encouraging self-control of seizures, but as yet no study has set out to determine which personal characteristics offer good prognosis for response to cognitive–behavioural interventions to reduce seizures. Even Andrews and Schonfeld (1992), reviewing patients' progress in their self-control-of-seizures treatment approach, only investigated seizure variables as predictors of success in the programme; despite their findings (see Chapter 7), they indicated that seizure-related predictors were only weak. Thus, by conducting well-designed treat-ment trials that include, as independent variables, psychological characteristics of patients as well as seizure variables, clinical psycholo-gists could contribute enormously to this area of research and lead to the development of evidence-based treatments which could be targeted at particular individuals. Important here, too, is the need for clear demonstration of which psychological seizure-reduction techniques can be applied to children and to people with learning disabilities; many of the published studies referred to in Chapter 7 have included individ-uals with learning difficulties, but it would be helpful ultimately for there to be guidelines as to which treatment approaches might opti-mally be used with children or with people with learning disabilities.

Within the area of psychological treatment of seizures also, clinical psychologists have an important educational role to play, not only in terms of the potential benefit of such treatments, but also in high-lighting other factors in the patients' ongoing care that may jeopardise the success of such interventions. Clearly, the use of self-control strate-gies by patients requires them to take responsibility for actions related to seizure management, over and above remembering to take their anti-epileptic drugs, and places on them the onus for change. Families, too, need to be receptive and readily able to support the individual in their endeavours and share the same attributional framework for the genesis of seizures (e.g. Reiter *et al.* 1987). In addition, if, while engaging in a psychological treatment approach, the patient is simultaneously being investigated for their suitability for epilepsy surgery, they may well see the locus for seizure control as residing primarily in the neurosurgeon. These 'mixed messages' to the patient (i.e. that they are on the one hand considered to be able to gain control of seizures, whereas on the other hand the implication of surgery is that they are unable to control their seizures) may make it less likely that the person will feel motivated to change their behaviour with respect to their seizures, unless they are not in favour of having neurosurgery. The clinical psychologist working in an epilepsy service is in an ideal position to identify these possible treatment conflicts and help streamline patient care so that treatment approaches can be attempted in a more scientific and rational manner.

Anti-epileptic drugs (AEDs)

It is clear that the evaluation of anti-epileptic drug effects on cognition and behaviour will continue, but the way in which the issue is addressed would benefit from some considerable refinement. Studies need to be more specific about the particular population they are involving with respect to age, ability level, seizure type, epilepsy syndrome, etc. As far as contributing to the debate about which drug is best to use and least likely to impair cognition/behaviour, this sort of information will only come from studies comparing one drug with another.

Perhaps, more importantly, clinical psychologists need to be able to make an informed opinion about the impact of an AED on the individual, as well as the effect of changes in medication regimens.

Quality of life (QoL)

We can anticipate that studies relating to QoL will burgeon in the coming years. Issues that we would like to see addressed would include the relationship between psychological disorder and QoL in people with epilepsy, the relationship between different types of service provision and QoL, and some investigation of the factors that are important to the QoL in people who have learning disabilities and epilepsy – not to mention children, who so far have not featured in any of the QoL studies reviewed by Kendrick (Chapter 8). The relationship between a successful outcome of psychological intervention and quality of life for the individuals concerned would be an interesting study. It is hoped that the QoL of life work will also be used to inform new service developments for people with epilepsy.

Behaviour problems in children

The intervention approaches outlined in Chapter 10 have yet to be evaluated in this clinical group. In many respects, it is essential that intervention/management programmes are developed and evaluated in order to enhance further our understanding of the nature of such problems in epilepsy.

The literature exploring the risk factors for the development of behaviour problems in children with epilepsy has highlighted possible approaches to intervention; these now need to be put to the test in order to determine both the appropriateness of the model and the efficacy of the treatment. As yet, we are not in a position to identify those children who are most likely to develop behaviour problems, but even without this knowledge, there is scope for developing early intervention programmes by looking, for example, at parental management.

Learning disabilities

We can only emphasise again how sadly neglected the area of learning disabilities has been in the epilepsy literature as a whole. As has been described in Chapter 11, we know very little about the impact of epilepsy in people with learning disabilities, or the significance of this to their carers. Is the concept of stigma applicable here? As yet, it is unclear whether there is a greater prevalence of behaviour problems in people with epilepsy and learning disabilities than in their counterparts without epilepsy. While Espie *et al.* (1989) suggest that there is, this is refuted by Deb and Hunter (1991) and in our own work in children (Jones and Cull 1993).

Indeed, in the latter two studies, adaptive behaviours were poorer in people with epilepsy, but there was no difference in respect of behaviour problems. This work needs to be expanded, as it may well be that there are differences between people with mild, and those with severe, learning disabilities in this respect.

At the time of writing, a growing interest in the needs of people with learning disabilities and epilepsy is very much in evidence and has been highlighted by Brown *et al.* (1993). It is hoped that this will have a major impact on both research opportunities and clinical practice.

Family issues

It is evident to the clinician that a diagnosis of epilepsy does not solely effect the individual concerned, but can have a major impact on their family, as has been described for children (West 1986) and for the families of adults with epilepsy (Thompson and Upton 1992). However, these effects have been the subject of very little systematic research interest, and the work that has been done has focused predominantly on children with epilepsy (see Chapter 10).

Questions that need to be addressed include how the family and/or other carers adapt to the diagnosis; whether the type of response depends on whether the diagnosis is made in childhood, or in adulthood, or whether the epilepsy is idiopathic or acquired following a brain injury; how parents, siblings and children react to the diagnosis, and how this affects their interactions with the person with epilepsy. While there is some limited information in this area, there is even less on family responses to the occurrence of non-epileptic seizures, although this is a developing field (see Moore *et al.* 1994). However, whether seizures are epileptic or non-epileptic, it is clearly important to have some understanding of families' attributions of seizure genesis and seizure control. Such information is essential for the practising clinician who may need to work in collaboration with the family when looking at the management of childhood behaviour problems, psychological approaches to seizure control, interventions for serious psychological disorders, and post-surgery adjustment. There is also a need to consider whether epilepsy presents an additional stressor in families caring for someone who also has learning disabilities, has suffered a traumatic brain injury, or has a neurodegenerative illness such as Alzheimer's Disease.

CONCLUSIONS

We hope that we have demonstrated how significant the contribution of clinical psychologists has been to date, and will be in the future, in furthering our understanding of the nature of epilepsy. In view of this, they need to be considered as essential members of any epilepsy service. In order to further develop the role of the clinical psychologist in this area, psychologists need to be undertaking relevant clinical work, but within the framework of formal research protocols based on sound experimental design, with a view to publishing findings in order to better inform subsequent clinical practice.

REFERENCES

Aldenkamp, A. P. and Vermeulen, J. (1991) 'Neuropsychological rehabilitation of memory function in epilepsy', *Neuropsychological Rehabilitation* 1: 199–214.

Alderman, N. (1996) 'Central executive deficit and response to operant conditioning methods', *Neuropsychological Rehabilitation* 6: 161–86.

Andrews, D. J. and Schonfeld, W. H. (1992) 'Predictive factors for controlling seizures using a behavioural approach', *Seizure* 1: 111–16.

Baxendale, S. and Thompson, P. (1996) 'Test of spatial memory and its clinical utility in presurgical assessment', *Epilepsia* 37 (Suppl. 4): S32.

Becu, M., Becu, N., Menzur, G. and Kochen, S. (1993) 'Self-help epilepsy groups: an evaluation of the effect on depression and schizophrenia', *Epilepsia* 34: 841–5.

Brown, S., Betts, T., Chadwick, D., Hall, B., Shorvon, S. and Wallace, S. (1993) 'An epilepsy needs document', *Seizure* 2: 91–103.

Deb, S. and Hunter, D. (1991) 'Psychopathology of people with mental handicap and epilepsy. I: Maladaptive behaviour', *British Journal of Psychiatry* 159: 822–6.

DiIorio, D., Faherty, B. and Manteuffel, B. (1994) 'Epilepsy self-management: partial replication and extension', *Research in Nursing and Health* 17: 167–74.

Espie, C. A., Pashley, A. S., Bonham, K. G., Sourindhrin, I. and O'Donavan, M. (1989) 'The mentally handicapped person with epilepsy: a comparative study investigating psychosocial functioning', *Journal of Mental Deficiency Research* 33: 123–35.

Gehlert, S. (1994) 'Perceptions of control in adults with epilepsy', *Epilepsia* 31: 81–8.

Gillham, R. (1990) 'Refractory epilepsy: an evaluation of psychological methods in out-patient management', *Epilepsia* 31: 427–32.

Goldstein, L. H., Bernard, S., Fenwick, P. B. C., Burgess, P. W. and McNeil, J. (1993) 'Unilateral frontal lobectomy can product strategy application disorder', *Journal of Neurology, Neurosurgery and Psychiatry* 56: 274–6.

Helgeson, D. C., Mitan, R., Tan, S-Y. and Chayasirisobhon, S. (1990) 'Sepulveda epilepsy education: the efficacy of a psychoeducational treatment program in treating medical and psychosocial aspects of epilepsy', *Epilepsia* 31: 75–82.

Incisa della Rochetta, A., Gadian, D. G., Connelly, A., Polkey, C. E., Jackson, G. D., Watkins, K. E., Johnson, C. L., Mishkin, M. and Vargha-Khadem, F. (1995) 'Verbal memory impairment after right temporal lobe surgery: role of contralateral damage as revealed by 1H magnetic resonance spectroscopy and T2 relaxometry', *Neurology* 45: 797–802.

Jones, S. and Cull, C. A. (1993) 'Behavior in children with a severe learning difficulty and epilepsy', *Epilepsia* 34 (Suppl. 2): S22.

Kirkpatrick, P. J., Morris, R., Syed, G. M. S. and Polkey, C. E. (1993) 'Cortical activation during a cognitive challenge in patients with chronic temporal lobe epilepsy – a dynamic SPECT study', *Behavioural Neurology* 6: 187–92.

Mathers, C. B. (1992) 'Group therapy in the management of epilepsy', *British Journal of Medical Psychology* 65: 279–87.

Miller, L. (1994) 'Psychotherapy of epilepsy: seizure control and psychosocial adjustment', *Journal of Cognitive Rehabilitation* 12: 14–30.

Moore, P. M., Baker, G. A., McDade, G., Chadwick, D. and Brown, S. W. (1994) 'Epilepsy, pseudoseizures and perceived family characteristics: a controlled study', *Epilepsy Research* 18: 75–83.

Ragan, C. and Seides, M. (1990) 'The synthetic use of movement and verbal psychoanalytic psychotherapies', *Journal of the American Academy of Psychoanalysis* (Special issue: 'Psychoanalysis and severe emotional illness') 18: 115–30.

Randolf, C., Golds, J. M., Zorora, E., Cullum, C. M., Hermann, B. P. and Wyler, A. (1994) 'Estimating memory function disparity of Wechsler Memory Scale–Revised and California Verbal Learning Test indices in clinical and normal samples', *Clinical Neuropsychologist* 8: 99–108.

Reiter, J., Andrews, D. and Janis, C. (1987) *Taking Control of Your Epilepsy. A Workbook for Patients and Professionals*, Santa Rosa: Basics Publishing Company.

Rousseau, A., Hermann, B. and Whitman, S. (1985) 'Effects of progressive relaxation on epilepsy: analysis of a series of cases', *Psychological Reports* 57: 1203–12.

Spector-Oron, S., Goldstein, L. H. and Cull, C. A. (1993) 'Self-control of seizures in adults with epilepsy', *Epilepsia* 34 (Suppl. 2): S79.

Tan, S-Y. and Bruni, J. (1986) 'Cognitive-behaviour therapy with adult patients with epilepsy: a controlled outcome study', *Epilepsia* 27: 255–63.

Thompson, P. J. and Upton, D. (1992) 'The impact of chronic epilepsy on the family', *Seizure* 1: 43–8.

Usiskin, S. (1993) 'The role of counselling in an out-patient epilepsy clinic: a three year study', *Seizure* 2: 111–14.

von Cramon, D. Y. and Matthes-von Cramon, G. (1994) 'Back to work with a chronic dysexecutive syndrome? (A case report)', *Neuropsychological Rehabilitation* 4: 399–417.

von Cramon, D. Y., Matthes-von Cramon, G. and Mai, N. (1991) 'Problem-solving deficits in brain injured persons; a therapeutic approach', *Neuropsychological Rehabilitation* 1: 45–64.

Walton, N. H., Goodman, C. S., Bird, J. M., Sandeman, D. R., Butler, S. R. and Curry, S. H. (1996) 'The Burden maze as a measure of nonverbal memory in epilepsy', *Epilepsia* 37 (Suppl. 4): S30.

West, P. (1986) 'The social meaning of epilepsy: stigma as a potential explanation for psychopathology in children', in S. Whitman and B. P. Hermann (eds), *Psychopathology in Epilepsy: Social Dimensions*, New York: Oxford University Press.

Wood R. Ll. and Eames, P. (1981) 'Applications of behaviour modification in the rehabilitation of traumatically brain-injured patients', in G. Davey (ed.) *Applications of Conditioning Theory*, London: Methuen.

Appendix

NEUROPSYCHOLOGICAL, COGNITIVE AND DEVELOPMENTAL TESTS

The tests listed below were referred to in Chapters 2, 3, 4, 5 and 9. The purpose of this appendix is to provide ease of access to these tests; dates of publication are given where indicated in publishers' catalogues, etc. The tests are listed in alphabetical order of test names, rather than authors.

'The Abilities of Young Children', (Griffiths, R. 1986) High Wycombe: Test Agency Limited.

'Adult Memory and Information Processing Battery (AMIPB)', (Coughlan, A. J. and Hollows, S. 1985), Leeds: St James' University Hospital, A. J. Coughlan.

'Autobiographical Memory Interview (AMI)', (Kopelman, M. D., Wilson, B. A. and Baddeley, A. D. 1990) Bury St Edmunds, Suffolk: Thames Valley Test Company.

'Bayley Scales II', (Bayley, N. 1993) Sidcup: Psychological Corporation.

'Behavioural Assessment of Dysexecutive Syndrome (BADS)', (Wilson, B. A., Alderman, N., Burgess, P., Emslie, H. and Evans, J. J. 1996) Bury St Edmunds, Suffolk: Thames Valley Test Company.

'Bender Visual Motor Gestalt Test', (Bender, E. 1946) Sidcup: Psychological Corporation.

'Benton Visual Retention Test, 5th edn', (Benton-Sivan, A. 1992) Sidcup: Psychological Corporation.

'Boston Naming Test, 2nd edn', (Kaplan, E. F., Goodglass, H. and Weintraub, S. 1983) Philadelphia: Lea and Febiger.

'British Ability Scales', (Elliot, C. D., Murray, D. J. and Pearson, L. S. 1983) Windsor UK: NFER-Nelson.

'British Picture Vocabulary Scale', (Dunn L. M., Dunn, L. M., Whetton C. with Pintilie D. 1983) Windsor UK: NFER-Nelson.

'California Verbal Learning Test for Children', (Delis, D. C., Kramer, J., Kaplan, E. and Ober, B. A. 1993) Sidcup: Psychological Corporation.

'California Verbal Learning Test (CVLT) Research Edition', (Delis, D. C.,

Kramer, J., Kaplan, E., Ober, B. A. and Fridlund, A. 1986) Sidcup: Psychological Corporation.

'Children's Category Test (CTT)', (Boll T. 1993) Sidcup: Psychological Corporation.

'Clinical Evaluation of Language Fundamentals' (revised edn, UK adaptation, CELF-R^{UK}), (Wiig, E. H. 1994) Sidcup: Psychological Corporation.

'Controlled Oral Word Association Test', (Benton, A. L. and Hamsher, K. deS. 1989) in Multilingual Aphasia Examination, Iowa City IA: AJA Associates.

'Diagnostic and Attainment Testing' (including 'Graded Word Vocabulary Test' and 'Graded Word Spelling Test'), (Schonell, F. J. and Schonell, F. E. 1956) Edinburgh: Oliver and Boyd Limited.

'Doors and People Test', (Baddeley, A. D., Emslie, H. and Nimmo-Smith, I. 1994) Bury St Edmunds, Suffolk: Thames Valley Test Company.

'Draw-a-Person. A Quantitative Scoring System', (Naglieri, J. A. 1987) Sidcup: Psychological Corporation.

'FePSY The Iron Psyche' v.5.0A, (Alpherts W. C. J. and Aldenkamp A. P. 1995) Instituut voor Epilepsiebestrijding, Achterweg 5, 2103 SW Heemstede, Netherlands.

'Graded Naming Test', (McKenna, P. and Warrington, E. K. 1983) Windsor UK: NFER-Nelson.

'Halstead-Reitan Neuropsychological Test Battery: Theory and Clinical Interpretation', (Reitan, R. M. and Wolfson, D. 1993) Tucson AZ: Neuropsychological Press.

'Leiter International Performance Scale', (Leiter, R. G. 1969) Florida: Psychological Assessment Resources.

'Luria-Nebraska Neuropsychological Battery', (Golden, C. J., Hammeke, T. A. and Purish, A. D. 1983) USA: Western Psychological Services.

'Multilingual Aphasia Examination', (Benton, A. L. and Hamsher, K. deS. 1989) Iowa City: AJA Associates.

'National Adult Reading Test' 2nd edn, (Nelson, H. with Willison, J. 1991) Windsor UK: NFER-Nelson.

'Oldfield-Wingfield Naming Test', (Oldfield, R. C. and Wingfield, A. 1965) MRC Psycholinguistic Research Unit Special Report No PLU/65/19: London: Medical Research Council.

'Pre-Verbal Communication Schedule (PVCS)', (Kiernan, C. and Reid, B. 1987) Windsor UK: NFER-Nelson.

'Recognition Memory Test', (Warrington, E. K. 1984) Windsor UK: NFER-Nelson.

'Revised Token Test', (McNeil, M. M. and Prescott, T. E. 1978) Windsor UK: NFER-Nelson.

'Rey Auditory Verbal Learning Test', in 'Neuropsychological Assessment' 3rd edn, (Lezak, M. D. 1995) New York: Oxford University Press.

'Rey Complex Figure Test and Recognition Trial (RCFT)', (Meyers, J. E. and Meyers, K. R.) Florida: Psychological Assessment Resources.

'Rivermead Behavioural Memory Test', (Wilson, B. A., Coburn, J. and Baddeley, A. D. 1995) Bury St Edmunds, Suffolk: Thames Valley Test Company.

'Rivermead Behavioural Memory Test for Children Aged 5–10', (Wilson, B. A.,

Ivani-Chalian, R. and Aldrich, F. 1991) Bury St Edmunds, Suffolk: Thames Valley Test Company.
'Speed and Capacity of Language Processing (SCOLP)', (Baddeley, A. D., Emslie, H. and Nimmo-Smith, I. 1992) Bury St Edmunds, Suffolk: Thames Valley Test Company.
'Standford-Binet Intelligence Scale – Manual (Form L-M)', (Terman, L. M. and Merrill, M. A. 1972) Trowbridge: Redwood Press Limited.
'Stroop Colour and Word Test', (Golden, C.) Florida: Psychological Assessment Resources.
'Stroop Neuropsychological Screening Test', (Trenerry, M. R., Crosson, B., DeBoe, J. and Leber, W. R. 1989) Windsor UK: NFER-Nelson.
'Symbolic Play Test' 2nd edn, (Lowe, M. and Costello, A. J. 1988) Windsor UK: NFER-Nelson.
'Test of Everyday Attention (TEA)', (Robertson, I. H., Ward, T., Ridgeway, V. and Nimmo-Smith, I. 1994) Bury St Edmunds, Suffolk: Thames Valley Test Company.
'Test for Reception of Grammar (TROG)' 2nd edn, (Bishop, D. 1989) Manchester: Age and Cognitive Performance Research Centre, University of Manchester M13 9PL, UK.
'Token Test for Children', (Disimoni, F. 1978) Allen TX: DLM Teaching Resources.
'Visual Object and Space Perception Battery (VOSP)', (Warrington, E. K. and James, M. 1991) Bury St Edmunds, Suffolk: Thames Valley Test Company.
'Vineland Adaptive Behaviour Scales', (Sparrow, S. S., Balla, D. A. and Cicchetti, D. V. 1984) Minnesota: American Guidance Services.
'Wechsler Adult Intelligence Scale', revised UK edn (WAIS-R[UK]), (Wechsler, D. 1986) Sidcup: Psychological Corporation.
'Wechsler Intelligence Scale for Children', 3rd UK edn (WISC-III[UK]), (Wechsler, D. 1991) Sidcup: Psychological Corporation.
'Wechsler Memory Scale', revised (WMS-R), (Wechsler, D. 1987) Sidcup: Psychological Corporation.
'Wechsler Pre-School and Primary Scale of Intelligence' revised UK edn (WPPSI-R[UK]), (Wechsler, D. 1990) Sidcup: Psychological Corporation.
'Wide Range Assessment of Memory and Learning (WRAML)', (Adams, W. and Sheslow, D.) Florida: Psychological Assessment Resources.
'Winconsin Card Sorting Test' (Grant, D. A. and Berg, E. A. 1981, 1993) Windsor UK: NFER-Nelson.

CONTRIBUTORS' ADDRESSES

Gus A. Baker
Lecturer in Clinical Neuropsychology and Health Psychology
University Department of Neurosciences
Walton Centre for Neurology and Neurosurgery
Rice Lane, Liverpool L9 1AE

Christine Cull
Clinical Psychologist, Learning Disabilities Service
Mid Anglia Community Health NHS Trust, Haverhill Health Centre
Camps Road, Haverhill, Suffolk CB9 8HF

Colin A. Espie
Professor of Clinical Psychology, Department of Psychological Medicine
Gartnavel Royal Hospital (Academic Centre)
1055 Great Western Road, Glasgow G12 0XH

Maria Fowler
Principal Psychologist, St Piers Lingfield
St Piers Lane, Lingfield, Surrey RH7 6PW

Ruth Gillham
Consultant Clinical Psychologist, Southern General Hospital
1345 Govan Road, Glasgow G51 4TF

Laura H. Goldstein
Senior Lecturer in Neuropsychology, Institute of Psychiatry
De Crespigny Park, London SE5 8AF

Anna Kendrick
Associate Lecturer, The Open University
24 Cathedral Road, Cardiff CF1 9SL

Susan Oxbury
Consultant Clinical Psychologist, Radcliffe Infirmary NHS Trust
Woodstock Road, Oxford OX2 6HE

Audrey Paul
Research Psychologist, Epilepsy Research Unit
Western Infirmary
Glasgow G11 6NT

Pamela J. Thompson
Head of Psychology Services, The National Society for Epilepsy
Chalfont St. Peter, Gerrards Cross, Bucks SL9 0RJ

Index

Reynolds, E.H. and Shorvon,
 S.D. 187
Ribbler, A. and Rausch, R. 20
Richens, A. and Perucca, E. 13–15
Ritchie, K. 174
Rivermead Behavioural Memory Test
 28, 47, 161
Rivotril 14
Rix, K. 179
Robertson, M.M. *et al* 99
Rodin, E.A. 151, 184; *et al* 132, 151,
 152, 156
Rosenberg, M. 136
Ross, E.M. *et al* 149
Roulet Perez, E. *et al* 170
Rourke, B.P. *et al* 152, 161
Rousseau, A. *et al* 105, 116, 206
Rugland, A.-L. *et al* 29, 162
Russell, W.R. and Whitty, C.W.M. 6
Rutter, M. *et al* 150
Ryan, R. *et al* 102

Sabers, A. 151
Sabril 14
Sagar, H.J. and Oxbury, J.M. 59, 62
Saling, M. *et al* 20, 22, 25, 60
Sander, J.W.A.S., *et al* 8; and Hart,
 Y.M. 87
Sass, K.J. *et al* 20, 21, 60, 61, 196
Scambler, G. 98, 102, 106, 107, 131;
 and Hopkins, A. 97, 98, 99, 132
Scheepers, B. *et al* 122, 123
Schonell Graded Word Reading
 test 67
Schonell Graded Word Spelling
 test 67
Scott, D.F. and Moffett, A. 85
Scoville, W. and Milner, B. 59, 63
Seidenberg, M. 154, 155; *et al* 20, 23,
 25, 26, 29, 150, 151
Seizure Severity Scale 136
seizures: absence 10; approaches to
 psychological management of
 115–21; atonic 10; and behaviour
 170–1; and biofeedback 121;
 classification of 9–12; and
 cognitive impairment 25–7;
 complex partial 9, 125, 190;

countermeasures for 118; evoked
 114; focal 54, 113, 205; frequency
 of 115, 152–3, 169, 187;
 generalised 10–12, 25; impact of
 on children 157–9; and lifestyle
 125–6; and memory loss 38–40;
 multi-component psychological
 approaches to 118–21; myoctonic
 10; partial 9–10, 25; practical
 guide to 124–6; psychogenic,
 primary and secondary 113–14;
 psychological treatment of 196–7;
 psychological understanding of
 113–15; psychomotor 117, 153;
 recording systems 124–5;
 refractory 116, 196; and relaxation
 techniques 116–18; self-induced
 114, 115, 185, 191–2, 197; simple
 partial 9; stress-induced 115, 117;
 tension/anxiety-induced 115, 117;
 tonic-clonic 10; *see also* epilepsy
Selai, C.E. and Trimble, M.R. 141
selective amygdalohippocampectomy
 (SAH) 57, 59, 62
Selective Reminding Test (SRT) 20,
 60, 61, 68, 89
self-esteem 102–3
Selwa, L.M. *et al* 24, 26
Serial Subtraction 83
serum drug levels 14–15
sexual abuse 122, 191
Sheth, R.D. *et al* 85, 172
Shortened Token Test 63
Shorvon, S.D. 7
Sickness Impact Profile (SIP) 135, 143
Sieblink, B.M. *et al* 27
Siegel, M. *et al* 114
Sieveking, E.H. 35
Silverstein, F.S. *et al* 172
Singh, B.K. and Towle, P.O. 184
Single Photon Emission
 Computerized Tomography
 (SPECT) 13, 204
Slater, E. and Beard, A.W. 101
Smith, D.F. *et al* 87, 88, 98, 99,
 136, 144
Smith, M.L. and Milner, B. 59
Snyder, P.J. *et al* 58

Crazy Love

ALSO BY LESLIE MORGAN STEINER

Mommy Wars: Stay-at-Home and Career Moms
Face Off on Their Choices, Their Lives, Their Families

Crazy Love

---◆---

A MEMOIR

---◆---

Leslie Morgan Steiner

St. Martin's Press New York

CRAZY LOVE. Copyright© 2009 by Leslie Morgan Steiner.
All rights reserved. Printed in the United States of
America. For information, address St. Martin's Press,
175 Fifth Avenue, New York, N.Y. 10010.

www.stmartins.com

Library of Congress Cataloging-in-Publication Data

Steiner, Leslie Morgan.
    Crazy love : a memoir / by Leslie Morgan Steiner.
        p. cm.
    ISBN-13: 978-0-312-37745-8 (alk. paper)
    ISBN-10: 0-312-37745-2 (alk. paper)
    1. Steiner, Leslie Morgan.   2. Abused wives—United
States—Biography.   3. Abused women—United States—
Case studies.   4. Family violence—United States.
I. Title.
    HV6626.2.S737 2008
    362.82'92092—dc22
    [B]
                                        2008034018

10   9   8   7   6   5   4   3   2

Crazy Love is a personal history. The events described in this book are real, backed up by police reports, restraining order documentation, family court, and other legal records. Many names, except for my own, as well as several geographic, chronologic, and identifying details, have been changed for the usual reasons of privacy and security. A few characters have been omitted and combined; the character of Winnie represents an amalgam of important friends.

To my husband, for understanding why I needed
to write this book

For Elin, who knew

In memory of Marilyn

For my mother, who was always there

IF YOU AND I MET AT ONE OF OUR CHILDREN'S birthday parties, in the hallway at work, or at a neighbor's barbecue, you'd never guess my secret: that as a young woman I fell in love with and married a man who beat me regularly and nearly killed me.

I don't look the part. I have an M.B.A. and an undergraduate degree from Ivy League schools. I live in a redbrick house on a tree-lined street in one of the prettiest neighborhoods in Washington, D.C. I've got fifteen years of marketing experience at Fortune 500 companies and a bestselling book about motherhood to my name. A smart, loyal husband with a sexy gap in his front teeth, a softie who puts out food for the stray kittens in our alley. Three rambunctious, well-loved children. A dog and three cats of our own. Everyone in my family is blond (the people, at least).

Ah, if only being well-educated and blond and coming from a good family were enough to defang all of life's demons.

If I were brave enough the first time I met you, I'd try to share what torture it is to fall in love with a good man who cannot leave a violent past behind. I'd tell you why I stayed

for years, and how I finally confronted someone whose love I valued almost more than my own life. Then maybe the next time you came across a woman in an abusive relationship, instead of asking why anyone stays with a man who beats her, you'd have the empathy and courage to help her on her way.

We all have secrets we don't reveal the first time we cross paths with others. This is mine.

Book One

———◆———

I MET CONOR ON THE NEW YORK CITY SUBWAY, heading downtown, twenty years ago. I was twenty-two. I remember it like yesterday.

— —◦— —

The window in Kathy's office was the only daylight I could see from my presswood desk in the hallway. I snuck a look. My ugly orange swivel chair squeaked.

It was a chilly, gray Monday afternoon in mid-January. The Midtown Manhattan skyscrapers were slick and dark with rain.

First thing that morning, Kathy—head of the articles department at *Seventeen* and the first boss I'd had in my life— held a meeting to dole out assignments for May. Then I interviewed a fidgety twelve-year-old Russian model who looked twenty-nine with makeup on. After that I ran out in the rain for lunch with the wacky British astrologer who wrote *Seventeen*'s monthly horoscope column.

I'd graduated from college the spring before on a day when Harvard Yard looked like the opening scene from a big-budget movie. Sun-dappled spring grass. My mom happy-drunk in a striped Vittadini wrap dress. My dad so proud I thought his

face would split open, beaming as only a poor Oklahoma boy with a daughter graduating from Harvard could.

The day so lovely I wanted to hold it forever in my hands.

Working at *Seventeen* was better than eating a Baskin-Robbins sundae. We read magazines all morning and talked about sticky teenaged paradigms on the clock. In the afternoons we raided the fashion closet—a huge room where the fashion editor kept designer samples that transformed gawky teenage ostriches into goddesses. I hated the few times I'd gotten sick and had to miss a day.

Outside *Seventeen* I roamed New York City as if it were my new backyard. Dinners at the Yaffa Café and Bombay Kitchen. Hours dancing with my roommate at Danceteria or Limelight. Even the most mundane activities—folding clothes at the fluorescent-lit Laundromat across Eighth Avenue, jogging through the Meatpacking District—became adventures.

But it was tricky getting the whole work thing down. Putting on panty hose like a uniform. No runs, my frantic morning mantra. Getting on the E train instead of the express to Harlem. Figuring out how to eat when my paycheck ran out six days before the next one was due.

Everything seemed so new.

I wrote and rewrote that afternoon at my desk in the hallway as the rain poured down outside Kathy's window. Every girl in America read *Seventeen* at some age. Nearly four million girls devoured each issue; some favorites became like

bibles for girls who had only a magazine to turn to for advice.

I should know.

Every day, often with little support or guidance, a teenage girl tackled staggering dilemmas. If your boyfriend offered drugs, did you do them? Did buying birth control make you a slut? Where did you get birth control at sixteen, anyway? What if your best friend drove drunk with you riding shotgun? Your stepfather came on to you? Your parents got divorced? Your mom got cancer?

My piece was slated for March, meaning I had to finish it by . . . Friday.

"Almost done?" Kathy barked as she whizzed by in her black patent-leather boots with three-inch heels. I jumped off my chair.

The story itself asked a simple enough question: Why do teenagers run away from home? But after poring over government statistics and interviewing social workers, psychiatrists, and the four runaways who would actually talk to me, I'd come to an awful understanding.

Of the estimated 1.5 million teenagers who hit the streets each year, the majority bolted because they thought any situation would be better than home.

Of those teenagers, 25 percent came from families with alcohol or drug abuse.

And 50 percent had been sexually or physically abused by someone in their household.

What kind of home was that?

The realization that broke my heart: All runaways start out fighting for a better life. The survival instinct that gave them the courage to leave bad homes made them try to turn the streets into a new home, the other runaways their families.

Within months, two-thirds were using drugs and supporting themselves through prostitution. Close to a third didn't know where they'd sleep each night. One-half tried to commit suicide. Two-thirds ended up in jail or dead from illness, drug overdoses, or beatings by pimps, johns, or other homeless people.

When I finally looked up from the computer, I was the only one left at the office, feeling like I'd been ditched by the cool girls after school in eighth grade. My watch read six P.M. It seemed like midnight as I trudged to the subway in the rain.

Winnie took forever to unlock the three deadbolts from behind her apartment door.

We hugged; she was only five feet two inches, so the top of her head butted against my chin. As always, her hair smelled like honeysuckle.

I dropped my purse in the foyer and started unlacing my L.L. Bean duck boots, indispensable during the snowy Cambridge winters and slushy springs. Ridiculous footwear now that I lived in the fashion capital of the planet.

"How was work?" she asked. Winnie (short for Winthrop—I'm not kidding) was wearing a white cotton shirt with a high ruffled collar, threaded with a pale cream sliver of silk, tucked into a long brown suede skirt.

"Great . . . I'm writing about teen runaways."

I shook the wet boots off my stocking feet. I had a harder time shaking off the images of the fourteen-year-old girl I'd interviewed for my story. The one who slept on a subway grate and blew her hair dry in a corner of the Trailways bus terminal next to the pay phone she refused to pick up to call home.

"So how was your work, Win?"

She was a salesgirl at the Polo Mansion at Seventy-second and Madison selling outrageously priced Ralph Lauren clothes to celebrities. She had to wear all Ralph Lauren clothes. Blond Wasp perfection every day.

"Oh, God, it's a long day when you're on your feet trying to smile at all those rich assholes."

Something on the stove started hissing like an angry cat.

"Fuck!" she yelled. Even in fourth grade, she swore like a thirty-five-year-old divorcée. I followed her into the tiny kitchen.

She took the pot off the burner and turned back, smiling. Even Winnie's teeth were cute. That was one of the first things I noticed the day she showed up at elementary school. Over the years she taught me the following life essentials: how to shave my legs with Vitabath Spring Green, sleep until noon, and look up sex words in the dictionary. I loved

wearing her preppy clothes, smelling like Winnie's laundry detergent even if just for a day.

The year I turned thirteen I grew four inches, began smoking pot, drinking tequila, and dating older guys. I totally outgrew Winnie's entire closet. Her Lacoste shirts wouldn't cover my belly button anymore.

When I drank, she was one of my favorite people to call late at night. "I love you, Winnie," I would slur into the phone. She was always pretty nice about those calls.

"Look!" She held out her left hand, fingers splayed, so I could get a full view of her sparkly new engagement ring.

"Congratulations, Win. I am so happy for you."

I was even happier for Rex, her fiancé. He'd get to smell her hair on their pillow every night for the rest of his life.

"I always knew he was right, even at that Trinity frat party when I first met him," Winnie said as she spooned fresh pesto into a blue enamel pasta bowl. She didn't say what I knew mattered most: Rex loved her, but not with that "My life is nothing without you" desperation that drove her crazy. A parade of high-school boyfriends had gotten Velcroed to her in exactly the same way I had as a kid. They always ended up needing her too much. I'd watched her peel them off one by one, like bubble gum stuck to her shoe.

I looked around their small apartment, filled with Winnie's Ralph Lauren fabrics and Rex's dark leather furniture. Winnie was supposed to live with me, our reunion following four years at different colleges, my chance to prove I'd be-

come sober and responsible and likable again, right? Then at the beginning of last summer, while she waited for me to move to New York, she stayed in this apartment with Rex. Just for a few weeks, she'd said.

Audrey, the roommate I eventually found in Chelsea, was great. But here's what I wanted to ask Winnie tonight: Couldn't she postpone marriage for a few years, so that we could be roommates, to give me a chance to catch up? If I wasn't right for her as a roommate, how on earth was I going to meet a man right for me? A man like Rex who might ask me to stay for a few weeks and then ask me to stay forever.

Instead I said, "Wow, the ring is beautiful." It was.

We sat down to eat and she gave me the blow-by-blow on how Rex proposed on the beach during their New Year's trip to St. Barts.

As we stood side by side in her miniscule kitchen afterward, washing the dishes in hot, soapy water that smelled like lemons, Winnie asked how my love life was.

"Kind of anticlimactic compared to yours," I said. "All that matters to men here is how much money they make and where they live."

"Trust me, every guy who walks into the Polo Mansion tells me within thirty seconds about his address and income bracket. Please." She shook her head and laughed, crinkling the snub nose that was the envy of every girl in high school, including me. I reached into the soapy water and grabbed a bunch of silverware.

"I meet them all over the place, Win. At parties and clubs, of course. Just last week I met a guy on the bus. Someone asked me out while I was standing in line for the bathroom at Isabella's. Another guy tried to pick me up while I was jogging around the Reservoir. They're *everywhere*."

She handed me a pot to dry.

"For the first time in my life, I have this rule—one of the things I learned when I stopped drinking—" My voice cracked. I bet my face looked like a tomato. I kept talking. "—is that I will never date a man to satisfy some need of mine or someone who wants me to fill a desperate need of his."

The words sounded like cheap cardboard. But Winnie nodded, her brown eyes big and reassuring.

"I don't have sex with them, Win. We don't even kiss. We talk. For hours. In restaurants I could never afford on my salary."

She laughed.

"You know, it sounds so innocent, Les. And really fun. It's just what you need right now, right?"

She flicked soap at my face and a few suds landed on my nose.

Yep, just what I needed. But not what I wanted.

After another congratulatory hug, I headed out into the cold rainy night, exchanging Winnie's warm, bright apartment for the manicured Upper East Side streets. The heavy doors of the million-dollar brownstones, locked and festooned with

polished brass knockers, seemed to declare that everyone in New York was safe at home.

Except for me.

Sleet slapped my cheeks during the long walk to the Fifty-third Street subway. Before I ran through the turnstile to catch the train, I glimpsed myself in the token-booth window. With my wet hair hanging in dirty-blond corkscrews and wearing my old blue down coat, I looked more like a kid than a magazine editor.

The subway doors opened and I squeezed into a slippery neon-yellow subway seat. I was sandwiched between a handsome, neatly dressed older man with thick blond hair and a heavyset Latina woman with grocery bags who smelled like day-old enchiladas and cigarette smoke. At Forty-second Street, she got off along with most of the car, heaving with the effort of carrying the paper bags.

The subway felt suddenly empty—except for the blond man whose arm was now touching my elbow. I didn't slide away from him into a free seat, as every other person who'd lived in New York for five seconds would. I thought it'd be too rude.

It meant something to Conor that I did not move away from him, he told me much later.

He was wearing a dark blue cashmere coat, the navy at

his throat cutting a sharp contrast to his wheat-colored hair and shiny, fresh-scrubbed farm boy face. He wasn't as old as I thought—maybe late twenties, early thirties. He smiled.

"Hi. What's your name?" He had clean, straight teeth. I'd been in New York long enough to know that if you encouraged men on the subway, things got ugly fast. But this man felt instinctively safe, strangely familiar. How bad could he be? I told him my first name and buried my face back in *Vanity Fair.*

"Leslie, hi. My name is Conor," he said politely.

I glanced up briefly, intrigued by his persistence. I looked like a sewer rat. What could he possibly see in me?

He smiled again. "Do you work in the city?"

For a second he looked like my dad asking how I liked Harvard.

I couldn't help responding with pride.

"I work at *Seventeen*—you know, the magazine?"

"Oh, interesting . . . I work at Block Moore—you know, the investment bank?"

The only reason I'd even heard of this bank was because my freshman roommate, Lee, had several ex-boyfriends who worked there. Harvard grads who'd been captain of the football team, the hockey team, the most confident, effusive men on campus. Not boys I ever would have dated for a million reasons—mostly because in college I could barely speak to guys, much less go on dates with them. They always called after Lee dumped them, to cry on the nicey-nice roommate's shoulder and get some vicarious thrill from talking to the next

best thing when Lee had gotten so sick of their pathetic late-night missives that she stopped returning their calls.

The train slowed as we entered Penn Station. I knew this man—Conor—had volunteered the name of his Wall Street firm to vouch for his credibility, proof that he wasn't a psycho subway killer. He stood and shrugged his body to straighten his expensive coat. Then he turned to me one more time, his left hand holding the silver subway pole for balance.

No wedding ring.

"I live in Jersey now, but I'm moving to a great place on East Eighty-second. My roommate and I are gonna have a party. Maybe I'll call and invite you."

"Sure," I said. The freckles across his nose made him look like a little boy, expectant, trying to seem cool and kind of arrogant. I didn't respond. I wasn't volunteering my phone number to someone I'd sat next to for six minutes on the New York subway. The doors closed behind him. I watched the back of his blond head through the cracked subway window as he walked away.

As the train pulled out, I saw a sign carved into the brick wall of the subway station, directing commuters left to Penn Station, right to Herald Square. I bet my grandfather Sammie—my mother's father—passed this same sign a hundred times on the way to his office on Thirty-fourth Street sixty years ago. After graduating from Harvard in 1929, he became a

vice-president at Macy's, a marketing boy wonder who lived in Strawberry Hill, a seventy-two-room fieldstone castle overlooking the Hudson River. He ordered custom-built automobiles from England during the Depression when most men couldn't afford to feed their families. I could imagine him walking through the brick subway tunnel, wearing the black coat and hat that Winnie and I used to play with on rainy days in my grandmother's attic.

When I looked up again, the train had screeched to a stop at my station. At the exit to Twenty-third Street, I stepped over a homeless man lying on a stained cardboard box. Even passed out, he clutched an empty bottle of Jack Daniel's with his unwashed hand, fingernails black with grime. Was he somebody's grandfather, too?

The rain had let up and the temperature must have risen ten degrees since I'd left Winnie's. Eighth Avenue was slick with iridescent pools of water and the night air had a humid feel as if the fog were wisps of cotton you could reach out and touch. I walked from the subway to my apartment on West Nineteenth Street, past couples spilling out of the corner diner, taxis splashing through puddles, the shuttered Off-Track Betting window, the funky, neon-lit Man Ray sushi place.

Whenever I asked about Sammie, Mom would smile and look away. She always repeated the same words: "I loved my father so much." Despite the fact that one December when she was eight, Sammie, searching for cash for a bender, stole the money she'd stashed under the ballroom rug to buy

Christmas gifts for her older brother and younger sister. Over the years he drank up all their money, and left my grandmother Frankie to support the family teaching at a local community college. Ten years later, after Frankie finally divorced him, he would walk the eleven miles from Manhattan to Strawberry Hill to visit Mom. His money went to alcohol, not train fare.

I'm not certain whether alcoholism killed my grandfather before or after I was born. I do know that he still worked at the Macy's Herald Square headquarters when he died. He lived there, too, in the basement. He was the janitor.

So I came by my predilection for addiction honestly, I suppose. I stole a pack of Marlboros from our fireplace mantel when I was twelve, held my nose while finishing off martinis at my parents' cocktail parties, and mastered inhaling when offered my first joint the summer after eighth grade. No one taught me these things. I just *knew*.

In high school, I wore myself down to a pencil nub by being an achievement-obsessed druggie, not the easiest combination to pull off. At school I pored over *Brave New World*, Maslow's hierarchy of needs, and derivative curves. I'd duck into a utility closet during study hall to make out with my boyfriend, whose main attribute was his ability to get me drugs on a regular basis. I craved numbing out the way some teenage girls love clothes shopping or lip-synching in front of their bathroom mirror.

On weekends, my father hid at his law office downtown and my mother tossed back rum and Cokes at our home in

Bethesda on a half-acre of hundred-year-old trees. My friends and I hit the bars in Georgetown—Scandal's, Mac's, the Saloon—where the drinking age was eighteen but girls as young as fifteen had no trouble slipping in. For the nights I stayed home, I kept a stash of treasures in my bathroom closet, behind a bottle of Herbal Essences shampoo and Tickle deodorant. A fifth of Spanish tequila, a Baggie of California sensimilla, and a carved wooden pipe sat nestled against a diaphragm from Planned Parenthood (I was a very responsible teenaged drug addict). When Mom and I were home alone, she'd eventually start calling me the Washington Whore, her idea of a good way to bring up a complicated subject. Although after a while I caught on that she was venting her own frustrations and childhood fears on me, at the time her rage cut like a razor.

Let's say it was clear something was wrong.

I tried to talk to my friends and teachers about Mom's drinking before I had any idea what addiction was, before I realized it was my problem, too. My first confidant was Robert Carrola, my friend Paul's handsome, disheveled father, who also happened to be my high-school chemistry teacher. I would find Mr. Carrola in the teachers' lounge in between classes. He always listened assiduously to each sobbing chapter of my troubled relationship with my mother. He came from a large, poor, close-knit Italian family. He blamed our problems on having had too much money for too long. If only it were that simple.

Mr. Carrola's willingness to listen was one of the acts of

kindness that saved me during my adolescence—the same way I tried to save the teenage girls who read *Seventeen*.

"Mr. Carrola," I sobbed one day, snot dripping out of my nose like a shoestring. "I am not going to hope anymore that she is going to stop drinking."

I was sixteen, hurt and angry and confused about Mom, finding solace in hash under glass and Marlboros encrusted with grains of white cocaine. I was proud of my attempts to become wise and jaded. My idea was to give up on Mom.

"Nah, Leslie," he said, shaking his head. He smiled; he looked like he'd been born with that smile on his face. He gave me a Kleenex and spread my hands wide open with his warm, callused ones as if trying to open up my heart as well.

"Hope is always good." He looked me in the face grinning, full of faith in me and in life. "You know, doctors always say the liver is the only organ that can regenerate itself. But they're wrong, Leslie. The heart can, too. Promise me you'll keep hoping."

Lucky I got into Harvard before I gave up St. Pauli Girls, drugs, and being an accomplished junkie. My freshman year, a woman named Hope—corny but true—took me to my first twelve-step meeting. I stopped drinking and using drugs cold turkey, right when most Harvard freshmen were discovering the joys of substance abuse. I ate three meals a day at the Freshman Union, went to class, took a lot of naps, and in between tried—awkwardly, desperately, with help from Hope and other people I met at meetings—to focus on how I felt on the inside, not what my life looked like from the outside.

This had the bizarre effect of making me feel like I was walking around campus stark naked. Back at home in Bethesda, things weren't much better: Spending more than forty-eight hours with my parents, their tinkling glasses of rum and Coke, and the ghosts of my childhood made me flee back to Cambridge with the hair standing up on the back of my neck. I ended up spending most vacations and holidays in my empty dorm.

After four years of this drama, I got a call from *Seventeen* offering to publish a piece I'd sent in a few months before about overcoming anorexia in high school (I know, I had so many problems it's hard to keep track of them all). Soon after, *Seventeen*'s articles department hired me to start work as an editor and writer following graduation.

Hope saw me off at South Station when I moved to New York. She'd spent months insisting that I could do this, I deserved this dream-come-true job, I needed to follow where life took me. As she said good-bye, Hope put her hands on my arms. Her fingers were warm through my cotton T-shirt. She squared my shoulders and looked into my eyes as if she were adjusting a picture frame with a carpenter's level.

"You know, Leslie, you've had a tough, but good, four years here," she told me in her cigarette-rough voice. "You worked hard to get sober—at eighteen, for chrissakes. You graduated from *Harvard*. The worst is behind you. You are going to be fine."

I hugged Hope good-bye.

Five hours later, I lugged a frayed black suitcase of my

dad's past the graffiti of Penn Station. Yellow cabs were honking and swerving crazily on Eighth Avenue in the summer twilight. More people than I'd ever seen at once, even at Fourth of July fireworks on the Mall in D.C., swarmed the streets around me. Everyone looked like they were in a big hurry to get wherever they were going. Except for me.

Six months later, it was like I'd been born again. None of the scars from my seedy teenaged druggie life showed on my face. I looked like an apple-cheeked girl straight out of college with a great job, a cool apartment in Chelsea, my first American Express card. Shockingly cute New York firemen at the station near *Seventeen* whistled at me as I walked home in a miniskirt and high heels borrowed from the fashion closet. Homeless people smiled at me. I went out almost every night on the cheap since I didn't need to buy drinks.

The kind of second chance almost no one gets.

I unlocked our basement apartment door, yanked off my boots, and hung up my drenched coat on the makeshift bookshelf in the hallway. My little Siamese slunk out of the bedroom and sniffed my wet laces suspiciously, as if conducting an inspection for microscopic and totally verboten specks of dog poo. My roommate from Savannah, Georgia— the one I found to replace Winnie—got up from our lime-green beanbag chair and handed me a stack of While You Were Out messages on one of the pink pads she'd snitched from the temp job she went to between auditions. She smiled the wholesome grin that was bringing in two-thousand-dollar residual checks from a Burger King commercial. Audrey had

become very skilled at answering the phone in a variety of character accents when the men I was dating called— Grace Kelly from *Rear Window*, Katharine Hepburn from *The Philadelphia Story*, Hattie McDaniel as Mammy in *Gone With the Wind*.

Oh, Hope was right. It was a fucking relief to start my life over, without drugs or alcohol just waiting to screw everything up. I was fine.

One afternoon a month or so later the chipped beige phone on my desk at *Seventeen* rang, the double ring that signaled an inside call. A woman named Lesley from the advertising department explained she had a guy on hold who must've been looking for me.

"He says he met you on the *subway*," Lesley chirped as if I were the only woman in New York who met men at places besides the library at the Princeton Club.

"The switchboard transferred him to me by mistake. I've talked to him for fifteen minutes. Fun guy. But I think he's got the wrong girl."

At least *I* meet men, I said to myself. I hung up and drummed my fingers while Snitty Face transferred the call.

"Leslie? Hi, this is . . . Conor. We met on the E train a few weeks back. . . . I've had a hell of a time tracking you down."

He paused to chuckle. His gravelly voice instantly brought back his attempt to be cool and arrogant on the subway, and the little-kid eagerness underneath. A delicious shiver went through me as I remembered how handsome he was and how he seemed so much older than he turned out to be. He'd tracked me down.

"So, my roommate and I are having that party, two weeks from Friday. I wanted to see if you'd like to make an appearance."

"Oh, I can't go that night," I explained nonchalantly. "An old client of my father's is taking my family to Vail for the weekend to thank him for some case that was just settled, that Dad worked on years ago before he became a judge."

In the moment of silence that followed, I could practically hear him raising his eyebrows. Of course I was trying to impress him: an expensive, athletic sport like skiing; a high-powered father; a weekend jaunt to Colorado.

Conor hesitated and then his voice deepened as if he'd cleared his throat.

"Well, why don't we get together some other time?"

Of course I was bluffing. What I'd said about my dad and the ski trip was true, but I'd left out a few facts. That my parents' thirty-two-year marriage was in free fall. That I'd spent most of my childhood cursing my father's devotion to his clients. That I was a lousy skier who often cried when confronted with steep moguls. That I was a drug addict, a slut, a liar.

I tried to remind myself that this guy called *me*, damn it.

"Sure." I kept my voice steady, casual. "How about a drink at P.J. Clarke's on Third?"

I was curious. One short drinks date near my office was no big investment.

"Great," he said, a little too quickly.

United Airlines lost my luggage and skis on the flight from New York to Vail. My father, brother Hugh, and sister Sylvia had all come along for the trip. For the first time I could remember, Mom stayed home from a family vacation, saying the autistic kids in her class would get rattled by a sub.

Mostly Hugh, Syl, and I hung out. They tried to trick me into skiing black diamonds when all I wanted were bunny slopes. My father was busy entertaining the client who'd brought us to Colorado. We saw him for maybe twenty minutes each day. I spotted him once from the chairlift, skiing his self-taught stem christies, and thought, "Wow, that looks like my father," before I remembered that *was* my father, he was in Vail, too.

On my way back to New York Sunday night, waiting in the taxi line at La Guardia Airport wearing my black Ray-Ban sunglasses and the rumpled jeans I'd flown/skied/slept in, I met a fortyish SoHo architect who looked just like Michael Douglas. We shared a cab into Manhattan. He asked for my number.

I couldn't remember what Conor looked like except for his navy cashmere coat and thick blond hair.

P.J. Clarke's was hot and crowded with loud young bucks in suits at the bar when I walked in a few minutes late. Conor was sitting alone at a small table for two. He was wearing a Brooks Brothers wool suit. A new leather briefcase sat on the floor by his feet. His hair looked freshly trimmed, his skin shiny clean as if he'd just scruffed it with Clinique Scruffing Lotion minutes before. He stood up when he saw me and took off his coat. Underneath he had on red suspenders and a carefully pressed red pinstripe shirt stretched tight across his chest as if he were trying to show off the size of his pecs.

Okay. Whatever.

He bought me a club soda. Then, instead of talking about himself incessantly like most men in New York on first dates, Conor asked me a string of questions, almost as if he were interviewing me, to be his—his what? I barely had time to breathe in between questions.

Where did you grow up?

What does your father do?

Do you have brothers and sisters?

Where did you go to school?

What'd you do in the summertime?

What sports did you play?

When I answered, of course I left out huge blocks of truth. Amazing how easy it was to make my childhood sound normal, idyllic even. The lovely springtime in Washington, Vermont summers, Harvard, skiing, tennis, blah blah blah.

In my defense, it *was* kind of difficult to explain to a first date my brilliant alcoholic mother, Dad the workaholic, how a whiff of Hawaiian sensimilla in a Greenwich Village park still made my knees buckle, and my double-digit one-night stands with teenaged drug dealers.

I drank my club soda and plotted a quick escape.

His face stayed locked on mine the entire time. I didn't have a chance to ask him one single question. After thirty minutes I drained my drink and got up to leave. Conor stood up so fast, he practically knocked over the table.

"Well, before you go, let me give you my number," he said, sounding like a used-car salesman.

Then, of all things, he pulled a résumé out of his brief-case. I stared at it in disbelief. The gang at *Seventeen* was going to *love* this one.

Right before I burst out laughing, he caught me off guard by laughing first.

"You can check me out," he said with a crooked, sexy smile, one side of his mouth grinning more than the other, showing his clean, strong teeth. "Then next time you can decide if you want to go on a real date with me."

Shouldn't he have been nervous that I was cutting the date short?

He laughed again, throwing his head back. He suddenly looked astonishingly handsome. The overeager boy had disappeared. The loud, smoky bar vanished behind him.

Too puzzled to say anything more than "Good night," I

folded his résumé and put it in my coat pocket before turning down Third Avenue to the subway.

When I got home, our garden apartment was cold and dark.
My Siamese was yowling her head off so loudly I could hear
her from the street. I'd gotten Criseyde the summer between
sophomore and junior year, my second year without beer and
a joint to see me through each day. I could barely carry on a
conversation with other human beings, which made roommates difficult. A cat, I could handle. Criseyde was so shy
the first time I visited the litter, I had to pull her out from behind a radiator. For the first week in my little studio apartment near the old Radcliffe dorms, she was a tiny lump
under my bedcovers. She ate by licking baby food off my finger. I was the only person she trusted. Now in Chelsea, she
went out into the backyard alone for hours, incredible bravery
given what a recluse she'd been in Cambridge.

A yellow note from Audrey stuck out from under the
brick we used as a doorstop, saying she was spending the
night at her boyfriend's.

I turned on some lights and taped Conor's cream-colored
résumé on the mirror of the massive mahogany bedroom set
Mom had given me, along with a jewelry box and a beautiful
old Hariz carpet, as part of my grandmother Frankie's estate
when she died the year I turned seventeen. I imagined what

I would have said to my grandmother if she were still alive. Like Sammie, Frankie died of alcoholism, at age seventy-six in a family where women traditionally lived alone and independently into their late nineties. She died in a hospital bed after breaking her hip in a drunken fall, killed twenty years too soon by alcohol withdrawal as much as by the infection that set into her hipbone. She was the first family member I knew who died. I was living in Madrid; the essay about that experience ended up front and center on my Harvard application. No one in my family suggested Frankie's death, or being there for Mom, might be significant enough to merit traveling across the ocean. I was too young to know better myself. I didn't come home for the funeral.

My father felt the annual real-estate taxes were prohibitive, so Mom had to sell Strawberry Hill, the childhood home Frankie had clung to after my grandfather disappeared into the streets of New York.

"You have to have something of hers," Mom had said a few months after the funeral, stroking the polished curves of the four-poster bed like you would a baby's soft head. She was as close to tears as I'd ever seen her. I went to hug her. She pulled back slightly, as if my touch would singe her skin.

"There were so many conversations I wanted to have with her," Mom said, looking down at the veins on her crossed hands. "She died too soon. You have to have this furniture to remind you of her."

Instead, Frankie's bedroom set reminded me of how my

mother found affection so unbearable. Mom always turned to alcohol, food, lavish birthday celebrations, cashmere sweaters on Christmas Day, wads of cash stuffed in my suitcase when I wasn't looking. As if words and physical contact were too powerful.

Or not powerful enough.

"So, been out with Subway Man much?" Winnie asked over the phone a few weeks later. She'd been in Italy on her first buying trip for Ralph Lauren. "I need a full update on your love life."

I put down the query from *Seventeen*'s slush pile I'd been reading when the phone rang.

"You know, that résumé move made me laugh every time I thought of it. We've been out a few times, once a week, I guess. He's cute, Winnie, but there's something . . . nervous under the surface."

"Such as?"

"He picks restaurants so carefully. It's like he's got a *Zagat's* guide: 'New York City—How-to-Impress-Your-Date Restaurants.' We've been to every one. Touristy places that try too hard. And he always pays cash . . . crisp twenties that look like he *ironed* them."

She giggled. "What's he like? Any fun?"

"He actually is fun—amusing in an offbeat, um, loner way. He hangs on every word I say. But it's weird, Win. I

can't tell you a thing about him. It's like he dropped out of the sky. He doesn't talk about family, friends. . . . All I know is he grew up in Massachusetts and graduated from college last year—which is strange because he's eight years older than we are. Lee's friends at his investment bank say he's a great guy, supersmart, the best trader on the desk, but they don't know jack shit about him either."

"I think he just got out of prison for abducting blond chicks he meets on the subways. He probably got his degree via one of those prison correspondence courses."

"Ha—very funny. At least he's not a product of Wasp inbreeding like some unmentionable recently engaged man I know."

"Touché," she snorted, trying to sound indignant, but I could hear her smiling on her end of the line.

"Anyway, I did have that architect I met at the airport wait in *Seventeen*'s lobby so Ann and Terri could walk by. They agree he looks just like Michael Douglas. He took me to lunch at Beekman Towers—you know, overlooking the U.N. in Midtown? He says he likes children but that they should be kept in a basement playroom, preferably soundproofed. 'Why not just get goldfish, then?' I asked him."

I'd made Winnie laugh. One of my favorite things to do.

"So then I met this investment banker at some party who took me to Smith & Wollensky—ever been there? I swear my steak lunch cost more than Audrey and I spend on food in a week. During lunch he asked me to test-drive his new Ferrari in Monza next month. How's that gonna work? Oh,

Winnie, Conor bores me. I am on the verge of not seeing him again."

"Boy, have you been busy!" she exclaimed. "I better not go on any more buying trips. I'll come back and you'll be fucking married with two kids."

Then she told me all about the fabrics she saw in Italy, and how all she could think about in Milan was what kind of silk she wanted for her wedding dress.

The March issue ran my runaways piece. I stopped by the newsstand at the Twenty-third and Eighth Avenue subway entrance just to stare at it in public. Perfect illustrations: shadowy silhouettes of teenage girls who should be in gym class instead of Times Square. True and gritty, not dark and glamorous like a slutty girl-band album cover.

Now I spent my days at *Seventeen* working on my first cover story. Kathy had assigned me a piece about why sex, drugs, and alcohol were actually harder on girls' bodies than boys'. Like the runaways piece, the facts told a decidedly unpretty story. As the head of the ob-gyn department at Mt. Sinai Hospital explained, women got V.D. more easily than men because of the moistness of our genital skin, alcohol hit us harder because of our lower body weights and higher percentage of body fat, and nicotine and other drugs mixed more potently with female hormones than male. Lovely.

The beauty editor stopped by my desk one afternoon to

ask if I had time to do a makeover. I thought she meant to write the copy. Then the stylist called to check dates at a local salon and I realized the makeover subject was *moi*. I felt like telling her that makeup and soft lighting couldn't compare to giving up alcohol and drugs.

I decided to deep-six Conor the next time he called. I met so many men, I was going out six nights a week. Sometimes lunch with one and dinner with another. Dating someone I wasn't completely into seemed silly.

Surprise. He didn't call. My old beige phone seemed never to ring. Did he somehow know I was bored with him? Was this a tactic to get my attention?

Then on a rare Friday night when I was too tired to go out and Audrey was snoozing at her boyfriend's, I had a dream.

Conor and I were driving in a beat-up, four-door vintage Ford, wide leather bench seats, no seat belts, cruising the empty streets of Wall Street and Lower Manhattan at dusk. The city was deserted. Conor turned the oversized, skinny steering wheel with one hand, looking like James Dean.

He kept his eyes on me as he drove, the blond hair falling over his left brow. I sat in the passenger seat mesmerized by the twists and turns the car took as if it were a Jet Ski gliding through placid water. Conor had lost all nervousness around me. We'd long ago stopped needing words to communicate. He pointed the nose of the car skyward and my stomach soared as we became airborne and flew around Manhattan's

skyscrapers as if the dream were taking place inside a blue-black Batman comic strip.

After driving for what seemed like hours, Conor slowly leaned over and smiled. His blue eyes never left mine. His right hand found the space between my legs, under the cheap black fabric of my miniskirt. I orgasmed beneath his hand, a rippling shudder, my entire body imploding from the hot touch of his fingers. At the same time the car exploded into tiny colorful bits like leftover confetti.

I woke up in my bed, alone in the sunny Saturday morning quiet. I lay under the covers almost unable to move. I hadn't had sex in more than four years—and never without being drunk or stoned. I'd only had a handful of orgasms in my life. Not ever in my sleep. Was such a phenomenon possible? I'd *never* heard of it, even when Dr. Ruth Westheimer came to Harvard Law School and talked about people who had sex with dogs and the importance of finding the right dildo.

Holy shit. Maybe I would go out with Conor again.

Seventeen shot my makeover on a Monday when the salon on Fifth Avenue was closed. The cut came first, really just a trim. Then the makeup. A muscular black man the size of a construction worker burst into the salon carrying a tiny bubblegum pink toolbox encrusted with fake jewels. He applied six to seven layers of makeup to my face along with dabs and

streaks of dark brown and black all around my eyes. I looked like a glamorous raccoon. A small crowd of tourists gathered outside the salon while we shot the photos. When I pushed open the heavy glass doors to leave, the crowd parted with a big "Ooh" as if I were a famous model. Either that or they were afraid I might grab one of their children to suck its blood.

The Friday before, Conor had finally called me at work. I could barely get the words out to tell him I was looking forward to seeing him. I agreed to a Monday night date. Tonight.

Suddenly, I felt tired of the new men in my life. Drained by the nervousness, the awkwardness, the lack of familiarity. I wanted one I could sit with in silence without twitching to think of witty stories or summoning up good night smiles so big and fake they hurt my cheeks. Someone who felt like family.

Speaking of family, I'd just gotten a huge cardboard box from my dad. Inside were five wool jackets he'd worn for the past twenty years, the way men rotate suits forever on a weekly basis, gray on Monday, navy blue on Tuesday. . . . After two decades the cuffs finally got frayed. He said he was going to throw them out. Then he thought about how I loved good fabric, how many new outfits I could buy on my puny salary, and sent the jackets to me instead of Goodwill. The suits were beautiful herringbone tweed in shades of black and blue and charcoal gray. I rolled up the sleeves and threw one on over a five-dollar T-shirt and a twenty-dollar

stretchy miniskirt, and presto! I could be in *Seventeen's* LOOKS UNDER $30 fashion spread. Best of all, the castoffs still smelled a little like him, that masculine wool-aftershave-cigar-smoke combination that made me feel as close to him as I was ever going to get.

On the way back to the office I jumped every time I saw my bizarre reflection in the Fifth Avenue store windows. Up on the ninth floor at *Seventeen,* I ducked past our security guard, Stitch, a retired postman, into the ladies' room before anyone spotted me. I went through an entire roll of cheap scratchy toilet paper before my face looked passably normal. I was noncommittal when Ann and Terri asked about the makeover.

"Oh, you'll just have to see," I told them. They groaned knowingly. Not a good sign.

A few hours later, I met Conor—my palms felt ticklish just thinking about him—under the clock at Grand Central Station. He was early again. I spotted him from across the cavernous amphitheater, leaning up against the clock post, reading *The Wall Street Journal.* I came up to him and kissed him softly. He made a sound in his throat like a soft moan.

We squeezed into the crosstown shuttle and then walked down Ninth Avenue, the street crowded with New Yorkers trying to get somewhere—home, the store, their kids' school, Central Park. Everyone else seemed to be heading uptown. We were the only ones going downtown.

Once we were finally alone, side by side in a booth at the old Empire Diner near my apartment, I kept remembering

the dream. Sitting next to Conor, smelling the clean scent of his soap, the wool of his suit mimicking my father's when he came through the front door every night, I couldn't stop looking at his hands. He kept them hidden—he was not a big gesturer and he never reached over to pat my thigh or arm, as so many men did way too early. But tonight I was looking for his hands and I got a thrill whenever I saw them.

Strong, quiet fingers. Round, manicured fingernails. Such elegant hands were a puzzling contrast to Conor's muscular chest and athletic waist.

I watched his hands all night long, holding his fork, picking up the check, resting easily on the table. In the dream they had gripped the steering wheel so confidently. His right hand had felt so hot beneath my skirt when he reached over.

Let's just say Conor had ceased to bore me.

He told me about work, his new roommate, the gym he'd found near his place, details about his daily life in Manhattan, the intensity of the trading desk. He was too old to be this excited. He had a few small wrinkles etched around his eyes that seemed to bespeak a wife, young kids, a mortgage. But at the same time, his face had the bright freshness of an eight-year-old boy running inside for a drink of water after baseball practice. I wanted to brush my fingers against his cheek.

I was not going to jump in bed with him tonight. I remembered all too well what it felt like to wake up next to skinny drug dealers or unshaven bartenders I could barely remember from the night before. Ugh. Dream or no dream, this time I was going to wait until I was ready.

Conor walked me home. He stopped to kiss me good night slowly, one hand on my waist, the other holding the wrought-iron security door to our basement apartment. He asked if I wanted him to come in, but backed off quickly when I shook my head and said, "Not tonight, Conor."

I think he knew I meant: *Not tonight, but soon.*

Inside my apartment, I headed for the bathroom to wash up. Pulling off my black Capri pants (yes, from the fashion closet), my fingers brushed my underwear. Soaked through. I'd totally forgotten what wet panties felt like. I'd never felt this flicker—like I was losing control and liking it. What would it feel like to make love to someone I truly cared about and trusted?

I brushed my teeth in front of the bathroom mirror I'd rescued from someone's sidewalk trash. YOU'RE GORGEOUS! spelled out in early-eighties pink, techno-square script. My mouth full of toothpaste foam, it occurred to me that maybe this was how it felt to fall in love, for real.

Monday, 5:30 P.M. I'd waited until I knew his secretary was gone so she couldn't screen his calls. Dad picked up on the first ring.

"Leslie! How's the working gal? Did you get the package I sent?"

"Yeah, Dad. I wore the gray one today. Thanks so much. You staying late tonight?"

He chuckled. "I've been here twelve hours already. I walked to work and I did not see one other person in all of downtown Washington." He pronounced "Warsh-ington" with a hint of Oklahoma twang.

My father grew up in south Oklahoma, a poor boy genius surrounded by an impoverished Baptist clan. He was the first in his family to finish high school. He was one-quarter Cherokee Indian, which explained why we all had high cheekbones, pigeon-toed feet, slightly golden skin, and nearly no body hair.

From the few stories he'd told me, his childhood was dominated—not in a good way—by his vagabond, zealously religious mother. She left her husband and moved the family as often as a dozen times a year in response to religious visions, eviction notices, and untimely visits from the police in response to late-night calls from neighbors. His older sister died from untreated leukemia, but Dad didn't talk about her much.

He graduated from a Chicago public high school and accepted a Navy R.O.T.C. scholarship at Harvard, a school neither he nor his mother had heard of before a teacher encouraged him to apply. He worked at a construction job all summer to save the train fare to Cambridge. When he left Chicago, his mother told him he was joining the devil.

He met Mom at Radcliffe. She was engaged to her brother's Kirkland House roommate, as close to incest as Wasps get. She broke it off to marry Dad under the old oak tree at Strawberry Hill. After a stint flying Navy planes to

38

repay his college debt, Dad went to law school. My mother paid his tuition by working as a phys ed teacher in Somerville.

I don't remember my father ever making it home from his job as a Washington lawyer before seven P.M. I doubt it occurred to him that we needed time with him as much as we needed new shoes and food on the table, the very things he must have considered as precious as myrrh when he was growing up a poor white-trash nomad. He became a judge in his early fifties. I read about his opinions in *The New York Times* and *The Washington Post* more often than I actually saw him. In my lifetime, we had only had a handful of conversations about anything besides the weather, tennis, or the Redskins. I remembered every sentence verbatim.

Today was different. I was not calling to tell him about Conor. I long ago stopped telling Dad about the guys I dated. He always got them mixed up. Nothing quite compared to having my dad call my shiny new boyfriend by an ex-boyfriend's name. Dad and I never talked much about Mom's tirades, my drug usage, anorexia, or drinking. He did not seem to notice my problems, no matter how grave. It struck me as simpler and kinder to let him think I'd always been fine. Especially now that I was.

I'd called to tell him I knew he'd moved out. At my urging, he'd given Mom an ultimatum: Stop drinking or else. Last night Mom had said, "So, did your father tell you he's rented a house?"

My heart dipped when I realized what it meant. She'd

refused to quit. She'd chosen alcohol over him. He'd probably mailed me those jackets when he was clearing out the closet they'd shared for more than three decades. Their separation had been ten years in the making, I'd guess. So what if Dad was too much of an emotional coward to tell me himself, that was no surprise. He had his reasons.

I was going to make this short and sweet for his sake. And maybe for mine.

"Dad, I just have a second, but . . . Mom told me you moved out. I know this is really a hard time and you don't want to burden me. But I'm here if you need me in any way. I'm really sorry. I know you tried . . . as hard as you could."

Silence. The sound of my father shuffling yellow legal pads on his desk.

"Well, Les." He cleared his throat. "I love your mother. Thirty-two years together. But I think the marriage . . . is over. I think it was actually over quite some time ago."

No shit, Dad, I thought as I hung up the phone.

As I was walking out to the lobby, I heard Conor and Stitch laughing. I stopped for a minute to put on Dad's gray herringbone jacket.

"Yeah, I bet it's not a bad job," I heard Conor say, in his confident man-to-man voice. "Watching seventeen-year-old models after thirty years at the post office."

Stitch laughed his deep belly laugh.

"Ah, they're a good bunch here," he said. "I just try to keep the crazies away."

I'd put my sleeve on the wrong arm and had to fumble in

the hallway to get the jacket on right. When I saw Conor standing next to Stitch, chuckling deep in his throat, crooked smile on his lips, I couldn't help but smile myself.

We headed downtown to Indochine. Conor had gotten more adept with restaurant choices. We sat at a low table in a cushioned, indigo corner. He asked if I'd like a glass of wine or a beer.

"No, thanks," I told him with a shrug. The way I always refused drinks. I didn't explain. My story would take ten years to tell. We weren't ready for that kind of drama.

"Hey, I've noticed you don't drink," he said curiously, leaning forward, smiling. His face was open, fearless: He wanted to know everything about me. "You haven't had one drink the whole time we've been dating. What's the story?"

To stall for time I studied the ornate inlaid ceiling of the restaurant.

"Well, there's just a lot of alcoholism in my mother's family, Conor. I haven't had a drink since my eighteenth birthday, the day I turned legal. Although trust me, I drank plenty before then. I don't want to turn out like some people I know who've become alcoholics."

Kind of the truth.

He pushed his glass of beer away. He gazed around at the flickering candles on every table in the restaurant. Conor smiled when he looked back at my face.

"Well, then I won't drink either."

I stared at his untouched beer glass. White foam oozed over the amber liquid, almost breathing. A few long white stripes of airy bubbles glistened along the cold, sweating glass.

I was touched. Kind of. What a lovely gesture. No alcoholic would stop drinking for someone he'd dated a half-dozen times. Break up with a girl because she *didn't* drink, sure. My sober friends would love this. Already I could hear the whole meeting laughing at how different normal drinkers were.

"No, Conor." I shook my head. "It doesn't bother me. I have friends—guys I've dated—who drink. It's been years since I've had a drink. Years since I *wanted* a drink. I have no problem going to bars. Being around alcohol doesn't make me have the slightest desire to drink again. There's no need—"

"Look, Leslie."

He stared over my head for a second, pausing as if to get the words just right. Then he looked straight at me.

"I like you. It's obvious that alcoholism disturbs you—you grew up with it and all. I know what it's like having something like that in your family. I don't want to do anything to . . . disrespect you. And I mean that in a really deep way."

He looked at me as if his blue eyes could cut through my flesh and bones to my heart. How did he know I could never trust someone who drank, ever again, because of Mom?

"Okay, it's a free country. But don't do it for me, Conor. It really doesn't mean that much."

I don't know why I lied.

After dinner, I told him I was too tired to go out to the jazz club as we'd planned. He took my hand—his smooth, warm—and started walking to my subway stop a few blocks from the restaurant. I needed to be alone, to think about Mom and Dad, apart for good. I couldn't concentrate on Conor or pretty jazz music. His vow not to drink just added to my distraction.

He walked me to the turnstile of the E train. We kissed good-bye as the station started shaking from the oncoming cars. Like all our kisses so far, this one was chaste—lips only. He squeezed both my hands long and hard as he kissed me. His hands felt like a broken-in catcher's glove. I wanted to be as close as possible to whatever it was inside Conor that made him *him* and made me feel so damn good when we were together. I was afraid to look at him. He believed in me. I couldn't handle it if something in his face destroyed the faith I felt coming through his hands like a blood transfusion.

He let me go. I pushed through the turnstile and slipped into the train just as the doors were closing. I slid into an empty subway seat and the car dissolved around me. Conor was gone.

The next Monday, Conor and I met after work under the clock at Grand Central. That afternoon, I'd gone to La

Guardia Airport to pick up six teenage girls from around the country, finalists in *Seventeen*'s teen model contest. I'd corralled them at baggage claim like a herd of young giraffes and brought them into Manhattan in a huge black limo. The doormen at the Park Lane on Central Park South had stared as a half-dozen six-foot-tall fourteen-year-olds climbed out of the stretch. The models were now ensconced with three chaperones from the beauty department, locked in for the night. As I'd left, one started jumping on the queen-size bed, her long blond hair flying toward the ceiling.

Conor was waiting patiently, a bouquet of pale pink roses in one hand, a bulky pink bag rolled up under his other arm. He was wearing khaki pants, loafers, a blue oxford shirt, and a surprisingly preppy knit vest, the kind a twelve-year-old would wear to church. His face lit up when he saw me.

"Hi," he said, still smiling, when I came up to him. He put his arm around my shoulders. His touch warmed my bones like a mug of hot chocolate thick with milk. Conor looked like he'd just showered, his clothes fresh and perfectly pressed, as if he'd been waiting all day for this moment.

"How ya doing?" He looked at me carefully.

"Okay," I said with a tired sigh. Nannying the wanna-be models had aged me ten years.

"Here, let me have that." He took my purse/sling/backpack. "Let's take a taxi back to your place so we can drop this off."

"You know what?" I asked. "Why don't we walk? I could use the fresh air. The bag's not too heavy for you, is it?"

"Nah." He laughed. "This is nothing."

So we walked the thirty-five blocks to my apartment, across Forty-second Street and through the grit and graffiti of Hell's Kitchen, a neighborhood that was probably safe only on early Monday evenings when everyone was hungover from the weekend. I shuffled for my keys outside the basement door. Conor had never been inside.

Once I opened the door, my cat rushed toward me, spotted Conor, and skidded in a panic through the living room, heading for the few inches of safety under my bed. She moved so fast all we saw was a skinny white blur.

"What was that?" He laughed. He put down my bag and handed me the flowers. Pink, long-stemmed, lightly scented. "I hope you like these."

"Oh, God, they're beautiful. That was my Siamese, Criseyde—she's kind of shy. Do you want a glass of water?"

"No, but the flowers do. Why don't you get them some and then I have something for you."

He motioned to the bag rolled up under his arm.

I put the flowers in a vase of water and got a glass for myself from our kitchenette. Criseyde's fiery eyes stared at Conor through the crack of the door to my bedroom, like a little girl watching her parents' dinner party when she was supposed to be in bed. Conor surveyed the books lined up in makeshift brick-and-plank shelves Audrey and I had put in the living room.

"Wow," he said when he noticed I was back. "You've read all these?"

"Hey, don't be too impressed. I was an English major. They're actually just my favorites, the ones I've kept."

He raised his eyebrows. Then he turned back to the bookshelf.

"What about these old-looking ones? *Beautiful Joe? Jim Jump? Black Beauty?* These don't sound like college books." He ran his finger along the spines of the books that were my favorites as a child. Even though the jackets were tattered now, I remembered how shiny each cover looked under the Christmas tree with a gold sticker that read FROM SANTA.

"Oh, you're going to make me cry now. Each one of those books is worth about a half hour of crying. Dead dogs, dead ponies . . . you know."

"No, not really. We didn't have books in my house."

How could anyone grow up with no books? He couldn't be serious. But true or not, this was the only time he had ever mentioned his childhood.

"Okay, now sit down," he said, turning back to the room.

I sat down on the pink futon couch.

"Close your eyes."

I closed them. Giggled nervously.

"Hold out your hands."

I stretched out my hands and felt a fabric like velvet, but lighter.

"You can open your eyes now."

In my hands was a beautiful pale blue dress with a pattern of tiny white flowers.

"Oh, Conor, you didn't need to do this . . ."

"It's silk. That's why it's so soft. It reminded me of you. Something in your voice last week made me think you could use a present."

I held the dress up. It had long sleeves, a V neck, a wraparound waist. The kind of dress I wanted to sleep in. I folded it carefully and put it back in the bag.

"Why are you frowning? Don't you like it?"

"Yes, yes. I actually love it, Conor. I just can't believe you found something that is exactly what I would have bought for myself. Thank you. It's beautiful."

He smiled slowly.

"I've always had a knack for this kind of thing. Now go try it on."

In my bathroom, I slipped off my work outfit, the usual miniskirt and wool jacket of Dad's.

I smoothed out the crumpled bag the dress came in. The store name, written in pink script lettering, looked oddly familiar. Yes—it was that store half a block from *Seventeen*. I'd stopped twice during my lunch hour, once to buy a pale fuchsia linen dress, another time when I bought the black wool number I was wearing when I met Conor that first time on the subway. What a weird coincidence.

"Hey, Conor!" I called from behind the bathroom door, where I stood naked, my nipples perking up from the chilly air, my toes curled away from the cold tiles. I heard rapid footsteps and within seconds he was standing in the hallway on the other side of the door.

"Yeah?"

"You're not going to believe this! You bought this dress at one of my favorite stores in the whole world, right near *Seventeen*."

He laughed, the lovely deep chuckle I remembered from his first phone call.

"I know. You mentioned on the phone once that you'd just gotten back from a great store nearby and that you'd eaten lunch across the street at some park with a fountain. So yesterday I cruised around the neighborhood near *Seventeen* until I found the right place."

How long did that take? How many side streets had he walked down? There were dozens of women's clothing stores in that neighborhood. Amazing how he found the right place. Amazing how special he made me feel.

"I didn't even know that store was open on Sunday."

"Actually, it wasn't. But the owner was inside taking inventory. I got him to open up for me and I told him all about you and what you like. He just got a shipment from Italy."

I pulled the blue dress over my head. It fit perfectly. There were three silk-covered buttons on the waist and a long, full skirt that made the dress look like it was made for me. The fabric was warm and soft as lingerie against my skin. I felt like Morgaine, the fairy heroine of *The Mists of Avalon*.

I smoothed my hair and came out of the bathroom. Conor was sitting on my pink futon, engrossed in John Rawls's *A Theory of Justice*, which he must have gotten from my bookshelf. Not exactly light reading.

"Oh." Conor made a sound when he noticed me standing

in the doorway. He put the book down but kept his thumb marking his place, as if he were afraid to let the book slip away.

"You can borrow that book, Conor. 'The veil of ignorance.' Amazing philosopher, Rawls."

"Oh, man," he said, shaking his head. "You look beautiful. Boy! Now let's get some dinner."

I sat on the smooth, chilly stairs of the Metropolitan Museum of Art at Fifth Avenue and Eighty-second Street, totally dwarfed by the massive concrete columns and a giant red banner that proclaimed 5000 YEARS OF ART! I rubbed the arms of my black cashmere pullover—Mom's thirty-year-old Radcliffe sweater that I'd machine-washed instead of dry-cleaning so many times that the finely woven cashmere had become more like that soft fuzzy material little-kid pajamas are made from. Mom always said that with a good haircut and nice shoes, you could get away with anything in between. Not that she was talking to me these days. She'd refused to call me back since she'd learned I'd talked with Dad about the separation agreement they were negotiating.

I stood up and waved to Conor when his blond head emerged from the shadows across Fifth Avenue. He took the steps two at a time. His mouth was soft and warm when he kissed me.

"Oh, those lips," he said softly in his whiskey voice,

making my heart pitch, his eyes closed, his long lashes forming half-moon fans.

Conor carried a small bag from an expensive Upper East Side deli, filled with four-inch-thick roast beef and chicken sandwiches and oversized green apples and navel oranges so perfectly formed they looked like they'd been plucked from a Manet still life. We spread out the food in Central Park on a grassy hill slightly north of the museum, surrounded by other picnicking strangers. The sun warmed my skin as we leaned back on the new green grass.

Suddenly, as if Barbara Walters had asked a question, Conor started talking.

"My neighborhood was real working-class Irish Catholic. Although my family is all Scottish—you know, from Scotland? Everyone there calls the place 'Southie.' You probably never knew Southie existed during those four years you lived across the river in Cambridge, right?"

I tried not to show how shocked I felt. He'd once said he grew up near Boston, but he'd avoided his childhood so assiduously on our dates, Winnie had begun to make up a past for Subway Man, calling his parents Mildred and Franklin.

He looked at me challengingly. No wonder he'd been fascinated by the details of my years at Harvard. He already knew all about Harvard. I didn't say anything.

"Never met my father. He left when my mom was about five months pregnant. Punched her stomach during a fight, something about how little money they had. Never came back."

He took a bite of roast beef. No wonder he'd avoided talking about his past for so long. Imagine hitting a pregnant woman. What was it like to be the son of such a man? I sat on the sloping lawn, mesmerized by Conor's words and the way his face twisted and softened as he talked.

"After my father left, my mother moved back in with my grandparents. She was twenty-two, six months pregnant with me, working as a checkout girl at Woolworth's. We lived with my grandparents until I was four. I remember so much of those years. I know it's hard to believe, because I was so young, but it's true. It was just the two of us together all the time.

"Then, I don't know when, sometime after I turned four, my mother—we've always called her Chickie, it suits her 'cause that's how big her brain is—she married a gas station attendant she met at Woolworth's. Secretly. My grandparents couldn't believe it. They were furious. They never trusted him, he wasn't from Southie, my grandfather always said he did not believe he went by his real name."

Conor shook his head incredulously. His face was flushed, pinpricks of red flaring under his skin.

"So, they started a new family right away. Four kids in five years. My stepfather—Wade—used to feed my brother and sisters and make me sit at the table without any food. He'd say 'Conor don't git none,' and make them say it, too. He used to ask me if I was hungry, sitting there watching them eat."

Conor said this all matter-of-factly. His face had turned its normal shade again. He took a bite of an orange slice

he'd carefully peeled and separated from the rest of the fruit.

It was hard for me to breathe. How could someone do that to a kid? My mom at least had waited until I was a teenager to go bat shit on me. His childhood was even more twisted than mine.

Conor took a drink of his Snapple tea. He kept talking, unable to stop, as if it were critical to tell me this story all at once.

"So . . . eventually I went to live with my grandparents. They were in their early seventies then, you know, because they'd had my ma so late. The greatest people."

A happy piece of the story. He reached into the back pocket of his jeans and took out his expensive crocodile-skin wallet. From behind several carefully folded twenties he pulled a small stack of cracked black-and-white photos with ridged white edges. His grandfather, stooped and wrinkled but with a smile that broke open his face, holding Conor on a tricycle. Conor's face, sprinkled with freckles, his blond crew cut sticking up in spikes. Conor and his tiny grandmother at the kitchen table, neither one's feet touching the floor, both drinking out of mugs that seem to dwarf them, in the tidy breakfast nook of his grandparents' South Boston walk-up apartment.

A kid-sized baseball glove lay on the table next to Conor. I could practically smell the leather. I pointed to the mitt, a question in my eyes.

"Little League. You know, in Boston, they worship the Red

Sox. I remember all my little eight-year-old friends, watching them practice for weeks with their dads in the concrete lots we used to play in. I'd hear them when I helped my grandfather water the flower beds in our yard at night. I was the only boy that didn't make the team."

Conor laughed, a handsome thirty-one-year-old man again, smiling as if recounting a treasured memory. I didn't want to insult him by feeling sorry for him, or to interrupt his story now that he was finally talking. So I glanced away and bit my lip to stop the tears coming out the corners of my eyes. When Conor wasn't looking, I wiped away the small puddles behind my sunglasses.

"So, eventually I had to choose—between going to school and taking care of my grandparents. They couldn't do anything after a while."

He was back in that time; he didn't see me anymore.

"I had to skip school to cash their pension checks, take them to doctor's appointments, fill their prescriptions at the pharmacist. They were so old. They just didn't understand I needed to be in school. So, after eighth grade was over, I decided not to go back."

When I was that age, on rainy summer days at the Vermont farmhouse my mother taught me exponential math. She drove me to the small-town library every afternoon; one summer I read forty books. She inculcated in me that A- was never an acceptable grade. By the time I graduated from high school I'd studied calculus for two years, lived in Madrid for six months to perfect my Spanish, and had been elected the

first female president of my class. By day I was Mom's golden child, trying to make up for being her Washington Whore. Until the magic day when I stared in wonder at the lovely fat acceptance envelope from Harvard stuck in the brass mail slot of our Bethesda front door. There was no way she'd be ashamed of me again.

"I got so lonely," Conor went on, as if still trying to apologize after all these years. "It was strange, being a teenager and spending all my time with two people in their seventies. I starting hanging out in the afternoons—you know, while my grandparents took their naps, they loved those naps—I started hanging around a real muscle gym in the neighborhood. The owner, Jed, was a guy only a few years older. He taught me martial arts. In four years I got a black belt in karate, a black sash in kung fu. He taught me how to lift weights. I could teach you."

So that explained his muscles and the graceful, athletic way he carried himself. He reached out to touch my slim shoulders, covered by my fuzzy overwashed sweater.

"In 1978 I competed for the Mr. Massachusetts title. Next year, Jed and I started a new gym, a mix of weight training and martial arts. I slept on the gym floor at night at first. Then we started another one, pretty soon we had three. We had more money than we knew what to do with."

He peeled the white membranes off another slice of orange and placed it in his mouth. The spring breeze ruffled his hair.

"So, one August a few years after my grandparents died,

I sold the business back to Jed. Chickie and Wade laughed when I said I was going to ——— college. They'd never heard of the Ivy League. I walked into the admissions office with my grades from elementary school and my GED. At first they would only take me into the continuing ed program—you know, night school? But after one semester my professors signed a letter to recommend my unanimous acceptance into the undergrad program. I graduated magna last spring. My whole family—Chickie, Wade, my sisters and brother, even Jed—they all came to my graduation. Chickie cried when I got my diploma."

He chuckled, looking down at his gently cupped hands as if expecting to find a small bird there.

"She said, 'You're our only hope now, Conor.' Sure, she knows a meal ticket when she sees one."

He looked at the curve in the road above us. An unending stream of Rollerbladers, joggers, and young couples pushing strollers went by. His face contorted; for a minute, I glimpsed how Picasso must have seen people's faces, jigsaw puzzles of ragged pain, disappointment, and hatred. Conor took a deep breath. Gradually, the lines on his face disappeared.

"So, anyway, by graduation I'd gotten four offers from Wall Street i-banks. Took the best one. I like this education gig. In fact, I just sent off my app for Harvard Business School."

He looked at me sharply, as if checking for a hint of ridicule in my eyes.

I nodded and put my fingers over his in the cool grass.

His hand was warm. I still didn't know what to say. We'd both ended up in the same place, with good college degrees, prestigious New York employers, bright shiny futures.

Conor looked at me again. The expression on his face—like a kid at the toy store asking if he's got enough money for a stuffed animal—made me want to look away. I forced myself to look back at him.

"Hey, we've all got crazy families," I said. "That's what family is for. Right? Let's go."

We stood up, brushed the crumbs and grass off our clothes, and threw away the remains of lunch. We walked around to the museum's entrance, up the steps and through the columns. The European sculpture galleries were empty except for the security guards. We stood together for a long time in front of the Italian marble nudes, rough, indescribably innocent statues meant to grace outdoor gardens in Tuscany. I didn't want to let go of his hand. We giggled together at the garish, brightly painted German porcelain figurines with elaborate china costumes, stark white faces, and smears of red for their lips.

The temperature inside the gallery was warm, as if the heat hadn't been turned down yet for spring. After about twenty minutes Conor took off his navy sports jacket. He had on his suspenders again, vertical maroon stripes with gold

clasps at pocket level. They were even more geeky as casual wear. I couldn't quite look at them.

His shirt was a white Brooks Brothers button-down cotton number, the same type he wore to work, I knew. Poking out were his surprisingly slim wrists, with a few blond hairs under the heavy cotton cuffs. Because it was Saturday he had the shirt unbuttoned at the collar, tucked into carefully ironed jeans, the seam crisp across his shins. What guy ironed his jeans? How, after everything he'd been through, could it matter to look perfect on the outside? I looked down at my wrinkled jeans that'd never once felt the heat of an iron.

The careful way he'd dressed for this casual Saturday afternoon reminded me of a young boy whose mother overdressed him to disguise humble origins. A mother whose hope was all in her son. Then it came to me: He'd dressed to look like the person he hoped to be, the Wall Street Ivy League wonder boy from an established family who'd never wear anything but preppy shirts and expensive loafers. It was like he had a page from a J. Crew catalog taped next to his mirror, and he was trying—too hard—to mimic the laughing, square-jawed models. The perfection of his execution betrayed him.

Of course what did not occur to me was what someone watching us in the sculpture galleries that day might have seen without even looking closely. Through Conor's eyes, a Waspy blond Harvard girl who knew which fork to use was even more seductive than a Brooks Brothers wardrobe.

All I could sense that day was that he trusted me, he needed me. That made me need him just as badly.

———❖———

The sun faded. The afternoon cooled. We wandered the Upper East Side holding hands.

We stumbled into Café Bianco, a tiny Italian restaurant on Second Avenue. As we stepped through the heavy brass double doors, New York City slipped away. Dark-haired waiters and waitresses chattering in thick Italian accents rushed by. We sat in a quiet garden courtyard with a fountain. The few people in the restaurant seemed to be finishing up very late lunches, in that languorous New York way where you might not eat lunch until five-thirty on a Saturday afternoon. We ate our pasta puttanesca in silence, tired from the sun and the museum and the talking we'd already done.

Holding hands, we walked slowly back to Conor's apartment, a fifth-floor walk-up at Eighty-second and York not far from Rex and Winnie's. His roommate was away for the weekend, he explained as we climbed the stairs. His apartment was spotless, modern, simply furnished with a sleek black leather couch, black-and-white-flecked granite kitchen counters, gleaming white Carrara marble in the bathroom. His half-open bedroom windows, overlooking York, let in the cool night air.

Conor sat on his bed in the twilight, moving around ner-

vously. I sat a few feet away in a chair by the windows. We talked for half an hour. Street noise, taxi horns, the occasional loud voice floated up to the fifth floor.

During a pause in our conversation, I beckoned to him with my finger. I whispered, "Come here." His eyes never left mine as he came to my chair with his hands outstretched, practically kneeling.

We took our clothes off. Quickly. The night was balmy enough that our bodies kept us warm on his queen-sized bed, carefully made up with pale peach-colored cotton sheets, crisply ironed (of course). We didn't say a word.

Later, when we came up for air, sweaty, out of breath, and refreshed all at once, our jeans and my cashmere sweater and his sport jacket and all our underwear were strewn on the floor. Conor tossed his head back on the pillow and laughed when I pointed out that we'd rocked the bed four feet away from the wall; an island in the dark room. I didn't explode from his touch, like in the dream. But I'd lost consciousness of myself in a way that was just as powerful.

The air around us was cool. I reached for my sweater and underpants. Conor had slipped under the soft sheets. I put my head on his shoulder.

"There's something else I need to tell you," he whispered. *Fuck,* I thought. Not exactly the words you want to hear ten minutes *after* having sex for the first time.

I needn't have worried.

"What I didn't tell you before is that Wade—my stepfather—he used to beat me all the time."

Oh, my God. My chest thickened. Fresh tears spit out the corners of my eyes.

"Put me in the hospital for days. Used to choke me until I passed out. Sometimes I still wake up from nightmares with his hands around my throat. Can't wear ties that are tight."

He twisted his neck against the pillow as if trying to throw off imaginary hands.

"Where was your mom?" I croaked like a tree frog, the only question I could think to ask.

"Oh, Chickie was there. Sure. He used to beat her, too."

Conor shook his head.

"In front of all of us. Smacked her, punched her, threw her down. Broke her ribs once by kicking her as she lay on the floor. I remember watching him break her nose. Blood all over the kitchen."

Conor suddenly brightened and sat up in the shadowy room. "You shoulda seen Wade the first time I came home after I got my black sash in kung fu."

I noticed with a start that he still called his mother's place "home." The edge to his voice, sharp like a paring knife, was back.

"I'd been weight lifting for about two years. Wade held up his fist to hit me 'cause of something, don't remember what, he never needed a good reason anyway. I said, real quiet, 'You better not try that with me anymore.'

"Then I pushed him, both hands on his chest, but you know, in exactly the right place, pushed him with my finger-

tips. He fell down, hard. I had gotten really strong, but you couldn't tell from lookin' at me."

Conor chuckled, his face blooming with joy. "Wade never came after me again."

Relief filled the dark room as he laughed. I felt like the bones in my face might crack apart. My throat ached from holding back tears. I'd have given several years of my childhood to make up for everything Conor had survived with no mother or father to protect him.

I couldn't find words to say that. Instead I put my hand on his smooth, hard bicep and brought him back down to me in his bed. His arms and chest formed a hollow around me that felt like a feathered nest in the dark. We stayed like that for a long time without talking. I didn't argue that neither of our pasts mattered now. I didn't explain that it'd been four years since I'd had sex, that in fact I'd never before had sex without being drunk or stoned. My cheeks and lips were rubbed raw from his beard stubble. My black sweater smelled like his skin; I wanted to sleep wearing it so I could smell him all night long and feel my own body under it, changed forever by the touch of his hands. I felt like Lucy in *The Lion, the Witch, and the Wardrobe.* I'd discovered an entirely new, magical world and didn't care if I never got back to the old one.

In the middle of the night, Conor walked me down to the empty street and hailed a cab. It felt too soon to spend the night, too early to wake up together with morning breath amid the harsh Sunday A.M. light. The asphalt was black

beneath our feet. The taxi glowed bright yellow. The lights from the streetlamps and traffic signals shone like jewels against the shadowy apartment buildings lining York Avenue. Conor gave the driver money and my address in Chelsea and kissed me through the open taxi window, his lips soft and dry as tissue paper.

"Bye, babe," he whispered as the taxi pulled away.

"Hurry up, Sandy!"

Even though she had her back to me, Mom's words bit through the damp air like the smack of a porch door slamming shut. She yanked repeatedly on our old dog's frayed red leash when he lingered by a boxwood still wet from the afternoon rain. I'd come to Washington a few days before Easter to research Health and Human Services data on teenage girls for a big AIDS education piece *Seventeen* had planned for the fall. It was early dusk, just after six P.M. I knew Mom would be home from her job teaching autistic kids at a Montgomery County public school. I parked Dad's red Mustang a few blocks away so she wouldn't know I'd borrowed it from him earlier in the day. Both he and I had left messages on her answering machine since Dad had moved out, but she had not called us back for three weeks straight.

"Mom, hi . . ."

She whirled around, her hair a silver halo. My hands

shook a little. I tried to focus on the smell of the rain in the air, the drops on the bush nearby, shifting the negative energy of my fear outward like a yoga teacher once taught me.

"What? You're here and you didn't call me in advance?" She looked sharply at me. Then she turned toward a neighbor's grizzled old Asian gardener trimming a privet hedge in his oversized yellow boots. She brushed some water off her slacks.

"Mom, I just didn't know if you'd want to see me." I tried to put my hand on her thin forearm but she pulled away with a fierceness that took me by surprise.

"This goddamn dog. You kids made me get him and now look, I have to take care of him all by myself. Have you talked to your father?"

"Yeah, Mom, I have. You know, you could always call him yourself."

"Not that bastard. He knows where to find me."

She chuckled ruefully and looked away again.

"I'm not drinking, you know," she said, scowling. "I even went to an AA meeting. I don't know how you stand those people, their smoking and all that talk about a 'higher power.' Honestly. I've found an alcoholism therapist who's better. It was idiotic to think I needed to go to a treatment center. Who would sub for me at school? Who would take care of Sandy? Not your father."

"Well, Mom, maybe Dad leaving was a good thing if it got you to stop drinking."

She lunged toward me, jerking the dog's leash inadvertently. Sandy yipped in surprise. Her teeth were clenched and the veins on her neck stuck out like those thick rubber hoses on Bunsen burners in chemistry lab. I took a giant step backward, away from her.

"Don't think that for a minute! And he told me *you* were behind it all. That was the most humiliating thing you have ever done to me. Don't think I'm really going to quit drinking. I don't have that big a problem. I'm just stopping now to show that your father was wrong when he called me an alcoholic. You are lucky I'm even talking to you."

She was blaming *me*? Why?

She stomped ahead in her little flat leather loafers from Pappagallo. I didn't know what to do, so I followed her down the street. Alcohol had been her best friend, closer to her than any of us, for more than thirty years now. Maybe it was easier for me to get sober; I'd been only eighteen. Maybe facing what makes you drink is too much for some people. Even if Mom stopped drinking for a few months, her liver might repair itself significantly, adding years to her life. Right now I'd settle for that if it meant she'd be civil to me and return my calls.

After striding along for a block, she slowed down and let me walk next to her. Yellow daffodils were blooming everywhere, popping up in bright profusion on the neighbors' velvety green lawns. Pink and purple buds on the azalea bushes that lined the sidewalks were just beginning to open up.

She didn't yell anything else, as if she'd said all she needed

to and now I could be her daughter again. She walked closer to me than she would if she were still mad. When I paused to get a pebble out of my shoe, she stopped, too, steadying me with her free arm when I lost my balance trying to slip the shoe back on.

Hope is always good, right?

When we got back to the house, I decided not to risk going inside. I tried to hug her good-bye at the top of the driveway. She let me. She smelled like lemon hand cream and Rave hair spray.

"Have a great Easter, Mom. You flying to Vermont like always?"

"Yes. My flight leaves from Dulles tomorrow afternoon. I have to get the garden plowed and make sure the house made it through the winter all right. I've got to resurrect that old place one more time."

She smiled at her Easter sardonicism and hugged me back in a sudden hard clutch. Then she pushed me away. For the first time she looked straight at me.

"Why don't you call me next time, before you come to town?"

She didn't ask where I was staying. I didn't tell her about the house Dad had rented. My guess was he'd never move back into the home he'd shared with her and us kids for so many years. I didn't tell her that Conor was taking the train down tomorrow, Good Friday, so the trading desk was shuttered, or that we were going to spend Easter with Dad. Mom didn't even know who Conor was. There was no point

in telling her that I'd met the man of my dreams right when she was losing hers.

I drove back to Dad's new house. He got home from work late, nine P.M., smelling like wool and reams of legal paper and one or two cigarillos. He looked ten years younger than before he'd left Mom. When I was brushing my teeth before bed I heard him laughing into the phone in his bedroom. A deep, knowing chuckle I'd never heard before. I had no idea who he could be calling.

As I climbed under the sheets on the sofa bed in the living room of his new house, it occurred to me for the first time that my encouragement to confront Mom about her drinking had offered him an escape from the Queen of the Wasps. He took with him the social prominence he'd gained from marrying her and the impressive, lucrative career she had helped him build.

The bonus was that he got to blame his departure on me.

My rusty old key still worked. The front door I had passed through hundreds of time as a child swung open. My footsteps echoed throughout the still hallway, the silence incongruous; this place was anything but calm when we all lived here. Conor carefully wiped his feet on the dingy welcome mat and followed me inside. He didn't notice what hit me instantly—Mom's stacks of old newspapers, the stench of cat pee, mounds of clean unfolded laundry sprinkled on the

gold silk Beidermeiyer couch and the wingback chairs by the fireplace.

Instead, in the foyer the first thing Conor spotted was a heavy gilt frame surrounding an old photo of my grandfather and his brothers and sisters, the Croton clan, dressed fabulously in the understated way that early-twentieth-century Wasps perfected. He didn't notice the inch of dust on the frame rim. His lips formed an O as he started to ask who those people were.

"Yip! Yack! Yap yap yap yap!" Sandy went ballistic in the kitchen where he got penned whenever Mom went away.

"That's my grandfather Sammie," I said over Sandy's machine-gun barking, pointing to the tallest man in the old sepia photo. Sammie wore his tailored suit with casual grace, as if each morning a properly bred person awakened to find oneself impeccably dressed by divine intervention. I hadn't told Conor much about my family yet. I'd brought him here on this sunny Easter morning because now I wanted him to know everything about me.

"Sammie was my grandmother's first husband. *Her* name was Frankie, well, her real name was Frances, but we always called her Frankie. She had three husbands. She died when I was in high school. Anyway, my grandfather was the only Harvard senior in the class of 1929 who owned *two* sports cars."

Standing across from me, Conor's eyes were wide and his face was so still it seemed he was not breathing. And I'd only just begun. I had to shout to be heard over the dog's incessant yapping.

"Sammie and Frankie married in August 1929. Good timing, right? It was eight weeks before Black Friday. They came home from their two-month European honeymoon to a totally penniless family. Sammie's father died a year later—financial ruin, social ruin, some strangely aggressive form of lung cancer. Sammie's mother—my great-grandmother—went crazy. Of course very quietly, genteelly. She did stuff like gave every person in the family a badminton set for Christmas, every Christmas."

We were still standing there motionless in the dark hallway. Conor seemed as mesmerized by my story as I had been by his.

"Look at them." I pointed back to the photo where my great-aunts and uncles posed with their arms looped together. "Look at those smiles. Not even the Depression and the loss of their parents can take away their belief in one another. And you know they all did fine. The girls headed to Wall Street. First they were secretaries, then they all married well; the boys headed to the military, the government, any place that would lead to respectability without the Harvard degrees they'd always thought they'd get."

Sandy had finally shut up. I could talk in a normal voice again. I took a deep breath.

"My mom barely ever talks about him," I said, pointing to Sammie. "But a few years ago at a family reunion, one of my great-aunts—my namesake, Leslie, this one right next to Sammie—told me about the last time she saw him. She and her husband were in New York City when they ran into

him by chance in the revolving door at the Plaza Hotel on Fifth Avenue. Aunt Leslie wore a fur coat and pearls, ready to go to the theater for the evening."

I smoothed my hair with my hands, tightening an imaginary fur coat around my neck, and put my nose slightly in the air.

"She told me that Sammie was dressed in an old suit and grease-stained hat, the only clothes he owned. She said she had to breathe through her mouth when she hugged him. He was a bum, Conor. He was coming into the Plaza to beg. Leslie bought him dinner and cigarettes at a diner nearby, blew off the show, and listened to Sammie tell funny stories about their childhood and watched his hands shake as he tried to hold his drink. She never saw her brother again."

Conor shook his head in wonder.

"God, Leslie, now I'm really starting to understand why you don't drink."

He looked one last time at the photo, all the pride and promise in my grandfather's handsome face. Then he looked curiously into our living room, crowded with antiques from Strawberry Hill. I took his hand, flicked on the light, and led him toward the middle of the old Oriental rug Mom cut down from the Strawberry Hill ballroom to fit this smaller oval room. It was the same rug she hid her Christmas money under the year Sammie stole her stash.

"Yeah. Many, many members of my own family had alcohol and drugs ruin their lives. I could have been one of them." For unknown reasons I gestured at the Chippendale chairs

lined up against one wall as if my dead alcoholic relatives were watching us. "I'm so lucky."

We walked through the formal dining room, lined with dark oil portraits of aunts and uncles, the messy sunroom. I took Conor into the kitchen, throwing the dog into another manic frenzy of barking. Sandy launched into frantic terrier sniffing of Conor's pant leg as if he were convinced a bomb lay hidden in the khaki folds and he had to find it before it detonated.

"Glass of water?" I asked once Sandy stopped yapping.

"Sure."

I handed him a Redskins glass filled with tap water.

"It's sad that your father wasn't here more. He just couldn't take it, huh?"

"I don't know. I never thought of it that way. It just always seemed like work mattered more. But at the end there he was leaving us to our own devices, to deal with Mom and her drunken rages. I guess that was a pretty sad thing to do to us kids."

What would Conor think once I dismantled the images of my idyllic childhood? Now that I'd started telling him, he had to know what my family was like behind the screen I painted when we were first dating. Would he understand why I'd created that facade?

"One afternoon in Vermont when I was eleven, Mom slammed her car door shut and said she was never coming back. I fed the other kids the only dinner I could make without turning on the stove—kielbasa and sliced cucumbers—

and sat on the front steps by myself, looking for the station wagon's headlights in the driveway. I crept inside when she pulled in at six A.M. I remember when I stopped asking friends to stay overnight. When I stopped having parties because Mom just used it as an excuse to get shit-faced and humiliate me in front of my friends. I have never heard my mother say she was sorry or that she loved me. When I left for college I knew I was not ever coming back."

Conor didn't say anything. I surveyed the kitchen counters. The beige Corian was crammed with grocery receipts and broken china that had been waiting to be glued back together for the better part of a decade. Sandy's canine heart medicine bottle sat next to Mom's allergy pills, a half-empty case of white wine, and a pile of unpaid bills.

"Anyway, that's all ancient history. But I wanted you to know it. Let me show you my room. It's here on the first floor. Everyone else slept upstairs."

I led him down a dark hallway into my old bedroom where my great-grandmother's hand-sewn quilt was still stretched tightly over my bed and my rectangular pillows were plumped up perfectly like hay bales. The room was clean and tidy like I'd left it the last time I'd stayed here. I'd mopped the floor myself every Saturday morning, a peculiar thing to do as an adolescent. Mom had hung my Harvard diploma over my desk. It was a bit crooked and Conor reached up to straighten it out.

"What was it like, Harvard?"

"Well." I rolled my eyes. "Believe it or not, I was terrified

of going to college, especially to Harvard. I tell you, Conor, I prayed to the college admission gods not to let me in so that I wouldn't have to go."

He frowned at me slant-eyed and suspicious, like I'd said I was abducted by aliens as a small child. He crossed his arms over his muscular chest and looked back at the crimson-edged diploma signed by Derek Bok.

Conor was frustrated; his forehead was still creased. Had he heard what I'd just said? Had he heard anything? He walked to the bay windows that curved along one wall of my old bedroom. "What a neighborhood!" he said. "Look at all these trees! I can't see any other houses. It's like a mansion on a private estate."

So what? I felt like saying. I wanted to go from room to room with Conor and say, "Here is the butcher knife she threatened us with," "Here is the spaghetti pot she dumped on the floor in the middle of my soccer team party," "Here is the bathroom rug I used to curl up on when I was crying and no one came." By telling him I'd feel not alone anymore. Because of his childhood betrayals he'd understand mine. But he still seemed irritated. Why? Suddenly I felt we had to get out of the house before it poisoned us, too.

"You want to go for a walk? Sandy could use some exercise—the dog walker only comes once a day when Mom's gone."

I clipped on Sandy's leash—more frantic barking—and locked the front door behind us. We took a shortcut across the lawn underneath our weeping cherry tree, the branches

covered with pink blossoms like a little girl's hair in bows. We retraced the steps of the walk Mom and I took three days before.

"Oh, Conor, I'm so glad you came down for the weekend. This is the best time to see D.C." I took his hand. "Isn't it gorgeous?"

The splendor of Washington in full spring bloom never failed to stun me. The flowering trees and bushes covering my neighborhood's steep hills, the cul-de-sacs, and the sloping lawns of old brick homes were so spectacular the scene looked fake. In college I'd hated the trip back to Boston after being home for Easter, abandoning these lush pastels for the drab brown of Boston's chilled version of spring. For several minutes we walked quietly, taking it all in, me thinking Conor was sharing my amazement at the show nature could put on. After a few shakes of his head, he finally spoke.

"I can't believe you grew up in a place like this," he said caustically. "Look at it! Even the fucking asphalt looks perfect. What do they do? Repave it every three months? Does everything have to be perfect here? I feel like I'm in Disneyland."

He sounded furious—at me. Like I betrayed him by growing up in such luxury. As if this type of neighborhood should not have been allowed to coexist in the same universe that let a young boy grow up fatherless among the concrete of Southie. He shook his head back and forth like we could not possibly have anything in common if this was what I took for granted every day.

"But, Conor—it's beautiful. Does a neighborhood have to be ugly in order to be real? And the whole point of my bringing you to see my house is that it never mattered how big the house was or how pretty the neighborhood because the real stuff happens behind closed doors anyway."

He turned to me quickly, holding up a finger accusatorily.

"Don't ever say we grew up the same. You don't understand. What you went without—that was just you feeling that. You had all this. Money. Parents who were educated. A fucking future. Harvard College, for God's sake! What'd you ever have to fight for? Poor baby, had to live in a messy house. Your mother drank too much. Your father worked too hard. You call those problems? You don't know anything about what it's like to fight for something you want and everyone tells you you can never have."

His nose was red; he looked close to tears. He spit out the words with such venom it was clear he was beyond such a simplistic, helpless reaction as crying. I took a step back, out of range. All I could think was: He was wrong. I did have to fight.

"Hey, I'm not the enemy here, Conor," I pleaded, putting my hands up. "I never took all this for granted." I swung my arms around the beautiful scenery. "Financial security and parents who went to fucking Harvard doesn't do much for you when all you want is for someone to say they love you, that you're good enough just like you are, parents who care enough not to get drunk or take clients out every night of your life. Maybe I was spoiled materially, but damn it, when

you're a kid, love means *much* more. I'd trade that house, Harvard, vacations to Florida, all that supposed privilege—I'd trade it all to hear my parents say they loved me once, to have my mother not act like Sybil every night. But I can't hate this place just to make you feel better. I love it here—I always have."

My face felt flushed like a child with fever. Now I was the one trying not to cry. It was as if the world all around had shrunk to this globe of crackling, angry space. Even the dog was outside the perimeter of anger that fused us together and shut everything else out. I walked mechanically for a few blocks in numb silence and then turned back to Mom's. Every time we came upon another perfect tulip bed, I looked up defiantly and Conor shook his head like if there was any justice in the world, we would stumble upon a really tacky garage sale or a Budweiser can lying on a front lawn.

Then right in front of us a big silver Mercedes sedan rolled into the driveway of an elegant Tudor home so stealthily Conor and I barely had time to pause on the sidewalk before the car skimmed our toes. A man and a woman a few years older than me—probably Conor's age—stepped out, all smiles. The couple was dressed for church, the man in a navy suit with a perky white carnation in his pocket, the woman in an expensively tailored, Creamsicle-orange linen dress and matching hat that covered most of her straight blond hair, which judging by the way it brushed her shoulders, probably cost $250 a month to maintain. They helped two angelic blond children out of the cavernous backseat of the Mercedes.

I could practically smell the leather interior. The whole family smiled at us as if posing for the cover of *Town and Country*. Conor's face twisted until he looked like he was either going to scream or throw up. His arms hung by his side and he clenched and unclenched his fists.

"Hi!" I managed to say to cover up the dumb-faced way we were both staring openmouthed at this Stepford family. "Happy Easter!" The kids ran up the flagstone path to the front door, their patent leather shoes tapping out happy sounds. The man and woman laughed in unison, taking each other's hands and walking inside after them.

"Conor, come on, let's go," I said, tugging on Sandy's leash before he pooped on their lawn. Conor's ashy face looked like he'd been slapped. Now I was outside the perimeter. He was alone with whatever he felt.

He stayed quiet for the rest of the day and during the long train ride back to New York. I felt horrified at the disparity between his childhood and mine. But I didn't see how the yawning difference in our pasts made a dent in our discovery of each other. I tried to read the whole ride, sneaking looks at him over the top of the page, but he was always looking out the window, away from me.

Once we reached New York, he dropped me off at my apartment. He got back in the cab to head uptown to his place without a kiss or backward glance. Okay, he needed space right now. I didn't call him that night even though it was hard not to.

Monday. Tuesday. Wednesday.

He called me at work on Thursday afternoon once the financial markets had closed.

"Hi. It's me," he said weakly.

"Hi! You okay?"

He laughed.

"Sure. How's my little rich bitch?" He laughed, making me laugh, too. I loved the way he said "my." It made up for being called a bitch. He must have meant it as a term of endearment, right?

"Oh, God, Conor. You had me worried. Can I take you to dinner tonight for a change?" I asked hurriedly. "I can't afford those places you've been wining and dining me at. But I know a great Middle Eastern place in Alphabet City . . . best food in New York for under five bucks . . . whatya say?"

I sounded much more confident than I felt, which was more like: *please, please say yes.*

"Sounds like a plan. I'll pick ya up at work. Usual time." I heard him grinning over the phone. The Conor I knew and adored—my Conor—was back. The relief and joy I felt as I hung up the phone surprised even me.

Last night I'd stayed at Conor's, like I did all the time now. He'd given me a key.

"I want you to have this," he'd said a few weeks after our trip to D.C. He put the small piece of brass in my hand.

I was so surprised I didn't say anything. I closed my fingers around the metal, warm from his body, and slipped it into my jeans pocket. "I want you to come here whenever you want, seven days a week if that's what you feel like."

So many of my friends from college and *Seventeen* bemoaned their boyfriends' fear of commitment. They ran around New York carrying panties and a toothbrush in a bag because their boyfriends wouldn't give them half a dresser drawer at their apartments. I thought for sure our Easter trip to Washington was going to make him reconsider, at least slow down our relationship for a few weeks. But after we'd made up, Conor liked it that I spent nearly every night at his apartment, running home to get clothes, do laundry, and feed my cat once a week.

I could not stand to be apart from him.

The morning air was still cool when I kissed him good-bye at the doorway to his building. It was a sunny spring Wednesday but it was cold here under the awning in the shadow of the apartment buildings lining York Avenue. I couldn't stop kissing him. A taxi headed uptown honked at us, like it was too early in the morning to be kissing in a doorway. Conor leaned back from me and laughed.

"See ya, honey. Can't wait till tonight. It's gonna feel like forever."

He put his hands on my face and gave me one last big smooch. He turned to catch a cab down the East River Drive to Wall Street. I walked away slowly because it felt wrong to be walking away from Conor.

I headed to Winnie's apartment to pick her up. Two weeks before, Winnie had taken a job I'd helped her get in *Seventeen*'s art department. She couldn't take life at the Polo Mansion any longer. Now I got to see her every day. We often walked to and from work together; Rex's apartment on Eighty-first Street was just a few blocks from Conor's apartment at Eighty-second and York.

In front of her brownstone, Winnie stood expectantly, wearing a Ralph Lauren black linen sheath and squinting at me in the morning light.

"Oh, Winnie, I love that man!" I shouted to her when I was ten feet away. "How am I supposed to wait until the day is over?"

She shook her head and rolled her eyes and we started walking to Third Avenue.

"It's like jet fuel, being with him. It's like we're one person."

Winnie nodded and smiled mysteriously like the Cheshire Cat.

"God, I know I sound sappy and sentimental," I said, tripping over a crack in the sidewalk because I could not be bothered to look down at the ground. "But I have never felt like this, Winnie. Is this how you feel about Rex?"

"Sometimes." She laughed. "Other times, I just want to kill him."

We laughed in unison.

She was still eyeing me sideways like I was slightly crazy.

"Well, what about the future?" she asked. "Isn't he going off to Harvard Business School in the fall or something?"

"Yeah, yeah, he applied for admission this fall. But frankly it seems so far away it might be another lifetime. And in some ways that makes the present far more precious to me. Oh, Winnie, I feel like the luckiest girl in the world."

Winnie looked at me like I just might be drunk again. She puckered her lips. "Okay, Mary Poppins. Just let me know if they cart you away to the fucking loony bin. I'll bring you old issues of *Seventeen* when I visit."

I left *Seventeen* right at five-thirty. Winnie was meeting Rex at some dinner for his job, so I walked uptown to Conor's alone. I was home before six-thirty, only a few minutes before Conor got there. I was in his arms one second after he opened the door. A sigh escaped from him and I knew he'd been thinking about this minute all day, too. His cotton shirt felt soft and warm as I unbuttoned it and pulled it off him, his chest smooth and cool underneath. We made love hungrily on his bed as if it had been a year instead of twenty-four hours. *I cannot live without this feeling,* I thought as I wrapped my legs around him. As we did almost every night, after making love we lay on the bed for a long while, listening to music, holding each other but not talking, until the room darkened. Then we changed into sweats and walked the twelve blocks to his gym, Pumping Iron, holding hands with our mesh-and-leather workout gloves on.

Pumping Iron at eight P.M. on a Wednesday night was packed. Pairs of muscular men in their twenties and thirties spotted each other on the flat benches and squat racks. Despite the sprinkling of women, the gym always felt like the gritty inside of the men's locker room.

Afterward we came back to his apartment, showered, and headed out into the warm New York City night to eat dinner at Café Bianco. We sat at our favorite table, next to the fountain in the quiet outdoor garden. Christy Turlington sat at the table next to us with a bunch of supermodel friends. She was one of the most beautiful women in the world—she'd stared out of *Vogue* at me all day—but Conor didn't give her a second look as he pulled out my chair. It was eleven P.M. by the time we ordered our pasta puttanesca. We both had work the next day but I wouldn't be tired; I was never tired these days.

We sipped ice water with lemon. Conor had not had anything to drink since that night he put down his beer. I still didn't know what to say or think about it. Of course I was wary of alcoholism. Of course I preferred to be with someone who did not drink. But his decision still made me vaguely uncomfortable in a way I couldn't articulate, even to myself.

We walked home in the blue New York night with our fingers loosely interlaced. We climbed the four flights of stairs with mock groans, me in front, Conor poking my butt with his fingers to make me go faster. The truth was that the weight lifting he'd been teaching me was making me visibly

stronger. The day before, I'd practically run up these stairs carrying two heavy bags of groceries. The week before, a group of models with skinny arms had asked me to try to un-stick the door to the fashion closet. I yanked on the handle and the door flew open. The girls all started clapping and I faked a goofy Arnold Schwarzenegger victory pose.

Conor made it to the top of the stairs first and he opened the door with his key. The apartment was dark and empty. His roommate Elizabeth was gone tonight as she usually was lately—she'd gotten a consulting job in Nashville during the week and the company flew her wherever she wanted on weekends.

Conor started kissing me in the foyer even before the heavy front door slammed shut and locked automatically be-hind us. His cold mouth tasted like Bianco's lemon ice water. Kissing all the way, we moved down the hallway into his room. I fell back onto his mattress. He pulled my jeans and panties off in one quick move and he spread open my legs and eased himself between my thighs. I could feel the cool Sea Island sheets under my legs, against my cheek, under my palms as I bunched the soft cotton up with my fists.

I could feel him get harder and his breath came faster as he got closer to climax. He closed his eyes; his long lashes brushed his cheeks. Then, without opening his eyes, he lifted his chest and rested his elbows easily on the bed to free his arms. His breath got shallow and rapid.

He carefully placed his hands around my neck.

He suddenly opened his cobalt eyes and looked into mine. His hands tightened around my throat. I could feel the excitement raging through his body like a freight train. I coughed; I began to choke. I tried to say, "Conor, no, stop, I can't breathe," but I couldn't make any sounds except for a croak deep in my throat. My eyes began to water. My body began to writhe involuntarily. Panic spread across my chest.

He mouthed three words slowly, under his breath, eyes unblinking. I could barely make out the words: "I . . . own . . . you." Then he shut his eyes and squeezed my neck even tighter.

Almost as if he had gone to another world, he came with a shudder deep within his body. He loosened his grip. His body crushed mine. Soon after, he rolled off and fell asleep.

Oh, my God. My throat ached. Somewhere deep in my stomach, practically as far down as where he was inside me, there was a cold, hard feeling, a kind of fear I'd never felt before, a block of ice in my womb. My lips were dry and cold. My hands shook slightly under the covers. I was going to throw up.

Oh, no, I thought, trying to banish the waves of nausea and fear. How weird. What was that? Kinky sex?

I went to the bathroom. Amid the gleaming Carrara marble I tried to reason with myself. Harmless, I guess. That's what all the sex columnists wrote, right?

Back in bed, I wrapped my arms and legs around Conor's warm body, trying to absorb the gentle rhythm of his breathing.

If I hugged him hard enough maybe the cold feeling would go away.

A lazy Sunday afternoon, Memorial Day weekend. The city was deserted. Conor took the phone off the hook.

His bedroom felt like a tree house far above the Manhattan streets. Spring had almost become summer and the weather had gotten hot, no more cool nights now. The miles of Manhattan concrete and pavement soaked up the sun's heat all day long, then the sidewalks bounced the heat back in the late afternoon and evening. Conor and I had been lying next to each other on the bed, naked, for hours, reading and dozing. The windows were wide open and Conor's white curtains billowed in the summer breeze. I couldn't hear the usual taxi horns honking down below. The drivers had probably all decamped to Coney Island.

I rolled over onto my stomach. The bedsheets were soft and cool under my naked belly. On the floor under his windowsill I spied a torn scrap of white paper. Part of the thin envelope he'd opened a few weeks before from Harvard Business School, a brief letter that politely yet unmistakably communicated he'd been rejected. The letter invited him to apply again in the future when he had more work experience. Hadn't they read the essay describing how he'd been working since he was eleven, that he started a successful business while still a teenager? Conor had torn the letter and

the envelope into small pieces and let them flutter out his bedroom window. This scrap must have blown back in.

"Rich kids half as smart as I am get in, that's why HBS does not require GMAT scores anymore," he'd said. "It's bullshit. But I have to go there. I'll apply again next year. Rat bastards."

He hadn't told anyone but me about not getting in. The guys on the trading desk would crucify him. He hadn't told his mother. He was trying not to call her as often and he told me he'd stopped sending her money. The day he got the letter was the first time I'd seen Conor angry since our trip to Washington. I had decided to hold off on telling him that Rex, who was one of those rich kids Conor thought were half as smart, got a fat envelope from HBS the same day Conor received his rejection. I hadn't known he was applying. He and Winnie were moving to Boston in the fall.

Conor rolled over and brushed my hair back from my face with his hand.

"Marry me, Leslie," he whispered. My stomach suddenly felt like a bottle with a genie coming out the top. With his blond hair, his big blue eyes, Conor looked so handsome, so hopeful—exactly like that man in the Tiffany ad proposing marriage with an eggshell-blue box hidden behind his back. Except that Conor was stark naked and he didn't have a box.

A surge of love like a current ran through me.

"Yes, Conor, of course," I whispered back. I kissed him.

What else could I say? It was like we were already married. I knew what it meant to him to have me as his girlfriend. As

his wife—his *wife*—I could help him overcome the years of abuse and neglect and pain. I could help Conor better than any woman on earth. And if I could make him whole, we'd be one person. He'd be mine forever.

The following Thursday night, we were walking up York Avenue to the gym, wearing our leather weight belts and holding hands.

"Hey, babe, you know my sublease expires June fifteenth. Let's find a place," Conor said. "We should live together. I wouldn't live with anyone unless—I don't think it's right unless you plan to get married. But with us, there's no reason to wait. We should be together all the time. We're a family."

Oh, God. A family. The taxis and buses and other people on York Avenue faded into quiet gray.

I hadn't told anyone about him asking me to marry him. It felt too soon. But I couldn't wait to tell people. I rehearsed over and over telling Winnie that I'd caught up, I'd found someone, too, even though Conor didn't much like Winnie and I knew he'd be upset if she was the first person I told.

"Sure, of course, that sounds great, Conor," I said, smiling up to my eyelids. I broke the news to Audrey. She spent all her time at her boyfriend's, too. She said she'd probably move in with him. Our Chelsea landlord shrugged and said we'd have to fork over thirty dollars so he could place a new

ad in the paper. I finally told Winnie one day over pizza at the Original Ray's across from *Seventeen*.

"So soon? You've only known him what . . . not even six months?"

"Well . . ." I pushed back my stool. It seemed to me like she'd moved in with Rex really fast as well, but the truth was they had been dating for more than three years. It only struck *me* as sudden.

"You know how I feel about him, Winnie."

"Yeah." She bit her lower lip like she wanted to say more. Then she smiled as best she could. "New York, you know. People move in together faster here. It's so damn expensive to keep two apartments when you're spending all that time together anyway."

I wished she could see, feel, how much I loved him. She'd understand then.

"Let me handle, it, honey," Conor said later that night when I showed him the apartment ads I'd circled in *The Village Voice*. He took the paper from me. "I'll get us the right place."

Sure enough, within two weeks, Conor found a small, charming sublet on Eighty-fourth and Lexington, with a balcony view of Central Park and the Metropolitan Museum of Art. It was even cuter than Rex and Winnie's place. *See, he's taking care of me already,* I wanted to say to Winnie. The lease started July 1. Filling out the sublet application, I included the trust fund Dad had created by putting a little bit of money aside for me on each birthday. It was very small money by

New York City standards, but it was more than twice what I made in a year and enough that no landlord would question my ability to contribute to our exorbitant New York City rent.

Conor also insisted on taking care of all the moving details. The day we moved, he took the day off and moved all of his furniture into the new apartment in the morning. He met me at *Seventeen* after work and we went together to my apartment in Chelsea. The Israeli movers he'd hired to move my stuff loaded it quickly into their beat-up truck.

We waved good-bye to the two men. Conor took my hand and we walked, for the last time, the four blocks up Eighth Avenue to the subway at Twenty-third Street. Only a few seconds after we got through the turnstile, the E train barreled into the station. The hot breeze whipped my hair back and blew my white sundress around like a parasol. The doors opened and we stepped into the train heading uptown, exactly the reverse of my path that night in January when I met Conor. Except now he held my hand like he would never let it go.

This time, we sat close together on the slippery yellow plastic seats. I looped my arm through his, my feet off the floor, my face buried in his warm neck, smelling his good smell. Conor gave me a well-timed shove as the train rounded a corner and I nearly slid off the seat. "Goofy!" he shouted, laughing. The other people on the train stared us down as if we were first graders misbehaving in class.

We got off at Eighty-sixth Street. Climbing up to the busy intersection at Lexington, the breeze blowing down from the

street felt cool and fresh compared to the stale subway air. We walked the two blocks down Lex to our new apartment, past New Yorkers busy shopping for dinner, heading to the Reservoir for an evening jog, locking up fancy little boutiques for the night. The cement sidewalk felt like sea foam under my sandals. I put my arms around Conor, thinking: This is the happiest day of my life so far.

The small moving truck was already double-parked in front of our new building. The two movers quickly unloaded my things, mostly boxes of books and clothes, my grand-mother's dresser and four-poster bed. Conor and I cracked up every time the movers called me "Lazlee" in their thick Israeli accents. I liked it, the small thrill of being a new and different person, if only in two strangers' eyes.

Conor and I left most of the boxes to unpack later. I changed out of my work clothes and together we set up Frankie's four-poster bed, threw on some sheets, laid out two bath towels, a couple of dishes, my cat's essentials, our clothes for work the next morning. The place was so cute in its shabby-chic way I felt giddy. I put a small picture of us—the only one we had—on the mantel of the little fireplace along an exposed brick wall.

We made dinner together quickly—our first homemade meal. Hand-cut pasta, fresh pesto from Winnie's favorite Italian market, a bottle of apple cider champagne Conor bought to celebrate. The woman we were subletting from had left her wrought-iron furniture on the small balcony overlooking Eighty-fourth Street, and I set the table out there. Looking

right, you could see the roof of the Metropolitan Museum of Art. I lit two candles but the soft evening breeze blew them out. Conor used a cutting board as a makeshift tray to carry out our plates, and shut the sliding glass door behind him with the back of his hand. We toasted the new apartment from the balcony, holding glasses filled with fizzing cider, eight floors above the honking taxis and the bustling New York summer twilight.

"Hey, you know who called me today?" I said casually in between sips. "That friend from college, Guy. He says the first year at HBS is not as bad as people say. He can't wait to meet you. He says if you need any help with your HBS application next year, he'd be happy to talk."

Conor's head suddenly jerked up. He put his glass down on the wrought-iron table. *Clink.*

I looked around the balcony. Conor looked so stunned I thought maybe a raccoon was hanging from the roof or he'd spotted a couple in an apartment having sex with the lights on (both of which we'd seen before). I didn't see anything unusual.

"He thinks you're a slut, Leslie," Conor said, his lips wrapped tightly against his teeth, looking down at his plate.

My head shot back in surprise as if he'd hit me.

Had I heard him right?

"He's the kind of guy who has a girl in every city waiting for him," Conor said in a low voice. "And he says he wants to meet me? To help me with my next Harvard application? What a snake."

Conor pushed his chair back so hard the table rocked and the chair legs scraped along the cement balcony. Something in him had uncoiled; the hands I loved jerked with anger as if he wanted to throw the furniture off the porch or smash it into the sliding glass door. He stormed inside and shoved the door closed behind him.

I was suddenly alone in the summer night. Our food lay uneaten on the table. In our glasses the champagne fizzed softly, sounding like bumblebees.

Sitting there, immobilized, I heard Guy's voice on the phone again. Around two P.M., he'd called from his dorm room in Boston, as he did every few months. Guy was the only undergraduate from our class of sixteen hundred students whom Harvard Business School had accepted right after graduation. We were friends who fooled around together occasionally, no fireworks but oh so nice, the only friend I'd ever had whom I did that with.

After I started seeing Conor, I stopped making out with Guy. Of course. Guy had started a serious relationship, too, with an older HBS student. He was happy that Conor and I were moving in together. I had told Conor this long ago. He hadn't shown a bit of anger or jealousy. I swear.

I sat there alone on our new balcony, my mercury rising. It was unfair of Conor to be so inexplicably possessive. Didn't he know he was ruining our first night together in our new apartment?

I pulled open the heavy sliding glass door and stepped inside. Conor sat on our lone chair in the living room, reading

The New York Times, his face cast down. He did not look up when I sat on a box next to him.

"Conor, we need to talk."

He looked up but did not put the paper down, as if my request were a casual one. Perhaps I was going to ask if he wanted some cappuccino. He raised his eyebrows and looked down again.

"I'm not a piece of property, Conor. I'm not looking for that kind of relationship. It's ridiculous that you're angry at me because one of my *friends* called me today. If you're jealous that I made out with him, or because he's at Harvard Business School and you're not, then that's your problem."

He stared at me. "Okay, if that's the way you feel, then why don't you leave now?" He looked down at the paper again.

How dare he. This was my place, too. I looked around the apartment at the packed boxes of his stuff, my stuff. The exposed brick wall and cute little fireplace with our picture on it. I couldn't figure out how or why in twenty minutes this evening had devolved from our most romantic night together to our most terrible one. I felt too angry to cry. Everything was happening too fast.

I ripped open one of my boxes labeled SHOES. I took the first pair, a set of white Tretorn sneakers. I pulled them on without socks. I was wearing pink flowered Gap shorts that looked more like men's boxers than women's clothing, and a white undershirt of Conor's. I grabbed my new keys and slammed the door of our new apartment behind me.

In the time it took to storm down to the lobby and out to the dark street my anger dissipated, smoke from a snuffed-out candle. I walked toward Central Park thinking: Was Conor scared that we were moving in together? So afraid that he'd lash out at me like this? Why hadn't I been calmer? I could have, should have, laughed it off. Told him I loved him more than any man on earth.

What was I going to do now?

As my anger cooled, the streets of our new neighborhood materialized around me. This was a nice block between Lexington and Park, quiet streets with big leafy trees, polished brownstone doors, shiny brass doorknobs and knockers. The gaslights lining the brownstone buildings flickered softly like fireflies. Across the street an older man with a potbelly walked slowly, smoking a smelly cigar, holding a fat bulldog at the end of a leash.

But this was still New York. I was a girl out alone after eleven P.M. Everyone who was coming home from work was already home. Even the doormen were all safely behind locked doors.

Wearing Conor's white undershirt, shorts that looked like boxers, and my stupid white sneakers, I started to wonder if other people might think I was homeless, a drug addict looking for a place to sleep. I had no purse, no money, no little green American Express card. A few taxis drove by. The people inside looked right through me. Conor's words about being a slut rang in my ears.

I walked for an hour slowly, aimlessly. People here were

always going somewhere, striding along purposefully. It was impossible to walk without a destination in New York City.

Where was I going?

I thought of my and Audrey's place in Chelsea. No furniture. And I'd turned the key into our landlord six hours before. Could I ring the buzzer at midnight at Winnie and Rex's happy little apartment? Winnie had just started to trust me again after years of my drinking. The thought of telling her about this fight filled me with shame.

Who could I tell that my boyfriend, my fiancé, for God's sake, whom I moved in with *today,* had kicked me out because I talked to another man on the phone? My body shook all over. My stomach felt as if it had dropped down a well.

I slowly headed back to the new apartment. I didn't know where else to go. I saw two rats, sleek as beavers, slip into a sewer at the corner of Lex and Eighty-fourth. The Korean market had moved its cut flowers and fruit inside and turned off the lights. There was no one on the street in front of our new building. I was frightened now, imagining a man with a knife jumping from the shadows, knowing no one would hear me scream. I race-walked past a narrow alley and a shuttered watch store until I got safely inside the lobby and the elevator doors closed behind me.

I turned my key quietly in our front door. I expected to find Conor waiting up, sitting in the living room staring at the front door, angry. But the kitchen and living room were empty. I peered into the bedroom. There he was, under the covers, asleep in Frankie's bed. Dried tears creased my face

like Saran Wrap stretched tight. I found a black ballpoint pen and a pad of yellow legal paper, the kind Dad always had lying around. I sat on a box in the living room, writing over and over again like a child being punished in grade school, "I am not a whore." Who was I writing to? Conor? My mother? God?

I left the paper on the butcher-block kitchen pass-through, under his coffee mug, imagining Conor finding it in the morning like a suicide note. Then I washed up in our new bathroom, my toiletries in my makeup bag like I was staying in a hotel. I tiptoed into the bedroom and crawled onto the far edge of my grandmother's bed.

I couldn't sleep. I lay there alone, listening to the unfamiliar noises, the honking cars on the street below. I started to cry, quietly, with my back to Conor, hoping until my chest ached that he'd wake up and put his arms around me and tell me he was glad I'd come back safe and that it was all going to be okay, that he had no idea why he flew off the handle. That he was sorry about the fight.

Finally I fell asleep.

The next morning, I woke up before Conor, feeling hungover. I went into the kitchen and crumpled the piece of yellow paper—evidence of my insanity last night—and shoved it to the bottom of my purse, chilled that it had actually felt good to write it. I took a long, cool shower, hoping I'd feel refreshed afterward. As I was toweling off, Conor came into the bathroom.

"God, you kept me up last night," he said, shaking his head

with a pseudo-smile and a rueful look on his face. He yawned and glanced around for his shaving kit. He did not look at me; it was as if I were too insignificant for him to acknowledge with eye contact. I felt desperate to connect with him.

"Don't cry like that in our bed if you expect to stay here with me," he said.

He'd lain awake, *choosing* to let me cry myself to sleep? My stomach dipped like it does when you stare into the pool from the high dive before jumping.

I got ready for work quickly and left without eating breakfast. I spent the morning in my orange chair trying to figure out what to do. Where could I go? This was New York. I made less than twenty thousand dollars a year. I couldn't take a hotel room or find another apartment quickly. I couldn't think of any friend I could tell this whole story to and then sleep on her couch for a week or a month or however long it took to find a place to live. Would my family help? No. What could they do anyway? This was not the time to ask Mom for help; and Dad still couldn't even remember Conor's name. This was my mess.

Everything *had* to be okay with Conor. *He* was my new family, my real family. I'd never felt so good in my life as I felt with Conor. How could a relationship fall apart in twenty-four hours? Yesterday, *yesterday* we were giggling like six-year-olds on the subway.

I went over and over the previous night's conversation, excavating each syllable. I racked my brain for the few other times I'd mentioned Guy just to see if there was something

legitimate that I'd missed. I hoped to find something, anything to validate Conor's anger. Then I could apologize and this would be over. You don't move in together for *one night* and then break up. How crazy.

As insurance, something to tell Conor if he asked, I dialed Guy's number in Boston and asked him not to call me again.

"Leslie, okay, of course I will do anything you want. But can you tell me—is this about me, something I've done to hurt you or offend you, or is it just . . . life?"

"Oh, Guy, Conor's just jealous, I think. This is a sensitive time since we're moving in together. I'll call you again when things are better."

"All right," Guy said, kind of sadly. "I won't call. But just know I'm here if you need me. I'll be thinking about you even though I'm not calling."

Somehow I got through the afternoon and distracted myself by doing a little work. I spent two hours in the fashion department surrounded by pretty fall cashmere sweaters. The editors didn't know me as well and wouldn't realize that something was wrong. I avoided Winnie's department scrupulously because she'd know in a second—God, I didn't want her to think that I'd fucked up my life again. I'd lose her, too. Crazy things like this happened when I was drinking and using drugs. They were not supposed to happen now that I was sober.

I realized with a jolt that I didn't know where I was going that night when I left work.

My desk phone rang about four P.M. just after the financial markets had closed.

"Hi, hon." It was Conor. He usually called at this time but I hardly expected him to call today. He was laughing. I could hear the noise of the trading floor behind him. "You won't believe what Psycho-Seiko lost today. Those Louisiana electric numbers came out and he bet on the wrong side of the flip. Over eight hundred K washed away."

Relief flooded my body. I wanted to jump through the phone to grab hold of him. It was the old Conor, back again.

"So what time are you coming home tonight, babe?" he asked. "Babe" is what my father always called me—only me, never my sisters—when I was a little girl. The easy way Conor used the endearment almost brought tears to my eyes. Plus he said "home."

"About seven, I guess."

The fight was over. I didn't ask any questions about why.

A few weeks later, the fight had shriveled up like one of those dried mushrooms you buy from a bin in Chinatown. I was too sickened—too afraid—to mention it to anyone. Maybe Conor was right—I did get too friendly with Guy. Maybe he was slimy.

Conor hadn't said anything more about it, thank God. For weeks I assiduously avoided mentioning HBS, other men I'd dated, and random phone calls from college friends.

I unpacked my things, but the apartment didn't feel like it was mine. Sometimes it seemed like Conor's harsh words had been soaked up by the walls, like in *The Shining*. I vowed to forget the fight. I tried to love coming home to him and the place that was ours.

Except that my Siamese cat drove Conor crazy.

Conor had liked her at first. He took her for walks in Central Park on her blue velvet leash. Now his litany of complaints made her sound like the Antichrist. Unnerved that she'd been shut out of my bed, she yowled outside our door at night like a dying donkey. She licked our overnight guests as they lay in our sofa. We had to keep the sliding glass doors to the balcony closed because she fancied teetering on the railings, eight stories above Eighty-fourth Street. Her litter box smelled.

Then Conor pulled the trump card: He thought he was allergic. Did I choose my cat over my boyfriend? I started asking around to see if anyone wanted to adopt her.

My sister Sylvia agreed to take her the next time she came to visit. I tried to think of it as sending Criseyde off to boarding school, a temporary change, a place I could visit frequently. Because I couldn't imagine someone I loved asking me to make this choice. And because someone like me would never get rid of a cat for a man.

August. On the Thursday before Labor Day, Dad and Sylvia drove up from Washington in the red Mustang. They were

coming to spend the night at our new apartment. Then we were all driving together to the farmhouse in Vermont for the holiday weekend. It would be Conor's first time meeting Mom, and Dad's first time visiting there since their separation.

Vermont. Summers started with sweaty, ten-hour car trips from Washington to the ramshackle summer farmhouse on Willow Street. Our green, wood-paneled station wagon was filled with suitcases, our Siamese cat, Sandy the dog, my two parakeets, a few snakes and turtles, Sylvia's smelly athletic equipment for every conceivable sport. The car did not have air-conditioning. After hours in the backseat, you had to peel your thighs off vinyl encrusted with a paste of cookie crumbs, apple juice, and sweat. One year our old Siamese stiffened in my lap as a Great Dane jumped onto the back window at a gas station, barked wildly, and pawed at the glass. She yowled and her eyes rolled back in her pretty brown head. The car filled with a sickening metallic scent as she died in my arms.

Climbing out of that hot, stuffy car into the cool, dry Vermont summer air was like emerging from hell into paradise. Then we would have long barefoot summers at the farmhouse, swimming in the cool river, playing Willow Street Wimbledon on the dirt road, having picnics on various mountaintops nearby, sleeping on the back porch with the Milky Way paving a path of stars overhead and the river gurgling nearby in the inky night. My dad stayed in Washington to work, coming up for a week in August.

One stultifying night I woke in a sleepy haze soon after Dad had arrived for his short vacation. "Get out of this house!" Mom screamed loud enough for the neighbors to hear. "My family's money paid for this all! Get the fuck out!" My father piled us, still in pajamas, into the green station wagon and drove us all the way home to Washington. Then he turned around to drive ten hours back to get my mother. We pleaded with him not to go get her.

"Teach her a lesson, Dad!" we shouted. "Don't let her treat us like this!"

"No, no, kids. It'll be better if I just go back." And he drove away.

Fifteen years later, he and Mom were still walking a rickety bridge together. Mom sounded mean and miserable, but dry. Dad and Sylvia lived in the nondescript suburban split-level filled with rented furniture. Dad took Mom out to dinner every Saturday night. Sylvia's descriptions of their encounters did not sound encouraging.

"Dad kind of slinks in from their dates," she said. "He sits out on the back porch smoking his little cigarillos for at least an hour. All I can see from my bedroom window is the orange tip glowing in the dark."

Mom as usual was spending the whole summer at the farmhouse, alone for the first time. She acted like nothing significant—such as Dad leaving her—had changed. It was like pretending she didn't have a boil under her armpit. She was too proud to imagine any man would quit *her*.

Conor and I and Dad and Syl walked in the swelter of the New York City summer night to El Pollo, blessedly air-conditioned. El Pollo served three things: salad, Peruvian chicken, and Peruvian-style curly fries the same color and curliness as Sylvia's long blond hair. Conor told dumb jokes throughout dinner. It felt like we were double-dating.

We emerged from the restaurant around nine. The night was still so hot our shoes sank into the soft tar on the streets. On the way back to our apartment, Sylvia leaned into an uncovered manhole on Eighty-sixth Street, and shouted "Hello" to hear the long booming echo. A homeless man, probably sleeping inside the manhole to escape the heat, answered back in a deep, scratchy, drunken baritone. Sylvia screamed and nearly jumped into the oncoming traffic as the three of us bent over laughing.

The next day, Friday, we left New York before eight A.M. Most people were asleep or at least still inside their refrigerated apartments. Already the streets were hot and damp with Manhattan dew—the runoff from doormen hosing down the sidewalks in front of their buildings. There was no traffic. We sped up the Major Deegan Expressway, past the exit to Strawberry Hill. No one lived in seventy-two-room houses anymore, and it was empty now, six years after Frankie's funeral, while the developer who bought it grappled with what he could turn the place into.

Sylvia piped up, leaning her head into the front seat to make sure Conor, sitting in the passenger seat next to my dad, heard her.

"You told him about Strawberry Hill?"

I turned to her in the backseat next to me. I shook my head and rolled my eyes. I snuck my hand under her seat belt and pinched her skinny little butt.

"Of course I've told him about Strawberry Hill. And Gasparilla. And Vermont. And how you are such a great soccer star. All the family highlights."

The car whizzed past the exit for the Mass Pike, the exit I took for four years driving back to Harvard from visits to my family in Washington and my interview trips to *Seventeen*. The same one Conor took to get to his mother's home in Southie. The same exit Winnie and Rex would take in a few days when they moved to Harvard's b-school dorms. When I finally broke the news to Conor about Rex getting in, he looked as if I'd helped Rex steal Conor's spot just by knowing them. I guessed we wouldn't be visiting Winnie and Rex in Boston anytime soon.

Dad steered the car left to follow the big green signs that read VERMONT. My brother had flown in the day before from Minnesota, where he'd spent the last year at Macalester College. Hugh had stayed in St. Paul for the summer to avoid hand-to-hand combat with Mom following Dad's departure. Smart. He'd agreed to fly in for Labor Day weekend because he knew how much having the family together at the farmhouse meant to her.

Once we crossed the Vermont state line, the temperature dropped ten degrees. Gone were the office buildings and McDonald's restaurants we'd been flying past. The highway

narrowed to a two-lane road cut out of jagged rock walls. Thick oaks, interspersed with pines, filled the median so we could not see or hear traffic going back to Boston. We passed a yellow MOOSE CROSSING diamond. After about twenty minutes, Sylvia spotted the blue-green outline of the mountains. At a toll booth Dad rolled down the white vinyl top. The mountain breeze smelled of pine needles, freshwater lakes, and worms.

The Mustang's wheels crunched onto the gravel driveway just before noon. Up at the top of a small grassy hill, the rambling yellow house and barn sat behind a dozen massive blue spruce trees. My mother had planted the trees too close to the house, so now, fifteen years later, their branches scraped the shingle walls and their roots crumpled the foundation a bit more each summer. We got out and brushed the wrinkles out of our clothes. I looked to Conor: Would he think I was crazy to love this old ramshackle place, or would he see its magic, too?

I heard the screen door slam and then Mom emerged from behind the trees that framed the front porch, a smile on her face, a glass of suspicious brown liquid in her hand, wearing her favorite old cutoff flowered jeans and a white T-shirt from some tennis tournament she'd won. I hugged her—filling my lungs with a mix of the industrial-strength SPF-45 sunscreen and the bug spray she wore all summer. I tried not to sniff for liquor on her breath. I didn't want to know if she'd started drinking again.

Conor shook her hand.

"It's nice to meet you, Ann. I've heard such wonderful things about you from Leslie."

"Yes, of course. Glad you could make it." She barely glanced at Conor, looking over his shoulder to Dad, the real prize, who stood awkwardly behind us, as if he wanted to be mistaken for a spruce tree. I could tell he was not sure whether to hug her or just get back in the car and drive off before she fixed him in her sights. She said, too cheerfully, "Hello, Stan!" He nodded nervously, like a fly caught in a spiderweb who was thinking, *So far, so good.* Sylvia—who could sniff out family strife like a canary in a coal mine— had quietly slipped out back to check out the river.

Conor got our bags out of the Mustang's tiny trunk. I led him through a break in the sweet-smelling trees along a small dirt path to the side entrance of the horse stables we called the sleeping porch. Dad had converted the stalls into a large bedroom. The horses' names were still etched into the planks of wood over the beds, and the swinging door to the barn had gnaw marks where the horses cribbed the wood in boredom during the long Vermont winters. Years ago Dad had cut holes into the barn to make windows along each wall. Through the largest one I could see Sylvia out in the back pasture, standing quietly by the river, surrounded by orange tiger lilies.

A few minutes later, she pried open the back door to the sleeping porch. "Hallo!" she called in a fake British accent as she came in. She flopped on the bed in the middle stall.

"Oh, don't worry, you lovebirds," she said. "I'm not sleeping

out here. I'll take over the loft. Come on, Conor, I'll show it to you."

We followed her through the crooked passageway to the wooden ladder at the bottom of the loft, a cavern with a peaked roof overlooking the summer kitchen. She scrambled up the ladder and disappeared through the rabbit-hole entrance my dad cut when the loft was where we kids slept. I showed Conor the farmhouse kitchen, complete with the original oak cabinetry and cast-iron sink, and took him up the steep, narrow staircase to the two tiny upstairs bedrooms. We trooped carefully back down the steep stairs and I pointed out the L-shaped indoor bathroom and the little door to the outdoor shower. Dad's suitcase was on the linen shelf outside the bathroom; he was probably unsure where he was supposed to sleep that night. I skipped my parents' bedroom, perpetually darkened by the enormous blue trees, dusty and messy due to my mother's typical "I have better things to do than make the bed" housekeeping.

After lunch, Conor and I swam across the cold river, carrying our shoes above our shoulders. We went for a long hike through the nearby Sand Piles, indigenous hills of white sand owned by a local construction company. As little kids we had played there for hours. When we grew too old for hide-and-seek and king-of-the-mountain, we rode ponies and bikes along the trails. Conor and I held hands as we walked on a sandy path to the neighboring farmer's grass airstrip. It was still common to hear a propeller plane land there every week or so. We picked two dozen ears from the

corn rows that lined the half-mile airstrip. In the hot after-noon sun I shucked one ear and we ate the sweet kernels raw off the cob.

That night, we all ate dinner by candlelight in the cool summer kitchen. Delicious white corn, fresh bread from a nearby bakery, salad from Mom's garden, steak grilled on our little barbecue that sat at the edge of the homemade beach out back.

I pointed to the rafters above that led to Sylvia's loft.

"See these rafters, Conor? One time our old cat—Powder—fell off one, got the wind knocked out of her when she landed twelve feet below on the wooden floor. She woke up with Sandy sniffing her—Sandy must have thought Pow-der was dead. Then Powder sank her claws into Sandy's nose until blood spurted all over the room."

Holding his fork carefully in midair, Conor nodded and smiled and everyone else laughed at the story they'd heard a dozen times before. I kept going. "Once Hugh, when he was ten, walked the length of the summer kitchen, rafter by rafter. Right, Hugh?"

My brother nodded, his mouth full of corn.

"Sylvia—she was about seven—saw him do it."

Conor looked around as if visiting Madame Tussaud's Wax Museum. He had no way of knowing whether the mis-matched antiques, three dozen old tennis racquets hanging on the walls, yellow oil bills from the 1920s stuck on a nail, constituted normal décor for a vacation home or an insane asylum.

"What a delicious dinner, Ann," he said nervously, looking for approbation.

"Mmm," she said, sipping the one glass of wine she allowed herself with dinner.

"Glad you like it, Conor," Dad filled in.

Later that night, hours after we'd fallen asleep with our arms wrapped around each other under a thick quilt in the double bed on the open-air sleeping porch, he woke me up excitedly.

"Leslie, Leslie—you've got to see this!"

I groggily climbed out of bed and followed him to the back porch, wondering what he'd seen. A deer? A skunk? A bear? I stepped onto the cold wooden planks.

"Brr," I said, rubbing my arms.

"I came out here to take a leak," he explained. "Then I looked up." He took my hand and leaned back to look up at the sky.

"Have you ever seen anything like that in your life? What is going on? Some meteorological phenomenon? I had to wake you up. Should we get everyone else?"

The Milky Way was so thick with stars it looked like you could walk across it. He craned his neck back while he spoke, afraid the magical night sky would disappear if he looked away.

"You know what, Conor?" I said, leaning into him. "The sky looks like this every night here. We're in the mountains, one hundred miles from any large city with lights. Sometimes it's even brighter in the winter."

"No way." He looked at me in astonishment. "I never could have imagined the sky could look so . . . big."

I stayed with him for ten minutes, gazing at the sky. The moon and stars shone so brightly we could count the vivid orange tiger lilies lining the riverbed. He stayed outside once I headed back in. When he finally climbed into bed, his icy feet woke me up as they searched out my warm ones at the bottom of our bed. We made love sleepily until the bedsheets were hot from our bodies moving together like one.

In the morning Mom made blueberry pancakes and then we climbed Little Sugarloaf together, an easy hike up a small mountain overlooking the pristine glacial lake below. At the top, we sat on smooth granite boulders the size of dump trucks and listened to the echo of swimmers splashing a half mile below on the beach. As kids, we'd always pestered Dad to lead a sleep-out on the top of Sugarloaf, but every time we attempted it, someone—eventually followed by everyone—chickened out as darkness fell, and Dad would lead us down the mountain in the early night, every twig snap surely the approach of a mountain lion. Today, we munched wild berries in the sunshine and slapped at the mosquitoes.

That afternoon, back at the farmhouse, I left Conor in the summer kitchen while I put on cutoff shorts, a tank top, and old black rubber riding boots to help Mom in the

garden. I pulled my hair off my face in a ponytail and covered all exposed skin in her special combination of sunscreen and bug spray. Despite the physical discomfort, this was one of the best places in the world to talk with her. A strange privacy existed, as if the garden were surrounded by twelve-foot-high invisible walls. In between spitting out gnats and digging our fingers deep into the soil to pluck out the long roots of the weeds, she told me how mad she was at Dad (she had made him sleep on the living-room couch the previous night) and she related a few funny stories about some gay friends she met at the one AA meeting she went to. I listened and asked a few questions, eager to show I was interested, glad she was confiding in me. I wasn't about to contest her version of Dad's betrayal or her opinion that she was not really an alcoholic.

After a long, hot two hours of weeding, I quit. I took off my boots and sat on the sandy riverbank, soaking my grimy feet in the cool water, washing the dirt off my hands and trying in vain to get the grit out from under my fingernails. Carrying my sweat-soaked riding boots, I came into the sleeping porch through the back screen door. Through the window I could see Conor had taken my place out in the garden, awkwardly trying to help my mom finish watering and weeding the corn.

A half hour later Conor came into the semidarkness of the sleeping porch.

"Your mother is a piece of work," he said.

She was a piece of work. Just about anyone would say that. I sat down on the edge of the bed, afraid to ask what he meant.

"She tried to tell me about what you were like in high school, how you were such a druggie slut. She tried to give me details. I wouldn't let her. No one should say things like that about their own daughter. I just left."

I was shocked that Mom would do such a thing, but it was not outside the realm of possibility for the woman who had nicknamed me the Washington Whore. Maybe she was trying to drive him away. Maybe she was jealous. Neither made much sense. After sitting with Conor for a few minutes, I headed for the main house to see if I could find anything out.

Mom was back in from the garden now, too. She stood in the doorway to the kitchen, three steps above me, her green eyes blazing as she wiped the garden dirt off her hands onto her cutoff flowered jeans. She had a glass of rum and Coke in her hand.

"Nice boyfriend," she said.

Behind her in the living room I saw my father's back. He pretended to look at some old books on the dusty shelves. He reminded me of a deer among trees, trying to camouflage itself from a hunting party.

"What?" I asked, not knowing what to say.

"Yes," Mom said, looking down at me from the kitchen where she'd cooked hundreds of meals for me as a child. "You always did like to bring home strays."

LESLIE MORGAN STEINER

I turned and left.

An hour or so later, Dad came out to the sleeping porch.

"So, Conor, I hear there was some . . . uh . . . trouble between you and Ann this afternoon," Dad said softly, one hand on his bony hip. I looked away. Conor folded his hands across his chest.

"Stan, your wife said some inappropriate, insulting things about Leslie. I don't know why she would say such things to me. After she said them, I left the garden. Maybe it was rude to leave, but it wasn't right for her to say those things about her own daughter to me."

Dad shook his head. He waved his hands in the air as if to acknowledge there was no easy way out of this. "Okay, I'll see what I can do."

He went back to the main house while Conor and I sat next to each other on the patchwork quilt that covered our double bed, waiting like defendants dreading a jury verdict. Dad came back ten minutes later. "Ann would just like you to apologize," Dad explained to Conor. "To get this first visit off to a good start, I think it's best to give in."

Give in, like you'd always done, Dad. Where did that get you, or us kids?

"I'll give you two some time alone to think about it," he said as he left, the old stall door squeaking behind him. Conor watched him go.

"She's crazy," Conor said, shaking his head. "She's just trying to bully you, and to bully me, too. She's saying she's in

112

charge here. She's trying to humiliate us. Like she's always done to you. And your dad—did you hear him? Leslie, I can't let anyone humiliate me, ever again. I can't let them denigrate you, either. I don't want this to be like my family all over again. It sets a standard if I go apologize."

Shit. He was right. Why couldn't this visit have just gone quietly, peacefully? My crazy family. I loved them. But it was time to stand up for Conor. And for myself.

We quietly packed our bags and straightened up the sleeping porch so that there was no trace we'd been there. Within thirty minutes we were standing on the front porch of my beloved farmhouse, just more than twenty-four hours after arriving. Mom, Hugh, and Dad gathered on the front step under the two biggest spruce trees. Sylvia had retreated to the loft. I folded my arms across my chest and looked straight at Mom, then Dad and my brother.

"Y'all, Conor isn't going to apologize for something he hasn't done," I said, looking from one to the other as I talked. "There are two sides to the story. We still want to see you for the rest of the visit. But we're going to stay at the Pasquani Inn instead of here."

I turned away. The three of them stood dumbfounded on the stoop, the sun in their eyes, either too satisfied or too surprised to respond.

"Dad, will you give us a ride?" I asked him.

He nodded, reaching into his shorts pocket for the keys.

We drove away in his red Mustang, shielding our faces

from the branches of the trees I used to leap over as a small girl. I didn't feel angry. Or sad. What I felt instead was simple: grown-up. Thanks to Conor, I'd finally stood up to the woman I loved, and feared, more than anyone in the world.

Book
Two

———◆———

A FEW WEEKS LATER, ON A CRISP FRIDAY IN SEP-
tember when the edges of the leaves in Central Park had
begun to crinkle into yellows and reds, I came home from
Seventeen to our tiny apartment. I turned my key in the door,
walked into the dark foyer, and set my purse and two grocery
bags down on the parquet kitchen floor. I put my keys and a
pile of mail on the butcher-block counter and started opening
bills.

"Hey, babe."

I jumped. Conor was sitting on the balcony wearing jeans
and a baby-blue Polo shirt, already changed out of his suit
and tie. He had a lit cigar in his right hand, the ash about to
fall off. Normally he didn't get home until after six P.M., even
on a Friday. I'd never seen him smoke a cigar.

He put the burning butt down on the wrought-iron
table and walked in from the balcony. He leaned through the
kitchen pass-through to kiss me. I could taste the cigar on his
breath—kind of like kissing your grandfather.

"Hi, honey . . ." I said quizzically. "What are *you* doing
home so early?"

"Oh, I left work early today . . . because I quit." He smiled
crookedly, like he'd brought home champagne-caliber news.
He winked at me.

"What? You quit? Why?" *I* was not smiling. He looked so cute, but he seemed buzzed, off-kilter, almost like he was drunk.

"I'd just had enough. I had to escape the stress of that job. It's just too intense. Like New York," he explained, looking away, as if of course anyone would understand this logic. "I've been fighting alone my whole life. Babe, now that I've found you, I want the bullets to go over my head for a while."

Oh, boy. I sat down on one of our wooden bar stools next to the kitchen counter, still holding a piece of mail. The warmth and trust in Conor's voice made me feel light and swoony. At the same time it was all I could do to stop myself shouting, *Are you crazy? Shouldn't we have talked about this before you quit?* I tried to be calm and stable for Conor.

"My boss made some calls and there's an opening at one of their subsidiaries. Guess where? Vermont. Can you believe that?"

I looked at him in bewilderment, unable to say anything.

This was all a bit fast. A voice in my head said: *We love New York. I have a terrific job that half the girls in America would push me off the Brooklyn Bridge to get.* A few months ago his lucrative Wall Street trading job—a job his street smarts made him naturally good at—represented the fulfillment of ten years of hopes and dreams. Hell, half the men from Southie would push *Conor* off the Brooklyn Bridge to get his job. Moving to a new company in a new state, he'd face new challenges, different scenery, but his demons would

dog him no matter where he went. As much as I loved summers at my mom's farmhouse, I couldn't trade life in New York for rural Vermont. What would we do there?

"Okay, Conor, okay. Give me some time to think this all through."

Instead I tried *not* to think about it as I put away the groceries, changed out of my work clothes, and held hands with Conor as we walked to the gym and then dinner at El Pollo. But another voice broke through, insisting: He needs you. He's much more important than any job or any city. As his lover, his best friend, his soul mate, I had to do what was right for him. This was what love was about. Wasn't it?

Sunday. As usual, a late breakfast with lots of coffee at our favorite diner on Madison Avenue. Red leatherette booths, black-and-white subway tiles on the floor, our regular waitress who had a crush on Conor. An awkward silence between us. The choice: him or New York. I couldn't imagine leaving New York and *Seventeen*. I couldn't imagine a day of my life without Conor.

This was all happening unexpectedly fast.

Every woman's magazine warned against being one of those reckless women who gave up everything for a man and got nothing in return. In the back of my head—okay, maybe the front—I'd been wondering why Conor had not gotten me a ring in the months since we'd talked about getting

married. I had to bring it up. I took a deep breath to get Conor's attention.

"Conor, you know how much I love you." I wrapped my hands around his on the cheap Formica tabletop. "You want me to go with you to Vermont, I'm there. But it's not right unless we are engaged—officially. It's been four months since you asked me to marry you. I don't need any proof of your feelings for me. But . . . I want to be engaged before we move. I want to get a ring and set a wedding date and tell our friends and family—before I give up my job and leave New York."

Now Conor seemed taken aback. He arched his blond eyebrows and stared into his coffee cup for a minute. He slipped his hands out from under mine and wrapped them around the chunky white ceramic mug. His tanned fingers looked like a teenage boy's. I imagined a gold wedding ring on his left hand. Our waitress rushed over with the pot as if her mission in life was to make sure Conor never, ever went without hot coffee.

"Okay," he said resolutely when the waitress left, giving me a big smile, exactly what I wanted and needed from him right then. As if his eyes were saying yes, of course, it was time to tell everyone what we had together. My stomach melted like butter on toast.

"Conor, I'm so glad you understand."

As long as I was with him—in Vermont, New York, or Timbuktu—nothing else mattered.

But then he looked away and took one of those quick inhales, like he was scared.

Did he understand?

"Yeah, babe, but the thing is, with leaving my job, we don't have the money for a nice ring now," he said, looking down at his hands and then up at me questioningly through the blond hair on his forehead.

Lack of money was why he hadn't given me a ring?

"Why don't I buy you a small ring now, one that we can upgrade later, you know, for a special anniversary when we have more money?"

My face suddenly felt made of Play-Doh. I tried to hide my dismay.

I didn't want a diamond as big as a doorknob. It was just— I wanted to be proud of my engagement ring. I wanted something that showed our commitment to each other. What if he went to the Wiz and came back with a diamond chip in a cheap gold setting? I could not wear something that ridiculed how I felt about him, that my family secretly made fun of, that made me feel embarrassed when I put it on.

"Let's think about it, Conor. This is really important."

And we left it at that.

A week later I went into my boss's office and shut the door.

"Kathy, Conor just accepted a job in Vermont."

"Wow, good for him," she said, looking down, shuffling some papers on her desk.

"Kathy, I'm going with him."

She looked up, her hazel eyes suddenly huge.

"*What?*" She stared at me in disbelief. She lit a cigarette to cover her shock.

"Leslie, you love this job. You're really, really good at it," she said, blowing out a bluish stream of smoke. "What could you possibly do in Vermont?"

"Well, I think I'll try being a freelance writer," I explained.

"You're talented, Leslie, but you're young. You're the most promising new editor here. You have a lot to give readers. You worked hard to get this job. Why would you give that up?"

"Conor really needs a break, Kathy. He wants to leave New York and I need to go with him. We're going to get married in a year," I said.

"I know you love him, Leslie. But you can't sacrifice everything you've worked for, just for a man. This is Feminism 101. You know that already."

This made me smile. Conor was not just any man. He needed me. She didn't understand.

"I am completely in love with him. I'd do anything for him. You've been really good to me, Kathy. *Seventeen* has been good to me. But I have to do this."

"Okay, okay." She blew out smoke with a big sigh and shook her head. "We'll give you lots of freelance assignments."

"Conor, how about this?" I said a few days later, standing by the butcher-block pass-through. I was looking up the number

for the Chinese place to order mushu pork and moo goo gai pan.

"I could take some money out of my trust fund to help buy the ring. My father always said the money should be used for something . . . permanent. Stitch—you know, the security guard at work—he has a childhood buddy who's a wholesale diamond dealer. I bet he'll give us a deal."

Sitting across from me on a stool, Conor held yet another white ceramic coffee mug in his hand. He shrugged and gave a small, noncommittal smile.

"Fine," he said. "Sounds like a plan."

On Tuesday during my lunch hour I walked ten blocks across Midtown to visit Marty Eiss, diamond merchant. In a small second-floor office, Stitch's "Ice Man" showed me loose diamonds like enormous mica chips glittering on black velvet. I picked one. The Ice Man pinched the small, sparkling stone in his callused, stubby fingers, held it up to the light and said he'd put it in a classic gold setting for me. A few days later I got the finished ring appraised, insured, and gave it to Conor to give to me the next weekend.

None of this struck me as strange. I didn't have to get engaged according to Emily Post. I wasn't my mother. I wasn't Winnie on the beach of a ritzy Caribbean island. Love was like a Persian rug: the backside of the tapestry with all the thread knots and loose ends was meant to be hidden. What mattered was the top side and the quality of the wool. Our love was real. The way Conor had proposed four months ago was incredibly romantic. It didn't matter that I'd paid for my

own ring, that he hadn't lifted a finger to get it for me. I was a realist, unusually mature for my age. Right.

That night I called my family. I twirled the phone cord around my finger while I looked over at Conor's blond head as he watched the Knicks game.

First I dialed Mom's number.

"Mom, hi, it's Les. Guess what? Conor and I got engaged. And we're moving to Vermont."

"Oh," Mom said. She was probably in the kitchen, clutching the wall phone that was covered with years of newspaper-smudge fingerprints.

"Well, ah, congratulations."

Her voice had an edge to it, like inbred etiquette alone forced her to go through the proper response to a newly engaged daughter. Did she despise Conor because he had the guts to stand up to her drunken bullying? Did she hate it that I now had the strength to face her, too? *Too bad, Mom. Get used to it,* I felt like telling her.

After an awkward silence, I said good-bye, hung up the phone, and called Dad. What he said sounded even more weird.

"Oh, well, Leslie, that's great," he remarked. The Sunday night Redskins game blared in the background. "He seems like a nice enough fellow. I guess if it doesn't work out, you can always get married again."

What?

Then Dad laughed.

I figured he must be thinking about divorce and remar-

riage a lot these days. Both of my parents were so screwed up, obsessed with their own problems. I felt like the only mentally healthy adult in the family.

Fortunately Sylvia, whom I called on her bedroom phone upstairs from Dad's TV den, was thrilled. She screamed "All right!" like I'd just slam-dunked a basketball to win the big game. Then she dropped the phone on her foot and I could hear her howling in the background.

A fresh start in Vermont, near the old farm where Mom took us for our barefoot summers, seemed a way to give Conor part of my childhood. How could I say no to someone who had such a terrible life before meeting me? How could anyone else understand this? I wanted him to have everything now that he was with me. He would have no reason to leave me, ever. It felt wonderful and selfless—like nothing I'd ever felt before. I had so much love in me that I never considered what moving for love would mean, what I might leave behind that could never be found again.

Conor's new company was headquartered in the suburban, flat part of Vermont, about one and a half hours from Boston, sixty-five miles from my mother's farmhouse. Conor lived alone in a motel while I tied up loose ends in New York. I gave *Seventeen* four weeks' notice. I wrote a twelve-page memo outlining—in excruciating detail—each project I was working on. I arranged to have our furniture put in storage until we

found a house to buy. Going through the motions of each day in New York without Conor felt like quitting heroin cold turkey. Our apartment felt unnervingly dismal, the city itself gray and colorless.

Columbus Day weekend, Conor drove down to New York in a rental car to get me. On Saturday morning we headed north together, giddy with our escape. We cheered as we crossed into Vermont, where the trees had faded to a dull russet, the finale of the fall foliage parade.

"Do you mind if we stop? I need to pee," I said just after we'd left Massachusetts. The parking lot at the next fast-food-bathroom-gas station complex was jammed with cars. Conor had to circle around to the back to find a space.

"I'll just come in to get a Coke and stretch my legs," he said.

I sat down with him for a minute in Arby's while he got his drink. It was close to two P.M. and the place felt like everyone was leaving just as we arrived, as if we were out of sync with the tourists visiting Vermont to see the trees. Under the dim lights, Arby's cheap plastic chairs and tables were a slippery black covered with ugly gray scuff marks, as if the employees had been playing soccer with them after-hours.

"Would you watch my purse while I go to the bathroom, hon?" I asked as I walked away from the table.

"Mmm . . . sure," Conor said midsip.

When I came back a few minutes later, my hands still wet from the bathroom dryer, he was hunched over the table, small pieces of crumpled colored paper spread out before him.

"Hey, what are you doing, Conor? That's all the junk that was in my purse. . . ."

He looked up, his eyes yellow. I stopped at the table's edge.

"I was looking for some Carmex in your bag . . . and I found all this stuff. What the hell are you doing keeping this crap? It's Guy all over again. Do you need to have someone else always waiting in the wings for you?"

"Conor, what are you talking about?"

I looked down in disbelief at the contents laid out on the Arby's table. Why would he go through my purse? What could he have found that would make him this angry?

I laughed. "Honey, I have nothing to hide. You can look in my purse anytime."

"What's this, then?" He shook a tattered piece of red cardboard at me furiously. His broad chest and muscular arms were coiled tautly like a lion poised to spring off a *National Geographic* cover. My brain flashed back to that fight in our New York apartment when he'd slammed the glass door to the balcony so hard I thought it would shatter.

"Oh, that." I laughed again, remembering how I got the torn red paper. "I never told you that story? Some guy working at the Bennington airport during Christmas last year—he must have been about fourteen—wrote me a love note on the claim tag on my skis. . . ."

Conor stared at me, furious. I sped up my explanation like a record on the wrong speed.

"It rained on Christmas—there was no snow—so I didn't

discover the note until three months later when I went to Vail. Isn't it cute? He says I'm the most beautiful girl he's ever seen, and that although he doesn't have his license yet I should call him the next time I come to town. He hadn't even started shaving. Oh, Conor, I kept it because it was such a sweet note . . . from a *boy*. . . ."

Conor was still not laughing. I started having trouble breathing.

"Don't keep shit like this if you want to be with me," he said coldly, not looking at me.

"What do you mean, if I want to be with you? I am with you. We're moving to Vermont together. We're engaged. Come on, Conor. I love you."

I waggled my hand to show him the ring, trying to get him to smile.

He held out the red luggage tag. "Throw it away if you want to get back in that car with me," he ordered.

"What? It's just a sweet note that always made me smile. I don't even know his name."

"Your choice."

I grabbed the tag and threw it into the black Arby's trash can a few steps away.

"Fine, Conor," I said, pissed. Who cared, it was just a note. I'd remember the boy, even without the red tag.

"And what's this?" he asked, smoothing out a piece of very crumpled, stained yellow legal paper.

"Oh, that must be . . ."

Holy shit. It was that piece of paper on which I wrote

"I am not a whore" over and over during our first night together in New York. I thought I'd put it in the kitchen trash. Instead I'd been carrying it around at the bottom of my purse since that horrible night.

"Are you fucking crazy?" he said, standing up, flapping the paper in front of my face. "Who are you writing to? What's your problem? You're a nutcase." He folded the paper and put it in the back pocket of his jeans.

"Give it back, Conor. That's mine," I pleaded through gritted teeth as he walked away.

An overweight woman taking her young daughter to the bathroom stared at us and then hurried by, grabbing the girl's hand. I couldn't bear the thought of Conor having that paper, like a dark piece of my soul, in his back pocket to pull out whenever he felt like it.

"Damn straight it's yours," he said, reaching into his pocket, crumpling the folded paper into a ball, and throwing it at me. I grabbed it in midair and ran back to the restroom. I flew through the door so fast, the handle smacked into the bathroom wall with a loud clang. The mother and daughter were washing their hands. The mother looked at me sideways, like I might be a kidnapper-cum-crack addict, and said softly to her daughter, "It's okay, honey. Let's just dry your hands and go back to Daddy."

I locked myself in the handicapped stall and sat on the oversized toilet tearing the sheet of paper into small pieces and flushing them away. What had set him off? He was so insecure and jealous—sometimes. If I'd shown him that

boy's note another time, I swear, he'd have teased me about robbing the cradle. Or if I'd explained about the yellow paper, he'd have rocked me in his arms. How could someone I loved and who loved me be so cruel, so randomly?

I washed up and patted my face with wet paper towels. Amazingly, my reflection looked normal in the mirror. I headed out to the main entrance, not sure if Conor would still be there. He was waiting in the rental car, the engine running. I got in without saying anything. We drove away in silence.

After twenty minutes, Conor made a comment about how many evergreens there were—he called them "Christmas trees"—this far north. He called me "babe," smiling as if nothing had happened.

At first we lived in the Vermont Star, a motel on the side of a highway between two small towns. The carpet had cigarette burn marks I covered with a bathroom towel. The bedsheets were dingy gray.

I spent my days house-hunting, the local realtor my new best friend. Our plan was that when Conor got into Harvard Business School next year—of course he would with a year more of what the admission committee considered "real" work experience—we'd resell whatever house we bought for a good profit and move down to Cambridge. Compared to the mountainous lakes region of my childhood, the part of

Vermont near Conor's new company was far more suburban, and ironically (because it was much less nice by my standards) far more expensive, due to its relative proximity to Boston and to companies like Conor's.

I'd dreamed we'd live in an old farmhouse like Mom's on acres of hilly land. Instead I looked at worn-down tract homes in our price range until my fingernails felt dirty. Then one day I found a 1950s ranch house in a sprawling small town dominated by a Pizza Hut, a Mobil station, and post office. The split-level ranch in a quiet neighborhood of half-acre lots about a mile from the turnpike was the best house we could afford. We put the property in both our names, despite the fact that the down payment and money for repairs cleaned out my trust fund. Conor's company paid to have all our furniture moved from storage.

I never imagined I'd spend my dad's hard-earned money on something as modest and unexciting as this ranch house. But I was happy to do it. After his lifetime of rental apartments and eviction notices, I wanted Conor to have a home. With me in it.

The house was spacious and airy, with good flow from room to room, structurally sound, but run-down and badly in need of cosmetic improvements. The plan was I'd tackle the surface work, steaming off old wallpaper, repainting some walls, replacing the linoleum in the kitchen and bathroom.

I'd held a hammer only three or four times in my life, but how hard could cosmetic repairs be? We'd sell the place for a profit in a year or two to pay Conor's business school tuition. After Conor left for work each morning, I walked around the empty rooms feeling very smart to have come up with this easy, clever way to make money.

In New York, having no furniture was normal and kind of chic. Here it made me feel like we lived in a trailer park. We spent five hundred dollars at a neighbor's yard sale to buy a few pieces of used furniture. We put an old wicker couch in the living room and a laminated maple dining set in the kitchen. I set up a white table and cheap bookshelf in a small back bedroom, my new office.

The walls throughout the house were a dull green, probably the original paint job from the 1950s. They were covered with years of cigarette smoke. My finger left a clean streak through the accumulated grit on the walls. I'd learned from a neighbor that the previous owners had both died of lung disease.

I rented a fifty-five-pound metal steamer from the hardware store on the main street of our new town. Wearing old jeans and long-sleeved T-shirts, I attacked the cancer walls in the kitchen, hallway, and bathroom. I spent hours alone in the empty house dragging the steamer around, loosening smoke-stained wallpaper off the kitchen and living-room walls, holding the steamer nozzle like an elephant's trunk. The days felt like years. As the water ran down the walls it turned brown from smoke residue. By early each morning I

was covered with dirty brown cigarette water thickened with old sticky wallpaper paste. After a week of steaming and scraping there were still scabs of wallpaper on the plaster walls.

The place looked and smelled worse than when I'd started.

One morning I pulled off my yellow gloves to read the paper and then moved on to the kitchen floor: scarred yellow linoleum which looked like an easier, more rewarding job than the walls. I tried mopping the floor clean. After two hours of scrubbing, down on my hands and knees, my fingers were deeply wrinkled and my body coated in sweat and lemon Mr. Clean. The green mop head was still coming up brown with fresh grime. I gave up.

After a quick lunch of Kraft Macaroni & Cheese out of a box (yum), I tackled the dirty, musty basement. The real-estate agent had called it "half-finished," which meant it had a cement floor and Sheetrocked walls. Old furniture and dozens of boxes of rusted tools, cracked jelly jars, and decrepit sewing supplies were piled in the corners. Some boxes were so heavy I had to drag them outside using Conor's leather weight-lifting belt. After two hours of dusty subterranean work, the afternoon broke into a glorious Indian summer day, turning the thick basement air into a golden yellow fog like Tinkerbell's fairy dust, only not all that magical.

I needed to open a window to let in the crisp fall air. To reach it I stood on tiptoe atop a small pipe sticking out of

the furnace oil tank. Before I could reach the window latch, the pipe snapped under my feet like a dead branch.

Black oil gushed out the spout, splashing the walls, creeping black and silent toward the electrical outlets. Would the house blow up when the black river reached electricity? My feet looked like they were covered in gooey, slippery black socks. I pounded up the wooden basement stairs, leaving black sneaker prints on each step. There was no time to call Conor. I grabbed the kitchen phone and dialed the number of the oil company which—thank God—was posted on a magnet on our crappy refrigerator.

I screamed the fiasco to the nice lady who answered the phone for the oil company: "The oil is *gushing* out! You have to come *right now!*"

"Ma'am, go outside," she told me calmly, sounding as if she got calls like this every day. "I'm sending the truck."

In less than ten minutes the oil company truck came tearing down the street like an ambulance. Men in jumpsuits and high rubber boots burst out each door, leaving the truck parked crookedly in front of the house.

"In there!" I gestured wildly toward the basement door. The men rushed through the garage entrance to plug the oil tank. I wanted to laugh, cry, and scream.

The house did not blow up. With my oil-stained fingers I signed an estimate for six hundred dollars for the company to suck up all the oil and repair the tank. The money was all I had in my checking account.

I picked Conor up from work at five o'clock in my oil-

stained clothes, smudges on my face, oil in my hair, my sneakers slipping on the clutch. In a rush I explained about the damage, the narrowly averted risks to me and the house, the money
to clean the basement.

Conor did not find my idiocy funny.

"You smell like oil," he said with disgust, sitting in the
passenger seat, staring at my oil-stained body. "You know,
that smell reminds me of my stepfather."

New York seemed impossibly far away.

November. The bright red and orange fall foliage was gone.
So were the tourists on the highway. Each morning the with-
ered grass in our neighborhood was covered with a layer of
white frost.

"Hi, this is Leslie Morgan. I'm a freelance writer and I'm
calling to suggest a story . . ."

Introducing myself to strangers had been easier when I'd
been able to add "from *Seventeen* magazine" after my name.
Now I had nothing to add.

The editor from *Vermont Sunday* interrupted me.

"Sure, I'm definitely interested," she said quickly, surprising me before I was through my spiel about my New York
magazine experience and English degree from Harvard. "Why
don't you send me the pitch in writing and I'll call you in a
week or so?"

I hung up the phone and leaned back in my chair in the

sunny former bedroom off the kitchen. Outside the two windows grew an old gnarled lilac tree. The neighbor across the
street told me it blossomed beautifully in the spring, that it
would fill the house and street in front with sweet perfume.
Conor rarely came in here.

In my first several weeks as a freelance writer, I'd found
an editing job two days per week at an irreverent weekly
magazine in Bennington, gotten a gig writing restaurant reviews for *New England Monthly,* and had been hired to write
articles for local publications about pagan witches, singles
facing Christmas in Vermont alone, and teen sexuality. Ironically, now that I lived in Vermont, New York magazine editors
seemed to think I represented a Middle American perspective. In addition to *Seventeen,* editors from *Mademoiselle* and
Ms. magazines had hired me to write for them. I was on track
to make as much as I'd made at *Seventeen,* still about half
what my Harvard classmates in consulting and investment
banking made, but I was proud. Of course, I knew I wouldn't
have checks to deposit for months—I used to put through
freelance paperwork at *Seventeen* and I knew how erratically
writers were paid.

When we moved to Vermont, Conor and I had set up a
joint checking account at the local bank. Seeing both our
names and the address of our new home in black ink on the
rectangular paper slips had excited me at the time. Then
Conor had, without explanation, left all bill-paying responsibilities to me. Every two weeks, he handed me his paycheck,
which after taxes, utilities, and our mortgage payment, was

astonishingly meager. The little checks I earned from editing barely covered groceries. The bigger ones from my national magazine articles came in sporadically with the glitter of late-arriving, beautifully wrapped Christmas presents.

I pushed my chair back and looked out once more at the twisted lilac. The skies had clouded up; the forecast was for our first snow. I thought of my view from the hallway at *Seventeen,* where I could see Manhattan skyscrapers looming out Kathy's window. I thought of her and the other editors putting together the January book without me. What if I called Kathy to ask for my old job back, and she said no, there wasn't a spot for me any longer?

Conor got dropped off around 5:30 P.M. by a coworker who lived three blocks away. He sat in the living room reading the paper while I fixed dinner. We ate in our bare kitchen with dark green walls, our elbows poking into the hard maple table because we didn't have place mats.

"I never told you this? Come on, I did so!" he grinned, his whole face lit up, fresh and smiling. He looked like a carefree man-boy, Oscar Wilde's Dorian Gray. Conor's unlined skin showed no trace of his childhood beatings at the hands of his stepfather or the emotional pain his mother had inflicted on him.

"Back in October, after my first day here, after I met Greg Mouse Brain, the other execs. It was that same day I had to wear those two left shoes."

Conor cracked up. I burst into laughter, too, remembering his first morning, how getting dressed for work at the

motel he'd discovered he'd packed only a mismatched set of black wing tips. He had to limp around the office all day, trying to impress his new bosses with his intelligence and New York business acumen while wearing two left shoes.

"I hadn't called the movers. You hadn't left *Seventeen*. You had just started that mongo memo. So that night I called the apartment in New York to tell you not to quit, that I was coming back, that it was all a stupid mistake. How could we ever be happy in rural Vermont? My boss was such a bozo. I couldn't find a deli for lunch or a restaurant open after eight P.M.

"When I called you, the phone was busy. You know what happened? I fell asleep!"

Conor threw his head back. The walls of the empty house echoed with his laughs.

Damn you, Conor. I gave up *Seventeen,* my life in New York, for this? I looked at our half-eaten spaghetti dinner. I was a terrible cook. I looked around the half-renovated empty house. I could hear cars roaring down the turnpike every time I stepped outside. It would be at least three months before I got paid for the jobs I was working on now. We'd barely be able to cover the mortgage and my health insurance until then. Heavy snow was falling silently outside. I would have to shovel it before Conor could back the car out tomorrow.

Easy for him to laugh. Part of me felt as trapped as the miniskirts and high heels put away in my office closet.

"Funny, Conor. Real funny." I got up and started to clear

the dishes. I wanted to break one over his pretty blond head. Conor laughed again and went back to reading the paper.

December. We needed a car. Conor's human resources department wouldn't stop hassling him about having a rental car for more than ten weeks, which they protested was longer than any new hire in company history. Conor wanted a stick-shift Volkswagen like the used one he'd driven in college. There was only one VW dealership in Vermont. We haggled with the dealer and then plunked down a down payment for a black Jetta with gray cloth interior—my first real car.

Of course, we didn't have the money to buy a new car. With Conor being employed fewer than three months and my erratic freelance income, we didn't qualify for a loan from the dealership.

I called my father at eight A.M. at the office, knowing he'd be there.

"Dad, hi, it's Les."

As usual, we tackled a safe subject—the weather. I could hear Dad stand up from his desk and walk to the picture window overlooking Pennsylvania Avenue and the White House.

"It's quite humid here. I played tennis this morning. If it keeps up like this, we'll play outside till Christmas!" he drawled, delighted, as if the good weather were a present just for him.

"It's snowing here again. You should see our front yard—the snow looks like a cement wall. But Dad, I'm actually calling to ask if Conor and I can borrow money to buy a car. It's not much—just for a Volkswagen. And I do mean a real loan, not a wink-wink-nod-nod parental disbursement."

He laughed.

"Okay, no problem. I'll charge interest, too. And you both have to sign a promissory note."

Ever the lawyer, my dad. But hey, it was his money, he more than earned it. A fair-and-square loan was the kind I wanted anyway.

"Sure, Dad. And thanks a lot. We both appreciate it."

"And, ah, don't forget about the oil, babe. I want you to protect my investment."

"Ha-ha-ha, Dad. See you later."

The last car I drove was a dinky secondhand white Chevette that all of us kids shared in high school. My father let me take the car to Cambridge my junior year. He did not tell me about checking the oil. I guess he thought intelligent beings were born knowing when to put oil in cars. One day as I was driving down Mass Ave. the engine blew up with a loud bang. I looked out my rearview mirror and saw a trail of neon green ooze lining the road behind us. I sold the car to the towing company for twenty-five dollars. My father retold this story with glee every single time I mentioned automobiles in his presence.

"So, babe, why don't you get some car mats for the car to-

day?" Conor asked when I dropped him off at work a few days later. "I want to keep the car really clean."

I nodded automatically. Car mats—those rubber things? I'd already promised to get the car washed every week because Conor explained that the Vermont winter and heavy salt on the roads corroded a car's undercarriage. I was happy to comply with Conor's requests; he knew far more about cars than "I blew up a Chevette" Leslie. Fair enough.

Of course I bought the wrong car mats.

"Too cheap," he said, kicking them over with the toe of his leather loafer when I picked him up at work that afternoon and showed off my purchase. "Too thin. Too short."

So the next day I went back to the car parts store and bought the only extra-long, extra-thick car mats the clerk had in stock. I could not return the first forty-dollar set of four, so I threw them in the trunk.

"How could you buy *brown?* The car interior is gray and black." Conor made me sound like a moron when I picked him up at work that afternoon.

"I've had cheap things all my life," he explained, as if this were news to me. "Some things, you really have to spend money on and do right."

I looked at him, astonished, thinking of all the things, like my engagement ring, our house, that we couldn't spend the "right" money on.

"You're an asshole," I said. Righteous, 100 percent justified anger—strangely pleasurable—flooded my body. "I've

driven around getting these goddamn car mats for you for the past two days. Who gives a shit! I've got better things to do than find you the perfect set of car mats! Go get them yourself!"

I unclipped my seat belt and stormed off into the maze of the employee parking lot. God knew where I was going.

I threw the keys to him. Well, okay, I threw the keys *at* him.

Then Conor did what he did best: He laughed. Dodging my throw, he caught the keys easily, and tossed them in the air a few times while looking at me. His blue eyes flashed and the corners of his mouth twisted up in small inverted Vs.

"Hey, Retard, I'll make a deal with you. Let's never, ever argue about car mats again, as long as we live. I love you."

He shook his head and laughed some more. My shoulder blades melted down my back, like I'd just gotten a Swedish massage.

"No more car mats, Retard, I promise."

He put his arms around me. He laughed again and kissed the top of my head.

Most Saturday mornings we headed two towns down the highway to our new weekend fort, a crowded breakfast-all-day place called Jake's. One day a Doberman sat tied with a red nylon leash outside the diner. Conor stopped to pet him. The dog looked up and whined with pleasure.

"Reminds me of Knight—you should have seen him," Conor said, shaking his head as we walked inside. I'd heard plenty about Knight, the big brown Doberman who'd been Conor's best friend during his twenties. "You'll love this—I remember once I had to leave him alone for twelve hours straight. When I got home and tried to open the front door, it wouldn't budge. I finally forced it open. Turned out Knight was blocking the door. I got in and saw a huge pile of dog poop on the floor that Knight was trying to cover with a towel he'd dragged in from the bathroom."

He laughed uproariously, overpowering the small, crowded diner. Conor was wearing a pale pink pin-striped shirt, perfectly ironed jeans, and expensive Italian loafers. Every other man at Jake's had on work boots. I doubt any other man in the diner—maybe all of Vermont—had a pink shirt in his closet.

"Another time, I'd been helping my stepfather on a job at the gas station—don't ask me why. I got home in the middle of the night, covered with gas and oil. I had to come in through a window because I'd left my key somewhere. I stuck my leg through first and Knight, without a single bark, swear to God, silently clamped his jaw around my shin. I yelled at him and he let go when he heard my voice—I guess the oil masked my scent."

Conor laughed again. Joy took over his entire face, his hands flew in the air, a tear appeared in the corner of his eye. Patty, our middle-aged waitress, was smiling at him from across the room, her arms folded over her blue apron.

I knew already that the story of the perfect dog had a

terrible ending. I remembered the first time I couldn't help ask, "So what happened to Knight?"

Conor had shaken his head and looked down like a kid without a costume on Halloween.

"Well, when Knight was five, I got into college. I couldn't take a dog. So I gave him to a former police officer who'd worked out at my gym. Had a big farm in western Mass. His kids thought Knight was like an older brother. He had the run of two hundred and fifty acres. I stopped by on my way home during spring break a year later and the farmer told me that Knight had been shot by deer hunters just after Christmas."

At the diner now, five years later, Conor sighed and leaned closer to me. He took my left hand, looked at my pretty engagement ring, and then glanced up at me.

"You'd love a Dobe, Leslie," he said softly. "They are such loyal dogs. You need someone to keep you company during the days that you're working at home."

I was not lonely working at home. We lived in *Vermont,* which last time I checked had a burglary rate one-hundredth that of Manhattan. For company my cat Criseyde would have been ideal, and she would have loved our rambling ranch house and the mice in the basement. It was useless to even bring up getting her back from my sister. Conor would just say he was still allergic, right?

"I love dogs, honey," I told him. "But I've always imagined a black Lab or a golden retriever. A Doberman, Conor? I am terrified of them. Everyone is. What will our friends and

family, even our neighbors, think? I don't want to have a dog that everyone is afraid of."

A few days later, Conor found a local breeder and took me for an afternoon to check out puppies. The father had huge, peaceful eyes and an easy grace to his action. The mother, smaller and darker brown, wagged her stub tail so hard it blurred.

On our way out to the car, puppy smell still on our hands, we saw a double rainbow arched over a stubbly cornfield across the road from the breeder's red ranch house. The colors, especially the yellow and violet, gleamed against the gun-metal gray of the sky. A sign of something good coming our way.

"See, Leslie? I knew you'd love them. You should trust me," Conor teased on the drive home. It wasn't that I trusted or didn't trust him. It was that I had no idea how to oppose someone as determined as Conor.

There was only one male in the litter. Conor insisted that a male would bond better with me. The puppy had patient brown eyes, too large for his head, and a coat so silky it had a blue-black sheen. We brought Blue home the day before our first Christmas together, our present to each other. The three of us huddled alone in our empty living room, the center-piece a scrubby tree decorated with a strand of lights from the hardware store. We bought Blue more presents than we bought ourselves, although Conor did surprise me with a big square box from Filene's that contained an elegant wool coat with a raccoon collar. The coat was more expensive than

anything I would have bought for myself. I loved it. At the same time I dreaded our January credit card bill.

Blue became my small, uncoordinated shadow. He slept on the floor of my office while I worked, chewing on a blanket he held between his huge paws as if it were an oversized baby bottle. I spent hours in the backyard teaching him to wear a collar and leash, to sit, lie down, come when called. I took him for long walks in the snow around our ugly little town, past old decrepit farms that had been neglected because the owners, whose families had cleared the fields stone by stone a century ago, couldn't afford repairs after paying property taxes. Blue waited on a blanket in the passenger seat when I visited clients or worked at the magazine in Bennington. Sometimes I even took him to New York when I had to meet with editors. After every absence, no matter how brief, he wagged his slinky body as if I were the savior he'd been awaiting his entire short life.

January. Conor and I stood in two feet of snow in our backyard with our hands on our hips, looking at the rotting wood of our back fence and the scraggly bushes that were taking over the yard, figuring out how to fight a half acre of Mother Nature. Suddenly a gruff voice called out over the wooden fence, "Don't be surprised if you hear my shotgun going off in the backyard. I'm after that goldurn groundhog there." A few

seconds later, a white-whiskered seventy-year-old man who looked like a skinny Santa Claus lumbered around the fence and introduced himself as our next-door neighbor. He carried a long, heavy gun, which he pointed toward the snow-covered ground. Red flannel long underwear peeked out under his belt. He hitched up his pants and stuck out his free hand.

"A shotgun?" I asked after we'd introduced ourselves. "For the backyard?"

"Sure, sure," Santa said, looking at me like a young 'un who didn't know any better. "Almost all of the neighbors 'round here have guns. Two retired police chiefs down the street. Guarantee ya they got more 'an one."

He gestured in the neighbors' direction with the long black nose of his gun.

"Aya, it was nice meeting you folks. Don't be scared if you hear that crack. Hope I get him this winta'." And he trudged back to his side of the fence.

I raised my eyebrows at Conor. "Whew!" I said quietly so as not to offend our gun-toting neighbor. "Can you believe that? He's got a gun! Do you think he's right that lots of people here own guns?"

"Well, it should be that way, Leslie," Conor said resolutely, almost excitedly, as if he'd been waiting to argue this new opinion. "It's cold as hell out here. Let's go inside." He turned toward the house. I mechanically followed him, stunned by this strange new reality: guns in our backyard.

"Everyone should have a gun if they want to protect

themselves," he said over his shoulder. "That's what this country is about. Guns are easy to buy here. You gotta love Vermont. My company even has a gun range for employees to use."

"What?" I looked at him like he was a two-headed snake. In New York, company perks were health clubs and taxi rides home if you stayed later than eight P.M.

"I actually have been thinking we should get one, too. I know how to shoot. . . ."

He did?

"I've always wanted to be able to practice on a regular basis. It would be good for you, too, so that you could protect yourself when I'm not around, all those days you spend alone in the house."

I looked at him sideways. He was holding onto the railing of the back porch, stomping his snowy sneakers on the wooden steps.

"Conor, I thought we moved here so you could escape the bullets. Why would you want to bring them into our life?"

Now he looked at me like *I* was deranged.

"Retard, I don't want some criminal to come in here and take away everything that matters to us, to humiliate and degrade us. You should have protection when you're home alone. Just you wait, you'll see that I'm right."

I was too surprised to say anything. God, I hoped he was not serious.

Turns out he was. On Saturday I stayed home to finish

an article for *Seventeen* while Conor drove to the Brattle-boro Trading Post and bought not one but two guns. Just like that. He laid out a Colt .45 and something called a Glock on our kitchen table, complete with four cardboard boxes of bullets, at least ten little brushes and several plastic bottles of cleaning fluid and oil and special chamois cloths. He also had an application to join the National Rifle Association.

Saturday night we stayed in for dinner. The kitchen table smelled like the lubricating oil from the guns and Conor's fingernails were rimmed with black grease.

"Those bullets I got?" he said, his mouth full of leafy lettuce. "Hollow points. They explode upon impact with flesh. And I think I should probably get a shotgun, too, next time I go to the Trading Post."

Hollow-point bullets? A shotgun?

"How much did those guns cost, Conor?"

Maybe logic about our finances would get through to him. We had no money for *guns*.

"It's a small price to pay for your safety, babe."

He had no idea how disturbing this topic was to me; or did he?

"If you make guns criminal, only criminals will have guns." He said this like he thought it up himself. Had he forgotten I knew how to read? This pithy NRA slogan was plastered all over the yellow application form he'd asked me to sign so we could get the family discount.

I got up from the table, unable to say anything more.

This was not a conversation I had ever imagined having with anyone in my life.

Conor never bought a shotgun, fortunately. But he put the Colt .45 under his pillow and the Glock into the car's glove compartment behind the owner's manual. Often he'd stuff it into his pocket when we went to breakfast at Jake's or walked around the neighborhood at night. When I was fluffing our pillows in the mornings after he left for work, sometimes I'd come upon the .45 like a scorpion in our bed. Who was this man I loved?

March. As we sometimes did on weekend mornings, one cold, overcast day we drove to Boston to escape the paralyzing quiet of Vermont winter weekends. On the way down, bundled in my new wool coat, I drove while Conor sipped his coffee in the passenger seat, the car filled with the blooming voices of Anita Baker and Sade. Blue sat in back with his head poking between us.

I nosed the car into one of the tiny, crooked spaces in Cambridge that I'd discovered as an undergrad when I knew every brick in Harvard Square. First we walked across the cobblestones to Memorial Church, where in June Conor and I would be married. We tied Blue's leash to the railing at the bottom of the steps.

Conor and I walked up the smooth wide stairs, between four elegant white columns into the empty one-room brick

building. The narrow crimson carpet led to a mahogany altar. In three months I would be on my father's arm walking past guests sitting in the simple wood pews underneath the creamy white walls inlaid with the names of graduates who died in World War II.

The last time I had sat in this church was during graduation two years before. All the English majors had gathered here, our black gowns heavy and awkward, the air in the Yard thick as fog with the pride and nostalgia of the thousands of parents, including my own, assembled to witness our coronation. A few weeks later, I'd moved to New York and *Seventeen*.

So much had happened in two years.

At the altar, Conor put his palms on my shoulders and kissed me softly on the lips. "I love you, babe," he whispered. "Thanks for loving me so much." He rested his forehead on mine. The altar became the world all around, Conor at the center.

We crossed the snowy, wind-whipped Yard arm in arm, the raccoon fur of the coat warm on my chin. Conor held Blue's leash. We walked to the Fogg Art Museum, where our wedding reception would be held in the inner courtyard. I took Conor through the Fogg's collection, pointing out my favorite Van Gogh self-portrait with green and yellow insanity swirls around his head; a delicate Degas dancer; a florid nymph by Titian. I showed him where the florist would place the bouquets, where the photographer wanted us to pose, the special changing rooms set aside for us.

"It's all gonna look great, babe," he said, looking around in awe. "You're gonna make us a beautiful wedding."

Although today was freezing, raw and gray, the early June weather would be sunny, I knew. I had luck in making everything look perfect on the outside. My graduation from high school was on a cloudless blue day. College, too. Every birthday. All perfect days. No one had ever told me that rain on your wedding day was supposed to mean good luck.

After leaving the Fogg we walked the crowded streets of Cambridge arm in arm, Blue trailing behind us. I kept my eye out for Winnie. Their HBS dorm was right across the Charles River. I hadn't called her much lately because Conor became enraged every time I did. He'd rant for an hour about Harvard's half-wit quota that made it easy for the richie-rich boys to get in instead of him. To make matters even worse, Winnie had taken a part-time job working in the HBS admissions office, which Conor took as an insult designed just to gall him. But I would have loved to run into Winnie, to see her smile, to hear her use a few inappropriate swear words in telling us about her life as an HBS spouse.

Conor, Blue, and I walked along Brattle Street as it curved through Harvard Square, window-shopping, passing the Brattle Theatre, which had been a church until my father and a classmate converted it to a movie theater in the late fifties and Dad hired Mom to be the candy girl. The loony, dynamic energy of Cambridge was a drug compared to the isolation of the empty ranch house with green cancer walls in snow-covered Vermont.

We ended up at the Coffee Connection overlooking bustling Mt. Auburn Street. We spent two hours drinking strong black coffee and silently reading the papers, our legs just touching, Blue asleep under my chair. We spent the rest of our cash on coffee beans to take home—one of our few luxuries.

Conor put down *The Boston Globe—The Glob,* Mom always called it.

"So, where should we go for dinner? The North End?"

We were only a few miles from Southie but going to see Conor's family was out of the question. We'd been there once, for a brief, horrifying visit to Chickie and Wade's essentially unfurnished apartment near the Expressway. I'd tried not to stare at the bare rooms, more like a cheap motel than a home. It was true, what Conor had said that day back in my Chelsea apartment so long ago—there was not one book, magazine, or newspaper in the entire place. Nor much of anything else, nothing on the walls, no personal knick-knacks or framed pictures of family, nothing but a television set on the cardboard box it came in. Wade and Chickie kept the TV on the whole time we were there. Conor said one day he'd take me by his grandparents' old apartment, show me his former gym, his favorite haunts when it didn't make him too angry to go back.

"Honey, we really should just go home," I told him.

I pictured the latest statements from our credit cards. Each balance was at or above the limit.

Conor gave me a cold stare.

"We literally cannot afford to go out to dinner tonight, hon," I tried again. I wanted to stay here, too. At times I wanted never to go back to Vermont and the house and our life there.

"Fine. Let's go then," he said brusquely, childishly, throwing his empty coffee cup into the trash. As if our credit card balances were my fault. Blue jumped up, shook his body to wake himself, and looked in puzzlement from me to Conor as if trying to figure out what the problem was here.

Conor took the wheel as we drove home. The roads going north in the early evening were empty. Southbound, they were crowded—everyone was going in the opposite direction, toward Boston, to dinner, the movies, a hockey game. Conor gripped the steering wheel with both hands, staring straight ahead. His ominous silence ate away at me more than words could ever have.

"Conor, God, it's not my fault."

He didn't say anything, didn't even look at me.

"We just don't have the money."

Again, nothing.

"I'm just trying to be responsible. We need cash for the mortgage, the car insurance, my health plan. American Express is going to cancel my card if I miss any more payments."

Conor still did not respond. He stared straight ahead at the empty road.

I leaned into the gray cloth seat and looked out the pas-

senger window. Old farms lined the quiet country roads. The sky was black overhead, carpeted with brilliant white stars. An ideal setting for the bullets to go over Conor's head. And mine.

"So who gets the car this Thursday night?" I asked, trying to change the subject. "You've got your finance class, right? And I have a puppy obedience class with Blue."

Conor barely glanced at me. Staring straight ahead, face expressionless, he shifted gears and the car decelerated smoothly down a long hill past an abandoned dairy farm, the white fence paint peeling off in long jagged strips.

Suddenly he spoke.

"I don't think I can marry you."

I stared at him, stunned.

He sounded defensive. He sounded scared. Worst of all, he sounded honest.

I held my breath. He couldn't marry *me*?

Conor kept driving, his strong hands steady on the wheel, his blond hair glinting in the light thrown off by the occasional street lamp. The white painted lines at the side of the road slipped by as I looked out the window, away from Conor's face. He said nothing.

After a few moments, I crawled into the backseat to get as far from him as I could. I wrapped my coat around myself, hugging Blue's warm body. How would I tell my family, my *Seventeen* coworkers, my friends, that he'd left me after I'd done so much for him? I started to cry quietly. Blue licked the

tears off my face for a few minutes. Then he gave up and went to sleep in my arms. Crying only made me feel more frantic and more desperate. I couldn't stop.

By the time we pulled into our subterranean garage, my throat ached and my face was swollen and cracked from the salt in my tears. Conor pulled in carefully and then got out and opened the back door. He stuck his head in.

"Come on, baby, stop crying. It's okay. I love you."

I heaved a huge sigh of relief, cleansed, saved. Forgiven—but for what, I didn't know. I smiled as I looked up at him. I let him help me get inside. All that mattered was being close to him. I never brought up what he'd said, or what it meant. Conor didn't, either.

Tuesday after Memorial Day weekend. Five days to go. Mom's thirty-year-old wedding dress lay folded in tissue paper in its original Saks Fifth Avenue box, perched atop Frankie's dresser in our bedroom. I'd found a six-foot-two German seamstress named Brunhilde—she looked uncannily like the hungry witch from *Hansel and Gretel*—to hand-sew intricate lace flowers into the original neckline and train. The caterer, the florist, the photographer all waited impatiently like shoppers outside Bloomingdale's art deco doors the morning of the summer white sale, except that my marriage to Conor was the white sale.

The early-morning sun slanted into my office, a yellow streak on Blue lying on the carpet. On my cheap wooden desk sat a slim, modern laptop computer, more expensive than we could afford. UPS had delivered it the day before.

"I need a laptop," Conor had insisted six weeks earlier. "For my financial management class. A nice laptop is gonna show people at work that I'm serious."

"But Conor, we can't afford it. We can't even afford a new washing machine. We don't buy more than three dollars of gas at a time."

"Come on, honey. Can't you just charge it to your AmEx and expense it as part of your writing business?"

I couldn't say no to Conor. So there I was in my nightgown, trying to get the new machine to work. I had to finish one last article before the wedding—for once, *Vermont Sunday* had agreed to pay me on the spot when I turned in the article. We needed the cash for the honeymoon. Two rooms away I heard the spray of water that meant Conor was getting into the shower.

This small thin machine seemed overwhelmingly complicated. What if I couldn't get the computer to work? What if I couldn't finish the article? How would we eat on our honeymoon?

To break the spell of my own panic, I stood up and slammed my open hand on the table.

"Shit! You stupid machine!" I yelled just after the noise of Conor's shower stopped.

Suddenly the house felt unexpectedly quiet. Conor burst into my office dripping wet, wrapping a blue towel around his waist. Hunched over the computer, I froze.

He grabbed my shoulder and turned my body to face his. His skin was stretched tight across his cheeks.

My heart seized as if I'd stumbled upon a snake on the path behind our house. I saw the pink blur of his hand as he slapped me hard across my face. My skin stung as my teeth cut through the soft, wet flesh of my mouth. My head jerked back. Conor grabbed my throat, pushed me up against the wall, and tightened his grip. He shook my whole body back and forth.

"*Don't. Scream. Like. That,*" he spit through clenched teeth. With every word my head hit the office wall, my neck bending like a Gumby doll.

I couldn't take my eyes off his face. I could smell his shaving cream but I could not breathe.

"My mother screams like that," he said. "Don't ever scream like that again," he said as if begging me. He pushed me to the floor and left the room. The front of my flannel nightgown was wet from his body.

I stayed on the cold wooden floor until I heard Conor go down the steps to the garage. The car engine rumbled. The garage door clattered open. The tires squeaked on the cement as he backed the Volkswagen out to go to his office.

Once I knew he'd gone, I took the yellow pages off my office bookshelf and looked up an 800 number for an abuse hotline, the kind of advice I'd offer in a sidebar for *Seven-*

teen. Wasn't this what you're supposed to do if your husband hit you? Your fiancé who was going to be your husband in five days? If any man hit you?

I was shaking from my fingertips to the pit of my stomach, feeling as if I were going to throw up. I dialed the 800 number from my office. Hot, hard tears like flax seeds sprang from my eyes as I gripped the phone and stared out the window at the lilac tree that smelled so sickly sweet.

What would I say when a voice answered? That it was 7:30 A.M., way too early for this to have happened? That Conor was the only man I'd ever loved this deeply? That he had driven off in our only car? That if it came to a choice between him or me I didn't know who I'd choose? That I might have bruises on my wedding day? That I was sure he was very sorry?

Did I tell the voice that although I was scared, I was not surprised?

The line was busy.

I let out a breath that I did not know I was holding. I walked through the house to make sure Conor was really gone. The house was quiet. I would take a shower to calm down and then call again.

I drank my coffee. I dressed and walked to the local library to finish the article on the public computer. I didn't call the hotline again.

I didn't call Conor either and I didn't answer the phone when it rang that afternoon. That was my big punishment for him. I left the house purposefully dark when he was due

home, to scare him into thinking I was halfway to Dad's house in Washington. Because no one hit me, ever, right?

In reality I was sitting in my office with my small lamp on, hunched over my desk, proofreading the article with my face five inches from the paper and my pen clutched tight in my right hand.

I pretended I didn't hear the Volkswagen pull in around six P.M. He came into my office holding the car keys, head down. I could smell fear on him, panic that I was going to vilify him for what he'd done or announce I'd canceled the wedding.

The dread on Conor's face offered a spider's thread of hope. If he were afraid, he'd never attack me again, right? I could leave anytime. And anyway, he just grabbed my throat. He couldn't have *hit* me. We were getting married.

Three days later, when my family and our wedding guests started arriving, the ten small reddish brown bruises around my neck were so faint no one noticed them.

As our wedding day accelerated toward us, it was easier than you'd think to avoid what had happened. Pulling off a flawless wedding for one hundred guests provided constant distractions—last-minute questions from the caterer, photographer, bridal party, minister, out-of-town guests who called to express their trepidation about Cambridge's notorious

maze of one-way streets and demonic drivers, the maintenance man at the church, the concierge at the hotel.

Yellow Post-it notes littered the kitchen like autumn leaves. Winnie: Hold bouquet during ceremony. Sylvia: Needs Bible for reading. Photographer: No pictures of Mom and Dad together! Aunt Nellie: Happy to wear lucky penny inside my right shoe. Minister Preston: Take "obey" out of the vows.

The gravitational force created by friends, family, and near-strangers, including myself, who expected me to get married seemed nonnegotiable. The fact that it was me marrying Conor, the man I loved who'd just choked me and bashed my head into a wall—in other words, the rest of my life that was at stake—seemed basically irrelevant.

What seemed far more pressing was that every detail fall into place. A fairy-tale wedding seemed like insurance against a turbulent marriage. There was no space for enjoyment or regret, reflection or reconsideration. It all happened too fast.

Conor did not apologize. Not a word to acknowledge what he'd done. I never caught him looking surreptitiously at the bruises on my neck. He carried himself exactly as if he'd never attacked me, never held his hands around my neck, never thrown me down onto the floor like an old rake.

My side of the family settled into the Embassy Suites on Storrow Drive, across the Charles River from the blue, green, and red spires of the Harvard River Houses. Conor's

family lived close enough that no one needed a hotel, fortunately, sparing Conor their proximity. The rehearsal dinner
was held at the Union Oyster House. Afterward, amid the
Friday night hustle of Fanueil Hall, Dad and I waited for
taxis to get the guests back to the hotel, awkwardly saying
good night to Conor's mother, Wade, and his stepsisters and
brothers.

"Dad, could we have breakfast tomorrow, maybe around
eight?" I suddenly asked him, my throat swelling, my stomach feeling liked I'd swallowed a tennis racquet. I wanted an
hour just with my father. Maybe I'd tell him what Conor had
done to me, if I had enough guts.

"Sure, babe," he said, smiling, a bit tipsy from his Old
Turkey bourbon, throwing his arm around my waist. "What
a perfectly lovely idea."

I felt like weeping with relief.

Conor and I had decided to honor the tradition of the
groom not seeing the bride until the wedding (or until the wedding photos, at least), so I didn't see Conor again that night.
Back at the hotel, I went up to Sylvia's room. She was already
asleep, wearing her basketball shorts and a Harvard T-shirt,
holding the old stuffed elephant she'd gotten for Christmas
when she was six. Conor crashed with his best man, Jed, his
partner from the kung fu schools in Southie, in the honeymoon suite.

Our wedding day dawned clear and sunny, a perfect June
morning. I slipped out of my soft hotel bed and took a quick
run along the Charles River, pounding the same paths I

learned to love in college. The early-morning sky was a powder-blue wash, the bright white sun just beginning to warm the cool, sweet-smelling air. I ran along the twisting dirt trail that skirted the slow-moving, polluted Charles. I thought about what I'd say to Dad. I pictured him telling me I couldn't possibly marry Conor; I imagined him making an announcement on the church steps while I hid in my sister's hotel room crying, devastated but sure it was the right thing to call everything off.

Shaking with adrenaline, I showered and changed quietly, tiptoeing while Sylvia slept. The lobby and restaurant were nearly empty when I went down just before eight. I waited by a window table at the hotel restaurant for nearly forty minutes. I couldn't admit that Dad had forgotten, or simply wasn't coming. A couple of times, checking my watch, I cried a few tears surreptitiously. Now I *needed* to tell him—but how would I find the time, the place, the courage?

On my way out to the lobby to call around, hoping maybe there was another restaurant where he just might be waiting, I spotted him sitting at a table by the buffet with some relatives, the remains of his breakfast in front of him, his thinning hair still wet from the shower. He looked up, his gray eyes like small manholes. He did not say, "Oh, there you are, I was looking for you." He barely acknowledged me. I didn't know what to do. Suddenly I couldn't imagine telling him or anyone what Conor had done to me; the attack didn't seem real, even to me. So I sat down and ate breakfast and pretended everything was normal.

Conor and I and the wedding party met the photographer at Memorial Church two hours before the ceremony was slated to begin. Harvard Yard was peaceful and quiet, the maniacal Cambridge traffic shut out by the high brick walls separating the Yard from the Square. I felt like I was behind bulletproof glass in a New York taxicab. The afternoon sun dappled the lawn outside the church across from Widener Library, where I'd spent many nights in a tiny cubicle surrounded by darkened stacks writing my thesis about twentieth-century vanguards like Edith Wharton, Virginia Woolf, and Margaret Drabble, writers who labored to capture the exquisite splitting-of-self compromises women face.

The wedding photographer looked like Georgia O'Keeffe, a tall, thin woman with a big toothy smile and a graying bun of hair. An artist who couldn't take a cheesy wedding picture if she tried. She arranged the dress, my hair, my flowers, my flowing ivory train, Conor and me in perfect symmetry.

"Okay! I've got enough. Beautiful shots!" she announced thirty minutes before the ceremony was supposed to begin.

I went inside the church to fix my makeup in the tiny upstairs bathroom. After about ten minutes, Winnie and Sylvia came to tell me that Conor had disappeared. Sylvia looked to me, uncertain, scared like she was on the nights Mom was reeking by five P.M. and getting to soccer practice meant risking her life with Mom behind the wheel.

"Every groom is late, last-minute cold feet, right?" I joked. The three of us made a face at our reflections in the

full-length bathroom mirror. The absence of a groom on your wedding day had to be just a minor detail.

A quiet voice inside said maybe *this* was the way out. Maybe Conor wanted to dodge the wedding as badly as I did. Perhaps if I hid in the bathroom, this wedding would vanish like a cloud wisp on a summer afternoon. From the tiny rectangular bathroom window, I looked out on my guests parading up the church steps in colorful wedding attire, decorating the white stone entrance like flower petals. To make myself stop shaking, I imagined they'd come to honor someone else's union.

Mom came in to tell us that Dad had gone off, too. Fifteen minutes after the ceremony was supposed to begin, I saw my father come up the steps, his face down. From my perch I saw his back bent over, his slightly pigeon-pointed toes, reminders of our Cherokee ancestors. Behind him walked Conor and Jed in their rented tuxedos and slicked-down hair. Conor looked as numb as I felt and he did not see me peering out the window as he passed below.

Mom returned to confirm that Conor was now waiting at the church altar.

"Look up," she said, giving me one final hair and lipstick check. She looked beautiful in her beaded blue mother-of-the-bride dress. A mother anyone would be proud to have.

"Mom?" I asked, hoping she could sense my distress through the same kind of mother-daughter osmosis that had prompted her, from four hundred miles away, to pick up the phone the night my junior year when I'd gotten food poisoning

so severe I'd been hospitalized. She'd also known something was wrong the afternoon I'd found out my creative writing thesis had been rejected by the English Department's stuffy, all-male review committee. These moments alone with her were my final toehold. But I couldn't begin to say any of that.

Instead I asked, "Do you have any last-minute advice?" My voice sounded like I was begging.

"Don't smile too much as you walk down the aisle," she said, looking away.

We were married. The ceremony took twenty-five minutes. It felt like twenty-five seconds.

You could hear the harp chords floating out from the Fogg courtyard like a princess's herald. The tablecloths were fuchsia, the flowers a medley of pink, white, blue, and purple, the champagne endless, the menu graced by delicate asparagus, salmon rounds, puff pastry shells. Our chocolate wedding cake would have held its own on a *Gourmet* magazine cover. My stomach felt like a locked safe. I didn't have time to eat or go to the bathroom and I hardly talked to Conor. The reception felt like a video where someone had pressed the fast-forward button.

There was a moment when time paused. The photographer, inspired by the dramatic setting of the Fogg's Italian Renaissance architecture, asked me to pose on the edge of the second-story balcony overlooking the courtyard below. Behind me, the marble walls were lined with paintings by

Titian, Ingres, and Cabanel, dark oils of frolicking nymphs and depictions of Venus in heavy gilt frames, celebrating the glory days before Manet's shocking *Olympia* and the explosion of Impressionism. As I sat on the wall feeling like Juliet, my ivory train fluttered almost ten feet below me into the courtyard space. The guests gathered to watch the photo arrangement. They were silent, clutching their drinks as they looked up at me, their eyes like matched sets of dark coins. Conor was not among them. The photographer told me not to smile, but to imagine I was Mona Lisa looking into the distance, into the future. Half a smile was probably all I could muster anyway. After a dozen clicks, the photographer helped me climb down. "This will be the one," she said, tapping her camera. "The perfect shot."

Later, after the photos and toasts and first dance and cutting the cake were all over—beautiful, everything—all I could fathom was that my feet were killing me and I needed to pee badly. I came out of the bathroom trailing my long wedding train to find the courtyard half empty. Many guests had left without saying good-bye. Why would anyone leave such a beautiful reception so early?

Mom followed me upstairs to the changing room where my green silk "traveling suit" was laid out. She unbuttoned the back of my—and her—wedding gown nimbly. Her dexterity made me realize she wasn't even tipsy. It'd been years, more than a decade, since I'd spent an evening with Mom where she was so tense that she'd refrained from getting

drunk. Was every single person at the wedding, including me and Conor and my mother, pretending this marriage was not a horrendous mistake?

"I'll take it now—that'll be easier," Mom said. From under a couch she took out the cardboard Saks Fifth Avenue box. She must have hidden it there earlier in the day, planning to take back my wedding gown even before I'd put it on. She covered the dress, still warm from my body, with tissue paper. She carefully closed the corners of the old box like a tomb.

Sylvia and I filled a taxi with flowers from the reception and we drove back to the hotel together, squeezed in the backseat with pink and yellow roses on our laps. Conor could not fit with us, so he left with Jed. I hugged Sylvia and headed up to the honeymoon suite carrying the biggest vase. The hallway was quiet and empty. I set down the flowers and slipped the keycard in the door, my hand shaky, not knowing what to expect.

Inside, Conor and Jed were sitting under the covers in the massive king-size bed, waiting for me. They had their arms around each other and huge grins on their faces. Jed stank of whiskey. He was wearing one of my long-sleeved flannel nightgowns, a Lanz sprigged with pink rosebuds, white lace and pearl buttons against his black chest hairs. He had my wedding veil on, too.

Conor sat next to Jed smoking a cigar, his broad chest stretching the ruffled front of his rented tuxedo shirt. As I took in the tableau, they burst into guffaws like teenage boys

in high-school French class. Laughing so hard the huge bed shook, Conor finally told me the story of why he was late to the ceremony.

"This guy"—he shot Jed a hard glance and burst into fresh laughter—"talked me into going to a bar across the street from the church. We had no idea what time it was. Don't know how your dad found us," Conor explained in the awed tone he always used when talking about my father. "Somehow he did. He sat down at the bar, chatted us up, said he didn't really have time for a drink because the wedding was about to start. So we went back with him."

"Ah, Les, you looked like an angel up there," Jed said, smiling like I was his little sister.

"Yeah, babe. You are the best. Come here," Conor chimed in. My body uncoiled. He slipped his arm around my waist and kissed me. "We're married." He had the same touch of awe in his voice.

He and Jed looked at each other and started laughing again. I changed into a pair of peach silk pajamas, a gift from Nellie. We bounced on the bed and took pictures of each other in my veil. Jed drank every miniature whiskey in our minibar, breaking the tiny gold seals with his large workman's hands, carefully lining up the empties on top of the burled wood TV console. They told me stories about Southie that made me laugh until the corners of the sheets were wet with my tears and stained with black streaks of my mascara.

At midnight Conor and I kicked Jed out and fell into bed. We didn't make love. It was a glorious relief just to forget the

events of the day and the week, to sink into the thick white hotel pillows and fall asleep with Conor's arms and body wrapped around me, warm and soft as a sheepskin coat.

———❖———

People complain—with enthusiasm—about the stress and expense and family tantrums that make up the drama of most weddings. But admit to an awful *honeymoon*? It'd be easier to open up the PA system at the local Wal-Mart and announce that your husband gave you herpes.

More than anything, Conor and I required a *cheap* honeymoon. In April, sitting at my white desk, I'd opened a distinctly unfriendly letter from the mortgage company about our myriad late payments. My American Express card had been canceled in May, via a form letter ordering me to cut up and return my card. I still kept the little green rectangle in my purse, a talisman from my New York life. But I knew it was useless. Our dire daily cash flow meant I could only take out twenty to forty dollars from an ATM at once, hardly enough to get traveler's checks for a romantic sojourn to Italy. I'd scoured my brain, scanning for affordable places that would still be marginally romantic.

One day a few weeks before the wedding, as I drove to pick up Conor from work, I'd thought of Martha's Vineyard, the secluded island off the Massachusetts coast. We could drive there, and take our car on the ferry. We'd continue the twenty-dollar-per-day local cash machine habit instead of

taking out lumps of cash in advance. We'd rent a cottage instead of an expensive hotel room. We could still make it sound and hopefully feel like a real honeymoon.

Once, with Winnie and her family, I'd come to the tiny pile of rubble at the tail end of the massive glacier that slid down from Canada. As a twelve-year-old, I took my first flight alone in a puddle jumper, up and away from the tiny Vermont airport near our cluttered, noisy farmhouse to Winnie's family's enormous Victorian estate, complete with tennis court, a pond with an island, a private beach, and a little bakery at the end of the winding, tree-lined driveway. Winnie and I and her babysitter stayed in our own guest house, listening to "Hot Child in the City" on her babysitter's boom box, French braiding each other's hair, talking about boys from school until we fell asleep in our sleeping bags. Winnie's family sold the estate when we were thirteen. She'd never been back. But as a college student, I took a bus from Boston and then the ferry to the Vineyard by myself, to spend a day visiting the island, going to the bakery, the private beach next door to her old house, standing at the bottom of the winding driveway to catch a glimpse of the house's peaked shingle roof above the trees.

Conor had never been to Martha's Vineyard, despite living his entire life less than three hours away. The treeless streets and gray concrete of Southie might as well have been two million miles from the Vineyard's private white beaches and Victorian "cottages." Conor, who had never said a word about our honeymoon or how we'd pay for it, agreed Martha's Vineyard would be fine.

The morning after our wedding, we packed up the Volkswagen in the driveway of the hotel on Storrow Drive, said our good-byes to our families, and drove south along Route 93. We risked missing the ferry due to Conor's insistence that we stop at multiple fruit stands along the way in search of great corn and tomatoes.

"Would you just relax and let me enjoy my own honeymoon?" he yelled from the passenger seat, his eyes hidden behind his dark sunglasses. "What is wrong with you? You're a bundle of nerves, you're killing me. I want to eat lunch at a real restaurant. We're passing all these great fruit stands. Chill out!"

"Conor," I said sternly, feeling like a schoolmarm, taking one hand off the wheel to point my finger at him. "I had to make these ferry reservations five weeks ago. You don't understand the way it works. If we miss our ferry to Martha's Vineyard in the peak summer times, we won't get there. We'll be spending our honeymoon by the side of the road."

"Yeah." Conor spoke like a rebellious ten-year-old determined not to take me seriously. He reached for the radio tuner.

I grabbed his hand, hard.

"Look, fuck you, *buddy,* for both your insults: that I don't know what I'm talking about, and that I'm a nag for trying to rush you. I planned every minute of this honeymoon and I'm not going to let you screw it up."

I couldn't see his eyes behind his sunglasses. He turned and looked out the window for the rest of the drive.

We arrived at Woods Hole three minutes before our ferry left and three seconds before I duct-taped Conor's mouth. But on the rollicking ferry ride across the ocean, the outline of the Cape Cod coast as well as the fight in the car receded in the background. Conor took my hand as we stood together at the front of the ferry. The salty wind, warm and fresh, blew our clothes and hair. The Vineyard came into view and I felt like skipping down the ramp. The island earth felt different, more solid; the sun was strong and bright, as if we were closer to it now. Conor pulled the car off the ferry ramp and we drove the few miles to our rented cottage, me pointing out all my favorite landmarks. Our little shingled house was neat and sparse, sitting atop a grassy hilltop in Gay Head, the deserted, wild tip of the island near Jackie Kennedy's estate. There were four tiny, barely furnished rooms and a long romantic porch with a view of the ocean. If you didn't look closely, you missed the rotted wood along the house's foundation and the white paint peeling off the porch swing.

Conor lay down for a nap. I started unpacking. I couldn't find his suitcase in the car or the house. I tiptoed into the little yellow bedroom, where white curtains embroidered with buttercups blew gently in the afternoon sea breeze.

"Conor? Are you awake?" I whispered from the doorway.

"Yeah . . . kinda," he said.

"I can't find your suitcase, honey. Did you bring it in from the car?"

"What suitcase, Retard?" he said groggily. "I thought you packed all my stuff in yours."

I stood in the doorway, astonished. He didn't pack for his own honeymoon. I thought of what he'd worn so far. The clothes he had on when we left the house in Vermont—the same button-down shirt and khakis he had on now. The only other clothes were the rented tuxedo he wore to the wedding.

"What are you talking about, hon? I never said I was packing your stuff."

"I just assumed you'd packed my clothes. Isn't that what a good wife does?"

"Oh, Conor," I said, turning away. Is that what a good wife did? There went another two hundred dollars we didn't have, just to buy him a bathing suit, some shorts, and a few shirts to get him through this week. But it was such a funny and stupid thing to have done, I forced myself to laugh as I carefully shut the door to the bedroom so he could go back to sleep.

When he woke up, we went into Edgartown and bought a few essentials. Then we took some old bikes from the cottage shed and went for a long ride along the narrow, winding country roads in search of Winnie's old summer home. That night after dinner I read short stories from F. Scott Fitzgerald's *Babylon Revisited* to Conor on the cottage front porch. He loved "The Diamond as Big as the Ritz" so much, I read it to him twice. In the twilight, the sky's red, pink, and orange streaks faded into the purple and blue night, the horizon disappearing as the ocean merged with the night sky.

The days went by slowly, lots of sleep and daytime sex in

the hammock out back and many cups of coffee on the front-porch swing. I sent pretty postcards to my family, Conor's family, Winnie, the minister who married us. We found a tick on Conor's forearm and put it in the microwave oven. We were little kids again. We ate out twice—all we could afford—but it was enough.

One afternoon we came home from a walk on the beach to find a handwritten note stuck under the cottage door from a woman we'd met outside a coffee shop in Oak Bluffs the morning before. She'd looked at us with longing as if we were a golden couple; she seemed personally elated that we were on our honeymoon. We discovered that she had rented our honeymoon cottage once many summers ago, before she bought her own small bungalow. The note was an offer to ride her horses on the deserted beachfront of her family's farm.

"C'mon, Conor. Let's go. This will be great!"

Driving there, trying to follow her little hand-drawn map, I got lost among the narrow dirt roads leading to the farm. I hated getting lost.

"Fuck," I yelled.

Before I saw his fist go up, Conor had punched me on the right side of my face. My head hit the glass of the driver's side window like a pinball. *Thwonk* went my skull against the re-inforced glass. I started to cry but I didn't even pull the car over. I just kept driving. Damn him. Not again. Not on our honeymoon.

The worst part was my lack of surprise.

A few minutes later we found the farm and our friend waiting by the weathered gray horse barn, the two ponies saddled and tied to the fence. I wiped my face and practiced a few quick grins to get my muscles going. I popped out of the car, a fake smile in place.

"Oh, thank you for letting us ride! Sorry we're late, we had a little trouble finding it."

I was pretty sure she wouldn't notice that my eyes were swollen and that there was a red mark on my right cheekbone the size of a fist. What was I supposed to do, jump out of the car and tell this total stranger, "Help! My husband just hit me because I got lost trying to find this place. Dial nine-one-one!" Unlike Mom's verbal attacks, which I blamed for years on myself, at least I knew what Conor did was wrong.

Conor didn't say anything.

We got on the pretty brown ponies, waved good-bye and rode off down a path to the ocean. We took beautiful, idyllic pictures of our long ride, the shiny ponies prancing in the foamy ocean in the afternoon sun. The sky turned orange and gold with the coming sunset. The light was purple by the time we came back to the barn and put the animals in their stalls.

The last three days went by and then our honeymoon was over. On our way back to Vermont, I drove while Conor slept. Everyone agreed getting married was stressful—maybe that was why he'd hit me. He always hated seeing his family— maybe it made him have flashbacks from the times his step-

father beat him. Was he acting out like the little boy he used to be? Our money problems, too much free time on his hands, the unfamiliar surroundings, all seemed like plausible excuses. I loved him. He loved me. He did not mean to hurt me. That made it okay.

Didn't it?

About thirty minutes before the Vermont state line a small neon-blue car that was going so fast it was shaking like a tin can appeared in my rearview mirror. The car pulled directly behind me and the driver started honking. Surprised, a little frightened, I looked in the mirror again. In the car were two young men dressed in ratty sweatshirts. I slowed down. They pulled up alongside me. The driver flashed a bronze badge that looked real. He kept pressing on the horn, gesturing wildly, his beat-up blue car rattling along the highway like it was made of aluminum.

If these two guys had taken on Massachusetts policemen and gotten away with a badge, I could picture what might happen if we pulled over on the highway for them. So I carefully moved to the right lane, slowed down to fifty miles per hour, and kept driving steadily, looking ahead. Conor woke up in the middle of this. The men badgered our car for a few seconds like a frustrated yellow jacket after a peanut butter and jelly sandwich. Then the car sped away.

"What the hell did you do to make those guys so angry at you?" Conor, barely awake, yelled at me. When I didn't respond to his accusation, he reached down to the floor. What was he doing? Something red, white, and yellow came toward

me. After the object hit me and fell apart, I realized he'd thrown the cold remains of his Big Mac from lunch at me. Small bits of onions and special sauce stuck to my hair, my ear, the steering wheel, and stick shift. This debris hardened during the rest of the drive. I left it there.

I didn't mention these details when friends and family asked how we enjoyed our honeymoon.

June, July, August. The summer passed.

We drove to the lake near Mom's farmhouse one time. She was away on a trip with her tennis team. We had to sneak onto a private beach because no dogs were allowed on the public one, and Conor wanted to let Blue splash around.

The lake was cerulean-blue. Its fingers spread into broad sandy beaches and dozens of secret coves. The moss-green mountains surrounding the water reminded me of Frankie's velvet ballroom couch that was so massive three kids could hide between the seat cushions. Only a few people besides my family and the local residents knew this lake. No place I'd seen—not Lake Como in Italy, not the alpine lakes in Switzerland—was more breathtaking. As a kid, I'd gotten eighteen summers here.

Conor complained that he needed to get home to study for his financial management class.

He would get sunburned because we (I) forgot sunscreen.

The sand bugs were biting his legs.

There was no place nearby to buy a sandwich, a good corned beef deli sandwich, like he used to get in New York.

We left after an hour and a half.

On the way home, we stopped by a spring I remembered near the highway. The water at our ranch house tasted like rust (and worse). Conor wanted pure water, even for Blue's metal drinking bowl, even for brushing his teeth at night. We couldn't afford bottled water. We filled up and tightly capped a dozen gallon milk jugs I'd rinsed out and brought along. I was a good and frugal wife.

One night, sometime that summer during a fight I can't remember, Conor pinned me on the pink futon in our little guest room and held the cold muzzle of the Colt .45 against my temple. He threatened to pull the trigger. I don't remember feeling scared. I did not believe he would fire the gun, although I knew it was fully loaded with hollow-point bullets.

The muzzle left a perfectly circular bruise on my skin for two days.

A bright Tuesday in September. I'd sold a big job to a Bennington printing company that afternoon, doubling my year's

earnings. Conor made dinner to celebrate. He set out candles and cloth napkins that I didn't think he knew we had. He charred a steak on the rickety grill the previous owners had left in the garage.

I leaned against the yellow counter in cutoff jean shorts and a University of Vermont sweatshirt, watching him look for the baked potatoes he'd put in the oven an hour before. They were definitely not in our 1950s oven. He opened cabinet doors and even the trash can. All the while he hummed his favorite Three Stooges ditty ("La Da Dee, La Da Daa"). "Hey, Retard, where'd you hide the potatoes?" he asked me, grinning. He finally looked in the freezer. The two potatoes were gently nestled next to the ice cube tray, at eye level with the top rack in the oven he had heated for the spuds.

Over the candlelit dinner, sans potatoes, he told me that his boss refused to let Conor buy coffee for him that morning in the company cafeteria.

"Greg just looked at me like I was crazy. Wearing his ninety-nine-dollar suit from Sears. Like in Vermont, you upset the world order if you spend thirty-five cents on your boss."

We looked over at Blue, who was gnawing on the bone from the steak, lost in dog nirvana. He noticed us looking at him, stopped chewing, eyed us suspiciously, and then got up and carried his bone out to the living room. Conor and I burst out laughing.

By nine, our street was quiet and dark. Conor cleaned the kitchen while I changed into one of my flowered nightgowns and washed up in the house's lone bathroom, tiny and narrow, covered in faded pink tile, with a small broken window that hadn't opened in several years.

I crawled under the covers to read in bed. The lights were on only in our bedroom, a first-floor room with three large windows that faced the street. Directly across from us was the neighbor's three-story white colonial, the largest house on the block, filled with two parents, three teenage girls, two hyperactive dogs, and an arthritic old Siamese cat. The husband had a subscription to *New England Monthly*. He read and liked my restaurant reviews and an article I'd just written about Frank Lloyd Wright's Usonian residences in New Hampshire. His chipper, sturdy wife wore red lipstick when walking the dogs at seven A.M.

We kept the shades pulled down in our stark little bedroom even during the day. Otherwise we could watch the neighbors' TV from our bed, which actually would have come in handy if our electricity got cut off. Conor came into our bedroom naked, his usual bedtime habit. He fumbled with the shade closest to the street. He hated the thin little crack of light in the morning. He jiggered the shade, trying to get it *perfectly* pulled down until—as if in defiance—it wildly, loudly rolled up.

Across the street, the faces of all three girls and their father, plus the red eyes of the Siamese, stared right at him,

the TV flickering in the background of their living room. Conor had gotten a bit fat here in Vermont. "Enjoying married life," he often joked as he patted his belly. His skin was a damp, pale white because he rarely had time for the nature and outdoors he told me he wanted to move here to enjoy. His profile in the lamplight looked like a naked Homer Simpson.

"Conor!" I shouted. He stood like a Popsicle frozen on a stick.

Like the Road Runner in a Looney Tunes episode, I tore to the light switch and flicked it off. Then I pulled the shade down myself. In the darkness we fell on the bed, holding onto each other, laughing until our cheeks and stomachs ached.

October. Winnie was driving up from Cambridge. I couldn't wait to see her, the first time since the blur of the wedding. A part of me wanted to hide from her, from everyone in my life. I didn't want to lie and say married life was great, even though sometimes it was.

"Doesn't she have anything better to do than drive all the way up here?" Conor asked as we walked Blue around the neighborhood in the morning before he left for work. "I want you to come have lunch with me. I'm your husband. She's just some friend."

"I haven't seen her since the wedding, Conor. She's one of my only friends around here," I explained, not for the first time. Winnie was planning to arrive in the morning, after he'd left for work. She was leaving in the late afternoon to visit some college friends in New Hampshire. I was grateful she wouldn't see Conor at all. Conor lobbed ambiguous insults about Rex in front of Winnie until I wanted to devour myself from shame. I was never sure whether he did it because (1) he was envious, (2) he wanted to push Winnie away, or (3) he knew it drove me crazy. Maybe all of the above.

Conor, Blue, and I turned the last corner of our walk and came upon our house—still puce green on the outside although I'd made sluggish progress repainting the inside walls a calm, unopinionated eggshell white. We walked into the dusty garage. Cobwebs hung from the old roof. I unclipped Blue's leash. Blue raced past Conor up the wooden basement stairs to the kitchen—one of his missions in dog life was to be first to the top of any stairs and out any door. A few weeks ago he'd jumped through the back door, shattering the glass and severing the tendons in his front legs but miraculously not killing himself. Sometimes I felt the same way myself, like I could understand jumping through glass to get to—or escape from—your family.

"This place still smells like oil," Conor said to me accusatorily as we passed through the laundry room on our way to the steps. The complaint was so routine, I missed the undertone that signaled he was still angry about Winnie's visit.

Watching my footing on the creaky, unpainted wooden stairs, I was about two steps behind him. Halfway up, he turned and said over his shoulder in the same coarse voice, "My laundry done yet?"

"No," I said, still looking down. "I think it's in the washing machine."

He turned again, blocking the stairway. He paused and gave me a look of hatred. I stopped, suddenly off balance. With a light push on my chest with both of his hands, just as he pushed his stepfather Wade so many years ago once he'd learned martial arts, he shoved me.

"Get it, then," he said through clenched teeth.

I stumbled backward, clutching for the handrail. My feet, clumsy in Birkenstocks, tangled. I fell halfway down the steps. As I caught my breath on the cold concrete floor, I thought, in amazement, that nothing hurt enough to be broken. Suddenly the basement went black.

When he'd gotten to the top of the stairs as I lay near the bottom, instead of coming to see if I was okay, Conor turned off the basement light.

I was sitting on the front steps drinking my second cup of coffee, listening for her car, when Winnie arrived in her old diesel Mercedes. She got out and we both start laughing because we were wearing identical yellow sundresses. I hugged her long and hard. My back was stiff from the fall and so the

hug hurt. At least I didn't have any bruises to cover up. I wouldn't—and did not want to—tell her the truth. But if she saw bruises, I could not have lied.

We talked over a long lunch of salad and pasta in the Indian summer sunshine on the back porch, surrounded by golden trees and green grass and chirping birds, like blond twins who'd stepped off the cover of a romance novel. Not one set in rural Vermont on the back porch of a cheap ranch house that had no furniture and smoke-stained, hospital-green walls.

"How did I get here, Winnie?" I asked incredulously. "Yesterday, I was single in New York working at *Seventeen*. Now I have a husband, a house, a dog. . . . How did this happen?"

She put her arm around me and laughed, but I meant it.

Conor had taken the VW to work, so Winnie gave me a ride into Bennington that afternoon before heading to Hanover. Conor was planning to pick me up around six P.M. at the magazine's offices. As we drove down the turnpike, Winnie's car coughed a few times and went silent. She pulled over and tried turning the ignition, but the ancient Benz wouldn't start. I walked to the pay phone at the nearest toll-booth and left a message for Conor at work. He left work to rescue us, but Winnie and I had already ridden away in the front seat of the tow truck by the time he got to the highway.

We sorted all this out when Conor picked me up at the entrance to *Bennington Magazine* that night. As soon as I was inside the car he started yelling.

"Goddamn it, Leslie, where were you? I had to leave work, I couldn't find you. I cannot do this kind of thing, Leslie! It's just not done."

He sounded like a kid stamping his feet in frustration. He was so angry that I was afraid to answer.

He got out of the car and said, "You drive," without looking at me. I took the highway to get home as quickly as possible. As I drove sixty miles an hour on the turnpike, he punched the right side of my face. I kept the car in its lane, looking straight ahead, cars all around me in the heat of rush hour.

"Are you crazy? I'm *driving*." I put on my blinker and eased the car to the far right lane and slowed down. He looked at me and smiled.

"I'll show you crazy," he said with something akin to pride. I watched, unbelieving, as he pulled the keys out of the ignition.

The steering column froze. The steering wheel made a soft click as it locked. The speedometer read fifty-five miles per hour.

"Conor!"

He was still jeering at me. I pushed the emergency flashers and applied the brake with caution. The car veered gradually to the breakdown lane. Cars whizzed by on my left, honking furiously. The Volkswagen slowed to a stop. I gripped the steering wheel to hide my shaking hands.

"Conor, give me the keys," I said as calmly as I could man-

age. When he handed them over, I held them in my sweaty palm, taking deep breaths. "That was really stupid, Conor. Do you want to kill us both?"

His plastic smile faded. "Just drive home," he ordered in a tone I had no desire to truck with. I started the car, eased our way to the next exit. I drove home slowly on back roads. Once in the house I quickly started making a pasta dinner. I tried not to think about what he'd done.

While the noodles were boiling on the stove, the phone rang.

"Winnie, hi, where are you? Did you make it to Dartmouth?"

I looked over my shoulder. Conor was in the living room, stroking Blue's back. I didn't think he could hear me.

"Yeah," she said. "I'm at Tamra's apartment. The bus came a few minutes after you left the station. I'll take another one home tomorrow. The mechanic says there's some problem with the engine that he can fix but it's going to take a week. Is there any way you can drive the car back to Boston the next time you come down?"

"Sure, sure, no problem." Did my voice sound normal? "I'll make it as soon as possible."

The pasta boiled over.

"Shit, wait a sec, Winnie." I grabbed the pot and set it in the sink.

"Hey, are you okay? You sound . . . distracted."

An understatement.

"No, I'm okay. Thanks so much for coming to visit. I'm sorry about all the problems with your car."

"Oh, it's not your fault," she said.

Conor had stopped petting Blue and he rustled the newspaper in annoyance that dinner was not ready. I was talking on the phone too long. I'd better get off before he realized it was Winnie. What if he thought I'd told her about the car keys or him pushing me down the stairs? He'd done so many things in such a short space of time. He seemed on a tear he couldn't control. No way I would chance making it worse.

"Oh, no, I'm fine, Winnie," I said loudly so Conor could hear. "Just tired. Long day. Hey, it was great to see you. Thanks for coming. Thank you so much."

I hung up and dumped the overcooked pasta into a colander. The noodles hung like strands from a limp mop. I was too "distracted," as Winnie would say, to care.

When I served Conor dinner, he took one bite and then brushed the bowl off the table with the back of his left hand. Stunned, I stared at the pasta and vegetables lying on the stained yellow linoleum floor.

Through clenched teeth, fists at his side, he said, "Leslie. I can't eat this shit. It reminds me too much of what my mother made me eat after Wade's kids were all done."

Without saying anything I went out to the porch to eat my cold dinner on the back steps, breathing in the cool fall air, trying to recapture the happiness I felt for a few hours with Winnie. Trying not to think about what could have hap-

pened on the highway with Conor. Our life would get better. It had to.

Conor was asleep by the time I'd finished cleaning up the mess.

I drove Winnie's car back to Boston the next week. We sat in the small living room of Winnie and Rex's apartment at Harvard Business School. Rex was in class.

With no preamble I said, "Winnie, I have to tell you something. Sometimes Conor hits me." I said just that—not that in a two-week period he'd choked me, pushed me down the stairs, taken the keys out of the ignition on the highway. I couldn't bear to recount the details.

Winnie gasped.

"Fucking bastard. Right now, Leslie, leave him now. Stay here."

I blew out a mouthful of hot air. "I can't, Winnie. I just can't. I love him. We're married. He doesn't mean it. He just does not know how to deal with his childhood. We're going to go see a therapist, to deal with it."

She was my friend. She knew about love. She tried to understand. She looked miserable.

"Okay, Leslie. I'm just so scared for you. It has nothing to do with him. I like Conor, and I know how much you love him. But he's sick, he needs help."

I could feel her fear. It was terrible to burden her with

the knowledge of what Conor did to me. She put her hands over her eyes.

"Winnie, I had to tell someone. You're the only one I can stand to tell. But I can't leave him."

Every other woman had given up on Conor. I wouldn't. He needed someone who loved him enough to help him. That was me. That's what Winnie couldn't understand, what no one would ever understand.

Winnie sighed and looked up at me.

"Just do this, okay, Leslie? Call me the next time. Come here anytime."

"I will, Winnie. I promise I will."

When Ed Horrigan walked through our front door, I knew right away he was different from the other men Conor worked with—as different as Conor himself. Ed had given Conor a ride home after work. He came inside to say hello; everyone else from the company who'd given Conor a ride dropped him at the end of the driveway. Tall and lanky with close-cropped dark hair and no-nonsense wire-rimmed glasses, he reminded me of my father, in a good way.

"Leslie, it's nice to meet you," he said, politely reaching out his hand.

"Come on, Ed, let me show you around the place," Conor said, waving around. Ed nodded to me as they left the room.

"Wait just a sec, Conor," I interrupted. "Ed, do you want some water, coffee, a Coke?"

"Oh, yes please, pop would be fine."

Pop? He must have been from Boston, too.

It turned out he was. I invited him to stay for dinner. He eyed the spaghetti I'd prepared hungrily. If he was salivating over *my* cooking, he must eat at Burger King and Pizza Hut. He didn't notice that we had no place mats.

I peppered him with questions as he ate.

"Next one over from South Boston, a neighborhood called Roxbury. Roxbury was just like Southie when I grew up. My parents still live in the same house. Ask them," he said, grinning, "they'll tell you nothing has changed. But the truth is our house is the only thing that's the same. Today our neighborhood is filled with graffiti-covered buildings and rusted-out cars. They're too lost in their books and my father's languages to notice a difference."

"Languages?"

"Oh, sorry. My father is a linguist. He speaks over ten languages. Most he taught himself from books. One or two, he doesn't know anybody else who speaks them, so he talks to himself. We hear him carry on conversations in his study for hours. You know that kind of ethereal brilliance that precludes mundane matters such as paying the mortgage or buying his children shoes that fit properly?" Ed laughed. I sat back in amazement to have heard *ethereal* and *preclude* used in the same sentence in the state of Vermont.

"Did you go to school in Roxbury?" I asked, puzzled by how the son of two intellectuals, with glasses and a beanpole frame, could have survived the Boston public school system.

"Well, when I was fourteen, I passed the entrance exam to Boston Latin. You've heard of it? Then I got a scholarship to Harvard. You went there, too, right?"

I nodded. "Class of '87."

"After my time. And anyway, I lived at home during college—to save money. I was probably the only Harvard student in history to pass from Roxbury to Harvard Square twice a day. I was a Dud."

"You were? You must be kidding! I was, too!"

Conor hadn't said a word the whole time. Now he was really lost. A Dud meant Dudley House, the Harvard dining hall for students who lived off-campus. Home of the eclectic, wacky transfer kids, foreign visitors, and shaky twenty-year-olds coming back from nervous breakdowns or rehab. An eccentric group even by Harvard standards.

"I knew there was something I liked about you, Leslie." Ed smiled. "When Conor told me you'd gone to Harvard, I was worried. But now that I know you're a Dud, you're okay by me."

Conor would get really pissed if we kept up with this Harvard-speak. But I couldn't help myself.

"How did you ever find your way to this outback?"

"I've been thinking the same thing about you and Conor. It's a long story . . . Nickelface . . . the Quand . . . a letter from Harvard Business School that sat on my father's desk

unopened for five months . . . I'll tell you the whole sordid tale when you've got nothing better to do. I've worked here—I'm the company's accountant—for the past five years. I send out résumés all the time but no one else wants me."

He smiled again. I felt like I'd found my long-lost brother. Ed turned back to Conor.

"Pal! Sorry about all this Harvard b.s. You married a good woman. You didn't show me the basement yet." Ed winked at me.

Conor took the bait and jumped up, man's work to be done. I cleared the dishes while Conor showed off his tools in the garage, his chain saw and circular blade. Tools he'd insisted on buying but had never, would never, put to use except to demonstrate to other guys.

After that night, Ed and Conor often came home together. The three of us spent long evenings around our dinner table in the ugly, half-renovated kitchen, which faded as we talked and laughed and told stories about work and Harvard and Ed's latest girlfriends. Ed brought me books by the bagful. He read all my article drafts.

One night he started laughing as soon as he saw me.

"Do you have a green dress?" he asked, cracking up. Conor gave him a wary look.

"Well, as a matter of fact, I do, Ed. But I hardly ever wear it around here."

What had Ed been doing? Looking in my closet?

"Mmm, well, last Friday I had lunch in town with Greg Mouse Brain."

Friday was the day I drove back from Manhattan wearing the tailored silk coat dress I had put on as my "traveling suit" after our wedding. I'd worn it last week in New York for my meetings with my new editor at *Seventeen,* the one who replaced Kathy when she went over to *GQ* the previous month.

"We were walking back to his car from the diner. I'd left my glasses at work and you know, I can't see three feet without them. Out of the corner of my eye I saw a blond woman in green, carrying a big pile of mail. 'There is only one woman in Vermont with a dress like that,' I told myself."

We were all out of place here.

I wrapped my scarf around my neck as I left *Bennington Magazine*'s offices after a long afternoon proofing the issue about to go to press. The cold October wind whipped a few shriveled brown leaves off the trees as I walked the two blocks to the big double-door entrance to the public library, which stayed open until eight P.M. on Thursdays.

That day was the one-year anniversary of my last day at *Seventeen.* Our second fall in Vermont. Winter was coming. We'd started seeing a new couples therapist, our third in three months. The first was an intake to get a referral within our health insurance network. Conor hated the second, an older woman who reminded him of Chickie. Now we'd found a third, a man who seemed acceptable. Neither of us had told any of the therapists about Conor's attacks on me. We'd never

spoken to each other about it, either. Amazing but true. Talking about it might have made it real; we both badly needed to believe the attacks were aberrations rather than predictable events that weren't going away by themselves.

I came to the library to conduct research. Some people believe abused women provoke the violence from their spouses. Not true. I'd conducted my own experiments.

Nothing I did made Conor hit me. Nothing I did made him stop. He acted like he knew what he was doing. I was sure he'd hit other girlfriends before me.

Conor always threw the first punch or kick. Sometimes, I hit him back as hard as I could. My one or two solid hits probably just made him angrier and violent faster, if he even noticed them.

Sometimes I purposefully said nothing, did nothing. He'd wind up. I'd shrink back, eyes open, body bracing. Passivity never stopped him, either. It didn't even slow him down.

"Do you have any psychology books on domestic violence?" I asked the middle-aged librarian. My voice cracked, surprising me as much as the librarian. A pink flush crept up my cheeks and down my neck. Without comment, she pushed her glasses up the bridge of her nose and looked at me. She led me to a stack in the back. She ran her wrinkled index finger along a row of thick, heavy books.

What a stupid euphemism. My situation wasn't "domestic violence." I grabbed four books and walked to a small, unoccupied reading room in the back of the library. I sat at a Formica table and opened one of the books.

I flipped through the introduction and the first few chapters, page after page of black-and-white type. I guess for obvious legal reasons, the book didn't have any photos of women who'd been abused or the men who'd abused them. No pictures to make the people real like me and Conor.

I read the opening to one chapter, looking for some connection:

> Despite the intensely apologetic "honeymoon" period following each domestic violence incident, every time a man hits a woman he's saying "I hate you."

Honeymoon period? I put the book down. Conor never apologized. It would be beneath him to acknowledge the violence was his problem by doing something predictable and sentimental like bringing me red roses with baby's breath the next morning. And hate? Our relationship was about love, not hate.

"I love him beyond words, Winnie," I'd said to her a few days before when she called to check on me. "I am lucky to feel this way. He's brilliant, funny, fascinating. I want to be with him *forever*. His mother never protected him, Winnie. Who can blame him for being so fucking angry? He needs help, my help. You don't abandon your soul mate."

Winnie breathed heavily on the other end.

"I know, Leslie. I think you are lucky to have found someone you love so deeply. But that doesn't make it okay

that he hits you," she said firmly. "He has to take responsibility for that, and to stop the behavior."

"How am I supposed to get him to stop, Winnie?"

"I don't know, Leslie, I don't know. Sometimes I think the only way you can get him to stop is to leave him. Not for good, but just until he figures this out."

"Maybe, Winnie. That actually sounds like a good idea. But it will never work with him."

Conor would cut me out of his heart forever if I left him, even "temporarily." He'd see it as abandonment. I didn't want to join the long list of women who'd left him.

I went back to my reading in the quiet library.

All the statistics were about women. Why wasn't any research done on why men became abusers? Did the world think violence in a relationship was the woman's fault? Because she caused it? Because she stayed?

I'd heard the question a million times: "Why would any woman stay in a violent relationship?" As if only someone really stupid, or with utterly no self-respect, would take that kind of abuse repeatedly.

Why did I stay? I had tried to leave. I'd gotten in my car in the middle of the night and started to drive away plenty of times. Leaving was easy. Then I'd get a few blocks and have no idea where to go. He lived in my home. He needed our car to get to work in the morning to earn money to buy groceries, to make our mortgage, to pay his student loans.

But the real reason I stayed was that I loved him. Leaving

meant abandoning our home, our life, our dreams, the best part of me, that part that was not afraid to love unconditionally. I couldn't leave that part of myself behind.

None of the books asked the question I thought about all the time: Why did Conor attack me? He knew I loved him and wanted to help him. Yet he was destroying what we had together. Conor still had trouble putting on a tie every morning because the tightness brought on flashbacks of Wade's hands around his neck, he'd told me. Now the turtleneck sweaters I wore to cover my bruises made me choke, too. The poison from Conor was spreading to me.

A single point in the books made sense: Many abusive men tried to isolate their partners in order to prevent them from leaving. Was that why Conor had wanted to move to Vermont? To get me away from New York, where I had friends and neighbors and coworkers? One chapter also warned that the most perilous time in an abused woman's life was when she decided to leave, because her abuser had nothing to lose by killing her then.

The librarian came into the reading room quietly and then whispered, "Did you find what you need?" I slammed the book closed and jumped up. "Yes, thank you," I managed to blurt out. She smiled and backed out of the room. I put the heavy books back on the shelf and then called Conor from the pay phone next to the bathroom.

"Hi. Just calling to check in. I'm at the library looking some stuff up."

I didn't tell him what stuff. And I didn't tell him how alone, and how scared, reading the books made me feel.

A few weeks later, after finishing up at the magazine, I went to the big Stop & Shop in Bennington and then it took thirty minutes to drive home in the frigid starry night. The moon was full and shockingly bright in the black Vermont sky. I drove with the sunroof open. Bracing cold air filled the car. I'd gotten adept at maneuvering through the tolls on the country highway. I glided through, flipped a coin into the basket without stopping, and started accelerating just as the gate rose. Hey, sometimes you had to take fun where you found it.

I parked the black Volkswagen in the basement garage and trooped up the wooden stairs in my winter coat and boots, my arms full of groceries. Yellow light spilled out the windows but the house was silent.

At the top of the stairs I heard the soft rustle of a page being turned. The sound came from my office. Curious, slightly bewildered, I put down the food at the top of the stairs and walked into my office, a place Conor rarely went, especially when I was not there.

My heart froze. Conor sat behind my desk, in my chair, with my tattered blue teenage diary open in front of him. I had not written a word in that diary or any other since

the night I was sixteen and Mom told me she'd been read-ing it. For the eight years since Mom had read that diary, I'd kept another in my head where no one could read it but me. But I'd never hated myself enough to throw the first one away.

Conor did not look up when I walked in.

My first confused question: How did he find it? I'd never mentioned this diary. I kept it in the bottom of my file cabi-net along with a few letters and souvenirs from high school, an article I wrote for the graduation issue of the school paper, my yearbook filled with friends' signatures. I hadn't looked at it in five years or more. He must have been looking for something (but what?), and then stumbled upon this. I felt like his dog Knight, trying to hide the shit on the carpet.

I could only imagine what Conor would say and do to me as a result of reading descriptions of my rampant drug use, drunken adventures, and sexual experimentation, culminat-ing with losing my virginity at an age I was sure he'd consider way too young (fifty would probably be too early in his mind). He sat quietly, contemplating the scuffed blue diary as if it were an original da Vinci notebook. Was he so angry that he was refusing to acknowledge me? He turned another page.

Memories of Mom screaming at me flooded my body like hot water from a tub faucet.

"No, no, no! That's *mine*!" I grabbed the diary from him and held it to my chest like a stuffed animal. It was so small my two hands covered it completely. I sank into the rug in front of

the desk, still wearing my coat and boots. Conor looked at me, stunned.

All I could think to do was call Dr. Joseph, the new therapist Conor and I had seen twice. He'd tell me to get in our car and leave, drive to a hotel, get away fast. I grabbed the phone off my desk and looked up his home number, written on the business card he'd given us. Conor stared at me from behind my desk, not saying a word.

The doctor answered the phone after two rings.

"Hello?" I could hear classical music playing in the background. I pictured him with a glass of white wine in his hand.

"Dr. Joseph, it's Leslie—you know, your new patient? I just got home from the supermarket and found Conor reading my diary . . ." I could barely stop crying long enough to get the words out.

"Okay. Okay," he said firmly. "Take a deep breath, talk it out."

I took a few breaths. Conor wouldn't hit me while I was on the phone with a doctor, would he? Once I calmed myself enough to start explaining what had happened, Dr. Joseph interrupted.

"Leslie, I think we should get you a prescription for tranquilizers." He sounded mildly annoyed. "I can call it into your pharmacy right now. We can all talk about this next week during our appointment."

"No! You don't understand. This is an emergency! You

don't know what he's going to do to me after reading this—"

I turned my back to Conor and moved as far away from him as the phone cord permitted.

"Now, come on," he interrupted again. "We're all adults here. What's going to happen between now and the appointment? We're going to have plenty of time to talk all of this through. I'll schedule you a special appointment for tomorrow or the next day if that will make you feel better."

Any mental health professional who assumed I was fine, who couldn't sense the danger I was in, who tried to invalidate my panic, who thought a tranquilizer would help, did not know much more about domestic violence than those idiotic books. I was alone. Again. Damn it.

"No, Dr. Joseph, that won't be necessary," I told him. "Don't bother with a prescription. I feel better now just talking to you. Thank you."

I wish I'd had the guts to say what I really felt: Go to hell, Dr. Fucking Joseph.

I hung up the phone. My tears were dry, my face tight from the salty residue. Conor was still sitting behind my desk, his arms folded in his lap. What was I going to do now?

"Leslie, just listen to me for a second." He was surprisingly calm and rational, the nice Conor. "I came across your diary when I was looking for some paper in here."

Right.

He kept explaining.

"I was actually reading the diary to try to help understand

you better. Isn't that what we're trying to do with this couples therapy? Understand each other better?"

Not exactly, I felt like saying. I thought we were aiming to get you to stop hitting me. I eyed him warily but he seemed sincere.

"Okay, Conor. Thanks for your attempt. But don't ever, ever read anything of mine again without asking me. I don't want you to mention to me what you read. It's off-limits, like evidence gotten in an illegal search."

"Okay, okay, fine." To my surprise he agreed, nicely, his face open and sympathetic. Something was fishy here; was he on Valium?

Then it dawned on me. Given that he was a fairly slow reader, he probably never got to the parts in my diary about losing my virginity. I felt like throwing my head back and laughing at my escape. He probably spent an hour reading about my fights with Sylvia and Winnie and Mom, my early drug experimentation, taking the SATs with a third-degree sunburn and open blisters on my face following a spring break tanning fiasco, the highlights of the 1982 Rolling Stones concert at the Capital Center during which I fell asleep. There was nothing that would set him off in the first thirty pages—the first two years I kept the diary. He did not realize what he'd missed.

I waited until Conor was in bed, then hid the diary in a file labeled "Maps and Travel Info" and crawled into bed quietly. The next day I called Dr. Joseph's office and canceled all our future appointments. I started thinking about how to find

someone or something that could really help us. It did not occur to me that I had to start with myself.

Ed Horrigan and Conor and I sat around the kitchen table, chairs pushed back, the remains of dinner in front of us. While we were drinking coffee, Conor got up to go to the bathroom. Ed turned to me suddenly, as if he'd been waiting all night for a moment alone. His eyes clicked onto me like a Nikon camera lens.

"Leslie," he said quietly, putting his long fingers over my hand on the table. "Do you know that your voice trembles when Conor comes into the room? What is going on? Can I help?"

My eyes widened but I couldn't get any words out. I tried to pull away but Ed increased the pressure on the back of my hand slightly, the way a teacher would if confronting a child about something she didn't want to admit.

"Listen to me, Leslie. It's a Pavlovian experiment. When Conor's here, your voice shakes. When Conor is out of the room, your voice holds steady."

"What?" I managed to squeak out. Holy shit. He *knew*.

"Are you okay, Leslie?" Ed asked steadily, unafraid, glancing down the hall to be sure Conor was still in the bathroom. He didn't mean was I okay now. He meant was I safe, day in and day out.

I looked away. My face felt hot. I snuck a quick look at him. The concern in his eyes startled me.

"Believe me—the last thing I'd do is undermine Conor. I thought long and hard before bringing this up. But I need to know—are you okay?"

How could it be so obvious that I was afraid of Conor? So fearful I couldn't even say what I thought in his presence without trepidation? Ed said my voice trembled. Who else had noticed? What else was I oblivious to? Before I could ask Ed any questions, Conor came back.

"Hey, buddy," he said loudly, slapping Ed on the back. Ed winced involuntarily. "Let's go smoke a stogie on the back porch."

I turned away before Conor noticed my face, which I figured must be totally crimson or ashy white, I hadn't a clue which. I cleared the table quickly, head down, and started washing dishes. On the metal sink I broke Ed's Coke glass and nearly cut the side of my hand.

I couldn't stop thinking about what he'd said. It was true: I was terrified of Conor. Being afraid had become my normal state. I was always tensed for my next mistake, his next attack. The only person I was hiding the truth from was myself.

I left a message at the farmhouse on Mom's answering machine, an electronic antique with a minicassette inside.

"Hi, Mom. We'll drive over for Christmas but I think it'd be easier—you know, with the dog and everything—if we just slept here. We'll get there as early as we can Christmas morning. See you soon! Bye."

I hung up the phone in our kitchen. My family was converging on Mom's Vermont farmhouse for Christmas—and sleeping miles apart. The rambling house could easily sleep more than a dozen people but all of us refused to stay overnight. My father couldn't—Mom didn't know it yet, but Dad had begun to date a young divorcée in D.C. Although Sylvia felt guilty about hurting Mom's feelings, she and Dad had reservations at a bed-and-breakfast about a mile from the farmhouse. Hugh had flown with a college friend to California, a place he was thinking of moving to after graduation, so he was off the hook. Conor had flatly refused to sleep at the farmhouse since the fight two summers earlier, so we would drive the ninety minutes back home Christmas night.

Just after ten A.M. on Christmas morning, we arrived at the farmhouse, which looked tiny perched up on the hill, surrounded by snow-covered blue spruce trees. The snowdrifts had piled up almost five feet in some places, covering Mom's empty flower boxes. We brushed off our boots in the rough-hewn summer kitchen, which felt even colder than outside. I stamped my feet loudly so Mom would know we were there. No one came out to greet us.

I pushed open the winter door to the kitchen, Conor trailing a few feet behind me. I could smell the roast beef Mom

had in the oven. Frankie's old, handwritten, batter-stained recipe and the ingredients for Yorkshire pudding—practically the only recipe my grandmother could follow—were laid out on the counter next to the cast-iron sink. Through the doorway to the living room, I saw a branch of the small Douglas fir Mom had decorated with a handful of favorite family ornaments, a fraction of the hundred-year-old hand-painted angels, doves, and Santas she kept in the attic in Washington.

"Hello?" I called from the kitchen. "Merry Christmas?"

"Oh, they're here," Mom said, as if to someone else in the living room. I walked into the room, stepping over the warped floorboards, to kiss my mom on the cheek. The fireplace was crackling even at this early hour. Mom didn't get up. She turned her face away and half-hugged me with her forearms.

"Merry Christmas, Ann," Conor said politely, without warmth. She leaned toward Conor and gave him a peck on the cheek, carefully holding him at arm's-length so he couldn't hug her back. She raised her eyebrows at me and took a sip of her coffee.

"Your father and Sylvia are out back, chopping wood," she said.

I tried ignoring her frostiness.

"Mom, the tree is beautiful," I said. "And that roast smells incredible!"

She smiled for the first time and looked around the room, thawing just a bit with pride. Beneath her thin-lipped exterior, I could feel that my mother was pleased I had come.

Christmas had always been her favorite holiday. She shopped year-round for presents, which she then hid under her bed and in the linen closet. During our childhood, every year the pile of presents grew more and more stupendous— proof that she loved us, despite the fact that Santa's wrapping skills and penmanship looked a little more sloppy-drunk each year.

I unpacked the presents we'd brought for everyone and took a deep breath of the sweet Christmas tree needles as I placed each gift under the tree. The house had its own smell—old wood, candle wax burnt down during summer nights playing Clue and Spades, wool blankets. It was good to be here.

At noon we crowded around the pine table Dad made more than twenty years ago, which was set with heavy silver and the blue-and-white china my parents received as a wedding present thirty-four years before. We dug into the roast and Yorkshire pudding and green beans and salad and little red potatoes my mom made every Christmas. She had always been a terrific cook.

After eating, we politely exchanged presents. Conor and I gave everyone gifts with a Vermont theme—maple syrup, hand-knit wool caps and mittens, sweaters from the White River Crafts Fair. Sylvia opened a camera with a series of heavy black lenses, a joint gift from Mom and Dad that probably cost nine hundred dollars. Then Mom handed me my unwrapped gift: a cheap watch with a fake black snakeskin band that looked like it came from the discount drugstore

she went to in Bethesda. She gave Conor a polyester tie with shiny black-and-gray stripes. The presents were so meager and ugly that I looked at her to see if this was a *Candid Camera*–type joke. Maybe she had our real presents hidden elsewhere. She gave me a look in return that said: *A lump of coal is all you deserve this year.* God, she could be so mean.

"Oh, thanks, Mom," I said, smiling. If nothing else, growing up in my family had taught me how to hide the hurt. I tried to look as if she'd just given me a string of matched pearls.

Dad didn't give us presents. "Ah, I'm sorry, Les, Conor. I was busy with a trial this week. I'll send you a check when I get back to Washington."

Later in the afternoon we piled into separate cars and headed to a nearby family-owned ski resort, a long Christmas tradition. We had the mountain to ourselves. Conor had never skied. My father tried to give him a lesson, attempting to ski with Conor between his long legs as he had when he taught us to snowplow as little kids. Despite the underlying awkwardness and Mom's crappy gifts, I was happy and grateful to see my family, even for a day.

We sat around the lodge after the chairlifts closed, our woolen socks resting on our chunky ski boots, the roaring fire warming us, drinking hot chocolate, a ritual that captured the happiest moments of my childhood. With a laugh, Sylvia looked at me with her blue beach-ball eyes.

"Les, do you remember that time I got lost?"

"Hmm, of course," I said, laughing.

Oh, to hide behind the past, when all was well with this family, when these stories were in the making.

Since Conor was the only one who hadn't heard the story, Sylvia told it to him.

"I was about eight," she explained, looking at Conor, beginning to laugh. "Taking the last run on a really cold day. It started to get dark around three-thirty. I took one more run when the rest of my family went inside." She wiped her nose with a napkin emblazoned with the red ski lodge logo. "I was going down Rattler—Conor, you didn't go down that one today, it's an expert—when I saw a roped-off trail. I don't have any idea why, but I decided to ski it, which was really stupid, because the ski patrols get mad if you go down closed trails. But I figured, last run, all they'd do was take away my lift ticket if they caught me. So, I was skiing down this run, all by myself, the drifts high as my knees, when I fell into a huge snowdrift."

She started to laugh so hard that tears slipped down her cheeks.

"I couldn't get up and it was getting dark and I just lay there moaning, thinking I was going to die."

By now she was laughing so hard her chair shook. I burst into laughter, too, because I could still picture what she looked and sounded like when I found her by following her tracks on my last run. Her eyelashes had been frozen with tears but she was too mad at her own idiocy to be grateful.

I could hear Conor's choked, polite laugh a half-second behind everyone else. A few minutes later, we all got up. My

face felt hot and chapped when I hugged everyone and piled our gear into our salt-dirty car in the empty parking lot.

I drove home through the steep, winding highways that led down from the mountains to our ugly little industrial town. Conor claimed he was too wiped out to drive. He dozed for much of the ride.

We pulled into the garage and trooped stiffly upstairs to the cold kitchen, our heavy snow boots clunking on the wooden stairs. Blue was overjoyed to see us after our twelve-hour absence. His happy body wriggling under my hands melted away some of my exhaustion and the ache of nostalgia, what my family used to be, what I wished it still were.

I let Blue into the backyard and then started rummaging for something for dinner. As I stood on a chair searching for matching types of spaghetti among the many half-empty boxes of pasta in our cupboards, Conor leaned against the stove with his arms folded.

"You know, how could you have just taken me to the top of that mountain without even teaching me how to do that snowplow thing?" His accusation might have sounded like an angry three-year-old's, if not for the edge to his voice. I knew better than to make light of his words. Underneath my ski sweater and turtleneck, my shoulder blades knitted together like wings sticking out of my back. "You set me up to be humiliated in front of your family! Your father actually tried to put me between his legs to teach me."

Still on the chair, I twisted to face him, my hands behind my back in tight fists.

"Conor, I really didn't do it on purpose. I am sorry. I didn't mean it."

I *was* sorry. He had a point. I learned to ski when I was two. It didn't occur to me until right that second how hard it would be to learn at thirty-three when the distance to the hard ground was considerably farther. It must have been terrifying and humiliating to be at the top of the hill wondering how to ski down by himself.

All this was irrelevant now.

With Conor in a foul mood, it was wiser to say little, to hope he blew himself out before he found a target. The best thing to do was to keep saying I was sorry, over and over. I stepped down and back.

Tonight my apologies did not slow him down.

"Just like my mother! You expect me to be able to do everything by myself!" He was shouting now. His face was red. He couldn't even see me. I stepped as far away as I could without being obvious.

"Do you know how that feels? Do you know how stupid I felt in front of your father? You just left me there all by myself! I would never do that to you!"

The pasta started to boil. I opened a plastic container of store-bought pesto and spooned it into a bowl. Breathe, breathe, I told myself. I just wanted to be at the farmhouse, with my family, safe, not alone here because he refused to even spend one night at my favorite place. Damn him.

"Look, Conor—you're right. I'm sorry. I said so twenty times. I've had enough!"

This was all the excuse he needed. He grabbed me and shoved me against the half-painted kitchen wall. The bowl, the pesto, the wooden spoon, one of the pasta boxes, all clattered to the floor. He grabbed my neck and started to squeeze. The water boiled over.

He shoved me to the floor and paused to catch his breath, wiping his nose with the back of his hand. While he was figuring out what to do next, I picked myself up, rigatoni stuck to my palm. I grabbed my car keys off the kitchen counter and ran down the basement stairs. As usual, it was beneath him to apologize, to follow me; he'd yelled many times that if I wanted to leave then he didn't want me anyway. The engine in the Jetta was still warm. I backed out of the garage and started driving.

Where to? Leaving was easy. The hard part was figuring out where to go.

Within a few blocks I had to make a decision, even if it was just to drive around town. I had no coat, no wallet, no money, no driver's license. Blue was outside in the cold night. Conor might or might not remember to bring him in. I wanted my dad. I longed to drive the two hours back to his bed-and-breakfast, wake him up and tell him what Conor had done to me. I stopped the car in front of the little bakery that sold homemade rhubarb muffins and leaned over the steering wheel, crying as if my whole body would break apart, thinking about how good it would feel to tell my dad everything and to hear him say, "Okay, babe, I'll take care of you, come back to Washington with me tomorrow."

Right—the man who'd forgotten to get me anything for Christmas. I imagined what my father's reaction would actually be if I showed up at his bed-and-breakfast at one A.M., waking the owner to get him out of his room. Shaming my father with my mistakes was worse than facing Conor. I couldn't stomach his disappointment and annoyance if I were to bring my problems to him instead of solving them on my own. And the ugliest possibility: What if he didn't believe me, or refused to help? Keeping Conor's attacks secret seemed my only way of preventing the violence from being real, the only piece of this ugly situation that I could control. I was alone again with the truth. I would be alone forever.

I straightened up, stopped crying, and slowly turned the car around. I drove home at five miles per hour, going slow, hoping that Conor would think I'd been gone a really long time, ashamed I'd only been gone a measly twenty minutes. I pulled into the driveway and waited until the light went off in our bedroom. I slipped back into the house. The stove had been turned off but the mess was still on the floor. I cleaned up as quietly as I could, let a shivering Blue in, and warmed him up with a long rub with a kitchen towel. I crawled halfway into his crate with him for a few moments. Then I got into bed next to Conor.

January. Frozen snow everywhere. Sidewalks covered with a permanent glaze of ice. Salt marks, like dried powdered sugar,

streaked every car on the highway. Time for Conor to reapply to business school. He said this time maybe he'd consider a few other schools in addition to Harvard, to hedge his bets.

"You should apply, too, babe," he said to me one night over dinner in our kitchen with Ed. I'd finally gotten to the point where I could conjure up a decent marinara sauce over al dente spaghetti. "You've got good business sense. I can see it in the way you've grown your writing business and advised your clients. Trust me—you'd do great at b-school."

He'd said this before. I'd always been suspicious that he just wanted a companion in this endeavor. But I had to admit the idea had grown on me.

Then Ed repeated the same thing. I was a natural for business school. He said maybe he'd go with us, too. Maybe he would—to watch over me, to stay close to Conor, to buffer the tension between us. He'd never said anything more about my fear of Conor since that night he'd held my hand down on the table.

"But the thing is," I told them, "I'm just not sure business school is right for me *now*—I don't feel quite ready to go."

They both looked at me like I was the big party pooper. Ed went so far as to stick out his bottom lip.

"Okay, okay, maybe I'll apply, too."

I spent most of the snowy winter in my office, proofing Conor's application essays in addition to my own late into

the night while Conor slept. Stripes of snow lay draped like long skinny blankets along the gnarled gray branches of the lilac tree outside my office window.

Late one night, like most nights when I couldn't write another word, I pulled on my boots and zipped my down parka over my flannel pajamas, and took a midnight walk down the middle of our snow-covered street with Blue. There were no streetlamps in our neighborhood. The pale orange glow of the moon behind the clouds provided eerie illumination for our walk. Our neighbors were long asleep, snug in their beds. The streets were so quiet I could hear the snow falling. The houses Blue and I passed looked like indigo shadows. The fresh powder was so white that the pine trees looked as if their branches were weighed down with frosting.

"The woods are lovely, dark, and deep . . ."

I crunched along in my boots, hands stuffed into my warm pockets, while Blue raced in front of me, behind me, all around me, a speedy brown locomotive blowing fluffy snow in his wake.

"But I have promises to keep, and miles to go before I sleep . . ."

Ed and Conor had bet I'd get in everywhere. At least one good business school had to take me, as proof that God or something in the universe believed in me and was directing me to leave this dark place, beautiful only when covered in virgin powder.

In early spring, when traces of dirty melted snow lined the mud of our front yard, we started receiving decisions

from the schools we'd applied to. Every afternoon, I walked to our mailbox feeling like an altar boy heading to the front of church while a watchful but invisible congregation looked on. Fat envelopes meant yes, thin ones no. As it turned out, Ed and Conor were right: I kept getting fat envelopes. I had to hide my pride because Conor kept getting rejections. More unfairness in the world. The worst was the day he got the thin envelope from Harvard. I left it buried in a pile of bills on the kitchen counter. I called Winnie at her part-time job in the HBS admissions office and asked her to withdraw my application before Conor got home from work and opened the mail.

"Christ, Leslie, are you *sure*?" she asked. "Harvard. Business. School. You know exactly what admission here would mean to your life."

I wanted to scream at her.

"Winnie, please, process it before the end of today, before the next mail drop."

"Okay. Just wait. I'm going to get your file."

I clenched my teeth and waited for her to come back to the phone to confirm she'd thrown away my forms.

Even so, I checked the mail with new urgency until I received the letter from Harvard confirming that my application had been withdrawn, which I waved quickly in front of Conor the night it came and said, "See, I didn't get in either, honey."

He finally heard good news from one of the schools that had accepted me. Fortunately it was one of the top programs

in the country. Not Harvard, but in the same dazzling universe.

It would have been a way out, to insist that I had to attend one of the schools he had not gotten into. Instead we decided—I decided, he decided, somehow we decided together—to go to the same school. He also convinced me to take out loans for his tuition in my name, because his spotty credit history meant red tape and higher interest rates. Did this prove that most of me wanted to stay with Conor? That I loved him despite his attacks? Was I a pathetic battered woman? Or was I scared, rightly so, of the rage my abandonment would provoke? Was I an idiot? A coward? A good and loyal wife?

Was I afraid of admitting the truth? That my so-called soul mate, the man I had chosen among millions of single men in New York City, the man my friends and family had suspected might be trouble, had turned out to be a man who held a gun to my head—when not telling me I was the wonder girl of his dreams?

I could not leave Conor. Even though I had no hope he would stop beating me down. Even though my voice shook when he entered a room.

When it came to a choice between him and me, I chose Conor.

Book
Three

THE WHITE AUGUST SUN IN THE VERMONT SKY
made it hurt to look in the rearview mirror of the U-Haul as
I drove away from the old ranch house. Blue sat next to
me on the truck's bench seat. The furniture, clothes, books,
wedding presents, kitchen paraphernalia, Blue's crate, bowl,
toys, dog bed, and Conor's guns—the sum of my and Conor's
life as a married couple—didn't even fill the small U-Haul
we'd rented.

Conor drove the Jetta behind us, the wind from the sunroof
ruffling his hair. His left hand, gold wedding band glinting,
hung out the driver's window. He looked like Jack Kerouac,
except that Kerouac would have driven a car far cooler than
our VW.

Ed had helped us pack. He'd decided to stay in Vermont
to wait for his next promotion. Maybe he'd apply to business
school or a Ph.D. program the next year. He'd bent over to
give us both identical good-bye hugs the night before, as we
stood in our cracked asphalt driveway next to the U-Haul, finally locked up after a long day packing. I knew he was still
worried about me. Maybe he thought, or hoped, I'd be okay
at business school.

I'd called Winnie a few nights before, while I was packing

dishes and Conor was out walking Blue, to tell her our moving date and our new number in Chicago.

"You excited?" she'd asked.

I looked around the empty kitchen and living room. The walls were finally white, and there was a new blue-and-white-checked linoleum floor under my feet in the kitchen. Even the outside walls were spanking white, the shutters and doors slate-blue. Now that we were leaving, the place looked great.

We'd tried to sell it. The depressed Vermont real-estate market kept sinking lower. So we'd put an ad in the local paper and rented the place to a nice lesbian couple with two dogs. The key was already in the mailbox for them.

"Relieved, I guess. But Winnie, what about leaving him, too? How can I? Do I just walk in one night and say, nice knowing you, let's get a divorce? Where would I go? Who would get Blue? Would I take our car? Leaving . . . it's a concrete wall."

Silence.

"Maybe our relationship will get better at business school."

"I fucking hope so, Les, I do," she said.

So we left Vermont. The road flew by underneath the U-Haul tires. Fewer than five hours later, we crunched into the gravel driveway of Aunt Nellie's house in Upstate New York a few miles from Strawberry Hill. Blue spent the night in the U-Haul on his blanket. We got off by nine the next

morning and made it to Chicago by nightfall. As we crossed from Indiana into Illinois, the lights of the Chicago skyline jutted up on the horizon. All told, it took less than two days to leave our old life behind.

As we drove through the South Side, I thought about my dad, who moved here fifty years before. In Oklahoma one day, while his father was at his electrician's job, his mother piled Dad and his brother and two sisters into the family's beat-up car. They stayed a year in Kansas City, then moved to St. Louis, then Denver, then Birmingham—I don't even know if I've got all the cities straight. One day, his mother opened her Bible and decided Chicago was next.

What did Dad think the first time he made this drive?

His mother found a job on an assembly line at a manu-facturing plant. They moved into cheap company housing on the factory grounds. By November, they were so poor, Thanksgiving dinner was a handout from their church. "We wouldn't have had anything to eat otherwise," Dad told me when I was in tenth grade. One day when he was about eight, my father rode his bike home from school to find that his apartment, with his mother and three siblings inside, had been quarantined for six weeks due to chicken pox. Some-how Dad found a place to sleep, in this unfamiliar Midwest-ern city where he had no relatives, until the quarantine was lifted.

He also told me that his older sister, Marilyn, was diag-nosed with leukemia here. Marilyn died when she was fifteen,

alone in a public Chicago hospital. Alone because my grand-mother would have lost her job if she'd taken time off to be with her.

Conor and I parked the U-Haul and the Jetta on the street in a leafy neighborhood filled with stately 1900s mansions with large front porches. A massive low-income housing project built about ten blocks away had precipitated instan-taneous white flight three decades before. In the b-school newspaper we'd found a listing for an old Victorian split into six dirt-cheap apartments. We'd rented one on the second floor with twelve-foot ceilings, crown moldings, expansive bay windows, a fireplace. Conor hired two young guys walk-ing by to help us unpack the truck. The dishes were in the cupboards and our bed made by midnight. We put my desk in the living room.

Now, instead of a view of the lilac tree, I looked out at a busy street corner glittering with a carpet of broken glass, used syringes, and condoms. The city grit and graffiti—and the people behind the spray-painted hieroglyphics, even if they might be thugs and homeless people—made me feel safer than I'd ever felt in the idyllic isolation of Vermont.

But what did I know about safety?

Classes began ten days later. My first two were finance and accounting. Gibberish spewed out of the professors' mouths—credits, debits, burn rates, turnover. The other stu-

dents had spent the last few years working eighty-hour weeks in Wall Street investment banks and consulting companies. *They* knew what alpha, beta, and delta meant.

My work experience at *Seventeen* and an undergrad degree in English left me at a stunning disadvantage. I scrambled to learn odd new rules: the laws of supply and demand, the psychology of marketing and advertising, the balance of accounting. I scored a 52 on the first accounting test—out of 800 possible points. Afraid I'd fail everything, I read every assignment, sat in the front row for every lecture, turned in every paper on time.

Each day I got up early, dressed quickly (and quietly), and snuck out to walk Blue around the block before I left for campus. Conor—sexy under the white sheets, but surreally distant and impersonal, like a Calvin Klein underwear model on a billboard—stirred in bed. Due to his Wall Street experience and economics background, he placed out of most first-year classes, and thus could sleep in.

I always had the same thought as I locked the apartment door before he woke up: *Phew*.

I usually had a muffin and coffee with my new friend Cherie in the sunny atrium of the business school, skimming *The Wall Street Journal*, which I struggled to comprehend, reviewing my notes with ink from the *Journal* staining my fingers. My section was 50 percent female, a bonus, because my year overall had fewer than 30 percent women. Business school felt like the first week of freshman year in college: Everyone was effusively cheerful and outgoing.

Soon I felt surrounded by more friends than I could keep track of. There were endless study group meetings, small mobs going to lunch at the local deli, intramural soccer games, corporate receptions almost every weekday, spontaneous raids on Baskin-Robbins, Thursday nights at the campus pub, where no one noticed or cared that I didn't have a plastic cup of beer in my hand. I stayed on campus as long as possible every evening, studying with classmates who knew I was married to someone at school but had never met him. Because of our different schedules, I rarely saw Conor during the day.

Night was different.

One evening close to Halloween, I stopped in front of our Victorian with its peeling paint and a dozen different mailboxes cluttering the front porch. Trash and dead leaves piled up on the sidewalk and street gutters. When Blue saw me from the second story he practically leapt out the window. The lights were on in the living room. Conor was home.

I turned my key in the door and put my bag on my big white desk. Blue nosed my pant leg, looking longingly at his leash on a hook by the door. I heard the TV in the bedroom; Conor did not come out to say hello.

After an hour I heard the shuffle of his slippers on the wooden floor. I stayed bent over my desk, highlighting a forty-page finance case it was unlikely I'd ever comprehend.

"Hey, babe," he said to my back. I turned around in my chair.

"Oh, hi, Conor. Didn't realize you were home," I lied. He

hadn't shaved or washed his hair. He held a coffee cup in his hand. Had he even left the apartment?

"How are you?" I turned back to the case.

"Hey. I want to talk to my wife," he said, coming to stand six inches behind me, like a subway panhandler about to ask for money, too close.

I paused, my highlighter poised, trying to gauge the anger in his voice.

"Sure, what's up?" I said, smiling, putting the pen down.

"I heard you joined Mike's study group for macroeconomics."

I nodded. How had he found out?

"Yeah, they just asked me today. It's a good group—Mike and Jim both worked at Lehman. You know how bad I am running numbers. I need those guys."

"I told you I want you to be in my study groups. This is the only class we're taking together."

He crossed his arms over his chest and locked his knees.

"But Conor, you said joining a macro group was a waste of time. You know that stuff from undergrad. I need a group that can help me out. That's what this school is about—teamwork and students teaching each other, right?"

"Well, then you can be the only one in my group."

"Oh, that will be fun. Winging a Nobel Prize winner's two-hundred-question multiple-choice exam. Not me."

He ignored my sarcasm. Conor aced every test, missing at most one or two questions, even though he did little homework and didn't take notes in class. "I don't write any of that

stuff down," he'd said when I'd asked why he didn't even take a pen to campus. "If I can't remember it right away, it's not worth knowing."

I was different. I wouldn't, couldn't, fail macro just to mollify him.

"Conor, I didn't come to b-school to be in a group with you. You hate teaching me this stuff, anyway."

I turned back around to the open case.

"Hey!" he barked. "I'm not finished talking to *my wife.*"

My wife. He said the words like he owned me.

I turned around and raised my eyebrows. We weren't in Vermont anymore. Part of the unspoken contract at b-school was that no one came to class without deodorant; no one argued with professors; no one fell down drunk at the Thursday night pub outings. Those with tattoos or socialist leanings or a penchant for beating their wives hid these failings.

In business, reputation meant everything, so something as innocuous as "I didn't know him well, but he had a reputation of having a bad temper," could doom one's chance of getting a job, could make an entire industry or career off-limits. I bet Conor knew it, too. He didn't want it to get out that he hit me; it would've destroyed our façade of the successful married couple who'd come to business school together.

I crossed my arms over my chest. From the corner of my eye I saw Blue put his head down and slink out of the room, his toenails clicking on the wood floor.

"I don't want you to be in any study groups with men," Conor explained, as if he were repeating something he'd made clear before.

I gave a short laugh, shook my head, and shrugged my shoulders.

"This school is seventy percent male, Conor. Over ninety percent of the professors are men. What are you talking about?"

I looked up at him. He could hit me tonight and I'd still escape to the safety of campus tomorrow. I stayed seated; I'd learned it was harder for him to go after me in a chair, especially a wooden one with arms. I grabbed the seat bottom, digging my nails into the wood so hard they gouged half-moon marks in the varnish. I tried to keep my voice breezy.

"We both need to network with other students, professors . . . it's an amazing program, that's why we're here."

"No!" he yelled, bending over me, his back curved, shaking his finger inches from my nose. "There can be only one person in charge of a family. That's me, *babe*. I am king of the castle here." He leaned closer; I could smell coffee on his breath.

The freedom I'd found at school had loosened his control over me. He was trying to find another way to tighten his grip. For a second, disgust trumped my fear.

"I can't believe I'm married to someone who believes such a stupid thing, Conor. What the hell? Should 'the king' set the time on our alarm clock, answer the phone when it

rings, decide what we eat for dinner? Or does being 'king' mean I am supposed to do all those things for you?"

He stared at me, furious, his eyes red. Then he leaned over my desk in front of me. Beads of sweat dotted his forehead. He still looked amazingly handsome, alive with anger.

He paused and looked around the living room as if trying to get hold of his rage with slippery fingers. He uncoiled his right arm and in one clean, purposeful sweep he brushed all of my finance notebooks across the living room. The metal binders snapped. Hundreds of pages of my notes and case study analyses scattered along the hardwood floor like an oversized deck of cards.

"Is that all you're going to do tonight, Conor? Or are you going to hit me, too?"

My voice broke, just a little. I tried to sound sarcastic but I guess somewhere in me I was still afraid. *You've got me now,* I felt like saying to Conor as he stood there, hands on his hips, while Blue huddled in his crate in the kitchen.

But you won't have me for long.

In one final gesture, he threw the massive finance textbook at my feet and then grabbed his leather jacket off the couch. He unlocked the front door and slammed it open. The brass knob went through the plaster of the foyer wall and stayed there, impaled on the cheap drywall.

I watched him go. He still had on his slippers.

"Leave," I whispered to his back disappearing down the

hallway, past the cheap pineboard paneling. "I don't know if I love you anymore."

I didn't say it very loud. He gave no sign that he heard me. Or that what I'd said made any difference. It wasn't true, anyway. I would still be there, waiting, when he came back.

It is strange what you don't forget.

In May, with money Winnie inherited from her grandmother, she treated me to a rendezvous in New York. The first night we stayed up until two A.M. talking nonstop in our room at the Palace on Madison. The next day we shopped nonstop until two P.M. At Bergdorf's we found a smoky blue Ferragamo interview suit on sale, something I couldn't dream of on a grad school budget. Winnie wanted to buy it for me.

"Oh, Win, you shouldn't," I pleaded, torn by guilt and delight, looking at myself in the three-way mirror. Like a wand from a fairy godmother, the suit transformed me into a confident, promising female executive.

"Oh, come on, Grams loved you, too. She'd want me to." I graciously accepted.

Dead-eyed from too much shopping and blabbing, we ate lunch at Bergdorf's outrageously expensive little café on the fifth floor. We were mostly quiet, chewing our salads. She looked around like she had some juicy gossip about one of the women at the table next to ours, and leaned toward me.

"I'm eight weeks pregnant," she whispered.

"Oh, my God!" I shouted. I half stood in my chair. She turned red. "Congratulations, Winnie!"

I felt so happy for her, I didn't notice that she wasn't smiling.

"What's wrong, Win?"

She looked like she was going to cry. Winnie hadn't cried since seventh grade. She bit her lip.

"It's just . . . you're the first person I've told, besides family. There were some tests, we thought there was something wrong with the baby. That's why I didn't tell you before. But I just found out Thursday that it's healthy. I'm so happy. But I'm still so scared that maybe there's something wrong."

I took her hand. "Winnie, it's going to be fine. You're pregnant! Wow."

Suddenly she asked me if I was going to stay with Conor for good. A complete non sequitur. But to me, the question made perfect sense.

"I can't have children with him," I said. "I have no idea what it's like to be pregnant, but I just could not do that to a child."

Looking down at her frisée, almost as if she was talking to herself, Winnie said quietly, "Well, then you have to leave him one day soon."

I knew she was right. But I had no idea how to say good-bye to Conor.

After lunch she told me she had to pee—that she'd been peeing a lot lately. We went down to Bergdorf's tiny bathroom

under the curved marble staircase in the basement. I spotted a pink baby's sock on the black-and-white subway tiles under the hand dryer. Impossibly tiny. I looked around for a baby girl in her mother's arms. When Winnie was washing her hands, I bent down and slipped the sock into my raincoat.

Back in Chicago, what stretched before me was a lifetime of contortion to avoid tripping Conor's temper. At times I'd succeed. I'd fail occasionally because how can you dodge something as unpredictable as rage?

I could not imagine being beaten while carrying a baby inside me, like Conor's mother had been beaten with him inside her.

I pictured jobs I couldn't take, lies I'd tell my friends, a life without children.

Mostly, though, I tried not to think about the future. The frantic acclimation to b-school distracted me plenty.

Then it would rain. I'd feel the sock in my coat pocket and remember that day at Bergdorf's and think: Would I ever have a baby girl too precious to be left at home on a rainy afternoon? What I was asking myself, I knew, was simple: Would I ever have a life without Conor?

Winnie's blue Ferragamo power suit—which I wore to every job interview—became my Cinderella ball gown. Every time I put it on, poof! I could smile, shake hands, answer tricky interview questions with aplomb. I changed into a woman

who couldn't imagine the day when Conor turned cold shower water on my naked body as I lay soaking in a hot bath. Or the Big Mac he threw at me as I drove home from our honeymoon on Martha's Vineyard. Or the time the previous fall that he poured dry coffee grinds on my head as I was making breakfast in our narrow galley kitchen.

To my surprise, corporate recruiters, a paradoxically picky, lemminglike bunch, offered me two marketing internships, one with American Express in New York City and another with Johnson & Johnson in New Jersey.

Conor did not send his résumé out, did not get invited to any interviews, and ended up with a last-minute summer job in Chicago.

Despite the irony of getting an offer from AmEx (maybe now I'd get my card back?), I took the job with Johnson & Johnson's New Brunswick corporate headquarters. I asked Aunt Nellie if I could live at her beach house on the Jersey Shore for the summer. This meant three months apart from Conor, seeing him only on a few weekends. He was not happy about it, but he didn't protest. I made the thirteen-hour drive to Jersey for the summer, alone with Blue. I could spend a summer without Conor, but not without Blue.

Rules seemed to govern everything for the 150,000 employees at J & J, the world's largest consumer health-care company. All the buildings were as white as a starched shirt. The grass was trimmed as short as a golf course. A dress code specified skirt and sleeve lengths. There was a memo on how to write memos. Every employee arrived before 8:30 A.M.

There seemed to be a policy about what cars you were supposed to drive—no flashy European luxury imports—and
what dogs you should have pictures of on your desk (there
were many golden retrievers; zero Dobermans). Working at
J & J was like drinking a vanilla milkshake.

Every night I arrived home at dusk at the rambling Victorian beach house. Blue and my twelve-year-old freckle-faced
cousin Lila, whom I officially chaperoned although she told
me when her curfew should be, welcomed me on the wraparound porch. After dinner, we'd walk barefoot a block to the
ice cream stand and eat our cones on the sidewalk. Conor
flew in occasionally on the weekends, along with Nellie, her
husband, and my two teenage cousins. There were too many
people around for Conor and me to fight. We had a few
blowouts in our hot parked car with the windows rolled up so
no one could hear us.

Three months alone, without being hit, without having
to hide bruises and swollen eyes, brought a tincture of clar-
ity, as well as questions that were too confusing to answer.
Why had I never directly confronted Conor about the violence? Where was my moxie, in such abundance in b-school
debates and job interviews? Of course, I'd always been
afraid of his reaction, but that wasn't my whole excuse. I'd
always thought it wouldn't do any good to question him, to
tell him the violence was unacceptable, to threaten to leave
him. Because I'd never leave him. And I knew it wasn't his
fault. He'd been abused far worse as a kid than the stuff he
did to me. Naming the violence wouldn't have stopped his

compulsion. It just would have made it more real. What was I going to do?

An article I'd written the summer before ran in *Seventeen's* August issue. When I saw the headline on the cover at a newsstand in New Brunswick near J & J, it occurred to me: I was a writer, I could *research* my future with Conor. Maybe I could find data that unraveled the dynamics of domestic violence, unlike the academic tomes I'd discovered in the Bennington public library.

I tracked down an assistant professor at a large state school in Maryland, working toward his Ph.D. on the behavioral psychology of batterers—a unique perspective in a field where research focused on the victims. I explained that I was a freelance reporter doing an article on abusive men for a woman's magazine. I misled him: (1) because I was afraid if I told him the truth, he wouldn't be as objective and clinical as I needed him to be; and (2) so I wouldn't cry during the interview.

My list of questions lay on a yellow legal pad on my desk at Johnson & Johnson. It was seven P.M. Everyone else had gone home. I clutched the gray office phone tight to my ear, afraid to miss one word of his answers.

I started with an easy, impersonal question.

"Why did you choose to study this population?"

He sighed heavily. There would be no easy, impersonal answers.

"I'm interested in the question of why men beat women. Not why women stay in violent relationships. I've spent a decade studying abusive men. In addition, as part of my own research, I run court-ordered self-help groups for batterers.

"I care about these men I am studying. They—and their responsibility for perpetuating violence—have been ignored for too long, to our society's detriment. I believe in their right to get help and I believe our society needs batterers to stop being violent."

I used my objective, edgy Barbara Walters voice to ask my first tough question:

"In your experience, why do men batter women they love?"

He sighed again.

"Every man I have ever studied who became a batterer as an adult was physically abused as a child by people he loved deeply. Usually an intimate family member who was also a role model for acceptable behavior. Often his mother or father or both.

"A batterer learns as a child that violence is an acceptable way to deal with strong emotions, and an effective way to dominate others in order to protect himself. The men I work with cannot separate intimacy from abuse. They do not think that their behavior is wrong. And they definitely have no understanding that it is criminal."

I thought of how deeply Conor loved his mother, and

what it had done to him when she allowed him to be abused.

"Do they love the women they are abusing?" It was getting harder to maintain my composure. The plastic phone slipped in my sweaty hand.

"Absolutely. They hit their partners *because* they love them," he said confidently. "I have yet to come across a batterer who lashes out violently at strangers. Part of the paradigm is that, to batterers, violence is a normal component of intimate relationships. The men I've studied would not get any emotional satisfaction or release unless they are intimately involved with the object of their violence. Their vulnerability terrifies and overwhelms them because of their learned behavior from childhood. They have learned—as a survival mechanism—that controlling the people they love is the only way to be certain they won't get hurt. And they know, through their own personal experience, that fear and violence are very effective ways to control people."

I always knew Conor's abuse had more to do with love and fear than hate. Finally, an expert who understood.

I looked down at my notebook. Next question:

"Do men who beat their partners, their wives, often abuse their children, too?"

"Yes. Almost always. Again, it's the intimacy and violence paradigm. And even if they don't physically abuse their children, by beating their mother they do two things: They terrify their children with the threat of 'You could be next' and they teach their children that violence against women is okay. Both

behaviors ensure that violent behavior is perpetuated in the next generation."

I took a deep breath as silently as I could. It was hard to get enough air in my lungs before I asked the next question.

"What are the positive signs you look for in the men in your group? The signs of hope?"

Now he took a deep breath.

"The most important thing, which frankly is rare, is honesty. Admitting that they have hit their partners, that this wasn't the first time, that they've hit other intimate partners, that there is a pattern of abuse that they have initiated."

Honesty? Conor had never admitted he'd hit me.

"The second thing, also critical, also rare, is taking responsibility for what they did. Saying this is my problem—not my partner's. Most batterers believe their partners provoke the violence. I work extremely hard to break through their denial and to get them to admit that violence is wrong and their fault. If a man can admit this, and truly believe it, then there is hope.

"But for most batterers this verges on impossible, because it requires them to admit that for many years they've been hurting other people, whom they love, in exactly the way they were hurt as small children. For most of the men I work with, denial of their problem has become a survival skill. For them to let go of this defense is devastating. But it's critical."

Conor was galaxies away from taking responsibility for the violence he brought into our relationship. The dull thud

inside my chest grounded me. I found my confident anchor-woman voice again.

"You say there is a pattern to the violence that spans different relationships. Could you tell me more about this?"

"Based on my quantitative research and learning from the men's groups I run, my hypothesis is that men who batter are like a subspecies whose behavior, as a group, is highly predictable. A relationship starts. The batterer has an uncanny sense for what the woman wants and needs emotionally, and he meets that need. I hear female partners use the phrases 'Prince Charming' and 'knight in shining armor' with incredible regularity when they describe what their partners were like in the early, courtship stage of the relationship. Batterers are like predators seeking prey."

How did Conor know, the night he met me on the E train, that I was so vulnerable? Was I still?

"You never hear of a batterer who introduces violence early on or too suddenly. No batterer hits a woman on their first date. He always waits until he's secure, which from the woman's perspective means until she is trapped, emotionally or financially, like getting engaged or pregnant, or quitting her job because he 'wants to take care of her.' A batterer intuitively knows when and how to lay the groundwork for a 'successful' violent relationship. The best cons, after all, are the ones that make the victim want to participate.

"Once the relationship is established and the batterer feels secure, he introduces the threat of violence. By a threat I mean something like punching a wall in the woman's pres-

ence, or saying, 'If I weren't such a gentleman I'd hit you for saying that,' during an argument.

"If the woman does not balk at the *threat* of violence, then soon the batterer actually hits or chokes or shoves her. Usually, it's something like a pinch that leaves a bruise or a controlled shove, not a full-blown beating. The batterer gradually escalates the violence, and increases the frequency, as the woman's denial and emotional numbness increase. By then, she's trapped and he feels free to do whatever he wants. He works on her emotionally, too, to make sure she does not tell people about the violence. It's critical that he convinces her the violence is somehow her fault or under her control. Her guilt protects the relationship so he can continue the battering."

I could not speak. This stranger on the phone had described my relationship with Conor in dreadfully accurate detail. Our first fight had been the night we moved in together—when I had nowhere else to go any longer. The first time he beat me was five days before our wedding. For two years I had let him beat me, in the name of "helping" him work through his childhood traumas.

I took a minute to write his words down on the legal pad. What I really needed was a decade to collect myself.

I looked at my next question. By this point, I knew what the answer would be. But I needed to hear it from him.

"The men you work with in your recovery groups, do they ever get better? Do they ever stop hitting their partners for good?"

His biggest sigh yet. I could practically see him shaking his head.

"No one I've studied has ever stopped being violent, all at once, for an extended period of time. I've seen batterers make a lot of progress toward controlling their anger and expressing it in more productive ways. But I've never seen anyone who didn't regress and beat their partners at regular intervals, even while making significant progress. There is no one I work with who I could say, this one is done, he'll never batter anyone again."

"Okay," I told him. "Last question. If one of the wives or . . . partners . . . of your batterers came to you and said, 'What should I do? Should I wait for him and help him work it out?' What would you tell that woman to do?"

He gave a short, humorless laugh.

"I would tell her that she is probably the last person on earth who could help him. First she should help herself and her kids, if she has them, to stay away from him—and I'd warn her to be extremely careful, because abandoning a batterer often provokes his deadliest rage. But leaving is actually the best way for her to help the batterer, too, and to help our society, because she is letting him, and the world, know that what he has done is wrong and totally unacceptable. By removing herself from the relationship, she makes it clear that she cannot help him, paving the way for him to realize that the violence is his fault, his responsibility, and that he is the only one accountable for his behavior."

I thanked him, told him I'd let him know when the arti-

cle came out, that I appreciated his time and insights very much. After I hung up the phone, I sat in the dark of my temporary office, staring at my blank computer monitor. Yeah, I knew *a lot* more now. But I didn't love Conor any less. And I still had no idea what to do.

At the end of August, Conor came to the beach to drive me and Blue back to Chicago. We went for one last walk along the empty Jersey Shore. Darkness was falling. We had to step over abandoned children's toys and sunscreen tubes in the sand. Conor's chest and feet were winter white. We moved next to each other in silence without holding hands.

Bringing up the abuse felt like explaining why I'd been speeding to a New Jersey state trooper. *I* felt guilty. I hadn't really talked to Conor in such a long time, my voice felt rusty.

"Conor, I've got something to tell you," I said, not looking at him, afraid I'd cry if I saw his face. The words came out as stiff and unappetizing as a frozen TV dinner on a tinfoil tray.

I stopped walking.

"If you ever hit me again, it's over. I love you and what we used to have together—too much to have . . . this . . . between us."

I looked at him as the wind blew my hair across my eyes. I needed to know he heard me. He looked at his toes in the sand.

"All right," Conor said a few seconds later, blue eyes still down. I could see his long lashes, half-circles over his cheeks. "I hear what you're saying. I promise I'll never . . . I'll never do it again, Leslie," he said, looking up, meaning the words. "I love you. I want to be happy with you and Blue—my little family. Let's go home."

November. The fall was a crazy blur of job interviews, classes, and study groups. I went through a dozen pairs of panty hose and just as many three-hour dinners with recruiters. The Ferragamo suit got lots of air. At the end of summer, the VP of marketing at J & J had asked me to work two days a week once school began. This meant money, an independent study credit, and two days a week away from Conor. Without talking it over with Conor, I'd said yes. Now I spent two days a week at Johnson & Johnson, flying away from Conor every Wednesday night, bringing in badly needed cash for food, household expenses, and more panty hose. I was so busy, I had no time to think.

Conor kept his promise. Thanksgiving came, marking three months since our beach talk, six months since he'd hit me. A few days later he came home on his bike with a small bag, a gift for me. Painted enamel earrings, two birds to wear in my ears, a matched pair. "Like us," he'd said.

One weeknight, after a fight that stayed only a fight, he

ran out in the rain to get my favorite pizza as a make-up gift.
He arrived home with the warm cardboard box, wet hair plastered to his forehead and a smile on his face. Late on a Friday, I stepped off the plane from New Jersey to find him
waiting for me at the gate, holding pink roses. When I saw
his face, my stomach unzipped like the old days in New York.

A few days later, he left a small package on my desk with
this note:

> To My Dear Wife—
>
> I found this on Saturday at a flea market. It's an
> antique jeweled peacock pin, a Chinese sign for prosperity
> and good luck. It's to wear on your interview suit. I just
> want you to know that your loves and ambitions are shared
> by me—what you care about I care about for you.
>
> Thinking of you always,
Conor

I came up with the idea to celebrate his thirty-fifth birthday and Christmas in Paris. "Sure, just us," Conor said, smiling when I told him. "Just us," he said again. His crooked
smile flickered. "Just us" had once been everything we'd
wanted. Maybe it could be again. I bought charter airplane
tickets and found a cheap, hopefully romantic Left Bank
hotel in a guidebook at the undergrad library.

The past two years were slipping behind us, a chapter
we'd talk about on our silver wedding anniversary: *Oh, yes,*

those first few years of marriage can be terribly rocky. You have to get through them, that's what commitment is about.

December. The day before his birthday, everyone left campus for three weeks of vacation, the last long break before graduation and our collective return to the working world. Christmas lights and decorations filled the storefronts and the windows of the apartments lining our street. Our neighborhood was deserted and eerily calm, reminding me of Vermont.

That afternoon while Conor was in the Loop buying something—new ties for job interviews, I think—the phone in our apartment rang. The rooms were shadowy in the early winter twilight so I had a hard time finding the receiver by our bed.

"Hello?" I shouted into the phone, breathless from the search.

"Les, hi, it's me, Winnie. I just wanted to say have a wonderful trip. Paris at Christmas? I'm so jealous. Think of me trying to keep Rex's family from pawing my belly while you're strolling the Champs-Elysées."

"Yeah, I am so excited. We'll be there this time tomorrow. Conor's gonna love it. Paris—it's a long way from Southie."

Winnie—almost nine months pregnant now, the baby totally healthy—laughed. It sounded like there was barely room in her lungs to draw a breath.

"Great, Les, sounds like this trip will be wonderful. I am so happy—for you and him and *me*—that you're okay. I have been so damn worried about you."

I looked out the kitchen window at the alley across the street. Someone had decorated her second-floor apartment with a wildly exuberant mishmash of cheap multicolored Christmas lights. I turned my back on the lights to face our dark bedroom.

"Win, you know, he still gets angry. That . . . pact or whatever we made on the beach doesn't stop him. At times it makes him angrier, I think; he's got no release. But there's been no . . . violence. He's trying so hard. I think we're going to make it."

"Sounds like it," she said. "It is fucking huge. He deserves a lot of credit. Sometimes I think the only way your relationship can succeed is if you live in different cities like you did last summer, or like you're doing now, away in New Jersey every week."

Fuck you, Winnie, I felt like saying. Damn her for speaking the truth so baldly. I still loved him, just as much. But if it came to a choice between him or me, I knew I'd choose me. And if you felt that way, didn't it mean part of you'd already decided?

I heard footsteps in the hallway. I half-wished the steps approaching our apartment would continue up to the third floor.

"Win, gotta go—he's back. Have a great Christmas. Thanks for calling—"

I hung up. A fleeting desire to never see Conor again in this lifetime flitted through me like a hummingbird skimming a lavender field. *No, he's your husband. You love him.* His key clicked in the lock. I went to turn on the light in the hallway.

"Hi, honey." I managed a smile.

"I brought dinner from the Italian place. Pasta with pesto. Your fave, babe."

"Yum, let's eat. I've gotta pack after dinner." We ate side by side on the couch in the living room, watching the news on TV like an old married couple. Blue lay at our feet, curled like a Pillsbury crescent roll.

After doing the dishes I went to the windowless bedroom in the back of our elegant but jaded city apartment—ground zero for countless nights of violence and mornings spent putting on cover-up and a high turtleneck. Those memories were fading like photos left in the sun.

Blue followed me, his nails clicking on the hardwood floor. With a grunt he jumped into his red fake-leather chair. I put on a white T-shirt and a pair of Conor's old boxer shorts so I could pack the clothes I'd been wearing. The living-room TV blared, punctuated by Conor's booming laugh at the sitcom's punch lines.

After I'd been packing for about thirty minutes, I looked up to see Conor standing in the doorway watching me. An inscrutable half-smile flickered on his lips.

"I've decided not to go," he said as he folded his arms across his barrel chest, still smiling. His words hung in the bedroom like a kite pausing in midair. At the sound of the

edge in Conor's voice, Blue got out of the chair and walked out of the room, his head down, wiggling his body in a half-hearted wag as he slid by Conor. A chill went through me.

The old Conor had canceled plans before, sometimes waiting until I stood at the door, dressed, made-up, perfumed. So I shouldn't have been surprised. But this time I was.

I knew better than to show how I felt. I put down the red wool sweater I was folding. He stood in the doorway, still watching me.

"I said we're not going."

I nodded to let him know I'd heard. I did not ask why he didn't want to go. Or tell him how hurt I was that he wanted to cancel his birthday trip. He went back to the living room.

I imagined holding hands with Conor on a Paris street, laughing while we drank café au lait at a small wrought-iron table, riding the Metro with the colors of the stations flying by.

He returned a half hour later. I was lying on our bed, staring at the inlaid white ceiling of this once grand, now shabby mansion subdivided into apartments. Our almost-packed duffel bags were still on the floor where I'd left them.

"So, have you called the airline to cancel the tickets?" he asked. A stupid question; as if the cheap charter airline was open at ten-thirty on a Saturday night. He meant: *I'm the boss here. Did you do what I ordered?*

I knew why Conor wanted to cancel our vacation. The

trip was my way to celebrate our starting over. But even good news had to be celebrated on his terms only. Even a joyous occasion frightened him if he couldn't control it.

The man I imagined in Paris was not the man in the doorway. That man was gone, if he'd ever even existed. There was no "old Conor." I'd been lying to myself since August. Maybe long before August.

"No," I said. I turned my head away from him, toward the white wall that divided our apartment from the one next door. I found my favorite crack in the wall plaster, the one that looked like a misshapen flower.

"I'm going," I told him, my back still to him. "Even if you're not, Conor. I've worked too hard this semester. We won't have a vacation again for a long time. I'd rather go with you, but I'm going anyway."

I closed my eyes. I suppose it was stupid to tell him the truth. But for the first time in three years I had to know what he would do if I told him how I really felt.

A long silence followed, a moment's pause like when you watch an infant sleeping, swaddled in the crib, and you're not sure whether she is going to take another breath or perhaps stop breathing forever. Silence that mesmerizes you.

A gentle whoosh of air came toward me. The room tumbled in a slow-motion blur. My head got stuck for a second in my tight T-shirt collar. With a grunt Conor yanked the fabric off. My head crashed into the hardwood floor.

"How dare you." His voice shot across the room like the punch of a fist. "You can't go without me. You selfish bitch."

From the bedside table he picked up my favorite wedding photo in an inlaid silver frame Frankie had given me the year before she died. No time to cover my face as he broke the picture over my head, so I closed my eyes to shut out the glass. Small bloody slits like paper cuts sprang up across my forehead and cheeks from the shards.

No, I pleaded silently as I covered my head with my arms. *Don't let this happen. I do still love him. He is my family.*

I didn't see Conor's foot pull back but suddenly my rib cage exploded as if hit with a sledgehammer. An ominous intensity I'd never felt before characterized his movements. Our small bedroom felt black with rage, as if Conor had been bottling up his anger since August, choreographing each punch and kick in advance, patiently knowing this moment would come even as I had hoped every day it wouldn't.

I looked at him, his jaw clenched, hands in fists, veins raised along his biceps like electric wires. It felt as if a complete stranger had broken into my home and was standing in my bedroom.

The phone. I tried to reach the rickety wooden nightstand next to our bed where I knew the phone lay in its cradle, the same receiver I'd picked up when Winnie called. It was only halfway across the room but Conor moved so fast that getting more than a few inches out of the reach of his arms and feet was impossible. Ludicrously so.

I heard the sounds of my own screams as if there was some other woman in our apartment screaming her head off.

He grabbed my neck with both hands, those fingers I'd

loved circling my windpipe easily. Using my head like a stopper he pulled me up off the floor and back onto the bed, forcing me into the mattress with the weight of his body and his hands around my neck. I could smell his sweat layered over our laundry detergent on his blue button-down shirt.

"*Shut up! Shut up! Shut up!*" I heard him yell.

He squeezed my throat until I could not make any more noise. What I could see of the room faded until everything before me went starry. I felt a deep quiet, a kind of peace almost, simplicity. My life was this room, this firm mattress, a soft, fading gray-black in front of my eyes.

When I came to, I had no sense of how much time had passed. Ten minutes? Ten seconds? Maybe my entire lifetime?

Conor stood by the head of the bed next to the phone, in front of the doorway. He watched me as if he were afraid to touch me again. He flinched—with relief?—as I opened my eyes and turned my face to him. His underarms were wet with sweat and his muscled forearms were crossed over his chest like a security guard blocking a bank vault.

My stomach and ribs felt as if an enormous hunk of ice lay wedged inside me. The old cliché came true and a parade of faces I might never see again passed before me. My mom. My sister. Winnie.

My love for Conor seemed completely irrelevant.

I heard a faint voice. It came from inside me.

You know this man. Use what you know.

The voice was calm. Its tone suggested a shrug: *Hey, it's*

up to you to decide the outcome here. It's okay if you want to give up right now. Him or you. Your choice.

I breathed. Out. In. I slowly sat up on the rumpled blue-and-white-flowered bedspread and raised my palms, laced with cold sweat, in the universal code for surrender. My body felt small and useless compared to his.

"Conor, I love you," I said softly, looking into his twisted face and red eyes. There were blisters of moisture on his shiny forehead. "I know you don't want to do this. Of course I won't go to Paris without you. Just stop what you're doing. I love you so much I'll do anything for you. I am so sorry."

I bowed my head. I didn't take my eyes off his face.

"We're going to be fine," I pleaded with a half-smile. My knees shook wildly. I tried to cover them with my arms. The iciness in my stomach made me fear I would throw up. He froze for a second, looking at me warily as if I might rush for the phone or the door again. My eyes tracked his. I tried again to smile.

Hope is always good, right?

Suddenly footsteps pounded in the hallway outside the apartment. Someone began hammering our front door, hard enough to splinter the wood. The person did not say anything. But to me the banging shouted out, "Stop it! Stop it! Can't you see you might actually *kill* her?"

The spell was broken. There was a world outside our bedroom again. I could feel glass in my face, a burn around my throat and fire in my ribs.

Conor bowed his face and began to cry. His shoulders

crumpled. His nose ran like a kid crying after breaking a trea-sured toy. He shook his head no as if trying to erase the last twenty minutes. His apartment keys jingled as he took them out of his pocket and carefully placed them on our bedside table on top of the broken wedding photo. A twisted peace of-fering. He picked his blue coat off the rack in the hallway.

"I'll call you tomorrow," he whispered as he left, still choking back tears.

As soon as the front door to the building banged shut, I reached for the phone. I was alive. I took a deep breath and picked up the receiver to call the police.

It felt as if entire years passed during the time I waited in our apartment, shaking with adrenaline, fingering the bruises on my ribs, trying not to throw up. But in actuality the two heavyset cops in uniform arrived surprisingly quickly. They might even have passed Conor on the street in front of the building.

I stood in the living room wearing an old terry-cloth bathrobe. I recounted the beating. The shorter cop wrote a few notes on a little pad, his stubby fingers moving the pen in quick jabs. I did not cry.

"We see a million cases like this," he said, shaking his head in a mixture of anger and disgust. "He'll apologize to-morrow, promise everything. Then we'll be back in a few weeks. Need a doctor?"

Despite the cuts on my face and the ache in my ribs, I shook my head no.

"Well, what ya have to do, is go—tonight, right after we leave—to city hall. Know where that is? You gotta file a restraining order. Tomorrow you gotta call our precinct, make sure a policeman issues the order. You hafta go with one of our guys to serve the order and verify his identity."

The trip to city hall, I might have been able to handle. But seeing Conor again, issuing papers to him, was a prospect too terrifying to contemplate. I shook my head again.

"He's your husband, right? You're married? Well, you gotta get a divorce lawyer. Start divorce proceedings immediately."

I stared at him. I felt the cops' invisible weariness like carbon monoxide filling the living room. They thought they'd be back in a few weeks to break up another fight, that I would be like every other woman who could not leave, women they nonetheless felt sorry for. They cared for me, a total stranger, in a way that Conor didn't—or couldn't.

As they left, the shorter cop paused at the door, as if giving me one last chance, talking to me like I was his daughter.

"Remember this when you think about how much ya 'love' him: He tried to kill you tonight. Next time, we might find you dead here."

He pointed a fat finger to the living-room floor to indicate where my body would lie. He and his partner walked out my door and took the stairs heavily. Like overweight synchronized

swimmers, each pulled a walkie-talkie out of his blue uniform pocket.

As I listened to their footsteps echo on the steps, I looked at Frankie's intricate, threadbare carpet and thought, *No one is ever going to find me dead on that floor.*

My throat so tight I could hardly force the words out, I left two identical, stilted messages for Sylvia and my study partner Cherie on their answering machines.

"I am okay. But please call me as soon as you get this message. This is an emergency."

I washed the blood off my face and changed into jeans and a heavy Norwegian sweater. I went into the kitchen. "Blue, Blue," I whispered. "It's okay, buddy." Blue walked cautiously out of his crate into my arms. I hugged his warm, silky body and clipped on his leash. We went out together into the cold Chicago night before I could think about what I was doing.

I drove the Volkswagen through the empty streets to city hall, a building I passed nearly every day. I parked at a broken meter in front. Blue curled up on the passenger seat to wait, his brown eyes liquid as I locked the car doors.

Inside city hall, the lone clerk on duty looked at me blankly, cracking her gum, her cornrowed hair decorated with red and green beads.

I robotically repeated my directions from the two cops. "I need to file a restraining order."

The clerk went wordlessly to a filing cabinet. My neck and rib cage and eye sockets ached as I stood at the gray metal counter waiting. She handed me the forms like a cashier at 7-Eleven passing me a Diet Coke.

I stood at a high linoleum table, like the ones in the post office, in the chilly, cavernous government building decorated with grimy plastic Christmas wreaths. One of the fluorescent ceiling lights was out. The clock on the wall said three A.M. Did it take more than three hours to change clothes, wash my face, make the phone calls, drive here? Where was Conor right now?

Forms. The slips of cheap shiny paper were oddly comforting. I was good at this, capturing information with a pen. In black ballpoint I described the kaleidoscope of times Conor held a gun to my head, the day he pulled the keys out of the ignition when I was driving sixty miles per hour down the turnpike, everything that had happened in the past few hours.

I needed to scrunch my words up to get it all down.

Whoever read these complaints would say I was the crazy one. That I imagined such bizarre stunts. It would be natural to think I'd made them up. Or worse, to believe I provoked them.

The day before, I had been taking my last accounting exam. I was supposed to be on my way to Paris with my husband. Instead I was standing in a government building in the middle of the night with cuts on my face describing the myriad times and ways my beloved beat me up during the course of our two-and-a-half-year marriage.

Blue and I climbed out of the Jetta and back up the apartment steps just before five A.M. The phone was ringing as I unlocked the door. The receiver felt like a ten-pound barbell.

"Les?"

Sylvia.

"I got your message when I got home from a party at two-thirty. I've been calling ever since. I'm going to get in my car and drive—"

It took almost an hour to tell her everything as I sat in my living room drinking a cup of lukewarm tea. "Don't come, Syl. I know you want to help. I want you to help. But this is my mess. I've got to take care of this part by myself. I'm . . . okay."

I could almost see her pale blue eyes reflecting the range of emotions I knew I'd inflicted: fear, anger, relief, sadness, confusion, concern. I thought of the time when she was four and I was eleven and I had to remove a cinnamon red hot she'd stuck up her nose. My sister.

Cherie called at seven A.M. I told her everything, too. She drove sixty miles back from vacation to take me to breakfast at the diner near our apartment. Later that day she called with valuable information—that Conor was staying with his friend Matt in the same building Cherie lived in. I needed his whereabouts so that I could direct the police serving the restraining order that afternoon.

I didn't call Mom or Dad or Hugh, Winnie or my cousins, all the people who'd want to know. Repeating what had happened would make the truth stand out like boldface on Page Six: Conor had almost killed me. Our marriage was

over. Feeling like a homeowner picking her way amid broken glass after an earthquake, I needed time without an aftershock. Before I could talk to anyone, I had to absorb the damage myself.

Plus I needed to conserve my energy for the afternoon's task.

Around two P.M. I walked in the chilly December sunshine to the police precinct. It was only six blocks from our apartment. Who knew? I gave the form from city hall to a police officer who looked as young and buff as one of those firefighters who'd whistled at me as I walked home from *Seventeen*. Using two fingers to jab at the keys on an old manual typewriter, he typed up a form labeled TEMPORARY RESTRAINING ORDER.

Then we drove in his squad car to the apartment building where Conor was staying, a building where dozens of other students lived. I prayed Conor would not be there. My palms broke out in a cold, nervous sweat that smelled metallic, of fear.

Conor answered the building's intercom on the officer's first buzz.

"Yeah, who is it?" He sounded like any other man, not someone who beat his wife last night.

"Sir, this is the Chicago police. Please come down to the lobby."

As we waited by the elevator, I noticed the officer had his right hand on top of his gun.

Less than thirty seconds later, Conor stepped out of the

elevator wearing the same jeans and gray sweatshirt he'd had on yesterday. His hair was wet from the shower.

He looked thinner than he did last night, too small for his clothes. Today was his thirty-fifth birthday. Our flight to Paris left in forty-five minutes with two seats empty.

I stood slightly behind the officer, who turned to ask if this was Conor. I nodded yes. He turned back.

"Are you Conor ——— ?"

"I am," Conor said. He sounded like an actor in a play.

The officer unrolled the restraining order and explained it.

"Your wife has filed a temporary restraining order against you. She says that last night—"

He glanced down at the typewritten order. My hands shook in my pockets.

"—at your apartment on ——— Street, at approximately 10:30 P.M., you beat her and choked her until she lost consciousness. She has detailed over a dozen similar incidents that occurred over the past three years. As a result, our precinct has prepared this temporary restraining order. You are not allowed to contact your wife via telephone or written letter or to get within sixty feet of her at any time for the next sixty days. If you do you will be arrested and imprisoned for violation of this order. Do you understand and agree with these terms?"

To my amazement, Conor nodded. He signed the restraining order without protest, without looking at me. My stomach lurched as he handed the forms back to the cop.

The officer tore off the bottom copy and handed it to Conor. Conor looked briefly in my direction and then down at the mottled brown indoor-outdoor carpeting. Less than three minutes after arriving, the officer and I left. Conor watched us go, standing in the middle of the mirrored lobby with his legs locked and his right hand clutching his copy of a piece of paper that said he'd tried to kill me.

The officer drove me back home. He double-parked his cruiser in front of my apartment. He handed me my copy of the restraining order.

"Call the police or have someone else call the police immediately if your husband violates these terms. And remember—you can't call him, have contact with him, either. The restraining order applies to both of you."

The officer's poker face as he went over the instructions helped keep my squirming emotions in their lockbox. Not what I would call calm, exactly, but able to limit the shaking of my arms and legs until I was inside our apartment, which felt cold and deserted and way too quiet.

The next afternoon, Christmas Eve, I left for Washington with Blue in the passenger seat. Twelve hours later I pulled up to my father's house. Sylvia's red Jeep was parked outside; Dad had taken his new girlfriend to Europe for Christmas a few days before. Sylvia opened the front door and put her arms around me without saying anything. Her hair smelled

of clove cigarette smoke and her skinny body was so warm, so alive, I never wanted to let go. She leaned back to look at me and touched the biggest cut on my face with her chilly index finger, not saying a word.

I spent Christmas Day at Dad's empty town house. My chest felt empty, too, like Conor had taken my heart with him when he left our apartment. Sylvia spent Christmas with Mom just a few miles away. Joining them was impossible for me. I wanted another day before this became real. I couldn't stand Mom telling me, "I told you so." I didn't want people, not even my own mother, to feel sorry for me, or to question my decision, or to suggest, out of malice or ignorance, that this turn of events was my fault or something I could rectify if I just tried harder next time. I felt made of Jell-O, jiggling as I walked around my father's home. I didn't turn on the lights even as darkness fell. Christmas was just another day. Everyone thought I was in Paris with Conor anyway.

On December 26 I sat on a black leather bar stool in the kitchen of Dad's empty house with a list of my closest relatives and friends. Mom's number was the first I dialed.

"Mom, hi, it's Les. I know you think I'm in Paris, but I'm actually here in D.C."

I didn't give her a chance to say anything.

"Conor and I have split up—because he was, ah, physically abusing me."

I stopped talking because I couldn't breathe. I heard her suck in a sharp breath.

"I am so sorry for you, Leslie." She said it like she really meant it. But not like she was completely surprised. "And for him. Because he's lost you now."

This last part undid me. Despite her cruel criticism of me over the years, from where she sat, I was anyone and everyone's prize. My bottom lip started quivering so hard, it was like there was a little motor in there.

"Oh, Mom." I gritted my teeth. "Thanks. I am glad you understand. I really need you."

I couldn't hold the tears back any longer and they dripped down my cheeks. A few slipped into the corner of my mouth. They tasted sweet.

"I'm here," Mom said. "No matter what. Anything you need."

I could tell the words were hard for her to get out, too. Maybe tears were coming down her cheeks as well.

I managed to work my way down the list. I faxed a letter to my father at his hotel in Switzerland. I called my cousin. My three bridesmaids. My best friend from camp. Kathy from *Seventeen*. Everyone sounded stunned, except for one person.

"I am so, so sorry, Leslie," Winnie said when I reached her at Rex's family house in Westchester. "I know how much you loved him. But you're better off now. He was so troubled no one could help him. Thank God it's over. I always thought he was a goddamn ax-murderer."

Oh, fuck, I thought. Was I such a fool?

Ed was one of the few friends I didn't call. He was

Conor's buddy first; it had to stay that way. I needed the division between Conor and me to be like two freshly painted yellow lines on the highway. Our life together, our mutual friends, were off-limits now.

Hanging up the phone, dialing it again and again, repeating the same words to different people, felt like peeling layers of skin off an open wound. Telling everyone was like building a barricade brick by brick, to stop me from giving him another chance, from crossing the yellow lines. The fact that I still loved Conor, would probably always love him, was a grave threat. I crawled into my dad's guest bed that night, afraid of the future. And of myself.

"Stay, Les, just a few more days," Sylvia begged. It was brutal to have someone whose diaper I'd changed worry about me. I told her I needed to go home and prepare for the future. Whatever that meant.

Blue and I drove off the morning of December 30 in the gray, post-Christmas letdown. The highways were deserted. I accidentally left my glasses inside Dad's house and had to drive back to Chicago trying to make out the hazy green-and-white signs along the highway. I nearly missed my exit into Illinois.

I made it home around ten P.M., parked the black Volkswagen in front of our apartment and carried in my duffel bag. Blue raced up the steps in front of me. I propped open

the apartment door with the bag while I checked to make sure Conor had not somehow gotten in. I noted with relief—tinged, I was ashamed to admit, with disappointment—that every room was exactly as I'd left it. He had not been there at all. *How can you possibly miss him?* I asked myself. But I did.

I got Blue food and water and fell into bed.

The next morning, I pulled on jeans and a sweatshirt from a pile of dirty clothes and walked to campus for some fresh air, to buy coffee and to check my mailbox. Afterward I took the cobblestone walkway toward home. I passed the bookstore, the recruiting center, the faculty dining hall, up the wide footbridge that divided the campus from our neighborhood. I cried as I realized it was not me who gave up on Conor or our marriage. I would have never given up. Conor gave up. He knew beating me that night guaranteed I would leave him for good. My worst fear, of Conor abandoning me, had come true long before December.

Tears ran down my face as I muttered to myself, looking down, not meeting anyone's gaze. At two o'clock on the afternoon of New Year's Eve, there were few people around; I couldn't have cared less about the strange looks I must have been getting.

Halfway across the arched footbridge I felt a cold, familiar presence. At first I couldn't quite see who it was because of my missing glasses. As I got closer I saw it was Conor. Of course. He was immaculately dressed in his blue cashmere coat, his throat wrapped in his maroon paisley scarf, his

hands thrust into his silk-lined coat pockets. He looked like a carefree young bachelor enjoying a stroll on this sunny winter's day, the last day of the year. *He* didn't have scabs on his face.

He stopped and stared at me in my dirty jeans, equally unsure of what to say. We were trapped on the footbridge, blocking each other's way.

One of the things I'd thought about during the dark days in Washington was that I had never screamed when he'd beat me—until that last night. Even when he held his cocked gun to my temple, I did not feel scared. When he pushed me down the stairs, I didn't remember feeling hurt anywhere on my body. I didn't remember feeling angry at him.

Exactly where had shutting myself down, never getting mad, trying always to see Conor's point of view, wanting to help him, gotten me? Right here on this narrow passageway facing Conor. The only thing good about being here was that Conor couldn't fight back. I would be safe no matter what. So it seemed logical to start screaming.

"You've ruined my life!" I shrieked. My wails echoed off the street below in the chilly winter air. "I fucking hate you!"

It didn't seem essential to go into the details about my lonely Christmas, the bruises underneath my turtleneck, how empty the apartment felt without him. How empty my life would always feel without him. It was enough to scream "You've ruined my life!" and "I hate you!" over and over. I clenched my teeth and stared at his magnificent face as if my anger could obliterate him.

Conor stood still. I felt like a giant wood chipper capable of shredding him into pulp. I imagined bits of his blond hair, his paisley scarf, the cashmere coat, being spewed across the bridge. He seemed afraid to get too close to me.

From my peripheral vision I saw passersby stopping. Nice-looking, well-dressed university people with open, curious faces. As they looked at me their faces darkened with anger. I was the enemy here, screaming at this tall, fresh-faced young man in such a nice blue coat. Mentally I put them through the wood chipper, too.

Finally I walked past Conor, who stayed frozen like a cardboard cutout of himself. I kept screaming and shaking my head like a schizophrenic bag lady released too soon from a state mental hospital. People stopped and stared at me as I sobbed the six blocks home.

By the time I put the key in the door of our apartment, my screams were screamed out. I felt curiously refreshed, better than I had in months. Go figure.

I opened the apartment door and Blue jumped me. I crouched down and he hugged me with his big front paws and licked the tears off my cheeks with relish. No one, not my sister or Winnie or the world's most understanding therapist, would ever sanction the wood chipper. But for once, I'd had the last word with Conor. Surprising how good that felt.

I held onto Blue with my whole body. I closed my eyes.

Then I started to laugh a little. Dry heaves that sounded like sandpaper scraping brick. I felt a shard of hope about my life, my future, the way you do when your fingers discover

something that just might be a Hershey's Kiss at the bottom of your purse. It never occurred to me that Conor had followed me back to the apartment, and was waiting until he saw the living-room light turn on so he could watch my silhouette from the street. I noticed him an hour later when I switched off the light. I crouched under the window in the dark, watching him watch me. When he still didn't leave, I dragged the dresser from the bedroom to the front hallway, blocking the door so I could fall asleep.

The next ten days dragged by like time spent underwater.

Days passed something like this: Eat breakfast, cry, take a shower, cry, go rent a sad movie so I could cry some more. I tried to absorb what had happened—*It's over with Conor, it's over.* And I struggled with an even dicier concept: What he had done to me was *criminal.* If our neighbor hadn't intervened, he might have killed me. It didn't seem possible. I slept from midnight to noon. My face felt like raw corned beef, salted with dried-out tears.

I had never felt so alone in my life. But stupidly, I wasn't scared. Despite what I knew about how dangerous it was to leave an abusive man, I felt far more shock and sadness than fear.

The few times I ventured out, I took Blue as my guardian, ridiculous because if we saw Conor, Blue would be delighted, not ferocious. But his companionship was all I had. One day

we stood together in the drama section of the video store two blocks from the apartment. I teetered between Jodie Foster's *The Accused* and Diane Keaton's *The Good Mother*.

Midway through *The Accused* a few hours later, sitting in our dark bedroom in the red chair, Blue cutting off the circulation in my legs like a sixty-pound lap puppy, I experienced an epiphany of sorts, the first posttraumatic aftershock. Watching Jodie Foster's character reliving the gang rape on a pool table in her local bar as patrons cheered, I dredged up the warning signs I'd ignored during the early days with Conor: the night he choked me during sex, his overreaction to Guy calling me, his possessiveness when other men even talked to me.

Part of me knew about Conor's dark side when we had dated only a few months. I had stifled my own fears, even after the attacks started. Conor had held a gun to my head and I had not been afraid. It was my elemental mistake that I did not listen to my own voice trying to warn me about the danger I was in.

Why didn't I listen then?

Would I listen now?

January. Happy New Year indeed.

I sat in a cushy business class seat on an American Airlines jet. I was headed for San Francisco for my first "callback" job interview. My destination was a large consumer company famous for its bleach and bug spray. The briefcase at my

feet was stuffed with the company's annual reports, marketing brochures, and market share analyses I'd memorized for
this visit. I was the only one of forty students interviewed
who had been asked back for this second round. The bruises
on my neck and tiny cuts all over my face had just healed.

An old friend from high school who was getting a Ph.D.
at Berkeley met me at the airport and drove me into the city.
We stopped by a funky San Francisco coffee bar, all granite
tabletops and exotic, aromatic blends. I could not bring myself to tell my friend what had happened with Conor or the
decisions I had to make, alone now. That I could be such a
good actress seemed a dirty secret. Faker. Liar. I felt numb,
an amnesiac.

The worst part was how much I missed Conor. I wanted
him there in San Francisco with me. This was loneliness:
The only person who would understand was the last person
I could turn to. One thought broke through the clutter in my
mind: I couldn't let loving Conor destroy the future, even if
I had to go into it alone. He chose violence. I chose me. I
walked the pastel hills of San Francisco from the coffee
shop to my hotel, jerking my heavy roll-aboard suitcase behind me, vowing that I would graduate from business school
and get every job offer I could. Damn him.

The company put me up in a spacious suite at the Ritz-
Carlton at the top of Nob Hill. I deserved this, I tried to per-
suade myself, pulling back the gauzy white curtains and
looking at a beautiful view of sunny, hilly San Francisco.
Not being thrown onto the floor of my apartment by my own

husband. Domestic violence? A husband who beat me? The truth just didn't seem possible. At the Nordstrom's a few blocks from the hotel, I bought a red coatdress that proclaimed a confidence I did not possess.

Fake it till you make it, I told myself as I put on my makeup and the new dress the morning of the interviews. Eight grueling hours later, the vice-president of marketing called me into his office. "It's unanimous," he said with a warm grin. "Everyone loves you. We never do this, but we're making you a job offer on the spot." I faced him across his large blond wood desk, the California sun shining so brightly I had to squint to make out the outline of his head and shoulders. I tried to smile. After all, he'd thrown me a life raft to the future, a guarantee that after graduation I'd have a place to go two thousand miles away from Conor. The man's lips moved but I couldn't hear what he said, like someone had pushed the mute button on the TV remote. All I could think was: nothing.

Alone in the elevator on the way out of the building, I covered my face with my hands, took a deep breath, and began to cry. Again.

One rainy, chilly Tuesday morning a few weeks later I sat across from a woman ten years older than I was. I sank into her soft corduroy couch under a watercolor of creamy white calla lilies, blue irises, and pink gladiolas, listening to the unseasonable rain and rush-hour traffic of the Chicago historic

district outside. She had brown curly hair, a little makeup, a naturally pretty face. A ready smile. She asked me what I was looking for in a therapist.

"I want someone to tell me, to help me find out, what went wrong here. What I did wrong. I want brutal honesty. I want someone to really help me see why I am so screwed up that I made such bad decisions—"

"What about kindness and respect? Do you want that, too?" she interrupted, the skin around her eyes crinkling with her easy smile.

I managed a grunt in my throat. "Well, some kindness and respect would be nice, too."

From everyone, I thought. Including myself?

I explained my history with Conor. She did not ask a single question about him. She did not dig into why I chose someone like Conor or why I still wore my wedding ring. She did point out that it might be difficult to reunite with Conor, given that I couldn't picture being alone with him for thirty seconds without beginning to hyperventilate.

"Let me give you some kindness and respect right now. First, it is amazing that you survived. Most women don't. Second, you haven't turned back to alcohol or drugs as a way to cope. Incredible. You are far stronger than you think.

"I've got a couple of mantras for you as you go through this recovery," she continued, amused. "Be honest with yourself. Trust your instincts. Ask for help when you need it." She ticked off three fingers. "And you will be fine."

I repeated the mantras silently, as if they were important new rules to follow. Her office was filled with colorful, over-sized books, photos of a small boy and a girl with her same curly brown hair, and a phone that rang quietly in a corner, burbling like water in a fish tank. I imagined that other patients who needed her as much as I did were calling and leaving messages of quiet desperation.

"Last thing," she said. "This is key. Don't *think* about what's happening right now, or what you went through with Conor. Feel it. Let what you feel guide you."

Later that afternoon, Cherie called to tell me that Conor moved into a studio apartment about eight blocks from me, on the other side of the rectangle of dirt everyone calls the Dog Park, because all the neighborhood dogs run free there most afternoons.

I tried to *feel* my reaction. Nothing.

"How's Conor doing, anyway?" Cherie asked.

"Oh, Conor's okay, I guess," I told her. The truth was I had no idea how he was doing.

"Hey, um, I thought you should know . . . people are talking about why you guys split up. People know he was physically abusing you. A few people were talking about how he follows you home and stands outside your apartment. We're scared for you, Leslie."

I didn't say anything. Don't cry, I told myself. All of a sudden, I was feeling a whole lot.

"You know, it's behind you now," she said in a determined, steady voice, as if there were nothing for me to be ashamed of. I was amazed to hear her talk about the devastation of my life so calmly. "I'm relieved that you've broken up for good. Now you have to focus on staying safe."

I didn't push the fact that I didn't feel the "for good" part yet myself.

Instead I took a big sniff.

"Don't you even think about getting back together with him," she said, as if she knew what I was thinking. "You wouldn't let *me* hit you, would you? You wouldn't take any abuse from a friend. So you know what? Apply those same standards to the men you get involved with. Pretend they are me. Don't take anything from a guy that you wouldn't tolerate from me. Call me anytime, anywhere if you even think about getting back together with him."

I didn't tell Cherie I thought about getting back together with Conor every day. I still slept in *our* bed, in *our* apartment, with *our* dog. Alone. And it didn't *feel* good.

February. Now that Conor had his own place just a few blocks from mine, I started finding presents from him on the front porch. A white mohair sweater in a fancy bag from a boutique nearby. A bar of my favorite Swiss chocolate. A

bag of freshly ground coffee. Pink roses. I tried to wear the sweater but it was so itchy I had to take it off immediately. I put the chocolate and coffee in the back of the freezer, behind some frozen bananas. The flowers wilted quickly and I was relieved to throw them away without feeling guilty.

He called about twice a week. Hearing his voice on the line felt like the cold suction of a meat locker shutting behind me. But the sound of his scratchy voice also thrilled me—as it always had. Our conversations were brief. No, I didn't need anything. No, I could not have dinner. (Was he crazy?) It was all I could do to refuse him.

He almost killed you, Leslie, I said to myself as I sat clutching the phone till my hand ached. This struck me as a pretty good reason not to see him. A second later it would seem irrational, paranoid—how could I think my own husband might try to kill me? But he had.

I did not ask for his new number because I was afraid I'd call him when I woke up crying in the middle of the night.

One morning he stopped me as I was leaving marketing strategy. He got so close I could smell his breath, feel the warmth of his body under his winter coat. In panic I looked around quickly to see if there was a pay phone nearby that someone could use to call the police. A few students bundled in down jackets walked past us, slowing down in disbelief that we were talking to each other.

"Leslie, wait a second, please. Don't leave. I'm trying so hard to be honest with myself." I could tell from his

cottonmouth and slightly swollen eyes that he was taking medication. His blond hair looked stringy and dirty, plastered to his forehead. The expression in his eyes—and his words—seemed sincere. So I listened.

"I have to admit all the wrongs I have done to you . . ."

I had never heard Conor speak about his problems with anger or allude to abusing me. This was as close to an apology as he'd ever gotten. I had to hear this.

"I'm going to a self-help group of men who have abused women. It's hard work."

Was that a teardrop in the corner of his eye? A glimmer of hope—for him, and maybe even for us together—shimmied through me.

"Will you come to family therapy with me? My group really recommends it. I told them I would ask you. Please, Leslie, I need to be with you."

Still in shock, I told him I wanted some time to think it over.

The next day, I left a message in his mail folder saying I'd try the therapy. Was I stupid? Hope was always good, right? Maybe therapy would help him. Maybe it would help me. Maybe I was still crazy enough about Conor to try anything.

On a Friday afternoon two weeks later, Conor and I arrived separately, but within seconds of each other, at the double doors of a nondescript building near campus for a three P.M.

appointment he'd set up. Conor went first into the therapists' comfortable, whitewashed basement office. He sat
down on a large oatmeal-colored couch, leaving room for me
next to him. I took a deep breath and walked past him and
sat on a cushy white chair with high arms.

There were two therapists, a husband-and-wife team prac-
ticing together. Conor looked like a little kid sitting across
from them. The female therapist, Christine, introduced herself and her husband. "We've found the two-on-two therapeutic model very effective at quickly getting to the root of issues
between couples," she explained. "It helps clarify the central
problems—and whether they can be solved—so that the couple can agree to stay together or end the relationship."

Conor leaned forward with his hands clasped on his knees.
"I love her—I love you, I need you." He turned to look at
me. "You are the girl of my dreams. Please, Leslie." He looked
down at the therapists' woven rug. "I will do absolutely anything if you give me another chance."

We all looked at each other. Small sweat streams flowed
along the fortune-teller lines of my palms and under my gold
wedding band, which I still couldn't bring myself to take off.
Before any of us could say anything, Conor spoke again.

"Therapy is helping me see that I am particularly vulnerable to stress and anger at night because of my childhood,
because Wade used to beat me at night when he got home
from his job," he explained matter-of-factly, leaning back on
the couch, his palms open. "If things are going to work out,
Leslie needs to be more careful in the evenings not to bring

up my 'hot button' subjects. I've made a list—money, academic performance, family stuff. I can't talk about those things. I've got a copy for you right here."

He reached into his shirt pocket and handed me a folded piece of paper.

I took it but didn't respond. I looked at both therapists. How could everything still be all about him? Did he have an inkling of how I had suffered—and was still suffering—because of what he'd done to me? I didn't say anything. Trust me, it was therapeutic enough to sit there.

I was exhausted when the ninety-minute session came to a close. We set a date for the next appointment. All I could think about was getting out of the basement and locking myself in my car before Conor left. I drove home. Miraculously, there was a parking space right in front of our apartment. On my way from the car to the building, I balled up Conor's list of "hot buttons" and jammed it into the trash can by the curb.

Three days after the first therapy session, Conor and I met again. This time the venue was family court, Monday morning at nine A.M. The sixty-day restraining order was expiring soon; a judge who'd never met either of us would decide whether Conor was still a threat to me. The courthouse was a 1960s urban renewal brick building in a rundown downtown neighborhood where garbage overflowed

from trash cans at the corners and lined the gutters along the sidewalks.

I parked the Jetta at a broken meter and walked two blocks to the courthouse. It was a bitter, windy day. The trash flew across the sidewalk and up against cars and buildings. A crumpled Dunkin' Donuts napkin stuck to my panty hose, underneath the raccoon fur coat Conor had given me during our first Christmas together.

The waiting room was lined with sad-eyed Hispanic women trying to watch too many children at once, clumps of working-class black men talking and laughing with their hands thrust in their pockets or crossed over their chests, and young cheaply dressed social worker types.

Before I could decide what to do, a thin woman approached me.

"Are you Leslie?" she asked, peering into a worn manila file. She wore no makeup, and had stick-straight, dirty-blond hair like Marcia Brady.

"Yes," I told her. How did she know my name? What else did she have in that file? I balled my coat under my arm to hide the fur trim.

"It says here that you don't have a lawyer," Ms. No-Makeup-Dirty-Blond-Hair Social Worker explained. She had a kind voice and clear, greenish brown eyes. I bet she knew how afraid I was. She was right about my not having legal counsel.

Last week I'd called my father to ask if he could recommend a divorce lawyer in Chicago. I'd seen his Harvard Law

School alumni directory, four inches thick, with graduates listed by city and area of legal expertise.

"Ah, you know, Les . . . I, um, I don't know anyone in *that* line of work," Dad stuttered back, sounding as if I had asked him to recommend a good dominatrix.

Stung by his antipathy, I stuttered, "Okay, thanks anyway, bye, Dad," and hung up the phone quickly. Standing in the living room, I burst into tears, crying so loudly I thought the downstairs neighbors would hear.

Was my own dad that ashamed of me? He sure was proud when I did something right. How could getting divorced, admitting that neither I nor my marriage were anything close to perfect, be *worse* than staying with a man who abused me?

Suddenly, still standing in my apartment, still holding the phone, crying my ass off, I choked on a new thought as if I'd swallowed a piece of gum by accident. Maybe my father *had* known about all my previous problems, Mom's alcoholic tirades, my drug and alcohol use, the anorexia, the terrible boyfriends, even Conor's abuse. Could it be Dad didn't have the stomach, or the heart, to hold me up when I wasn't quite so perfect?

I wanted my dad there, physically there in my apartment, to help me. For a second, through the tears, maybe because of them, I could see clearly: My dad had never been there. Even when I'd badly, obviously needed him. It was terrifying to admit, even as a twenty-six-year-old, that the responsible adult, the only one I could rely on as a child, had actually been the one who was drunk every night. But at least she'd

been home. Dad had always been at the office, taking a client to dinner, traveling on my birthday, forgetting about our wedding breakfast, proofreading documents late into the night the time I broke my wrist in sixth grade or the evening Mom first called me the Washington Whore.

Dad had always seemed like the parent I could trust. For twenty-six years I'd misjudged both my parents. My father's love rested on my being perfect far more than my mother's; if I screwed up, he was as reliable as a ghost. Mom had far more obvious faults, but she had always been there for us kids.

Outside the Family court chambers a week later, I nodded to the social worker. She explained that she was a law school student. "An advocate" is what she called herself. She said I didn't need my own lawyer for today's proceeding. Thank God for that.

"You don't have to talk to your husband—Conor? The most you'll have to do is tell the judge what happened to make you file the original restraining order, and why you want it made final. Trust me, it's a brief, routine proceeding. When your husband gets here, I'll talk to him so I can explain both sides to the judge if necessary. I am here to moderate—I'm paid by the Women's Legal Defense Fund—and to make sure the judge hears your side in addition to your husband's."

Although in good legal fashion she was trying to be objective and factual, I sensed that she was trying to protect women like me who might be intimidated by a judge or by speaking against their husband in a court of law. Women like me—whose husbands had tried to kill them.

Conor showed up just a few minutes before our appointment. The advocate went to him and jotted down a few things in her file. Conor did not smile, toss back his hair, or lean in toward her once. Either he was just as sickened by being here as I was, or she was tough enough that she wasn't wooed by his charisma and looks. She came back, her shoes clacking efficiently on the tile floor, and announced, "We're set."

She strode into the court, Conor and I in tow. The judge called our names. Conor and I stood next to each other like penitent children. The young lawyer explained matter-of-factly that I wanted the restraining order made final and that "her husband" had no objection. The judge asked me and Conor in turn if this was correct.

"Yes," I said.

"Yes, sir," said Conor.

The judge waved us away. Dismissed. I picked up my paperwork at a small bulletproof glass window. The Xeroxed form with our names blocked in said that Conor could not come within ten yards of me and must refrain from calling, writing, or talking to me. It was renewable in six months if I proved to the court that Conor was still a threat. It was a thin piece of paper, similar to cheap notices and junk mail letters I threw away every day. I folded it carefully and slipped it into the small wallet I took everywhere. To me it was precious.

I looked around the courthouse waiting room. The young

lawyer was holding another file and talking earnestly to a black woman with a red-and-yellow Caribbean-style head-kerchief who looked about twenty and was holding the hands of a small boy and girl.

I looked around again. Conor was gone.

———◆———

Dogs look at paper clips and candy wrappers and rocks and think: *Sure, I can eat this.* Blue was no exception. He'd always been skinny and prone to vomiting in the car. But lately he'd been throwing up every morning like a pregnant woman with morning sickness.

One Monday, he did not eat the Reese's peanut butter cup I bought him at 7-Eleven, a regular pit stop on our morning walk, his daily treat to go along with my coffee. This dog would eat chocolate in his sleep. What was wrong?

We walked home slowly and I settled him on the red chair, covering him with a blue-green mohair throw. I went to my two morning classes, wondering about him the whole time. When I came home to check on him, he had not moved. I hugged him, shook him, and called his name. Blue didn't even open his eyes. Then I noticed a small pool of di-arrhea dripping onto the floor.

I rolled him into the mohair blanket and somehow car-ried him to the VW, which was fortunately (1) parked right outside and (2) not about to run out of gas. Like an EMT

entering an emergency room, I burst into the vet's waiting room carrying Blue on my makeshift stretcher.

The vet, a hulking, bearded forty-year-old man wearing a white coat, appeared quickly.

"He's a three-year-old male Doberman pinscher. He has not eaten for three days," I told him. The vet wrote it down on a chart. "He's been throwing up. I found him lying in his own diarrhea. I can't get him to wake up."

The vet told me to bring Blue into a private room. I placed him, still wrapped in the blanket, on a chrome examining table. The vet pinched Blue's silky black coat. "Extreme dehydration," he said. He rolled back Blue's eyelids. "Jaundice," he continued. He turned to look at me.

"What have you done to this dog?" he said accusatorily. "I have never seen a three-year-old animal in such terrible condition. How long has he been like this?"

"Just since Friday," I whined, almost unable to speak. "He ate less and less each day. Then he started throwing up. I took him for his walk this morning and he wouldn't even eat his treat from 7-Eleven. Then by noon he wouldn't wake up. I didn't do anything. I have no idea what's wrong."

The vet's face softened as I talked. "Okay, okay," he said, patting my shoulder with one hand as he ran his other hand gently along Blue's flank. "I'll do everything I can to help him. He is in a coma—he's not in pain. But I need to be honest with you that he's pretty far gone."

I lay my body over Blue and stroked his beautiful head, his soft ears, his velvety lips and throat. How could this be

happening? I sent out a short, simple message to the God of Sick Pets, a combination of an order and a prayer: *No.*

The phone rang when I'd been home just long enough to make peppermint tea. The vet.

"He held on for about twenty minutes after you left," he said. "I'm sorry. I think he was just sticking it out because you were with him. Once he realized you were gone, he let go. I still don't have any idea what was wrong. With your permission I'd like to conduct an autopsy, at my own expense, just to understand what happened. He was a perfectly healthy dog."

I heard my voice telling him yes, thank you, of course, I have to know why as well. I felt like asking: Did he die of a broken heart, will that show up? As I was about to hang up, the vet interrupted, apologized, he had one more question.

"Afterwards, do you want to pick up his body, or do you want us to take care of it? We could arrange for a private cremation or we could have him cremated with several other dogs."

The words themselves would have been hideous, if not for the kindness in the man's voice. I thought of Blue's happiest moments at obedience school in Vermont and the Dog Park around the corner, places where he was surrounded by dozens of other dogs of all breeds.

"Please cremate him with the other dogs," I said. "He would like that best."

I hung up. While drinking my tea, I realized I had to tell Conor. It came to me unexpectedly—like loud music suddenly blasting from your neighbor's stereo—that I had not thought of him, had not needed him, during this ordeal.

I called information to get his new number. He answered on the first ring.

"Conor, I have something really sad to tell you," I said.

"Yeah, what?" Conor said warily.

"Blue died today. He had been sick for a few days and I took him to the vet this afternoon. He died after I left. The vet has no idea what happened but is going to try to find out."

"What the fuck? What are you talking about? He's dead? Why didn't you take him to the vet earlier? Why didn't you call me a few days ago when he first got sick?"

"Blue didn't seem that sick. I had no idea it was serious. I am so sorry. The vet says that at least Blue didn't suffer. I am really, really sorry, Conor. I know how much you loved him."

Then I was quiet. As much as we loved Blue together, I refused to let grief glue us back into one person, even for a few hours. Another tie to Conor was gone. A strange, beautiful, awful gift from Blue.

"Okay, Retard." Conor's voice held a mix of exasperation, grief, and anger. He hung up.

March. Spring had gotten a toehold on the city. Birds chirped outside the basement windows, rectangles filled with pastel

tips of crocus buds. Conor twisted his hands as he sat across from me on the therapists' oatmeal couch during our second appointment. I had no words to describe how I felt about being with Conor again.

I perched on the edge of my chair, drying my sweaty palms on my old jeans, which I wore along with ratty sneakers and Sylvia's faded high-school volleyball sweatshirt. Conor looked like he belonged on an Armani billboard instead of a couch in a therapist's office. Pressed jeans, crisp white oxford shirt, polished brown Italian loafers. His hair looked like he just had it trimmed in some expensive hair salon. He'd lost about ten pounds since Christmas, I guessed. He looked like his old self again. In the waiting room before the appointment he'd told me that he'd gone back to working out two hours a day at the gym. *The peacock is starting to preen again,* a voice inside me said.

The four of us mumbled a few inane pleasantries until the male therapist cleared his throat.

"So, you've both had time to think about your relationship since our last meeting. How do you feel? Are you committed to staying together?"

His businesslike candor startled me. He looked at us with his eyebrows arched in a question mark, first at Conor on the couch, then at me several feet away in my chair with the high sides. Conor answered first, without looking at me.

"We want to stay together," he said with a pair of confident nods of his chin. "We've had some hard times, but we

belong together. I've never loved anyone so much. I need her—I need you, Leslie."

Yuck.

I had not talked to Conor about our marriage since the last session. How could he speak for me? His face reddened and his eyes watered as he leaned forward to look at me.

Before I even knew what I was going to say, I opened my mouth.

"Well, actually, I don't feel that way."

Both therapists froze. Their eyes turned to me. I couldn't look at Conor but I imagined he was staring at me, too. I was having trouble getting air into my diaphragm. My lips were dry. To my surprise, however, I was too angry to cry.

"I want to get divorced," I said to the two therapists sitting on their couch. I couldn't look at Conor.

The therapists stared at me with identical, surprisingly placid expressions on their faces.

Weren't they going to ask me to explain why I wanted a divorce? To justify my decision with ten reasons? Did they expect me to cry about how Conor destroyed me? To say any woman would be crazy to get back together with a bastard like him? To explain how sorry I felt for him?

I thought they'd at least insist I needed to meet Conor's gaze when I said I wanted a divorce, something I would not be able to do.

Instead, both therapists looked at each other and nodded in unison.

"Okay, Leslie," the male therapist said. Christine smiled

at me and patted my knee. "You can go. We'll stay here with Conor for now."

As if in a dream, I gathered my pink windbreaker, purse, and car keys. Five minutes after I'd walked in, I passed Conor on the couch. I looked down at the gray wall-to-wall carpeting as I placed one foot in front of the other and walked toward the door, the shiny nickel doorknob beckoning to me. As I went by, all I could see were Conor's hands, one closed into a fist, pounding his other hand like a baseball in a mitt.

I drove home with all four windows rolled down to fill the car with wind noise and strong gusts of cold spring air. Once inside my apartment, I locked and bolted the front door. Checked it twice. Unplugged my phone.

Then I sat in the chair reading a case study for international marketing Cherie had highlighted for me. A bit of helium floated in my blood, making me feel light and airy, as well as slightly trepidatious about what I was going to feel like when the giddiness wore off. I got to bed early, around nine P.M. I slept well.

In the morning in the campus coffee shop, I ran into a friend of Conor's as I stood in line to buy a croissant.

"Is he okay?" the friend asked, clutching a folded *Wall Street Journal* under his arm. He was dressed in a suit and tie for a job interview. I got a whiff of his aftershave.

"What do you mean?" I said.

"You don't know?" he asked, looking at me strangely. "Matt found Conor at the train station in the middle of the night. He'd been there for something like six hours, just walking around in a daze like a homeless person. Matt took him to emergency health services. He's gotta stay for an evaluation. That's the last I heard."

"I don't know anything about it," I whispered, stunned. "I'm sorry to hear that."

He's not your husband, I told myself, turning so that Conor's friend wouldn't see me cry. *You can't help him anymore.*

The morning of December 21 Conor and I had sex for the last time. Of course I did not know at the time that it would be the last time. I guess you don't usually know that. It was memorably boring sex. We had a houseguest staying with us, a friend of a friend who was applying to business school. While she was in the shower he insisted we make love. I did it to avoid a fight. I climbed on top of him, did my thing, and it was over long before our houseguest was finished in the bathroom.

April. I spent two hours each week with my therapist. At the end of every session I expected her to proclaim, sadly, that

years of therapy were needed to fix me up so I never married a psychopath again.

Instead, we talked about my future, my life going forward. We laughed a fair amount, which always took me by surprise.

As I left one appointment, she gave me homework: I needed to make a list of the top ten things I wanted from a relationship, the next time. "The next time" was a concept that caught me completely off guard. I couldn't fathom going on a date with another man.

So instead of reading cases and studying for tests, I spent long evenings at home working on the list. Sitting at my white desk in my quiet apartment, imagining Blue curled at my feet, I typed on my computer keyboard. I picked out a fancy italic script, as if I were designing a wedding invitation. I revised the list obsessively in my head as I walked the streets around campus.

The day before our next session I printed my top ten list on the creamy white paper I used for résumés:

1. Must be kind, good, uncomplicated, a nice person.
2. Must be successful at life in general (work, relationships, sports, or whatever is meaningful to him).
3. Must be crazy about me.
4. Must have a good relationship with his mother.
5. Would make a good father (acid test: if I were an unborn baby choosing a father, I would choose this person to be my father).

6. Must value independence in himself and in me.

7. Must like animals.

8. Must enjoy watching and playing sports.

9. Must have great friends.

10. Must enjoy books and writing.

Except for being crazy about me, Conor had never fit any of these criteria.

Late one weeknight, my phone rang. I was half-asleep in bed. The clock read eleven P.M. I picked up the phone.

"May I speak to . . . Leslie?" a polite, official-sounding male voice asked.

"Yes," I answered, puzzled.

"This is Sprint phone service calling," he explained. "I was calling to confirm that we have permission to release your phone records to Mr. Conor ——— ."

"Excuse me?" I asked, fully charged now.

"Yes, ma'am. We received a request for all of your local and long-distance phone calls from the past six months. Honestly I thought it was an unusual request, so I am calling to confirm. I apologize for disturbing you at this hour, but I had the feeling this might be important."

"Thank you. Thank you for calling. No, you may not release my phone records to anyone," I said, trying to quell the shaking in my voice. What was Conor doing? Why would

he want our phone records? Did he think I had been having an affair?

The man paused.

"I'm going through a divorce from a man who physically abused me," I explained, choking out *divorce* and *physically abused*. This Sprint employee, a stranger, was trying to help me, across the phone lines, from wherever he was working, hundreds or thousands of miles away from my dark bedroom. "I think he is trying to dig up information he can use against me."

"Yes, ma'am, I understand. I had the feeling there was something . . . aggressive . . . about his request. I just talked to him a few minutes ago."

"Can you put a note in my account? So he can't try this again? He might call back and see if he can get the records another way."

"I'll do that right away. And don't you worry, ma'am. We won't give out any of your information."

I hung up the phone, still puzzled. Afraid. I didn't sleep again that night, wondering about Conor's next move, his brilliant mind, all the places and people he could call to hurt me in whatever way he could. The next day I had the apartment's locks changed, even though Conor no longer had a key. When I got in my car, I started automatically locking the doors before I started the engine. I stopped leaving my apartment after dark if possible, and when I did I turned on every single light in the place to illuminate a safe return. I mapped every pay phone between my apartment and

school. The restraining order was always in my wallet. My new job, the only one that mattered, was keeping myself safe from Conor.

A few days later, I called a lawyer. I had waited, I supposed, because hiring a divorce lawyer was an unambiguous admission that one wants to get divorced. Also I was still hoping that the phone would ring one day and it would be my father.

"You know," Dad would say. "I was thinking you must feel quite alone right now. You probably feel lost and scared. And angry at Conor that he beat you for the past three years, spent all your money, and convinced you to take out all his business school debt in your name. Since I am your father and one of the best judges in the country, I will be your divorce lawyer! We're going to humiliate that bastard for what he did to you!"

Yeah, right. Time to go to the dance alone.

How was I supposed to find a divorce lawyer? I knew no one in this city outside b-school. Who could I ask for a recommendation? One of my marketing professors? My landlord? The Somali guy who I bought coffee from every morning at 7-Eleven?

There was only one person I could think of who knew divorce lawyers in Chicago. My therapist. She recommended someone other clients had used. I called his office and over

the phone reduced our marriage to a glib three-minute syn-opsis: I fell in love with this guy, he beat me for three years, he's acting kinda crazy these days, I think it's probably best to never see him again. I cried for thirty minutes after hang-ing up the phone.

Two days later I went in person to the lawyer's office downtown. Before I left my apartment, for the first time I took off my wedding ring and put it in Frankie's old jewelry box. The streets of Chicago were exploding into spring, cherry blossoms, green grass, and dandelions everywhere, people walking around on their lunch hours with silly smiles plastered across their faces. The lawyer's office was in the Loop right next to a dentist I went to once, in one of Chicago's newer buildings on Wacker Drive, thirty stories of gleaming granite overlooking the obtusely green Chicago River.

Greg Bandy, Esquire, came out to the small reception room to greet me with his hand stuck out for a shake. I looked at him in disbelief. He stood six inches below me, Thumbelina's lawyer, fortyish, well on his way to being 100 percent bald, wearing a miniaturized, precisely tailored wool suit and highly shined wing tips. Not a man you'd bet on against Conor, with his muscles, black belt, and Mr. Massa-chusetts title.

Once we were seated across from each other in his office, he asked a few routine questions about where we were mar-ried, when, what kind of ceremony, where our families lived, our parents' occupations, our religions, financial history,

and current sources of income. He jotted down the answers in quick, left-handed jerks.

"We'll be able to dissolve your relationship," he told me matter-of-factly, like marriage was an Alka-Seltzer tablet, "in such a way that I'm confident your husband will never have legal cause to bother you again. It will cost you roughly ten thousand dollars plus expenses like notary signings, copying forms, courier services." Even though ten grand about equaled my tuition this semester, Greg Bandy made it sound like I was getting a bargain on a used car.

Where was his outrage? How could he not be appalled, horrified at what I went through? Maybe he just didn't understand.

I took the restraining order out of my purse, unfolded it, and handed it to him like it was an original copy of the Declaration of Independence. He glanced down and handed it back. I launched into a detailed, impassioned description of the last four months, trying to make my outrage contagious with lots of hand gestures. "What I want," I told Greg, shaking my finger at him, "is to *fight* Conor."

I wanted an Oklahoma-sized lawyer who jumped onto his desk and shouted out to the world that we would get Conor back! This groundbreaking domestic violence case would save the lives of thousands of other women! We would take it to a judge, the Supreme Court, organize a March on Washington!

But here I was, stuck with little Greg Bandy, whom I realized had started talking again.

"We're going to convince him that he has won, once and for all," Greg said, as if he hadn't heard me. "That he has truly beaten you, forever. Give him the money he wants. Give in on everything you can afford to give in on."

I leaned back in the wingback chair, agog.

Greg folded his hands in his lap and looked at me humorlessly as if I were a naïve ten-year-old who'd gotten in greater trouble than she realized. He looked pained, as if much against his will, he had become the guardian for a hapless child whom he was obligated to extricate from this mess.

"This is what's going to happen if you go to court. First, it is going to take years. *Years,*" he said emphatically but without raising his voice. He was probably incapable of raising his voice. "The Illinois divorce court currently has a waiting period for unmediatable cases of two to three years. These are cases involving children, complicated assets, thirty-year marriages. These are considered urgent cases that have precedence over simple, no-fault cases like yours."

No fault? I wanted to scream, clutching the restraining order. I bit my tongue, literally.

Greg continued. "You want to move on with your life, don't you? Five years is a very long time to have this man bothering you. It's not a complicated divorce. The best thing is to get it over with.

"Second, get this guy before a judge and this is what might happen—the judge might believe Conor. Young, disadvantaged youth, apparently he must have some powers to

charm . . . versus you." He gestured to me with his hands up. I filled in the blank in my head: versus spoiled rich Harvard girl whose father was a big-shot judge in our corrupt nation's capital and whose mother was a gorgeous Wasp alcoholic. "The judge might believe Conor, not you."

I wanted to strangle Greg Bandy right then. I didn't because then how would I find another lawyer? The yellow pages?

Greg Bandy stood up and put out his hand for me to shake again. This time I squeezed it as hard as I could, wanting to break his little bones. Then I headed to the lobby.

Getting divorced on paper was the least of my battles right now anyway, I told myself as I took the elevator down to the street. I could only devote so much time and emotion to the legal side of this self-inflicted disaster. I tried to absorb some measure of confidence from the arrogant, angular skyscrapers rising above me as I left the Loop.

Once home, I called my therapist to tell her about Greg's approach.

"Leslie, I know this is hard to hear. It might take you years to accept, but Greg probably has the right strategy. Conor was abusive and manipulative throughout your marriage. You should expect him to continue to be abusive and manipulative during your divorce. Greg's approach—avoiding hand-to-

hand combat—actually sounds pretty rational to me. Pretty wise."

Shit.

Greg and Conor's lawyer met alone a week later. Conor had recovered nicely from his shock that I wanted to get divorced. He'd hired a female lawyer, of course. Someone who had a chance of falling for him, someone he knew how to deal with. Someone whose implicit betrayal of me as another woman would demoralize me even further. It did.

Following their meeting, Greg called me to pass on several new pieces of information. I sat down on our living-room couch like someone preparing herself for dreadful news. I turned off the music on the stereo.

"You might want to know that Conor has listed a new official residence."

My God, I thought. Why? Where would he go with less than two months of school left? Was he going to drop out so close to graduation?

"He's kept his apartment, but he's changed his official mailing address to 12 Main Street in Ocean Grove, New Jersey."

Aunt Nellie's summer house? Impossible. That seaside beach home with its wraparound porches and widow's walk was my refuge during my summer apart from Conor. The rooms were filled with pictures I drew for Nellie as a child, sappily signed "your ever-loving niece," books I wrote for my cousins, pictures of our childhood holidays together. Why

on earth would someone who had loved me since I was born let a man who beat me list her house as his residence?

I couldn't speak.

"I also wanted to let you know that apparently Conor visited your father in Washington three weeks ago. Your father gave Conor a thousand dollars to help him get back on his feet. Did you know this?"

"No." My stomach dropped a few floors. I had spoken with my father—the same man who couldn't trouble himself to help me find a divorce lawyer—every few days for the past month and he'd never said anything about seeing Conor or giving him money.

"Conor used that money to hire his attorney."

Sitting on the couch, I shook my head back and forth wordlessly. Getting divorced was turning out to be far harder than getting married. Couples should be read a Miranda-like warning right before they say, "I do":

Any love that you feel at this point may be used against you in the future. Studies have shown that in divorce, the craziest person always wins, regardless of who was harmed most by the relationship. Do you understand that although it takes only five minutes to get married, to get divorced can take years, cost you your life savings, destroy your friendships and family relationships, and forever undermine your emotional health and faith in humanity? Do you realize that you are blind with love and hope right now, and can't possibly know what you're doing?

Greg Bandy interrupted my thoughts.

"There's more?" I asked incredulously.

"Conor's attorney believes that you should be paying him temporary alimony in order to support Conor in the manner he became accustomed to living with you. We can delay this for a few weeks with a counter-request, but it may be wise for you to pay it for a few months just to assuage him—"

"What? I don't even have any money!"

"Well, your father does."

I stopped. "I'm not paying him alimony. What else, Greg?" I wanted this conversation to be over.

"One last request. Conor would like his guns back. He believes you still have them. Is this true?"

"I'll have to get back to you," I told Greg woodenly as I hung up the phone. The pain in my abdomen felt like someone was scraping a rake along the inside of my stomach. My father. My mother's family. A female lawyer. My financial future. He wanted his *guns* back?

And these were just Conor's first moves.

As I went through the motions of daily life, reeling from the emotional sucker punches from people I loved, I was struck by the kindness of people I barely knew. The vet. My therapist. All the people at school who did not ask questions.

Would the cops who came that night ever know how grateful I was? Did the family court advocate realize how much I appreciated her respect? Every time I came into my building I thought: Who pounded on the door that night? The Indian couple downstairs? The law school student upstairs? Did that person know they may have saved my life?

My high-school English teacher left a voice-mail message almost every day. The locksmith bumped his wait list and changed my locks the morning I called. Not a single classmate mentioned my sordid situation to a company recruiter. Every time I thought of Blue, I knew I'd had the best dog in the world. Wherever he was now, Blue knew it wasn't my fault, that I was going to be okay when this was all over, Conor or no Conor, perfidious father or not, alimony or no alimony.

I thought of what I'd done with Conor's guns back in February. I couldn't bear to have them in our apartment. Giving them back to Conor had been out of the question. I thought about putting them in a paper bag and dropping them in Lake Michigan. Instead I turned them in at the police station, which of course I now knew was only a few blocks from our apartment. The cop saw my hands shaking as I gave him the shoe box with the guns inside. "I need to give you this. They're not mine." He gave me a short form to fill out. He smiled and nodded. "You're doing the right thing," he told me.

When I'd called the Ice Man, the diamond jeweler in New York, he'd been remarkably kind as well. I mailed him a small

padded envelope containing my wedding and engagement rings. He sent me a check I used to pay Greg Bandy's retainer.

A marketing professor I barely knew, a short, plump woman whose red hair was always pulled back in a bun, came up to me in a deserted campus corridor one afternoon. "I've heard some rumors about your situation," she said obliquely, almost whispering. "I was in the same thing a few years ago. You'll get out. You are going to be fine. You won't believe how much better you're going to feel a year from now. Hang in there." She touched my arm and left me speechless as she hurried down the hallway to teach her class.

One night the phone rang while I was trying—and mostly failing—to read a financial accounting case.

"Leslie, hi."

It was Ed.

We talked awkwardly for a few minutes. I hadn't spoken with him in four months. He'd always been best as the funny man, hard to pull off under the current circumstances.

"I called, uh, really to tell you one thing, Leslie," he said, his gravity fitting like a bulky homemade sweater. "I know you probably feel awful now. And I need to be there for Conor. But I want you to know that you are a great girl, any guy would be lucky to be with you. In a year, this will be like a nightmare that happened to someone else. In five years, you're going to be married to a wonderful man, two kids, totally happy. I guarantee it."

These kindnesses did not deaden the pain of Conor's

betrayal, my aunt's puzzling hospitality-cum-disloyalty, and my father's emotional abandonment. But they did give me hope for the future. And, as Mr. Carrola said, hope is always good.

In the midst of the death of my dog, trips to my therapist, and calls from my lawyer relaying Conor's latest kicks to my ribs, good news came into my life daily, links to the future. Job offers. Lots of them. Phone calls, follow-up letters confirming salary, title, and responsibilities, good news on the answering machine and in my mailbox, every single day.

By late April I had five full-time offers. Multiple jobs were rare during the second year of a national economic recession; the school had forecast that only 60 percent of students would get any offers by graduation.

Three different times I overheard classmates talking about my good fortune when I passed in the hallway outside the career development center. I felt grateful they were not gossiping about me and Conor. My friends would probably never understand that luck had nothing to do with my success; anger was the magic ingredient. Each phone call and letter from a recruiter was a vote against what Conor had done to me. A promise that, if I could hold out long enough, I was going to have a future, a safe future, without Conor.

It didn't matter which job offer I took. Each company was hundreds of miles away from Conor, far enough that he couldn't stalk me or impulsively track me down. Back in Vermont, when I'd accepted Ed and Conor's challenge to go to business school, I'd never for one second imagined an M.B.A. degree would be my underground railroad away from Conor. I could hardly believe it now.

If I could have, I would have sewn the thick corporate offer letters to my shirt like armor for the days I passed Conor in the halls, the time I heard he had started dating an old girlfriend who had recently moved to Chicago, the night I spotted him pacing the block in front of my building, looking up at the living-room windows as I drove past him, looking for a safe place to park our car.

The vet called about a month after Blue had died, in the late afternoon as I sat in the living room sipping yet another mug of peppermint tea. On the mantel was a picture of Conor holding Blue back when he was an eight-week-old puppy. Blue's fat belly faced the sky as Conor cradled him in his arms in our backyard in Vermont. Conor smiled down at Blue like a newborn baby.

"The blood work we did last month came back from the lab yesterday. I finished the autopsy paperwork two hours ago. Your dog died of liver cancer. I have never seen such a

young, strong, and . . . beautiful animal die of liver cancer, so suddenly. I don't know what to tell you."

He paused.

"By any chance did he eat a lot of grass?"

"Grass?" I ask. "No, not really, we live in an apartment. I've never seen him eat grass. There's no grass around here. Even the Dog Park—you know the one, near the university? It's all dirt there."

"Okay, that rules out fertilizer poisoning. What about chocolate?"

"Yes, every day. He loved Reese's peanut butter cups. I gave him a miniature one every morning."

Long pause.

"I'm sorry to tell you this. But chocolate is a poison for dogs. I assume you didn't know that."

What?

"He . . . he was my first dog. I had no idea. He *loved* chocolate."

"Well, the only reason I can think that such a healthy dog would have developed liver cancer so quickly, and have died so suddenly, is that he might have been poisoned. I was thinking lawn chemicals or rat poison. But even a little bit of chocolate every day might have built up in his system and caused his liver to fail."

My face froze and the tears on my cheeks evaporated.

I thanked the vet in a daze and hung up the phone. I remembered one night in Vermont when Conor threatened to

take Blue outside and fire the .45 into his brown head. Instead, I had killed him through a daily treat that I thought showed Blue how much he meant to me.

I got up from the living-room couch, took a sip of cold tea, and went to splash water on my face in the bathroom. I looked in the mirror. My eyes stared back blankly like blood-shot marbles.

Out of thin air, my father's older brother Jimmy called to say he was coming to Chicago for an electricians' convention. I hadn't seen him in five years. My dad had never invited his family to any of our graduations or special family occasions, or to my and Conor's wedding. He said it was too far for them to travel, they didn't have the money for plane tickets. So I'd seen Uncle Jimmy sporadically when business brought him to wherever I lived.

Jimmy left a message on my machine, his voice soft in his lingering Okie accent, asking whether he could take me to dinner the last night he was in town. I met him at a small Italian restaurant near the convention center, the kind with red-and-white-checked cloths and marinated peppers in a jar on the table. Jimmy sat waiting for me at the bar, a shorter, stockier, blue-collar version of my dad with his tailored wool suits and cigarillos in his elegant fingers.

We talked about his business, an electrical service company he'd started at seventeen. He was thinking of selling it and retiring. I blushed when he asked my advice. I didn't need the Ferragamo suit any longer. My M.B.A. gave me permanent, instant credibility, even to someone who'd been working fourteen-hour days since before I'd been born.

We both ordered spaghetti and Caesar salad, laughing about how unimaginative our choices were. Over coffee, the candlelight flickering from the small white tea lights on the table, his face softened as he glanced at me.

"Ah, hon, you look just like her," he said, reaching out to cup the side of my face with his worn, callused hand. "She's buried just a few miles from here. I went to her grave today."

I realized he was talking about Marilyn, his sister who had died at fifteen. No one in my family had ever told me I resembled her. My father had never mentioned it, or shown me a picture of her.

"What was she like?" I asked.

"She was the sweetest thing," he said, looking up at the ceiling. "Like an angel." He took a deep, shuddering breath. Fat tears began rolling down his weathered cheeks. He did not wipe them away.

"You know, your father's probably told you, but we had very little money growing up. Sometimes we had no food. And Marilyn, she was so skinny. I know she was as hungry as the rest of us. But she gave us her food, almost every day. Es-

pecially your dad. He was a scrawny thing. Still is." He tried to laugh, patting his own gut.

The tears were still coming. He acted like he barely noticed them, as if he cried every day over Marilyn, even though she'd been dead for forty-seven years.

"Our mother used to beat her, I never knew why. Because Marilyn was the least trouble of all of us. Mother had a hard life. She had to take it out on someone. Sometimes I think Marilyn knew that, and she made sure Mother beat her so she wouldn't go after us. But it was terrible to see Marilyn with bruises all over her legs and arms, especially when she was so good to the rest of us."

I sat in paralyzed silence. I'd never imagined violence so similar to Conor's in my own family. How crippling for my father. Despite leaving poverty behind, he had to see me trapped, by love, like Marilyn had been.

"Your father never got over it, Les. You have to understand. It was terrible not being able to help her, not being able to stop Mother, never having enough food, not having a real home. His way was to escape, into his studies at school, to Harvard God bless him, into his law firm. He can't help it if he got so far away from people he forgot how to reach out, even to his own children. He loves you, hon. He just doesn't know how to show it. Since she died, he never did. Especially when people need help the most, like Marilyn did."

Something in me cracked open and spilled out onto the

LESLIE MORGAN STEINER

red-and-white tablecloth as Jimmy talked, his blue shirt collar wet with tears like navy-blue polka dots. A piece of me lay with my teenaged aunt, beaten, hungry, dying alone at fifteen in a public hospital bed. Another piece was lodged in my dad as a smart, sensitive ten-year-old boy, helpless to help anyone but himself, soldering off his heart to survive the pain of growing up the way he did.

Damn it, Jimmy was right. I couldn't muster any more anger against Dad—a boy with a sister who'd died so he'd make it out of a world she couldn't survive. My dad suffered an incalculable penalty for his escape, same as Conor. To leave behind a childhood as traumatic as theirs, most pay with a piece of their soul.

Right then I knew I was done with Conor for good. No matter how sorry I felt for him. No matter how much I still cared. You might have thought, naturally, that I had been "done" when I mailed my rings back to New York or hired a divorce lawyer. But this felt different, subcutaneous, deep in my gut. Almost in a karmic way, I was finished forever, in this lifetime and any to come, with loving bad boys.

I never wanted to be in a relationship with another man who'd shut down part of his heart, even though I understood that neither my father nor Conor had done so voluntarily. I couldn't bear to love another man who couldn't love me back. I wanted someone kind, with a generous heart, one that could regrow itself. Like my uncle, crying unashamed in public about a fifteen-year-old girl who'd been dead for almost five decades.

I had no idea how I'd go about finding such a man. I'd take my sweet time figuring that part out.

May. Two weeks before graduation, late on a Thursday, I drove home blasting R.E.M. with the windows open to take in the fresh spring air. I'd spent the evening with my finance study group. All we did was copy spreadsheet files from one another's computers while everyone but me drank monstrous margaritas. I turned up the radio.

"Losing my religion . . ."

The car felt empty without Blue on the passenger seat.

The street was deserted, no cars on either side of the road.

Except for one. A nice new white Honda, the interior lit, the door open. I slowed down.

A well-dressed black woman about twenty-five years old was walking away from the car, brushing off a tall, handsome young black man wearing a sports coat and jeans. Wet tracks ran down her face. The man walked closely behind her, alternately cajoling her and a second later raising his fists. I could hear the car beeping *ping . . . ping . . . ping* because she'd left the keys in the ignition.

Suddenly she turned and tried to run. He grabbed her with his long arms and shoved her up against a dirty storefront. Even from my car I could see the fear on her pretty face.

Without thinking, I jerked my car over and parked in front of the white sedan.

"Hey, what's going on?" I yelled as I climbed out, jangling my keys like some kind of badge.

By this time the man had let the woman go and she'd slid behind the wheel of the car. He stepped back as I approached, his anger displaced by uncertainty and shame at being interrupted. I didn't look at him. I leaned into the car as she sat clutching the wheel, crying and staring straight ahead. The car smelled like new leather.

"I just left a husband who beat me for three years," I said. "You do not have to put up with this. You do not deserve to be treated like this."

"I know," she whispered as fresh tears poured down her face. She sniffed loudly and shook her head. She wouldn't look at me. Her eyes were rimmed with red, but I could see resolve in them.

"You're right," she said. "It's just taking me longer than I thought."

She bent her head on the wheel. I put my hand on her arm. She squeezed my fingers hard enough to hurt.

"You're going to be okay. I promise." I handed her a clean tissue from my pocket. "No one can treat you like this if you don't let them."

She nodded again, gave a loud sniff, wiped the tears away. "Thank you," she whispered.

As I left, I gave the man a long stare. The spell had been broken and his face was open, sorrowful, filled with hope

and fear—a look I saw dozens of times on Conor's face. How long would that look last before he got angry again? I could feel the woman's determination as I got back into my car. I knew she would be all right, one day. The man I was less certain about.

Graduation dawned sunny, breezy, a surprisingly cool day for May. Mom flew in from Washington for the ceremony. Although she didn't put it this way, she wasn't flying seven hundred miles merely to celebrate my graduate degree. She was coming to be there, to make certain I closed out my life with Conor, to make sure I did what we both knew I had to do. Despite our problems, she had always been there— physically there—for me.

If that's not love, then I don't know what love is.

I hadn't sent an invitation to my father. He had never asked when graduation was, or whether I wanted him there. He did not offer financial or legal help with my divorce proceedings. Not a word of kindness, respect, or sympathy regarding the dissolution of my marriage and my attempts to start a new life. I tried not to hold this against my dad. Jimmy had been right.

As I stood on stage accepting my diploma, I saw Mom in the audience. With her silver hair juxtaposed with a jade-green silk shift, she created a brush stroke of colors against all the other parents. When I came up to her holding my

rolled-up diploma, she embraced me with one of her stiff little mini-hugs and a whiff of lipstick and perfume.

After we left the auditorium, she asked strangers to take pictures of us at various spots on campus. The way she wore her pride reminded me of the day I got my SAT scores back, the time I came home to announce I'd been elected junior class president, the evening I showed her the acceptance letter from Harvard as she stirred a pot of lamb stew in our kitchen. If I became the first female president of the United States, she'd take the same nonchalant pose as the queen of England: Of course, you're my daughter.

The present she handed me while we sat on a bench next to the campus library told me the backstory. Inside the small velvet box lay a gold ring inlaid with tiny green and red stones that formed the shape of a butterfly. I got it right away: caterpillar, cocoon, butterfly. The only way she knew how to tell me I was going to be okay, transformed by ugliness into something more beautiful in her eyes.

How could she see so much sometimes, and so little at others?

I put the ring on my left hand where I used to wear my wedding band. The butterfly felt heavy, an anchor. The stones sparkled in the sunlight. I held out my hand so she could see how it looked.

"Mom, thank you. Thank you for everything."

For giving me the money to finish my last semester of school. For answering fifty late-night calls. For hating Conor when what I felt was far more complicated than hate.

I tried to look right in her eyes so she could know how much she meant to me. She met my gaze for a second and then turned away with a small smile, like a shy eight-year-old girl.

It was just enough.

She took a taxi to her hotel to wash up and change clothes for dinner. I headed home in my black patent leather high heels, still wearing the dark gown and silly headboard with its cheap tassel, my costume for the day. The sunlight dappled the cobblestone campus walk as I slowly picked my way toward our—my—apartment. Squirrels ran fearlessly across my path. I imagined Blue in doggie heaven, chasing squirrels, eating Reese's peanut butter cups without dying from it, looking down on me from a cloud like he used to look down from the window of our apartment when I came home at night, his huge paws hanging out the windowsill like oven mitts. The leaves on the trees lining the campus walkway shimmered a fresh apple-green, as if they'd just burst out of their buds. I could smell cut grass, the first mowing of the summer.

It was the prettiest day I could remember since coming to business school.

I stopped by the student center for one last check of my campus mail folder. The only thing inside the bin was a tattered manila envelope, the official kind the university used for sending, and resending, interoffice mail. It was empty. I turned it over.

On the back, a note was scribbled in black ballpoint,

along with a stick figure of a little boy like a kindergartner would draw for his mom. Above the note Conor had written my maiden name, instead of the name I'd taken when we'd married.

Good-bye Retard—
I wish you all the best.
Sorry we didn't make it together.
I'll always think of you.

Conor

I cried there in the darkened b-school hallway, alone. Those five lines made for the shortest, saddest good-bye ever. How could he think a few banal phrases could capture the end of our relationship? His note made my love for him and all we'd been through sound trite, easily dismissed on a scrap of paper. My tears splashed on the orange manila envelope.

We'd come here together, embittered but still a makeshift family, less than two years before. How could it be that I planned to depart alone, Blue dead, Conor a cipher I feared passing on the street? After a few weeks of visiting friends and bumming at Rehobeth Beach with Sylvia, I would move out of the apartment we'd lived in as a married couple. I'd start a new job, a new life, hundreds of miles from Conor, with an unlisted phone number and a post office box instead of a published address, on the same day I turned twenty-seven. As alone as I'd ever been.

I kept walking on the campus pathway until I got to the dean's crowded cocktail party, silly-drunk classmates spilling out of the flagstone courtyard. I could see the foot-bridge where five months before I'd screamed at Conor until I thought my screams would tear me apart. Surrounded by Cherie and dozens of other friends, I sipped a club soda and scanned the crowd of my fellow M.B.A.s, all of us poised to scatter in different directions to seek whatever the future held.

Across the sea of graduates, I glimpsed the back of Conor's blond head above a knot of people talking together. My heart seized.

He didn't see me. He was wearing the same navy-blue Brooks Brothers sport coat he wore on that magical spring day only four years before, when we picnicked at the museum and later made love for the first time. I clenched my jaw and looked down at the butterfly ring on my wedding finger. Tried to breathe.

I had to look at him one more time. It would probably be the last time I saw my husband, my supposed soul mate, the man who almost killed me.

He held a drink in his hand. There was a blond woman standing at his side, a woman I did not recognize from our class. As I watched, he rested his hand possessively on her slim waist and she leaned in toward him. Conor moved his head closer and his lips brushed her smooth golden hair in a caress that paralyzed the muscles in my face.

It was impossible to break my gaze. I could tell by the

way his head moved that Conor was laughing. I could practically hear his strong, confident laugh ring out across the
courtyard, just as it had that night at P.J. Clarke's in New
York when I'd started to fall in love with him.

Finally, I looked away. I took off my glasses, so that he'd
get lost in the blur of classmates in the crowd.

Good-bye, Conor.

I never saw him again.

Epilogue

CONOR STANDS TOO CLOSE TO ME IN A SQUARE,
shadowy room. His face glows like a candle in the dark. Thick
wheat-colored hair, freckles across his nose. People always
said we seemed more like brother and sister than husband
and wife. His eyes search mine.

Conor doesn't care that I have three young children
whom I love in exactly the way I used to adore him: without
demanding anything but love in return. I can feel Conor's
certainty that what he wants trumps the devastation his actions will wreak upon my marriage, my kids, my life. I don't
resist when he starts kissing me.

I wake with a start, sickened, lying next to my husband in
our warm bed.

It takes a minute to realize I am safe, behind locked doors
in an old house in one of the most crowded cities in the
United States. Sheltered by our blue down quilt, my head
deep in a pillow that covers a menagerie of Beanie Babies,
earplugs, and cough drops. My husband's breath comes in

rhythmic whooshes like waves on a beach. I've been safe for years.

Trying to shake off the nightmare, I slip from the warm bed and tiptoe into my daughters' room, the polished wood floor cold beneath my bare feet. Next door in the darkness our boy sleeps on the bottom bunk, sprawled sidewise, clutching the basketball he holds all night in lieu of a stuffed animal. One of the girls stirs in her narrow bed. Even when she was an infant, a profusion of strawberry blond ringlets surrounded her tiny, heart-shaped face. Her red hair was a surprising and welcome resurgence of my charismatic, auburn-headed grandmother Frankie, dead from alcoholism almost twenty-five years now.

I slide into the rocker between the twin beds and softly glide back and forth, listening to my daughters breathing, my husband snoring. To distract myself, I review message points for a television interview I have to give the next day about stay-at-home moms who return to full-time work after years raising children. The neighbor's automatic sprinkler comes to life, whirring like a dentist's drill in the yard out back.

Two floors below me, in our dusty boiler room, there is a small cardboard box that's been duct-taped shut for more than fifteen years. The box holds fragments of my life with Conor, once-precious objects I can't consign to one hundred years of biodegradation amid the East Coast's cigarette butts, old lawnmowers, and dirty diapers. Our wedding album, bound with creamy, sweet-smelling leather. An envelope with several black-and-white pictures of five-year-old

Conor and his grandparents that I found after I no longer had an address to send them to. Still in Frankie's silver frame but with only a few shards of glass left is the wedding photo he broke over my head the last time he beat me. On top of the stack lies my folded wedding veil, the lace probably yellow and brittle by now. I kept Conor's résumé from our first date. Another piece of paper is there, too—the permanent family court restraining order against him dated four years later.

For a long time after I left Conor, I struggled with how I fit our society's stereotype of an abused woman. Exactly why and how had I lost myself to a man who I was intelligent enough to see was destroying me? I kept silent during cocktail party debates about why women—Mary Winkler, Nicole Simpson, Farrah Fawcett, Laci Peterson, or whoever was in the news that week—stayed in violent relationships. I walked away after the inevitable pronouncement that women who let themselves be abused are weak, uneducated, self-destructive, powerless.

I fit none of those stereotypes. I never met a "battered woman" who did.

I paid for loving Conor. For years I lived with an unlisted phone number and took my mail at a post office box. I sold the Vermont house at a 40 percent loss. It took me almost a decade to settle both our business school debts.

I imagine I will always flinch when a man, any man, raises his voice, whether it's in a boardroom or my backyard.

I've had to tell everyone I dated about Conor. I've had to

tell every employer, too, so their security desk would know to turn Conor away if he ever came looking for me. And although I don't have to, nearly every time I speak publicly I briefly mention that I was once married to an abusive man—because I never know who is listening, who my words might help.

I don't imagine I will unpack that cardboard box very often. But I can't deny that our story is part of me, my life, who I am. It's taken me years to understand the particular, dangerous chink in my self-esteem that let Conor slip in. But in one profound way I was lucky: While still in my twenties, I learned to spot—and stay away from—abusive men.

Some women don't learn from their mistakes. Most people don't get second chances in life. I was able to marry again, to raise children with a stable, loving man, and to pursue a career that has given me financial freedom and professional rewards beyond my childhood dreams.

Conor is gone. He may appear in my dreams every few years, but he'll never have power over me again. I don't regret loving him. But I'm happy to bury our past in a corner of my basement, next to the furnace, where it belongs.

Acknowledgments

This book was difficult to write. Sharing this story is either one of the stupidest or bravest things I've ever done. But I wrote it for women, like me, who are in violent relationships and don't know how to leave, and for their families and friends, who also suffer. And for those who have left but are too scared or ashamed to tell their stories. You are not alone.

I owe thanks to many people who believed in me when I did not believe in myself: Scott Adam, Helen Allen, Kristin Auclair, Skippy Redmon Banker, Linda Baquet, Mary Anne Baumgold, Larry Benders, Cheryl Yancey Biron, Martin and Sennait Blackman, Missy Everson Blum, Brooke Boardman, Mel Bornstein, David and Katherine Bradley, Beth Brophy, Jennifer Brown, Vivian Brown, the Caiola family, Ellie Callison, Julie Chavez, Susan Cheever, Gay Cioffi, Sarah Crichton, Patricia and Burt Davidson, John and April Delaney, Hermine Dreyfuss, Michele Dreyfuss, Dawn Drzal, Sarah Patton Duncan, Charlie Esposito, Brooke Evans, Page Evans, Donna Farnandez, Will Fuller, Heath Kern Gibson, Sarah Gordon, Don Graham, Michael Gray, Anne Hunter Greene, Rolf Grimsted, Brett Groom, Julie Gunderson, Dan and

Betsy Habib, Bobby and Mary Haft, Cathi Hanauer, Bunkie and Anne Harmon, George Harmon, Grant Harmon, Miriam Harmon, Janet Heezen, Jack Henry, Steve Hills, Monica Holloway, Jamie Hull, Kurt Inderbitzen, Martha Inman, Bo Jones, Willie Joyner, Therese Kauchak, Leonard King, Janet Kinzler, Julia and Barry Knight, Benn and Linda Konner, Anil Kothari, the Kressy family, Lew Kunkel, Carol Kurilla, Elisabeth LaMotte, George Lardner, Ethan and Karen Leder, Micki Leder, Gene and Mary Legg, Leslie Lehr, Nancy Lewin, Jody Levinson, Caroline Little, Sara London, Ann McDaniel, Leslie McGuirk, Adam Mansky, Ruth Marcus, Aaron Martin, Carolina Martinez, Susan Mathes, Chris Mathna, Sabrina Maxine, Terri Minsky, Stephanie Modder, Julia Harmon Morgan, Perri Jae Morgan, Tim Morgan, Robbie Myers, John Nicholas, Bill Nielsen, Jeremy Norton, Kelly O'Brien, Susan and Tim O'Leary, Dale and Melissa Overmyer, Tallie Parrish and family, Paula Penn-Nabrit, Jodi Delhi Peterson, Nancy Kline Piore, Carmen Pitarch, Neil Polo, Brian and Gwen Potiker, Elin Rachel, Ivan Ramirez, Marissa Rauch, Katherine Russell Rich, Bradford Hamilton Richardson, Midge Turk Richardson, Catherine Rose, Ann Sarnoff, Ania Sender, Susan and Roger Smith, Sarah and David Steinberg, Erna Steiner, Joseph and Marilyn Steiner, Marjo Talbott, the Taney family, Jake and Carrington Tarr, Jeri Curry Thorne, Jim Thornton, Sarah Tomkins, Ken and Karen Troccoli, Ampy Vasquez, Jackie B. Walker, Kate Wallis, Elsa Walsh, Pat Walsh, Judith Warner, Anne Terman Wedner, Katherine Weymouth, Laurie Wingate, Sarah Woolworth and

the Culture Club crew, Natalie Zett, my friends at Longacre Farm, the Westside Club, *The Washington post,* Johnson & Johnson, Leo Burnett, D.C. Heat, Little Folks, Harvard University, the Radcliffe Institute, Down Dog Yoga, and the Maret School. I am lucky and proud to know you all.

Special thanks to my agent, Alice Fried Martell, and the team at St. Martin's Press led by Jennifer Weis, for believing in this book from the beginning. Thanks also to Bruce Vinokour at CAA, and his talented partner, Stephanie Vinokour, for having faith in my story.

Most of all, I owe thanks to my husband, Perry Winter Steiner, and my children, Max, Morgan, and Tallie, who have made my dreams of a happy family come true at last.

IF YOU OR SOMEONE YOU KNOW MAY BE SUFFER-
ing from family violence, help is available. If you are in immediate danger, call 911. Relationship violence is a crime.
You deserve immediate protection from the police in your
community if you are being abused.

For advice and support, call or visit the following free,
anonymous helplines:

- National Domestic Violence Hotline: 1-800-799-SAFE
  (7233), TTY 1-800-787-3224, www.ndvh.org
- National Sexual Assault Hotline: 1-800-656-HOPE
  (4673), www.rainn.org
- Family Violence Prevention Fund: 1-888-RX-ABUSE,
  www.endabuse.org
- National Teen Dating Abuse Helpline: 1-866-331-
  9474, TTY 1-866-331-8453, www.loveisrespect.org
- Childhelp National Child Abuse Hotline: 1-800-4-A-
  CHILD, www.childhelp.org
- Gay, Lesbian, Bisexual, Transgender National Help Center: 1-888-843-4564, www.glbtnationalhelpcenter.org
- National Center for Victims of Crime/Stalking Re-
  source Center: 1-800-394-2255, TTY 1-800-211-7996,
  www.ncvc.org
- National Center on Elder Abuse: 1-800-677-1116,
  www.ncea.aoa.gov
- Resource Center on Domestic Violence, Child Protection and Custody: 1-800-527-3223, www.ncjfcj.org
- National Network to End Domestic Violence: www
  .nnedv.org

DILLINGER

DILLINGER

A NOVEL

HARRY PATTERSON

Thorndike Press • Thorndike, Maine

Library of Congress Cataloging in Publication Data:

Higgins, Jack, 1929-
  Dillinger.

  1. Dillinger, John, 1903-1934—Fiction.
  2. Large type books. I. Title.
[PR6058.I343D5 1983b]   823'.914   83-13098
ISBN 0-89621-470-2

Large Print edition available through arrangement with Stein and Day,
Publishers.

Cover design by Eileen Rosenberg.

For Geoff and Irene —
not forgetting Sarah,
Kate, and Rebecca.

Early in March 1934, John Dillinger, the most notorious criminal in American history, made a spectacular escape from Lake County Jail, Crown Point, Indiana. What happened to him in the period following his escape has always been a matter of speculation. He was reported to have been seen in Chicago, New Orleans, California, New York, even in London, England. And there were those, of course, who insisted that he was safe over the border in Mexico. Perhaps it went something like this . . .

ONE

Dillinger lay on his bunk in one corner of the cell, his head pillowed on a hand, staring up at the ceiling. His cell mate in the "escape-proof" new section of Lake County's three-story brick jail, Herbert Youngblood, a big black man, stood at the window gazing out through the bars down into the street in front of the jail.

Dillinger said, "What's it like out there?"

"Must be two, maybe three hundred people," Youngblood said. "Hell, it's worse than the State Fair. They got National Guard out there in uniform, like they were going to war." He turned, smiling. "Maybe they think you're planning on taking a trip?"

"It's a thought," Dillinger said calmly.

There was the rattle of a key in the lock

9

of the sliding cell door, a row of vertical bars. They turned to see an old man wearing faded denims, holding a tray, Sam Cahoon, the attendant.

"Coffee, Mr. Dillinger?"

"Why not?"

Dillinger sat up, and the old man placed two tin cups on the small table and filled them, the pot shaking a little in his hand so that some coffee spilled.

"You been across to the hotel this morning?" Dillinger asked as Cahoon passed him his cup.

"I sure have, Mr. Dillinger," Cahoon said. "They're sleeping on the floors. More folks coming in all the time. They've got reporters, radio people, a newsreel cameraman. You should get a commission from the hotel, Mr. Dillinger."

He smiled in a strained, anxious way as if conscious that he might have gone too far. Dillinger sipped his coffee thoughtfully, and it was Youngblood who answered for him.

"A great idea, Pops. Next time you're over there, you tell the guy who runs the joint Mr. Dillinger was asking about his cut."

"I sure will," Cahoon said eagerly. "More coffee, Mr. Dillinger?"

"No thanks, Sam. This is just fine,"

10

Dillinger told him.

The old man picked up the tray. On the other side of the bars was one of the trusties with a mop stuck in a bucket.

"I was told to bring this here," the trusty said.

Cahoon slid the bars to the side just enough to let the man squeeze by and put the bucket and mop down next to where Dillinger was sitting. Quickly Youngblood said, "I'll do that."

The trusty, who looked very nervous, said, "I was told to give it to Mr. Dillinger." He scurried out, followed by Sam, who locked the sliding bars behind him.

"Idiots," Youngblood said. "What good's a mop and bucket without water?"

Dillinger held a finger up to his lips. He went over to the bars and checked right and left, and, then, with his back to the bars in case anyone came along unexpectedly, he squatted down and carefully lifted the mop end from the bottom of the bucket and took out something wrapped in flannel.

"Stand next to me," he whispered to Youngblood.

Their backs making a screen in case anyone happened along, Dillinger unwrapped the flannel. In its center was a blue-black

11

.32 caliber Colt Automatic. Quickly, Dillinger checked the clip, saw that it had all eight rounds, and jammed it back into the handle.

"Let's have your knife," Dillinger said.

Youngblood produced a bone-handled pocket knife from the top of his right boot and handed it across. Dillinger sprung the blade, instinctively tested it on his thumb, and told Youngblood, "Stand by the bars. Anyone comes, you tell me fast."

As Youngblood leaned backward against the bars, Dillinger reached under the mattress on his bunk, slit it, and shoved the Colt into the slit. He tested to see if the gun was far enough away from the cut not to fall out accidentally. Only then did Dillinger look up at Youngblood with a smile.

There was amazement in Youngblood's eyes. "Jesus, Mr. Dillinger," was all he said.

The lounge of the hotel was crowded, with reporters three deep at the bar, and the noise made it necessary to shout to be heard. The young woman sitting alone at the bamboo table by the window where she could view the street looked out of place in the neat two-piece black suit and cream oyster-satin blouse, her blonde hair framed by a close-fitting black velvet hat.

The man who approached her, glass in hand, was perhaps thirty-five, with a world-weary, sardonic face. A gray fedora was pushed to the back of his head.

"Hello," he said. "Mike Jarvis, A.P. I hear you're with the *Denver Press.*"

"That's right. Martha Ryan."

"Can I get you a drink?"

She lifted her cup. "Coffee's just fine, thank you."

He sat down and offered her a cigarette. "They sent you up here to get the woman's angle, I suppose?"

"That's right. Only it doesn't look as if anyone's getting in to see him," she shrugged.

"Well, there's the sheriff," Jarvis said, nodding toward the large window.

"Oh, where is he?" Martha Ryan said, standing.

Jarvis laughed. "He's a she," he said, pointing to where a middle-aged woman flanked by two male deputies was crossing the street. "Her husband was the sheriff of Lake County. When he got himself killed, she took over for the rest of his term, like they did in the olden days."

The door opened. Lillian Holley entered

13

and was immediately surrounded by excited newsmen, all talking at once. The two brawny deputies started to push a way through the crowd for her and she called in exasperation, "Can't a girl get a cup of coffee in peace round here?"

Jarvis, watching the sheriff speculatively, turned suddenly to Martha Ryan. "She won't let any of the guys see Dillinger at the moment, but what if I persuaded her to let you in?"

Martha Ryan stared at him skeptically. "You think there's a chance?"

"Maybe, only one thing. You share your story with me and no one else. Is it a deal?"

She reached across and pressed his hand. "A deal, Mr. Jarvis."

He stood up as Lillian Holley pressed forward. "Hey, Lillian! Over here!"

She paused, glancing toward him. "Mike Jarvis, you still here? You don't give up, do you?"

Her eyes considered the young woman. She came forward, and Jarvis held his seat for her. "Here, take this."

She sat down. The two deputies stood guard, backs toward her, arms folded, and the crowd of reporters retreated to the bar.

"Introduce me, Mike," she said.

"Miss Martha Ryan of the *Denver Press.*"

Mrs. Holley frowned. "Your editor must be crazy, expecting a kid like you to hold her own with a bunch of villains like these guys. Just out of college?"

"That's right, Mrs. Holley."

A waiter appeared with fresh coffee. Lillian Holley said, "I get it, he wants a fresh angle. Why, thousands of red-blooded American women have the hots for Johnny Dillinger."

Martha Ryan blushed, and Jarvis said, "It's the little lady's first big assignment, Lillian."

"Next thing, you'll be telling me her aging mother's in the hospital and she needs the money."

Jarvis grinned and turned to Martha. "Hey, you didn't tell me."

Martha Ryan smiled. "I won't lie to you, Mrs. Holley. Any kind of story from here would get me a byline and could make my career."

Lillian Holley looked her over calmly. "Well," she said, "it's nice to see a woman ambitious for a change, instead of all these hustling men."

Martha Ryan said, "Just five minutes with

him? Please, Mrs. Holley, it could be my break."

Jarvis patted Martha Ryan's hand. "Too much to expect, angel. I mean all these guys here have been hanging around for days trying to see John Dillinger. They'd go crazy. No, it can't be done."

Lillian Holley noticed how Martha Ryan gently moved her hand away from Jarvis' condescending pat. "You men," she said to Jarvis, taking his bait, "think you know everything. Who the hell do you think is in charge around here? If I say this girl sees Dillinger, she sees him, and there's nothing those creeps can do about it."

"Sorry, Lillian, no offense meant," Jarvis said hastily.

Lillian Holley leaned across the table to Martha Ryan. "I'll give you five minutes, that's all, you understand?"

The girl stared at her in amazement. "You mean it? You really mean it? Five minutes with Dillinger."

"Hey, you got a great title for your feature there," Jarvis told her.

Lillian Holley said, "I'm leaving now. Give me a couple of minutes, then report to the back entrance of the jail. You'll be expected. And keep it to yourself for now."

"Oh, I will, Mrs. Holley," Martha Ryan said.

Lillian Holley stood up and turned to Jarvis. "And that goes for you, too. Keep your mouth shut on this one, Mike, or don't come back."

She nodded to the two deputies and followed them to the door.

Martha Ryan said, "I can't believe it." She turned to Jarvis as he sat down again. "Have you any idea what this could mean to me, Mr. Jarvis?"

"Sure I do," he said. "New York, next stop." He lit another cigarette. "And what I said about sharing the story. Forget it. This one's yours. Who knows, maybe you could get a Pulitzer."

She was almost in tears. "But why are you doing this for me? I don't understand?"

"Simple," he said. "I work out of A.P.'s New York office myself. Maybe if you get there, you'll let me buy you a cup of coffee some time." He smiled and reached across to pat her hand.

Instead, Martha Ryan took his hand and pumped it. "Thank you, Mr. Jarvis," she said.

"Call me Mike."

"Thank you, Mike."

Jarvis smiled. "Now get the hell out of here and get your story."

Youngblood, leaning against the door, watching, now made a quick gesture. "Someone's coming."

Dillinger quickly lay on the bed. As he lit a cigarette, the key rattled in the lock, the sliding bars opened, and a guard stood to one side as Lillian Holley entered, followed by a young woman.

"On your feet, Johnny," Mrs. Holley said. "I'd like you to meet a lady. This is Miss Martha Ryan of the *Denver Press*, and I've told her she can have five minutes with you."

"Hell, Mrs. Holley," Youngblood said, "I could do with five minutes there myself."

As Youngblood spoke, there was the most extraordinary change in Dillinger. He was on his feet in an instant, his face pale, his eyes very dark, so that Youngblood recoiled as from a blow in the face.

"Sorry, Mr. Dillinger," he whispered.

Dillinger turned to Martha Ryan, his charming half-smile on view again. "Miss Ryan, what can I do for you?"

She was, for a moment, almost overcome. He was not what she thought he'd be.

18

Though he was shorter than she'd expected, his shoulders were those of a bigger man. His restless, intelligent face and pleasant, courteous voice carried a curious authority.

Her throat was dry, but she managed to speak. "Well, I know your background, Mr. Dillinger, everyone does. Your family, that kind of stuff. I just wanted to ask you some other kinds of questions."

He pulled a chair forward. "Fire away."

She took a pad and pencil from her purse. "They say you intend to escape from here. Is that true?"

The question was so naive that Lillian Holley laughed harshly and answered it for him. "This section of the jail, honey, the new section, is escape-proof. That's the way the architect designed it. Even if he got through that door he'd have to pass through God knows how many gates and armed guards."

Dillinger turned to the girl. "Satisfied?"

"But they say your friends are coming to get you out."

"What friends? If I had friends, they wouldn't be stupid enough to try to crash Mrs. Holley's Indiana Alcatraz, would they?"

The half-smile was still firmly in place, as if he was laughing at the world and everyone in it. "However, if an attractive honey like you'd come along for the ride, I might decide to try for the outside." He winked at Mrs. Holley. "Course, Mrs. Holley could come along as chaperone."

Martha Ryan wasn't sure whether he was making a pass or a joke or both at the same time. She tried again. "Have you any interest in politics, Mr. Dillinger?"

"Not until Mr. Roosevelt came along. You can say I'm for him all the way, and for the NRA – particularly for banking, only he'll have to hurry."

She looked genuinely bewildered. "I don't understand, you're a . . ." She hesitated.

"A thief?" he said helpfully. "True. I rob the banks, if that's what you mean, but who do they rob, Miss Ryan? Indiana, Kansas, Iowa, Texas – take your choice. People thrown off their farms wholesale while the banks foreclose, then sell out at a huge profit to the big wheat combines."

"Business, Johnny," Lillian Holley said dryly. "Just business."

"Oh, sure, the kind that makes me feel clean," Dillinger said. "Six million unemployed out there, Miss Ryan. You ask them what kind of a thief John Dillinger is."

Martha Ryan sat there staring up at him. He didn't sound that much different from some of the editorial writers she'd met. Lillian Holley said, "O.K., angel, that's it," and pulled her up, a hand under her elbow.

Martha Ryan held out her hand. "Thank you, Mr. Dillinger and good . . ." She swallowed the words, blushing.

Dillinger laughed. "I wouldn't put that in your article if I were you. They mightn't understand." And then he smiled gently. "Don't worry about me, Miss Ryan. I know the road I'm taking, I know what's at the end of it. My choice! No one else's."

Martha recoiled instinctively. Dillinger's courtly smile had changed into a stone mask. She went out, wanting to glance back. Lillian Holley followed. The door closed behind them. Dillinger stood there for a moment, then felt inside the mattress and took out the pistol.

"Are you with me?" he asked Youngblood.

"You crashing out, Mr. Dillinger?"

"That's it."

"The guy I killed was trying to stick a knife in me, but I could still get the chair, Mr. Dillinger, him being white. That don't leave me much choice, so I'm with you."

"Good. When the time comes just do as I

say, and I'll get you out of here," Dillinger told him.

He took his jacket out of the cupboard, put it on, and slipped the pistol into his right-hand pocket. Then he lay on the bed and closed his eyes, thinking of his father. Boy, that old son-of-a-bitch would be surprised if his bad boy walked in the door.

As one of the deputies unlocked the door at the rear of the prison, Lillian Holley said, "Well, what did you make of him?"

Martha Ryan was bewildered and showed it. "I expected a monster, not a . . . ladies' man."

"I know. It's very confusing. You know there are people who argue that he's never even killed anybody."

"I can't believe that."

"I'll tell you one thing. He's an Indiana farm boy, born and bred, and wherever he travels in the back country, people know, but they don't turn him in, not for any reward. Can you explain that to me?"

"No."

"Well, when you can, you'll have your real story."

She shook hands and Martha Ryan passed outside and the door closed behind her.

When Cahoon unlocked the door of Dillinger's cell, he was carrying a bucket full of soapy water that he put down by the wall.

"Okay, Herbert," he said to Youngblood. "Cleaning time." He straightened and found himself staring into the muzzle of a Colt automatic, steady in Dillinger's hand. "Jesus Christ," he said softly.

Dillinger got off the bed. "Just do as I say, Sam, and we'll get along. Understand?"

"Anything you say, Mr. Dillinger," Cahoon told him eagerly.

"Who's out there?"

"The cleaning detail, all trusties. They won't give you no trouble."

"Any guards?"

"No."

"What about down in the old jail?"

"I saw Deputy Sheriff Blunk down there a few moments ago."

"Fine, we'll get to him in a second."

Dillinger moved out into the long corridor, which had cells opening off it. There were about twelve men out there, all trusted prisoners as Cahoon had said – the cleaning detail starting the day's work, talking cheerfully among themselves.

Dillinger moved closer and paused. The man nearest to him saw him almost at once and stopped in the act of squeezing out his mop in the bucket, an expression of astonishment on his face. His stillness passed through the others like a wave. There was silence.

"Everyone inside."

Dillinger motioned with the pistol to his own cell and stood back as they filed past him into the cell. There was no trouble, but then with men like these, he didn't expect any.

He said to Youngblood. "You stay here. I'll be back." He nodded to Cahoon. "Let's go."

When Deputy Sheriff Ernest Blunk, on duty on the first floor, heard Cahoon call to him, he went up the stairs without hesitation to find Dillinger waiting for him, gun in hand.

"Oh, my God," Blunk said, more frightened than he had ever been in his life before.

Dillinger relieved him of the pistol he carried on his right hip and slipped the gun into his pocket. "Is anyone else down there on your landing?"

Blunk, a prudent man, saw no reason to argue. "Nobody, Mr. Dillinger."

"And the warden?"

"Mr. Baker's in his office on the ground floor."

"Okay, then we go down and get him." He pushed Cahoon along the corridor toward Youngblood, who was standing outside the locked door of their cell, holding the key. "Put him in with the others and wait here."

As Blunk had said, the corridor below was deserted. They moved along it and paused at the top of the stairs leading to the ground floor.

Dillinger said, "Go on, you know what to do."

Blunk sighed and called. "Hey, Lou, you're wanted up here."

"What the hell for?" a voice called back. Warden Lou Baker appeared at the bottom of the stairs and started up briskly. He was almost at the top when he looked up and saw Dillinger standing there, gun in hand.

He stopped dead in his tracks and, in the circumstances, stayed surprisingly cool.

"Johnny, what in the hell do you think you're playing at? You ain't going anywhere. You got at least ten National Guardsmen at the front entrance armed with machine guns."

"Well, that should make things interesting," Dillinger said calmly. "Now upstairs, both of you."

A few moments later Youngblood was putting the warden and Blunk in the cell with the others. He locked the door. "Okay, what happens now?"

"Stay here," Dillinger told him. "I'll be back."

Youngblood said, "You wouldn't leave me, Mr. Dillinger?"

"The most important thing you should know about me," Dillinger said, "I never ran out on anyone in my whole life," and he turned and moved away along the corridor.

The man on duty that morning at the barred gate, which gave access to the jail offices at the front of the building, was a trusty who sat at his desk, reading a newspaper. The headline said: *Public Enemy Number One Finally Caged.* There was a photo of Dillinger to go with it. A slight tapping sound caused the trusty to look up, and he saw the man himself peering through the bars just above him, a gun in his hand.

Dillinger said softly, "Open up!"

The trusty almost dropped his keys in his eagerness to comply but a moment later had the gate open. The office door stood partly ajar, and someone was whistling in there.

"Who is it?" Dillinger inquired softly.

"National Guardsman."

"Just the one?" The man nodded and Dillinger said, "Call him out."

The trusty did as he was told, and a second later the door opened and a young National Guardsman in uniform appeared. There was instant horror in his eyes, and he got his hands up fast.

Behind him on the table were two loaded Thompson submachine guns. Dillinger moved past him and stared down at them for a moment. "Well, I'll be damned," he said. "Thank you."

He slipped the pistol into his other pocket, picked up a machine gun in each hand, and turned to the two men. "Okay, now we're going to go upstairs, all the way up to the top landing in the new wing. You fellas see any problems in that?"

"No, Mr. Dillinger," they assured him eagerly, and the trusty turned and led the way.

A few minutes later, Youngblood, clutching one of the machine guns, was shepherding them into the cell on the top landing with the others. Dillinger said, "Let's have Blunk out here again."

27

Youngblood pulled the deputy sheriff out and closed and locked the door. "Now what?" he asked Dillinger.

"We're clear, all the way down to the jail office and the front entrance, only that's too public by far."

"So what do we do?"

"Walk right out of the back door, and this is the man who's going to show us the way, isn't that so, Mr. Blunk?"

Ernest Blunk sighed heavily yet again. "If you say so, Mr. Dillinger."

"Oh, but I do," Dillinger said. "In fact, I insist," and he pushed him along the corridor.

It was raining when they emerged from the door at the rear of the prison ten minutes later and moved along the alley. Dillinger and Youngblood wore raincoats taken from two local farmers whom they'd found eating in the kitchen. The farmers were now locked in a washroom.

"The garage?" Dillinger said to Blunk. "How far?"

"Right down there, a hundred and fifty yards," the deputy told him.

"Okay," Dillinger said. "You lead the way and just remember what I'm holding under this raincoat if you feel like calling out."

He raised the machine gun slightly, the muzzle poking through, and Blunk said hastily, "No trouble, Mr. Dillinger, not from me. We got this far, haven't we? All I want is to see you off my hands."

He led the way, following a route which took them past the Criminal Courts building, and a few moments later the men entered the side door of a large garage. There was a single mechanic in oil-stained overalls working on his own.

He glanced up. "Hello there, Mr. Blunk."

It was apparent that he didn't recognize Dillinger. Blunk said, "Ed Saager, the best mechanic in town, Mr. Dillinger."

Saager looked shocked as Dillinger produced the machine gun from under his raincoat. "Which car here's in the best shape?"

"Why, that would be the Ford here," Saager told him. "Mrs. Holley's car."

"Engine tuned?"

"Like a watch."

"Fan belt okay?"

"Replaced last month."

"Pickup?"

"Best in the lot."

"Then that's what we'll take. You get in

the rear with my friend and you, Mr. Blunk, can take the wheel."

Saager opened his mouth as if to protest, thought better of it, and got into the rear seat with Youngblood. Blunk took the wheel and started the motor as Dillinger got in beside him.

"Nice and easy, Mr. Blunk," he said as they turned into the main street. "No need to hurry."

He leaned back and lit a cigarette calmly.

Mike Jarvis and Martha Ryan were sitting in a booth at the rear of the hotel lounge enjoying a late breakfast when there was a sudden excited murmur and a voice called, "Dillinger's escaped."

Jarvis jumped to his feet and moved out. Martha Ryan sat there, suddenly cold, aware of the excited hubbub of voices outside.

Jarvis came back a moment later and sat down. "My God, would you believe it. That place was supposed to be escape-proof. Not only did he walk right out, he's used the sheriff's car for his getaway." He threw back his head and laughed. "Jesus, will Lillian be mad."

But Martha Ryan simply sat there, the coldness growing within her, aware only of

Dillinger's final words to her. That he knew the road he was taking. That he knew what lay at the end of it.

It was still raining, and they were over the border into Illinois when Blunk, on Dillinger's orders, pulled up at the side of the dirt road they had been following.

"Okay," Dillinger said. "This is where you two get off."

They got out of the car reluctantly, uncertain as to his intentions, but Dillinger just drove away, the wheels of the big Ford churning mud, and Dillinger hoping some of it would land on Blunk's suit.

Youngblood started to sing loudly in the rear seat. A few miles further on, Dillinger stopped the car to light a cigarette and then took a few crumpled bills from his pocket and counted them.

"Fourteen dollars isn't going to get us very far."

"And that's a fact," Youngblood said. "I guess there's only one thing to do. You'll just have to rob a bank, Mr. Dillinger."

He started to laugh, and Dillinger, loving the feel of being behind the wheel of a fast-moving car, feeling as exhilarated as a kid, tossed him the cigarette pack and drove

31

away through the rain, wondering what the newspaper headlines would be saying in the morning.

TWO

Doc Floyd came up out of the hollow and followed the overgrown path through the trees, pausing at the edge of the swamp to light his pipe. He was seventy years of age with a worn and wrinkled face, his gray mustache stained with nicotine. His straw hat was frayed at the edges, and the old alpaca coat hung from bony shoulders.

The garden on the other side of the track was also overgrown, the fences broken, and the clapboard farmhouse beyond dilapidated, shingles missing in places from the roof. There was an atmosphere of decay about everything.

An old hound dog nosed out of the undergrowth and limped toward Doc Floyd, who leaned down and fondled its ears.

"All wore out, Sam, just like you."

He straightened at the sound of a car approaching and said softly, "Looks like they're here, Sam. Let's go." He went up through the broken fence toward the house, the dog trailing him.

When he went around to the front, a DeSoto sedan was parked there. The man in the dark suit who leaned against it, wiping sweat from his face, fanning himself with his hat at the same time, was middle-aged and overweight. His name was George Harvey, and he was manager of the Huntsville National Bank. The man beside him could have been any one of a hundred local farmers to judge by his faded jeans and sweat-stained felt hat. The only difference was the deputy's badge on his chest and the pistol in the holster on his left hip.

Harvey said, "Ah, there you are, Doc. You know Larry Schultz?"

"Sure I do," Doc said. "Mary okay now, Larry? I heard she was under the weather."

"It was nothing. She's fine now." Schultz was embarrassed, and it showed.

"Okay, let's get down to business," Harvey said. "The bank's been very patient, Doc, but enough is enough. I have to ask you formally now. Are you in a position to settle?"

"You know damn well I'm not," Doc told him flatly.

Harvey turned to Schultz. "Serve your papers."

Schultz produced a folded document from his shirt pocket and held it out to the old man who took it from him. "Sorry, Doc," he said.

Doc shrugged. "Not your fault, Larry, we all got to eat."

Harvey got behind the wheel of the DeSoto and switched on the motor. "Okay, Larry, let's go. I'm a busy man."

Schultz went around to the other side and got into the passenger seat. Doc ran a finger over the gleaming paintwork. "Some car, Mr. Harvey. I suppose a car like this must cost a heap of money?"

"Seven days, that's what you've got," Harvey said. "Then the bank forecloses, and that means everything, Doc, so don't you move a damn thing out of here."

He drove away very fast, spraying dirt, and disappeared along the track through the trees toward the main road. Doc Floyd stood there for a long moment, then turned and mounted the steps to the porch and went inside, the dog following him.

He found a half-full bottle of whiskey and

a glass and sat at the table in the untidy, shabby room, drinking slowly, savoring it as if it might be the last drink he was likely to have.

His eyes roamed around the room, taking in the sagging furniture and the worn carpet and finally came to rest on the photo of his wife in the old silver frame.

"Not much to show for forty years of living, old girl," he said softly.

He toasted her, emptied the glass in a quick swallow, and poured another.

It was perhaps an hour later that he became aware of the sound of a car approaching up the track outside. By then he was drunk enough to be angry.

"The bastard, Sam," he said softly to the dog. "Back already."

He stood up, took an old double-barreled shotgun down from the wall, found some cartridges in a drawer, and loaded it as he went to the door. The hound dog whined anxiously and followed.

Doc stood on the porch outside, the gun ready in his hand, only the car that had stopped in the middle of the yard wasn't the DeSoto. It was a Ford coupe, and the man in the black felt hat and neat dark blue suit who slid out from behind the wheel was definitely not George Harvey.

"Hello, Doc," he called softly. "That's a hell of a welcome."

Doc lowered the shotgun in astonishment. "Jesus Christ," he said. "Johnny Dillinger. You shouldn't be here. They come looking for you just day before yesterday."

"Who's they?"

"A bunch of lawmen. Come in two cars. The fellow who asked about you stutters. Tall, wiry, big fellow."

Dillinger laughed. "That must be Matt Leach. He runs the Indiana State Police."

"I wouldn't laugh, Johnny. He said he'd break my ass if I was lying to him about you being here. He said he'd break your ass when he caught you."

"Somebody sent him a dime book called *How to Be a Detective*," Dillinger said. "He thinks it was me."

"Was it you, Johnny?"

Dillinger rolled his eyes like Al Jolson. A picture of innocence.

"Oh you're a terrible man, Johnny."

Somewhere thunder rumbled, and there was that sudden quiet moment before a storm when everything seemed poised for a terrible downpour.

Dillinger said, "Mind if I come in? I think it's going to rain."

"Sure, sure, Johnny, but what if Leach comes back."

"I'll just bring my insurance policy into the house with me if you don't mind." Dillinger went back to the Ford. Doc watched him bring in the machine guns as if death were being carried into the house under both of Johnny's arms.

And then the rain came, a heavy relentless downpour that churned the yard to mud as Dillinger sat on the porch, drinking Doc's coffee and cleaning his tommy guns to perfection. The old man's plaint was getting to him, making his eyelid tic.

"Three thousand lousy bucks by next Monday," Doc was saying, "or they take over — even the furniture."

"Can't you sell some of your land off and settle up your debt to the bank?" Dillinger asked.

"Not possible," Doc said. "Not under the terms of the mortgage. And there isn't enough time. That bastard George Harvey is collecting as many small farms as he can and hoarding them for resale when times get better."

The old man poured another drink.

"Anyway, enough about me. What about you? That break from Lake View prison the other month must have been really something, wasn't it Johnny?"

"For them, not for me," Dillinger said. "It was a breeze."

"You're really number one, Johnny," Doc said. "I've known them all one time or t'other. None like you. I heard you was in California. The radio said you robbed a bank in Los Angeles last week."

"Sure wish I did. I heard I was in Houston and New Orleans doing the same thing on the same day. It's okay with me. Just keeps the cops confused. What about your wife, Doc, she leave you on account of your drinking, the way she always swore she would?"

"She left me all right, Johnny. Died last year. Top of that, my girl Carrie, who married a guy from Miami, well, he got himself killed asleep at the wheel last year, and Carrie took the baby with her to the Florida Keys. She runs a café down there."

"Why don't you join her?"

"I couldn't do that to her. I'd just be a burden. A dried-up old man with no money."

Dillinger said, "I remember when this was

the best hideout in Kansas. A man could get anything here. A night's sleep, a change of car."

Doc chuckled. "Remember the night I took that bullet out of your arm after the Fort Harris job?"

Dillinger smiled faintly. "You were a pretty damn good doctor for a country vet."

"Oh, I had my moments." He poured another whiskey. "It's funny, Johnny, but when you reach my age, you get to thinking what it's all supposed to be about."

"Any answers?"

"Oh, sure — three thousand dollars, that's what my whole life adds up to. Only I ain't got it, which means my life adds up to nothing. That's a hell of a thing to contemplate."

Dillinger sat there staring at him for a moment, then he stood up, picked up the old man's yellow oilskin slicker, pulled it on, and went down the steps to the Ford.

"Where you going in the rain, you damn fool?" Doc yelled after him.

When Dillinger came back, he was carrying a small case that he carried inside and placed on the table. He opened it carefully. Inside, there was a stack of money, each bundle neatly banded in a bank wrapper.

The old man's eyes widened.

"Fifteen grand there, all I have to show for a misspent life," Dillinger smiled. "Keep it for me. If I don't come back, use it any way you see fit."

"No, Johnny, I couldn't," Doc whispered. "God, where are you going?" the old man demanded.

"To see a man about a bank loan," Dillinger said, his back to the old man as he went down the steps to the Ford, got behind the wheel, and drove away.

George Harvey glanced at his watch. It was just after two-thirty, and it occurred to him that an early finish might make sense today. The relentless rain that had cleared the streets of Huntsville hammered ceaselessly against the window of his office and filled him with acute depression. He was about to get up when the door opened and Marion, his secretary, looked in.

"Someone to see you."

Harvey showed his irritation. "I don't have any appointments."

"No, he knows that. A Mr. Jackson of the Chicago and District Land Company. Says he's only in town by chance and wonders if you could spare him a few minutes."

"Does he look like money?"

"I'd say so."

"Okay. Bring him in, give it five minutes, and then come in to remind me I've got another appointment."

She went out and returned a moment later to usher Dillinger in. He held the yellow slicker over one arm, and Marion took it from him.

"I'll hang it up for you."

"That's very kind of you."

She felt an unaccountable thrill as she went out, closing the door behind her, and Dillinger turned to face Harvey.

"It's good of you to see me, Mr. Harvey."

Harvey took in the excellent suit, the conservative tie, the soft-collared shirt in the very latest style, and got to his feet.

"That's what we're here for, Mr. Jackson. Take a seat and tell me what I can do for you. You're in the property business?"

"That's right. Chicago District Land Company. We're in the market for farm properties in this area — suitable farm properties. Our clients, the people we represent in this instance, intend to farm in a much more modern way. To make that pay, they need lots of acreage. Know what I mean?"

"Exactly," Harvey said, opened a box on

his desk and offered him a cigar. "I think you'll find you've come to the right place, Mr. Jackson."

"Good." Dillinger took the cigar and leaned forward for a light. Harvey frowned. "You know, I could swear I've met you some place before."

"That could be," Dillinger said. "I get around. But let's get down to business. I need a bank down here."

"No problem."

"Good, then I'd like to make a withdrawal now."

"A withdrawal?" Harvey looked bewildered. "I don't understand."

"Yes," Dillinger said. "Twelve thousand dollars should do it, what with my expenses and all."

"But Mr. Jackson, you can't make a withdrawl when you haven't put anything in yet," Harvey explained patiently.

"Oh, yes I can." Dillinger took a Colt .45 automatic from his pocket and placed it on the table between them.

Harvey's whole face sagged. "Oh, God," he whispered. He looked at the man's face, and it came to him. "You're John Dillinger."

"Pleased to meet you," Dillinger said. "Now we've got that over with, you get twelve grand in here fast, and then you and me will take a little ride together."

Dillinger walked over very close to Harvey so that the banker could feel Dillinger's breath on him.

Harvey was not a religious man. He went to church Sundays because his customers went to church. But he found himself hoping that his Maker was looking down right now to protect him.

"Are you going to kill me?" Harvey asked.

"You're going to kill yourself, Mr. Harvey, if you keep shaking that way."

They both heard the door open. Quickly, Dillinger pulled his gun arm in and turned so that it wouldn't be seen from the door. It was Harvey's secretary, saying, "Your next appointment is here, Mr. Harvey."

There was a slight pause. Dillinger waited, and Harvey took a deep breath. "Cancel it. They'll have to come in tomorrow. Tell Mr. Powell I want twelve thousand dollars in here." He glanced at Dillinger. "Will fifties be okay?"

"Just fine," Dillinger said amiably.

The woman went out. Dillinger put the Colt in his right-hand pocket, stood up, and walked around the desk behind Harvey. "You got a briefcase handy?"

"Yes," Harvey said hoarsely.

"When he comes, put the money in that. Then we leave."

The door opened a moment later, and the chief cashier, Sam Powell, entered, carrying a cash tray on which the money was stacked. "You did say twelve thousand, Mr. Harvey?"

"That's right, Sam, just leave it on the desk. I'll clear it tomorrow." He improvised fast. "I'm into a situation that requires instant cash."

"Too good an opportunity to miss," Dillinger put in.

Powell withdrew, and Harvey took his briefcase from under the desk, emptied it, and started to stack the cash inside. He looked up. "Now what?"

"Get your coat," Dillinger said patiently. "It's raining outside or hadn't you noticed? We walk right out the front door and cross the street to the Ford coupe."

"You're going to shoot me?" Harvey said urgently.

"Okay if you make me. If you behave yourself, I'll drop you outside of town. You can have a nice long walk back in the rain to think about it all."

Harvey got his coat from the washroom

and put it on. Then he picked up the brief-case and moved to the door. "Now smile," Dillinger said. "Look happy. Here, I'll tell you something funny. You know what guys in your position always say to guys like me in the movies? They say, 'You'll never get away with it.'"

And Harvey, nerves stretched as tight as they would go, started to laugh helplessly, was still laughing when they went out to Marion's office and picked up Dillinger's oilskin slicker and felt hat.

Sitting at the table, the screen door propped open, Doc Floyd heard the car drive up outside. He straightened, glass in one hand, the other on Dillinger's case and waited fearfully. Dillinger appeared in the doorway, the briefcase in one hand. The dog whined and moved to his side, and he reached down to scratch its ears.

He tossed the briefcase on to the table. "Three thousand in there plus a little interest. Twelve thousand in all. That seem fair to you, Doc?"

The old man placed a hand on the brief-case and whispered, "You kill anyone, Johnny?"

"No. I found your friend Harvey a real

cooperative fellow. Left him ten miles out of town on a dirt road to walk back in the rain." He unfolded the paper from around a stick of chewing gum. "You can pay what you owe on this dump now, Doc, or take the money and run all the way down to the Florida Keys and that daughter of yours." Dillinger popped the gum into his mouth. "Want some?"

"What about you, Johnny? That fellow Leach . . ."

"To hell with him."

Doc wrung his hands. Just then they both heard a car in the distance.

"That coming this way?" Dillinger asked.

"Any car you can hear ain't on the main road. Get in the back room, Johnny, quick. Take the briefcase. Take the guns. Anything else around here yours?"

Doc turned clear around, spied the coffee cups, put them in the sink. The only thing he saw in the room that frightened him was the look that came into Dillinger's eyes.

"Please go into the back room. If you shoot it out with someone here, win or lose, I'll never get to see my grandchild in Florida, Johnny. Please?"

Dillinger went into the back room, taking the briefcase and guns. As soon as he slammed the door, Doc rushed out of the house. Thank heavens the rain had stopped, he thought. He wanted to meet the car as far from the house as he could.

He could see it was a Model A, black as they all were spewing a cloud of dust behind it. The man driving didn't look familiar. Then Doc saw that a woman was sitting beside him.

The man turned the engine off and got out. "Evening," he said.

Doc nodded. He'd seen traps before, man and woman in the front, three men hiding behind the seat.

The man said, "Me and the Mrs. kind of got lost."

"Where you headed?"

"Moline."

"You got a long ways to go."

"Know that. We figured to stop in a hotel someplace tonight. Or thought maybe we could pay someone to stay over."

"You don't want to stay here," Doc said. "My woman has black fever."

The man didn't know what black fever was any more than Doc did, but he took a step backward.

"I can get you some water," Doc said.

"No, thanks," the man said. "We'll be

shoving off. When I get to the road, I turn left or right?"

"Left's the only way that'll head you toward Moline. There's a town an hour down the road got rooms above the general store."

"Thank you kindly. You want us to tell the sheriff or anybody to send a doctor for your wife?"

"I'm a doctor."

The man got back into his car. He didn't believe Doc was a doctor any more than he believed in the man in the moon.

"She's dying," Doc said, "and we want to be left alone for what time's left."

"I appreciate that," the man said, got in the car, and drove off slowly so as not to scatter too much dust in Doc's direction. Doc hurried to the house, opened the door of the back room, and said, "It's okay, Johnny. Travelers. Sent them on their way."

"I hate this."

"Hate what, Johnny?"

"Hiding like a rat. I wasn't made for it. I want to walk around like a free man."

"You'll sure be able to do that," Doc said, "soon's the heat's off. Johnny, I'm old enough to be your father. You been real good to me, so I'm going to chance saying something."

He wished Dillinger wasn't looking at him with those stony eyes.

"Say it!"

That man was sure on edge, Doc thought. "You take too many chances. You've got to head south, I don't mean Texas, I mean all the way to Mexico, where they can't catch you, Johnny."

"That means getting across the border."

Doc poured whiskey into a spare glass and pushed it across to him. "Listen, Johnny, a few years back I had dealings with a man who ran people into the country from Mexico illegally. European refugees, people like that."

"So?"

"West of El Paso, there's a small town called Sutter's Well. Used to be a silver mine. It's a ghost town now. The back trail out of that town crosses the Mexican border. No border post, no customs, no police. That's the way we used to bring them in."

"Will it take a car?"

"Oh, sure. Dirt road, but sound enough. You need to carry plenty of spare gas. Six or seven five-gallon cans in the trunk should cover you. Couple of spare fan belts. I can let you have a set of tools. Know your way around an engine, Johnny?"

"I know my way around a car, Doc, the way a cowboy knows his horse."

"Good. I can give you the address of a Mexican in El Paso, big fat fellow called Charlie, can get you a passport that looks better than the real thing, just to cover you in case you get picked up."

"I'm not planning to get picked up."

"I know you're not planning to get a bullet hole in your radiator either, Johnny, but be damn careful."

"That Ford out there is going to be hotter than hell when Harvey gets back to town. I'll need to switch cars."

"I can help you there," Doc said eagerly. "You take me down to the south barn in the woods. I'll surprise you. Here, better take your fifteen thousand back. And take your hardware. You might need both in Mexico."

He carried the case for Dillinger, who carried the machine guns. They went out and got into the Ford. Dillinger drove around to the rear of the farm and took the track down through the trees beside the swamp, following the old man's directions and finally braked to a halt beside an old dilapidated barn in the trees.

They got out. Doc unbarred the double doors, Dillinger helping him, and pulled them back. A white Chevrolet convertible stood there. It looked brand-new.

"And where in the hell did you get that?" Dillinger wanted to know.

"Kid called in here about six months ago named Leo Fettamen. You heard of him?"

"I don't think so."

"Strictly small stuff, but as car-crazy as you claim to be, Johnny. Fettaman robbed a bank in Carlsberg. Bought this and an old Ford with the cash. Went into Huntsville in the Ford with a guy who called himself Gruber. They intended to take the bank, come back here, and use the Chevy as their getaway car. The kid had a theory that the more imposing you looked, the less the cops were likely to stop you."

"What happened?"

"Killed in a gun battle with the sheriff and his deputies. Hell, I think half the town put a bullet in them before they were finished. The righteous are terrible in their wrath, Johnny."

"So I've noticed," Dillinger said.

"Obviously I couldn't start riding around in it. That would have caused talk. Seeing's you got eyes for it, Johnny, I'll make a deal with you. It's yours for twelve thousand dollars."

Dillinger smiled and slapped Doc's hand. "Doggone, you got it."

"One thing you'll need from that Ford is the battery. The one in the Chevy couldn't be deader."

Dillinger drove the Ford into the barn beside the Chevrolet, then got a wrench from the tool kit and removed the battery. It was only five minutes' work to substitute it for the battery in the other car, then he slid behind the wheel, pulled the choke, and applied the starter. The Chevrolet's engine started instantly, purred like music.

As he got out, the old man was already transferring his belongings from the Ford. "Anything I've forgotten?"

"You could say that."

Dillinger lifted the rear seat of the Ford, revealing a shotgun and two automatic pistols.

"You going to war, Johnny?" Doc asked.

They stowed the shotgun and pistols along with the rest of the arsenal under the rear seat of the Chevrolet. "That's it," Dillinger said.

The old man shook his head. "No, the Ford, Johnny. That's got to go." He nodded across the track to the swamp. "In there." He slapped the car on the roof with the flat of his hand. "Seems like a waste, but when a man gets too greedy, he can end up on the end of a rope."

Dillinger reached in and released the hand brake, then went round to the rear. The two men got their shoulders down and pushed. The Ford bounced across the track, gathered momentum, and ran away down the slope, plunging into the dark waters below. They stood there watching it disappear, Dillinger lighting a cigarette and offering the old man one. Doc shook his head and put his empty pipe in his mouth, chewing on it until the roof of the Ford had disappeared under the surface.

"That's it."

They went back to the barn and got into the Chevrolet. Dillinger drove back to the farm, braking to a halt at the foot of the porch steps. He started to open his door, but Doc shook his head.

"You've got to get moving, Johnny. Let's cut it now."

"Whatever you say, Doc." Dillinger held out his hand.

Doc said, "I want you to know I'm going to take your advice. I'm going south to the

Florida Keys with money in my pants, and it's all thanks to you." He got out of the car and closed the door, leaning down to the window. "I'm going to get some warmth into my old bones before I die, and that's thanks to you as well, Johnny."

Dillinger smiled. "Good luck, Doc." He drove away through the rain.

The old man stood there listening to the Chevrolet's sweet sound fade into the distance. Then he trudged across the muddy yard to the barn and opened the doors. An old Ford truck stood inside. He started it with the handle and drove it across to the front of the farm and went into the house.

When he reappeared, he was carrying a suitcase and the briefcase, no more. He put them into the cab and went back up the steps into the living room. The hound dog moved restlessly beside him. It was very quiet, with only the rain humming on the roof.

"Quiet, Sam," he said gently. "We're leaving now."

He took out his pipe, filled it methodically from his worn tobacco pouch. Then he picked up the photo of his wife in the silver frame and slipped it into his pocket.

He struck a match on the side of his shoe

and put it to the bowl of his pipe, then took the cowl off the oil lamp on the table and touched the match to the wick. The lamp flared up, and he reached forward and very gently turned it on its side. It rolled, coal oil spilling across the table and dripping to the floor, tongues of flame leaping up.

"Why, damn me, Sam," Doc said to the hound. "We appear to have a fire on our hands. Time to leave, I'd say."

He went out to the truck, holding open the door so that the old dog could climb up on the passenger seat. He walked round to the front, swung the crank, then got behind the wheel and moved into gear. As he drove away, he started to sing softly:

John Dillinger was the man for me,
He robbed the Glendale train,
Took from the banks, gave to the poor,
Shan't see his like again.

Behind him, flames burst through the shingle roof, and black smoke billowed into the air. Doc hadn't been happier in years. Then he remembered the man who'd come calling, Leach. The son-of-a-bitch had the whole of the Indiana State Police to catch one man. He hoped Johnny would be across the state line by now. Or real soon.

In his Washington's office, J. Edgar Hoover had seven grown men standing around his desk as if they were page boys instead of high-ranking G-men. Hoover's voice was calm, but the men who had worked with him knew that he was furious.

"He phoned me," Hoover said.

Of course they knew already. It was the scuttlebutt of Headquarters.

"He phoned me collect. He said I should tell the President not to close any more banks."

The men standing there kept straight faces because they knew what Hoover's fury would be like if they so much as smiled.

"He's made more headlines than movie stars. I don't want the kids in this country growing up emulating that man. Understand?"

They all nodded.

"The local boobs can't catch him, and when they do, they can't hold onto him. I want John Dillinger taken by the Bureau. Dead or alive."

It was the man standing next to Purvis from Chicago who said, "Any preference?"

Hoover laughed, so they all thought it was okay to laugh too.

Hoover stood up for the first time. "Here's my plan."

THREE

In Texas he'd driven with the top of the white convertible down, hoping the breeze would help. Maybe not feeling safe yet was adding to his discomfort. But once he was across the border he felt safe, though the hot sun seemed to bear down on him even more, and he finally pulled over to the side of the dusty road and raised the top to keep the sun off his head. He put the turned-down panama hat beside him on the seat to let the sweatband dry out a bit, damn glad he'd bought the panama and thrown the straw hat away. He didn't want to look like an American from a mile away.

With his fingertips he felt the mustache he'd started to grow on the ride down. He glanced in the rear-view mirror. It was coming in black. All he needed was a better suntan.

Above the town the Sierras floated in a purple haze. He bet it was cooler up there, but he had to find a decent hotel, if there was such a place. Across the Plaza Civica that fronted the church, he saw it, the Hotel Balcon, a squat pink building with a crumbling facade. It had been used as a strong point during the Revolution, and the walls were pitted with bullet holes.

He pulled the white Chevrolet up in front of the hotel, aware of the eyes watching him from the park. Maybe from windows up there too. Should he have stuck to a black car like most other people drove, not a white convertible that called attention to himself? He loved the goddamn car and didn't care about anything except that it was now covered in dust and grime. These people sure had lousy roads compared to the States.

Dillinger put on his linen jacket, took the one suitcase. Everything else was safely stowed in the trunk.

He noticed but didn't pay any attention to the old man who sat on the bench in front of the hotel, smoking the stub of a cigarette the way people who can't afford cigarettes do, dragging smoke out of the last half-inch.

As Dillinger passed, the man said, "Hi."

Dillinger stopped. He certainly didn't recognize the old fellow in the crumpled linen suit. He had the face of a man who'd lived hard all his life. A grizzled beard framed his wide mouth.

Dillinger'd been worried about knowing only a few phrases in Spanish, and here was this guy saying, "Hi." Then, "Can you spare two bits?"

Dillinger put his suitcase down. "How'd you know I spoke English?"

"You walk like an American. And I never saw anybody down here drive a job like that." He pointed at the convertible. "Besides," he said with a small-time laugh, "Illinois plates don't grow on cars down here. Two bits, and I'll watch your fancy job while you check in."

"What's it need watching for?"

"The kids around here'll be down on it three seconds after you walk in that front door. I'm cleaned out. Two bits and nobody gets near your car."

Dillinger took out his wallet and extracted a five-dollar bill. "Watch it real good."

The man examined the bill, his face lighting up as if he'd just won a jackpot. "Thank *you*," he said, stretching the "you" out.

Dillinger was picking up his suitcase again when he heard the man say, "Don't I know you from somewhere, mister? You been in Laredo?"

"No."

"San Antone?"

"No," Dillinger said, and headed up the steps to the hotel entrance.

"Hey, I know who you look like," the old man said. "You look like John Dillinger."

Dillinger looked around to see if anyone was standing within ear shot. The only person close enough to have heard was a fat Mexican woman carrying a basket on her head. No chance she'd know the name even if she'd heard.

"I seen your picture," the man said. "You're him, ain't you?"

Dillinger turned slowly and moved back to face him. "You're mistaken, friend. The name's Jordan — Harry Jordan." He parted his jacket slightly so the old man could see the butt of the Colt pistol holstered under his left arm. "You should be more careful, old-timer. Americans should stick together in a place like this."

The old man said, "I guess I made a mistake. I'm sorry."

"Make them myself every day," Dillinger

said and went into the hotel.

On the balcony above the hotel entrance, sitting well back out of the sun, the man who'd rented the best room in the hotel had listened to the exchange with interest. He hadn't heard the actual words, but the new *gringo* spoke with an authority he liked. He picked up his malacca cane, and, straightening his wide-brimmed hat, he headed down to the lobby, walking with the confidant gait of a man who knew what he wanted.

Dillinger, waiting at the desk for his key, saw the onlooker coming in the mirror. He was tall with good shoulders, his temples brushed with gray, and the broken nose looked out of place in the aquiline face. There was an elegance about him, a touch of the *hidalgo* in the way he carried himself. He was a breed the revolution had almost destroyed. The proud ones who never gave in. Who had to be broken.

He removed the long cigarillo from his mouth. "Senor Jordan?" he inquired in careful, clipped English.

Dillinger froze. How did the man know the name on his passport? No point in denying it. The hotel clerk knew. The old man in front knew. "Yes," was all Dillinger said.

"Allow me to introduce myself. Don Jose Manuel de Rivera."

Dillinger could tell from the way the hotel clerk nodded to the man that he was a wheel.

"My business can be stated quite briefly, senor," Rivera said. "Perhaps I could accompany you to your room? We could talk as you unpack."

"We can talk right here in the lobby," Dillinger said, gesturing to a glass-topped wicker table with two chairs beside it.

"As you wish," the man called Rivera said.

Just then they both heard the commotion outside, and a cracked voice yelling, "Scram! Vamoose! Get the hell out of here!"

"Excuse me," Dillinger said, and walked quickly to the front entrance, where, as he suspected, the old man was trying to chase away three shirtless teenage Mexican boys, one of whom had already opened the near door of the convertible and was peering into the glove compartment.

With quick strides Dillinger was at the car. He grabbed the kid by his hair and yanked him out of the car, then twisted the kid's arm behind his back, paying no attention to the stream of Spanish invective. Calmly, Dillinger looked at the other two boys, who were standing on the running board on the other side. Whatever they saw in his eyes, plus the yelping of their friend, sent them dashing down the street.

The old American came around so he could yell at the captive's face. *"Ladron! Ladron!"*

"What the hell does that mean?" Dillinger asked.

"Thief."

"Tell him I'm going to break his arm so he won't steal anymore."

The old man translated it into rough Spanish. The kid looked frightened.

Then, with one motion, Dillinger flung the kid to the ground, giving him a chance to scamper away.

Dillinger laughed, and only then did he notice that the whole scene had been observed by Senor Rivera from the doorway.

"Bravo, Senor Jordan," Rivera said.

"I apologize for the intermission," Dillinger said, "but I really like that car the way it is."

"Understandable."

The old man, his face a mask of disgrace, was holding out the five-dollar bill Dillinger had given him. "I guess you want this back. I didn't do too good watching your car for you."

"You did fine. If you hadn't yelled, I wouldn't have come out. Just what I wanted." He reached under the front seat of the car and pulled out a big flannel rag. "Here. Why don't you clean the dust off the car while I talk to this gentleman. If you're dusting it, I don't think anybody else will bother it."

"Absolutely, Mr. Jordan," the old man said, taking the rag and hastily pocketing the five-dollar bill again.

Rivera said, "Perhaps now we can talk in your room where it will be quieter, senor?"

Dillinger hesitated and then shrugged. "Why not?"

Dillinger got his suitcase at the front desk, led the way up the broad wooden stairs to the first floor, and unlocked the door at the end of the corridor. The room was like an oven. The fan in the ceiling was not moving. Dillinger yanked the pull chain; nothing happened. He flicked both switches on the wall. One turned on the light. The other did nothing.

"Mexico is not like the United States," Rivera said.

Dillinger moved to open the French windows and nodded toward a table on which stood a pitcher of ice water and several glasses.

"Help yourself. If you don't mind, I'll wash up."

When Dillinger took his jacket off, Rivera noticed with interest the under-arm holster and gun. No wonder the man could act with such authority. So much the better!

Dillinger put the holster down within easy reach. This Rivera looked rich. Dillinger trusted rich people less than poor people.

He stripped to the waist, poured lukewarm water from a pitcher into the basin on the washstand in one corner, and sluiced his head and shoulders.

Rivera said, "If you have not been to Mexico before, I recommend you order bottled water, Senor. American stomachs do not like our water."

Dillinger nodded his thanks. Rivera sat down in a wicker chair by the table, and Dillinger walked to the window, toweling his damp hair. A steam whistle blasted once, the sound echoing back from the mountains across the flat roofs, and a wisp of smoke drifted lazily into the sky from the station.

Rivera put down his glass and said, "I'd

like to offer you a job, Senor Jordan."

"What kind of a job?" Dillinger was amused. This guy sure didn't know who he was.

"I've reopened an old gold mine near my hacienda at Hermosa. That's a small town in the northern foothills of the Sierra Madre, toward the American border. Hermosa and the area around it is rough country. The peasants are animals, and the Indians who work the mines. . . ." He shrugged. "But you will find this out for yourself. What I need is a man of authority, who will work with me for six months or a year. Keep discipline. You know what I mean?"

This guy was fascinating, Dillinger thought. "Who keeps discipline for you now, Mr. Rivera?"

"Ah," Rivera said. "I had a good man, also an American, very tall, very strong. He didn't want to go back to the States, the police bothered him there and so he had an accident, and now I have to replace him. I hope with you."

"In one sentence," Dillinger said, "not a chance."

"You have not heard my terms, senor. Two thousand dollars in gold for six months, five thousand dollars in gold for a year."

Dillinger was really tempted to tell this fancy jerk that he'd made that much in five minutes by vaulting over a counter and emptying a teller's drawer.

"En oh," Dillinger said. "That spells no. But how would you like to work for me while I am in Mexico? You could be my guide. I'll pay you a thousand dollars for a month, how's that?"

Anger blazed in River's dark eyes. The jagged white scar, bisecting his left cheek that Dillinger hadn't paid attention to before, seemed to stand out suddenly against the brown skin. Rivera took a cigarillo from his breast pocket and lit it. When he looked up, he had control again.

"I know you did not mean to insult me, Senor. You do not know the ways of Mexico." He took a slow puff. "I usually get what I want, Senior Jordan. We have a saying: *A man must be prepared to pay for past sins.* I will pay you double what I paid the other American if you return to Hermosa with me. My final offer."

"Thanks, but no thanks," Dillinger said gently. "I'm really here on a kind of vacation."

He was aware of the sweat trickling from his armpits, soaking into his shirt. He poured himself a glass of ice water, then remembered Rivera's warning about the water.

Rivera said calmly, "Your final word?"

"Yes. Sorry we can't do business."

Rivera walked to the door and opened it. "So am I, Senor Jordan. So am I."

Rivera closed the door behind him, descended the wide wooden stairs to the lobby, and went outside. He found the old man who was guarding Dillinger's convertible sitting on the bench, a small bottle of *tequila* in hand. So, he'd spent some of the money already.

"Hello, Fallon, I thought I recognized you. Having a difficult time of it lately?"

The old man looked at him sourly. "You should know, Mr. Rivera!"

"You needed a lesson, my friend," Rivera said, "but that's history now. You can come back and work for me at Hermosa any time you like."

"That's not work, Mr. Rivera. It's slavery."

"As you choose. Who is this Senor Jordan?"

"Jordan?" The old man stared at him blankly. "I don't know any Jordan."

"The one you were talking to. He owns

the convertible. Who is he? What's his game?"

"I ain't telling you a damn thing," Fallon said.

Rivera shrugged and walked along the terrace. Two men were sitting at the end table eating *frijoles*, a bottle of wine between them. One was a large, placid Indian with an impassive face, great rolls of fat bursting the seams of his jacket. The other, a small, wiry man in a tan gabardine suit, his sallow face badly marked from smallpox, got to his feet hurriedly, wiping his mouth. "Don Jose."

"Ah, my good friend, Sergeant Hernandez." Rivera turned and glanced toward Fallon. "I wonder if you might consider doing me a great favor?"

Hernandez nodded eagerly. "At your orders, as always, senor."

Twenty minutes later, Fallon surfaced with a shock as a bucket of water came hurling onto his face. One side of his face hurt from his eye to his jaw. He was lying in the corner of a police cell. The big Indian who stood over him must have hit or kicked him. Fallon's side hurt as much as his face. Sergeant Hernandez sat on the bunk. Fallon recognized him instantly and went cold.

"What is this? What have I done?"

"You are a stupid man," Hernandez told him.

"I'm an American. You have no right to put me in here," Fallon said.

"If you don't like our ways, why don't you go back? You want me to escort you to the border and turn you over to your Federalistas?"

Fallon shook his head.

"You are here because to go back there you have to spend fifteen years in jail, is that not so?"

The massive Indian moved within kicking distance of Fallon.

"You see," Hernandez said, "he only knows one thing. Kicking."

Fallon rolled away from the Indian, which brought him closer to Hernandez.

Hernandez leaned down and whispered to Fallon, "I think you will now stop being stupid. Now I think you may even try to be sensible? Is this not so?"

"Sure," Fallon muttered.

The cell door opened and Rivera entered. He glared down at Fallon.

Hernandez said, "Senor Rivera has some questions to put to you. You will answer them. You understand?"

"Yes," Fallon moaned.

"Excellent," Rivera said and sat on the bunk. "Let's start again then. This man,

Harry Jordan. Who is he?"

A slight wind lifted the edge of the dingy lace curtains in Dillinger's room. The place had that strange, derelict air common to rooms in cheap hotels the world over. It was as if no one had ever really lived there. As Dillinger lay on the bed, he heard the great bell of the church toll, and it reminded him of Sunday mornings in Indiana when he was twelve. He'd led his neighborhood gang – all sixth-grade boys – in a foray to steal coal from the Pennsylvania Railroad and sell it to the women in town. He remembered the happy days in Gebhardt's pool hall, and the even happier times playing baseball. He loved baseball because it was two games being played at the same time, winning against the other team, and being watched by the girls, who after the game always went after the boys who played best. Some of those older girls had terrific figures, not like these Mexican women. Jesus, was he getting homesick so soon?

He had to wait it out till the hunt for him cooled off. He had to be steel, like the time in prison he found strength to pour acid on his heel so he could get transferred to yard duty. They owed him nine years!

He remembered how good he felt – like he was flying – when he got out of jail that first time. He wasn't going to spend any more time ever behind bars.

The knock on the door stopped his reverie. He hoped it was the damn bellboy with the bottled water he'd asked for more than an hour ago. God, things moved slow in Mexico!

"Come in," he yelled. "The door's open."

What came in wasn't the bellhop but a small, wiry man in uniform with a pockmarked face.

"Police, senior," pockmarks said. "I am Sergeant Hernandez. May I see your passport?"

Dillinger looked across the room to the dresser where his Colt automatic lay in its holster. The sergeant followed his eyes.

Dillinger swung his feet off the bed, went to his jacket, took out the Harry Jordan passport, and handed it to Hernandez, who went through it page by page, his face expressionless.

"How much did you pay for this passport, Senor Jordan?" Hernandez asked.

"Same as anyone else," Dillinger said.

"I must have you accompany us to headquarters, senor."

"Would you mind explaining what this is all about?"

Hernandez straightened, his jacket falling open, and drew a revolver from the holster on his left hip. "Please, senor, let's be sensible about this. No fuss, eh? We must think of the reputation of the hotel." He pulled Dillinger's Colt automatic from its holster and pocketed it. "We can drive to police headquarters in my car, or my driver can follow us in your car in case you do not wish to leave that beautiful automobile unattended in front of the hotel. You see, the man who was watching it, he is no longer watching it because he is in jail. Like you, Mr. Dillinger, he doesn't want to be turned over to the Federalistas on your side of the border."

FOUR

In the courtyard, a troop of Mexican Federal cavalry was exercising. Dillinger, with Hernandez beside him, waited till he could drive the convertible into the courtyard. He wasn't about to leave it in the street.

When they parked, Hernandez held his hand out for the keys.

Dillinger started to separate the trunk key from the ignition key on the ring.

"Both keys, Senor Jordan," Hernandez said. "If you please."

Dillinger decided not to make a fuss about the trunk key. Considering what was in the trunk, he'd just as soon not call attention to it.

Inside, Dillinger was told to sit down on a tough wooden bench in the whitewashed corridor, watched over by Hernandez's Indian. Through the open window, he could hear the shouted commands to the cavalry. If he had to shake loose of this place, he wasn't going to leave the convertible behind, which meant he'd have to be able to get it out of the courtyard. He'd get his keys back, or he'd wire the ignition. Getting into the trunk would be a bitch. He was beginning to be sorry he hadn't left the car in the street and got a second set of keys made to keep under the bumper as he used to do back home.

He stood up to make sure nobody was bothering the car, but the Indian put a heavy hand on his shoulder and made him sit back down.

"Nobody does that to me," Dillinger said, uselessly. The Indian didn't understand him. "You're going to be sorry you were born."

Finally he heard a murmur of voices from down the hall, and Hernandez beckoned to him. They passed many doors, Hernandez leading, the Indian behind, until they came to a door that was open, as if they were expected. Hernandez gestured, and Dillinger went in.

The office was sparsely furnished with two chairs and a desk. There was a rush mat on the floor. The one luxury was the ancient fan which revolved listlessly in the ceiling.

The man behind the desk wore a rumpled khaki uniform. He was middle-aged and balding, a small black mustache brushing his upper lip. He smiled, and Dillinger saw that most of his teeth had been capped in gold.

"I am Fidel Santos, Chief of Police," he said in English. "Please sit down, Senor Jordan."

On the desk before him he had Dillinger's wallet and the false passport.

"What's this all about?" Dillinger asked.

"As with most things in life it is a question of money, senor." Santos nodded. Hernandez placed a small black suitcase on the desk and flipped it open, revealing the neat rows of bank notes. "Just over fourteen thousand American dollars to be precise. We found it in the trunk of your car."

Bastards, Dillinger thought.

"How have you earned this money, senor?"

"My father died three months ago and left me a small farm in Kansas, which I sold."

Hernandez stood by the window cleaning his nails with a knife. He paused and looked across. Dillinger was aware of the Indian behind his chair, of the faint creaking of the fan in the silence.

Santos said, "You know that there is a government tax on foreign currency brought into this country?"

"No, I didn't know that."

"Strange. According to your passport, you crossed our border at Solernas. One would have thought the custom officials there would have made this plain to you when you declared the money."

There was another slight silence. Hernandez finished cleaning his nails, snapped the blade shut, and slipped the knife into his pocket. Outside, a bugle sounded, and the cavalry clattered across the cobbles into the plaza.

They seemed to be waiting for him to make the next move. Dillinger said, "No one is sorry about this little misunderstanding more than I am. I'll be glad to pay the necessary tax to the proper authorities."

"Unfortunately there is the question of the fine," Santos said.

"All right, I'll pay the fine and put it down to experience."

"I'm afraid that won't be possible, senor," Santos said patiently. "In such cases it is usual for the entire sum involved to be forfeited and then, of course, there is the question of a fine."

Dillinger thought, these guys are thieves in uniform. He could feel the blood rising to his face. He had to keep his control.

"And how much would the fine be?" Dillinger asked.

"A difficult question in your case, senor. You see, there is also the matter of certain firearms discovered under the rear seat of your automobile. Another serious infringement of our laws, almost certainly leading to their confiscation and also of the vehicle itself."

That hit Dillinger between his eyes.

He managed to keep control of his voice as he said, "Folks, we have a saying in the States. You can take everything away from a cowboy except his horse. That automobile is my horse."

There was a pause.

Then Santos said, "Perhaps you don't realize the position you are in. A prisoner at present in custody here, an American just like you, insists that your name isn't Jordan at all. Does that surprise you?"

Dillinger managed to look astonished. "You've got my passport, haven't you?"

"Passports, senor, may be bought. Oh, I'm sure this is a nonsense, of course. The man concerned is an old drunk. He insists that you are the bank robber, John Dillinger, who recently escaped from prison in Indiana."

Dillinger worked his way from an expression of total bewilderment to one of outraged laughter. "Jesus, this guy must be out of his head."

Santos laughed sympathetically. "A drunken old fool, as I said. I foresee no problem in clearing the matter up, but you will, of course, have to remain in custody until we have an opportunity to check with our *compadres* to the North."

There was silence. Santos lit a cigar and nodded to the Indian. The Indian touched Dillinger on the shoulder and motioned him toward the door.

The Indian took Dillinger out and along the corridor and down a flight of stone steps to an iron door outside which a guard was sitting reading a newspaper. He unlocked the door.

The room was about forty feet square, with only one small window high in the opposite wall, and contained twenty or thirty other prisoners. Through the door came the strong odor of urine, human excrement, and stale sweat. The Indian pushed Dillinger inside and shut the door with a clang.

Most of the prisoners were Mexicans in ragged trousers, shirts, and straw sandals. Several of them came crowding around to look at the strange new prisoner. Someone touched his jacket. He felt a hand slide into his pocket. Dillinger grabbed for the wrist and twisted it with an easy strength that sent the man staggering across the cell. The others moved back to a respectful distance. He pulled a drunk from a bench against the wall, sat down, and lit a cigarette, hoping it would counter the stench around him.

There was more to this situation than met the eye, he thought, more even than Santos confiscating the money to keep for himself. If Santos had simply wanted to do that, it would have made more sense to let him go.

A man got up to relieve himself in an overflowing bucket in the corner. The stink was terrible.

"Spare a butt, Mr. Dillinger?"

Fallon eased on to the bench beside him. A livid bruise stretched from the corner of one eye to the edge of the jaw.

Dillinger shook a cigarette out for him. "What did they use, a sledgehammer?"

"Sergeant Hernandez has an Indian sidekick called Valdez." He rubbed his jaw.

"Built like the side of a house."

"You told them I was John Dillinger." It was a statement of fact, not a question. Dillinger sat there staring at Fallon calmly, and the old man said, "They made me tell them, Mr. Dillinger, beat it out of me."

Suddenly there was a scuffle between two prisoners on the bench next to theirs. Dillinger stood, and with a voice that cut through the commotion like a sword shouted, "Shut up!" Nobody needed to know what the words meant. The two scuffling prisoners returned to their places. The others stared at the *gringo* who spoke with an authority not even the chief of police had. Now, when they talked, it was in whispers.

"That's better," Dillinger said.

Fallon coughed. "I saw you with that man Rivera. Do you know who he is?"

"He offered me a job at his mine."

"He's the original walking bastard, that guy. When I first skedaddled into Mexico one step ahead of the cops, I went to work for Rivera."

"You told him who I was."

"I kind of let it slip that there was more to you than the name Jordan, but I wouldn't tell him no more than that."

"Then the cops picked you up?"

"They sure did. Beat the hell out of me, then Rivera came in the cell, and Hernandez said I'd better start talking or else. I had to agree to go back on the payroll at Hermosa, too. I didn't have a choice.

"That's okay, old-timer." There was one more cigarette in the pack. Dillinger broke it in two and offered him half.

Fallon put his half in his wallet.

"Saving it for later?"

"Saving it forever. What a souvenir, half a cigarette given me by Johnny Dillinger."

"What's that?" Dillinger asked, pointing to a picture postcard that came part way out of Fallon's wallet as he put the half-cigarette away for safekeeping.

Fallon unfolded the card. It was an advertisement in Spanish for a hotel in Hermosa. Standing in front of it was the most exotically beautiful woman Dillinger had ever seen.

"Who's that?"

"That's Rose. Runs the hotel now that her mother and father are both gone."

"What makes her look that way?" Dillinger asked.

"You mean the eyes? She's half Chinese, half Spanish."

"Is she as good-looking in person as on that card?"

"Better. And a nicer woman you never met. It's hard to believe she's Rivera's niece. Her father and Rivera never got on. Rivera didn't want his kid brother marrying a Chinese woman. If he hadn't, there wouldn't have been Rose. Last year when her father died, Rivera wouldn't go to the funeral. You know what she did, just to rub his nose in things? She had a new sign painted. Had them hang it above the front door of the hotel."

"What's it say?"

"Shanghai Rose."

Dillinger laughed out loud.

"Every time Rivera goes into town he sees that sign. Oh, that Rose, she's something special."

"You're not sweet on her, are you now?"

"Me?" Fallon said. "She's a lady. 'Sides, she wouldn't look at anyone's as decrepit as me. In Hermosa, she's like a princess waiting for a prince to come along."

Dillinger thought they'd have come for him by now. Fallon had dozed off, but was waking up. Dillinger asked him, "Why does Rivera have such trouble getting help for the Hermosa place?"

"The mine's a death trap. Least five cave-ins I know of. Christ knows how many dead Indians. He uses Apaches up there."

"Apaches? I thought they went out with the old West."

"Not in Sierra Madre. That was their original stronghold. Still plenty around up there."

"If it's that bad, why'd you agree to go back? Why not cut and run when they let you out?"

Fallon shrugged. "I don't have a *centavo* more than the change for the five dollars you gave me. In this country a *gringo* without money in his boot . . ." He shrugged.

The door opened, and Hernandez looked in. "Senor Jordan, will you come this way, please."

Dillinger picked his way between the Mexicans and followed Hernandez. They mounted the stone steps, passed along the whitewashed corridor, and paused outside the office. Hernandez knocked and motioned Dillinger inside.

The air was heavy with the aroma of good cigars. Santos had one clamped firmly between his teeth. He took it out and grinned cheerfully. "Ah, Senor Jordan. Sit down. I am happy to tell you that your troubles are over."

Dillinger hardly noticed Santos. He had eyes only for Don Jose Manuel de Rivera as he turned slowly from the window and smiled. "We meet again, Senor Jordan."

"Seems so."

"I am pleased Don Jose has employment to offer you," Santos said, smiling. "He has agreed to pay the balance of your fine out of his own pocket."

"I came the moment I heard at the hotel that you'd been arrested," Rivera said.

"That was real kind of you."

"After speaking with Senor Santos it occurs to me that you may now review my earlier offer of employment in a somewhat different light."

"I think you could say that."

"Then you will be prepared to accompany me to Hermosa on the evening train?"

"What about my car?"

Rivera turned to Santos. "It is his pride."

"Mexico," Santos said, "has a generous heart. Senor Jordan may have his beautiful white automobile, without its arsenal, of course."

Rivera picked up the passport. "I will see that this is returned to Senor Jordan at a more suitable time."

"Of course, Don Jose. I regret, however, that in the matter of the confiscated money, the law must take its course. However, in the circumstances, and as Senor Jordan is now, as it were, in your custody, we will say no more about the fine."

"How will I get my car to Hermosa if I go with you?" Dillinger asked.

"As I do with mine," Rivera said. "It travels on the flatbed railroad car reserved for automobiles. You are then prepared?"

Dillinger thought, I am prepared to see if Shanghai Rose is as beautiful as her picture. If she hates this son-of-a-bitch as much as I do, we ought to get along real fine.

FIVE

Dillinger was amused by the idea that, for a change, he was being taken for a ride. In spite of all the coal he'd stolen from the Pennsylvania Railroad, he's never traveled any distance on a train before. Just an hour out he'd had the crazy idea of getting into his convertible on the flatbed and staying in it for the rest of the train ride because a car was a natural place for him to be.

The train was fun. He was following the conductor along the narrow corridor of the Pullman car and had to brace himself every couple of steps as the train swayed and rocked. The attendant knocked on a compartment door, opened it, and moved inside.

There were two bunks, but Rivera had the place to himself. A small table had been pulled down from the wall, and the remains of a meal were on it.

"Come in, Jordan."

He obviously intended a master-and-servant relationship, and the dropping of the "senor" was merely the first step. Dillinger leaned against the door and took out a packet of Artistas. The Mexican poured cognac into a glass, held it up to the light, and sipped a little.

"So I'm Jordan again?" Dillinger said.

"I should have thought that the sensible thing for everyone concerned," Rivera said. "Your true identity is of no consequence to anyone but me."

"Fallon knows."

"Fallon will do exactly as he is told."

"And that Chief of Police, Santos?"

Rivera smiled faintly. "He has the money. I have his silence."

"The money was mine," Dillinger said.

"And from whom did you appropriate it? Let us concentrate on the future, not the past," Rivera said. "I need a man to take charge of a rather difficult mining operation. A hard man to keep those Indians of mine in order. A man who is capable of using a gun if necessary. I should have thought you and your experience would fit the bill admirably."

"Has it occurred to you that I might have other plans?"

"Hermosa is twenty miles from the nearest railway, and there is a train only once a fortnight. The roads, I am afraid, are the worst in Mexico. However, we are linked to civilization by an excellent telegraph line, and Santos did assign you to my care. If you misbehave, Santos is prepared to fill the last part of our bargain."

"And what is that?"

"To turn you over to the American authorities at a border crossing — under your real name, of course."

Dillinger dropped his cigarette into Rivera's brandy glass.

Anger flared in Rivera's eyes. "Do your work, that's all I want from you. Do it well and we shall get along. Do it badly . . ."

Dillinger opened the door and went out. In a way, he'd won. In the end it had been the Mexican who had lost his temper.

The second-class coach was crowded, mostly peasant farmers going to market, and filled with great heat, heavy with the stench of unwashed bodies. This was not the way Dillinger liked to travel.

He spotted Fallon in a corner by the door, playing solitaire with a pack of greasy cards. Fallon looked up, his face wrinkling in disgust. "It's enough to turn your stomach in here, Mr. Dillinger."

"Which explains the second-class tickets," Dillinger said. "He wants us to know exactly where we stand." He pulled his two suitcases from under the table. "Let's get out of here. There's plenty of room in the first-class end. Another thing, it's Jordan, not Dillinger. Remember that."

"I'll try," Fallon said.

They went into the first empty compartment they came to. Fallon produced two bottles of beer from his canvas grip, and sprawled in the corner by the window.

"This is more like it. What do we do if the conductor comes?"

"What do you think?"

Fallon opened one of the bottles and passed it across. "What did Rivera want?"

"Mainly to let me know who's boss."

"He must be the great original bastard of all time."

Dillinger tried the beer. It was warm and flat, but better than nothing. He put the bottle on the floor, lit a cigarette, and placed his feet on the opposite seat.

"How come Rivera survived the revolution? I thought men like him were marched straight to the nearest wall."

"I guess some did, some didn't. Some fish always escape the net."

Dillinger awakened with a start. The train had begun the cautious descent of a narrow canyon, the coaches lurching together as the engineer applied the brake. Dillinger's watch said 4 A.M. He got up quietly and went past the sleeping Fallon into the corridor.

He stood by the window and shivered slightly as the cold mountain air was sucked in. The sky was very clear, hard white stars scattering toward the horizon, and a faint luminosity was beginning to touch the great peaks that towered on either side. A moment later the canyon broadened, and he could see the lights of a station.

He heard Fallon behind him saying, "La Lina — only a whistle-stop for mail and passengers. Another couple of hours to where we're going."

"I didn't even know we'd passed through Chihuahua."

"Didn't seem any point in waking you. We were only there for twenty minutes while they changed the engine."

La Lina swam toward them out of the darkness as the train coasted in and slowed to a halt. There was a small station house with a couple of shacks behind it and nothing more. The stationmaster came out carrying a lantern, and three mestizos in straw hats and blankets, who had been crouching against the wall, got to their feet and came forward.

Fallon and Dillinger jumped to the ground and walked toward the rear of the train. A couple of boxcars had been linked on behind the flatcar on which the Chevrolet had been roped into place. When the men paused to light cigarettes, they heard a low whinny and the muffled stamp of hooves.

"When did they join us?" Dillinger said.

"Chihuahua. The guard told me they were thoroughbreds going up to Juarez for the races next week."

When they turned to retrace their steps, the three mestizos were standing patiently beside the train, hands in the air, while the stationmaster and guard searched them thoroughly.

"What's all that about?" Dillinger said.

"They say that the train's been robbed three times in the last four months," Fallon told him. "Bandits get on at way stations, dressed like dirt farmers. Last year in Sonora they shot the engineer of the night express and left it to freewheel down a gradient. Ran off the track after five miles."

They boarded the train again, and the guard closed the door. He turned and said in English, "I notice, senors, that you have moved into a first-class compartment."

Dillinger replied, "It's too crowded in the other coach."

"It is also cheaper, senor. You are prepared to pay the necessary addition?"

"Now there you put me in a delicate position," Dillinger told him.

The guard shrugged and replied with perfect politeness. "Then I'm afraid I must ask you to resume your former seats. I have my duty — you understand?"

"I knew it was too good to last," Fallon said.

They got their cases from the compartment and moved back into the second-class coach, where most of the occupants were sleeping. They sat down in their original seats in the corner by the door that led to the luggage van.

Fallon laid his head on his arms. Dillinger lifted his hat forward and saw a young Indian girl in a red skirt, a large cloth bundle on the floor between them. She stared past him into the wall, blindly, as if in a trance.

He finished his cigarette and closed his eyes. A few moments later he was aware of the girl moving. He glanced up and saw that she was looking back along the coach at the three mestizos who had boarded the train at La Lina. One of them nodded briefly.

The mestizo removed his blanket and stood up. He was of medium height, with broad shoulders bulging beneath the faded khaki shirt, and the Indian blood showed in the high cheekbones and broad nose.

The girl went forward without a word, placed her bundle on the table, and untied it. The three men immediately reached inside and took out revolvers. Dillinger nudged Fallon with his elbow.

"Hey, this is terrific. We've got company."

Fallon sat up and cursed softly. "Well, I'll be damned. Juan Villa."

"You know him?"

"Used to be one of Rivera's peons. Stuck his knife into a foreman a couple of years back. A real firebrand. You ever hear of Pancho Villa?"

"Sure."

"Juan claims to be his nephew. That's bullshit, but it goes down big with the peasants."

On seeing Fallon, Villa's face was illuminated by a smile of great natural charm. He raised a hand warningly as his two companions went toward opposite ends of the coach.

"You would be wise to place your guns on the table, old friend," he said in halting English. "It would desolate me to have to kill you."

"We aren't armed," Fallon told him.

"Then stay where you are, and don't try to interfere."

Villa raised his revolver and fired once through the roof. The effect was astonishing: a sudden eruption of sleeping passengers, a stifled scream, then frightened silence.

"We will now pass around the hat," Juan Villa said. "You would do well to contribute generously."

Dillinger thought banks were a helluva lot better than trains. Less risk, more loot. Maybe Mexico didn't have enough banks.

The door beside Dillinger opened and the conductor stepped in. He hesitated for no more than a second before turning to run — too late. The bandit who had been standing at that end of the coach shot him in the back.

Now that's not sporting, Dillinger thought.

A child screamed, and its mother placed a hand over its mouth. In the passage between the coach and the baggage car the conductor was moaning. Dillinger started to his feet.

These guys are doing it all wrong.

Immediately the barrel of Villa's revolver swung toward him, and Fallon cried out frantically, "No, Juan, no!"

Villa hesitated and then shrugged. "I owe you a favor. This cancels it." He turned to the bandit who had shot the conductor. "Lock them in the baggage car and come back."

Fallon gave Dillinger a shove. "Get moving!"

The conductor had stopped groaning. Fallon and Dillinger stepped over his body. The bandit bent down to pick up the bunch of keys the man still clutched in his right hand, then followed them into the baggage car.

"Stinking gringos," the bandit said. "A bullet in the head is better, I think." He threw down the keys and thumbed back the hammer of his pistol.

"Villa won't like that," Fallon cried in a panic.

"So I tell him you tried to jump me."

The bandit pushed the barrel of the

revolver into Dillinger's back. Dillinger had practiced the maneuver a hundred times. He had anticipated a policeman's gun in his back, marching him somewhere he didn't want to go. Dillinger raised his hands, pivoting on his left foot, his left arm coming down on the man's gun arm as Dillinger's right hand, now formed into a fist, continued the movement by smashing into the side of the man's face. With his left arm tight around the bandit's gun hand, Dillinger raised his left arm up sharply, hearing the crack of bone. The man dropped the revolver and collapsed with a groan.

Instantly, Fallon grabbed the gun up from the floor.

"You stay here," Dillinger said. "I'll work my way back to the Pullman car. See if we can catch them between two fires."

Dillinger opened the door, and the cold air sucked it outward, sending it crashing back against the side of the coach. The train was moving at no more than twenty miles an hour, and he stepped out on the footboard, reached for the edge of the roof, and pulled himself up.

There was a catwalk running along the center, and he worked his way to the end of the baggage car and sprang across to the roof of the second-class coach. The stars were pale, and in the east the dark peaks were already tipped with fire, as he jumped to the roof of the Pullman and lowered himself down through the open window to the door.

When he reached Rivera's compartment, he knocked softly. It opened almost immediately. Dillinger pushed Rivera back in and stepped inside.

Rivera had obviously just awakened. "What is it?"

"Bandits got on at La Lina. We're having a little trouble back there. Have you got a gun?"

Rivera looked at him suspiciously, then pulled a suitcase from under his bunk, opened it, and produced a revolver. "How many bandits?"

"There were three, but Fallon's looking after one of them in the luggage van. The leader's a man called Villa. Fallon said he used to work for you."

"Juan Villa?" Rivera's face hardened. "That man is a murderer!"

He brushed past Dillinger and moved along the corridor quickly. The noise of the train effectively cloaked any disturbance that

100

was taking place inside the second-class coach as the two men passed through the empty first-class compartments. Rivera paused at the door to listen for a moment, then opened it.

Juan Villa was halfway along the coach, his hat held out to a group of people at a table. The third man stood a couple of feet away with his back to the door. Rivera took a quick step forward and placed the barrel of the gun against his neck. The man's whole body seemed to go rigid. Rivera plucked the revolver from his hand and passed it to Dillinger.

Rivera moved forward and said, "Villa!"

Villa looked up sharply. For a moment his face was washed clean of all expression and then he smiled. "Eh, *patrón*. We meet again."

"Put down the gun," Rivera said.

As the bandit hesitated, Dillinger shouted to Fallon. A moment later, the first bandit lurched in from the luggage van holding his head, Fallon behind him.

Villa shrugged and dropped his gun on the table.

"Take them to my compartment," Rivera said.

Fallon pulled the young Indian girl up

from the end table and pushed her after the others. "She was in it, too."

"What about the conductor?" Dillinger said.

"Dead."

As they reached Rivera's compartment, the engineer sounded the steam whistle three times — the emergency signal — and braked sharply.

The train slowed to a halt, and Dillinger looked out of the window. A bunch of steers were milling across the track, a dozen or fifteen peons on horseback vainly trying to urge them on. Suddenly the peons turned and galloped forward with shrill cries, drawing revolvers and firing as they came. When they reached the train, they dismounted.

Dillinger ducked back inside and turned to Villa. "Friends of yours?"

The bandit grinned. "I don't think they're going to like the way you've been treating me, amigo."

There was an outburst of firing from the rear of the train. A mounted trooper galloped past the window and then another. Rivera pushed Villa forward. "Three times they've made this trip to Juarez, my friend. They were beginning to lose faith in you."

Dillinger looked out and saw mounted

troopers of the Federal cavalry emerging one by one from the boxcars at the end of the train. Most of the bandits were still trying to remount when they were surrounded. They tried firing back, but it was no use. They were outmaneuvered and outnumbered. It was all over.

Rivera pulled on his jacket and turned to Fallon. "You stay here with Villa. If he makes the slightest move to escape, shoot him." He nodded to Dillinger. "Bring the others outside."

As he jumped to the ground, the young officer in command of the troop walked forward and saluted. "Lieutenant Cordona. They informed me in Chihuahua that you were traveling on the train, Don Jose. It would seem we have been completely successful."

"Not quite," Rivera said. "They murdered the conductor."

"Which one is Villa?"

"He is at present under guard in my compartment. He, of course, must be held for public trial in Chihuahua, but the others . . ."

Cordona shouted to his sergeant. "Bonilla, how many have you?"

"Fifteen, Lieutenant."

Cordona looked at the two bandits from

the train. "These also?" Rivera nodded and pushed them forward. "What about the girl?"

Dillinger swung around quickly. "She's only a kid."

"Like all Americans you are a sentimentalist," Rivera said. "I would remind you that it was the girl who carried the arms on board, relying on the fact that she wouldn't be searched. She is directly responsible for the conductor's death."

Cordona grinned. "What a pity. I could find a better use for her." He sent her staggering toward Bonilla. "Six at a time. Detail ten men."

The windows of the second-class coach were crowded with faces, but there was no sound as the troopers pulled carbines from their scabbards and dismounted. They marched the bandits a short distance from the train and lined up the first six at the edge of a small hollow.

Cordona strolled toward them, paused, and barked an order. The sound of the volley echoed back from the mountains.

Cordona and Sergeant Bonilla drew their revolvers and moved forward as two of the fallen started to scream. Dillinger glanced at Rivera's impassive face, then looked across at the Indian girl.

Dillinger turned, climbed up into the train, and went along to Rivera's compartment. Villa was sitting on the bunk and Fallon lounged in the doorway, the barrel of his revolver propped across his left forearm.

"I'll take over here," Dillinger said.

"If you think I'm going to get any pleasure from watching that bunch outside, you're mistaken."

"Then go and have a smoke or something. I'd like a word with our friend here."

"Suit yourself," Fallon said, and he went away along the corridor.

Out of the silence, as Villa and Dillinger looked at each other, Cordona's voice drifted, sharp and clear on the morning air. There was no fear on Villa's face, only strength and a blazing intelligence.

"In case you have failed to discover the fact for yourself, I should inform you that the *patrón* enjoys this sort of thing."

"He called you a murderer."

"Quite true, senor. He had a foreman at his hacienda, and I had a young wife who killed herself. It did not take me long to discover the reason. It seemed to me that I was justified in putting my knife between his ribs. The *patrón* thought otherwise."

"I thought it would be something like that." The silence was broken by another volley. Dillinger moved out into the corridor and opened the door on the other side. He turned to Villa. "You'd better get going. You haven't much time."

"For what, a bullet in the head, senor?"

Dillinger took the remains of his packet of Artistas from his pocket and tossed it across. "You can keep them."

Villa's face split in a wide grin. "Sometimes God looks down through the clouds, senor. It is almost enough to give a man faith again."

He jumped down to the ground and ran for a narrow gully that curved up into the scrub that covered the lower slopes. Dillinger watched him disappear, then broke the revolver and emptied the rounds into his hand. He threw the rounds away and turned as the third volley crashed out.

A moment later Rivera climbed up and immediately frowned at the sight of the open door. "What has happened?"

"I'm afraid Villa got away," Dillinger said.

Cordona appeared in the doorway at ground level and stood there listening. Rivera said, "Why didn't you shoot him?"

"I tried to," Dillinger took the revolver from

his pocket and handed it across. "Unfortunately, the damned thing wasn't loaded."

As Dillinger turned from the rage in Rivera's eyes, Cordona ran for his horse, calling to his men. Dillinger moved along the coach between the staring people and sat down beside Fallon.

"What's all the excitement?" Fallon asked.

"Villa got away."

As the train moved forward with a sudden jerk, Fallon said, "Johnny, I kind of think you and that fellow you just let get away have a few things in common."

SIX

Dillinger had had enough of the train to last him. "I can't wait till they get my Chevy on the ground again," he told Fallon. "I want to pay my first call on what's-her-name – Rose – the lady at the hotel."

"First may be last if Rivera catches you. He doesn't like his people consorting with his enemies."

Dillinger grabbed Fallon by the front of his shirt. "Don't ever refer to me as one of his people. I don't belong to anybody."

"I'm sorry," Fallon said. "Meant no harm."

Dillinger released him. "Let's get one thing straight, Fallon. You're an American and I'm an American and nobody else around here is an American, which gives the two of us some common ground. That's one helluva lot more important than the fact that we are temporarily working for Rivera."

"What do you mean temporarily, Johnny?"

"Do you intend to stay? I don't intend to stay. Your problem is you can't go home and you need some dough to live on this side of the border, right?"

Fallon nodded.

"I intend to solve your problem just as soon as I solve my problem. My problem," Dillinger continued, "is that you blew my cover."

"You know I didn't want to."

"Some people who talk lose the use of their tongues."

"But Rivera knows."

"Well," Dillinger said, "he might just lose something else."

"What might that be?"

"The thing he values most."

"His life?" Fallon asked.

"His gold."

"We're almost there," Fallon said to Dillinger, who was getting more and more restless by the minute.

In the far distance a feather of smoke marked the train's progress, and a faint whistle echoed back eerily. The only signs of man's presence were the telegraph poles that branched from the railway line, marking the rough track which led over the lower slopes of the mountains to Hermosa.

The canyon floor was a waste of gravel and rock, bright in the morning sun, dotted with clumps of mesquite and sage. Already the fierce heat of this dead land was beginning to rise from the ground.

At the station, Rivera took charge of the flurry of activity, getting the luggage off, then supervising the unloading of the convertible.

"Tell them anybody scratches the paint on that car is going to get personal retribution from me," Dillinger told Rivera.

"You better learn some Spanish," Rivera said, "because as soon as we get to the mine, you're going to have to give your own orders."

"*Avanca*, hurry your ass, *vamos*, let's go, *vete*, get out of here. See," Dillinger said, "Fallon's been teaching me real good."

As the Chevy was driven down the ramp and came to rest on the solid but dusty ground, Dillinger patted the hood as if it was the nose of a horse. He drew some water from the station's outside pump, unscrewed the hood ornament and topped off the water in the radiator, then seated himself behind the wheel as if it were a throne.

"He is a child," Rivera said to Fallon.

"I wouldn't let him hear you say anything like that, Senor Rivera," Fallon whispered.

Just then a large buckboard came over the hill, pulled by two horses. Its ironbound wheels rattled over the stones in the dirt road.

The driver was an ox of a man. Under his wide-brimmed straw hat was a coarse and brutal face. A revolver and cartridge belt were strapped to his waist. He jumped to the ground and hurried forward, hat in hands.

"You're late, Rojas," Rivera said. "I've been waiting for at least half an hour."

"There was trouble at the mine, *patrón*," Rojas said in his harsh voice.

"Anything serious?"

"I took care of it." Rojas held up a fist like a rock.

"Good," Rivera said. "You got my wire?"

Rojas nodded and glanced at Dillinger. "Is this the one?"

Rivera said, "Senor Jordan will operate under my direct orders when circumstances require it. You, Rojas, will still control the men."

It was part of Rivera's plan never to let just one man be in charge of disciplining the work in the mine. Rojas would seek his favors as he did in the past. And the *gringo* would keep Rojas on his toes — as did the *gringo* before him. Rivera ruled by the oldest precept of all: divide and conquer.

"Hey," Rojas shouted, spotting Fallon, "the old fool has come back." He strutted over to Fallon, only to find Dillinger barring his way.

"The old fool's name is Mr. Fallon. My name is Mr. Jordan. Your name is?"

"Rojas!" Rojas shouted.

"Pleased to meet you, Senor Rojas." Dillinger smiled, extending his hand.

"Enough of this nonsense," Rivera said. "Get the buckboard loaded. We've wasted enough time."

Dillinger and Fallon stooped to raise one of the packing cases between them. Rojas, to show off, lifted the other easily in his great arms.

"We haven't got all day to waste while you two fool about like a couple of old washerwomen," Rojas shouted.

He pushed Fallon out of the way, grabbed at the packing case, and tried to pull it from Dillinger's grasp. Dillinger held on tight, and with the point of his right boot caught the Mexican on the shin, where a small blow will go a long way. Rojas staggered back with a curse. Dillinger lifted the packing case into the buckboard and turned to face him.

"Sorry, I didn't see you there," he said calmly.

The Mexican took a single step forward, his great hands coming up, and Rivera cried, "Rojas — leave it!"

Rojas reluctantly stepped back, eyes smoldering. "As you say, *patrón*."

"Follow us with the buckboard, Rojas," Rivera said. He got into the rear seat of the convertible as Fallon slipped in beside Dillinger at the wheel. As they went over the brow of the hill above the railway line, Dillinger offered Fallon a cigarette.

The old man said in a low voice, "What are you trying to do — commit suicide?"

"Rojas?" Dillinger shrugged. "He's like a slab of granite. Hit it in the right spot and it splits clean down the middle."

"I hear everything you say," Rivera said from the back seat.

"I intended you to hear it," Dillinger replied, winking at Fallon.

Dillinger knew that few men would survive a real brawl to the finish with Rojas. But that in itself was a challenge, something a man like Fallon would never be able to understand. You don't protect yourself from a bully by kissing his ass.

Dillinger leaned back in the seat, the heat of the day enfolding him, narrowing his eyes. Already the mountains were beginning to shimmer in the haze and lose definition. As they progressed higher into the Sierras, they passed through the tortured land of mesas and buttes, lava beds and twisted forests of stone — a savage, sterile land that, without its gold, was no place, Dillinger thought, for a good, clean-living bank robber.

"I've got six cans of gas in the trunk," Dillinger shouted to Rojas over the roar of the engine, "but they won't last forever. Where do you get gas out here?"

"You get it from me," Rivera said. "There is a tank at the hacienda."

Dillinger made a mental note to get some of that spare gas hidden somewhere. He didn't want the oats for his horse in Rivera's exclusive control.

"We haven't passed another car," Dillinger said.

"You miss the traffic back home?" Fallon said.

"Miss the paved roads is what I miss," Dillinger said, laughing. To Rivera he shouted, "When's this road going to get paved?"

"When hell freezes over," Fallon said low enough so that Rivera couldn't hear, and they both laughed.

"What are you two laughing at?" Rivera asked.

They both shrugged their shoulders at the same time. That made them laugh again, and this only aggravated Rivera more. As far as he was concerned, all Americans were just grown-up children.

An hour later they came around the shoulder of a mountain and saw an immense valley, a vast golden plain, so bright with heat it hurt the eyes to look at it. At the side was a great hogback of jagged peaks lifting into the clear air, incredibly beautiful in their savagery.

"The Devil's Spine," Fallon said, "is what they call it."

"Looks more like an impregnable fortress," Dillinger said.

"That's what it was in the old days. They say there's a ruined Aztec or Pueblo city somewhere on top."

Then the shot rang out, its sound dying away quickly. Dillinger instinctively jammed on the brakes. Shading his eyes with both hands, he examined the landscape.

Rivera said, "Probably a hunter."

"Hunter my ass," Fallon whispered.

Two Indians came over the hill riding small wiry ponies. They wore red flannel shirts and breech clouts, almost like a uniform, their long hair held back with bands of red flannel. Both of them carried rifles in the crooks of their arms. One of them held the carcass of a small deer across his blanket saddle.

"I told you it was a hunter," Rivera said.

"Hunting for *him*," Fallon whispered, indicating Rivera.

The Indians came down the slope. Instead of reining in their ponies, they let the animals crowd the stopped car, as if getting a message across.

Dillinger started to inch the convertible forward. One of the Indians raised the barrel of his rifle slightly.

"We don't want any trouble with these now," Rivera said, but Dillinger noticed in the rearview mirror that Rivera had slid his revolver out of his waistband onto the car seat beside him. Dillinger felt naked without his Colt.

Suddenly a voice called out, high and clear in a language that Dillinger was not familiar with, and a third rider came over the rim of the hill and moved down toward them fast. The first two Indians backed off slightly.

The new arrival reined in beside the Chevrolet and sat looking at Rivera, a fierce Indian with a wedge-shaped face that might have been carved from brown stone. He wore his black hair shoulder length under a shovel hat of the kind affected by some priests. A faded black cassock, pulled up to his knees, revealed untanned hide boots.

There was a silence, dust rising in small whirls as the ponies danced. Rivera had turned quite pale. He sat there staring back at the man, a muscle twitching in his jaw. The Indian returned the gaze calmly, the sunlight slanting across his slate-colored eyes, and then he abruptly turned his pony and went galloping away, followed by his companions, leaving the Chevy in a thin cloud of dust.

"One day I shall kill that animal," Rivera said, as Dillinger shifted gears and resumed speed.

"He didn't look like a man it would be too easy to kill," Dillinger commented.

"Filthy Apache," Rivera said.

"Name's Ortiz – Juan Ortiz," Fallon said. "His people call him Diablo. Ever come across Apaches before?"

Dillinger shook his head. "Only in the movies."

As Dillinger drove, Fallon filled him in.

"I guess you don't know too much about Apaches. Even their name means enemy. In the old days what they really lived for was war – against other tribes, against the settlers, against anybody. The ones in the States have been pretty much tamed. Lot of them shipped off to Florida somewhere. But the ones who came back down here . . . you don't want to tangle with them. Ortiz was what they call a Broncho Apache, the kind that stick to the old ways. When he broke his back in a riding accident, he ended up in the mission hospital at Nacozari. The Jesuits started educating him."

"Madness," Rivera interjected.

"Now he's a kind of lay brother or something," Fallon went on. "Works with the priest in Hermosa, Father Tomas. I think the old man would like the Indian to take his place when he's gone."

"Over my dead body," Rivera shouted. "Ortiz is a Chiricahua Apache, cruelest savages that ever set foot on God's earth."

"Geronimo was a Chiricahua," Fallon said. "It's only forty-five years since the American cavalry chased him right into these mountains and forced him to surrender."

"They should have been exterminated," Rivera said. "Every last one of them."

"He's doing a pretty good job of that right now up at the mine," Fallon whispered.

Rivera glared at them. "What are you whispering?"

"Don't get suspicious," Dillinger said. "Just two Yankees shooting the breeze." To Fallon he said, "The Indians at the mine are Apaches?"

Fallon nodded. "Mainly Chiricahua with a sprinkling of Mimbrenos."

"Where'd you learn all this?"

"From Chavasse. He's only a kid, mid-twenties, I'd guess, but he knows more about Apaches than any man I know. Came here from Paris to write a book about them and ended up being manager of Rose's place."

"Ah, Rose's place," Dillinger said.

A moment later they topped a rise and saw Hermosa in the valley below. There was a single street of twenty or thirty flat-roofed adobe houses, with a small whitewashed church with a bell tower at one end. The hotel, clearly visible, was the only two-storied building in the place.

Ragged, barefoot children ran after the Chevrolet, hands outstretched for coins. Rivera tossed some loose change to scatter them as the Chevy pulled up outside the hotel. On the crumbling facade, eroded by the heat of the desert, was a weathered sign board: SHANGHAI ROSE.

They climbed down and Rivera said, "I've had enough of this damned heat. I'll go out to the hacienda in the cool of the evening."

Rivera preceded them inside.

Fallon said to Dillinger, "I hope he doesn't run into Rose first thing. They hate each other's guts."

"Come on," Dillinger said, "I need to wet my whistle."

Inside there was no sign of Rivera. Fallon led the way into a large stone-flagged room. There were tables and chairs and a zinc-topped bar in one corner, bottles ranged behind it on wooden shelves. A young man poured beer into two glasses.

"Lord God Almighty's just been in to tell me you were here. He's gone up to his room," he said in English with a pronounced French accent.

Fallon picked up one of the glasses and emptied it in one long swallow. He sighed with pleasure and wiped his mouth with the back of one hand. "Another like that and I'll begin to feel human again. André Chavasse, meet Harry Jordan."

They shook hands, and, grinning, the young Frenchman put two more bottles on the counter. "We heard you were coming, courtesy of Rivera's telegraph. All the comforts of civilization, you see."

Chavasse was perhaps twenty-five, tall and straight with good shoulders, long black hair growing into foxtails at his neck. He had a handsome, even aristocratic face. The face of a scholar that was somehow relieved by the mobile mouth and humorous eyes. A man whom it would be hard to dislike.

Dillinger turned to Fallon. "What happens now?"

Fallon shrugged. "I suppose he'll want us at the mine tomorrow."

"Where do we stay?"

"Not at the hacienda, if that's what you're thinking. Rivera likes to keep the hired help in their place. There's a shack at the mine."

"You're staying here tonight," Chavasse

put in. "Rivera booked the room. It's the brown door at the top of the stairs."

Dillinger swallowed his beer and put down the glass. "If it's all right with you, I'll go up now. I feel as if I haven't slept in two days."

Fallon grinned at the Frenchman. "We had ourselves a rough ride in. Villa and his boys tried to take over the train, then we ran into Ortiz on the way. That didn't improve Rivera's temper, I can tell you."

"You saw Ortiz?" Chavasse asked eagerly. "How did he seem?"

"Had blood in his eyes, if you ask me. One of these days Rivera's going to do something about him."

"I would not like to be Rivera when that day comes," the Frenchman said gravely.

"You think he's dangerous?" Dillinger asked.

Chavasse took a cigarette from behind his ear and struck a match on the counter. "Let me tell you something, my friend. When you speak of the Apache, you speak of the most dangerous fighting men who ever walked the face of the earth. Rivera will find one day that he has pushed Ortiz once too often."

"And André should know," Fallon said.

"He's forgotten more about Apaches than I'll ever know."

"Right now," Dillinger said, "the only thing I'm interested in is about eight hours' sleep and whatever passes for a bath around here."

He walked out into the dark hall and paused to remove his jacket, blinking as the sweat ran into his eyes. A step sounded on the porch, and a spur jingled as someone entered.

He turned slowly. A young woman stood in the doorway looking at him, the harsh white light of the street outlining her slim figure. Booted and spurred, she wore Spanish riding breeches in black leather, a white shirt open at the neck, and a Cordoban hat.

But it was her face that blinded him, slightly Oriental eyes that were unusually large, the nose tilted, a sensuous mouth. There was about her a tremendous quality of repose, of tranquility almost, that filled him with a vague irrational excitement.

"You are Senor Jordan?" she said. "Harry Jordan, who is to run the mine for my uncle? I am Rose Teresa Consuela de Rivera."

She removed her hat, revealing blue-black

hair in braids coiled high on the back of her head. She put out her hand in a strangely boyish gesture, and he held it for a moment, marvelling at its coolness.

"You know, for the first time I actually feel glad I came to Mexico," he said.

The look that appeared on her face lasted for only a second, and then she smiled. Laughter erupted from her throat and the sound of it was like a ship's bell across water.

SEVEN

It was evening when Dillinger awakened. The coverlet had slipped from him in his sleep, and he lay there naked for a moment, watching the shadows lengthen across the ceiling, before swinging his legs to the floor. The window to the balcony stood open, and the curtains lifted in the slight breeze.

The courtyard at the rear of the hotel seemed deserted when he peered out. He quickly filled the enamel basin on the washstand with luke warm water from a stone pitcher, went out on to the balcony, and emptied the basin over his head.

He toweled himself briskly, pulled on his pants and shirt, then examined his face in the cracked mirror, running a hand gingerly over the stubble of beard. He opened one of his suitcases, took out razor and soap, and got to work.

125

There was a knock at the door, and as Dillinger turned, wiping soap from his face, Rivera entered. He carried Dillinger's shoulder holster and the Colt .32. He dropped them on the bed.

"Well, the world is full of surprises," Dillinger said.

"There are eight rounds in there, my friend, as you know. If we have trouble with Ortiz, do you think eight rounds are enough?"

Dillinger twirled the Colt around once by the finger guard. "One round is enough. Eight can be too few. Depends on the circumstances."

"Am I wrong to trust you?"

"You are wrong to trust anybody."

Rivera laughed. "Here are some pesos in case you want to indulge yourself in the saloon downstairs. It is not a gift, but an advance against your pay. Don't lose it at poker."

"I don't lose at poker," Dillinger said, "or anything else. What about gas for my car?"

"I trust you with a gun because I have two, and I have Rojas. But I do not trust you yet with gas, which would give you ideas of leaving Hermosa. Perhaps you will learn to ride a horse, Americano," Rivera said, laughing again as he closed the door behind him.

Somewhere, someone was playing a guitar, and a woman started to sing softly. Dillinger put on the shoulder holster, finished dressing, brushed back his hair, and went outside.

Rose de Rivera leaned against the balcony rail at the far end of the building, her face toward the sunset as she played. In Chicago, he had once heard a woman singing in Spanish in a night spot, but nothing like this. Rose's voice was as pure as crystal.

His step caused her to turn quickly, the sound of the last plucked string echoing on the evening air in a dying fall. She wore a black mantilla and a scarlet shawl was draped across her shoulders. Her dress of black silk was cut square across the neck. A band of Indian embroidery in blue and white edged the bodice.

She smiled. "You feel better for your bath?"

"You saw me?"

"Naturally I turned my back."

"My compliments on the dress. Not what I'd looked for."

"What did you expect, a *cheong sam?*

Something exotically Chinese? I wear those, too, if I'm in the mood, but tonight the Spanish half of me is what I feel."

"Are you more proud of your Chinese half or your Spanish half?"

"When I am feeling Chinese, I am proud to belong to an ancient and wise civilization except for one thing."

"What's that?"

"They invented gunpowder," she said, and she came close. He didn't know what to expect, but all she did was touch his side where the shoulder holster showed. "Who are you?" she said.

"What about your Spanish half?" he said, avoiding the question.

"My father used to tell me a Rivera sailed with the Spanish Armada."

"Didn't they lose against the English?"

"Is winning always everything?"

"The Americans beat the English."

"You are all terrible — vain, proud, impossible. What do you do for a living when you are not being strong man for my uncle? You know he is only playing you off against Rojas?"

"Yes."

"You know what happened to the last American who worked for him?"

"Yes."

"You think God gives you special protection that others do not have?"

"Yes," he said, laughing.

"You haven't answered anything I've asked you. Why are you being so mysterious?"

Dillinger thought how different she was from the pushovers back home. If he'd seen her in Indiana, he'd have thought of her as a stranger. His girl friend, Billie Frechette, was part Indian, really a dish, but nothing like Rose.

Dillinger kissed Rose lightly, the way he'd seen in the movies, keeping his chest away from her so she wouldn't feel the holster pressing against her. When he'd kissed Billie, she always put her hand down there right away, but Rose just smiled and turned away just enough so he wouldn't try again.

For a scond he thought it was his heart beating loudly, but it was a drum pulsating through the dusk. Voices started an irregular chant, the sound of it carrying toward them on the evening breeze. There was a flicker of flame from a hollow about a hundred yards away, and he noticed an encampment.

"Indians?"

"Chiricahua Apaches. They sing their evening prayer to the Sky God asking him to return the sun in the morning. Would you like to visit them? We have time before supper."

A flight of wooden stairs gave access to the courtyard, and they moved out through the great gateway toward the camp. Rose took his arm, and they walked in companionable silence.

After a while she said, "Fallon told me about how my uncle tricked you. He is a hard man."

"That's putting it mildly. How do you and he get on? Your uncle would like to see you go?"

"My presence is a continual irritation. He's offered to buy the hotel many times."

"But you don't want to leave?"

She shook her head. "When I was twelve my father sent me to convent school in Mexico City. I was there for five years. The day I returned, it was as if I had never been away."

"Why should that be?"

"This countryside," she said, "it's special. I don't like cities. Do you?"

"Not too much," he said.

"You are lying to please me."

He wanted to tell her that out in the countryside the banks were far apart and didn't have all that much money lying around. You had to go to the towns and cities for the big loot.

"In Mexico the people make heroes of their bandits. In the States, they make heroes of gangsters."

Was she guessing? Did she know something?

"Your uncle," Dillinger said, "is a bigger bandit than Villa."

"Yes," she said, laughing, and took his hand, but just for a moment. He felt desire again, and hoped it didn't make him crazy in the head the way it used to, the longing he couldn't stand.

"In the countryside here," she said, "have you noticed that the rocks shimmer, the mountains dance, and everything is touched with a blue haze? I think the countryside is like the face of God. Something we are not meant to see too clearly."

Her hand was on his arm, an unmistakable tenderness in her voice. He looked down at her. She flushed, and for a moment her self-assurance seemed to desert her. She smiled shyly, the evening light slanting across her face, and he knew that she was the most beautiful woman he had ever seen.

There was something close to a virginal fear in her eyes, and this time he squeezed her hand. Her smile deepened, and she no longer looked afraid, but completely sure of herself.

Without speaking, they turned and moved on toward the encampment. There were three wickiups, skin tents stretched tightly over a frame of sticks, grouped around a blazing fire. Three or four men crouched beside it singing, one of them beating a drum, while the women prepared the evening meal.

Several children rushed forward when they saw Rose, but then they stopped shyly. She laughed. "They are unsure with strangers."

Rose moved toward them, and the children crowded around, wreathed in smiles. She spoke to them in Apache, then beckoned to Dillinger. "There is someone I want you to meet."

She led the way to the largest wickiup. As they approached, the skin flap was thrown back. The man who emerged looked incredibly frail. He wore buckskin leggings, a breech clout, and a blue flannel shirt, a band of the same material binding the long gray hair.

His face was his outstanding feature. Straight-nosed, thin-lipped, with skin the color of parchment, there was nothing weak here, only strength, intelligence, and understanding. It could have been the face of a saint or a great scholar. By any standards he looked like a remarkable man.

Rose bowed her head formally, then kissed him on each cheek. She turned to Dillinger. "This is my good friend, Nachita — the last chief of the Chiricahuas."

Dillinger put out his hands in formal greeting and felt them gripped in bands of steel. The old man spoke in surprisingly good English, the sound like a dark wind in the forest at evening.

"You are Jordan, Rivera's new man."

"That's right," Dillinger said.

Nachita kept hold of his hands, and something moved in his eyes like a shadow across the sky. The old man released his grip, and Dillinger turned away, looking out across the camp.

"This is quite a place."

Behind him, Nachita picked up a dead stick and snapped it sharply, simulating the distinctive click of a gun being cocked. Dillinger instinctively reached for the gun under his arm and turned, crouching, the Colt in his hand as if by magic.

Nachita smiled, turned, and went back into his wickiup. His lesson was for Rose.

Here was a man who handled guns as if they were his hands.

Dillinger found Rose watching him, her face serious, the firelight flickering across it. He laughed awkwardly and put the gun away.

"Nachita certainly has a sense of humor," Dillinger said.

There was a pause as she looked at him steadily, and then she said, "We must go back to the hotel. Supper will be ready."

Dillinger took her arm as they left the camp. "How old is he?"

"No one can be sure, but he rode with Victorio and Geronimo, that much is certain."

"He must have been a great warrior."

They paused on a little hill beside the ruined adobe wall, and Rose said, "In eighteen eighty one, Old Nana raided into Arizona with fifteen braves. He was then aged eighty. Nachita was one of the braves. In less than two months they covered a thousand miles, defeated the Americans eight times, and returned to Mexico safely, despite the fact that more than a thousand soldiers and hundreds of civilians were after them. That is the kind of warrior Nachita was."

"Yet in the end the Apache were defeated,

as they were bound to be."

"To continue fighting when defeat is inevitable, this requires the greatest courage of all," she said simply.

Funny she should say that. He'd imagined himself one day coming into a bank he'd cased, but not well enough, and finding himself in a trap, every teller a G-man waiting with a gun instead of a wad of bills. He'd imagined himself backing out of the bank, shooting machine guns from both hips, knocking out the G-men like ducks in a gallery. He'd walked out of three movies where he could tell that the gangster was going to get killed in the end.

After supper Dillinger went into the bar and joined Fallon, who was sitting with Chavasse at a small table in the corner. Fallon produced a pack of cards from his pocket and shuffled them expertly.

"How about joining us for a hand of poker?"

"Suits me." Dillinger pulled forward a chair and grinned at the Frenchman. "Shouldn't you be working?"

Rose arrived, carrying bottles of beer and glasses on a tray. "My manager is permitted to mingle with special guests," she said.

"As always your devoted slave," Chavasse said dramatically, grabbing her hand and kissing it with pretended passion.

She ruffled his hair and disappeared into the kitchen.

Dillinger felt a sting of jealousy. He said, "She just introduced me to old Nachita. Quite a guy."

Chavasse said, "Everything that's best in a great people. He taught me more than anyone else about the Apache."

"Fallon tells me you're quite an expert on the subject."

The Frenchman shrugged. "I studied anthropology at the Sorbonne. I decided to do my field work for my thesis as far away from home as I could get. I meant to stay six months. But where in Paris could I get a job like this?" He laughed. "And such a nice boss."

Dillinger felt the sting again, wondering if there were some kind of relationship between the Frenchman and Rose. She had ruffled his hair as if it were nothing.

When they had finished their beer, Dillinger took some of Rivera's pesos from his pocket and slapped them on the table. "How about another round?" he said to Fallon.

"With pleasure," the old man replied, and left.

Dillinger lit a cigarette and leaned back in his chair. "This man we met on the road today, the one they call Diablo? Juan Ortiz. What do you make of him?"

"I honestly don't know. When he was younger, he had a bad reputation. They say he killed at least three men. Knife fights, things like that. There isn't much law in the mountains. I think in the old days he'd have made a name for himself, but that was before the Jesuits at Nacozari got their hands on him."

"And you really think he's changed?"

"What was your impression?"

Dillinger frowned, thinking about it. "I got the feeling he was trying to provoke Rivera in some strange way. It was almost as if he was inviting him to lose control."

"But why would he do that?" Chavasse asked.

"I don't know. Maybe to give him the excuse to strike back."

"This is a country saturated in blood. First the Aztecs, then the *conquistadores*. In four hundred years, nothing but slaughter."

"Yet you stay."

"I stay."

As Fallon returned with the beer, Dillinger spied Rivera sitting down at a small table. He wore clean clothes and smoked one of his usual cigarillos. When he rapped on the table with his cane, Chavasse got up and went across. He listened to Rivera and went into the kitchen. He returned with a tray containing a bottle of champagne and a glass. He placed them in front of Rivera and came back to the others.

"Champagne?" Dillinger said blankly. "Here?"

"Kept especially for Lord God Almighty," Chavasse explained. "One of his favorite ways of publicly indicating the gap between himself and others."

At that moment Rojas swaggered into the bar, looking as if he'd been drinking. When he saw Rivera, he pulled off his hat and bowed respectfully. Rivera called him over and murmured something to him. Rojas nodded and after a moment crossed to the bar and hammered on it.

"What about some service here?"

Before Chavasse could get up, Rose appeared from the kitchen. She walked round the counter and stood facing him, hands on hips. "In the first place, lower your voice. In the second, take that thing off and hang it in the hall with the others." She pointed to the revolver strapped to his waist.

Rojas turned meekly and went outside. He came back without the revolver, and she placed a bottle of tequila and a glass on the counter.

Rojas filled his glass with tequila and swallowed it down, the spirit slopping out of the corners of his mouth. Dillinger looked at Rivera, who returned the gaze coolly, filled his glass with champagne, and sipped.

Dillinger drank some of the lukewarm beer and put the glass down firmly. "How much is that champagne?"

"Twenty-five pesos a bottle," Chavasse said.

Dillinger sighed, pulled off his right boot, and extracted a folded bank note from beneath the inner sole. He pulled the boot back on and flicked the note across to the Frenchman.

"Twenty dollars American. Will that do?"

"I should imagine so."

"Then get a bottle and glasses. Ask Rose to join us."

Chavasse looked at Rivera and grinned, pushed back his chair and went into the kitchen.

"There goes my mad money," Dillinger said ruefully.

Chavasse hurried back, followed by Rose

with a bottle of champagne and glasses on a tray. Suddenly everyone seemed to be laughing, and there was an atmosphere of infectious gaiety. Dillinger glanced at Rivera, the Mexican returning his gaze.

"To the provider must go the honor of opening it," Fallon said.

As Dillinger reached out, a shadow fell across the table. Rojas pushed Chavasse out of the way and wrapped a huge hand about the bottle. "I always wanted to try this stuff."

Dillinger grabbed the neck of the bottle firmly. "Then go and buy your own."

"Why should I, Yankee, when you are here to provide it for me?"

The Mexican tried to lift the bottle from the table. Dillinger exerted all his strength to keep it there. Rojas grabbed the edge of the table and tried to turn it over while Dillinger leaned his weight against it.

As Dillinger half turned in his chair, he had a glimpse of Rivera still sitting calmly on the other side of the room sipping champagne. Only now there was a smile on his face, and Dillinger knew that the whole thing had been arranged. Rojas imagining he was going to teach Dillinger his place on the *patrón*'s orders. Rivera intent on discovering just how good he was.

Rose took Rojas by the arm and tried to pull him away. "Please," she said. "No fighting in my place."

Rojas, his hand still on the champagne bottle, turned toward Rose and spit in her face.

Chavasse was livid. All Dillinger's repressed anger boiled up. A hard ball of fury rose in his throat, choking him. With a swift movement, he leaned back, removing his weight from the table, and Rojas lost his balance, releasing his grip on the bottle as he sprawled on his hands and knees. Dillinger smashed the bottle across the back of the bull neck and stood up.

The others moved hurriedly out of the way. Rojas shook his head several times and started to get up. Dillinger snatched up his chair and smashed it across the great head and shoulders once, splintering the chair like matchwood.

Rose was wiping her face, crying.

Rojas shook his head, wiping blood from his face casually. He got to his feet, his eyes never leaving Dillinger.

He stood there swaying, apparently half out on his feet, and Dillinger moved in fast. Rojas took a quick step backwards, then smashed his bull fist savagely into Dillinger's face.

141

Dillinger lay on the floor for a moment, his head singing from the force of the blow. Rivera laughed, and, as Dillinger started to his feet, Rojas delivered a powerful blow to his stomach and hit him again on the cheek, splitting the flesh to the bone.

Rojas came in fast, boot raised to stamp down on the unprotected face. Dillinger grabbed for the foot and twisted, and Rojas fell heavily across him. They rolled over and over, and as they crashed against the wall, Dillinger pulled himself on top. He reached for Rojas's throat and was suddenly thrown backward.

As Dillinger scrambled to his feet, Rojas rose to meet him. Dillinger feinted with his left and smashed his right fist against the Mexican's mouth, splitting the lips so that blood spurted. Dillinger moved out of range, then feinted again and delivered the same terrible blow. As he stepped back, his foot slipped so that Rojas got home a stunning punch to the forehead that sent Dillinger staggering back against the open window, where he almost went over the low sill. As he straightened up, Rojas lurched forward again. Dillinger ducked, twisted a shoulder inward, and sent the Mexican over his hip through the open window in a savage cross-buttock.

Dillinger scrambled across the sill, almost losing his balance, and arrived on the board-walk as Rojas rose to his feet. Dillinger, enjoying the best fight he'd had since he was a kid, hit him with everything he had, full in the face, and Rojas went backward into the street.

For a little while he lay there as Dillinger hung on to one of the posts that supported the porch. Slowly, the Mexican got to his feet. He swayed in the lamplight, his face a mask of blood, eyes burning with hate, and then his hand went around to the back of his belt. As he came forward, a knife gleamed dully.

Behind Rojas, old Nachita appeared from the darkness like a ghost. The Indian's hand moved in a single smooth motion, and a knife thudded into the boardwalk at Dill-inger's feet.

There was a mist before Dillinger's eyes. He felt as if he had little strength left in him. He picked up the knife and went toward Rojas, the knife held out in front of him.

He heard a voice say, his own voice like that of a stranger, "Come on, you bastard. If that's the way you want it."

Rojas, who had been prepared to fight

knife-to-hands, not knife-to-knife, stumbled away into the darkness.

Dillinger swung around, the power in him like a white-hot flame. They were all there on the boardwalk, looking at him strangely in the lamplight, fear on their faces. Rivera stood at the top of the steps, and Dillinger went forward, the knife extended.

Rivera staggered back, almost losing his balance, and hurried into the hotel. Dillinger was aware of a grip of steel on his arm. Old Nachita took the knife from him, supporting him at the same time, and Rose appeared on the other side.

She was still crying, and Dillinger couldn't understand why. As they led him forward, he frowned, desperately trying to concentrate, and then, as they reached his room, Fallon appeared and opened the door, his face ablaze with excitement.

"Jesus, Johnny, I never seed anything like that in my whole damn life. You really took that big ox apart."

"Johnny?" It was Rose's voice. "I thought your name was Harry. Who are you?"

He turned to her voice, smiling foolishly and trying to speak, and then the lamp seemed to revolve into a spinning ball that grew smaller and smaller and finally disappeared into the darkness.

This time J. Edgar Hoover had only one operative standing in front of his desk. He'd just finished reading the man's report.

"You've got a pretty good fix on him."

The man said, "He didn't do the California job or the Chicago job. The woman we picked up in Kansas swore she'd seen a white Chevy convertible in Doc's barn. If Doc didn't take it to Florida, maybe Dillinger took it south."

"You think it's Mexico."

"Mr. Hoover, if there was this scale manhunt on for me, I'd get out of the country."

"Okay. Send a wire to Mexico City. Ask them to query the chiefs of police in all northern provinces if a white Chevrolet convertible has been seen driven by an American. Ask them to keep it confidential. Just say the car is stolen and the man who's driving it is probably armed and dangerous."

EIGHT

The desert was a dun-colored haze reaching toward the mountains, the canyons still dark with shadow. It was the best hour of the day, the air cool and fresh before the sun started to draw the heat out of the barren earth.

Dillinger, behind the wheel of the Chevrolet, Fallon beside him, seemed to ache in every limb. He drove slowly over the rough trail, both to spare himself and because Rose was cantering along beside them on a bay horse.

"How do you feel?" Rose asked.

"I guess I'm not very handsome today." The right side of his face was disfigured by a large purple bruise.

"Do you think it was worth it?"

He shrugged. "Is anything?"

She said to Fallon, "Do you think he tries to commit suicide often?"

"Only on his bad days," the old man replied.

The trail wound its way between a forest of great tapering pillars of rock and entered a narrow canyon. In the center it widened into a saucer-shaped bowl, then narrowed again before emerging once more into the plain.

At this point the track branched off in two directions, and Rose halted. "Here is where I leave you. I'm going straight to the mine. Father Tomas is staying at the village for a few days and I promised to take him some medicine. Perhaps I'll see you later?"

Dillinger switched off the motor. "I think maybe we should have a talk first."

She sat there looking down at him and then nodded, "All right."

The horse ambled forward. Dillinger got out of the car and walked beside her, a hand on a stirrup. "I hope you don't think I – well, you know, was too pushy last night."

"As long as you understand that a kiss is not necessarily a promise of better things to come."

"I'm used to, well, a different kind of woman."

"You're blushing."

"I don't blush," Dillinger said sharply.

"Perhaps it is the sun," she smiled. "I think I'd better tell you something."

He felt that jealous ping again. He was certain she was going to tell him that she and the Frenchman were involved.

"Harry — or Johnny — whatever your real name is . . ." She looked over at Fallon to make sure he was out of earshot. "I was in the telegraph office first thing this morning. There's a police alarm out for a white Chevrolet."

"From Santos or Hernandez?"

"To them, from the F.B.I."

"Damn. Who knows about this?"

"The telegrapher. He hasn't seen your car. But he is paid by Rivera to tell him everything that comes in over the wire."

"Are there police in town?"

"Two. Both old. They won't see the message if Rivera doesn't want them to. Why are they looking for you?"

"Not me. My car. I must have lent it to a bootlegger."

"You are very charming when you lie." She patted her whinnying horse's neck. "Till later then. Perhaps I can put something on that poor face of yours."

"What?"

"My hand," she said, cantering away.

Half an hour later the white convertible came over a rise, and the track dipped unexpectedly into a wide valley. Below them stood a brown, stone hacienda built in the old colonial style.

The place seemed prosperous and in good repair, with well-kept fences around a large paddock. A worker in riding boots and faded Levis was saddling a gray mare. He turned and looked up at them, shading his eyes with one hand, then went toward the house.

Dillinger drove into the courtyard and pulled up at the bottom of the steps. As he got out, a little girl ran out of the front door, tripped, and lost her balance. As she started to fall, he moved forward quickly and caught her.

She was perhaps three years old and wore a blue riding suit with a velvet collar and brass buttons. She was frail, her brown eyes very large in a face that was too pale for a land of sun.

Dillinger set her on her feet gently, and a woman moved out on to the steps and gathered the child to her. "Juanita, how many times have I told you?" She looked up at Dillinger. "My thanks, senor."

She was a slender woman with graying hair and a black dress buttoned high to the neck. She wore no jewelry, and her face was lined and careworn, the eyes moving ceaselessly from place to place as if she were continually anxious about something.

As Dillinger removed his hat, Rivera appeared on the porch. he stood there looking at his wife, saying nothing, and she took the child by the hand and hurried inside.

Rivera turned to Dillinger. "I'd intended coming with you to the mine, but there are matters I must attend to here first. Rojas is already there. He'll show you over the place. I'll be along later."

He went back inside.

Too bad, Dillinger thought. If he'd known, Rose could have driven with them instead of taking the horse. She could have sat between him and Fallon up front, her left thigh against his right thigh.

Dillinger drove away, following Fallon's directions up out of the valley. The heat was increasing. He could feel the sweat from his back soak through his shirt.

Finally, they came over the crest of a hill and saw a valley below. Dillinger had seldom seen a more dismal sight in his life. There were perhaps twenty or thirty crumbling adobe houses with a dungheap at one end and what appeared to be an open latrine running straight through.

There was a well in the center of the village, and a woman was lifting a pitcher of water to the ground as they approached. She was in an advanced stage of pregnancy, her belly swollen. She paused, obviously tired, and Dillinger got out of the car.

He took the pitcher from her and said *"Donde su casa?"* surprising himself at the bits of Spanish he had picked up by just listening.

She pointed silently across the street. He walked before her and opened the door. There was only one room, and it had no windows. It took several moments for his eyes to become accustomed to the half-light. When they did, he saw an old woman stirring something in a pot over a smoldering fire. A few Indian blankets in the corner were obviously used for bedding, but there was no furniture. He put down the pitcher, his stomach heaving at the smell of the place, and went outside.

"That place isn't fit for a dog to live in," he said to Fallon as he climbed back into the car. "Isn't anyone doing anything for these people?"

"Rose does what she can. So does Father Tomas. He's the best friend they've got, but they're like zombies. Rivera has the men doing a fourteen-or fifteen-hour day. They're worked so hard they don't give a damn about anything anymore."

Rose's horse was tethered beside a buckboard outside a house at the other end of the village, and Dillinger braked to a halt.

"Is the mine far from here?"

"Just over the rise, three or four hundred yards."

"You walk on up. I'll join you later."

Fallon trudged away up the street, and Dillinger approached the hut just as Rose, hearing the car, came out. She looked tired and pale, and there was sweat on her face. Dillinger took the canteen from the Chevrolet and handed it to her. "You don't look too good."

"There's not much air in there, that's all." She poured a little water into the palm of one hand and rubbed it over her face.

"Who's inside?"

"Father Tomas. I'd like you to meet him."

Dillinger followed her inside. The place was exactly the same as the other, the room half-filled with acrid smoke from the fire of dried dung. A man lay on a filthy blanket in the corner, an Apache woman crouched at his feet.

A white-haired old priest sat beside him on a small stool, gently sponging the damp forehead. Dillinger leaned closer. The skin on the man's face was almost transparent, every bone clearly defined. He was obviously very ill.

The priest clasped his hands together and started to pray, his face raised to heaven, a single shaft of sunlight through the smoke hole lighting upon the white hair.

Dillinger made his way outside, Rose following him. From his pocket he took the flat bottle of tequila that Chavasse had given him against emergencies. He unscrewed the cap and swallowed.

He turned to look at her. "Can't anything be done?"

"My father had a plan, a wonderful plan. At the far end of the valley, above the hacienda where the streams run down from the snows of the sierras, he wanted to build a dam. With its waters, the whole valley would have flowered."

"And your uncle doesn't see things that way?"

"I'm afraid not, senor," Father Tomas said, emerging from the house behind them. "Don Jose is interested only in obtaining as much gold as these wretched people can squeeze from the mine. When he is satisfied that the well has run dry, he will leave for what to him is a more favorable climate."

"This is Senor Jordan, Father," Rose said. "The one my uncle forced into coming here."

The old man took Dillinger's hand. "I heard what happened in Hermosa last night, my son. God moves in His own good time. Perhaps Don Jose made a mistake when he tricked you into coming here."

Before Dillinger could reply, two horsemen galloped down the hill, one behind the other, and turned into the street. Rojas was slightly in front. He reined in so sharply that his horse danced sideways on its hind legs, crowding Dillinger, Rose, and the old priest back against the wall, splashing them with mud.

His companion was a mestizo in a battered red straw hat. A man who had turned against his own people. He had coarse, brutal features, and a hide whip dangled from his right wrist.

Rojas sat there glaring at Dillinger. Two of his teeth were missing, and his lips were twice their normal size. A livid green bruise stretched from his chin across the left side of his face to the eye, almost closing it.

"What do you want?" Father Tomas said.

"I've come for Maco. The swine's not turned up for work again."

"He's too sick," the old man said.

"They're always too sick." Rojas dismounted. "They know we need every available man at the mine, and they take advantage of it."

He took a step forward, and Dillinger put a hand against his chest. "You heard what Father Tomas said."

Rojas moved back, and his right hand dropped to the butt of his revolver.

"I wouldn't do that if I were you," Dillinger said calmly.

Through the stillness they could hear the rattle of the steam engine that operated the conveyor belt up at the mine and the thin, high voices of the Indians calling to each other. The mestizo with the whip fidgeted nervously, avoiding Dillinger's eye. Rojas turned without a word, scrambled into the saddle, and lashed his horse into a gallop.

Dillinger turned to Father Tomas and Rose. "I think it's time I took a closer look at this mine."

Rose climbed into the saddle of the horse. "I'm returning to Hermosa now. Will you be coming in this evening?"

"You sure you want to keep company

155

with a desperate character like me?"

"Perhaps I can make you see the error of your ways."

"I doubt it, but I tell you what you can do."

"What's that?"

"You can buy the champagne this time."

She smiled and he slapped the horse on the rump and it galloped away.

He drove out of the village, followed the track up to a small plateau that was like a shelf in the face of the mountain. Water, splashing in a dozen threads from the snow-capped peak, had been channeled to run through a stoutly constructed shed, open at both ends.

It was a scene of great activity. An old steam engine puffed smoke near the mouth of the mine, drawing in a steel cable that hauled ore-laden trucks along a narrow track.

Dillinger got out of the Chevrolet and headed toward the ore shed. Fallon emerged to beckon him in. "Come see this," the old man said.

Inside the ore shed the only piece of machinery was a steam-operated crusher. Two Indians fed its flames with wood. The heat was unbearable. The water ran into a great tank lined against leakage with clay, and there were several cradles and two puddling troughs. The Indians who worked at them were stripped to the waist, their bodies shining with sweat.

"Why doesn't he bring in more machinery? If the mine's producing anything like a return, it would pay him."

"I told you they closed it in 1893 after the rock came down on more than fifty Indians. Since I've been here we've had so many cave-ins I've lost count. Men get killed all the time."

"Then the timbering must be at fault. Don't tell me Rivera's trying to save money there, too?"

Fallon shook his head. "The mountain's just waiting to come down on all of us. Every time you cough in the tunnel, a rock comes down. That's why we daren't use any more machinery. The vibration might be all that's needed."

They paused beside three wooden cabins, and Fallon opened the door of the first one. "This is where we live."

It was plainly furnished with table and chairs, two bunks, and an iron stove in one corner.

"Who uses the other two cabins?" Dillinger asked.

"One of them is the powder store. Rojas lives in the end one."

"Where is he now?"

"Went into the mine about five minutes ago, looking like murder. I pity any poor devil in there who gets in his way."

They walked beside the rails past the steam engine and entered the mouth of the tunnel. Dillinger had expected it to be cooler in the tunnel. Instead, the heat was worse.

"What's wrong with the ventilation in here?"

"The air shaft was blocked by a rockfall a couple of months ago," Fallon replied. "Rivera gave orders to leave it alone and concentrate on bringing the ore out."

"Hell, that sounds dangerous to me. Didn't you tell him that?"

Fallon shrugged. "He said we didn't have time to waste."

They turned a corner and the sunlight died, leaving them in a place of shadows illuminated by lanterns and guttering candles. When they reached a fork, Fallon hesitated. "There are two faces, north and south. Rojas could be at either."

They stood to one side as a truck pushed by half a dozen weary, dust-coated Indians moved past them. Fallon lifted a lantern from a hook in the wall and led the way into the darkness.

Gradually, Dillinger was conscious of faint sounds, and a light appeared. The tunnel narrowed until they had to stoop, and then it opened into a low-roofed cavern, badly illuminated by several candles.

Ten or twelve Indians crouched at the rock face, swinging short-handled picks. Others gathered the ore into baskets, which they emptied into another truck. The air was heavy, thick with dust and almost unbreatheable.

Dillinger turned away and moved back along the tunnel. He paused once, leaning against the wall, and coughed harshly, trying to clear the dust from his lungs. There was a sudden slide of pebbles from the darkness above.

"See what I mean?" Fallon said.

Dillinger didn't reply. He turned and moved back along the tunnel. Suddenly a man cried out in pain, the sound echoing flatly through the darkness.

Dillinger started to run. Gradually the light increased as he came out into the main tunnel, and he saw several Indians crouched against the wall, their truck tipped onto its side, ore blocking the track.

With one hand Rojas kept an old gray-haired Indian down on his knees. In the other he wielded a whip. It whistled through the air and curved around the thin shoulders, drawing blood. The old man cried out in pain.

When the whip rose again, Dillinger spun Rojas around and sent him crashing back against the wall. The Mexican gave a cry of rage and came up from the floor, drawing his revolver.

Dillinger moved in fast, ramming one arm against the man's throat, grabbing the gun hand and forcing the barrel toward the floor. For a moment they swayed there, and suddenly the revolver went off.

The sound re-echoing in the confined space was like a charge of dynamite exploding, and the earth seemed to tremble. As the Indians cried out in alarm, the mountain rushed in on them.

NINE

Dillinger remembered thinking, "This is it," as everything seemed to cave in all around him. He'd thought that once before in a small bank, an easy job; as he'd gone out the door carrying a bagful of bills, he saw ten feet ahead of him a man too old to still be a cop pointing a .38 at him from a distance nobody could miss at. "This is it," he'd thought, but the policeman's gun clicked, a misfire, and Dillinger had just kicked the weapon out of the cop's hand and jumped on the running board of the waiting car that took him on the git road to safety. That was the time he decided never to do a job without the protection of a bulletproof vest.

A bulletproof vest, even if he'd had one on, is no protection against a mine cave-in. Dillinger lurched forward, groping his way through clouds of dust. He tripped and fell on his hands and knees. He lay there for a moment, coughing and choking, and then scrambled up a sloping ramp of rubble to where light gleamed between stones.

He pulled at the stones with his fingers, and Fallon and Rojas appeared on either side of him, the Mexican obviously gripped by fear. A few minutes later the gap was wide enough, and they crawled out into the sunlight followed by four Indians.

A crowd was already running toward them from the ore shed, and Father Tomas came over the hill behind them in his buckboard. He reined in a few yards away and jumped to the ground.

"How bad is it?"

Fallon's face was a mask of dust. "I think the whole damned mountain's fallen in."

Dillinger took the bottle of tequila from his pocket, swallowed some, and passed it to Fallon. Rojas was sitting on a boulder, his head in his hands, dazed. Dillinger handed him the bottle of tequila and said roughly, "Get some of that down you, and pull yourself together."

Rojas took a long swallow, coughing as the fiery liquid burned into his stomach. He got to his feet and wiped his mouth.

"How many men are still inside?" Dillinger demanded.

"I'm not sure. Twenty or so."

Fallon scrambled on top of the boulder and addressed the crowd in Spanish. "Those men in there haven't got long. If we're going to do anything, it's got to be now. Get pickaxes, shovels, baskets — anything you can lay your hands on."

Dillinger and Fallon led the way up the slope and started to pull boulders away from the entrance. Everyone joined in, even the old priest, forming a human chain to pass the earth and stones backwards as they progressed farther into the tunnel.

The gap through which they had made their escape was widened until it would admit a dozen men with equipment. Lanterns were passed through. Dillinger stripped off his shirt and examined the wall of rock that filled the rear of the tunnel.

It was hot. The air was heavy with the settling dust. Fallon moved beside him. "We've got to keep on digging. At least we've got the tools."

Rojas crawled through the darkness to join them. He reached up and touched the ceiling. Immediately several flakes of stone peeled away.

"It wouldn't take much to bring down the rest."

"We'll be all right if we're damn careful," Fallon told him, trying to sound confident.

They labored feverishly in the weird, dust-filled light, stripped to their waists, sweat glistening on their naked backs. Rojas proved to be a pillar of strength, his great hands lifting, unaided, rocks which Dillinger and Fallon together would have found difficulty in moving. Behind them formed a line of Indians, passing the baskets of stone and earth backwards.

They worked in shifts, supporting the roof with fresh timbering as they advanced, but progress was slow. The lack of air and the great heat made it impossible for anyone to last at the face for longer than half an hour at a time. By the middle of the afternoon they were no more than forty feet into the tunnel.

Just after three, Rojas, in front, let loose a groan.

"What is it?" Dillinger demanded.

Rojas turned, the whites of his eyes shining in the lamplight. Dillinger crawled forward into the narrow cutting they had cleared in the heart of the rockfall. An immense slab of stone weighing at least five or six tons was stretched across their path.

Fallon crouched at his side and whistled softly. "We haven't a hope in hell of moving that by hand."

"What about dynamite?" Dillinger said.

Rojas sucked in his breath sharply. "You must be crazy. Half a stick would be enough to bring down the rest of the mountain."

"If there's anyone still alive back there, they're going to die anyway," Dillinger said. "At least we'd be giving them a sporting chance."

He crawled back along the tunnel past the line of Indians and emerged into bright sunlight. The whole village seemed to be there, women and children included, some squatting on the earth, others standing as they waited patiently.

Dillinger thought, Whoever thinks robbing a bank is dangerous ought to try this sometime.

An Indian handed him a bucket of water, and he raised it to his lips, drinking deeply before pouring the rest over his head and shoulders. Then he noticed Rivera.

"How bad?" Rivera asked.

"We've gone as far as we can with pick and shovel. There's a five-ton slab blocking our way."

"Have you tried splitting it?"

"It would take hours by hand," Dillinger

said. "Dynamite is the only answer."

"It could also bring the whole place down."

"Maybe, but there are at least twenty men in there according to Rojas. If we don't get them out within three or four hours, they'll be dead."

"You don't even know that they are alive now."

"For Christ's sake, we've got to try," Fallon said.

"He's right," Dillinger said. "They deserve some sort of chance."

Rivera said, "I am not going to destroy the source of gold to save a few Indians. You can try to reach them with pick and shovel. On no account will you use dynamite."

"We'll see about that," Dillinger said.

As Dillinger turned to go, he heard Fallon's "Watch out!" Rivera had leveled the revolver in his hand at the back of Dillinger's skull.

"One false move and you're dead," Rivera said. Then he called out, "Are you there, Rojas?"

"Yes, *patrón*." Rojas had three mestizos beside him now, all armed.

"Excellent. Now this is what I want. You, Fallon, get back into the mine and keep the men digging around the big slab. No dynamite!"

"Yes, senor," Fallon said like a beaten man.

"As for you," Rivera said to Dillinger, "your friend Rojas will sit alongside you as you drive your pretty white car back to Hermosa where you will be turned over to the authorities, who will advise their American counterparts that they have captured the man in the white convertible. Understood? You are finished here."

Dillinger looked around at what "here" represented. A crowd of rescue workers and their women. Rose, watching him helplessly from less than fifty feet away. Next to her, in black, Father Tomas. And far behind them, standing on an outcrop of rock, Ortiz and two of his warriors.

Dillinger knew instinctively how men like Rivera control a community by their harshness in public. He would not hesitate to shoot "as an example to others." The easiest one to shoot and get away with it was the big-shot *gringo* who was an escapee from the law in his own country.

To Dillinger's surprise, it was Father Tomas who came forward.

Immediately Rivera waved his revolver in his direction. "Do not come closer, Father."

Father Tomas did not miss a step until he was close enough to Rivera to touch him. He touched the left arm, the one without the gun, and said, "Please, Senor Rivera, this man from

America is right. We must try quickly to save the lives of those souls who are entombed in the mine. If the only way to work quickly is dynamite, let it be dynamite. If God wills, the men will be rescued alive."

"And if God doesn't will, the mine will collapse, and not another ounce of gold ore will be got out of there. Let go of my arm, Father. Tend to God's business, not mine."

"Please, let the men be rescued," Father Tomas said, "and put that thing away." He reached for Rivera's gun arm, and in that same instant, Rivera turned to face him and point-blank shot Father Tomas in the forehead. The force of the bullet sent Father Tomas back into the dirt, as people gasped and cried out.

"Rivera," Dillinger said, "you are a son of a bitch and a coward."

Rojas was about to strike Dillinger when a voice, louder than the crash of thunder, was heard. It was Oritz, standing on the rock with his two warriors. "Rivera," he boomed, "as God is my witness, you are a dead man!"

Ortiz and his men clambered off the rock, mounted, and with a war cry as of old, galloped off.

As Dillinger drove slowly back to Hermosa, trying for the second time in a month to hatch

Checkout
Check us out on Facebook
and Instagram!
740.349.5500
Title: Dark souls [VIDEO GAME (Nintendo Switch)] : remas

Due: 4/3/2023

Title: Dillinger [large print]

Due: 4/24/2023

LCL DOWNTOWN NEWARK
740-349-5500
Follow us on
Facebook and Instagram!

lickingcountylibrary.org

an escape plan, he could see that Rojas, sitting in the passenger seat, would much rather find an excuse for drilling him than for turning him over to the authorities as Rivera had ordered.

Suddenly there was the sound of hoofbeats, and catching up with the car were Ortiz and his warriors on their ponies. Ortiz's rifle was in his saddle, but he knew it was useless to draw. The hated Rojas would kill the American before Ortiz's bullet would reach Rojas.

"American," Ortiz yelled. "Rivera should let you use dynamite. The men in the mine are my people," the Apache said. He dug his heels into his pony and went over the ridge toward the village in full gallop.

"Catch up to him," Rojas ordered.

"I don't dare," Dillinger said. "The radiator's boiling. Can't you see the steam? We have to add water."

"You have a water can in the trunk?"

"Only gasoline."

"Don't get nervous," Dillinger said to Rojas. He stopped the car, and then he did a trick that he'd learned when he was sixteen years old, what they used to do in Indiana if an old car boiled over far from a gas station. He unscrewed the radiator cap, stood on the hood, unbuttoned his trousers, and in full view of Rojas, urinated a stream three feet straight into the steaming radiator.

As they entered the town, Dillinger and Rojas could see a huge milling crowd around Ortiz in the main square.

"He's getting them roused up," Rojas said. "Why are you stopping?"

"Too many people."

"Keep going!" Rojas barked.

"I'll hit somebody," Dillinger said, the car now going at a snail's pace.

"Faster," Rojas said. "Run the vermin down!"

As Dillinger applied the brakes, the crowd turned as if it were one person, and everyone, women, children, some men, all came toward the car. These were not a beaten people, but an aroused mob.

Dillinger could hear Ortiz yelling, "There in the car is Rivera's man Rojas, the murderer's murderer, who will not use dynamite to free our trapped people."

Rojas knew how to read faces.

"Back this out of here," Rojas ordered.

"You drive it," Dillinger said, putting on the hand brake and getting out of the car.

"I don't know how to drive, you idiot!" Rojas yelled. "Get back in here."

"Put the gun down in the driver's seat. Gently."

Rojas was livid, but when he turned to face the mob, he knew that however many people he might shoot, before he could reload they would be at him like ants, choking him, stomping on him, then stringing him up. Carefully, he put the gun down in the driver's seat. Dillinger picked up the gun as he slid behind the wheel and slowly backed the car away from the mob, then turned. He sped out of town, holding the wheel with his left hand, the gun aimed at Rojas in his right, and at the top of his voice singing the song that was on the Hit Parade when he left home, "Who's Afraid of the Big Bad Wolf?"

Ortiz rode hard for almost half an hour before reaching an encampment of five wickiups grouped beside a small pool of water in a horseshoe of rock that sheltered them from the wind.

The carcass of a small deer roasted over a fire on an improvised spit, and three young Indians squatted beside it smoking cigarettes.

Ortiz dismounted and tethered his pony. He gazed at the men impassively for a moment, then went into his wickiup, lay on his face, and closed his eyes.

In the darkness there was only a deep satisfaction and a hate that burned like a white-hot flame, so pure that it was an ecstasy, a mystical reality as great as any the Fathers at Nacozari had told him about.

Ortiz decided what he must do. He left the peace of the wickiup and assembled his warriors.

He said, "I have worn a priest's cassock in the hope that I would one day be received as a man of God. Today, I saw Father Tomas, a man of God, shot in the head by that butcher Rivera. Before everything, I am an Apache," he said, and with one rent of his powerful hands ripped the cassock from his body and flung it aside. Underneath he was wearing the breech clout, and on his head he now put the headband of an Apache warrior.

He continued, "This is what we must do. Chato and Cochin, go for those of our brothers who would join us in this thing. Ride to the north pasture, break down the fences, and slaughter some of the cattle. You will not harm the herdsman. He must be spared to carry the news to Rivera."

He turned to the third man. "You, Kata, get as many rifles as we have hidden and come back here to me."

They moved to do his bidding, and within a few minutes he was alone listening to the sound of them vanishing into the dusk.

He stood for a while, thinking, then picked up a handful of dust and tossed it into the fire. In his veins, he felt the fire of vengeance.

TEN

As he drove, Dillinger was lecturing Rojas. "When I was a kid," he said, "I learned that some people have big fists and small brains. Other guys have lots of brains, but their fists are useless. And some have brains and fists and know how to use them both. I been trying to pigeonhole you, Rojas, and I figure you for the first kind, big fists, small brains."

"Gringo, I will get you to the Federalistas, sooner or later, just as Senor Rivera wants."

Dillinger applied his right foot to the brakes so hard that Rojas went flying into the windshield, hurting his nose and forehead. "Sorry," Dillinger said, "I thought I saw a snake in the road."

"You drive this car like a crazy madman."

"Then I guess you'd better just get out,"

Dillinger said, waving Rojas's gun at him. "Out!"

"You can't make me get out here. Take me to the hacienda."

"I can take you back to town, how about that?"

"No."

"Well, that's where I'm going, Rojas. Out!"

"Suppose no one comes by?" Rojas said, getting out of the convertible.

"Someone'll come by. If it ain't people, it'll be your own kind, vultures, coyotes, somebody," Dillinger said, laughing, as he swung the car around, sending up a cloud of dust to envelop Rojas.

A couple of miles toward town Dillinger spotted some desert wild flowers growing out of an outcropping of rock not too far from the road. He stopped the Chevy, picked an even dozen of the flowers, put them carefully in the back seat.

The town seemed deserted.

Inside the hotel saloon Chavasse greeted him with a wave.

"Rose upstairs?"

Chavasse nodded. Dillinger didn't see any reaction of jealousy in Chavasse's face. Wouldn't he have if . . ?

Upstairs, he knocked on Rose's door, keeping the bunch of wild flowers behind his back.

"Who is it?" came her voice. Amazing how just her voice could get him going.

"Your favorite outlaw," he said, touching his mustache with his free hand.

Wearing a dark green kimono, with silver and gold bands around the sleeves, she opened the door. With one hand she clasped closed the front of the kimono, but the top of one breast showed just a smidgen. It was enough. He remembered how the girl before Billie Frechette would sometimes greet him at the door with nothing on top. This woman was different. His feeling was different.

"I thought you were being turned over to the authorities?" she said.

"You sound like an authority to me. Can I come in?" He whipped the flowers around, startling her.

"Oh, they're beautiful," she said, turning to find something to put them in. She used a pitcher as a vase. "Your face looks better from your fight with Rojas," she said.

"Your face looks better to me all the time, too," he said.

And then he put his arms around her.

"You'd better close the door," he said. "It's all right. I'm on good behavior." But his heart was beating like a tight drum.

Fallon, waking, gave a long, shuddering sigh, rubbed his knuckles into his bloodshot eyes, and pushed himself up. After a while he swung his legs to the floor and padded across to the window. In the gray light of dawn the mountains seemed forbidding, and in the village great balls of tumbleweed crawled along the unpaved road, pushed by the wind.

He shivered, aware of the coldness, of the bad taste in his mouth. He was getting old, that was the trouble. If you had to hide out in a place like this, at least it could be for doing something worthwhile, like Johnny, instead of the petty junk he'd gotten into trouble for.

They'd stopped work at the mine last night just before midnight because no one had the strength to continue. They should have used dynamite the way Dillinger had said. It would have long been over, one way or t'other. Rivera had sentenced them to death to save his damn gold.

Now the Indians at the mine knew something he didn't know. That was always the case when they whispered among each other.

Fallon pulled on his hat and coat, opened the door, and went outside onto the porch. It was still and cold, the only sound the wind whistling through the scrub, and a strange air of desolation hung over everything. It was as if he had stumbled upon some ancient workings long since abandoned. He frowned and went up the slope.

The ore shed was empty. Usually by this time it was filled with Indians crouched together against the wall, waiting for the first shift to start. The old steam engine was cold, something that was never supposed to happen. One of the watchman's regular duties was to keep it stoked during the night.

He returned to the cabin, led his horse from the shed at the rear, and saddled it quickly. The first thing he noticed as he went down into the village was the absolute stillness. No smoke lifted into the sky from early-morning cooking fires, and there was a complete absence of life. Not so much as a dog crossed the street as he rode up to the well and dismounted.

He opened the nearest door and peered inside. The room was bare — even the cooking pots had gone — and when he touched the hearth, it was cold.

He tried the next house and the next, with the same result, and returned to the well slowly. As he stood there beside his horse, a dog howled somewhere out in the desert, the sound echoing back from the mountains. Was it a dog? Or was it one of those Indian signals? In the first moment of irrational fear, Fallon scrambled into the saddle and galloped out of the village.

Whatever was wrong had succeeded in frightening every man, woman, and child in the place. He pushed his mount hard. Half an hour later he reached the head of the valley and rode down to the hacienda.

As he went across the courtyard, the door opened, and Donna Clara appeared. Her hair was plaited like an Indian woman's. She seemed considerably distressed.

"Senor Fallon, thank God you are here."

Fallon looked down at her without dismounting. "Isn't Don Jose here?"

She shook her head. "I'm quite alone except for Juanita and Maria, my maid. My husband went up to the north pastures with Rojas while it was still dark. His herdsman brought the news that some of the cattle had been slaughtered."

"What about the servants?"

179

"Usually the cook brings me coffee in bed at six. When she didn't come, I decided to look for her." She shook her head in bewilderment. "The kitchen is cold, there is no one there. It is like a house of the dead."

"It may be something to do with what happened yesterday at the mine," Fallon told her. "I'll ride down to the servants' quarters. There must be somebody who can tell us what's going on."

He galloped round to the rear of the house and down the slope toward the cluster of adobe huts beside the stream. When he kicked open the first door and went inside, it was the same story. The servants had taken their belongings with them.

As he scrambled into the saddle again, someone up at the hacienda screamed, and he dug his heels into the horse's flanks and urged it up the slope. When he entered the courtyard, a buckboard was standing at the front door. Donna Clara leaned with her face to the wall, and Felipe, Rivera's vaquero, stood on the steps, hat in hands.

Fallon dismounted. "What is it?"

Felipe came down the steps slowly, his face very pale. "See for yourself, senor."

In the back of the buckboard, behind the

rear seat, lay something covered with a brightly colored Indian blanket. Fallon moved forward and drew in his breath sharply. Father Tomas gazed up at the sky, his faded blue eyes retracted only slightly. The mortal head wound had turned his face into a grotesque mask.

Fallon covered the priest's head with the blanket. "Where did you find him?"

"No more than a hundred yards from my hut, senor. The strange thing was that the horses had been hobbled."

"They didn't bury him. They sent the body here as a message."

Donna Clara turned from the wall. Her face was drawn and very white, but she had obviously regained control of herself. "Senor Fallon, tell me the truth. What does this mean?"

"What has Don Jose told you?"

"He tells me nothing. Please, I must know what is going on."

"There was a dispute at the mine. Twenty or so men were trapped by a cave-in. The new American suggested dynamite to move a huge rock that was blocking our rescue work. Don Jose refused and ordered the American turned over to the authorities. Father Tomas pleaded with Don Jose. So —

I am sorry, Donna Clara – Don Jose shot Father Tomas as an example."

"I don't believe you!" she cried.

"There were many witnesses."

"Is that why the cattle have been slaughtered?"

Fallon shrugged.

"Is that why the people have run off?"

Fallon didn't answer her.

"Senor Fallon," she said, "I would like you to escort us into Hermosa."

"Don't you think we should wait for your husband to return?"

She shook her head. "No, we'll be safer in town. We can go in the buckboard and take Father Tomas's body with us. Felipe can drive."

She turned without giving him time to reply and went into the house.

Fallon looked up at the mountains as the early-morning sun slanted cross them and shook his head.

"Have you got a gun, Felipe?"

The vaquero shook his head. "The *patrón* keeps all firearms locked in the armory in the cellar. He alone has the key, senor. We would need sledgehammers to break down the door."

Donna Clara emerged from the house, a

shawl wrapped around her head and shoulders. Behind her the maid carried little Juanita. The women sat on the rear seat with the child. Fallon climbed back on his horse. They turned through the gate and went up through the trail toward the head of the valley.

The sun moved over the top of the mountains, chasing the blue shadows from the desert, and Felipe cracked the whip over the horse's backs, urging them on.

Already the heat lifted from the land like a heavy mist, and Fallon wiped sweat from his face with a sleeve.

They dropped down through a dry arroyo and moved toward the place where the trail from the mine joined the one to Hermosa. Beyond this point the big trail wound its way between great, tapering needles of rock and entered a canyon so deep that the bottom was shaded from the sun and unexpectedly cool.

Through the silence a jay called three times, and Fallon glanced up sharply. Or was it a jay? Usually jays stayed close to water, and there was none here. At that moment there was a spine-chilling cry from behind that re-echoed within the narrow walls of the canyon, and two Apaches galloped in from the desert, blocking the buckboard's retreat.

Felipe threw one terrified glance over his

shoulder and curled his whip out over the horses. The canyon widened into a deep, saucer-shaped bowl with sloping sides. If they could get to the other end, they would be in the clear. Felipe whipped the horses again. He made out three specks ahead, and, as they closed the distance, the specks were clearly three Apaches on horseback. Felipe tried reining the confused horses, but now the Apaches in front were close enough so that one raised his rifle in almost casual gesture and fired. The shot bruised Felipe and again he tried reining the frightened horses, but a second shot rang out and found its mark. Felipe cried out sharply and went over the side.

As the women screamed, the buckboard sleued, the rear wheels bouncing over a boulder. The terrified horses reared up, snapping the lead traces, then burst through the Apaches as the buckboard turned over, spilling its occupants to the ground.

Fallon reined in as Maria rolled beneath him. He lost his seat and went backward over the animal's rump, falling heavily to the ground. He rolled over and over, half stunned, and landed beneath the wrecked buckboard beside Father Tomas's body.

Donna Clara was running for the narrow entrance to the canyon, clutching Juanita in her arms, tripping over her long skirts, her mouth open in a soundless scream. An Apache in an old blue coat with brass buttons galloped behind her, laughing, holding his rifle by the barrel. He swung it in a circle and Fallon could see it curving toward Donna Clara's head. He could do nothing to stop it as the Apache's rifle splintered bone, and Donna Clara pitched forward onto her face. Juanita clutched at her mother's body, screaming, trying to shake her back to life.

Fallon looked about him desperately, but there was no retreat. The sloping sides of the bowl lifted smooth and bare into the sky out of the white sand. Rough hands dragged him from under the buckboard.

The Indians lashed him to the rear of the buckboard, his hands behind him. Maria crawled over to her mistress, weeping, then tried to take Juanita in her arms, but the child would not let go of her mother. Felipe leaned against the rock, clutching a bloody arm. The Apaches were armed with repeating rifles, and two of them had revolvers in their belts. Their faces were painted in vertical stripes of blue and white.

What happened then was like something out of a nightmare. One of the Apaches turned Donna Clara over. She was mercifully dead. He went over to the frightened Maria. She was begging him for mercy, but his face impassive, the Apache lifted his rifle and smashed her head again and again. He picked up little Juanita, who was now kicking and screaming, and when Fallon yelled, "Leave the little girl alone," he lifted Fallon's chin and spat in his face.

Meanwhile, the others had built a fire from pieces of the buckboard. When the fire was going well, they removed one of the wheels, lashed the screaming Felipe to it in the form of a St. Andrew's Cross, and roasted him alive. All because they belonged to Rivera.

As the sun rose, the stench of burning flesh became unbearable. Fallon hung there, waiting for his turn to come, and his head dropped forward on his chest.

A thunder of hooves caused him to look up as Ortiz rode into the bowl followed by a dozen warriors. Ortiz dismounted and walked forward, pushing aside those who crowded around him excitedly. Unlike the others he wore no war paint, but Fallon took in the red flannel shirt and headband, the rawhide boots. It was enough.

He tried to moisten dry lips. "Juan?" he said. "What is this ?"

"No more Juan Ortiz," the other said. "You see only Diablo now. You understand me?"

"Diablo?" Fallon croaked.

"That's right," Ortiz said. "Now say it again. I want you to know that Juan Ortiz exists no longer."

"Diablo," Fallon whispered.

"Good," Ortiz said, and he took out his knife and sliced through Fallon's bonds.

Fallon swayed slightly, dazed and stupefied, and they brought a pony and pushed him onto its back. He groped for the halter and Ortiz put a hand on his arm.

"You will tell Rivera I hold his daughter, old man. For that I will let you live, understand?"

Fallon lashed the pony and galloped away.

ELEVEN

When Dillinger went out on the balcony, the sun was just beginning to appear over the rim of the mountains. Rose had let him stay the night, but on the couch in her sitting room. He stood there breathing in the freshness of the morning for a while before going downstairs. He had understood love when he was a boy in Indiana because he had loved his dog. But the feeling he had now was different from the feeling he had had toward the many other women. He was happy, yet his heart hurt with the pain of his happiness.

The bar was empty, but there were sounds of movement from the kitchen. He leaned in the doorway. Rose stood at the stove, dressed for riding.

"Whatever it is, it smells good."

She smiled over her shoulder. "I'm short on eggs this morning. You'll have to make do with refried beans. There's coffee in the pot."

He found a cup and helped himself.

"Are you going out to the mine?" she asked.

"If Rojas or Rivera tries to grab me again..."

"I saw you had a gun last night."

"It belonged to Rojas. I'm sure he has another by now. Rose, I want to trust you with something."

"My uncle says never trust a woman."

"I trust you. When I was a kid, I landed in reform school. That's a jail for kids. And then I was transferred to a worse place. I put in nine years, do you know how long that can be? I didn't hurt anybody. I didn't steal much. But I swear to you, I am not spending nine years or nine days in anybody's jail any more. Rivera knows who I am."

"Better than I do?"

"He knows my identity. Which is why if he and I can't live in the same place, I've got to move on."

"That will be sad for me."

"Unless you decide to come with me." It was out of the bag. He watched her eyes,

189

those beautiful, slightly slanted eyes, larger than any he had ever seen.

"This hotel," Rose said, "is all I have in the world. If I cannot move the hotel, I cannot move. I am like a prisoner, too."

Just then Chavasse came in and placed a large stone pitcher on the table. "I don't know what is happening. There is not one Indian left in the place. I had to milk the cow myself."

Rose turned. "What are you talking about?"

"They've all moved out. Only the mestizos are left and they seem to be frightened out of their wits."

"What have they got to be frightened about?" Dillinger demanded.

Rose frowned. "I thought it was strange when Conchita didn't bring me any eggs this morning."

She put down the pan and went through into the bar. Chavasse and Dillinger followed her. The town seemed strangely still in the early-morning sun. Old Gomez, the crippled railwayman Rivera had imported to work the telegraph, came out of his office and locked the door. He stumped down the street and paused to raise his hat to Rose.

"Where is everyone this morning, Rafael?"

"The good God knows, senorita. I have troubles of my own. The line is down again."

"Are you sure?"

Gomez nodded. "At six each morning I get a signal from Chihuahua, just to check that everything's working. Then I reply. It didn't come through this morning."

"What happens now?" Dillinger asked him. This man must know they're looking for someone driving a white Chevrolet convertible.

Gomez shrugged. "They give me three days to find the break and repair it. If they don't hear from me by then, they send a repair crew from Macozari. That's how it works. In theory. Last time it happened it was ten days before they did anything."

As he went off down the street, a crowd of thirty or forty mestizos emerged from the church and came down the street toward them.

The spokesman was a large fat man with a graying beard. He removed his straw sombrero and said to Rose, "Senorita, in the night the Indians have stolen away with our burros. Why is this?"

"We don't know, Jorge," she said.

"Perhaps it is something to do with the disaster at the mine. Perhaps they thought that Don Jose would force them to labor for him in place of those who have died."

Jorge shook his head. "There is more to this, senorita. We are afraid."

"But what is there to fear, Jorge?"

As if in answer there came a whooping yell from many throats. A bullet suddenly splintered the post at the side of the door, and before the echo of the shot could reach them, a second one rang out and shattered one of the windows. As Dillinger swung round, mounted Indians came over the ridge on the far side of the town, howling like a wolf pack as they moved down among the houses.

The people scattered, most of them fleeing in panic to their homes. Dillinger pushed Rose through the door of the hotel, and Chavasse followed.

As Dillinger slammed and barred the front door, Chavasse ran into the kitchen to do the same at the rear. Several Indians thundered along the street, and shots crashed into the building as the Frenchman returned.

"They've gone crazy," Rose said. "That hasn't happened in fifty years."

Dillinger peered out of the window, his face blazing with excitement. "Apaches painted for war. I never thought I'd see anything like that in my life."

Another bullet shattered glass and thudded into the opposite wall. Dillinger drew his Colt automatic. He scrambled across to Rose, who crouched by the window. Her face was very pale, and there was blood on her cheek from a splinter of glass. "Haven't you any weapons in the place at all?" he said.

She seemed slightly dazed and wiped the blood away mechanically. "There's an old revolver in the top drawer of the dresser in my bedroom."

He handed her the Colt. "You know how to use this thing?"

Something clicked in her eyes, and she came back to life again. "Of course I do."

"Okay. Hang on here. I'll be back."

Dillinger went up the stairs on the run, turned along the corridor, and kicked open the door to her room. He found the revolver at once, an old Smith and Wesson .45. It was empty, but there was a box of cartridges. He loaded it quickly, then crossed to the door leading out to the balcony.

As he stepped out, three Apaches rode

into the courtyard, one of them carrying a burning brand. Dillinger dropped to one knee, rested the barrel of the Smith and Wesson across the rail, and aimed low. The heavy slug lifted the Apache from the saddle as he started to throw the brand toward the stables. His two companions flattened across their ponies' necks and rode for cover.

Dillinger went back inside, closed and barred the shutters in all the bedrooms, and hurried downstairs. As he dropped to one knee beside Rose, she turned, her face pale. "Ortiz is leading them. I just saw him ride past. He wasn't wearing his cassock. He was all Apache." She shivered.

"Your friend Ortiz has become Diablo again."

He peered over the sill. Most of the mestizos had managed to reach the temporary safety of their homes and had barred the doors. Three or four lay in the street. An Apache was standing over one of them, his rifle butt ready to smash down. Dillinger shot him in the back.

Flames flickered over the dry woodwork of the stables opposite. An Apache galloped past and tossed a great bundle of burning brushwood onto the porch of the hotel.

"Oh, no! please, not our home," Rose cried.

Flames ran like lightning across the bare

boards, flaring up toward the windows so that Dillinger and Rose had to draw back.

More Apaches rode by, firing wildly. Dillinger pushed Rose down to the floor.

Chavasse crawled forward. "We can't stay here."

Flames licked in through the window, crackling the remaining glass, and Rose got to her feet. "We'll be safe on the roof. The rest of the hotel won't burn. The walls are made of stone."

She led the way upstairs. As they passed along the corridor, there was a thunderous crash from below as the roof of the porch collapsed.

At the end of the corridor a wooden ladder in a storeroom gave access to the flat roof through a trapdoor. Chavasse went first and turned to help the others. There was another burst of firing from the street outside.

When Rose had gone up, Dillinger moved to follow. There was a sudden splintering crash outside in the corridor. As he ran to the door, the wooden shutters to the window opposite burst open, and an Apache swung a leg over the sill. Dillinger shot the Indian in the face. The man dropped his rifle and diappeared backward, screaming as he fell.

The rifle was an old Winchester carbine, and Dillinger picked it up, ran back into the storeroom, and scrambled up the ladder. As he came out on the roof, Chavasse pulled the ladder up after him and closed the trap.

The roof was surrounded by a three-foot parapet. Dillinger tossed his revolver to Chavasse and moved across to the side that fronted the street. A heavy pall of smoke drifted across the town as the stables and other buildings burned.

The Chevrolet was parked in the alley at the side of the stables opposite. An Indian turned his pony into the alley, crowding in against the automobile. As he pulled an axe from his belt and raised it to smash the windshield, Dillinger raised the carbine and shot the Apache out of the saddle. The now-riderless pony whirled and galloped away.

The Apaches were now attacking several houses at the same time, directed by Ortiz, conspicuous in his scarlet shirt. Three of his men swung a beam of wood against the door of the general store, which stood next to the stables. Dillinger fired once, picking off the man at the back. The Apache screamed, staggering forward into his companions. They dropped the beam and ran for cover, and Dillinger fired after them. He caught a hurried glimpse of Ortiz pointing toward the roof of the hotel and ducked behind the parapet.

Rose and Chavasse crawled beside him.

"Ortiz has gone mad," Rose said. "He must be stopped."

Chavasse, who knew the Apache better than anyone, said, "Only another Indian can stop him now."

"They will not stay for long," Rose said. "In a little while when the excitement is over, they will realize what they have done and the price that must be paid. They will ride into the sierras as their fathers did before them."

"I'm not so sure," Chavasse said. "Ortiz is like Geronimo back from the grave."

Someone screamed in the street. The Apaches had succeeded in breaking down the door of a house, and one of them was dragging a woman into the street by her hair. Dillinger took careful aim and shot him. He immediately ducked behind the parapet as answering fire thudded into the wall.

Suddenly all the shooting ceased.

In the stillness that followed, the only sound was the screaming of the woman lying in the street. When Dillinger peered cautiously over the parapet, he saw that the Apaches had moved into a group, looking up at the mountains. Dillinger raised his eyes and saw a line of khaki-clad riders come over the ridge and start down the slope in a cloud of dust.

"They look like Mexican cavalry," Chavasse said.

Dillinger nodded. "Could be the bunch looking for Villa." Or for a white convertible, he thought.

Ortiz called out sharply. Those of his men who were on foot mounted, and the whole troop galloped along the street into the smoke.

Dillinger opened the trap and let down the ladder.

Consumed by the fierce flames from the burning porch, the front door had fallen from its hinges, and Dillinger kicked the charred remains into the street. As the others moved out to join him, the soldiers came past the church and galloped toward them, Lieutenant Cordona leading.

Cordona flung up his hand and dismounted. There were twelve troopers with him and Sergeant Bonilla, who had a length of rope looped to his right wrist, the other tied around Juan Villa's neck.

The bandit sat on his horse with ease in spite of the fact that his hands were tied in front of him. He grinned at Dillinger. "We meet again, amigo."

He flung up his hand and dismounted.

Cordona came forward excitedly, his elegant uniform coated with dust. "What has happened here?"

"During the night every Indian in the place moved away," Chavasse said. "Before we had time to find out what it was all about, the Apaches hit us."

"Why should they do this thing?"

"There was a cave-in at the mine yesterday," Rose told him. "About twenty Indians lost their lives. This American wanted to use dynamite to try to get them out, but Don Jose refused, and when Father Tomas pleaded with him, Rivera shot him. Ortiz has sworn vengeance."

Cordona crossed to the store and with his foot turned over the Apache whom Dillinger had shot from the roof. He looked down at the painted face. "How many were there?"

Dillinger looked inquiringly at Chavasse and then shrugged. "A dozen or fifteen, certainly no more. We killed four of them. They cleared off fast when they saw you coming."

"Then we must teach them that there are

laws now," Cordona said briskly. "Water the horses, Sergeant. We move out at once."

"What about the prisoner?" Bonilla demanded.

"We must leave him." Cordona turned to Dillinger and smiled faintly. "Perhaps this time, senor, you could contrive to make sure that he does not escape?"

He didn't see Dillinger winking at Villa.

Cordona saluted Rose gallantly. "The pleasure of seeing you again is marred by the distressing circumstances, Senorita de Rivera. We shall lay them by the heels, never fear."

Chavasse said, "They can run a long way. They know every arroyo, every water hole in these mountains."

"So do my men," Cordona said. "Half of them are Indians themselves, remember."

"But not Apache," Chavasse said.

Sergeant Bonilla turned from the water trough and led Cordona's horse forward.

Cordona mounted, adjusted his chin strap and smiled. "Before dark, my friends, I promise you Juan Ortiz. Either riding a horse or across one."

Watching him canter away into the smoke, followed by his men, Villa sighed. "What a pity that in life we do not profit by the experience of others."

He slid to the ground and held out his bound hands to Dillinger with a smile. "Would you mind, amigo? There is really no place I would care to run to at the moment, and I find this rope most uncomfortable."

Ignacio Cordona had held his present rank for only six months and had little prospect of receiving a captain's bars in less than three years. It seemed only reasonable to assume, however, that the destruction of Diablo and his band would bring his promotion significantly nearer. That thought pushed every other consideration from his mind.

Half an hour after leaving Hermosa they topped a rise and saw a bearded scarecrow riding toward them on an Indian pony. When Fallon caught sight of the uniforms, he slid to the ground with a hoarse cry and waited for them.

He was still terribly shaken by his ordeal, and Cordona dismounted and held a canteen to his lips. When he had drunk his fill, the old man stammered out his story in a few graphic sentences.

Cordona turned to Bonilla. "Four in the ambush at the canyon and perhaps twelve or fifteen have joined them from the town."

He grinned. "Fair odds."

Cordona mounted quickly and galloped away, followed by his men. Within a few moments they were only a cloud of dust traveling fast across the desert. Fallon shook his head, climbed back on his pony and rode off toward Hermosa.

At the entrance to the canyon Cordona halted and sent Bonilla and a trooper forward. The two men rode through into the great bowl and reined in their horses sharply at the scene which met their eyes.

The fire still smoldered, its heat making things lose definition, and the charred body of Felipe, with its unrecognizable face, was sprawled across the embers.

Bonilla rode on through to the other side, where a broad trail of pony tracks turned into the desert. He dismounted for a moment to examine the tracks and then rode back to his companion.

"Tell the lieutenant to come on in. They've cleared off."

He dismounted and lit a cigarette while he waited, gazing up at the steeply sloping sides of the bowl, at the rocks above, imagining the poor devils trapped in here with no hope of retreat.

He shuddered and turned to meet Cordona as he rode in with the rest of the men. The young officer dismounted and walked forward. He examined the bodies, Dona Clara's, Maria's, Felipe's, and Father Tomas's, then turned, his face expressionless.

As part of his equipment, each trooper carried a small military trenching shovel. The men unstrapped them from behind their saddles, stacked their carbines, and got to work.

Cordona and Bonilla stood watching them without speaking. When the wide grave was about three feet deep, the lieutenant nodded, and they carried the four bodies across and laid them side by side. The men turned expectantly, grouping round the grave, and Cordona removed his cap and started to pray.

From the rocks above, Ortiz brought the sights of his rifle to bear on the base of the lieutenant's skull and squeezed the trigger. It was the signal to begin. As Cordona pitched forward into the grave, the Apaches fired at each of the men below.

Within a few moments it was all over. Here and there an unfortunate trooper still moved or tried to shelter behind the bodies of his friends, but there was no escape. The shots continued until no limb moved. Finally, Ortiz held up his hand and scrambled to his feet.

As he stood gazing down at the carnage, one of his men ran between the boulders and tugged at his sleeve excitedly. Ortiz followed him across the hillside to a point where he could look across the desert. Two riders were galloping along the trail from the direction of the hacienda.

He ran between the boulders, motioning his men to silence, and they crouched in their original positions. Several minutes later Rivera and Rojas rode into the bowl below.

They dismounted quickly and stood, gazing about them, horror on their faces. Suddenly Rivera caught sight of his wife and stumbled into the grave, pulling away the bodies that half-covered her. He fell to his knees. Then, like a man demented, he looked everywhere for the body of his child, but could not find it.

Standing beside Ortiz, Kata raised his rifle and turned inquiringly. Ortiz shook his head.

"He is the one we want," Kata said. "Then it is over."

"He must suffer first," Ortiz said. "That is why we took the child."

TWELVE

Rojas and a work party of mestizos brought the bodies back to the hacienda in a large wagon.

For Rose the saddest sight was watching her uncle pulling himself up onto the wagon and looking at the corpses again.

"Has Juanita been found?" Rivera asked frantically.

"No, *patrón*, she is not there," Rojas replied.

Rivera looked past the bodies of Dona Clara, Maria, and Felipe, and fixed on Cordona as if it was in the troopers that his hopes had lain. But suddenly Rivera was crying, something Rose had never seen in her life, nor imagined he could do. And so, when Rivera jumped off the wagon, Rose, out of the kindness of her heart, put her arm around her uncle's heaving shoulders.

"I am not grieving for the dead," he said. "It is for my *angelita*, Juanita,"

"We will get her back," Rose said.

"Who will get her back?" Rivera asked. "The troopers are dead. I can send someone to the next telegraph station, and they will send twice as many Federalists to avenge Cordona's death, but by that time who knows what that Ortiz will have done to the child."

"We will get her back now." It was Dillinger, standing at Rose's side. "Provided you do not send for the troops."

Rivera looked at them, Rose and the American, and he could see what had passed between them.

"Rose," Rivera said, "in this moment of my greatest sorrow, I must tell you who this man is."

"I know he is not Harry Jordan. His name is Johnny."

"He is a wanted man."

Rose said, "He is wanted by me."

"He is wanted by the police in North America. He is a gangster, a robber of banks!"

Dillinger looked at Rose as if to try to read what was going on in her mind.

She said, "Uncle, I have known for some time what kind of man he is. That he takes money from banks that take money from the people may be an act of justice that is against the law. Johnny," she turned to him, "have you ever taken a life?"

"No, except in self-defense."

Rose whirled on Rivera. "Yet just yesterday, uncle, you took twenty lives that he wanted to save. Who killed the priest? And how many lives have you taken over the years in order to pry gold out of the mountain? If there is a gangster here, it is you!"

Rivera, his eyes like dark steel, looked at her and at Fallon and Dillinger, all stepping back from him as if he were a pariah.

"I want my daughter back," he said.

Dillinger said, "Rivera, you are a businessman. I want to make a business proposition to you."

Slowly, Rivera turned to fix his gaze on the man he had just reviled, "Yes, Senor Dillinger."

So, it is "senor" again, Dillinger thought. Out loud, he said, "I'll take a small group into the mountains. Fallon, Rojas, Villa, Nachita as a guide. You can come, too, if you want to, but get this straight. I'm in charge."

"Continue," said Rivera.

"Rojas has got to obey my orders like everybody else."

Rojas started to object but was immediately silenced by Rivera.

"Continue," Rivera said.

"We'll need guns from your storehouse. Including my Thompson submachine gun. I'll need gas from your cache for my car, and horses. We'll get done what the stupid cavalry couldn't do."

"And what is the other side of your proposition?" Rivera asked.

"If I get your kid back alive, I want twenty thousand dollars of your stored gold and safe conduct to a place on the border where I can cross safely back into the United States. Fallon gets another five thousand dollars of your gold and stays with you only until he gets a prearranged message from me that I am safely over the border."

Rivera thought for a moment.

"I warn you," Dillinger said, "don't bargain with me about the price."

"It is agreed. You can trust me, Senor Dillinger."

"I'm not a fool, Rivera. The kid and Rose come with me to the border. They go back if I cross safely over."

"What if Rose decides to go with you?"

Dillinger looked at Rose.

"Nachita can come with us. He can bring the kid back."

"I accept your proposition," Rivera said, approaching Dillinger, extending his hand.

Dillinger ignored the offered hand. "Come on, Rojas," he ordered. "Let's get the guns."

The child Juanita sat in the sand and listlessly played with an old doll, pretending not to be frightened by the Apaches sprawled around her. They were as uncomfortable with the Spanish child in their midst as she was with these strangers with painted faces. Behind them the foothills dropped steeply to merge with the desert. To the west, a great canyon sliced into the heart of the mountains.

Ortiz went up the slope above them, a vivid splash of color as he moved through the brush. He climbed onto a pillar of rock and looked east. In the far distance he looked for the tracer of dust that he was expecting.

Below, away from the others, Chato and Cochin were whispering. Chato said, "I know how much Ortiz hates Rivera, but now that we have killed Federal troops, it will be like war. We will be killed if we fail, and even if we win for a while, there are thousands of them, and they will drive us into the mountains."

"You speak the truth, brother," Cochin said. "I had hoped with the coming of better times to go north into New Mexico, to find some kind of work, to send my own son to school. Now all that is fleeing on the wind because of Ortiz's lust for revenge."

"If we leave, brother," Chato said, "we will be deserters."

"If we stay," Cochin said, "I may become an assassin."

"Of whom?" said Chato in alarm.

Together they turned, because Ortiz had come down from the mountain.

Rose said to Rivera, "I wanted to see you privately, uncle, to tell you that despite the angers that have crossed us with each other over the years, I am pleased that you are letting my friend try to find Juanita for you."

"Sometimes a tragedy brings people together," Rivera said. "After this is over, do you plan to go north with your friend?"

"Nothing has been decided, uncle."

"Thank you, my dear, for coming to talk to me after all these bitter years," Rivera said.

As she turned to go away, Rivera thought, Once Juanita is back in my hands, there will be no one for Rose to go north with. Dillinger will be dead and no one will miss him. Not even Rose after a time.

Rivera led Dillinger, Rose, Chavasse, Villa, and Fallon to the company office, fifty yards up the street from the hotel. The sign over the door said *Hermosa Mining Company*. Rivera unlocked the door. The main room was furnished as an office with a desk and filing cabinets. In one corner was a metal cabinet, which when unlocked by Rivera revealed an assortment of arms.

Dillinger pointed to an all-steel door toward the back. "What's that?"

Fallon, who knew damn well what was behind the door, flicked Dillinger a look that said maybe he shouldn't have asked the question.

"Oh," Rivera said, "the gold from the mine, after it has been processed, is stored there before being shipped to Chihuahua. There will be enough in there for your fee, and Fallon's, when the time comes."

The very way he put it made Dillinger uneasy. But he had no time for such thoughts now. On the top shelf of the metal cabinet he found his favorite weapon, the Thompson submachine gun. He picked it up, as if shaking hands with an old friend, and loaded it with one of the hundred-round circular magazines.

"Nice to get this back," he said. "I can recomend that shotgun if anybody wants something reliable for close quarters work."

Chavasse picked it up. "Just the thing for me, the worst shot in the world." He also selected a revolver and pushed it into his waistband.

Dillinger felt funny about Rose's taking a revolver and an ammunition belt and strapping it around her thin waist. He handed her a rifle. "Better take this, too. Don't know if we'll get close enough for a hand-gun." What he was really hoping that she would stay as far back as possible.

"I've always had to take care of women," Dillinger said. "I never thought there'd be one watching out for me."

At the hotel a couple of mestizos were using Rose's horses to clear the debris of the burnt-out porch.

"Careful," Rose was saying. "Don't damage the main part of the building."

Just then she saw what she had been waiting for, a single rider coming fast. Within seconds, Nachita was pulling up alongside her, his breathless pony stomping and whinnying.

"What did you find out?" she asked.

Dillinger and Fallon both came over to hear, Chavasse and Villa joining them.

"Ortiz is clever. From where he is, he can see you coming at a great distance. The closer you get to his camp, the harder it will be for you to retreat rapidly. It is a natural fortress of stone, high ground that overlooks the path up."

"Will he harm Juanita?" Rose asked.

"Not until he gets what he wants."

"And that is . . .?"

Nachita nodded toward Rojas, who was aproaching with his *patrón*.

"Would he harm her after he got what he wanted?" Rose asked.

"To a man like Ortiz, the wife of an enemy is a piece of the enemy. That is why he killed Donna Clara. The child of an enemy is the same. He has not killed her because she is the meat, the goat tied to the stake that makes the mountain lion come within the range of his gunshot."

Dillinger, who had been silent, now spoke. "I hope to hell you've got a good plan."

"In my many moons," Nachita replied, "I have learned that a plan that succeeds is a good one, and a plan that fails is a bad one. This one seems to depend on whether we can trick Ortiz, or whether, as he plans, he can trick us."

THIRTEEN

They were making last-minute plans to leave Hermosa. Nachita was to be on the lead horse, with Villa, who also knew the territory, immediately behind him. Then Rivera and Rojas, Fallon and Chavasse, all of them armed. Rose offered Dillinger one of her horses, a gentle mare, for the ride into the desert.

"I don't care how gentle the goddamn horse is," Dillinger said, "I can't ride."

Rose said, "I can't believe there is something you can't do, Johnny."

"I never said I was perfect. How about joining me for the ride in the Chevy."

For Rose, who had learned to ride when she was very young, sitting on a horse was second nature. "I don't know," she said.

"The car smells better than a horse," he said.

"Not to me. I hate the smell of gasoline."

"Don't you drive?"

"No," she said.

"You've never driven?" he repeated unbelievingly.

"Never."

"Then we're even. Come on, I promise not to try to talk you into the back seat, so help me Hannah." He held up his right hand as if taking an oath.

Up ahead, she could see that the others were getting restless.

"All right," she said, tying up her horse and sliding into the passenger side. "I don't know how far you will get with this up the mountain."

"Far enough." He'd checked everything that was checkable on the car to make sure it was in as good running condition as it could be. He'd cleaned the air filter. He'd vented the gas cans in the trunk so there'd be less danger of an explosion. He'd put in a jerry can of spare water, remembering when he hadn't had any. Though he loved to ride with the top down, he prudently raised it because of the heat and because they might be observed from above and he didn't want Ortiz to know how many people were in the automobile.

"Let them get a head start," Dillinger said. "We'll catch up easily."

"Are you afraid?" Rose said.

"Afraid of what?"

"I guess that answers my question."

"Sure, I'm afraid of getting bullet holes in this beauty. I haven't seen a body shop since arriving in Mexico."

"Shouldn't you be more concerned about a bullet in one of those cans you're carrying back there?"

"A bullet hits one of those, you and I don't have to worry one bit. Would you rather take your horse?"

"I'll stay where I am."

"Even in this dangerous, gas-carrying heap?"

Rose laughed. "You have such an expression on your face. What are you thinking? What are you wishing?"

"I wish we were setting out to rob a bank," he said.

The night sky was clear, and the moon bathed the desert in a hard white light, making it easy for Nachita to follow the tracks that Ortiz's band had made in the dust and sand of the valley floor.

They pressed on without a halt, pushing

their mounts hard. Just after midnight the trail turned into the foothills of the mountains. Nachita halted them for a rest, and Dillinger got out of the Chevrolet and walked across to a slight rise.

The view was spectacular. The desert stretched to the horizon, and its hollows and canyons were dark and forbidding, thrown into relief by the white moonlight which picked out the higher stretches of ground.

"Beautiful, isn't it?" Rose sat on a boulder beside him, taking off her hat and shaking loose a switch of long hair.

"It is now."

She smiled momentarily and then gazed out over the desert. "In a way, I feel that you came because of me. Juanita, my uncle, Ortiz, what do any of them mean to you?"

"Ever since Fallon showed me the picture postcard, I've headed here like I was pulled by a magnet. Your worries are my worries, Rose."

She turned, her face grave. "You could still turn back."

He smiled slowly. "I never go back to anything. An old superstition."

"You'll go back to the States, won't you?"

"That's different. That's home."

"Why are they looking for your car? It sounds like they really don't want you at home."

"Oh, I'm wanted all right," Dillinger said, laughing. "By my friends and by my enemies."

He put a cigarette in his mouth, and Chavasse called out softly, "No lights. That's one thing we can't afford."

Dillinger put the cigarettes back in his pocket. "I wonder just how close we are. We must have come better than twenty miles."

"Nachita thinks they may have sent scouts down to the foothills," she said. "From now on progress will be slower. An hour, perhaps two? Who knows?"

Above them, stars swam in the hot night, and Dillinger was aware of the heat like a living thing crowding in. He wiped sweat from his forehead. "It's too damned hot."

Fallon moved across to join them and stood looking to the far mountains. In the distance the stars were already being snuffed out as clouds moved across the sky.

"I think we're in for a storm."

"In these mountains?" Dillinger said in surprise.

Fallon nodded. "The heat builds up the

pressure during the day. It has to give sometime."

"What's the going likely to be from here on in?" Dillinger asked. "Will the Chevrolet take it?"

"Wagon trains did in the old days," Fallon told him. "Mines all over these mountains then, even a ranch or two. Desert again on the other side."

Dillinger moved back to the Chevrolet and got behind the wheel. "They'd sure as hell like to know about you at the factory," he said softly to the car, switched on the motor, and took up his position at the rear of the small group.

They ascended into a country of broken hills and narrow twisting waterways long since dry. The slopes on either side of the trail were covered with mesquite and greasewood, and, as they climbed higher, a few scattered piñions, rooted in the scant soil, thrust their pointed heads into the night.

On one occasion, Dillinger and Rose had to stop and call to the others for assistance to roll a boulder out of the way so that the car could pass. Later, thunder rumbled in the distance, and the sky over the peaks on the far side of the valley was momentarily illuminated by sheet lightning. The air seemed charged with electricity, vibrant and humming with a restless force that threatened to burst loose at any moment like water running over a dam.

For a while Nachita had been on foot, moving slowly, sometimes even feeling for the trail while Chavasse led his pony. By now the sky was overcast and the moon clouded over. As a precaution, Dillinger drove without lights.

"I think a horse would be safer," Rose said.

They came over a ridge through the piñion and found themselves on a small plateau surrounded by heavy brush. The old man turned and held up a hand.

"We stay here till morning. No fires, no lights. We are very close."

They dismounted, and Dillinger pulled the Chevrolet under some pines. Rivera was impatient. "Why can't we move in now and take them by surprise?"

Nachita shook his head. "They would smell our horses on the night air even before they heard them, and we are lower down the mountain. A bad position from which to attack. There would be no surprise. In the dark they would hunt you one by one through the brush."

"I thought Indians didn't like fighting at night?" Dillinger remarked.

"Someone must have forgotten to tell the Apaches," Chavasse said grimly, and he turned to Rivera. "There are seventeen of them up there. Long odds for a dark night on a mountainside with a storm brewing. Nachita knows what he is doing. What he says goes as far as I am concerned."

"And that stands for the rest of us," Fallon put in.

Rivera turned and faced them. "So it would seem I am not in command here?"

"You never were," Dillinger said softly.

For a long moment there was silence as thunder rumbled overhead, the sound of it rolling heavily across the mountains. Rivera abruptly started to unsaddle his horse.

They tethered the horses at the edge of the small plateau. Chavasse and Villa beat among the bushes for snakes. Rose moved to the rear seat of the Chevrolet so she could stretch out. The others grouped around her, chatting, except for Rivera, who sat in lonely isolation on the far side of the clearing, and Rojas, who seemed to prefer the company of the horses.

They talked quietly, their voices a low

222

murmur on the night, occasionally choking back laughter as Chavasse bantered gaily with Fallon. Rose knew that the men were deliberately trying to relieve the tension, to make her feel more secure, and she was filled with a sudden rush of tenderness for all of them. And then a match flared in the night in the direction of the horses. Rojas had lit a cigarette.

Chavasse stifled a cry of dismay and rose to his feet, but Dillinger was already halfway across the clearing. He swung backhanded, knocking the cigarette from the Mexican's mouth, sending him off balance into the brush. As Rojas started to get up, Villa pushed him back down and held a knife under his nose.

"One more thing as stupid as that, amigo, and I shall cut your throat."

He stood up and Rojas got to his feet, glaring at them, a sullen, dangerous animal about to explode. Rivera saw what was happening, took three quick paces forward, and stuck Rojas heavily across the face. "Idiot! It is not just us you endanger. You risk the life of the child."

Rojas turned without a word and stumbled into the brush.

"He will do as he is told from now on, I

will see to that," Rivera said, and returned to his place. At least he could be in command of Rojas, if of no one else.

Nachita moved to the edge of the clearing and stood listening, head turned slightly to one side. "Any harm done?" Chavasse said.

Nachita shook his head. "We are well hidden here. We must post a guard, though."

Chavasse volunteered to take the first watch. Rose curled up in the rear seat of the Chevrolet. Dillinger made himself as comfortable as he could on the front, and the others bedded down in the brush around the car. It still hadn't rained. As Dillinger closed his eyes, a great rush of tiredness swept over him, and he slept.

He was awakened by Fallon shortly after 3 A.M. "Your turn, friend. Better take your poncho. I think we might get rain soon."

Dillinger checked to see if Rose was okay in the back seat. She looked like a little girl, asleep with her hands under her cheek. He then went to sit on a boulder beside the horses, his rolled-up poncho under him, the Thompson across his knees. There was a dull ache just behind his right eye. He could have used some more sleep.

No more than ten feet away, Rojas sat

glaring at him through the darkness. He was no coward, and yet he had seen what Ortiz was capable of. He was not here for sentiment, but because the *patrón* had ordered him to come. Now, for the second time, he had been publicly humiliated.

His last shred of loyalty to Rivera had vanished with that smack across the face. An hour earlier he had made his decision. To hell with them. He would ride out, taking the other horses with him. If the others had only the stupid convertible for transportation, they couldn't all fit in. Some would have to go on foot. If the Apaches caught them, his revenge would be complete.

Rojas had waited only for the American to take his turn on guard duty. He got to his feet, pulled out his knife, and moved forward quietly.

In the darkness on the other side of the clearing Nachita had been watching Rojas, and now he called out urgently, "Jordan, watch out!"

Rojas flung himself forward. Dillinger turned, bringing the barrel of the machine gun down across the Mexican's wrist so that he dropped the knife. They came together breast-to-breast, Rojas exerting all his considerable strength in an effort to wrench the Thompson from Dillinger's grasp. Dillinger hooked a foot behind the Mexican's ankle, and they fell together, rolling between the horses into the brush.

Suddenly Rojas released his hold and drew his revolver. As Dillinger pushed him away, the Mexican fired, the bullet ricocheting from the stony ground into the night. As the rest of the party rushed forward in alarm, Rojas ran headlong into the brush.

As Dillinger scrambled to his feet, the others crowded around. "What happened?" Fallon demanded.

"If it hadn't been for Nachita, Rojas would have put his knife in me." Dillinger turned to the Indian. "Does the gunshot mean trouble?"

Nachita nodded. "They know where we are. We must be ready for them."

At that moment, a great zigzag of light struck the rocks, followed moments later by the crash of thunder. The deluge of rain came with a sudden great rush, filling the night with freshness.

Rojas kept running in a blind panic, expecting at any moment to hear shots behind him in the brush. It was impossible to see his hand in front of him. He moved forward, half-crouching, holding his left arm high to protect his face from flailing branches.

Suddenly he tripped over something, lost his balance, and went over the edge of a small gully, the revolver flying from his hand into the darkness. He would never find it now. He could feel the apron of shale sliding beneath his weight, and he clawed desperately for a secure hold. As his hand fastened on a tree root and he pulled himself to safety, rain started to fall.

He had to get off the mountain, that much was certain. He blundered forward into the darkness through the greasewood and mantinilla, losing his balance, stumbling from one gully into another until he had lost all sense of direction.

When he finally paused for a rest, he was hopelessly lost. The rain was still falling heavily, drowning all noise, but behind him loose stones tumbled down the slope. He stood peering into the darkness, his throat dry. As another shower of stones cascaded down, he turned to run.

Someone thudded into his back with stunning force, sending him staggering to his knees. He turned, flailing desperately, feeling hands reach for his throat.

There were hands everywhere, forcing him down against the ground, twisting his arms behind him. He started to scream, and something was pushed into his mouth, half-choking him, leaving only the rush of the heavy rain and the sound of unfamiliar voices.

Cochin said, "If we deliver this one to Ortiz, perhaps it will satisfy him. He was the worst against our people in the mine."

There was a grumbling from the others, then Chato said, "Only Rivera will satisfy him."

"Then what are we to do with this one?"

"Glad I brought the Chevy now?" Dillinger asked, with everyone except Nachita crowded under the raised top of the convertible. "Like college kids crowded into a phone booth."

He didn't mind, because to make room for the others Rose had to sit in his lap.

"Look at Nachita's umbrella," Fallon said.

The old Indian had pulled two flat pieces of what looked like thatch from his pack and had angled them over his head so that they formed a roof-like peak and sloped down to either side.

"He's got a portable roof," Dillinger said.

Chavasse chimed in, "You don't expect Indians to ride around with umbrellas, do you?"

Suddenly all their attempts at humor stopped. The cry of an owl had pierced through the rain.

"That's no owl," said Fallon.

"Everyone out of the car, quick," Dillinger said. "It's too easy a target."

They scrambled out into the diminishing rain. Nachita was staring to the north. Something seemed to flit between the bushes on the far side of the clearing.

Fallon's instinct was to head for the horses. Crouching, he ran for the greasewood on the far edge of the thicket where the horses were tethered. Damn, he thought, puffing, he was feeling his age in his bones.

The horses moved restlessly, stamping their feet and snorting. Fallon strained his eyes searching the darkness, his rifle at the ready.

A tremendous flash of lightning seemed to split the sky wide open. A crash of thunder made the mountain seem to tremble. Then a second flash of lightning laid bare the hillside. In its brief light Fallon saw an Apache among the animals.

He gave a hoarse cry of alarm. The Apache rushed at him, and Fallon fired blindly again and again, but the Indian kept coming, his right hand swinging upward. Fallon was aware of the knife, but it was too late to do anything about it. The point caught him under the chin, penetrating the roof of the mouth, slicing into the brain.

In the next brief moment of illumination, Dillinger saw what was happening. He ran to save Fallon, but it was too late. The Apache and Fallon were sprawled over each other in death.

Gradually the thunder moved away, across the mountains, and the rain stopped. As dawn began to edge away the darkness, Nachita slipped into the brush. When he reappeared, he reported, "They have gone now."

It was Villa, on his knees beside Fallon, who pulled out the knife and wiped it on his pants leg. Rose gazed down in horror.

"He wasn't a cautious man," Rivera said solemnly.

"If it wasn't for you, he'd be a live man," Dillinger replied.

Rose put her arm around Dillinger's shoulders.

They took a short-handled miner's pick

that had been strapped to Fallon's saddle and dug two shallow graves as best they could, covering the thin soil with rocks for protection against animals.

It wasn't a time to conduct a service. "There's one American who won't make it home," Dillinger said to no one in particular.

They moved out.

It was perhaps half an hour later when Dillinger noticed smoke up ahead, rising on the damp air. He stopped the car and got out.

Nachita moved cautiously down through the trees, and they followed to where a white tracer of smoke lifted into the morning from a clearing in the brush.

They found Rojas, or what had been Rojas, suspended by his ankles from a dead thorn tree above a fire.

FOURTEEN

The Indians were all assembled around Ortiz.

"We started out with more than twice as many as they did," Ortiz said, "and none of us is a woman. Now they have lost two to our one. The gods are turning in our favor."

It was Chato who said, "Killing Rojas was enough. It was wrong to kill the old man."

"Silence!" Ortiz said. "Manilot was told by me to turn the horses loose. The old man saw him and would have shot him. Now they are both dead. The next one to be dead must be Rivera."

"Do we wait for them here?" Kata wanted to know.

Ortiz shook his head. "First we must confuse them a little." He turned to a small, swarthy man in a green shirt and leather waistcoat. "Paco, take my horse and six men. Ride to Adobe Wells, then circle back here. We will take the pack trail through the canyon and across the mountains to the Place of Green Waters. We will wait for you there."

"How can we be sure that Nachita will follow Paco and not us?" Kata said. "The old one is cunning."

"Which is why he will follow the band led by my horse," Ortiz said.

"Perhaps they also will split into two groups?"

"There are too few of them." Ortiz shook his head. "They sleep lightly enough as it is."

Paco had already selected his men. He mounted Ortiz's pony and rode quickly down toward the desert.

Ortiz turned and looked to the east again. The dust was a little more pronounced, and he thought of Rivera, a smile touching his lips. It would not be long now. The pleasure he was beginning to find lay in the contemplation of his enemy's destruction.

He swung onto the back of Paco's pony, nodded to the others and led the way up into the canyon.

By noon the party from Hermosa had moved into a broken wilderness of rock and sand, crisscrossed by dried-up water courses. Despite the lack of wind, hot air rose to meet them like the blast from a furnace door, lifting the sand into dust devils.

The line of riders was strung out along the trail, their faces covered by scarves against the dust, Dillinger for once, leading the way. The grisly discovery in the clearing had had a chastening effect on everyone. Even Chavasse, whose high spirits were normally well in evidence, was strangely subdued as he rode, lolling in the saddle, half-asleep.

Dillinger couldn't get his mind off Fallon. He'd gotten to like the old guy without ever knowing much about him. He wondered if Fallon had any relatives back in the States. He had to have somebody, a son or a daughter someplace, a cousin, a niece or nephew, somebody. Nobody would ever know he had died, or where. Maybe he could be reburied when this was all over, with a proper marker. Shit, what a lousy way to go.

He glanced back at the others. The trail

was much better now as it descended. On impulse, he increased speed and went off after Nachita who scouted in front.

He came over a small rise and went down to a sloping plateau of sand and shale dotted with mesquite and cactus trees. Several hundred yards away a shoulder of the mountain lifted sharply toward the vast, sprawling peaks of the sierras.

On one side a canyon cut through sand-polished stone. On the other the slope was open to the desert, dropping through the tangle of catclaw and brush over shale and tilted slabs of rock to the desert below.

Nachita had dismounted below the shoulder of the mountain. When Dillinger drove up in the white convertible, which now had a film of sand and dirt on it, Nachita was squatting on his haunches beside his pony, examining the ground. Dillinger and Rose both got out of the car.

The barren soil was crisscrossed by tracks. Dillinger dropped to one knee and frowned.

"They have separated," Nachita said. "Nine of them have gone through the canyon, the others down to the desert."

"Why would they split up?"

Nachita shrugged. "Perhaps they have quarreled. Some of the young men, remembering what they have done, will already be afraid. Chato and Cochin confided in me. They think Ortiz is mad to go back to the last century, always fighting, always on the run. If Ortiz kills, they can be punished too."

Dillinger took out a pack of chewing gum and offered a stick to Nachita, who shook his head. "Which way has Ortiz gone?" Dillinger asked.

"Into the desert. His pony has led all the way. Its tracks are easy to recognize."

The others rode up and dismounted. Rivera came forward, beating dust from his coat. "What has happened?"

"They've split up," Dillinger told him. "Ortiz and a party of six have ridden down into the desert. The rest have gone through the canyon. God knows where it leads to."

"How will we know which party Juanita is with?" Rivera asked.

Nachita said, "With Ortiz. He is no fool."

"I've been this way before," Villa said. "A long time ago. An old pack trail goes over the mountains. It's hardly used these days. There's a little chapel in the pine trees on top. Santa Maria del Agua Verde, it's called. Our Lady of the Green Water, because of the spring that bubbles up inside. It's the nearest water for forty miles."

Nachita shook his head. "There is water not a dozen miles from here where the foothills of the mountains run into the desert. Once there was small *rancheria* there. Now there are only adobe walls and a well."

"And that is where Ortiz is going?" Rivera asked.

Nachita nodded, and Chavasse said, "It makes sense. He's obviously made those who refused to follow him any longer take the tougher trail. Their tongues will be hanging out before they reach Agua Verde."

Rivera nodded. "This time he's played right into our hands."

"It's too easy," Dillinger said.

"You give Ortiz too much credit," Rivera said.

Chavasse shook his head. "I agree. It does sound too easy." He turned to Nachita. "Ortiz knows we're following. How can we hope to surprise him?"

The old Apache permitted himself one of his rare smiles. "There are ways, but we must wait and see. First I shall scout the trail." He mounted his pony and rode away.

Dillinger got the canteen from the back seat and offered it to Rose. She drank, then he did. As he wiped his mouth with the back of his hand, he noticed that she was looking at him in a different way.

"Johnny," she said. "Your friend Fallon knew who you really are. Now the only one is Rivera. If your enemy knows, shouldn't a friend know?"

Dillinger looked at her eyes, the feature that had first attracted him to her. Would the truth blow everything up?

"Come on, Rose," he said matter-of-factly, "you know who I am."

"I know you robbed banks up North. I know you are too familiar with guns. The Federalistas are looking for this car, but *who* are you?"

Women always find out, sooner or later. He knew that. "If Johnny is the first part," she said, "is Dillinger the second?"

"You win the big prize."

"If I had to fall in love with a thief, why not the best?"

"The best are the bankers. They steal from the people every day and get away with it. When I unload them once in a while, all it does is raise their insurance rates a bit. It doesn't stop them from stealing."

"You are justifying breaking the law because others break the law, too?"

"That's the whole point, Rose. Those bastards don't break the law, they steal legally. We break the law taking it away from them. Is your uncle any different from a bank robber?"

"Yes," she said.

Was she challenging him? "How?"

"He's worse. To him, killing is a normal part of business, of getting what he wants."

"Yet you talk to him like there was nothing ever bad between you."

"Only until Juanita is found."

"And then?"

"I must see if I have caught a thief."

It was perhaps half an hour later that Dillinger saw the old man galloping toward him, and braked to a halt. Nachita pulled up alongside.

"I have found them," Nachita said. "Follow me slowly."

There was a place in the distance where a narrow spine of rock ran out into the desert like a causeway. As they approached, the old man led the way to the shelter of a narrow ravine. Dillinger killed the engine.

Nachita dismounted from his horse and started up the steep slope. Dillinger and Rose followed. It was hard going, and the old man pulled him down just before they reached the top.

"Careful, now."

They stayed in the cover of a dead pine, and Dillinger peered over. Several hundred yards away a ridge lifted out of the ground, dipping in toward the mountain.

Nachita said, "The ruins and the well are on the other side in a hollow."

"You're sure they are there?"

"There is a sentry posted in the hillside in a mesquite thicket below the first gully. An open attack would be useless."

Rose said, "Why attack, anyway? Can't we just negotiate whatever it is Ortiz wants for the child?"

Nachita paused before answering. "It is possible," he said, "that I can approach the camp openly. I can cry out to the sentry from cover, say I am Nachita come to powwow with Ortiz."

"What would happen?" Dillinger asked.

"Ortiz would either kill me or powwow."

"We can't take that chance," Rose said.

"Even if we were to talk," Nachita said, "Ortiz is likely to ask for something we cannot give him."

"Like what?" Dillinger asked.

"Rivera's life." Nachita sighed. "We will wait for the others.

Dillinger, sitting on the running board of the Chevy next to Rose, could see them coming for quite some distance. For the moment there was only the heat and the desert. A small green lizard appeared from the bush a few feet away, life in a dead world. He watched it for a while. It disappeared with extraordinary rapidity as the others rode up.

Rivera stood in front of a boulder, his arms crossed. The others squatted in a semicircle before Nachita and Dillinger, who explained the situation.

"It would seem that we haven't a hope in hell of surprising them," Chavasse said.

Nachita nodded and rose to his feet. "We must make them come to us. It is the only way."

"And how do we do that?" Rivera demanded.

"I will show you."

They followed him out into the desert toward a ridge with a narrow gully through its center that made a natural entrance. The spine of rock petered out perhaps a hundred yards further on.

"Two riders must go out into the desert. Once beyond the point they will be seen."

"And Ortiz will give chase?" Chavasse asked.

The old man nodded. "The rest of the

party will be hidden behind the ridge. Once Ortiz and his men follow their quarry through that gully, the rest will be simple."

"Why two riders?" Dillinger asked.

Nachita shrugged. "One man alone might look suspicious, but two might indicate that we also have split our party."

"And my daughter?" Rivera demanded.

"She will undoubtedly be left with a guard. I will work my way across the mountainside on foot and enter the camp from behind while you occupy them here."

"It's a good plan," Rivera said slowly.

"It only remains to decide who is to act as a decoy," Villa put in softly. "An unenviable task."

Dillinger sighed. "I think the bait would look a whole lot stronger if I drove out there in the convertible with the top down as if I didn't have a care in the world."

There was silence, then Nachita said, "I agree, but there should still be someone with you. If you are alone, it would be suspicious."

Rose said, "He is not alone."

Chavasse tried to object. "I'll go, not Rose."

"Wrong," Rose said. "If we've been observed before this . . ."

"I'm certain we have," Nachita said.

"Then we should seem the same. I will be the passenger."

Nachita said, "Good, it is settled. Give me fifteen minutes, then move out."

He turned and ran lightly across the broken ground, disappearing into the jumbled mass of boulders that littered the hillside. The rest of the party started to make ready.

Dillinger took the magazine drum out of the Thompson, checked that everything was working, and fitted it carefully back into place. Then he took the clip from the butt of the Colt, emptied it, and reloaded again with care, as if his life might depend on it. He put the Thompson on the floor to the right of the accelerator, next to Rose's rifle.

Rose leaned over and kissed his cheek. "For luck," she said.

"I told you we'd come out of this thing, didn't I?" He grinned. "Besides, I've been chased before." he replaced the Colt in its shoulder holster and put the top of the convertible down. Getting behind the wheel, he said, "Let's go."

He turned on the ignition and drove away slowly, waving to Chavasse behind a boulder. Rivera and Villa had taken up positions directly opposite.

Far out in the desert the parched earth faded into the sky, and the mesquite glowed with a strange incandescence as if at any moment it might burst into flame.

They rounded the point and moved across a wide plain. A high ridge swelled from the ground between them and the ruined *rancheria*. Dillinger glanced casually toward it, but no sound disturbed the heavy stillness.

"Now you know what it is like to be a fox," he told her.

"This could get on my nerves very easily," Rose said.

At that moment they heard baying. Rose turned to see six Apaches sweep over the hill and plunge down toward them, in full cry.

Dillinger slammed on his brakes, throwing up a cloud of dust, momentarily concealing them, as he turned the Chevy, backed up, and then turned back the way they had come, straight at the Apaches pursuing them.

As the bone-dry dust boiled beneath the hooves of the Apaches' horses, the Indians suddenly saw their quarry in the white automobile disappear in a cloud of dust and a moment later emerge heading toward them. They reined in the frightened horses, but the car kept coming right at them, and as the Apaches turned their horses' heads to retreat, they were met by Villa and Chevasse and Rivera firing directly at them.

Dillinger stopped the car sideways across the road. Rose took the first shot at the attackers, hitting one of them, whose riderless horse kept wheeling around. Dillinger was afraid to use the Thompson at that distance, so he gunned up the Chevy and, his foot all the way down on the gas, ran it straight at the nearest of the Apaches, who lost his balance trying to get his horse out of the way of the charging automobile and slid from the saddle, only to have Villa's bullets thud into him as he hit the ground.

It was all over. Miraculously, none of Dillinger's group had been hurt. Rivera quickly checked out the dead Indians. None of them was Ortiz.

FIFTEEN

There was no sign of the child at the camp. Rivera was furious. Somehow Nachita had made a mistake. They had followed the wrong group.

Dillinger and Rose left the Chevy at the side of the road down below and climbed up to the camp in the hollow beside the well. Nachita had lit a fire and squatted before it, waiting for coffee to boil. He glanced up, and Dillinger walked past him to the crumbling adobe walls.

It was strangely quiet, the heat blanketing all sound, and then a small wind moved across the face of the plain, rustling through the mesquite with a sibliant whispering that touched something inside him.

Was the kid dead? Was all of this useless? He remembered his own childhood, full of hope. When he'd enlisted in the Navy, his heart was high, but he'd hated the regimentation. He didn't want to be ordered around by anyone. That's when he went AWOL, got sentenced to solitary for ten days, his first imprisonment. Was all life like that, the smashing of good hope? Or was he just too damn tired now to think sensibly?

Rose came toward him, the Cordoban hat dangling from her neck. Instinctively, she put an arm around him, a bandage around his pain. When she spoke, there was a strange poignancy in her voice.

"There's nothing quite so sad as the ruins of a house."

"Hopes and dreams," Dillinger said. "Gone."

He turned, looking out over the desert again, and she moved beside him. Their shoulders touched. She started to tremble.

There were so many things he could have said as he held her close for a moment.

"Let's go and have a cup of coffee," he said.

The others were sitting round the fire as they approached. Chavasse and Rivera had obviously been having words.

"What's wrong now?" Dillinger demanded.

"All at once, everything's Nachita's fault," Chavasse said.

"He's supposed to be able to follow a trail, isn't he?" Rivera said.

Dillinger poured coffee into a cup, gave it to Rose, and glanced across to Nachita. The old man smiled faintly. "We followed the right pony, but the wrong man was riding him. A game Ortiz is playing. He knows that I am leading you. That eventually we must meet. He wishes it to be on his terms in a place of his own choosing. And now six of my brothers are dead."

Dillinger said quietly to Rose, "We think of our side, their side. I thought we just won. But for Nachita it means the opposite when Apaches die."

Rose squeezed Dillinger's hand, but Rivera didn't want to hear any of this. He stood over the squatting Nachita, his voice raised, saying, "Where has Ortiz taken my daughter?"

Nachita shrugged. "Perhaps he will cross the desert to the mountain we call the Spine of the Devil. Near its peak there are the ruins of an ancient city. Men lived there long before my people came from the cold country in the north. In the old days it was an Apache stronghold."

Villa nodded. "I have heard of this place. Pueblo — or Aztec. They call it the City of the Dead."

"But to get there Ortiz must stay on the old pack trail across the Sierras," Nachita said. "The well at Agua Verde is the only water before the desert. If he camps on the trail tonight, he should reach there by noon tomorrow."

"Then what are we sitting here for?" Rivera demanded.

Chavasse helped himself to more coffee. "It would take us two days to catch up with him now."

"Not if we go over the mountains." Nachita pointed to the great peak that towered above them. "Agua Verde is on the other side. Perhaps twenty miles."

Dillinger looked up at Nachita, shading his eyes. "Can it be done?"

"As a young man, I rode with Geronimo over the same trail to escape from the horse-soldiers who chased us across the Rio Grande."

"A long time ago."

"It was a great ride." Nachita turned and looked up at the mountain again. "There is a place near the peak where we could spend the night. It is even possible that we could reach Agua Verde before Ortiz."

Dillinger looked at Villa. "What do you think?"

Villa nodded. "The well at Agua Verde is inside the chapel. By the time Ortiz and his men arrive they will need water badly."

"Perhaps even enough to bargain for my child," Rivera said.

"If we are going, we must go now," Nachita said. "We have perhaps four hours left until sunset."

Dillinger nodded. "There's no way I can get the Chevrolet over there."

"I show you." Nachita took a stick and drew in the sand. "Ortiz comes from the west. We go straight over and cut across his path in front of him, if we are lucky. You, my friend, take your automobile out into the desert to the north, skirting the base of the mountain. The long way round. A hundred miles at least, but in the cool of the night." He shrugged. "And your automobile can travel faster than the wind, is it not so?"

"And what if it breaks down out there in the desert?" Rose said. "The sun in the heat of the day can fry a man's brains. Or a woman's."

"A horse could break a leg going over the mountain," Nachita said. "Or a man. This way, we have two chances of reaching Agua Verde before Ortiz."

"That settles it," Dillinger said. "Anyone

250

want to chaperone Rose and me?"

"I will come, senor," Villa said. "I know this country, you don't."

Dillinger said to the girl, "Rose? You want to take Villa's horse and go with the others?"

She glanced at her uncle. "I will come with you."

"Okay, let's get moving."

He and Villa put the top up on the convertible. Dillinger got behind the wheel and pressed the starter as Villa scrambled into the rear seat. "Lead my horse," he shouted to Chavasse.

Dillinger waved. "See you at Agua Verde," he called, and drove down into the vast desert.

Nachita led them up the slope of the mountain without hesitation, zigzagging between the mesquite and cacti. After an hour they went over a ridge and faced a shelving bank of shale and thin soil held together by a few shrubs.

Rivera, who had been bringing up the rear, now joined them, his face lined with fatigue. "Why have we stopped?"

Nachita had ridden to a point where the ledge turned the corner of the bluff, and now he came back and dismounted. "From here it will be necessary to blindfold the horses. Use strips from your blankets."

Nachita went first, and the rest followed at spaced intervals. When the ledge turned the corner, Chavasse sucked in his breath. At this point the trail narrowed to a width of perhaps five or six feet. On his right hand there was nothing, only clear air to the valley floor below.

The ledge lifted steeply, following the curve of the wall, and he climbed after Nachita, holding his horse as close to the wall as possible.

And then the ledge narrowed until there hardly seemed room for man and animal together. Chavasse pushed forward frantically and came out on a small plateau. He led his mount up and over the edge of a gentle slope thinly scattered with pine trees to where Nachita waited.

Rivera came over the edge after them, and the Frenchman leaned against his mount, wiping sweat from his face. "Something to remember till my dying day." He turned to Nachita. "Can we rest here?"

The old man shook his head. "From now on it is easy, and we can ride. There is a good campsite in the forest on the far side of the summit."

Nachita mounted, and they rode after him.

The desert was purple and gray, turning black at the edges, and in the desolate light of evening the peaks were touched with fire.

It was cooler at this height, the air pleasant with the scent of pines, and the climb already seemed remote and impossible.

The ultimate ridge lifted to meet the dark arch of the sky where already a single star shone. They went over and a little way down the other side to a clearing in the pine trees. Nachita held up his hand, and they dismounted.

Chavasse felt weariness strike through him. It had been a long day. He carried the saddlebags across to where Nachita was already building a small fire of twigs and pine cones in a deep hollow between three boulders.

Everyone looked worn down to the bone. Rivera gazed into the fire vacantly, lines of fatigue etched into his face.

For the first few miles out into the desert, the going wasn't too bad, a flat, sun-baked plain over which the Chevrolet moved fast. At one stage Dillinger pushed the car up to sixty, and Villa tapped his shoulder, laughing like a kid.

"This is better than riding, amigo," he shouted.

Dillinger had to slow down as they came to a flat brown plain that was fissured and broken.

It was like driving your way through a maze, turning from one ancient dried-out water course into another, traveling at no more than ten or fifteen miles an hour. They ran into one dead end after another, frequently having to turn back and try again, and progress was painfully slow and darkness was falling before they finally emerged onto salt flats.

The heat and the dust were unbelievable. They stopped beside a clump of organ cactus, and Villa gathered a few dry sticks for a small fire to make coffee while Dillinger topped up the Chevy's tank with gas from the cans in the trunk. Then, checking the radiator, he groaned.

"We must have been boiling away more water than I thought." He got out the jerry can. "I was saving this in case the canteen ran dry and we had to drink this." He poured what was left in the jerry can into the radiator carefully, not wanting to spill a drop.

He and Villa sat with Rose on the running board and drank coffee as darkness descended. Dillinger said, "Good to give the old car a chance to rest."

"Just like horses, eh?" Villa said.

Dillinger patted the side of the Chevrolet. "If she lets us down, I wouldn't give much for our chances when the sun comes up tomorrow."

"Death, my friend, comes to all of us. The dice was thrown a long time ago. The result is already known, but then, you know this, I think, Mr. Dillinger."

Dillinger looked at him calmly. "Rose knows, but how did you find out?"

"I saw your picture in the paper in Durango a couple of months back. I recognized you on the train, in spite of your new mustache. When we spoke, privately. When you let me go."

"You told nobody?"

"I owed you, my friend, and besides, we are, after all, in the same line of business. Life is a pretty wild poker game."

Villa tilted his hat and closed his eyes, turning his back so that Dillinger and Rose could lie side by side through the dark night.

It was in the middle of the night that Dillinger awoke because he felt a hand on his shoulder. He was about to leap up, ready to draw or fight, when he realized it was Rose's hand.

"You are a restless sleeper," she whispered. "I only wanted to say I love you."

Dillinger turned over on his back. The sky was full of unexpected stars.

They got a good early start, the Chevy making time, when there was a sudden loud bang as the left front tire burst. The Chevrolet slued wildly, and Dillinger fought with the wheel as the car spun around and finally came to a stop.

They sat for a moment in silence. Dillinger said, "Anybody hurt?"

Villa said, "I think I just spat out my heart, a saying we have, but never mind."

"I'm okay," said Rose.

"Let's inspect the damage."

The tire was in shreds, but worst was the fact that the rear axle was jammed across a sizable rock.

"Jesus!" Villa said. "The horse is dead."

"Not so fast," Dillinger said, getting down on his hands and knees and inspecting the situation. He glanced up. "It seems to me that if we raise her off the rock with the jack and give her a good push, she should roll clear soon enough."

It was a solution so ludicrously simple that Rose laughed out loud in relief.

Dillinger got the jack from the trunk and positioned it under the part of the axle that was free. Villa started to pump. Gradually the Chevrolet lifted.

"Okay," Dillinger said. "Let's try."

It took both of them and Rose all their strength. For a moment, it looked as if the plan wasn't going to work, and then the jack tilted forward and the Chevrolet ran free.

Dillinger had a spare, and the tire change took only minutes.

"Okay, let's push on."

Villa said, "One thing, my friend. I know Rivera of old. Even if we succeed in this matter, he will send me back to prison to face a firing squad."

"And me?" Dillinger said.

"My observation tells me that it would be unwise to turn your back on him."

They got back into the car. Dillinger said, "So why don't you make a break for it while the going's good?"

"Because there is the child to consider. Because I am a man, and Rivera is not," Villa said simply. "The same for you, I think."

Dillinger smiled. Knowing Rose was

listening to their exchange, he said, "It's what we think of ourselves that's important."

He pressed the starter and drove away, singing another of the Hit Parade tunes that reminded him of home, "Brother, Can You Spare a Dime?"

SIXTEEN

Dillinger waited for Villa beside the Chevrolet, the Thompson ready in his hand. There was the sound of falling stones, and the Mexican came down the slope through the brush above him, his clatter waking Rose in the back seat.

"Nobody there," Villa said. "We've beaten all of them to this place, amigo."

"Great," Dillinger said. "So what if Ortiz and his band arrive first? Long odds for the two of us."

"Three of us," Rose said.

"True, but the only well is inside the chapel," Villa said. "He will need water before trying the desert. If we are inside and he is out . . ." He shrugged.

"Okay. What about the car?"

Villa glanced at the steep walls of the

arroyo on either side. "We leave her here and go the rest of the way on foot."

"The hell you say. Look, Villa," Dillinger said. "Those Apaches find this heap, they'll burn it or kick it to death. I want this car. I love it."

Rose had wandered around a bend. "Hey, car-lover," she called out. "Come and see."

Villa followed Dillinger past the curve to where there was a huge recess between the stones, a shallow natural cave. "Drive your true love in here," Rose said. "If you throw a few branches over it, they'll never see it unless they smell the gasoline first."

It was, both Villa and Dillinger agreed, a perfect hiding place. Dillinger impulsively kissed Rose on the cheek. "Leave it to a woman."

Dillinger drove the car in as far as he safely could, and then the three of them, like kids, threw brush and branches on till it nearly disappeared from view.

"Let's go," Dillinger said.

"Our leader leads," Rose said to Villa.

"I meant it," Dillinger said. "We don't want to get caught here, the three of us against a mob of them."

And so, over the barren mountainside, through brush and shale, they finally came over the rim of an escarpment. With a rush of feeling, Dillinger saw the chapel.

It stood foursquare to the winds, firmly rooted into the ground at the very edge of a small plateau perhaps twenty-five yards wide and bordered by a few scattered pines and a tangled thicket of greasewood and mesquite.

The chapel itself was built of granite with a roof of overlapping stone slabs about twenty feet above the ground. The door was of heavy oak bound with iron, and there were two narrow arched windows on either side and a row of similar windows under the eaves.

Villa opened the door and stepped inside, and Dillinger followed him. There was a small altar with a wooden cross, a lantern hanging from a chain, and two benches against the rear wall. It was very quiet, the pale dawn light slanting down from the upper windows. Villa took off his hat and crossed himself as he went toward the altar.

The well was sunk into the center of the floor and was constructed of some strange, translucent stone shot with green fire that tinted the water, giving the place its name.

Dillinger turned slowly, examining everything. There was a stout locking bar on a swing pin behind the door, and the lower windows had wooden shutters that fastened on the inside.

"Anyone would think the place had been built to stand a siege," Dillinger remarked.

"In the old days it was a refuge for the mule-drivers on many occasions," Villa said. "It is a mystery why the water should come up here and nowhere else. That is why they built the chapel in the first place, more than two hundred years ago."

Through the windows on the other side the view was magnificent. The chapel stood on the extreme edge of the shelf looking out across the desert to the Devil's Spine, and there was a drop of almost a thousand feet to the valley floor.

"I feel as if I could almost reach out and touch it," Dillinger said, nodding across at the mountain.

Villa grinned. "You would need a long arm, amigo. It is at least fifteen miles away. The desert air plays strange tricks."

They slept the sleep of the dead. When Dillinger finally awoke, he saw Rose still sleeping, and he imagined what it might be like waking up in a real house in Indiana late on a Sunday morning and seeing Rose in the bed beside him.

There was the slightest breath of wind, a dying fall. But in the sound he detected a footfall. And then another. He reached for his Thompson, got up noiselessly, and then kicked open the chapel door. Nachita was standing in the open doorway, rifle crooked in his arm.

Nachita and Chavasse led their horses in through the door. When all the animals were hobbled together at one end of the building, the old Apache cut a switch of brush from the thicket and walked backward to the chapel, smoothing all tracks from the sand.

He barred the door and turned to face them. "When they come, no one must make a move till they have dismounted. Then, with all of you taking aim, I will call out in the Apache language. I will go out and bargain with Ortiz while he and his men are in your gun sights."

"That's crazy," Rivera said, shaking both fists. "We should kill as many as possible with the first volley. Then bargain with Ortiz."

"And kill the child," said Nachita in anger.

"I didn't say shoot at the child?" Rivera shouted.

"It could be hit by accident. Or any one

of them we missed could throw the child off the mountain," Nachita said. "I am here to set free a child who is paying for your sins. I am not here to idly kill my fellow Apaches who are following a leader who is as mad as you are."

Rivera looked ten years older than when Dillinger had first met him. A muscle twitched in his right cheek. He gripped his rifle tightly. Dillinger was ready to let loose the second that Rivera made a wrong move.

Rivera looked at each of their faces. Then to Rose he said, "What about you? What do you think?"

Calmly, Rose said, "In all our years, this is the first time, uncle, you have asked my opinion as if you meant it. I think all these younger men believe that Nachita, who led us here, should have a chance to do things his way. As he said at the outset, a good plan is one that works. If his fails, there are always the rifles."

Dillinger had to restrain himself from actually clapping his hands in applause, just as he did in movie houses when an actor said something he agreed with strongly. He'd never thought he would meet a woman who was more than his equal, and here she was, as brave as a man, and saying the right thing with an eloquence he never had.

Suddenly they all heard the sound of trotting horses.

A moment later the first Apache turned the corner of the bluff and moved into the clearing. Ortiz was almost directly behind him.

He sat on his horse with an insolent and casual elegance, a supremely dangerous figure in his scarlet shirt and headband. The moment he appeared, Rivera gave a sort of strangled cry, and raised his rifle.

"Don't do that, you idiot!" Dillinger shouted.

The shot, badly aimed, caught the pony in the neck, and Ortiz pitched forward into the dust. He rolled over twice, came to his feet with incredible agility, and plunged into the thicket as Rivera fired again.

His companion was already wheeling his pony to follow him when Chavasse, Dillinger, and Villa all fired at once. The Indian toppled from the saddle, and his pony galloped back along the trail.

Rivera kept firing into the brush, pumping the lever on his rifle frantically, until Chavasse pulled the weapon from his hands.

"It's too late, you damned fool. Can't you understand?"

Rivera stared at him, his face pale, a translucent film clouding his eyes. Suddenly, eight rifles blasted at once from the thicket, bullets passing in through the windows and thudding into the plaster on the opposite wall.

Chavasse pushed Rivera to the floor, and Dillinger and Villa crawled beneath the windows, closing the shutters. In each shutter there was only a small loophole, but plenty of light still slanted down from the upper windows. One or two more bullets chipped the outside wall or splintered a shutter. Then there was silence.

Dillinger peered cautiously through a loophole. Ortiz's pony and the dead Apache still lay in the center of the clearing. Everything was still.

He started to turn away, but from the next window Chavasse asked, "What's that?"

A branch was being held out into the open, a rag of white clothing dangling from the end. Villa said, "They want to talk terms."

"That remains to be seen," Dillinger said. "It could be a trap." he turned to Nachita. "What do you think?"

Nachita shrugged. "There is only one way to find out."

He unbarred the door and walked outside. For a moment he held his rifle above his head, then he leaned it against the wall and went forward. Ortiz emerged from a thicket to meet him.

Rivera took a single step forward, and Villa swung his rifle toward him. "I think not, Don Jose."

For a moment Rivera glared angrily at him, and then something seemed to go out of the man. He turned away, shoulders sagging.

Nachita and Ortiz were talking in Apache, their voices carrying quite clearly in the stillness. There was a sharpness to their exchange. After a while, Nachita turned and came back, leaving Ortiz standing there, shouting things after him.

"What is it?" asked Rose, taking old Nachita's hands into her own.

"Ortiz does not wish to deal with me. He says that because I consort with all of you, I am a traitor to the Apache nation."

"What does he want?" Dillinger demanded.

"You," Nachita replied. "He says you of the white car are the leader."

"No." Rose moved forward. "He can't be trusted now. He might do anything."

Her concern was plain for everyone to

see. Dillinger smiled and put down his submachine gun. "Hell, angel, you take a chance every day of your life."

Rivera said, "I am the one who should be discussing the terms."

Dillinger looked at him calmly. "Thanks to you I'm not sure we're in shape to do that anymore."

He stepped into the hot sun and walked across the clearing. Ortiz waited for him, hands on his hips.

Dillinger halted a few feet away, and Ortiz said in English, "So, you came over the mountain. I had not thought it possible."

"You haven't asked me out here to exchange pleasantries," Dillinger said. "What do you want?"

Ortiz said, "Take a message to Rivera. Tell him that if he gives himself to me, I shall hand over the child. The rest of you can go free."

"How can we be sure she's still alive?"

"See for yourself."

He stepped into the thicket, and Dillinger followed. The two men pushed their way through the brush and emerged into a clearing in the pine trees where the ponies were tethered. An Apache squatted on the ground, the only one in sight. Juanita de

Rivera sat on a blanket a few feet away from him playing with her doll.

She looked pale, the eyes too large in the rounded childish face, and Dillinger dropped to one knee beside her. "Hello, Juanita, remember me?"

Her velvet suit was torn, bedraggled, and covered with dust. She passed a hand across her eyes and said, "Will I be seeing Mama soon?"

Dillinger patted her on the shoulder and stood up. "How much water have you got?"

"Enough," said Ortiz.

Dillinger shook his head. "You've come fifty miles at least since your last water hole, and you were expecting to find plenty here."

"Tell Rivera he can have half an hour," Ortiz said. "After that there will be no more talking. I have allowed him to live long enough."

Dillinger pushed his way through the thicket, aware of the unseen eyes on either side, and crossed the clearing to the chapel. he stepped inside and closed the door.

Rivera moved forward eagerly. "What does he want?"

"You!" Dillinger told him bluntly. "If you hand yourself over within half an hour, he'll give us the child and let us go free."

"You have seen Juanita?" Rose demanded. "How is she?"

"A little the worse for wear, but otherwise unharmed." He turned to Rivera. "What about it?"

The Mexican's face was deathly pale and beaded with sweat. He struggled for words and said in a low voice, "Is there no other way?"

"From the moment you ruined Nachita's plan for us we lost any real advantage we might have had."

"But what about the well? They must need water badly."

"They could last for a couple of days," Villa put in.

Dillinger turned to Nachita. "What would happen if we did turn him over? Would Ortiz keep his word and let us ride out?"

"I'm not sure," Nachita said. "He is in this thing too deep. He has nothing left to lose. To a man like Victorio, honor was everything. Ortiz is a different breed. Besides, I think he is mad now."

"What about water?"

"I would say they have none. I noticed the condition of Ortiz's pony when I went to speak with him."

Dillinger nodded, a slight frown on his face as he considered the situation. He said slowly, "Do you think he might kill the kid if we turn down the exchange?"

Nachita shook his head. "If he had intended to kill her without reason, he would have done so. I think he will keep her with him now until what happens happens."

There was a short silence as they all considered his words. It was finally broken by Villa. "It pains me to admit it, but it would seem that a grand gesture from Don Jose would appease Ortiz only for a moment."

"I'll test the water one more time." Dillinger said.

He picked up a canteen, filled it from the well, and went back outside. As he crossed the clearing, Ortiz stepped from the thicket.

Dillinger stopped a few feet away. "Nachita says you have no honor."

No anger showed on Ortiz's face. He shrugged and said calmly, "So be it. What happens now is on your own head."

Dillinger held out the canteen. "For the child."

"You would trust a man without honor?" Ortiz said. "How do you know I will not drink this myself?"

"Only you can prove that you are still a man."

"Then follow me," Ortiz commanded.

Once again he led the way into the thicket to where Juanita sat on her blanket. She seemed happy to see Dillinger so soon again. Ortiz knelt and held the canteen for her as she drank. When she finished, the canteen was still more than half full.

"You can have the rest," Dillinger said.

Ortiz turned the canteen over and spilled the rest of the water to the ground. "I will drink," Ortiz said, "when Rivera is exchanged for the child."

He handed the canteen back to Dillinger and said, "Go now!" You have fifteen minutes left."

Dillinger returned to the chapel. The others gathered around him to hear what had happened. Suddenly he stopped talking because he, like the rest, had heard the muted throbbing of a drum.

"It is their way of trying to frighten you," Nachita said.

Then came the sound of an Apache chant, voices rising and falling like waves coming in across a beach.

"It is the courage chant," Nachita said.

"If they attack," Chavasse said, "they will drug themselves with mescaline first. They will think they are invulnerable."

Villa nodded. "You could empty your gun into one of them, and he'll still keep coming."

"Bullshit," Dillinger said. "I've made up my mind. Rivera will be exchanged for the girl."

"No," Rivera said from the corner. "I will not do it!"

Nachita stood facing all of them. To Dillinger he said, "You believe Ortiz because he spilled the rest of the water."

Dillinger nodded.

"You think he will act with honor?"

"It's a chance worth taking."

"You Yankees," Nachita said, "are naive. You believe what you want to believe."

Dillinger turned to Villa. "You bring Rivera out. I'll come with you to take the kid. She's just seen me, she'll be less frightened if I pick her up."

Villa twisted Rivera's arms behind his back and pushed him out the door.

Outside the chapel Dillinger made himself fully visible so that Ortiz could see he wasn't armed. The chanting stopped. There was a rustling in the thicket across the clearing, and Ortiz appeared. Near him, the thicket opened and a young Apache was visible, carrying Juanita in a blanket.

"Put her down!" Dillinger barked.

The young Apache didn't understand him, but Ortiz said something, and the Apache put Juanita at Ortiz's feet. It was at that moment that the child recognized Rivera, who was being held and pushed by Villa from behind. She got up to run to her father, but Ortiz grabbed her hand.

"Sit!" he commanded. "Not yet."

Then Ortiz advanced to the center of the clearing. "At last, Rivera," he said. Then to Villa, "I will take him."

No man in the history of the world could have looked more frightened than Rivera did at that moment, or more pathetic.

Ortiz said, "Rivera, you died when you shot Father Tomas. You died when you let twenty Apaches die in the mine. Today I merely carry out the sentence."

Dillinger said, "Let's cut the palaver. Have the kid brought forward."

Ortiz motioned to the young Apache, who picked up Juanita in her blanket and again moved her to where Ortiz now stood.

"We will now exchange justice for justice," Ortiz said, "life for life."

"No you won't," Rivera said, suddenly lunging for the child, trying to take her up in his arms. Villa, taken by surprise, made a try at holding Rivera back.

In one swift movement Ortiz reached into his clothing and pulled out a long-barreled Smith and Wesson. His eyes like a madman's, he aimed at Rivera, pulling the trigger again and again. Rivera dropped the wriggling, screaming, frightened child. As Rivera crumpled, Ortiz raised the Smith and Wesson and emptied it at Villa's chest. Then he swooped up the screaming Juanita and ran with her back into the thicket, leaving her blanket behind.

Dillinger could see that Ortiz's perfidy had taken the young Apache completely by surprise, for he stood like a statue for a second before dashing after Ortiz into the bushes.

Dillinger, betrayed, waited for bullets to thud into him from either direction, the thicket or the chapel. He glanced down at the bodies. Rivera was clearly dead. Villa was still breathing, so Dillinger knelt beside the man whose breath came in bubbles. His eyes said, It is the luck of the game, and he died.

Chavasse, Rose, Nachita, were all coming across the clearing from the chapel, armed with rifles but not firing into the thicket after Ortiz, for fear of hitting the child.

Dillinger tried to say something to Rose,

but she averted her face.

Nachita said, "You all go back to the chapel. I will be back soon," and he went off in the direction in which Ortiz had vanished.

SEVENTEEN

They buried Rivera and Villa in a shallow grave in the pine trees. When they had finished, Dillinger returned to the chapel.

He stood at the window and looked out across the desert at the mountain. Strangely enough, he didn't feel tired, but as if he had just awakened from a long sleep.

A small wind blew in through the door, setting the lantern creaking on its chain above the altar, carrying with it the scent of pine, and he could almost hear the stillness.

Chavasse slept peacefully, all strain washed from his face, and Rose lay on a blanket beside the gray ashes of fire, her head pillowed on one arm. Dillinger stood for a long time looking down at her. Then he filled two canteens at the well, picked up his submachine gun, and went outside.

Nachita was just emerging from the thicket across the clearing, sweat on his brow.

Dillinger crossed quickly to meet him. "You are breathing hard," he said.

"My horse is breathing harder," Nachita said, "and he is far younger than I am." He sat down on a rock.

"Are you angry because I believed Ortiz might be a man?"

"Anger is like rust in the heart. It destroys not the enemy but he who is angry. If I come north to your country, I will trust your judgment about the people. Here, you must trust mine. I bring good news."

Dillinger offered him one of the canteens. Nachita unscrewed the cap, then drank his fill. "The news," he said, "is that the others have deserted Ortiz. In his dishonor, he dishonored them."

"Where have they gone?" Dillinger asked.

"Where has the wind gone? The Federalistas, if they come, will never find them. It doesn't matter. Ortiz is now alone with the child, on his horse, heading into that part of the desert that is near the great rocks in the direction away from Hermosa.

He has no reason to keep Juanita now except as a shield from bullets. Where are you going?"

Dillinger checked his Colt in its underarm holster and swung the Thompson over his shoulder by its strap. "It is my fault he got away. This time he won't."

"Come back," Nachita shouted after him. "You don't know your way about this countryside. Two wrong decisions do not make a right one!"

But it was too late. The American had rushed downhill too fast to hear his words.

Inside the chapel, Nachita knelt beside Rose and shook her gently. Her eyelids fluttered, then opened slowly, and she gazed at him. In that brief moment of waking she knew at once that something was wrong.

"What is it?"

"He has gone into the desert."

Her eyes widened. "Alone?"

Nachita smiled. "Men will do foolish things."

Her nostrils flared, the face becoming hard and full of purpose.

"We'll go after him."

"Good. We'll take the spare horses. We can move faster if we can change mounts along the way." He looked down at

Chavasse. "Shall we wake him?"

Chavasse opened his eyes, blinked. "What is it?"

"Dillinger has gone after Ortiz on his own."

Chavasse struggled onto one elbow. "The bloody fool. They'll spread him on an ant-hill and watch him die by inches."

Nachita said, "They do not exist. The young Apaches have abandoned Ortiz because he lost his honor. Ortiz is alone."

"And Juanita?" Chavasse asked, getting up. "Jesus, we'd best move fast."

Dillinger threw the brush and branches off the camouflaged car like a madman. He was sure he could catch up with Ortiz if only he could get going, but it took twenty minutes before the car was clear enough to be carefully backed out of the cave-like crevice. If it shot back in reverse, he'd have gone over the side.

He couldn't wait till he got it back down on the desert so he could pick up speed.

The desert smoldered in the sun, heat rising from the ground to enfold him, and the bushes seemed to shimmer with fire. He wondered how far ahead his quarry was. If he did not know now that he was being followed, he soon would. The noise of the convertible's engine echoed back at him from the hills.

He realized how much Ortiz must hate Nachita. The old man possessed the same qualities of strength, courage, and intelligence. He could be cruel, that was true, but only in the way that life itself was cruel. He had fought for his nation and seen it defeated. Still, he had retained his honor, and Ortiz had not.

The sun beat down mercilessly, but Dillinger obstinately refused to put the top up. He drove down into a shallow depression and up the other side, pasusing to reach for his canteen. He tilted his head, the cool liquid spilling across his face. As he straightened, the desert seemed to move and the mountain to float before him.

There was no sound. Only a great silence. For a moment Dillinger was part of it, fused into a single whole. He sat at the wheel as if turned to stone, hardly daring to breathe. Then there was a slight rattle, the faintest of sounds, as a lizard passed between two rocks. Life in the barren wilderness, the second time such a thing had happened to him. If Rose had been there, she would have taken it as an omen.

He didn't realize that Ortiz could observe him. But in fact Ortiz was only six hundred yards from the car, about a hundred and fifty feet higher among the rocks that bordered the desert. He had been giving his horse a rest. The child was asleep on the ground, exhausted. But he had his energy still, and his pride, and now, in his sight, the white convertible, standing still.

Ortiz leaned his left elbow on the rock to steady his arm as he sighted along the top of the rifle. It was too far for accurate fire, but if he hit the car at least, the stupid American would drive closer, close enough perhaps for Ortiz to put a final bullet between his eyes.

Carefully, Ortiz squeezed the trigger.

Dillinger jumped in his seat instinctively when the bullet his the hood ornament and ricocheted into the right side of the windshield, spidering the glass. In an instant, he turned on the ignition, accelerated like a demon, and became a fast-moving target. But no further shots came.

His hatred for Ortiz doubled because of the damage to the car. It was as if the car's virginity had been taken. It would need a new hood ornament. It would need a new windshield. And where in all of Mexico would he find someone who could make it new without asking too many questions? Damn.

Ortiz saw the car moving fast in his direction and kept his finger ready on the trigger. Suddenly, the car disappeared from his view. He frowned, then seeing that the child was still asleep and his horse safely tethered, he moved quickly toward a new position. And sure enough, within minutes, looking between two large rocks, he saw the Chevrolet, not racing as before, but parked, its engine still running, the sound of it now echoing. But of Dillinger there was no sign.

It had been a momentary flash of scarlet from the rocks that had warned Dillinger of Ortiz's new position. He'd parked the car, left the engine running, and got out carrying his Thompson. He figured he'd have to climb two hundred feet to get well above Ortiz, so the hunter could become the hunted.

Rose, Chavasse, and Nachita had been

able to make faster time down the mountain than Dillinger, aided by the old Apache's unerring eye for the trail. Once on the plain, they had ridden hard, changing mounts when the horses tired.

It was Rose who spotted the stopped Chevrolet. Nachita had motioned them to slow down, then stop also. It was then that they heard the shot, and even from that distance they could see that the car had been hit.

Rose didn't know whether Dillinger had been hit or not, but when that shot rang out, she was certain she loved this man who led an impossible life.

Nachita also decided on the advantage of the higher ground, and so they tethered their horses and started to climb. Soon they reached a flat outcrop, and Nachita motioned Chavasse and Rose to lie flat. He crawled forward, then motioned them to crawl forward too.

He pointed. They saw Ortiz's tethered horse and something very small just waking up. "Juanita!" Rose's heart sang.

"Careful," Nachita cautioned, pointing to a position in the rocks almost directly below them. Ortiz was in a sniper's position, waiting. They could not see Dillinger anywhere.

"You and Chavasse go for the child now.

When you are almost there, I will get Ortiz."

Dillinger, recovering his breath, now moved into position where he would be able to see Ortiz. There he was! If he only had a rifle. he had to get closer so that the Thompson would be sure to get Ortiz with the first burst.

He climbed down as quietly as he could. Suddenly, there was a noise off to the right. It was Ortiz's horse whinnying. Rose was clearly visible, running ahead of Chavasse. In a moment she had put down her rifle and scooped up Juanita into her arms.

Ortiz saw this also, and cried out like a madman whose property was being stolen. Dillinger pulled himself up on the rock in front of him, ready to fire his Thompson, but Ortiz, screaming indecipherable words in Apache, was running toward Rose and Juanita. Dillinger saw Chavasse fall to one knee to take better aim at the zigzagging Apache. The Frenchman fired once, the bullet skimming off a rock, and then a second and third time in quick succession. If he'd hit Ortiz, it hadn't slowed the Apache down a second. Dillinger was scampering breathlessly down the rocks, hating the Thompson for the first time in his life because it was too inaccurate to use with Rose and Juanita now just beyond Ortiz in the line of fire.

Why didn't the kneeling Frenchman fire again, Dillinger thought as he moved quickly over the sharp rocks, trying not to trip. Chavasse was looking at his rifle as if it had jammed, when Ortiz came close enough to kick the rifle clear out of Chavasse's hands. Out of the corner of his vision, Dillinger saw that Rose had put Juanita down to pick up her rifle. She should never have let go of the kid. She should have run with Juanita in the opposite direction.

Ortiz saw his chance. Instead of stomping on Chavasse as he had planned to do, he ran toward the child. Dillinger knew the danger. Once the Apache had the kid in his arms, the Thompson'd be useless. Dillinger ran as he'd done the hundred-yard dash in high school, at the last moment flinging the Thompson away as he risked everything in one flying tackle, hitting Ortiz just at the back of the knees, crumpling him to the ground.

Ortiz in his rage summoned up the

energy of a giant, and with a mighty heave rolled over and pinned Dillinger to the ground.

"Get the kid!" Dillinger yelled at Rose, then felt the Apache's fingers tighten on his throat.

Rose, standing ten feet away, rifle in hand, didn't know how to shoot Ortiz without hitting Dillinger.

"Get the kid and run like —" Ortiz's hands, the strongest Dillinger had ever felt, tightened on his windpipe, cutting off his yell to Rose and his air. At least the kid was safe, he thought, but what a way to go.

And then, staring up at Ortiz's face whirling against the sun, Dillinger suddenly felt the hand-grip on his throat loosen.

"Scum!" he heard Nachita saying as he twisted Ortiz's head in an arm lock. "Geronimo wouldn't even have let you hold the horses."

Dillinger saw Nachita's knife as if in slow motion go in and out of Ortiz twice, and then Ortiz's eyes rolled upwards. As Nachita stepped back, Ortiz rolled off Dillinger and sank to the ground.

Somewhere Dillinger could hear Juanita crying. Then Chavasse was standing over

287

him, and then a moment later Rose was kneeling beside him. His breath was coming back, and he knew, like a man redeemed, that everything would be all right.

EIGHTEEN

Rose accepted custody of Juanita as if she were her own. As Rivera's closest adult relative, she used her authority to see that Dillinger got the $20,000 of gold that Rivera had promised him. And when Dillinger suggested that Fallon's $5,000 go to Chavasse so that he could stop being a hotel manager and barkeeper in a strange land, Rose accepted that also. What she could not accept as easily was that with the passing of weeks, Dillinger had decided to return home.

Nachita accompanied them to the border because he knew a place that was absolutely safe from detection. Rose rode along with Nachita, but for the last few miles she let Nachita lead her horse and she sat with Dillinger in the convertible, both of them aching with their feelings for each other.

"If only I'd have met you in Indiana," Dillinger said.

"If you'd met me in Indiana, you'd have taken no notice of me," Rose replied.

"I'd have noticed you anywhere," he said.

When they reached the border, a desolate place with cactus and bramble, Dillinger pulled over, took Rose by her shoulders, and said, "Please come with me."

"I love you, Johnny," she said. "but I cannot go with a man who doesn't know where he is going."

And so he offered her his white Chevrolet as a gift. "This way," he said, "you'll know I'll come back."

"Because you love the car."

"Because I love you both. Put Mexican plates on it, have it painted black or red, and nobody'll ever bother you."

"You forget," Rose said. "I can't drive."

Dillinger looked at Nachita on his horse. He didn't drive either.

And so he said his good-byes to both of them. "You know what you need here in Mexico? More banks."

Without looking back, Dillinger drove across the invisible line that separated Mexico from home. As quickly as he could, he got onto a good road, and then came to a place in New Mexico called Las Cruces, by which time he had decided that he couldn't go on driving a car that the FBI and God knows how many policemen were on the lookout for.

On the side street he spotted a black Ford roadster that looked like a thousand other black Ford roadsters. He parked the white convertible right behind it, and within minutes had wired the Ford to start without a key. Nobody was looking, so he transferred the suitcases containing his gold and the Thompson and some extra clothes and the picture of Rose she had given him that was too big to put in his wallet.

As he drove the Ford away, he looked once in the rearview mirror. That white convertible was a helluva car.

He parked in the business district, and asked a policeman if there was a nearby ice cream parlor.

"Yes, sir," the cop said. "Right around the corner."

Dillinger saluted the cop in thanks.

There were four teenagers at the counter, drinking ice cream sodas. When the soda jerk came over, Dillinger said, "I'll have a black and white."

The chocolate soda with vanilla ice cream tasted like all of his childhood memories together.

"Ten cents," said the soda jerk.

"That," said Dillinger, "was the best ice cream soda I've had in a long, long time."

The soda jerk beamed. "Those kids," he said, pointing to the teenagers, "never say nothing nice about my sodas."

Dillinger put two bits on the counter. "Keep the change."

"Gee, thanks," the soda jerk said, hoping the stranger would become a steady customer.

But the stranger hit the road like there was no tomorrow, driving through Roswell, Portales, Clovis, and then into Texas, through Amarillo and Phillips and Perryton into Oklahoma, past Hooker and into Kansas, where he pulled up at a gas station in Meade, and used the public phone booth to make the one call he had to make.

The secretary said, "Mr. Hoover, there's a collect call from John Dillinger. Shall I accept?"

J. Edgar Hoover nodded, because you didn't need to put a tracer on a collect call. The operator could tell you where the call was made from. He got on the line and motioned the secretary to pick up the extension so she could write down what was said.

"Mr. Hoover," Dillinger said. "You can find that white Chevy convertible you're looking for in a town called Las Cruces in New Mexico. I don't want you to say I've never been helpful to you."

Hoover thought Dillinger was very helpful because a line could be drawn from Las Cruces to wherever he was calling from now and they'd know which direction he was headed in.

"Thank you," Mr. Hoover said.

"Don't hang up," Dillinger said. "I'm not finished."

"Good-bye," Hoover said, thinking, You *are* finished."

"Don't hang up, you son-of-a-bitch," Dillinger yelled. "I'm the best thing that ever happened to you."

But the line was dead.

Three months later, on Sunday, July 22, 1934, John Dillinger was shot dead outside the Biograph Movie Theater in Chicago by agents of the Federal Bureau of Investigation. He was betrayed by a woman.